"An amazing and fascinating study. . . . Pastors might well commit to spending a year with this book — in conversation with others, if possible. It will preach!"
— *Presbyterian Outlook*

"Before we can get to the glorious resurrection, we must take full account of the tragic necessity of the cross. . . . Penetrating and unflinching in its insistence on Jesus Christ, condemned, crucified, dead, and buried, this book powerfully demonstrates that the crucifixion of the Son of God is good news of cosmic and comprehensive scope."
— Leanne Van Dyk
Columbia Theological Seminary

"In this amazingly complex but clear book Fleming Rutledge goes deftly where few seem willing to go — to the variety of imaginations shaping early Christian explorations of the significance of Jesus' death. She is one of the few theologians who not only preach inclusivism but practice it by inviting *all* points of view into the discussion."
— Scot McKnight
author of *The Jesus Creed*

"Though I have been thinking much about the cross of Christ for a half-century now, Fleming Rutledge has taught me many new things in this wonderful book. And where she addresses matters that I have long cherished, she has inspired me anew. This book is a gift to all of us who pray for a genuine revival of crucicentric preaching and cruciform discipleship!"
— Richard J. Mouw
Fuller Theological Seminary

"Fleming Rutledge here lays out the horror of the cross with unflinching honesty and with a patient, full exposition of the rich themes of Christ's redeeming death. She does not shy away from the demands of her theological vision, taking up motifs of satisfaction, substitution, rectification, and divine wrath in turn. Throughout, Rutledge draws on the rich storehouse of a preacher. The whole world stands under her gaze — literary examples, political folly and cruelty, horrendous evils of war and torment and torture, religious timidity and self-deception, human faithlessness and sin. But always the gospel rings out. Christ's cross has won the victory, and it is all from God. This book is a moving testimony to the courage, intelligence, and faithfulness of one of the church's premier preachers. Every student of the Scriptures needs this book."

— **Katherine Sonderegger**
Virginia Theological Seminary

"Demonstrating impressively wide reading, incisive observations, and a passionate concern for clear thinking and faithful preaching, this book is a big read but well worth the effort, especially for clergy — but also for thoughtful laity."

— **Larry W. Hurtado**
University of Edinburgh

"To those who think they want a maximally mellow God who overlooks our faults and accepts us just as we are, Rutledge's challenge is to 'get real.' Twentieth-century atrocities bear witness: there is something drastically wrong with the human condition, which only God can fix. Setting things right calls for crucifixion, not only Christ's but also ours. Rutledge has given us a very Pauline book, full of information and observations to provoke clergy to preach the cross to their congregations."

— **Marilyn McCord Adams**
Rutgers University

"Here is the kind of strong theology that will undergird strong preaching. Preachers who take this book to heart could well revitalize the church."

— **George Hunsinger**
Princeton Theological Seminary

"A deeply probing and richly evocative exploration of the central mystery of the Christian faith. This is a book to contemplate, to savor, to reread. . . . It is easy to glibly repeat Paul's claim that Jesus' death is a scandal and stumbling block. It is quite something else to let that claim transform how you perceive the world and the triune God who created it. This book confronts all that is glib and evokes that life-giving transformation."

— **John D. Witvliet**
Calvin Institute of Christian Worship

"To read this book is to share in a work of joyful, honest, evangelical thinking done right at the foot of the pulpit steps for the sake of the one thing that finally matters in the church — the hearing and proclamation of the word of the cross in all its scandalous power."

— **Philip G. Ziegler**
University of Aberdeen

"I can hardly think of a book more necessary for our time. Many well-meaning attempts to summarize the good news today barely allude to the cross, and we're left with an anemic if not a false gospel. Read, mark, and inwardly digest this book if you want to learn about the cross that truly rectifies the ungodly, even the likes of you and me."

— **Mark Galli**
editor of *Christianity Today*

"Brilliant. . . . Persistent readers will find their hearts transformed. Preachers will be emboldened to speak more frequently of the cross, contributing to the gospel renewal of the church."

— **Paul Scott Wilson**
University of Toronto

"The word that came to my mind as I read Fleming Rutledge's book *The Crucifixion* was 'bracing': the book is bracing in its vigorous affirmation of the centrality of Christ's crucifixion in the Christian proclamation, bracing in its description of the unspeakable horror and shame of the crucifixion, bracing in its affirmation that we are one and all sinners, bracing in its identification and rejection of the many forms of theological silliness now inhabiting the church. Though meant for pastors and laypeople, this book will also benefit scholars. It carries its deep learning with eloquence and grace. I will be returning to it."

— **Nicholas Wolterstorff**
Yale University

"In the crucifixion we sense anew the intersection at which Christian *drama* and Christian *dogma* meet one another with announcements that are emphatically universal and nothing less than cosmic. At that intersection we are truly fortunate to have the voice of Fleming Rutledge, one of the most gifted theological preachers of our time. In her writing we encounter the confluence of high drama and arresting dogma, as they work together to strengthen the preacher and provide a high-protein diet that will nourish the congregation to vigorous health."

— **J. Louis Martyn**
Union Theological Seminary

"Richly illustrated with examples from literature and current events, this book should prove a gold mine for preachers at the same time as it invites the careful reflection of every reader on the mystery of salvation."

— **Stephen Westerholm**
McMaster University

"Rutledge's work on the crucifixion is not only broad but also deep. Thought-provoking, often moving, this book offers a genuinely novel approach to a topic on which it often seems nothing new can be said."

— **David Bentley Hart**
author of *The Beauty of the Infinite* and
Atheist Delusions

"This justly celebrated preacher has been digging into the doctrine of atonement for many years. Here is the rich harvest of her labors — a resource especially for preachers like herself."

— **Robert W. Jenson**
Center for Catholic and Evangelical
Theology

"In this bold, uncompromising, nuanced, and expansive work Rutledge takes us through — and beyond — theories of atonement, avoiding all merely individualistic, spiritualized, religious, moralistic, and therapeutic reductions of the meaning of the crucifixion. Rutledge resolutely proclaims the truth of Christ crucified. To all priests, preachers, and professors: if you care about the church and its mission in history, read this book!"

— **Douglas Harink**
The King's University, Edmonton, Canada

" 'Who put the roses on the cross?' asked Goethe, who in fact preferred that the brutal cross be covered in roses. Fleming Rutledge brushes the roses aside and asks us to *look* at the cross and, even more so, at Him who hung upon it for our sake. This is a book marked by outstanding exegesis, theology, and pastoral sensitivity — a book for thinking Christians and even thinking unbelievers."

— **Joseph Mangina**
University of Toronto

"In this thoroughly readable book, preacher-theologian Fleming Rutledge demonstrates that she is also a fine exegete. Through careful exegetical study of the Bible in dialogue with a range of interpreters, she has produced a book that merits a wide readership among theologians, biblical scholars, and preachers."

— **Martinus C. de Boer**
VU University Amsterdam

"In the rich tradition of the preacher-theologian, Fleming Rutledge in her own incisive voice gives testimony to the rectifying significance of Christ's crucifixion with detailed exposition that is at once deeply reflective and full of deep conviction. From a wealth of scholarly references and observations ranging from Scripture, the history of church imagery and its critics, literature, modern theology, and the daily news, readers will find much to ponder in this commendably studied yet vitally proclamatory gospel treatise."

— **Christopher Morse**
Union Theological Seminary

"In this remarkable study of the cross Fleming Rutledge weaves together many metaphors, motifs, and themes into a hermeneutically well-reasoned synthesis. She has mastered an incredible amount of material, including biblical scholarship, the history of theology, and contemporary systematic theology. And she is a master communicator. This is a great book."

— **Arne Rasmusson**
University of Gothenburg, Sweden

"Fleming Rutledge's reputation as a preacher is widely known, her rhetorical skills — of logos, ethos, and pathos; of content, engagement, and passion — widely respected. This treatment of the crucifixion — the fruit of almost two decades, and indeed of a lifelong journey — could in fact also be read as one long sermon. . . . What does it mean to say that Jesus Christ died for us? Honestly facing her own resistance to many traditional and contemporary framings of this question, Rutledge consults widely and delves deeply into biblical, historical, and interpretive material in search of her own answers. We do not hear enough about the working of God nowadays, she claims, only a great deal about our own human working, especially our religious working and imagination. Rutledge here tells the rich and surprising story of *God's* working, weaving its significance into the stories of our own lives, as reflected in scholarship, literature, film, and the daily news. . . . Informing, reminding, critiquing, illustrating, unmasking, challenging, reassuring, encouraging, and inspiring, she writes for both preachers and listeners. The question *Will it preach?* is in fact her major concern. The answer can only be a resounding and grateful *Yes!*"

— **Dirk Smit**
Universitıy of Stellenbosch, South Africa

And so he was raised on a cross, and a title was fixed, indicating who it was who was being executed. Painful it is to say, but more terrible not to say. . . . He who suspended the earth is suspended, he who fixed the heavens is fixed, he who fastened all things is fastened to the wood; the Master is outraged; God is murdered.

Melito of Sardis (d. c. A.D. 180)

THE CRUCIFIXION

Understanding the Death of Jesus Christ

Fleming Rutledge

WILLIAM B. EERDMANS PUBLISHING COMPANY
GRAND RAPIDS, MICHIGAN

Wm. B. Eerdmans Publishing Co.
2140 Oak Industrial Drive NE, Grand Rapids, Michigan 49505
www.eerdmans.com

Hardcover edition 2015
Paperback edition 2017
Printed in the United States of America

23 22 21 20 19 18 17   2 3 4 5 6 7

Library of Congress Cataloging-in-Publication Data

Rutledge, Fleming.
    The crucifixion: understanding the death of Jesus Christ / Fleming Rutledge.
        pages   cm
    Includes bibliographical references.
    ISBN 978-0-8028-7534-1 (pbk.: alk. paper)
    1. Jesus Christ — Crucifixion.   I. Title.

    BT450.R88   2015
    232.96′3 — dc23
                        2015010111

This book is dedicated
to those who did the most to help bring it into being:

Reginald E. Rutledge
servant of Christ
and my husband of fifty-six years

and
Wallace M. Alston, Jr.
who designed and directed the pastor-theologian program
at the Center of Theological Inquiry in Princeton
from 1996 to 2007
and the resident scholars at CTI in 1997-98 and 2002

About the Cover

The large stained-glass window depicted on the cover of this book is generally known as the "Wales Window." It was presented to the 16th Street Baptist Church in Birmingham, Alabama, by the people of Wales, as a response to the historic terror-bombing that became a major turning point in the civil rights movement. On Sunday morning, September 15, 1963, a month after the March on Washington, four little black girls attired in their best white dresses were killed in their church building by a Ku Klux Klan bomb. (A reenactment of this event was the opening scene of the acclaimed 2014 film *Selma*.)

The people of Wales raised funds to commission a stained-glass window for the church. The designer, John Petts, produced a unique image of the crucifixion. It depicts a brown-skinned Christ in an unusual position; his body is in the cruciform position but seems to be moving off the cross as though he were not captured on it, but is freely present in every tragic human situation. His head hangs at the same angle with the same facial expression as in a striking Byzantine ikon called "Utmost Humiliation." This expression conveys not only his own suffering and anguish, but also unspeakable sorrow on behalf of the sinful world.

Petts states that one powerful arm of the crucified Jesus is turned against the demonic powers that brought him to the cross, while the other is extended to embrace the whole creation. Petts does not explain the unusual garment that the Lord is wearing, but to me it suggests a prison suit or chain-gang uniform. His boots are blackened as if he has been marching in the mud, but his body appears transfigured in white light. The composition conveys utter helplessness and victimization, yet in the same image we seem to see a dimension of power and transcendence.

The inscription, "You do it to me," is taken from the parable of the Last Judgment in Matthew 25:40. The choice of words in the window is striking, because Jesus' saying takes on a different meaning in the context of his crucifixion. The acts of mercy commended by the Lord in Matthew 25 as done to him in the persons of "the least of these" are, here, depicted as their opposite: the full force of universal human depravity is turned upon him. All of humanity is involved in that "you."

This image encompasses much of what I have sought to say in this book, and more besides.

When a visitor completes her journey through the deeply moving exhibits in the Birmingham (Alabama) Civil Rights Institute museum, the final thing she will see, through a very large clear window, is the Sixteenth Street Baptist Church directly across the street and park, restored and active. It is a stunning sight and a perfect conclusion to the pilgrimage.

Contents

Preface

When someone asks me how long I have been working on this book, I usually say that I started it when, after twenty-one years, I retired from parish ministry — in other words, about eighteen years ago. In the truest sense, though, it has been the work of a lifetime. When I was about thirteen — that would be 1950 — I was already beginning to wonder what it meant to say that Jesus died for the sin of the world. I knew the impassioned saying of Paul, that "I decided to know nothing among you except Jesus Christ and him crucified" (I Cor. 2:2), but was not sure what that meant. Did Paul really intend to place the cross at the exclusive center of his message? What about the incarnation, the ministry of Jesus, and the resurrection? If "Christ crucified" is indeed the heart of the gospel, what does that signify?

Another issue troubled me. When I was about fifteen, I wrote a letter to a sort of theological Dear Abby column in the *Episcopalian*, which came to my parents' house on a regular basis. "Dear Dora Chaplin: If God is good, why is there so much evil in the world?"[1] Such is the naïveté of youth that I thought this question originated with me. Dora Chaplin was kind enough to treat my question with the utmost seriousness. If I remember rightly, her answer was a version of the free-will defense, which was enough to satisfy me for a few months before it all started up again, lasting all through college and beyond. What does Christian faith say about evil in the world?

During the early years of my marriage and child raising, the urgency of these two issues persisted in my mind, though it was not until *after* three years at Union and General Seminaries in New York City that the need to understand much more about the cross of Christ became pressing and inescapable.

During my active ministry, I had the great privilege of preaching on Good Friday all over the United States for an uninterrupted thirty years. This made it necessary to develop a theology of the cross, and it set in motion my resolve to write a book that would help preachers. At the turn of the twenty-first century, however, the Good Friday three-hour preaching services, once so well attended and so carefully prepared, were disappearing. In the Episcopal Church, the sermons and meditations that were the centerpieces of these services have now been largely replaced by prayers and litanies, substantial interludes of music, short homilies (optional), and liturgical practices such as reverencing the cross and receiving the reserved sacrament. This devaluation of the preaching of the cross is, I believe, a serious deprivation for those who seek to follow Jesus. Palm Sunday theoretically presents an opportunity to preach the cross, since the passion narrative is appointed to be read in liturgical churches, but in actuality so much is going on in the services that day that there is little time for a substantive sermon. Therefore it is quite possible for a pastor to go through an entire year of Sundays and never once preach Christ crucified in any expansive way. The *skandalon* (offense) of which Paul the apostle spoke, and the difficult and controversial issues surrounding the interpretation of the cross, have gone missing from the heart and center of our faith. This is a grave deprivation affecting not only evangelism but also the shaping of the Christian life.

In spite of, or perhaps because of, these obstacles, my intention all along has been to help not only those who preach sermons, but also those who listen to sermons. If there is a dearth of preaching about the cross in the churches today, perhaps it is not entirely the fault of the preachers and liturgists. It may be partly because lay church members are not asking for it.

---

1. Dora P. Chaplin was the first female professor (of Christian education) at General Theological Seminary, and a widely respected church leader in the '40s and '50s.

There should be an urgency about this; the Christian faith is empty at its heart if congregations habitually skip over Good Friday as if it had not occurred. This volume is an attempt to redress the balance.

It is a challenge to address such a profound topic in easily accessible terms and still take account of the wide spectrum of the church's teaching about the crucifixion of Christ. These pages attempt to be a bridge between academic scholarship, on the one hand, and local congregations, on the other. Along those lines, I assure readers that, despite the apparatus of footnotes and bibliography, this does not pretend to be a history of doctrine. I happily yield that territory to those who are qualified. What I have attempted — as a pastor and a preacher — is a series of *theological reflections* on Scripture and tradition that I hope add up to a coherent account of the death of Jesus Christ for the church — to the people of God visible and invisible.

It is the *living significance* of the death of Jesus, not the factual details concerning it as a historical event, that matters. Books about the crucifixion in its own time, the method and its history, the current theories about Jesus' execution, and so forth are of potential interest to general readers; these subjects, however, interesting though they are, are of peripheral importance. The historical event will always be the indubitable fact on the ground, but the declaration of the apostle Paul that the word of the cross is the power of God for salvation (I Cor. 1:18) is not a statement about a mere historical event. The preaching of the cross is an announcement of a living reality that continues to transform human existence and human destiny more than two thousand years after it originally occurred.

It is a fundamental presupposition of what follows, therefore, that the message of the crucifixion is not accessible from outside the living event. For those who are unconcerned about its inner significance, it will remain a "stumbling block" and "foolishness," as Paul wrote. The cross reveals its meaning as it takes shape in the experience of believers. In the final analysis, then, this is a book written "from faith for faith."[2]

By the grace of God, however, there may be readers who think they have no faith, or have inadequate faith. The very existence of such doubts are themselves a sign of the divine action that elicits the cry, "Help my unbelief!" (Mark 9:24), words to which our Lord himself responded with immediate, sovereign favor. It is such readers that I have especially in mind.

---

2. I Cor. 1:18, 21-25; Rom. 1:16-17.

Now for Some Practical Interpretive Comments

Some may wonder about denominational bias in this book. I am an Episcopalian — indeed, a descendant of generations of Episcopalians. Certain portions of this book inevitably reflect particular emphases and priorities within the American Episcopal Church. During the whole time of writing, however, I have had my eye on the larger church. My experience of the mainline Protestant denominations has been wide and deep, and I have had many significant contacts with Roman Catholics as well. I have been a guest preacher and teacher in churches and theological colleges in Canada and Great Britain. As for the global South, where Christianity seems to be especially vibrant, though I lack hands-on experience, I trust that the Holy Spirit might inhabit these pages and make the universal message of the Lord's suffering and death strike the hearts of some of those he loves in the wider world.

In my wish to present a book that will be useful to a general readership as well as academically trained pastors, I have had to make some tricky decisions about how much scholarly discussion to include. One of the reasons this project has taken so long is that I have spent years and years chasing down all sorts of interpretive controversies, only to discover belatedly that I will never be able to do this like a "real" academician. My good friend Will Willimon recently related a funny (what else?) story about how Stanley Hauerwas told him to quit with the footnotes already, because he was never going to convince the scholars that he was one of them. Or something like that. In any case, Will's version of this story helped me to get on with the writing. Although my footnotes take up a lot of space, the book can be read by the interested pastor or layperson without reference to them.

At the end of my select bibliography I have listed a representative number of more or less *theological* commentaries on the books of the Bible for the use of preachers and other students of the Scriptures. There are any number of excellent commentaries on the biblical texts, but more rare are commentaries with an overt theological bent. In the heyday of the historical-critical method, many scholars with theological interests were constrained to keep them under wraps, but the academic landscape began to change in the 1960s and 1970s, and there are now once again a number of "biblical theologians" — as well as some notable systematic theologians who are gifted exegetes as well. Many of them were there all along, but they have recently become bolder, to the great benefit of the church. These are the scholars I, as a preacher, find most useful.

Of all the chapters in this book, the one that means the most to me personally is "The Descent into Hell." Those occasions of Good Friday preaching became more and more a time for reflection on the relationship between the problem of evil and the crucifixion of Christ. In the end, I spent more than two years writing that one chapter. I wrote it in protest against horrors, in memory of the victims, and in solidarity with those who mourn inconsolably. As I am putting the last touches on this preface in the early weeks of 2015, the signs of seemingly invincible evil are unusually pronounced around the world. Scanning the news brings less diversion and more alarm. Anyone occupying a pulpit these days needs plenty of fortification. If our preaching does not intersect with the times, we are fleeing the call to take up the cross. We can learn from the example of Dostoevsky, who in *The Brothers Karamazov* used material that he read in the newspapers to give a human face to the problem of evil.

FR

Acknowledgments

There are two powerful influences in the background of this book, one having to do with the academy and one with the church. At Union Theological Seminary in New York in the 1970s, warm personal relationships and mutual respect among a number of professors and doctoral students in two distinct fields — biblical studies and systematic theology — resulted in a rich soil in which M.Div. students like myself could develop. After I graduated in the midseventies, I continued to be involved for several years with a discussion group of faculty and doctoral students from both those fields, meeting at Union, to discuss the letters of the apostle Paul. Having observed this dynamic between the two disciplines at work, I have never again been satisfied with anything less.

The second influence was my fourteen years at Grace Episcopal Church in New York City. When I arrived as a member of the clergy staff in 1981, the booming, youthful congregation was gripped by a renewal that had occurred specifically as a result of the preaching of the cross during the '70s.[3] Far from being a culture-bound notion peculiar to dead white males, the message of "Jesus Christ and him crucified" (I Cor. 2:2) was for numerous young New Yorkers of various extractions the source of life itself. The experience of ministering for fourteen years within a congregation of God's people being shaped by this gospel convinced me more than ever that there was unique power in it, not only for conversion but also for a new way of living.

Over the twenty years or so that this book has been in the works, many people have helped me in ways that I can never repay or sufficiently acknowledge. It almost stuns me as I recognize the hand of God in this fellowship

3. The preachers in those renewal years 1975-1981 at Grace Church were FitzSimons Allison, Paul F. M. Zahl, and James G. Munroe.

of mutually encouraging servants of the Word. If I list them here without detailed acknowledgment of their generosity, their knowledge, and their support — of one another as well as myself — it is because I simply do not know how to say how profoundly grateful I am to have known them.

From seminary days there were several professors who later became not only mentors but also friends. Their influence pervades the entire book. They are Paul L. Lehmann, J. Louis Martyn, Raymond E. Brown, and Christopher Morse. Richard A. Norris, Cyril C. Richardson, and Samuel Terrien also played a significant part in my theological education. In the early years after my graduation, the aforementioned group that met at Union Theological Seminary for several years to study the letters of the apostle Paul brought me into conversation with several doctoral students who went on to become professors in their own right — Martinus C. de Boer, Nancy J. Duff, and James F. Kay among them.

During my two residencies at the Center of Theological Inquiry (CTI) in Princeton (1997-1998 and 2002), many distinguished scholars took an interest in my project and read parts of it, with helpful comments: Patrick Miller, Mark Reasoner, George Lindbeck, David Tracy, and the two South Africans Etienne de Villiers and Dirk Smit, among others. Joseph Mangina, in particular, has been a partner for years. His learning, his literary imagination, and his friendship have been a constant joy, along with his dear family.

In particular I thank those others who read chapters, or portions of chapters, and took time to make lengthy and constructive comments; primary among those are J. Louis Martyn, George Hunsinger, Jim Kay, Kate Sonderregger, Susan Eastman, and Jordan Hylden. A special mention is owed to Adam Linton, rector of the Church of the Holy Spirit in Orleans, Massachusetts. Adam is unique among my colleagues, combining as he does a degree from Gordon-Conwell, experience as a Navy chaplain, twenty years in the Russian Orthodox Church, ordination as an Episcopal priest, fluency in languages, and profound knowledge of Karl Barth's *Church Dogmatics*. He has been an encourager and partner for years. To him and his wife Lori, and his exceptionally interesting and vibrant congregation on Cape Cod, my deepest gratitude and warm admiration.

Three theological seminaries have meant much to me since I left parish ministry in 1997. The *first* is the Duke Divinity School, where I have been privileged to preach, teach, and lecture many times. Ellen Davis, Susan Eastman, Richard Hays, Richard Lischer, and Joel Marcus have been partners in this enterprise in ways that they might be surprised to know. The *second* is Princeton Theological Seminary, where the encouragement of Beverly Gaventa, Pat and Mary Ann Miller, Paul Rorem, George and Deborah

Hunsinger, Ellen Charry, Iain Torrance, and Dan Migliore, among others, has meant a great deal to me — not to mention the stalwart friendship of Wentzel van Huyssteen. Jacquie Lapsley and Pat Miller helped me with Hebrew, and Nancy Lammers Gross with Paul Ricoeur. I imagine that Kate Skrebutenas, the skilled reference librarian at Princeton for many years, has been thanked by more people than any other person in the world of theological research in America, and I am honored to add my name to that list. As for the *third,* I have made three visits — as lecturer, preacher, and teacher — to Wycliffe College in the University of Toronto School of Theology. I will always be thankful to Principal George Sumner for inviting me to be in residence and teach homiletics for a term, one of the most challenging and rewarding periods of my life. Through Wycliffe and other channels, I have been invited to preach, lecture, and teach in four of the Canadian provinces, and the support of the saints in Canada has been a joy to me. Among colleagues at Wycliffe I especially salute David Demson. His wife Leslie and I share enthusiasm for the biblical word that we believe should always be translated "Behold!"

There are certain witnesses, now across Jordan, who are present in this book in ways that many of them could not have imagined. Some of them made contributions from their writing and are footnoted accordingly in the book, but even more important was the impression all of them made in their persons. It means much to me to write their names. Roughly in chronological order of their influence in my life, beginning with my early adolescence, these departed saints are: John M. Gessell, Albert T. Mollegen, Samuel J. Wylie, Dean Hosken, Lawrence G. Nelson, Richard R. Baker, Charles Perry, Paul L. Lehmann, Raymond E. Brown, Cyril C. Richardson, Richard A. Norris Jr., Reginald H. Fuller, Will D. Campbell, J. Christiaan Beker, Furman Stough, and Arthur Hertzberg. (If all but one of these are men, that's a comment on how far we've come since I was young.)

During the last stages of writing, I retreated from everything several times. Without these breaks from distractions, I could never have finished. Kathy and Nat Goddard, devoted members of the Episcopal Church of the Holy Spirit in Orleans, Massachusetts, allowed me to use their guest house in the Cape Cod National Seashore for two weeks. I will always rejoice to remember this gracious time of writing, interrupted only by dune walks and seabird watching. The following year, as the book approached completion, I spent two periods of time working in the new Princeton Seminary Library. I am grateful to Ellen Charry for her hospitality in her elegantly furnished house on Mercer Street, and for the stimulation of her company. I give thanks for the late Dana Charry, whose contributions also appear in these pages.

It had been forty years since I used a theological library, having amassed a little theological library at home. Obviously, it was very difficult for a nonacademic person born in 1937 to negotiate the new technology all at once. At the last minute I was firing off e-mails every hour or so in every direction, trying to get help with footnotes and bibliography. I divided up these panicky requests among Jim Kay, George Hunsinger, Richard Hays, Ellen Davis, Susan Eastman, Joel Marcus, Pat Miller, Christopher Morse, and especially Joe Mangina, whose patience and wide-ranging intellectual resources seemed inexhaustible. (Susan Eastman and Joel Marcus will recognize and remember the above references to Grace Church in New York. They are among the most distinguished "alumni" from the '70s and '80s.)

I think I have always operated on the principle of Athanasius: "We expound the same sense in more than one form, lest we should seem to be leaving anything out — for it is better to submit to the blame of repetition than to leave out anything that ought to be set down" (*De incarnatione* 20). With all due respect to the great Athanasius, this was a mistake on my part. At the very last stage of writing, I received a piece of crucial advice. Robert "Jens" Jenson, an encourager since my first residence at CTI, generously read the entire manuscript, which was some 150 sprawling pages longer than it is now, and put the fear of God into me about sending it out into the world full of repetitions and digressions.

At this crucial moment, when I was close to despairing, divine Providence in the form of Jason Byassee led me to a talented young editor, Adam Joyce, who turned out to be exactly the right person to help me not only to pare the manuscript down but also to get it into better order. Robert Dean, a shining star in my advanced homiletics class at Wycliffe and a newly minted Ph.D., also read the whole thing with a particular eye to theological nuance. Words simply cannot express my gratitude to these two young men, not only for doing the tedious work and bearing with my push-back, but also and even more important, for believing in the project and encouraging me every step of the way. It was a humbling experience — a good many of my favorite passages had to go — but my readers will be thankful for the greatly streamlined (believe it or not) result.

Others have contributed to this enterprise in other, less definable ways. Some of them are outside the community of faith but curious about the gospel. I have had these potential readers in mind all along — persons who count themselves unbelievers but are nevertheless drawn to learn more about Christian belief. Friends of this description have been my companions in this endeavor from the beginning. To some extent this book is a dialogue with these unnamed but very real conversation partners.

I have neglected my close friends and other relationships shamefully during these last months, not answering calls, not communicating, not being available. They have all been very forgiving. There is one friend in particular who is dear to everyone in our family and extended family, and that is Pennie Curry — a formidable Christian witness and exemplar. Her love of the Lord, care for the church, and tireless efforts on behalf of the Hispanic community and of young people in need of guidance have borne witness to the crucified and risen One wherever she goes.

There is one other person and program that I want to single out. When I left my last parish post, I was already beginning to sketch out this book, but the great leap forward did not occur until 1997 when I received an offer that might as well have dropped directly from heaven. Wallace Alston, whom I had known only slightly as a fellow student of Paul Lehmann, called me out of the empyrean and invited me to be the first pastor-theologian in residence at the Center of Theological Inquiry in Princeton — a program that he envisioned, designed, and enabled. This project involved not just the resident scholars in Princeton, but also many scores of pastors meeting in local groups all over the United States. This book would have been an impoverished enterprise if it had not been for my introduction to the international fellowship of biblical and systematic theologians who were at CTI during my two periods of residence in 1997-1998 and 2002. Many have become lifetime friends. It is simply not possible to overstate the importance of those gifts of time, space, and comradeship. That time, and those people, more than anything else, by the grace of God made this book possible.

The house of Eerdmans has published all of my previous seven books, but until I sent in the manuscript of this one, I had no idea what was involved in the preparation of a volume with more than 1,500 footnotes and hundreds of Scripture references, every single one of which had to be checked. When I first began working on this book eighteen years ago, I was not always as careful about my citations as I should have been. The process of polishing up my manuscript has been an extraordinarily tedious job and I am in awe of Tom Raabe, my copy editor, whose patience and skill during the three months that he had to work daily with me (not to mention many previous months working on it by himself) have been remarkable. I also thank Mary Hietbrink and Laura Bardolph-Hubers for essential support. I am proud that Willem Mineur has designed all eight of my covers; he is a master, and a joy to work with. Finally, I salute Jon Pott, longtime senior editor, whose retirement came just as this manuscript was being completed, and William B. (Bill) Eerdmans Jr., who continued to cheer me on even when it seemed I would never finish.

It's customary to thank one's spouse and to say it couldn't have been done without his or her support and so on, but in this case it is almost impossible to say how much Dick Rutledge has contributed. Indeed, it simply couldn't have happened without him. Just to begin with, writing a book like this costs a lot of money. Without institutional support, I was high and dry for most of the years of work, except for the blessed twelve months at CTI and the rewarding term at Wycliffe. Ten years into the writing, it was a tremendous help when the Louisville Foundation gave me a large grant, which paid for two years of a rented office. Almost all the credit in this regard, however, belongs to Dick, who not only paid for my entire three years of theological education in the first place, but on his own initiative and without my knowledge went out and searched for an office where I would be protected from distractions. He found the perfect one, and paid the rent for nine more years after the grant ran out. But his financial support was the least of it. Who can count the dinners prepared and eaten alone, especially during the last six months? Who can imagine the loss of companionship when I pretty much dropped out of sight and hearing? Who can evaluate the amount of irritability endured while I struggled with the manuscript? Who can calculate the management of problems like a broken refrigerator and a flooded garage, with no help from me, during those critical last months? But none of that can compare with the precious gift of a lifelong companion who truly knows and truly loves the Lord, and who serves the Lord's church with total devotion. I just don't know how to even begin to say what this partnership has meant to this book and to our marriage. May God be praised for all his bountiful gifts.

Alford, Massachusetts   FLEMING RUTLEDGE
January 15, 2015

Introduction

Christianity is unique. The world's religions have certain traits in common, but until the gospel of Jesus Christ burst upon the Mediterranean world, no one in the history of human imagination had conceived of such a thing as the worship of a crucified man. The early Christian preaching announced the entrance of God upon the stage of history in the person of an itinerant Jewish teacher who had been ingloriously pinned up alongside two of society's castoffs to die horribly, rejected and condemned by religious and secular authorities alike, discarded onto the garbage heap of humanity, scornfully forsaken by both elites and common folk, leaving behind only a discredited, demoralized handful of scruffy disciples who had no status whatsoever in the eyes of anyone. The peculiarity of this beginning for a world-transforming faith is not sufficiently acknowledged. Too often, today's Christians are lulled into thinking of their own faith as one of the religions, without realizing that the central claim of Christianity is oddly *irreligious* at its core.[1] Dietrich Bonhoeffer wrote that the weakness and suffering of Christ was and remains "a

---

1. Testimonies to this factor are numerous. Martin Hengel writes of "the utterly unique event of the passion and crucifixion of the Messiah of Israel which is without any parallel in the history of religion" (*The Atonement: The Origins of the Doctrine in the New Testament* [Philadelphia: Fortress, 1981], 41). Roy A. Harrisville is even more specific about the universal religious impulse when he notes that "Jews and pagans alike were ready to affirm resurrection or immortality. That lay at the heart of their conceptuality; what they could not believe was that a messiah or *kurios* could die" (*Fracture: The Cross as Irreconcilable in the Language and Thought of the Biblical Writers* [Grand Rapids: Eerdmans, 2006], 276-77). It is not only academic scholars who have noticed this. In one of his quirky, allusive fantasies, Donald Barthelme has Cortés and Montezuma talking about religion. Montezuma is learning about Christianity. "I especially like the Holy Ghost," he says, and the Father is all right too, but "that the Son should be sacrificed seems to me wrong. It seems to me he should be sacrificed *to*" ("Cortes and Montezuma," *New Yorker*, August 22, 1977).

reversal of what the religious man expects from God."[2] This use of "religious" and "religion" will inform much of the discussion in this book.[3] As defined in these pages, "religion" is a set of beliefs projected out of humanity's needs, wishes, longings, and fears. The religious imagination seeks uplift, not torture, humiliation, and death. Therefore the principal purpose of this book about the crucifixion will be to strengthen the reader's surmise that the cross of Jesus is an unrepeatable event that calls all religion into question and establishes an altogether new foundation for faith, life, and a human future.[4]

The apostle Paul, writing a letter to the Christians in Rome, brought his ringing introduction to a climax with these words: *I am not ashamed of the gospel.* Why should he be ashamed? we might ask. Why would it be necessary to issue this disclaimer? A person opening the Bible in search of spiritual guidance, inspiration, or instruction might well be puzzled to find so blunt a reference to being ashamed. One might search religious literature for a long time and never find any such language as this.

In the letter to the Romans, Paul seems to assume that his hearers will know what he means when he says he is "not ashamed." About the Corinthians, however, he can't be so certain, so he goes into more detail. It is

---

2. Dietrich Bonhoeffer, *Letters and Papers from Prison,* ed. Eberhard Bethge, enlarged ed. (New York: Macmillan, 1972), 360. As Bonhoeffer's situation under the Nazis became more and more perilous, he drew ever closer to the crucified One. We still await a fully theological examination of Bonhoeffer's musings from prison, but when he floated some thoughts about "religionless Christianity" (280-82), he was resisting the idea that Christianity could be co-opted for any human purpose. That is why he said he spoke freely of God to unbelievers, but felt uneasy about doing so in conversation with "religious people." If humanity had "come of age" — a notion that Bonhoeffer provisionally entertained — it was because humanity after the Enlightenment was able to see that "religion" no longer served its needs. This is a position taken by most of the intellectual leadership in the West today. Therefore, the more that Christians recognize the irreligious nature of their faith in the sense meant here, the more we will recommend the *skandalon* of the gospel, which overturns our notions of our needs altogether through the irreligious "word of the cross" (I Cor. 1:18).

3. When John Calvin wrote *The Institutes of Christian Religion,* the post-Enlightenment issues pressing upon Bonhoeffer lay in the future. Calvin would have agreed with the definition of religion given here, however, because he wrote that "the human mind is a perpetual forge of idols" (*Institutes* 1.11.8).

4. Throughout this book, the use of the terms "religion" and "religious" will be informed by the critiques of Ludwig Feuerbach (*The Essence of Christianity,* 1841) and Sigmund Freud (*The Future of an Illusion,* 1927), both of whom, from their different perspectives, defined religion as a purely human construction. Robert Jenson considers this in his chapter "The Identification of God": "The true God knows we project our values on to him and so conceive of him idolatrously, and is unmoved by our childishness. He is intent on giving us new values and contravening our identity" (*Systematic Theology,* vol. 1, *The Triune God* [New York: Oxford University Press, 1997], 53).

the crucifixion as a means of execution, he says, that would normally cause shame for anyone associated with the victim. Paul is quite specific about this in the Corinthian letter. "It pleased God through the *folly* of what we preach to save those who believe," Paul writes. "We preach Christ crucified, a *stumbling block* to Jews and *folly* to Gentiles. . . . For the *foolishness* of God is wiser than men, and the *weakness* of God is stronger than men" (I Cor. 1:21, 23, 25). The words here italicized are piled up by Paul to remind the Corinthian Christians of the scandalous nature of the faith they claim. The Christians in Corinth were a boastful group, full of pride in their supposed spiritual superiority. Their braggadocio is misplaced, Paul tells them, for the "word of the cross," in its very scandalousness, is the only legitimate ground for Christian confidence. Thus Paul, surely one who in his previous existence as Saul the Pharisee did not suffer fools gladly, robustly declares that he and his fellow apostles "are fools for Christ's sake" (I Cor. 4:10).

The Singularity of the Crucifixion of Christ

Now to be sure, the theme of divine foolishness expressed by Paul is found elsewhere in religion. This in itself is not peculiar to Paul's message. The utter uniqueness of the New Testament gospel is not the foolishness itself, but the linkage of holy foolishness to an actual historical event of government-sponsored torture and public execution — a happening, it must be emphasized, *without any spiritual overtones or redeeming religious features.* It is not easy to gain a hearing for this crucial point, because so much American Christianity today comes packaged as inspirational uplift — sunlit, backlit, or candlelit. Furthermore, we are so accustomed to seeing the cross functioning as a decoration that we can scarcely imagine it as an object of shame and scandal unless it is burned on someone's lawn. It requires a considerable effort of the imagination to enter into the first-century world of the Roman Empire so as to understand the degree of offensiveness attached to crucifixion as a method of execution.

We can begin with the oddity of the universally recognized signifier, "the crucifixion." It will help us to understand the uniqueness of Jesus' death if we can grasp the idiosyncrasy of this manner of speaking. There have been many famous deaths in world history; we might think of John F. Kennedy, or Marie Antoinette, or Cleopatra, but we do not refer to "the assassination," "the guillotining," or "the poisoning." Such references would be incomprehensible. The use of the term "the crucifixion" for the execution of Jesus shows that it still retains a privileged status. When we speak of "the crucifixion," even in this secular age, many people will know what is meant. There is something in the strange death of the man identified as Son of God that continues to command special attention. *This* death, *this* execution, above and beyond all others, continues to have universal reverberations. Of no other death in human history can this be said. The cross of Jesus stands alone in this regard; it is *sui generis*. There were many thousands of crucifixions in Roman times, but only the crucifixion of Jesus is remembered as having any significance at all, let alone world-transforming significance.[5]

Thinking about the deaths of other famous people will illuminate this point further. Genuine martyrs, like Bonhoeffer, are raised in death to a level of sanctity and fame they could not have had in life. Similarly, the premature deaths of glamorous figures such as Eva Peron, John Lennon, and Diana Spencer convey upon them a permanent aura of mystical stardom. Jesus' death, however, is not like any of these. Even people who do not believe in Jesus, or who have only the most tenuous knowledge of Christianity, will have some residual impression that Jesus' death, unlike that of other martyrs and victims, is supposed to have an extra degree of significance. Attenuated though our knowledge of Christian theology might have become, we still retain a memory that his death by crucifixion was thought to have some sort of unrepeatable significance. From that unique event, the deaths of his followers drew their own consequent meaning.

An Appeal to the Reader

It is remarkable that there has been no major study of the crucifixion specifically for pastors and lay students since John Stott's *The Cross of Christ*, published in 1986. Much has happened on the interpretive front since then. The writing of this volume began eighteen years ago, when the concept of the death of Christ as an atoning substitution had been under attack for some time.[6] Since then, the atmosphere surrounding this motif has become

---

5. It is recorded that several thousand slaves were crucified after the failed rebellion of Spartacus, but we do not know the name of a single victim.

6. In certain Protestant circles, as Green and Baker point out, the penal substitution model has been hallowed by long use and has had no real competition until recently (Joel B. Green and Mark D. Baker, *Recovering the Scandal of the Cross: Atonement in New Testament and Contemporary Contexts* [Downers Grove, Ill.: InterVarsity, 2000], 23-26). However, this consensus is breaking down even in circles where it has long been regnant, partly because of pressure from the academy, partly (and unfortunately) because of widespread lack of interest in doctrinal matters, but perhaps mostly — and rightly — because critiques of the *exclusive* and *rigidly schematic* use of this model have begun to hit home.

even more heated. An active and sometimes even belligerent opposition has probably been a factor in widespread losses in the preaching and teaching of the cross. A number of significant books and essays about the theme of atonement have appeared in recent years, many of them highly critical of the "substitutionary atonement" and "penal substitution."[7] A person familiar with this perspective may very well glance through the present volume and decide to read no further, believing that it is just one more defense of the theme of substitution. This would be a serious misapprehension concerning the author's intent, which is to deal seriously with the entire spectrum of biblical imagery and theological interpretation.

The reader is therefore asked to consider this volume in its totality and not draw premature conclusions about its theological bias. Its most important goals are to expand the discussion about what happened on the cross of Christ and to encourage the return of that subject to the center of Christian proclamation.

This volume is designed for potential readers both lay and ordained, Catholic and Protestant, of all denominations. The subject itself transcends all boundaries. The book is perhaps most particularly directed to busy pastors who are burdened with duties yet serious about preaching the gospel and seeking help for their sermons. It is also for inquiring laypeople who want to understand their faith better and might read portions of this book either individually or in study groups. It may be useful for theological seminary students in introductory courses. Most of all, it should speak to the reader who is drawn to the figure on the cross but does not quite know what to make of him.

Worldwide Christianity faces a portentous array of challenges. Many voices from within the church are calling for a complete recasting of the foundations to suit the new era. This is often accompanied by expressions of disdain for those who still find the traditional forms a source of vitality. The traditionalists, on the other hand, are frequently discovered doing variations on the old circle-the-wagons maneuver. On the ecclesiastical left, self-righteousness and cultural trendiness for its own sake are constant dangers; on the right, reaction and fear are often the principal motivations. Lines are therefore drawn where engagement would be more profitable.

In the current theological struggle, many people are being hurt. Much damage is done by stereotyping, labeling, and pigeonholing. This is often

---

7. A helpful overview of recent publications is given by Michael Hardin in "Out of the Fog: New Horizons for Atonement Theory," in *Stricken by God? Nonviolent Identification and the Victory of Christ,* ed. Brad Jersak and Michael Hardin (Grand Rapids: Eerdmans, 2007), 54-77.

noted and lamented, but there have been few effective antidotes. A serious effort needs to be made by all parties to understand the nuances of the positions of others. Struggling to understand another's perspective so as to engage it sympathetically and accurately is a Christian action. The argument of this book will be polemical at various points, to be sure, but its purpose is to make a contribution to the conversation and to continue it, not to repel those who may hold otherwise — let alone those who have not made up their minds.

The Role of Sympathetic Imagination

One of the most respected Protestant theologians of his generation, William C. Placher, has written of the complications involved in interpreting the crucifixion. In an article about the theme of the cross as substitution or exchange, he offers an anecdote from his own experience that he hopes will illustrate what Christ has accomplished and then writes, in some frustration, *"I do not know how to make this story, or for that matter any purely human story, work."*[8]

As Placher well knew, there is no analogy from the side of the fallen creation that "works." None of the symbols, images, motifs, and themes "work" in any logical way, either as analogies or as theories to explain what God in Christ is doing on the cross. They are figures of speech, and as such require imagination and participation. As people of faith, we do not *interpret* them so much as we *inhabit* them — and indeed, as Scot McKnight points out, they inhabit us.[9] The truest way to receive the gospel of Christ crucified is to cultivate a deep appreciation of the way the biblical motifs interact with each other and enlarge one another.

In the final analysis, specialized theological knowledge can take us only so far; we need to know the *story*. The revered American writer Joseph Mitchell was raised in the church in the South and knew its language. In the last decades of his life he attended Grace Church in New York with some frequency. He told a group of parishioners of a conversation he had with his dying sister in North Carolina.[10] As he sat by her bedside, she asked him, "Buddy, what

8. William C. Placher, "Christ Takes Our Place: Rethinking Atonement," *Interpretation* 53, no. 1 (January 1999): 13.

9. Scot McKnight, *A Community Called Atonement* (Nashville: Abingdon, 2007), 37. I am indebted to Robert Dean for pointing me to this reference.

10. A year before he died, Joseph Mitchell gave me permission to tell this story.

does Jesus' death on the cross a long time ago have to do with my sins now?" Mitchell, who was an instinctive theologian though certainly not a trained one, struggled to find the right words, as you would expect a meticulous writer to do, and finally said, with his characteristic occasional stammer, "S-s-somehow, he was our representative." Academic inquiry must hold its peace for a moment in the space between that question and that response.

Joseph Mitchell and his sister were, in a sense, better readers of the Bible than many highly trained scholars, because her question and his answer were wrenched out of their guts, not coolly considered in a classroom. Yet the work of scholars is necessary also, because there has to be analysis. It was necessary for Joseph Mitchell to say something to his sister. The story of salvation is not "beyond words." The New Testament is from beginning to end a living witness to the apostolic preaching. The cross was meant to be preached. In every new generation, the various theories will be examined again as more people come up against the question for themselves: *What does Jesus' death on the cross a long time ago have to do with us now?*

Much depends upon our response to the scriptural word-pictures. Imaginative writers like Mitchell spend their whole lives in the world of open-ended and fluid metaphors.[11] The Old and New Testaments give us images — drawn from many sources — making a kaleidoscopic, inexhaustibly rich storehouse from which to draw meaning and sustenance for all times and all generations. No one image can do justice to the whole; all are part of the great drama of salvation. The Passover lamb, the goat driven into the wilderness, the ransom, the substitute, the victor on the field of battle, the representative man — each and all of these and more have their place, and the cross is diminished if any one of them is omitted. We need to make room for *all* the biblical images. We will be best enriched by the meaning of the crucifixion in *all* its manifold aspects, not just as an intellectual construct, but as dynamic, living truth empowering us for the living of these days.

The Need for Interpretation

The action of God in the cross of Christ has elicited various theories because the New Testament speaks about it in various ways. Take, for example, a seemingly simple sentence like this: "Walk in love, as Christ loved us and

11. Mitchell was not at all unhappy when reviewers interpreted his descriptions of the bottoms of rivers and the abandoned, empty rooms of hotels as descents into the depths of the unconscious.

gave himself up for us, a fragrant offering and sacrifice to God" (Eph. 5:2). This lovely verse is known to many churchgoers because it is often said at the time of the offering. Its words and rhythms are so familiar to some of us that we do not really stop to think about them. In the context of a search for an explanation of Jesus' death, however, such a verse calls for closer examination. Why did Christ "give himself up for us"? To whom was this "offering" made? What did this "sacrifice" accomplish, if anything? When we contemplate Jesus on the cross on Good Friday, what do we see? There is no dramatic rescue scene in view. Jesus does not seem to be taking anyone's place. There is no obvious reason for his being where he is. All indications are that he is suffering a penalty for something *he did not do;* that much is clear. But what would lead us to conclude that he was being punished on behalf of someone else? Why does Jesus need to be sacrificed in the first place, and why, in the words of the familiar verse from Ephesians, is he being sacrificed *for us?*

Many Christians would say, repeating words they have often heard, that the death of Jesus on the cross shows us how much God loves us. This is plainly stated in Ephesians 5:2 and in many other places in the New Testament. Jesus himself says in the Gospel of John, "Greater love has no man than this, that a man lay down his life for his friends" (John 15:13). But why would it be necessary for God's Son to die *in such a peculiarly horrible way* in order to show us this greater love? This is a question of surpassing importance and must not be waved aside.

Faith Seeking Understanding

Since Anselm of Canterbury at the turn of the first millennium, and especially since the Reformation, the history of the church has been marked by disputes about the message of the crucifixion. This state of affairs is a sign that something is amiss. There have been times when groups of Christians — especially Protestants of an evangelical persuasion — have rated themselves genuine or false by adherence to, or rejection of, a given "theory" of what happened in Christ's death. This is a difficult stance to maintain, since the great church councils that succeeded in defining the nature of Christ and the Holy Trinity left us with no equivalent conciliar definition of the cross.[12] This fact in itself is suggestive. Does anyone think that the great minds of the early church were

---

12. Jaroslav Pelikan, *The Christian Tradition: A History of the Development of Doctrine,* vol. 1, *The Emergence of the Catholic Tradition (100-600)* (Chicago: University of Chicago Press, 1971), 141.

not up to the challenge? It seems wiser to posit that there is a reason for the silence of the sources in this respect, and that the reason favors a multifaceted understanding rather than favoring one theory over against another.

Our chief witness for this case is the Bible itself. Ironically, it is precisely because of the rich variety of the biblical testimony that a number of interpretive "theories" and "models" have grown up around the cross. A significant number of evangelical Christians still insist upon one version or another of the "penal substitution" theory. Anselm of Canterbury's "satisfaction" theory is well known and often attacked; it will be discussed at length in the bridge between chapters 3 and 4. Gustav Aulén, in his classic work on the atonement called *Christus Victor,* rejected the suspiciously rationalistic word "theory" altogether, preferring the terms "motif" and "idea."[13]

Indeed, "theory" is a poor word to choose when seeking to understand the testimony of the Bible.[14] The Old and New Testaments do not present theories at any time.[15] Instead, we find stories, images, metaphors, symbols, sagas, sermons, songs, letters, poems. It would be hard to find writing that is less theoretical. Even Paul, perhaps the most intellectually gifted of the biblical writers, is highly contextual and unsystematic in his presentation of the Christian gospel. This does not mean that there is no thinking to be done. Rather, what we are seeking here is a creative balance between doctrine and artistry, responding not only to the problems put by the biblical text but also to its narrative structure, poetry, and language. The phrase of Anselm, *fides quaerens intellectum* (faith seeking understanding), still speaks to us today.[16] The work of theology is the process by which the church continually rethinks its message.[17]

The terms "motif," "theme," and "image" will therefore be used more or less interchangeably in order to emphasize the metaphorical power of the biblical language rather than force it into a rationalist, reductionist approach. Stephen Sykes, in his examination of the atonement, shows us how to analyze without losing the poetry. "Theories arise because there are questions

13. These topics will be discussed in chaps. 11; 3–4; and 9 respectively.

14. Hans Urs von Balthasar writes, "Our aim is not to erect a system, for the Cross explodes all systems" (*Theo-Drama: Theological Dramatic Theory* [San Francisco: Ignatius, 1994], 4:319). His title "theo-drama" encapsulates what we are saying here.

15. References to biblical "principles," often made in conservative evangelical circles, are equally unsuitable.

16. A widely used introduction to systematic theology by Daniel L. Migliore is called *Faith Seeking Understanding* (Grand Rapids: Eerdmans, 1991).

17. "Systematic theology is the Church's continuing communal effort *to think through* her mission of speaking the gospel" (Jenson, *Systematic Theology,* 1:22, emphasis added).

to be asked," he writes, and therefore theories do "have explanatory value." In a charming understatement, he writes, "What God did about human sin is . . . extremely surprising," and therefore requires explication. Sykes seeks to do this, however, by emphasizing wide-ranging imagery rather than theory. He refers to related biblical passages as "hints and suggestions," using the example of song with its "snatches." He has, furthermore, chosen to frame his argument in the form of narrative, calling his book *The Story of Atonement*.[18]

God

*Christ*ology is reflection on the past, present, and future of Jesus the Messiah (*Christos* in Greek). Such reflection is necessary for the discussion of his crucifixion. It would be a mistake, however, if this book were construed exclusively as Christology. It is a *theo*logy of the cross (*theos* — God; *logos* — word or speech). When we talk about the cross, we are not talking exclusively about Jesus, but about *God*.

A fundamental problem is that it is not at all clear exactly who God is. We have not become a secular society so much as we have become a generically religious one. Undifferentiated spiritual objects, therapies, and programs are widely marketed. Popular religion in America tends to be an amalgam of whatever presents itself. Discerning observers have noted that these new forms of spirituality are typically American; highly individualistic, self-referential, and self-indulgent, they are only feebly related to the history or tradition of any of the great world faiths.[19] There is no more important calling for the church in our time than claiming the self-identification of the God who is the Father of the Lord Jesus Christ.

Who, then, is this God of whom we speak? The following three points are listed in the chronological order of the biblical history of Israel and the church.

First, God is the God of Abraham, Isaac, and Jacob.[20] This is God's own

---

18. Stephen Sykes, *The Story of Atonement*, Trinity and Truth Series (London: Darton, Longman, and Todd, 1997), 50 and passim. Among recent treatments, Bruce Longenecker has drawn out the narrative structure of Paul's letters in *Narrative Dynamics in Paul*, as has A. Katherine Grieb in *The Story of Romans*.

19. Towns in northern India where Tibetan refugees have settled must endure an influx of "spiritual tourists" from the West. A Tibetan Buddhist leader complained, "When I listen to these people, I have to laugh. Buddhism is a fad to them" (Stephen Kinzer, "As the World Heals, Tibet's Exiles Feel Forsaken," *New York Times*, June 24, 1999).

20. I have given much thought to the current trend toward calling God the God of "Abra-

self-identification: this is the way God chooses to be known. "[God] said [to Moses], 'I am the God of your father, the God of Abraham, the God of Isaac, and the God of Jacob'" (Exod. 3:6). As Robert Jenson has memorably written, "God is whoever raised Jesus from the dead, having before raised Israel from Egypt."[21] This is the God who established his covenant on Mount Sinai, who sent the prophets to announce the apocalyptic Day of the Lord, who preserved his people throughout the exile with the promise of a new covenant (Jer. 31:31). The particularity of this God is startling; the God of Israel aligns himself with specific mortals with individual names who live in identifiable places on the map. They have life stories unique to themselves, by no means always edifying. This God, unlike the gods of the religions, has chosen of his own sovereign free will to elect a discrete group of people simply because he wills to do so. The *irreligiousness* of this election is that it has nothing to do with any spiritual attainments by the chosen ones. The opposite is true — they are selected, we might say, in spite of themselves, for if there is one thing certain about the children of Israel, it is that they did not deserve their election. This factor of *undeserved election* is in view whenever God is called "the God of Abraham, Isaac, and Jacob."

Second, God is the God who is revealed most fully and definitively in the crucifixion and resurrection of Jesus of Nazareth. The interlocking, twofold nature of this definitive event displays the uniqueness of the God proclaimed in the Bible. Resurrection in and of itself was not unheard of; after all, gods who died and rose again were ubiquitous in the ancient Near East.[22] The

---

ham and Sarah, [Isaac and Rebecca, Jacob and Rachel]." There are a number of problems with this. What about Hagar? and how to fit in Leah? For that matter, the twelve tribes of Israel are descended also from Bilhah and Zilpah (Gen. 35:25-26). When we reflect upon these complications, the simplicity of "Abraham, Isaac, and Jacob" may come as a relief. There are many places in Scripture where women are given a place of startling prominence by any standard, let alone the standards of that culture and time. It is not necessary to force them artificially into the given name of God; there are other ways of emphasizing the equality of men and women in the story of salvation (we need far more sermons and teachings on Deborah, Miriam, Abigail, Ruth, Esther, as well as the numerous less well-known women of the New Testament). Jesus himself, with his well-documented regard for women, nevertheless repeats God's Old Testament name without qualification: "Have you not read what was said to you by God, 'I am the God of Abraham, and the God of Isaac, and the God of Jacob'?" (Matt. 22:31). I am sorry to disappoint anyone, but I do not wish to go beyond the name given by Jesus to his Father.

21. Jenson, *Systematic Theology*, 1:63.

22. The myth of the dying and rising god under various names — Attis, Tammuz, Osiris — was one of the most prominent features of the numerous mystery religions of antiquity. The all-important difference between these deaths and Jesus' is that his happened as a certifiable event within history. The gods of the Near Eastern religions "died" and "rose" repeatedly as part of the natural cycle of nature. The death of the god was never presented as a historical

unique feature of the Christian proclamation is the shocking claim that God is fully acting, not only in Jesus' resurrected life, but *especially in Jesus' death on the cross*. To say the same thing in another way, the death of Jesus in and of itself would not be anything remarkable. What is remarkable is that *the Creator of the universe is shown forth in this gruesome death*.

Third, God is the triune God. He is one God in three persons: Father, Son, and Holy Spirit. Jesus of Nazareth was not a free-floating holy man. If he is not the second person of the Trinitarian Godhead and the only-begotten Son attested in the Nicene Creed, then God's self was not directly involved at Golgotha. In that case, Jesus would be detached from the eternal plan of God shown forth in the history of Israel, and the cross would be a random event of no more than passing interest.[23] Many people are attracted to contemporary attempts to depict the human Jesus without realizing the price we pay for cutting Jesus loose from the Christology of the early church councils. The Chalcedonian Definition remains the measure by which we test our proposals: Jesus was *both* fully divine *and* fully human, but if the fully human Jesus is not God incarnate, then salvation is not from God after all. To be sure, the doctrine of the Trinity is a notoriously complex subject, and the church has not helped by encouraging its clergy and people to dismiss it as though it were a useless abstraction. One of the happier theological trends of our time is the current revival of interest in talking about and worshiping God as triune.[24] The Christ event derives its meaning from the fact that the

---

event. This is a widely researched phenomenon in studies of the ancient Near East; a recent study is Tryggve N. D. Mettinger, *The Riddle of Resurrection: "Dying and Rising Gods" in the Ancient Near East* (Stockholm: Almqvist & Wiksell, 2001).

23. The here-today gone-tomorrow books that have been written in recent decades proposing Passover plots, faked deaths, last-minute substitutions, Judas-centered conspiracies, Zealotry gone wrong, etc., are good examples of "passing interest."

24. It is not possible within the scope of this book to go into a full discussion of the revived debate about the economic versus immanent Trinity. However, the doctrine of three persons in one is indissolubly related to soteriology (from *soteria*, "salvation"). Is it really *God* who saves us in Jesus Christ? The way to speak of both the immanent and the economic Trinity at the same time is to say "Father, Son, and Holy Spirit." The name of the Trinity incorporates them both. It's the way God is in himself (immanent), and the way he is toward us (economic). One of the currently popular substitutes for the name of the Trinity, "Creator, Redeemer, Sustainer," cannot serve this function because God does not create, redeem, or sustain himself. These terms describe God in relation to us but not within himself, so God's being *(ousia)* is not affirmed. When we say "Father, Son, and Holy Spirit," however, we are saying that what God is in himself, he also is toward us. The doctrine of the Trinity is therefore a working out of what it means to say that God is love. It tells us that God is love within his own three-personed self, and he is love toward us as we see his action in the Son's incarnation, crucifixion, and resurrection. As Catherine LaCugna writes, "The whole point of the original doctrine of the Trinity was that

three-personed God is directly acting as one throughout the entire sequence from incarnation to ascension to Last Judgment.

The Word of the Cross as Power

It is Paul the apostle who, most explicitly, insists upon the cross as the central content of the gospel. The first two chapters of I Corinthians are at the heart of our subject. Paul is concerned because the behavior of the Corinthians does not correspond to their vaunted faith. He seeks to recall them to their foundation in the gospel of Christ crucified (1:17; 2:2). The cross, he forthrightly declares, is indeed an offense *(skandalon)* and foolishness to those who wish to escape from it, as the Corinthians do. He draws a contrast between the two ways that the gospel is received: "*The word of the cross* is folly to those who are perishing, but to us who are being saved it is the power of God" (1:18). We will deal with this important verse in more detail later, but here we take up the phrase "the word *(logos)* of the cross." This is odd phraseology. Why doesn't Paul just say "the cross"? Perhaps it will be clearer if we translate, "the preaching of the cross." The problems in the Corinthian church are manifold, but Paul believes that the underlying difficulty is their neglect of the preaching of the cross. There is a presupposition behind Paul's use of the term "word of the cross" that needs to be spelled out.

When the power of the apostolic preaching first exploded upon the world scene, it was anchored in an event already past, but its meaning was not imprisoned there. When Paul writes, "The word of the cross is the power of God," he means that God is present and powerful specifically *in the message.* He writes further in the same letter, "Just as we have borne the image of the man of dust, we shall also bear the image of the man of heaven" (15:49). With this, Paul shows that in the cross and resurrection the death of Adam, the man of dust who represents us all, is assimilated to the future of Jesus, the man of heaven who represents us all *that much more,* thus guaranteeing our future with God. This *past-future* dialectic has everything to do with ethical life *in the present,* so that Paul concludes his letter with these words: "*Therefore,* my beloved brethren, be steadfast, immovable, always abounding in the work of the Lord, knowing that in the Lord your labor is not in vain" (15:58).

God (God's *ousia*) simply does not exist except as three persons. Vice versa, the divine persons are not other than the divine *ousia,* they *are* the *ousia*" (*God for Us: The Trinity and Christian Life* [San Francisco: HarperSanFrancisco, 1993], 369). God's inner being or essence *(ousia)* is interrelational, intradynamic, interpersonal. In other words, "God is love" (I John 4:16).

Here is an important distinction with far-reaching implications for Christian behavior. The deeds of Christians in this present time — however insignificant they may seem, however "vain" they may appear to those who value worldly success — are already being built into God's advancing kingdom. In other words, Christians do not simply look to the cross of Christ with prayerful reverence. We are set in motion by its power, energized by it, upheld by it, guaranteed by it, secured by it for the promised future because it is the power of the creating Word that "gives life to the dead and calls into existence the things that do not exist" (Rom. 4:17). Our labor is not only "not in vain" but also has eternal significance because it is being built into God's future in ways that we presently see "through a glass, darkly," but in the fullness of time, "face to face" (I Cor. 13:12 KJV).

The Word of the Cross as *Skandalon*

There is a dearth of preaching and teaching about the cross in both mainline and evangelical churches, and the twenty-first-century emergent church in its various manifestations also tends to lean away from the cross.[25] In view

25. The term "mainline" will be used throughout to denote the Protestant denominations that were foremost in the United States until the mid-1950s. The principal ones are the Presbyterian Church (PCUSA), the United Church of Christ (UCC), the United Methodist Church (UMC), the Evangelical Lutheran Church in America (ELCA), and the Episcopal Church in the United States (TEC). Other groups would be the American Baptist Churches in the USA, the Evangelical Covenant Church, the Reformed Church in America (RCA), the Christian Reformed Church (CRC), and a few others; in this book the first five are generally meant. The term "evangelical" as applied to churches is much harder to define. In Europe, it used to mean simply "Protestant," whereas in the United States it has a more political connotation and can sometimes (not always) tilt toward fundamentalism. Not all evangelicals in America are "conservative," however; a significant number are "liberal" or even "radical," who identify themselves as politically left-wing while being committed to the Bible and to classical Christianity. In this volume, "evangelicals" will ordinarily be used sociopolitically to identify a party within the larger church in the United States. The African American churches, as we will have frequent opportunity to observe, are to some extent in a class by themselves and do not really fit into any of the above groups. Likewise, the presence and power of the Pentecostal churches should be acknowledged; these churches are making an increasing contribution to biblical theology (Gordon Fee and Amos Yong in particular). It is too early to discern what sort of impact the loose confederation called "the emerging church" will have.

That is the Protestant landscape. The Roman Catholic Church, while beset with controversy to be sure, can still be identified and discussed as itself *per se* without reference to its factions (a fact much to be envied). The same is largely true of the Orthodox, certainly in comparison to Protestantism. These branches of Christendom will not be ignored in these pages, though the Protestant influence will predominate. Since all three branches have inherited the same apostolic

of the unique significance of the crucifixion at the heart of Christian faith, it is not entirely clear why this should be so. One reason, however, is surely related to controversies about its interpretation, which undermine the confidence of those who would proclaim it.

Paul was also affected by the unease, if not outright hostility, of those who heard his preaching. As noted earlier, he felt called upon to say, "I am not ashamed of the gospel; it is the power of God for salvation" (Rom. 1:16). These words reflect Paul's proactive stance vis-à-vis his critics. According to the apostle's Corinthian correspondence, there was something about the gospel of a crucified Messiah that attracted the scorn of the worldly and the sophisticated. This was true not only of those without but also of those *within* the church — the Corinthian congregation in particular. Therefore, it is to the Corinthian church that he writes to defend his cross-centered preaching in these foundational words:

> For the word of the cross is folly to those who are perishing, but to us who are being saved it is the power of God. For it is written, "I will destroy the wisdom of the wise, and the cleverness of the clever I will thwart." Where is the wise man? Where is the scribe? Where is the debater of this age? Has not God made foolish the wisdom of the world? For since, in the wisdom of God, the world did not know God through wisdom, it pleased God through the folly of what we preach to save those who believe. For Jews demand signs and Greeks seek wisdom, but we preach Christ crucified, a stumbling block to Jews and folly to Gentiles, but to those who are called, both Jews and Greeks, Christ the power of God and the wisdom of God. For the foolishness of God is wiser than men, and the weakness of God is stronger than men. (I Cor. 1:18-25)

There is something disingenuous about this, since Paul himself was a trained scholar, supremely competent to discern stupidity. However, he is deadly serious in what he says about wisdom and foolishness, and this should actually increase our appreciation for his courage. To become an apostle to the Gentiles, he had to turn away from his rarefied existence as a leader among the religious elite to a life of almost unimaginable danger and affliction as he traveled the world over, preaching Christ crucified to people of every sort, including slaves and those at the bottom of the socioeconomic heap.[26]

---

and patristic traditions, we are bound together in spite of ourselves, a cause for thanksgiving in the midst of our "unhappy divisions" (1928 Book of Common Prayer, 37).

26. See especially I Cor. 4:8-13; II Cor. 1:8-10; 4:8-12; 6:4-10; 11:23-29. It was the Corin-

This extraordinary aspect of Paul's apostolate is not always sufficiently appreciated. As he says himself, he was not only "a Hebrew born of Hebrews" (Phil. 3:5) but also an intellectual of the highest order, so it was no small thing for him to move out of his comfort zone. Not only did he put his life on the line repeatedly, but more to the present point, he cut his ties with the Jewish intelligentsia to become an evangelist of the crucified Christ in the midst of a helter-skelter assortment of converts, many from the very dregs of society. When we think of ancient Rome, our imaginations are engaged by members of the upper classes, the emperors and senators. We have not been taught to envision the miseries of the "head count," the landless masses of the Roman Empire, who were less than nothing to the lordly rulers of that society.[27] The modern reader needs to bear this in mind when reading Paul's words: "Consider your call, brethren; not many of you were wise according to worldly standards, not many were powerful, not many were of noble birth; but God chose what is foolish in the world to shame the wise, God chose what is weak in the world to shame the strong" (I Cor. 1:26-27).

This is no light thing for Paul to say. He possessed the great distinction of being a Roman citizen, and we know from Philippians that Paul could be vain about his status: "If any other man thinks he has reason for confidence in the flesh, I have more" (Phil. 3:4). In the Spirit of the crucified Lord, however, he wrestled himself down from this superior position: "But whatever gain I had, I counted as loss for the sake of Christ. Indeed I count everything as loss because of the surpassing worth of knowing Christ Jesus my Lord. For his sake I have suffered the loss of all things, and count them as dung, in order that I may gain Christ and be found in him" (3:7-9).

Any person seeking to understand and expound the meaning of the cross today must undergo a similar divestment. The "worldly standards" referred to by Paul are no longer useful in the new era of the Lordship of Christ. Something has happened that has changed everything. In the words of the apostle's celebrated christological passage in Philippians 2:7-8: "[He] emptied himself, taking the form of a slave *(doulos)*, being born in the like-

---

thian congregation with its elitist, escapist bent that needed to hear about what Paul and his fellow apostles endured for their sake.

27. The "head count" (Latin *capite censi*) is the Roman equivalent of the Greek *hoi polloi*. The great orator and writer Cicero owned a run-down *insula* (apartment block). We tend to think of Cicero as our humane contemporary, but he and his contemporary Crassus, who owned many *insulae*, may have deserved the designation "slum landlord." This gives us an inkling of the remarkable appeal of early Christianity to those who were invisible to the upper classes. See Neil Elliott, *The Arrogance of Nations: Reading Romans in the Shadow of Empire* (Minneapolis: Fortress, 2008), 36-40.

ness of men. And being found in human form he humbled himself and became obedient unto death, even death on a cross."

This final phrase, "even death on a cross," was probably inserted by Paul into a confession that was already in circulation. He wants to emphasize the *skandalon* of the crucifixion. This was not a popular topic in Paul's time, and it is not a popular topic today. This is hard to understand, especially in view of Paul's declarations, "I decided to know nothing among you except Jesus Christ and him crucified" (I Cor. 2:2) and "Far be it from me to glory except in the cross of our Lord Jesus Christ, by which the world has been crucified to me, and I to the world" (Gal. 6:14). It sometimes seems as though the church has willfully decided to ignore the radical content of such passages, concentrating instead on a more generic, less offensive interpretation of Jesus' death — for example, "Jesus died to show how much he loved us." That is true, certainly, but it has a bland sound and falls far short of accounting for the particular horror of crucifixion. The question this raises is this: On the cross, was Jesus was simply "showing" us something, or was something actually *happening?* This question will be a major factor in our discussion.

The Necessity of Interpretation

Paul's argument is that the preaching and teaching of the "word of the cross" cannot be done without offense. The four Gospels, each in its own way, make the same point by depicting the hostility that Jesus evoked on his way to his trial and execution. The challenge is to understand *why* his death is offensive, and what this signifies. The event demands explanation. In a few striking sentences, Joel D. Green and Mark D. Baker declare that the death of Christ was so dissonant that it could not be simply appropriated. They cite the story of the two disciples on the road to Emmaus to show that *the crucifixion does not easily explain itself and requires interpretation:* "The death of Jesus on a Roman cross was an event that lacked within itself a self-evident, unambiguous interpretation. [The two disciples'] affect and their words together communicate the presumed incongruity between the nature of Jesus' ministry and the manner of his end. . . . In the early decades of the Christian movement, the *scandal* of the cross was far more self-evident than was its *meaning.*"[28]

What is the universal, world-transforming significance of the crucifixion? It is not self-evident. Anyone visiting a museum and listening to the comments

---

28. Green and Baker, *Recovering the Scandal,* 11, 15, emphasis added.

of visitors looking at paintings of Jesus on the cross will learn that visual depictions of the event are ambiguous. In a secular culture, there is no way for people to understand what is going on with that figure in the painting, cruelly pinned to the wooden posts. If one looks at a painting of — for instance — the crucifixion of Saint Andrew, this becomes clear. Except for the fact that Andrew's cross is in the shape of an X, the viewer cannot notice any significant difference between one crucifixion and another. Why should portrayals of the death of Jesus have more resonance than depictions of the deaths of others? Ultimately no painting, no movie, no television program can explain the saving significance to us; we must hear the words of the Bible in faith. This is, or should be, a primary goal of Christian preaching and teaching.[29] The cross of Christ does not interpret itself by itself. Indeed, as some of the Protestant traditions recognize, the symbol of a cross *per se* can all too readily become a mere token or amulet leading to superstition and magical thinking. Even worse, when detached from its significance, it can and often has become a sign denoting allegiance to a cause that mocks the very One who died in that way — the cross of Constantine, the Crusaders, and the Ku Klux Klan.

The Trinity, the Cross, and the Word of God

The scandalous "word of the cross" is God's own Word. The link between scandal and God is in itself irreligious; this is another aspect of the uniqueness of the Christian message. The word of the cross is, moreover, the Word of God in three persons — a notion as offensive to the uninitiated intellect as is the spectacle of a crucified God to the religious sensibility. Nothing less than the Holy Trinity — Father, Son, and Holy Spirit — is at work in the event of the "word of the cross," bringing the past event of crucifixion into the present (as in Gal. 3:1) with the same cosmic power that brought the creation itself into being *ex nihilo* — out of nothing. The word of the Father (Gen. 1:3), the Son as Word and agent of the creation (John 1:3; Heb. 1:2), the descent of the Son into the world in the form of a slave (Phil. 2:7), the Spirit giving life (Ezek. 37:9-10; John 3:5-7; Acts 4:31) — all this is happening

---

29. I do not wish to retract this point, but at the same time I acknowledge (and repudiate) the hint of Pelagianism. Karl Barth is entirely right when he writes, "He [Christ] speaks for Himself whenever He is spoken of and His story is told and heard. *It is not He that needs proclamation but proclamation that needs Him.* He . . . makes it possible. He makes Himself its origin and object. He is its basis and truth and power" (*Church Dogmatics* IV/1 [Edinburgh: T. & T. Clark, 1956], 227, emphasis added). In other words, although the cross calls for interpretation, it is the Spirit that does the interpreting through the human agent.

in Jesus' cross and resurrection. It is God's new creative act, his great reclamation project that is even greater than the creation itself, because whereas we are "wonderfully created," we are "yet more wonderfully restored."[30]

Understanding the cross and resurrection as *a single event,* undertaken from within the Trinity itself, is of utmost importance and will continue to inform the discussion throughout.[31] The scandalous "word of the cross" is not a human word. It is the Spirit-empowered presence of God in the preaching of the crucified One. The Holy Spirit, so central to New Testament writings as diverse as those of Paul, John, and the author of Acts, inhabits the message and empowers the speaker, so that the proclamation of God's act in Christ is the new occasion of creation, issuing from the Trinitarian power of the originating Word itself.

A commitment to the engendering Word of God is based upon a "high" view of the threefold Word. *First* and foremost, Jesus Christ himself is the incarnate Word; *second,* God's Word written as Holy Scripture is the trustworthy yet dynamic and explosive witness to God in Jesus Christ; and *third,* the preaching of the gospel is the Spirit-created event of the Word in the present moment.[32]

The "Word of the Cross": Not Passive but Active

The "word of the cross" was first heard in the preaching of the apostles. The early Christian preaching was like no other form of human speech ever heard before.[33] To understand the nature of gospel preaching, we need to under-

---

30. Book of Common Prayer (1979), Second Sunday after Christmas Day. Derived from the seventh-century Leonine Sacramentary.

31. F. W. Dillistone nicely calls the cross-resurrection event the "double-sided saving act" (*The Christian Understanding of Atonement* [Philadelphia: Westminster, 1968], 88).

32. It would be a misreading of the author's intent to think that this emphasis on the Word is meant as a diminution of the sacraments; indeed, the Lord's Supper has a major part in the very first chapter, and baptism is at the heart of the last two chapters. What is being proposed here, rather, is that the Word and sacraments are of equal and interlocking potency in an era when preaching has become less central in many churches. In the Episcopal Church, for example, the liturgical movement, with its emphasis on eucharistic ritual, has succeeded so well that biblical preaching has been increasingly devalued, being replaced by brief homilies. This encourages congregations to think that Scripture can be read almost mechanically, as though the mere recitation of the words were enough, without interpretation. In this incantatory view of the Word, there is insufficient understanding of the Word as an *event,* recurring with fresh power whenever it is expounded and heard in each new situation.

33. Amos N. Wilder, *Early Christian Rhetoric: The Language of the Gospel* (Peabody, Mass.:

stand the nature of the Scripture itself.[34] There is a fundamental syntactical distinction between saying "we question the Bible" and "the Bible questions us." It is common, in congregations, to hear of subjects like "Using the Bible in Small Groups." But we do not "use" the Bible; if we attempt to do so, it will slip away from us, leaving something opaque and very much less dynamic in its place. Contrary to the story line in many "spiritual" journals, the biblical narrative does not tell of our journey toward God; it is the other way around. The right approach is not "What questions do I have to ask of the Bible?" but *"What questions does the Bible have to ask of me?"* God does not wait for Adam to start looking for him; it is God who comes looking with the question, "Adam, where are you?" — the first words spoken to fallen humanity. God says to Job, "Gird up your loins like a man; I will question *you,* and you will answer *me."* God is the one who says, "I will shew thee great and mighty things, *which thou knowest not"* (Jer. 33:3 KJV).

In other words, the new understanding imparted by the Bible comes from *a source lying beyond our ability to frame questions.* Again, Jesus constantly displayed this coming-from-beyond quality in his own ministry, so that people said, "What is this? A new teaching!" (Mark 1:27). The message is that this Word is beyond human capacity and must be received from its Author. Nowhere is this more true than in the interpretation of that unthinkable event, the crucifixion of the Son of God by human agents.

In interpreting Scripture, therefore, we do our best to set aside our own presuppositions, insofar as we are able, coming before the text to hear it speaking to us, rather than the other way around. Wonders occur in groups that study the Bible together, because the Word has power to create a community of discovery that is much more than the mere sum of its individual parts. In the final analysis the Bible is intended to be read with faith — or, if not, at least with an openness to the idea that faith might happen, since faith is not a human achievement but a gift from God. One of William Stringfellow's enduring contributions to the church has been his exceptional grasp of the might of the Word to effect what it requires — as in his Romans class, which produced a Bible leader from a group of tough New York street

Hendrickson, 1999). A central thesis of Wilder's book is that "the speech of Jesus and his first followers broke into the world of speech and writing of their time . . . with a novel and powerful utterance" (9). His first chapter is entitled "The New Utterance." Wilder stresses the nature of the early Christian preaching as a "speech-event."

34. In a review of Northrop Frye's estimable *The Great Code,* the writer and critic Naomi Bliven, who happens to be Jewish, wrote: "The Bible is *kerygma* . . . its literary pretensions are secondary to the conviction of its authors that *it is revelation"* (*New Yorker,* May 31, 1982, emphasis added).

kids.[35] The gospel is not inert; it has power to evoke both faith and action. Thus, in Colossians 1:5-6, the Word is described not as the *content* of the apostles' preaching and mission, but as the *active agent,* the *subject* of the verbs: "the word of the truth, the gospel which has come to you, as indeed in the whole world it is bearing fruit and growing."

For these reasons the cross cannot be interpreted as though it were an ordinary or even an extraordinary historical event. The case of Jesus is in a class by itself. We can study the historical facts, ponder the motives of Pilate, debate the role of "the Jews," and propose alternative interpretations until the fourth millennium, and we will be no closer to the reasons for the utter uniqueness of this death. Paul writes in Romans 1:17 that the gospel is "revealed through faith for faith." This has never been an easy presupposition to defend. Like the "word of the cross" itself, the uncompromising nature of the Scriptures is a roadblock, a *skandalon* (I Cor. 1:23). Yet we cannot allow ourselves to be reduced to mumbling, "Well, you just have to take it on faith." We have evidence from within Scripture itself that scholarship, reflection, and wrestling with the text are part of our calling as God's people; the profound engagement of the Evangelists and apostles with their own received Hebrew Scriptures bears witness to this.

It remains true, however, that the Scriptures themselves are a scandal. How can we take this human book (which it is) seriously as the Word of God? Here we come up against the doctrine of revelation. The meaning of the life, death, and future of Jesus Christ has been entrusted to human witnesses. The whole enterprise of preaching is built on this trust in the witnesses. It is not always understood that the confidence of the biblical preacher, teacher, and witness is not personal arrogance. Such confidence arises out of the paradoxical faith in the sufficiency of God to override the insufficiency of human beings. As Paul wrote, "Who is sufficient for these things? For we are . . . commissioned by God[;] in the sight of God we speak in Christ" (II Cor. 2:16-17). In an earthier style, the African American preacher Johnny Ray Youngblood, whose lapses and deficiencies were well known to his con-

---

35. Stringfellow wrote about his experience of leading a group of Hispanic inner-city youths in a study of the Epistle to the Romans. First of all, though it is hard to imagine, he says that he simply had them read passages over and over. Eventually he asked them just one question: "What does this say?" Not, "Do you agree with this?" or "What does this mean to you?" or "How do you feel about this?" but simply, *What does this say?* (Stringfellow, *Count It All Joy: Reflections on Faith, Doubt, and Temptation* [Grand Rapids: Eerdmans, 1967], 62-72). Few are as confident in the power of the Word to speak for itself as the remarkably assured Mr. Stringfellow, but the unusual character of his best writings owes largely to his radical trust in the Word. His work is distinguished by its insistence on the Scriptures both as revelation and as power.

gregation, declares: "This thing [the Word of God] is a two-edged sword. It whips back and cuts the hell out of me and then comes forward and cuts y'all. And the truth of God's Word is not predicated on my lifestyle. It is predicated on God's word itself. He sends sinful men to preach to sinful men. I'm just another beggar, tellin' other beggars where to find bread."[36]

Interpreting "the Word of the Cross" by the Spirit

This book is being written at an auspicious moment in the history of biblical interpretation. We all owe a profound debt of gratitude to the generations of gifted, dedicated, and godly men and women who labored in the historical-critical school of interpretation. We will never again be able to work without their insights and tools. However, this method of explicating texts has probably taken us as far as it can take us.[37] There has been a marked shift in academia, little noted thus far by the ordinary person in the pew, but offering much hope for the ordained or lay Christian who is really interested in mining the Scripture for a faith that will stand the test of these times. In recent decades we have seen a turn toward a more literary style of interpretation that gives greater prominence to the text as it stands, and to the canon of Scripture as a whole, becoming more responsive to the "plain meaning" of the text as well as its metaphorical and rhetorical qualities.[38] This shift owes much to what is called "postmodernism," an admittedly shape-shifting but

---

36. Samuel G. Freedman, *Upon This Rock: The Miracles of a Black Church* (New York: HarperPerennial, 1994), 13.

37. I came through seminary at the precise moment (the mid-1970s) that this seismic shift was taking place. A few of the most important historical-critical scholars were able to see how significant this movement was, even though it meant they would have to turn away from much of what had been the bedrock of their work. A particularly impressive example is Raymond E. Brown, by any standard one of the giants of the historical-critical era, trained in the school of the great W. F. Albright. In his last major work, *The Death of the Messiah,* Brown demonstrated his range and freedom as a scholar by making a definitive turn toward the more literary approach of today. Reflecting on this in a later lecture at Fordham, he said, "I began to doubt the tools of my trade" (from my lecture notes, Fordham, March 8, 1984). Many, perhaps most, scholars of his generation were unable or unwilling to make such a shift. He was proud of having done so, because he believed it would benefit the church and the ordinary Christian in the pew, and he was annoyed that many who reviewed *The Death of the Messiah* did not notice the change in his approach (letter to the author, 1998).

38. It was not so long ago that ministers felt bound to instruct their congregations in the mysteries of J, E, and P; the Deuteronomic editor; Q; Proto-Luke; etc., as though these scholarly hypotheses were more interesting and important than the text itself.

important phenomenon that, though feared and resisted by many, has in fact assisted us as the professional scholars have begun to move away from "scientific" textual analysis to a far more productive appreciation of narrative, metaphor, imagery, and the canonical shape of the text. These contributions of postmodernism have brought us back in touch with our premodern forebears in faith, so that pastors today, unlike those of the recent past, may be found reading biblical commentary written fifteen hundred years ago.

One of the principal purposes of this book of "biblical theology at work," therefore, is to strengthen the nerve of preachers and teachers within the church, most especially in regard to preaching "the word of the cross." This volume is designed to honor the complexity of the New Testament witness while, at the same time, encouraging the reader to trust that the message of the crucified Lord is directed straight to every heart with the enabling and liberating power of the Holy Spirit. The meaning of the cross is not hidden from the simple. It is not an arcane subject fit only for scholars. No one needs to feel that he or she is cut off from the meaning of the text, for it is the Spirit, given to all believers, who will interpret. Here is another aspect of the *Trinitarian* nature of the word of the cross.[39]

The Relationship of the Four Gospels to One Another

To be sure, interpreting the story of the crucifixion responsibly will always be a challenging and subtle task. Each of the Evangelists presents it differently, with significant variations and even contradictions occurring among the four. When we add the voices of Paul and the author of Hebrews, we have a complex picture; Martin Hengel calls it "a multiplicity of approaches."[40] Concerning the differences, Raymond Brown gives this brief summary:

---

39. Nowhere is the work of the Spirit in interpretation more clearly delineated than in the Gospel of John. Jesus says to the disciples, "The [*parakletos*], the Holy Spirit, whom the Father will send in my name, he will teach you all things.... When the Spirit of truth comes, he will guide you into all the truth" (John 14:26; 16:13). This volume about the cross is therefore undertaken with hope and trust in this promise of the Lord that the Spirit will interpret all that belongs to Jesus. This project of interpretation and confirmation is undertaken by the three-personed God, and the importance of this is underscored by Jesus' repetition two verses later: "All that the Father has is mine; therefore I [the Son] said that he [the Spirit] will take what is mine and declare it to you" (16:15). Above all, the Spirit of the triune God is power — power to create interpreters with a new understanding that transcends that of all humanly established authorities (3:1-8; 14:26; 16:13-14).

40. Hengel, *The Atonement*, 53.

In the passion narratives of John and Luke one does not have the extreme turmoil, unanswered prayers, and abandonment by God found in Mark and Matthew. Jesus remains united with his Father. If one were to put gospel Christologies on a spectrum showing the extent to which they allow the human weakness or the divine power of Jesus to become apparent, Mark would be at one end and John at the other, and in between Matthew would be closer to Mark and Luke closer to John. Yet the portrayal of Jesus in John and in Luke is not the same. The Johannine Jesus does not manifest the forgiveness and healing bestowed by the Lukan Jesus; the Lukan Jesus does not exhibit the hauteur and the power evident in the Johannine Jesus.[41]

These variations present interesting challenges and opportunities for interpreters and preachers.[42] Many of the greatest preachers, whose sermons on the entire Bible have been collected, have managed to give full attention to the differing witnesses in ways that remain valuable today.[43] In the background, however, there always lies one overall perspective or another, which led Alexander McLaren, for instance, to skip over Romans 9–11 entirely. Every serious interpreter must sooner or later, consciously or unconsciously, decide whether to read Luke-Acts through the eyes of Paul, or Paul through the lens of Luke-Acts. In the pages that follow, the central purpose will be to expound the message about the cross as it was most radically defined by Paul, but refracted throughout all four Gospels and the other epistles as through a prism. As for the Fourth Gospel, John has a unique perspective on the cross as well as almost everything else. He emphasizes the completion of Christ's work as he dies ("It is finished" [John 19:30], superbly rendered by the Latin *consummatum est*). The view taken in this book is that while John is compatible, in varying degrees, both with Paul and with Luke-Acts, it retains a special christological authority unique to itself.

---

41. Raymond E. Brown, *The Death of the Messiah: From Gethsemane to the Grave; A Commentary on the Passion Narratives in the Four Gospels*, 2 vols. (Garden City, N.Y.: Doubleday, 1994), 90-91.

42. An impressive presentation of the crucifixion from the different perspectives of each Evangelist was given by New Testament scholar Joel Marcus from the pulpit of St. Mary's Cathedral in Glasgow on one Good Friday, published as *Jesus and the Holocaust: Reflections of Suffering and Hope* (New York: Doubleday, 1997).

43. I refer regularly to the multivolume collections of Calvin, Spurgeon, and Alexander McLaren when preparing to preach.

The Supposed Problem of the Apostle Paul

The "theology of the cross" *(theologia crucis)* is rightly traced to the influence of Paul. Strangely, this in itself may be one reason for its neglect today. The great apostle to the Gentiles is widely misunderstood, impugned, or ignored.[44] Many church members not only lack understanding of his letters, but often direct a distinct animus against Paul himself, personally, and read his letters through hostile lenses if they read him at all. His personal idiosyncrasies and liabilities have been magnified in the popular mind to the point that he has become a caricature of himself. His confidence is regarded as conceit, his passion for the gospel as intolerance, his attitude toward the Jews as anti-Semitism, his views about women as misogynist, his teaching about sexuality as benighted, his preaching of Christ as obsessive. It requires some degree of effort to begin to understand that most of these characterizations are both unfair and inaccurate.[45] It is certainly true that Paul was disliked, even feared, by many in the early church. That is clear in his letters, especially Galatians and II Corinthians. However, Paul was also greatly loved and revered in his own time (this is clear in the letters and also in Acts).[46]

An additional problem is that the letters make demanding reading, a fact recognized by another New Testament writer: "There are some things in them [Paul's letters] hard to understand" (II Pet. 3:16). The Gospels, cast as they are in narrative form, are more accessible than Paul's knotty communications. Many Christians do not realize that the authentic voice of Paul is not found in the book of Acts, and as a consequence the atypical speech about the unknown God in Athens (Acts 17:22-31) is given too much prom-

---

44. This is true not only in the mainline churches (with certain exceptions), but also in conservative-evangelical circles in America where Paul is often invoked, especially as he appears in Acts, but is seldom allowed to speak with his own distinctive voice.

45. I continue to meet these complaints everywhere I go in the churches. The only one of these objections to Paul that has some foundation is his teaching about sexual love, in which he seems to have little interest. For a full exposition of the Bible's teaching on sexual matters, we must look elsewhere in the Scriptures — the Song of Songs, Mark 10:2-9, and Eph. 5:22-33 in particular.

46. A noteworthy testimony to the persisting power of Paul's message is that of Fay Weldon, the recognized British novelist, playwright, and essayist. In a recent piece, "Converted by St. Paul," she described how reading Paul brought her back to the church, having discovered that Paul was nothing like the caricature she had previously known. "I had assumed St. Paul was the woman's enemy . . . but reading [the letters] I found this extraordinary person, this witty visionary, with the most amazing, God-given tale to tell, and I believed him" (Weldon, "Converted by St. Paul: Unconvinced by the Modern Church of England," in *Why I Am Still an Anglican,* ed. Caroline Chartres [London: Continuum, 2006], 134).

inence.[47] For many, the apostle's own voice in the genuine letters is known only from a very few familiar passages — the *agape* chapter of I Corinthians 13 and the final portion of Romans 8. These famous verses are justly beloved, but often for the wrong reasons. When portions of Paul's letters are detached from their polemical contexts, they are all too easily sentimentalized and domesticated. Many Christians today are more drawn to an oversimplified picture of the apostle Simon Peter. It is curious that we are more than willing to overlook Peter's flaws of character, indeed to love him for those very flaws, and yet be very hard on Paul.[48]

For whatever reasons, then, Paul's letters, and his theology of the cross, are little understood in many of today's congregations. The focus on the four Gospels to the neglect of the Epistles is an impoverishment so serious as to threaten the theological foundations of the church.[49] That sounds like an overstatement, but it is not, for reasons that should become apparent as we proceed. In subsequent chapters we will address some of the charges against Paul in turn, but the present context calls for a vigorous defense of Paul's preaching of the cross, in particular.[50]

47. Many preachers and even trained theologians proceed as though there were no tension between Acts and Paul's epistles. It could be argued that this is an example of the unfortunate lack of mutually constructive conversation between theologians and biblical scholars. The preaching attributed to Paul in Acts is not much like the preaching of Paul himself, which we know firsthand from his letters. We all have to choose which to emphasize, Acts or Paul's epistles. We must, willy-nilly, read one through the lens of the other. The propensity of the church at large is to read Paul through the lens of Acts, which has had the unfortunate result of drastically de-radicalizing Paul.

48. The popular author Phyllis Tickle sometimes, in her addresses to church groups, makes her appeal for an "emergent church" based on a warm, embracing Peter versus an intolerant, dictatorial Paul. Her apparent ignorance of Paul's universal gospel is striking; she seems not to know of Paul's account of the debate at Antioch where it was Paul, not Peter, who was "inclusive" (Gal. 2:11-16).

49. The practice in liturgical churches of carrying a Gospel book in procession, sometimes with torches, and having a passage from it read by a member of the clergy (never a layperson), sends a distorted message about the relative importance of the Gospels and the Epistles. Furthermore, in many churches the Gospel reading is usually the sermon text of choice and is featured in the bulletins distributed to the children — as though the Old Testament and the Epistles scarcely existed.

50. It is undeniable that some struggle with the material is required. Generally speaking, it takes several years of study, whether in a local Bible study group or in an academic setting, before Paul's basic assumptions begin to become second nature for Christian people. The reason for this is that our default position is *anthropo*centric; that is to say, we are so accustomed to thinking in terms of human capacity that the radically *theo*centric stance of Paul (and of the Bible as a whole) takes a lot of getting used to.

Paul as Interpreter of the Gospels

Many churchgoers do not realize that Paul's letters were written only twenty or thirty years after the resurrection when many who had known Jesus "according to the flesh" were still very much alive and active. Christians who think that the Gospels bring them closer to Jesus have placed a premium on what they take to be greater chronological and physical proximity. The author of the Gospel of John is at pains to correct this misconception. For instance, in the third portion of Jesus' high-priestly prayer, the Lord prays specifically for "those who believe in me through their [the apostles'] word" (John 17:20). The believers of the future will be brought into the near presence of Jesus, not just in the sense that the stories of his life will be retold, but because *the apostolic preaching, by the action of the Spirit, makes Jesus present.*[51] Paul, the apostle *par excellence*, does this directly in his letters.

Thus, the Pauline letters contain virtually no mention of the teachings of Jesus. It is "the word of the cross" that conveys the *dunamis* of Christ. "Jesus Christ and him crucified" was the content of the powerful message that flamed across the Gentile world (I Cor. 2:2). Paul distilled the gospel in a way that we would not have known without him. A further claim, therefore, can be made for Paul's teaching. Without his letters, we would not know how to interpret the four Gospels. Paul is not the spoiler who took the simple lessons of Jesus and made them intellectual, abstract, and opaque, as in the familiar popular misconception. If all we had of Jesus was his parables dealing with judgment, we would all be turning gratefully to Paul. Indeed, if it were not for Paul, we might not know how to assess Jesus' ministry; there was serious dispute among the closest disciples themselves about central issues, as we know from Paul's vivid description of his argument with none other than Peter, the chief of the apostles (again, Gal. 2:11-14).

Take, for instance, Jesus' well-attested practice of taking his meals with unsavory characters. In today's cultural environment, this has become one of the most admired, most cited, and least questioned of all Jesus' deeds, yet it is open to various interpretations. What does it signify? In later chapters, we will examine *the problem of impunity* — people being absolved from heinous crimes without consequences. Is that what Jesus is doing? We learn from the

---

51. "Jesus Christ is . . . present in the kerygmatic occasion . . . not as an empirical object, but as the saving power of the gospel known only to faith in and through the humanity and temporality of preaching. He is present not simply as a figure who is proclaimed but as *the abiding agent of Christian proclamation*" (James F. Kay, *Christus Praesens* [Grand Rapids: Eerdmans, 1994], 61, emphasis added).

Gospels that Jesus "came not to call the righteous, but sinners" (Matt. 9:13 and parallels)[52] and that the last shall be first and the first last (Matt. 19:30; etc.). It is Paul, however, who gives us the phrase "the justification of the ungodly." It is Paul who speaks unambiguously of Sin as a Power, not an accumulation of misdeeds. It is Paul who shows that "all [human beings], both Jews and Greeks, are under the power of sin, as it is written: 'None is righteous, no, not one'" (Rom. 3:9-10). It is Paul who shifts attention from repentance to justification as a more radical way of proclaiming the unconditional grace of God in Christ. It is Paul who in Romans 11 gives us the most comprehensive view of God's future, allowing us to put the Gospels' references to hellfire and damnation into a new perspective. And it is Paul whose treatment of the Jewish question is the portion of Scripture that stands up best under post-Holocaust scrutiny. The early church leaders knew what they were doing when they collected Paul's letters and allotted more space to him in the New Testament than to any other writer. The experience of being grasped by Paul's message of *the justification of the ungodly* is not one that a person ever forgets.

The "Jesus of History" and the "Christ of Faith"

Closely related to the Jesus-Paul question is the modern problem of the relationship of the historical Jesus to the Christ of faith. The exploitation of this perceived discrepancy by publicity-seeking scholars reached unprecedented proportions in the 1980s and 1990s. There has been a ceaseless flow of print and talk about the unreliability of the New Testament witness concerning Jesus. Never in the history of Christianity has there been such a widespread attack on the church's faith in Jesus as divine Messiah and risen Lord. Many leaders in the mainline churches have joined in this campaign to persuade their own members to give up their supposedly outdated, unenlightened trust in the Scriptures and the historic creeds. These texts are, it is suggested, to be supplanted by the work of the scholars of the Jesus Seminar as well as many others who have their own quarrels with the church.[53]

---

52. Luke, particularly, seems to want to guard against any suggestion of impunity or general amnesty. The saying in Matthew has been amended in Luke 5:32 to read "but sinners to repentance." This is a Lukan characteristic that serves as an important corrective, although we will see that the Lukan preference for the theme of repentance is significantly different from Paul's apparently deliberate omission of it.

53. The Jesus Seminar, a group of biblical scholars whose success in drawing attention to their agenda can only be envied by quieter scholars, began putting forth its pronouncements, typically timed for Christmas and Easter, in the 1980s and 1990s. The seminar succeeded in

Few outside academia would know that the incongruities so frequently cited today as proof of the Bible's unreliability were noted many centuries ago by such as Origen and Calvin. It seems more than a little disingenuous for skeptical scholars of today to act as though they were the originators of newly minted insights made possible only by their supposed discoveries and intellectual fearlessness.[54] It cannot be emphasized too strongly that those writers who seek to reduce and diminish the figure of Jesus are creating a Jesus to suit their own preferences just as surely as Thomas Jefferson did when he took scissors and paste to the Gospels.

The key to Jesus is now, as it has always been, his crucifixion and resurrection. Nothing whatever is known from first-century extrabiblical sources about Jesus as a historical figure. The New Testament is the only witness we have. Any modern reconstruction of the "historical Jesus," therefore, is certain to be a product of the cultural environment that produced it, whereas the Jesus proclaimed as Lord in the New Testament comes closer than any other figure known to human history to being universal, transcending time and historical location, belonging to all cultures and all people everywhere and forever. That is a big claim, but Christians need not be ashamed to stand by it. This proclamation of Jesus as Lord, as we hope to make clear in chapter 1, arose not out of Jesus' *ministry,* which after all can be compared to the ministry of other holy men, but out of the unique apostolic *kerygma* (proclamation) of the crucified and risen One. As Luke Timothy Johnson writes,

> Christian faith has never — either at the start or now — been based on historical reconstructions of Jesus, even though Christian faith has always involved some historical claims concerning Jesus. Rather, Christian faith (then and now) is based on religious claims concerning *the present power of Jesus.* . . . Christian faith is not directed toward a human construction about the past; that would be a form of idolatry. Authentic Christian faith is a response to the living God, whom Christians declare is powerfully at work among them through the resurrected Jesus.[55]

---

getting itself on the covers of the major newsweeklies, on cable television talk shows, and into the headlines of newspapers all across the country. The headlines included "Scholars Say Jesus' Words Invented by Evangelists," "Jesus Never Predicted His Return, Scholars Say," "Scholars Cast Doubt on the Resurrection," "Scholars Speculate That Jesus' Body Was Eaten by Dogs."

54. A telling comment on the Jesus Seminar was made by Dorothy Scherer, the widow of Paul Scherer, the noted Lutheran pastor and preacher, later a member of the faculties of Union (New York) and Princeton theological seminaries. Speaking of Seminar member Marcus Borg, Mrs. Scherer said quietly, "He seems to want to take Jesus away from us."

55. Luke Timothy Johnson, *The Real Jesus: The Misguided Quest of the Historical Jesus*

There is indeed an element of mystery and intractability surrounding the figure of Jesus. It would be irresponsible to proceed as though this difficulty did not exist. The portraits of Jesus in the New Testament have been shaped by the resurrection. The honest inquirer into Christian believing may be assured, however, that there is not a shred of evidence that the men and women closest to the events described in the New Testament ever perceived any discrepancy between the human being who walked the roads of Galilee with them and the risen One they proclaimed as *Kurios* (Lord). According to the apostolic witness, the Jesus of Nazareth who preached the kingdom of God in first-century Palestine is the preexistent Son and Messiah now reigning at the right hand of God.

In view of all the noise the naysayers are making, therefore, it is all the more vital for Christian teachers and preachers to expound the Scriptures day in and day out "through faith for faith" (Rom. 1:17). No other antidote will be effective against those who, as Jesus said, "know neither the scriptures nor the power of God" (Matt. 22:29; Mark 12:24). The drift away from the Bible has weakened the church. Many people are ready to believe but have been intimidated into thinking that no educated person with any pretense to cultural sophistication could actually take the testimony of the Bible seriously. The one antidote to this is a robust exposition of the apostolic gospel.

The stance of this book, therefore, is confessional. The crucified Jesus of Nazareth has been revealed in his resurrection to be the living Lord of the church in the present, and the One who is to come (*ho erchomenos* — Rev. 1:8) in the future to be the judge of the entire *kosmos*. This confession does not preclude doubts of the most serious sort. Many believers have a crisis of faith every few days, yet in the midst of grave misgivings they continue to build their lives upon the confession of faith in Jesus Christ as found in Holy Scripture. We may trust that Paul and the other witnesses were neither dupes nor deceivers, and we may claim for ourselves the words Paul wrote, "Far be it from me to glory except in the cross of our Lord Jesus Christ, by which the world has been crucified to me, and I to the world. . . . Henceforth let no man trouble me; for I bear in my body the marks of Jesus" (Gal. 6:14, 17).

---

and the Truth of the Traditional Gospels (New York: HarperCollins, 1996), 133, 142-43. Anyone seeking a description of the Jesus Seminar will be rewarded by Professor Johnson's survey in *The Real Jesus.* As his subtitle indicates, his treatment is highly polemical, but it is always entertaining and informed by serious scholarship in its own right. From my perspective, the most serious defect in his work is his lack of appreciation for the Tübingen school of New Testament studies (and for the Protestant project in general), but on the whole the book remains one of the best critiques of the Jesus Seminar and its allies.

Locating the Right Dynamic Tension

Certain issues should be addressed briefly but emphatically before we launch into our full discussion of the crucifixion:

- What is the relation of our theme to the resurrection?
- What about the life and ministry of Jesus?
- Where does the doctrine of the incarnation fit?

1. As regards the **resurrection**, I Corinthians 15 is a central source. When Paul speaks of the cross, he presupposes the resurrection as part of the same event. As noted earlier, in the same letter that begins with the announcement, "We preach Christ crucified, a stumbling block to Jews and folly to Gentiles" (I Cor. 1:23), we find this: "If there is no resurrection of the dead, then Christ has not been raised; if Christ has not been raised, then our preaching is in vain and your faith is in vain" (15:13-14), and this: "If Christ has not been raised, your faith is futile and you are still in your sins" (15:17). Surely these powerful declarations should lay to rest any suspicion that concentration on the cross detracts from the *sine qua non* of the resurrection. Perhaps the strongest statement we can make about the resurrection in this book about the crucifixion is that *if Jesus had not been raised from the dead, we would never have heard of him.*

2. And what of Jesus' **life, ministry, and teaching**? By focusing on the cross, are we failing to honor them? No, because the life of Jesus is single-mindedly directed toward his self-offering. As John Donne wrote, "All his life was a continual passion."[56] One of the traits that continues to compel us about this man Jesus is that, unlike anyone else who ever lived, he was entirely directed toward others at every moment of his life. Calvin inquires, "How has Christ abolished sin [and] banished the separation between us and God . . . ?" and responds, "To this we can in general reply that he has achieved this for us by the whole course of his obedience. . . . [F]rom the time when he took on the form of a servant, he began to pay the price of liberation in order to redeem us."[57] The life and the death were of a piece. His death, far from being an unfortunate error or derailment of his purpose, was the willed culmination of that life of self-giving for our good.

---

56. John Donne, "Death's Duel," February 25, 1631.

57. Calvin, *Institutes* 2.16.5. T. F. Torrance uses this same phrasing, "the whole course of his obedience," in *The Mediation of Christ,* rev. ed. (Colorado Springs: Helmers and Howard, 1992; orig. 1983), 79.

3. The **incarnation** is the other essential pole of the Christian confession.[58] God's own self is totally, unreservedly, unconditionally invested in the self-offering "even to death on a cross" of the man Jesus. If God is not truly incarnate in Jesus as he accomplishes his work on the cross, then nothing has really happened from God's side and we are thrown back on ourselves. If there is no incarnation of the Godhead in Jesus' sacrifice, then there is no salvation apart from what human nature can contribute.

We come full circle to Christology. The incarnate One is fully God and fully human at the same time. The Council of Nicaea determined that Jesus was of one substance *(homoousia)* with the Father, not just of similar substance *(homoiousia)*,[59] and the Council of Chalcedon declared in its Definition that "Our Lord Jesus Christ . . . is recognized in two natures, without confusion, without change, without division, without separation . . . not as parted or separated into two persons, but one and the same Son."

---

58. Joseph Mangina has pointed out to me that Eastern patristics scholars John Behr and Khaled Anatolios have recently been insisting that for the Church Fathers there is no incarnation that is not oriented to the cross. (In Eastern iconography it is traditional to depict the newborn Jesus already dressed in a winding sheet.) The Son's becoming flesh and his movement toward death are two aspects of the same divine *telos*. This point about the inseparability of the cross and the incarnation is a corrective to the tendency (prominent in some Anglican circles) to speak of the incarnation as a hallowing of creation, without acknowledging the bloody gash that the crucifixion cuts across the picture. This is particularly noticeable in contemporary Celtic movements.

It is often claimed that an incarnational emphasis is traditionally Anglican. This is not strictly accurate. It does not date from the origins of the Church of England in the Reformation. To be sure, Thomas Cranmer's Book of Common Prayer (1549 and 1552) drew extensively from pre-Reformation, "catholic" sources for its prayers and liturgy, but its overall theological trajectory was Augustinian and Reformed, much influenced by the Reformer Martin Bucer, who came to England from the Continent in 1549. The 1559 book was reestablished under the Protestant Elizabeth I. In the seventeenth century, two distinct theological/ecclesiastical positions can be identified within the Church of England: (1) the Reformed/Protestant and (2) the catholic/ Laudian. William Laud, who became archbishop of Canterbury in 1633, was one of those who opposed the then-prevailing Calvinist theology and sought vigorously to retain pre-Reformation liturgical practices and the divine right of kings. He was executed by order of Parliament in 1645 — such were the times — but today, Laud and his confreres can stand in as the victors in the battle for the heart of the American Episcopal Church. Eighteenth- and nineteenth-century Latitudinarianism also played a key role in the great success of the Anglo-Catholic movement in the nineteenth century and the sweeping reforms of the late twentieth. All this resulted in a de-emphasis on atonement — a primary Protestant theme within the Church of England — and a greatly increased emphasis on the incarnation in the Episcopal Church (for a brief synopsis, see Paul F. M. Zahl, *The Protestant Face of Anglicanism* [Grand Rapids: Eerdmans, 1998], 1-8).

59. Thus, as theologian and ethicist Paul L. Lehmann used to tell his students, the salvation of the human race hung by an *iota*.

A summary, then, of some of the principal balances undergirding the plan of this book:

- Each of the major biblical motifs concerning the death of Christ, and to some degree the minor ones, will be expounded.
- The incarnation, the ministry, the cross, and the resurrection of Jesus Christ are assumed to be fully integrated aspects of the Christian message as a whole.
- The orthodox confession that Christ is both fully divine and fully human in the same person is affirmed.

Many more such balances will emerge as we proceed. Perhaps, however, "balance" is not quite the right word. For instance, the christological affirmation about the divine/human nature of Jesus is not a "balance"; it is a paradox. There is no midpoint compromise between paradoxical affirmations; the way ahead is found *in the tension itself.* This is not the same thing as "having it both ways" by seeking a bland, safe position in the center between two poles.[60] Christian theology and the Christian life are best found on the frontiers, where our thinking and doing are engaged by the dynamic tension between two seemingly contradictory truths. At all times, our tendency to want to smooth over this tension is undercut by the self-correcting confession of the apostle when he declared, "I decided to know nothing among you except Jesus Christ and him crucified" (I Cor. 2:2).

Two Principal Thought-Categories

Speaking of dynamic tension, there are two undergirding categories proposed in this volume to interpret the crucifixion of Christ. In the biblical testimony they overlap, but for the sake of clarity we propose to distinguish them from the outset. These two thought-complexes are as follows:

---

60. In a different context, Arthur Schlesinger Jr. observed, "The middle of the road is definitely not the vital center; it is the dead center." The original quotation was in his 1949 book *The Vital Center: The Politics of Freedom,* but it has had a long and varied life. He protested against the misappropriation of "the vital center" to mean "middle of the road" in his introduction to the second edition ([Cambridge, Mass.: Da Capo Press, 1988], xiii). He also protested indignantly in *Slate* (January 10, 1997) against President Clinton's misuse of the term to mean "middle of the road." This complaint could equally well be lodged against the use of the term *via media,* often used by Anglicans/Episcopalians to describe their tradition.

1. Atonement for sin (treated particularly in chapters 4, 6, 7, 8, and 11)
2. God's apocalyptic invasion and the conquest of the Powers (prefigured in chapters 3 and 5, fully developed in chapters 9 and 10 as *Christus Victor*)

In these pages it is proposed that all other doctrinal and ethical concerns find their place in these two categories. This includes especially the triplet dear to many mainline churches today: (1) creation, (2) incarnation, and (3) the kingdom (reign) of God. These emphases have tended to displace the *theologia crucis* at the heart of much Christian teaching today, but in fact they are part of it. We have already begun to address the central doctrines of creation and incarnation. The indisputably major theme of the kingdom of God, so prominent in the Synoptic Gospels, does not and should not float free of Christology, as is especially clear in the Gospel of Matthew when it is read *in toto.*[61] Jesus' announcement, "The kingdom of God is at hand," presupposes an apocalyptic eschatology that will be fully revealed in the crucifixion and resurrection. We will see how the proclamation of the kingdom risks being understood as another — albeit higher and better — human project when it is not essentially and uniquely yoked to the righteousness *(dikaiosyne)* of God conclusively revealed in the Christ event.

These two thought-complexes will not be mentioned on every page, but they will be presupposed at all times as we proceed.

A Brief Guide for the Reader

The Table of Contents

As the table of contents will indicate, the present volume is constructed as follows:

> *Part 1: The Crucifixion* is a four-chapter section designed to give a broad overview of (1) the nature of crucifixion as a mode of execution and its unique place in the Christian story, and (2) some of the major issues raised by the fact that Jesus died in this particular way. A special chapter on Anselm bridges chapters 3 and 4.

---

61. Dale Allison has shown that when Matthew is read from beginning to end, the high Christology of the Evangelist becomes clear and is connected to the proclamation of the kingdom of God (called the kingdom of heaven in Matthew). Jack Dean Kingsbury's *Matthew: Structure, Christology, Kingdom* is an extended treatment of Matthew's high Christology.

Chapters 3 and 4 focus on injustice and the overarching category of Sin. There is a specific reason for moving the theme of Sin forward into the first major section instead of postponing it to part 2. Sin, understood as a Power, lies at the very heart of the underlying meaning of the cross, and that is the reason for tackling it at the outset.

Part 2: The Biblical Motifs lays out the richness and variety of the biblical material. The introduction to part 2 outlines the way that the New Testament writers use numerous motifs of great depth and richness to expound the meaning of the cross. The following eight chapters examine each of the principal motifs in turn.

Each of the first four chapters stands partially on its own, and together with the "bridge" chapter on Anselm, the four chapters are meant to hold together as a semi-independent whole. They are therefore grouped together as part 1. The most important chapters in part 1 for the entire argument of the book are probably chapters 1 and 4.

The bridge chapter on Anselm is particularly recommended for theological students and clergy who have been encouraged to dismiss the work of this controversial but indispensable theologian.

Part 2 will be of interest especially to those who want to probe deeply into the biblical material. To some extent each chapter stands by itself. This section is very important, but if one is not inclined to read every word, the individual chapters can be used as references by topic (see table of contents). *If only a few chapters in part 2 are to be read, let them be 8 through 12,* because they contain the most important and original work.

A Few Technicalities

Capitalization

Readers will notice right away that sometimes "Sin" and "Death" are capitalized and sometimes not. When they are capitalized, this will signal to the reader that the context requires that Sin and Death be understood as Powers (also capitalized) over which human beings have no control. The word "Power" (or "Powers") is capitalized to denote the existence of the unique, semi-autonomous agency whose status as the Enemy of God means that it operates from a sphere that lies outside of and beyond human control. The word "Law" will sometimes be capitalized, to indicate its status as a bondservant of the Powers. That is the way Paul uses the word "Law" in Romans 7 and, especially, in the whole of

Galatians. This use of capitalization for "Sin," "Death," "Law," and "Powers" has become more or less standard among many Pauline scholars.[62]

When the word "sin" appears without capitalization, it is being used in the more ordinary sense of transgression, which prevailed until the recovery of New Testament apocalyptic in the twentieth century. It will never be capitalized in quotations from the Bible or from commentators who do not capitalize it. Similarly, "Powers" will be capitalized when quoted authors capitalize it. Despite the strong emphasis on the presence of evil in this book, I do not capitalize the word "evil" because, unlike Sin and Death, it is not specifically personified in the New Testament as one of the Powers. Although in the present day, "evil" has become the preferred word, Sin and Death with their captive the Law are, for the apostle Paul, the sum of all evil.

Inclusive Language

Eschewing "he" and "him" and "men" whenever possible comes naturally to most of us nowadays, and in my own writing I generally do this as a matter of course, but I am not slavish about it. When I am quoting from a poet, novelist, or pre-1960 scholar, or if I want to preserve the cadence of someone's English ("for us men and for our salvation," for instance), I use the generic "man" without apology.

Biblical Translations

I have used the Revised Standard Version throughout, except when otherwise noted. From my perspective, the gains in the New Revised Standard Version are outweighed by the loss of literary quality and powerful sentence structure (compare "For as in Adam all die, even so in Christ shall all be made alive" [RSV] with "as all die in Adam, so all will be made alive in Christ" [NRSV]).

Looking Ahead

The cross of Christ is the touchstone of our faith. From the beginning it has caused offense, as we have seen in Paul's statement that the cross is a stumbling block to Jews and foolishness to Gentiles. It is typical of Amer-

---

62. This capitalization is common practice especially among biblical theologians in the line of Ernst Käsemann (J. Louis Martyn, Beverly Gaventa, Douglas Campbell, Susan Eastman, and many others).

ican Christianity, as of American culture as a whole, to push the cross out to the margins, because we prefer a more upbeat and triumphalist form of proclamation and practice. The Great Recession put a crimp in our style for a brief time, but it has not canceled out the disturbing trends in our culture toward self-centered lives based on consumption, sensation, and instant gratification — all this coinciding with the exponential growth of the gap between the superrich and the struggling middle class, not to mention the gap between those barely holding on and the truly poor. The "word of the cross" (I Cor. 1:18), in contrast, calls the Christian community to embrace struggle on behalf of others as the way of discipleship.

This is not a grim and joyless vocation. Even in the midst of suffering, Christian pilgrims on the cruciform path will find themselves drawn into the very heart of God. Jesus himself, in his most famous sermon, promised everlasting beatitude to those who would take up the cross: "Blessed are you when men revile you and persecute you and utter all kinds of evil against you falsely on my account. Rejoice and be glad, for your reward is great in heaven" (Matt. 5:11-12). "Whoever would save his life will lose it; and whoever loses his life for my sake and the gospel's will save it" (Mark 8:35).

May this volume, an attempt to unfold some of the incomparable riches of Christ crucified, be a present source of strength and encouragement for those who seek to understand and receive the Lord's gifts. May it serve the gospel of the One who suffered and died to deliver the cosmos from its bondage to death, and to incorporate each and every one of us into his own full, true, and eternal humanity.

PART 1

The Crucifixion

CHAPTER 1

The Primacy of the Cross

The inner criterion of whether or not Christian theology is Christian lies in the crucified Christ . . . we come back to Luther's lapidary statement, the cross is the test of everything: Crux probat omnia.

JÜRGEN MOLTMANN, *The Crucified God*[1]

The Preeminence of the Passion Narrative in the Four Gospels

Long before the advent of critical biblical scholarship as we know it today, it was observed that the four Evangelists tell the story of Jesus' life in four quite different ways. The four passion narratives vary greatly in details and in theological emphasis. For example, the "seven last words from the cross" so beloved by generations of Good Friday preachers are strikingly different in the various accounts, with only Matthew and Mark concurring.

Where all the Evangelists agree, however, is in the massive attention they give to the passion narrative and the way they aim their Gospels toward the cross as the climax to the story of Jesus.[2] In all four accounts, the events prior to the passion are structured to be a prologue to it and to find their culmination in it — with the resurrection as vindication and victory. All four Gospels pointedly include three solemn predictions of the passion by Jesus himself. In this, they are somewhat like Wagner's musical drama *The Ring*

---

1. Jürgen Moltmann, *The Crucified God: The Cross of Christ as the Foundation and Criticism of Christian Theology* (New York: Harper and Row, 1973), 7. *Crux probat omnia:* The cross is the test of everything.

2. Indeed, Martin Kähler went so far as to define the genre "gospel" as a passion narrative with an extended introduction. *The So-Called Historical Jesus and the Historic, Biblical Christ* (Philadelphia: Fortress, 1964), 80 n. 11.

of the Nibelung: a particular leitmotif (musical theme), generally known as "redemption through love," is planted early in the story so that when it recurs at the end, we will respond to it with our emotions fully engaged. Not to push the analogy too far, the passion predictions of Jesus function in a somewhat similar way.

Looked at from the opposite perspective, each one of the four Gospels presents the passion narrative as the dénouement, the climactic revelation that shapes the character of everything that has gone before it. The Gospels are designed, each according to its own perspective, to show, after the fact, how Jesus' sacrificial life led to his sacrificial death. Jesus' healing of a man on the Sabbath is an early warning to the law-abiding Pharisees who will turn against him (Mark 2:1-4). His deliverance of a possessed boy astonishes the onlookers, whereupon he says, "Let these words sink into your ears; the Son of man is to be delivered into the hands of men" (Luke 9:44). The parables promising the riches of the kingdom provoke intense hostility from the religious leaders, who say, "'Where did this man get this wisdom and these mighty works?' . . . And they took offense at him" (Matt. 13:54, 57). Jesus' gift of sight to the man born blind throws him directly into conflict with those who will conspire against him (John 9). And so it goes throughout; as the hymn puts it,

> Why, what hath my Lord done? What makes this rage and spite?
> He made the lame to run, he gave the blind their sight.
> Sweet injuries! Yet they at these themselves displease and 'gainst him
>   rise.[3]

The portions of the four Gospels dealing with the life and teachings of Jesus were divided into short, discrete units (pericopes) suitable for reading and exposition in the context of worship in the early church. Once the Last Supper begins, however, the method changes. The portions describing the arrest, trial, suffering, and execution of Jesus are quite unlike the rest of the Gospels. These sequences are staged as long dramatic narratives, differing noticeably from the division of the earlier material into brief pericopes. The passion stories take up one-fourth to one-third of the total length of the four Gospels, and biblical interpreters generally agree that the material was shaped by the church's oral traditions prior to being put into written form, in a way that forever indicates the surpassing importance of the suffering of Christ for the life of the earliest Christian communities.

3. Hymn by Samuel Crossman (1624-1683), "My Song Is Love Unknown."

Jesus' three passion predictions in each of the four Gospels offer an illustration of the method. These passages fall upon the ear with extraordinary gravity. "From that time Jesus began to show his disciples that he must go to Jerusalem and suffer many things from the elders and chief priests and scribes, and be killed, and on the third day be raised" (Matt. 16:21). These predictions, deliberately spaced at intervals by all four Evangelists, gather weight and momentum as the narratives proceed inexorably toward their climax. Mark and John, in particular, have arranged their Gospels to leave no doubt that the passion is the main event. For this reason the climactic christological statement in Mark's Gospel ("Truly this man was the Son of God" — 15:39) is not uttered until the moment of Jesus' death on the cross. As for the Fourth Gospel, Jesus' repeated references to his *hour of glory* signify the "lifting up" on the cross that he makes a keystone of his teaching about himself.[4] The entire Gospel turns on the moment in chapter 12 when Jesus stops saying "My hour has not yet come" and begins to say, "My hour has come." From that moment he begins his return to the Father, which is accomplished as he is "lifted up" on the cross.[5] The Evangelist makes this clear in other ways as well, as for example in 7:30, "No one laid hands on him, because his hour had not yet come." When the hour of glory does come, Jesus voluntarily and deliberately gives himself up: "Jesus, knowing all that was to befall him, came forward and said to them, 'Whom do you seek?' They answered him, 'Jesus of Nazareth.' Jesus said to them, 'I am he'" (John 18:4-5).

The Cross as the Center of Christian Understanding

The place of the cross in Christian theology has been at issue from the very first days of the new faith. We know this because the Corinthian and Galatian letters of the apostle Paul were written within twenty or twenty-five years of the resurrection — and those letters stake out the unique meaning of the Lord's death. Paul had his work cut out for him, for as Jürgen Moltmann writes in the very first sentence of *The Crucified God,* "The cross is not and cannot be loved." As a general rule, the *theologia gloriae* (theology of glory)

---

4. "Jesus said, 'When you have lifted up the Son of man, then you will know that I am he'" (John 8:28; also 3:14; 12:32-24).

5. I am not suggesting that John has a theology of the cross *per se* as does Paul (and Mark also). The Johannine literature has a perspective all its own. I am pointing out that the Fourth Gospel, like the other three, is structured toward the passion and death, beginning with "Behold, the Lamb" and culminating in the words, "It is finished (*tetelestai,* 'completed')" (John 1:29, 36; 19:30).

will drive out the *theologia crucis* (theology of the cross) every time in a comfortable society. We will often observe that this is particularly true in America, where optimism and positive thinking reign side by side.[6]

Teaching about the cross is very hard work. We see something of this in Paul's second letter to the Christians in Corinth, where Paul drains himself of every mental and emotional resource in hopes that their trust in the gospel will be renewed. Taking up the cross, as Jesus himself called us to do, means a total reorientation of the self toward the way of Christ. Long before he knew his own destiny, Dietrich Bonhoeffer memorably wrote, "When Christ calls a man, he bids him come and die."[7]

The crucifixion is the touchstone of Christian authenticity, the unique feature by which everything else, including the resurrection, is given its true significance. The resurrection is not a set piece. It is not an isolated demonstration of divine dazzlement. It is not to be detached from its abhorrent first act. The resurrection is, precisely, the vindication of a man who was crucified. Without the cross at the center of the Christian proclamation, the Jesus story can be treated as just another story about a charismatic spiritual figure. It is the crucifixion that marks out Christianity as something definitively different in the history of religion. *It is in the crucifixion that the nature of God is truly revealed.* Since the resurrection is God's mighty transhistorical Yes to the historically crucified Son, we can assert that *the crucifixion is the most important historical event that has ever happened.* The resurrection, being a transhistorical event planted within history, does not cancel out the contradiction and shame of the cross in this present life; rather, the resurrection ratifies the cross as *the* way "until he comes."

The Corinthian church is an important test case because that congregation seemed unable to locate itself correctly with regard to the crucifixion. They placed themselves either *beyond* the cross, as though already raised from the dead (like the superspiritual *pneumatikoi* of I Cor. 2:15 and 14:37), or *above* the cross, as though suffering was behind them and beneath them (the "superapostles" of II Cor. 12:11), rather than *in* the cross. These problems, in Paul's judgment, were the cause of the Corinthian Christians' de-

6. There have been numerous studies of optimism as an American trait, but there is a significant exception to these generalizations about American Christianity. Black slaves produced a moving body of song about the Lord's suffering and death. One may legitimately wonder whether "Were you there when they crucified my Lord?," sung every year during Holy Week in many affluent white congregations, has not been misappropriated to some extent, absent the circumstances in which it was originally sung.

7. Dietrich Bonhoeffer, *The Cost of Discipleship* (New York: Macmillan, 1963), 7. In more recent translations, the syntax of this celebrated statement is not nearly as powerful.

ficiencies with regard to love. That is why he wrote the famous thirteenth chapter of I Corinthians ("Love [*agape*] bears all things, believes all things, hopes all things, endures all things" — 13:7). Sentimental, overly "spiritualized" love is not capable of the sustained, unconditional *agape* of Christ shown on the cross. Only from the perspective of the crucifixion can the true nature of Christian love be seen, over against all that the world calls "love." The one thing needful, according to Paul, is that the Christian community should position itself rightly, at the juncture where the cross calls all present arrangements into question with a corresponding call for endurance and faith.

The fact that the English word "witness" is, in Greek, the same as the word "martyr" is a semantic indication of how quickly the apostolic witness-martyrs came to understand that their testimony would be costly. Paul summons his churches to "interpret the signs of the times" (Jesus' own expression in Matt. 16:3). They are watching for God-given opportunities to meet the "works of darkness" while wearing the "armor of light" (Rom. 13:12). Surprisingly, the liturgical season of Advent, rather than Lent, best locates the Christian community. Advent — the time between — with its themes of crisis and judgment, now and not-yet, places us not in some privileged spiritual sanctuary but on the frontier where the promised kingdom of God exerts maximum pressure on the present, with corresponding signs of suffering and struggle. As if to clinch the point, Paul writes at the very heart of his resurrection chapter that he is in peril every hour. "I protest, brethren, by my pride in you which I have in Christ Jesus our Lord, I die every day!" (I Cor. 15:30-31). He wants them to understand that the resurrection life in this world, though free and confident "in sure and certain hope of eternal life," must always be marked by the signs of the cross.

The Challenge of Gnosticism to the Theology of the Cross

Gnosticism in its numerous and various forms has always been far and away the most pervasive and popular rival to Christianity — particularly in connection to the *theologia crucis*.[8] This was so in New Testament times,

---

8. "Modern-day gnosticism is the natural religion of Americans, including American Christians. . . . Feel-good religion and spiritual pills to elevate our consciousness and enhance our sense of comfort with our presumably 'real' selves — these are American specialties of long standing." Richard John Neuhaus, *Death on a Friday Afternoon: Meditations on the Last Words of Jesus from the Cross* (New York: Basic Books, 2000), 117.

and remains so today.[9] Defining this philosophy is no easy task, because gnosticism is, by its very nature, diffuse and mercurial; brief descriptions will of necessity be oversimplified. A few basic concepts, however, can be set forth.

Actually, the first step into the complexities of gnosticism is very simple. We begin with the Greek word *gnosis,* meaning "knowledge." All the various forms of gnosticism are grounded in the belief that *privileged spiritual knowledge is the way of salvation.* This is such a familiar religious idea that, on the face of it, no warning flags appear.[10] After all (many would say), Jesus himself gathered a privileged group that he taught privately. The difficulty begins to appear with the suggestion that the privileges are not for everyone. Take, for example, a saying of the Buddha, speaking of his own teaching: "This doctrine is profound, recondite, hard to comprehend, rare, excellent, beyond dialectic, subtle, *only to be understood by the wise.*"[11] Jesus' teaching of the Twelve, even when it was "in parables" that others did not grasp, was the opposite of esoteric doctrine; it was to prepare them for their post-Pentecost role of preaching a gospel of radical leveling. What Jesus taught them privately was to be made known to the entire world, for as he said, "Nothing is covered that will not be revealed, or hidden that will not be known. What I tell you in the dark, utter in the light; and what you hear whispered, proclaim upon the housetops" (Matt. 10:26-27).

Gnostics, in contrast, are mystery-mongers; they claim to know things that other people don't know.[12] Elaine Pagels, the celebrated author of *The Gnostic Gospels,* said perhaps more than she intended when she stated in an interview that sin, repentance, and the Last Judgment appeal to the masses, whereas gnostic illumination is for the elite.[13] As Paul warns the Corinthian

9. Gnosticism is the *most pervasive and popular* alternative to Christianity. Stoicism is the *most worthy* alternative, but those who embrace the noble and austere tenets of stoicism have always been few.

10. Many popular Christian speakers and writers mine the theme. Richard Rohr, for instance, habitually refers to the "deeper wisdom teaching" of Jesus that is the "goal of religion," the "contemplative seeing" that is "so important for anyone on a serious spiritual journey." This is typical gnostic language, quoted from Rohr's own publicity material.

11. Quoted in Huston Smith, *The Religions of Man* (New York: Harper, 1958), 115.

12. Note from a lecture by R. A. Norris at the General Theological Seminary, 1974.

13. Interview with Joseph Roddy, *Rockefeller Foundation Illustrated,* April 1980. I mean no disrespect, but thirty years later as this book is being written, Elaine Pagels, despite disclaimers, is still recommending gnosticism and disparaging orthodoxy. She continues to encourage the perception, widely held, that little was known of splits and divisions in the church until the Nag Hammadi finds in the 1940s. In fact, we know of these divisions and struggles from the New Testament itself. This is not to negate the importance of the Nag Hammadi texts, which

Christians, "Not all possess *gnosis*" (I Cor. 8:7). Paul's sarcastic references to the supposed "wisdom" of the Corinthians (3:18; 4:10; 6:5) are part of his attempt to correct gnostic snobbery in that congregation. He hopes to win them back to his message of God's subversive plan to *make foolish the wisdom of the world.* In particular, Paul redefines *gnosis.* The Corinthians have apparently sent a message to the apostle that "all of us possess *gnosis.*" Yes, Paul replies, but there are limits to *gnosis* (knowledge). " 'Knowledge' puffs up, but love builds up. If any one imagines that he knows something, he does not yet know as he ought to know. But if one loves God, one is known by him" (8:1-3). In just these three sentences, Paul does two things: (1) he shifts the emphasis from *knowledge* to *agape,* and (2) he reverses the direction of knowing. It is *God* who has knowledge of *us,* through love. Paul brings all this together in I Corinthians 13:

> If I have prophetic powers, and understand all mysteries and all *gnosis,* and if I have all faith, so as to remove mountains, but have not love *(agape),* I am nothing. . . . Love never ends; as for prophecies, they will pass away; as for tongues, they will cease; as for *gnosis,* it will pass away. For our *gnosis* is imperfect and our prophecy is imperfect; but when the perfect comes, the imperfect will pass away. . . . For now we see in a mirror dimly, but then face to face. Now I *know* in part; then I shall *understand* fully, even as I have been fully *understood* [*gnosis* is the root of all three italicized words]. So faith, hope, love abide, these three; but the greatest of these is love. (vv. 2, 8-9, 12-13)

A careful reading of I Corinthians 13 *in its context* reveals that it is a strongly anti-gnostic text, specifically on ethical grounds. The whole concept of privileged spiritual *gnosis* is called into question by the impending Day of God; Paul's double pairings of "now/then" point to the second advent of Christ when human *gnosis* will be subsumed into the perfect *gnosis* of God, the One whose knowledge *of us* is incarnate in the *agape* love of Jesus Christ.

Gnostic emphasis on esoteric knowledge has a number of ramifications. Where there is gnosticism, there is spiritual hierarchy. This is not always obvious at first, because the gentle spiritual paths typical of many gnostic programs promise well-being, personal enrichment, and access to the divine for all, often with special emphasis on women, gay people, people with disabilities, and others who may feel marginalized. Sooner or later, though, the hierarchy will make itself known, for in gnosticism higher reality is "spir-

---

are indeed extraordinary, but they do not add as much really new information about early Christianity as is often thought.

itual," so that religious advancement depends on achieving degrees of spiritual enlightenment. Masters (of either gender) lead disciples through various stages of evolved consciousness. Naturally, this results in stratification, with adepts at the top. Those who do not find meditation, spiritual exercises, or consciousness-raising congenial find themselves left behind.[14]

The Corinthian church was a particularly striking example of these divisive gradations. In I Corinthians 12, Paul shows how spiritual virtuosity can disrupt a congregation when greater honor is shown to those who are considered specially gifted. In "charismatic" congregations today, those whose gifts are more worldly (administration, housekeeping, financial oversight, social action) can be made to feel inferior to those who are praying extemporaneously, laying on hands, speaking in tongues, and exercising other flashy "spiritual" gifts. Even in noncharismatic mainline congregations today, it is not hard to find people who feel spiritually inferior to those who advocate and practice contemplative disciplines. To counter this attitude, Paul writes that "God has so composed the body, giving the greater honor to the inferior part, that there may be no discord in the body, but that the members may have the same care for one another" (I Cor. 12:24-25).[15] As J. Louis Martyn puts it, God's new creation is "the church that leaves behind all marks of religious distinction."[16]

When Paul says "inferior" in the verse just quoted, he is not expressing his real opinion; he is reflecting the Corinthian gnostics' views back to them. Action taken in the world, these particular gnostics thought, was a matter

14. In 1916, the Episcopal bishop of Pennsylvania, Philip J. Rhinelander, delivered the Paddock Lectures at the General Theological Seminary in New York under the title *The Faith of the Cross*. His words would not have been unusual a century ago in the Episcopal Church, when the notion of spirituality had not yet become a central preoccupation. His reflections are in tune with much of what is being argued here. Here, for example, is his response to the gnostic tendency to make Christian faith a matter of insider knowledge: "The secret of the Cross is not abstruse nor difficult, the despair of most, the privilege of few. A key is needed, but the key is presumed to be ready in each hand. The reading of the mystery of Calvary is . . . easily within the compass of each child who has not thrown away his birthright" (Philip J. Rhinelander, *The Faith of the Cross*, Paddock Lectures, General Theological Seminary, 1914 [New York: Longmans, Green and Co., 1916], 15).

15. Some of the Christian gnostics of the postapostolic period, especially the Valentinians, thought very highly of Paul. They read him ingeniously, as though he were a gnostic himself. On this interpretation, Paul would be recommending a lower level of written knowledge *(exoteric)* for the masses, and *esoteric* oral teaching to be communicated privately to the elite initiates. It is not uncommon to hear Paul described in gnostic terms today, with emphasis on the supposed "mysticism" of his conception of being "in Christ," but this is to misread his radical leveling of all such distinctions.

16. J. Louis Martyn, *Galatians,* Anchor Bible 33A (New York: Doubleday, 1997), 27.

of indifference, since those possessing *gnosis* were thought to be already living on a higher plane. The concept of *redemptive suffering in the world,* so central to the *theologia crucis,* is foreign to gnosticism, which, though it often recommends acts of mercy along the spiritual path, places little value on suffering for the sake of the world. Since gnosticism considers material reality unspiritual, conduct in the world cannot be at the ethical center, as it is in Christianity.[17] First John is an anti-gnostic letter in its entirety, with its emphasis on the materiality of Christ's incarnation (I John 1:1-2) and the keeping of the commandment to love as the one true test of "knowing" Christ. "He who says 'I know [the *gnosis* word-group] him' but disobeys his commandments is a liar, and the truth is not in him; but whoever keeps his word, in him truly love for God is perfected" (2:4-5). "He who says he is in the light and hates his brother is in the darkness still" (2:9). First Timothy is explicit: "O Timothy, guard what has been entrusted to you. Avoid the godless chatter and contradictions of what is falsely called knowledge [*gnosis*]" (I Tim. 6:20).

Virtually all human religion is gnostic. The eclectic religiosity of America today emphasizes individual spiritual experiences with a corresponding lack of interest in the human struggle for justice and dignity.[18] The great Eastern faiths have many gnostic tendencies, with rigorous spiritual disciplines for the elite and popular, undemanding rituals like prayer wheels, amulets, and idols for the masses.[19] It seems likely that the versions of Buddhism so popular in America today are actually types of gnostic spirituality.[20] The

17. This same gnostic indifference to the earthly, material body led the Corinthians to devalue the Christian proclamation of the resurrection of the body in favor of the much more widely held notion of the immortality of the soul. This mistake lies behind what Paul is saying in I Cor. 11.

18. A great many secular American Jews, however much they may be estranged from the God-language of their Scriptures, continue to maintain the prophetic tradition in their active support of justice and peace. That includes the strong minority of Jewish voices raised in criticism of Israeli policy in recent years as the Palestinian-Israeli standoff becomes ever more dangerous and ethically challenging. This impetus toward criticism-from-within is a notable characteristic of biblical faith.

19. This is not peculiar to Eastern faith. It became, obviously, a major focus of conflict between Protestants and Catholics during and after the Reformation. No one, including Christians, is immune to superstition and the transfer of religious devotion to idols of every sort. One of the admirable features of Islam is its refusal of images and other distractions from strict monotheism.

20. Buddhist Thich Nhat Hanh, widely regarded as a spiritual leader, once told the religion editor of *Newsweek* that the crucifixion "is a very painful image to me. It does not contain joy or peace, and this does not do justice to Jesus" (*Newsweek,* March 27, 2000).

Dalai Lama continues to attract adoring crowds wherever he goes, but there are many points of difference between what he has to say and the theology of the cross. In an interview with Gustav Niebuhr of the *New York Times,* he sought to explain his appeal with this observation: "We all desire happiness and wish to avoid suffering."[21] How many American Christians, hearing this, would realize how different it is from (for example) Martin Luther King's often-repeated summons to "redemptive suffering"? Let us be clear, however: Christianity does not recommend suffering for its own sake, and it is part of a Christian's task in the world to alleviate the suffering of others. By no stretch of the imagination, however, could Christianity ever be said to recommend the avoidance of suffering in the cause of love and justice. Perhaps the clearest way to sum this up is to say that Christian faith, when anchored in the preaching of the cross, recognizes and accepts the place of suffering in the world for the sake of the kingdom of God. "Blessed are those who are persecuted for righteousness' sake," said Jesus on the mount (Matt. 5:10).

To summarize: three characteristics of gnosticism reflected in the New Testament are:

1. an emphasis on spiritual knowledge *(gnosis)*
2. a hierarchy of spiritual accomplishment
3. a devaluation of material/physical life and a corresponding avoidance of ethical struggle in this material world

Gnosticism differs from Christianity in a number of other ways as well. For instance, the various gnostic systems hold no clear distinction between God and humanity, or God and the creation. Thus, for a gnostic, Jesus is a son of God, but all of us, potentially or actually, are children of God. This idea seems, on the face of it, to be far more appealing than orthodox Christianity's teaching that God is the Creator and we are the creatures, made in God's image but not of God's substance.[22]

21. Gustav Niebuhr, "For the Discontented, a Message of Hope," *New York Times,* August 14, 1999.

22. An easy way to illustrate the eroding effect of gnosticism is to point to the devaluation of the theological essence of baptism by the widely held view that we are all children of God by nature. This teaching has deeply penetrated the church. The classic Christian position, that we are children of God by adoption and grace, made effective in baptism, is now suspect in many quarters. Ironically, the de-sacramentalizing of baptism in the Episcopal Church — baptism is no longer required to receive Holy Communion in many parishes — has coincided with a new emphasis on the baptismal covenant.

The statement Jesus makes in John's Gospel, "Flesh and blood cannot inherit the kingdom of God," can be interpreted in a gnostic sense (meaning that *the body itself* is nonspiritual), but the Fourth Evangelist intends it as an *anti*-gnostic utterance, meaning that the unaided human being has no "natural" or innate potential for spiritual knowledge but can only receive it as an unmerited gift of God. The words of Jesus to Nicodemus, "That which is born of the flesh is flesh, and that which is born of the Spirit is spirit" (John 3:6), can easily be interpreted, gnostic-style, to mean that material "flesh" is evil (or insignificant) and the higher "spiritual" world is the way to God. However, the word "flesh" *(sarx)* is never used in this way in the New Testament, neither in John nor in Paul. In John, flesh carries the connotation of *incapacity* but not of evil ("It is the spirit that gives life, the flesh is of no avail" — 6:63). Indeed, it is precisely his flesh *(sarx)* that, in a profoundly anti-gnostic teaching, Jesus gives us to eat: "For my flesh is food indeed, and my blood is drink indeed. He who eats my flesh and drinks my blood abides in me, and I in him" (6:55-56). It is notable that "after this many of his disciples drew back and no longer went about with him," in part because they found his materialistic teaching offensive and irreligious (6:66).

A lot of Christians have "drawn back" from classical Christian teaching and "no longer go about" with the faith of the church. This includes a good many leaders and teachers.[23] There are many reasons for the great popular appeal of gnosticism. Much of it is in tune with today's American attitudes. It seems to offer greater openness and flexibility to those who experience Christian orthodoxy as rigid. It promises "a way to detach religious and creative impulses from any entrenched creed."[24] It is thought to be more welcoming to women, artists, freethinkers, and free spirits. It is attractive to those who think of themselves as offbeat, antiestablishment, adventurous,

23. The appeal of gnostic spirituality pervades much theological education today. During the late '60s and early '70s, life in the liberal seminaries — especially the interdenominational ones — was dominated by the call to revolutionary social action. It was not uncommon to hear clergy boast that they rarely prayed and spent little time preparing sermons because they were too busy on the barricades. With whiplash-like speed, the emphasis in the '80s and '90s, which continues today, shifted to "spirituality," a word and concept virtually unknown in Protestantism until quite recently. The suddenness of this change from social action and liberation theology to spirituality has been enormously confusing to faithful Christians who are served a smorgasbord of enneagrams, labyrinth-walking, and all things Celtic, with a heavy dose of the Jesus Seminar mixed in. Classical and biblical Christianity is lost in this unmoored environment.

24. Frederick Crews, "The Consolation of Theosophy," *New York Review of Books,* September, 19, 1996.

or iconoclastic. It definitely seems more "spiritual," and it offers a selection of paths to follow, techniques to master, knowledge to gain — yet without restrictive dogma. For example, gnostic devaluation of the material world offers two views of our sexual nature, both of them conducive to a libertine style of life. Either the sexual act is thought to be intensely spiritual, offering access to the divine, or it is a matter of no importance one way or the other, since the flesh is unspiritual. Either way, the gnostic is free of sexual restrictions. Paul seems to have some such teaching in mind when he says to the Corinthians, "Do you not know that your bodies are members of Christ? . . . Shun [sexual] immorality. Every other sin which a man commits is outside the body; but the immoral man sins against his own body. Do you not know that your body is a temple of the Holy Spirit within you, which you have from God?" (I Cor. 6:15-19). The biblical view of sexual relations is earthy and "fleshy" in a way that is utterly foreign to most "spiritual" thought. Paradoxically, the freewheeling sexual attitudes often seen in the various forms of gnosticism arise out of indifference to the lasting importance of the body. The idea that the indwelling Holy Spirit, God's gift in baptism, puts a different valuation on the body (understood literally), with consequences for sexual behavior, is Christian, not gnostic. It is therefore not difficult to understand why some variation of the gnostic view would be very appealing in our permissive society.

In the final analysis, however, the most serious incompatibility of gnosticism with the apostolic faith lies in gnosticism's claims for human religious capacity. It is remarkable that Christianity is widely believed to be a gnostic system. A professor of psychology at Brown guilelessly declares, "All religions assume that certain individuals have special access to *divine, esoteric, or transcendental knowledge* . . . believing it is part of the religious perspective itself. . . . The idea of *privileged access among a select few* is among the last to die when people fall away from a religious tradition."[25]

Allowing for all of gnosticism's varieties, we can safely say this, in summary: in gnosticism's portrayal of salvation, the power to redeem (God's power) has been subsumed into *our capacity for being redeemed.*[26] Therefore the crucifixion becomes unnecessary.

---

25. Joachim I. Krueger, "Holy Celebrity," *Psychology Today,* September/October 2013, 33, emphasis added.

26. Roy A. Harrisville, *Fracture: The Cross as Irreconcilable in the Language and Thought of the Biblical Writers* (Grand Rapids: Eerdmans, 2006), 276.

Religious Gnosticism versus the Fresh Wind of Irreligion

Dietrich Bonhoeffer wrote from his Nazi prison cell: "By *this-worldliness* I mean living unreservedly in life's duties, problems, successes and failures, experiences and perplexities. In so doing we throw ourselves completely into the arms of God, taking seriously, not our own sufferings, but those of God in the world."[27] The high value thus placed on the earthy, worldly, material, physical dimensions of life is one of the most striking characteristics of the Judeo-Christian tradition, marking it out from religious gnosticism. It has been well argued that secularity itself was made possible by Christianity.[28] Bonhoeffer was surely working with this concept when he began to write about "religionless Christianity" and the gospel in a secular world. One of the most powerful passages in his letters goes as follows: "God as a working hypothesis in morals, politics, or science has been surmounted and abolished; and the same thing has happened in philosophy *and religion*. . . . God would have us know that we must live as men who manage our lives without him. . . . The God who lets us live in the world without the working hypothesis of God is the God before whom we stand continually."[29]

Bonhoeffer did not live to work out these ideas fully, but he is here arguing against having God "smuggled in at some last secret place" as though God were irrelevant to anything but religious desperation. He wanted also to communicate that God is not a "working hypothesis." God is the living God who is already ahead of us in all our modernity, our sense of mastery, our worldly life at its strongest. He urged that the biblical message was not just something to fall back on in moments of weakness; "we shouldn't run man down in his worldliness, but confront him with God at his strongest point."[30] This is of the highest importance for Christian theology if we ever

27. Dietrich Bonhoeffer, *Letters and Papers from Prison,* ed. Eberhard Bethge, enlarged ed. (New York: Macmillan, 1972), 369-70, emphasis added.

28. "At the heart of the Christian gospel . . . is a tendency toward radical secularity." Richard K. Fenn, *Beyond Idols: The Shape of a Secular Society* (New York: Oxford University Press, 2001).

29. Bonhoeffer, *Letters and Papers,* 360, emphasis added.

30. Bonhoeffer, *Letters and Papers,* 346. This section is, in part, an attack on psychoanalysis. In all fairness, Bonhoeffer did not live long enough, nor was he temperamentally suited, to come to terms with the new phenomenon (although, or perhaps because, his father was the chair of psychiatry and neurology at the University of Berlin). He was concerned that it placed all the emphasis on the "inner life" and was therefore an enemy of "the whole person in relation to God," including ethical life and community responsibility. The passage is quoted here because it accords so well with the point we are making about the irreligiousness of the crucifixion.

hope to command the respect, if not the assent, of the unbeliever. It is this very passage from Bonhoeffer that ends with his often-quoted words, "God lets himself be pushed out of the world on to the cross." We are on safe ground to argue that the crucifixion of Jesus was the most secular, irreligious happening ever to find its way into the arena of faith.

The space thus opened up for irreligion at the very heart of the Christian message clears the way for all kinds of people in a way that the various forms of gnosticism simply cannot do. In gnosticism (including Christian gnosticism such as that in Corinth) there is always an inner circle, there is always a spiritual elite.[31] Gnosticism promises mysteries that only the illuminati can fathom.[32] It subtly or not so subtly suggests that "the capacity for being redeemed" is a condition for redemption. By contrast, the Christian gospel — when proclaimed in its radical New Testament form — is more truly "inclusive" of every human being, spiritually proficient or not, than any of the world's religious systems have ever been, *precisely because of the godlessness of Jesus' death.* In fact, the "word of the cross" is far more sweeping in its nullification of distinctions than many by-the-book conservative Christians are willing to admit. The Christian gospel, in slicing away all distinctions between "godly" and "ungodly" (Rom. 4:5), spiritual and unspiritual, offers a vision of God's purpose for the whole human race, believers and unbelievers alike, so comprehensive and staggering that even the apostle Paul is reduced to temporary speechlessness (Rom. 11:36). We will return to this theme at more length later in this volume, as we examine Paul's concept of justification, or rectification *(dikaiosis),* and the righteousness of God *(dikaiosyne).*

Gnosticism and the Cross

Why are we spending so much time on gnosticism? Here is the reason. Gnosticism in all its many forms prevents us from understanding the biblical witness to the crucifixion. Of all the characteristics of gnosticism that we have

31. This problem manifests itself in different ways. For example, in some circles those who are able to practice meditation consistently are considered farther along in their spiritual journeys than those who repeat a mantra a couple of times and then find their minds wandering like Winnie-the-Pooh's to the next snack. In a different context, I was once dis-invited to preach in a charismatic congregation because I was deemed to be insufficiently Spirit-filled.

32. Dr. Tom Moore in Walker Percy's *Love in the Ruins* says, "Beware of Episcopal women who take up with Ayn Rand and the Buddha and Dr. Rhine formerly of Duke University [the parapsychologist]. . . . They fall prey to Gnostic pride . . . and develop a yearning for esoteric doctrine." Walker Percy, *Love in the Ruins* (New York: Farrar, Straus and Giroux, 1971), 94.

surveyed, none is more important for our study than gnostic Christianity's studied lack of interest in the cross. Luke Timothy Johnson is a good guide to this matter. In commenting on the gnostic gospels, he first points out that unlike the canonical Gospels, they lack narrative structure, and then continues: "Even more strikingly, the Gnostic Gospels lack passion accounts. The death of Jesus is either omitted or touched on only lightly. Their emphasis is on the revelation of the divine. In the canonical Gospels [by contrast] the passion accounts play a central and decisive role. The emphasis of the canonical Gospels is on the suffering of the Messiah."

Johnson then makes precisely the point being emphasized here about religious teaching that recommends personal "spiritual" satisfaction without the cost of struggle and conflict: "In Gnostic Christianity, *the enlightenment of the mind enables the avoidance of suffering.*"

He continues: "The canonical Gospels view Jesus from the perspective of the Resurrection.... [B]ut in sharp contrast to the Gnostic Gospels, which have *only* that perspective, the canonical Gospels hold that vision of power in tension with the reality of Jesus' suffering and death.... In none of the canonical Gospels is the scandal of the Cross removed in favor of the divine glory. In each, the path to glory passes through real suffering."[33]

This absence of passion narratives from the gnostic gospels speaks volumes about the difference between gnostic Christianity and apostolic Christianity. This is insufficiently understood in the churches. A good dose of the Corinthian correspondence would be a healthy antidote. In these letters, especially the ones combined to make up II Corinthians, Paul writes at length and in some detail of his apostolic sufferings, not to boast — quite the opposite — but in a last-ditch bid to help the rebellious Corinthian Christians to understand that the life of the resurrection, while uniquely life-giving, has a not-yet dimension that cannot be manifested in this present world except by taking up the cross of Christ.[34] Church leaders, especially, should be mindful of Paul's description of the cruciform life: "We [apostles] are afflicted in every way, but not crushed; perplexed, but not driven to despair; persecuted, but not forsaken; struck down, but not destroyed; always carrying in the body the death of Jesus, so that the life of Jesus may also be manifested in our bodies. For while we live we are always being given up to death for Jesus'

---

33. Luke Timothy Johnson, *The Real Jesus: The Misguided Quest of the Historical Jesus and the Truth of the Traditional Gospels* (New York: HarperCollins, 1996), 150-51.

34. William Stringfellow, writing in the 1970s, offers a compelling defense of the "charismatic movement" when it is not detached from sociopolitical contexts but brought to bear upon such issues and struggles (*An Ethic for Christians and Other Aliens in a Strange Land* [Eugene, Ore.: Wipf and Stock, 1973], 143-51).

sake, so that the life of Jesus may be manifested in our mortal flesh. So death is at work in us [apostles], but life in you [Christians]" (II Cor. 4:8-12).

The Centrality of the Passion Narratives

Nowadays the debate about Jesus seems to be focusing largely on the question of his divinity, or lack thereof. The mainline churches tend to be on the defensive about the creedal claim that Jesus is the only-begotten Son of God. The situation was the reverse in the early church. The denial of Jesus' full humanity (the heresy called Docetism) was a principal enemy of orthodoxy in the first centuries. In those early days, in a religious milieu full of divine redeemers and saviors, it was much easier to claim Jesus as another deity than to argue for his concrete, suffering humanity. The opposite is true today; the humanity seems almost taken for granted over against the divinity (in secular and theologically liberal circles, at any rate). It was not always so. It was necessary, in the early centuries, to be militant against the powerful currents threatening to draw Jesus out of the world altogether. Churchgoers who regularly recite the Apostles' and Nicene Creeds in our time are so accustomed to naming Pontius Pilate there that they do not realize what an oddity this is in a theological manifesto. The name of this otherwise obscure provincial governor has been preserved forever at the heart of the Christian confession because it battens down the startlingly specific, historical nature of God's incarnate appearance among us — an anti-gnostic move if ever there was one. This "profane figure in the history of salvation" is there to close off argument about the geographical, chronological, and historical particularity of this human life and death.[35]

In the Apostles' and Nicene Creeds, the only word used in connection with the entire span of Jesus' life is "suffered." "Born of the Virgin Mary, suffered under Pontius Pilate, was crucified, dead, and buried." Who, today, notices how extraordinary this is? What a way to describe the life and ministry of a man so famous for his teachings, parables, healings, exorcisms, and other works! None of these things are even mentioned in the creeds, and very little is said of them in the various New Testament epistles. The wording of the creeds is a vivid demonstration of the early Christians' conviction that the passion was the culmination and consummation of everything that Jesus accomplished, so as to subsume everything else in the magnitude of

---

35. Jan Lochman, *The Faith We Confess: An Ecumenical Dogmatics* (Philadelphia: Fortress, 1984), 118.

its significance. Yet various versions of Christianity stripped of suffering and devoid of crucifixion are more common than ever in affluent America.

A North American theologian who has made important contributions to the theology of the cross is the Canadian Douglas John Hall.[36] He speaks of the crucifixion as a "conquest from within" the human condition, particularly emphasizing the human condition of pain, limitation, abandonment, and despair. He insists that the Christian community is identified by the *theologia crucis* as by nothing else. If we are to claim our true identity, we need to renounce our relentlessly upbeat orientation.[37] He calls for the church to understand itself as the community of the cross, the community that *suffers-with* (*com*-passion), the community that willingly bears the stigma of the passion in service to others. He declares that "the basic distinction between religion and [Christian] faith is the propensity of religions to avoid, precisely, suffering: to have light without darkness, vision without trust and risk, hope without an ongoing dialogue with despair — in short, Easter without Good Friday."[38] Here, Hall makes the same distinction between Christianity and religion that we opened up in the introduction. Feuerbach and Freud said, variously but with great intellectual courage, that "theology is anthropology" (Feuerbach) and that religion is wishful thinking, "born from man's need to make his helplessness tolerable" (Freud).[39] If avoidance of suffering is the aim of religion, it is no wonder that so many are drawn to its various manifestations and repelled by the cross.[40]

---

36. Douglas John Hall, *God and Human Suffering: An Exercise in the Theology of the Cross* (Minneapolis: Augsburg, 1989). Hall's more recent work has gone off on another track, but this particular monograph has much to offer on the subject of the cross.

37. We should always remember that statements like this describe the white churches more than the black. The black church has taught us much about how to integrate suffering with faith.

38. Hall, *God and Human Suffering*, 126. As a Canadian, Hall speaks of "North America," but after spending some time in various parts of Canada, it seems to me that he is largely addressing the United States.

39. There has never been a more trenchant argument against religion than that of Freud in *The Future of an Illusion*, which should be mandatory reading for every intellectually curious Christian. Discussing "the psychical origins of religious ideas," Freud writes that "they are illusions, fulfillments of the oldest, strongest, and most urgent wishes of mankind. The secret of their strength lies in the strength of those wishes" (*The Freud Reader*, ed. Peter Gay [New York: Norton, 1989], 695 and 703). Just so; it is the argument of this book that no human wish could have come up with a crucified God.

40. The central event of Christianity is too offensive and too much against the grain of religious thought as we know it ever to have emerged out of human religious imagination, no matter how philosophically subtle or humanly moving that religion might be. I personally find parts of the Qur'an and the Bhagavad-Gita quite stirring, but no one has been able to persuade

Jürgen Moltmann is even more incisive than Hall. The theology of the cross, he writes, "is not a single chapter in theology, but the key signature for all theology."[41] The names traditionally associated with this *theologia crucis* are Paul the apostle and Martin Luther. In our own time, it is not possible to deny or ignore the voices emerging from the underground to testify of the power of the theology of the cross. Thus Bonhoeffer, Moltmann, J. Christiaan Beker, and many others who have spoken out of the subhuman depths of World War II have guided us forward to a new understanding of the cross as *crux probat omnia* (the test that proves everything). When Moltmann, for instance, calls for attention to Good Friday in all its "profane horror," he speaks as one who has observed profane, horrible, and godless events firsthand and has determined not to turn away from them to a *theologia gloriae* (theology of glory). Moltmann has described his experience of returning to his theological classroom in Göttingen after World War II, together with other "shattered and broken" survivors, and being restored to life by lectures on the crucifixion. "A theology which did not speak of God in the sight of the One who was abandoned and crucified would have had nothing to say to us then."[42] Ernst Käsemann, arguably the most important New Testament scholar of the generation after Rudolf Bultmann, lost a daughter in the Argentine "Dirty War" of the 1970s; his later theology of the cross is wrung out of acute pain.[43] Japanese American theologian Kosuke Koyama has observed, "Jesus Christ is not a quick answer. If Jesus Christ is the answer, he is the answer in the way portrayed in crucifixion."[44] We cite Moltmann in summary of these observations: "Christians who do not have the feeling that

---

me that there is anything in them equal to "the word of the cross." Islam teaches that Jesus was not really crucified at all (Qur'an 4:157). John Stott has written, "I have entered many Buddhist temples in different Asian countries and stood respectfully before the statue of the Buddha, his legs crossed, arms folded, eyes closed, the ghost of a smile playing round his mouth. . . . But each time after a while I have had to turn away. And in imagination I have turned instead to that lonely, twisted, tortured figure on the cross . . . plunged in God-forsaken darkness. That is the God for me! He laid aside his immunity to pain. He entered our world of flesh and blood, tears and death. . . . There is still a question mark against human suffering, but over it we boldly stamp another mark, the cross which symbolizes divine suffering" (*The Cross of Christ* [Downers Grove, Ill.: InterVarsity, 1986], 335-36).

41. Moltmann, *The Crucified God*, 72.

42. Moltmann, *The Crucified God*, 1.

43. Martin Hengel's book, *Crucifixion*, is dedicated to the memory of Elisabeth Käsemann. The horrific story of her imprisonment and last days can be found online at htpp://memoryinlatinamerica.blogspot.com/2011/07/argentina-elisabeth-kaesemann.html.

44. Kosuke Koyama, *Mount Fuji and Mount Sinai: A Critique of Idols* (London: SCM, 1984), 241.

they must flee the crucified Christ have probably not yet understood him in a sufficiently radical way."[45]

The "Real" Jesus: The Crucified One

For some years now, the "third quest of the historical Jesus," driven by the publicity-loving Jesus Seminar and its satellites, has dominated media coverage of religion.[46] The ringing statements of the apostle Paul about the world-transforming significance of the cross/resurrection event are written off by these reconstructionists as theological accretions. Paul is construed as a mythmaker whose theological writings have no truthful relation to Jesus as these scholars present him — variously, as an Essene mystagogue, a Galilean Chasid or charismatic wonder-worker, a healer and sage, a political revolutionary, a peasant Cynic, a teacher of an alternative spirituality.[47] None of these interpretations of Jesus ascribes any transcendent significance to his crucifixion. His execution is generally interpreted in terms of the inevitable fate that awaited anyone who represented a threat to the order and authority of the divine emperor — an emphasis that should indeed play a significant part in any account of Jesus' death, but does not fully account for the message of the New Testament that, taken as a whole, presents Jesus' crucifixion, validated by the resurrection, as *the* defining feature of his entire life and mission.

It is essential to remember that it was the preaching *(kerygma)* of the apostles and early Christians that created the church in the first place. Men and women did not forsake their former ways of life because they were offered spiritual direction or instructed in righteous living; they became converts because of the explosive news that they heard. The apostolic preaching makes up most of the New Testament.[48] The Spirit-driven proclamation of

45. Moltmann, *The Crucified God*, 38.

46. The first "quest" was in the nineteenth century and was effectively brought to an end by Albert Schweitzer's landmark (albeit idiosyncratic) classic *The Quest of the Historical Jesus* (1906). The so-called second quest in the 1960s was associated with a group of Rudolf Bultmann's students, including Günther Bornkamm, whose *Jesus of Nazareth* (1956) was influential at the time, although the "second quest" flamed out in the 1970s. The Jesus Seminar and its spin-offs have been called the "third quest." Figures associated with the third quest include Robert Funk, Marcus Borg, John Shelby Spong, John Dominic Crossan, James M. Robinson, and many others. A parallel development is the work of E. P. Sanders, which has increased interest in Second Temple Judaism.

47. Summarized in Johnson, *The Real Jesus*, chap. 2.

48. The Pastoral Epistles and James only intermittently exhibit the ringing kerygmatic note (a notable passage in this regard is II Tim. 4:6-8, which sounds like the authentic voice

the new faith pivoted on the cross/resurrection event.[49] The overwhelming impression given by the apostolic *kerygma* is that of a revolution in human affairs. The first epistle of Peter speaks of this new preaching as "the things which have *now* been announced to you by those who preached the good news to you . . . things into which angels long to look" (I Pet. 1:12). The word "now" is often used in the Epistles to indicate the brand-new state of being that exists as a result of Christ's crucifixion and resurrection. This radical newness, this transformation, is epitomized by the very frequent appearance in Paul's letters and the epistles of Peter of the phrase "but now" *(nuni de).* Paul uses it six times in Romans; for example, "*But now* the righteousness of God has been manifested apart from law . . . the righteousness of God through faith in Jesus Christ for all who believe" (Rom. 3:21-22). We see striking occurrences of *nuni de* in I Peter 2:10 and 2:25. A passage from Ephesians, couched in the sweeping language typical of that great letter, puts it this way: "Therefore remember that at one time you Gentiles in the flesh . . . were . . . separated from Christ, alienated from the commonwealth of Israel, and strangers to the covenants of promise, having no hope and without God in the world. *But now* in Christ Jesus you who once were far off have been brought near in the blood of Christ" (Eph. 2:11-13).

These selections and dozens of other such passages make it clear that the new situation heralded by the "but now" is not a result of Jesus' teaching in and of itself. To be sure, the teaching and ministry were the inaugural events of God's new deed, as evidenced by Jesus' own announcement, "The time is fulfilled, and the kingdom of God is at hand" (Mark 1:15). The messianic nature and significance of Jesus' deeds are unforgettably described by him in his inaugural address in Luke 4:16-21. The testimony of the Gospels

---

of Paul), but their value should be construed differently, as commentary upon the *kerygma.* The Epistle of James is in a category by itself, though not entirely without kerygmatic features. This sort of distinction-making within the New Testament may seem illegitimate from a canonical perspective, but everyone must make some sort of decision — whether consciously or unconsciously — about which strains within the Bible are chosen to interpret and measure the other strains.

49. Ascension and Pentecost, though liturgically separated from Easter, are actually seamless parts of the cross/resurrection whole. The chronological separation observed in the church's calendar is based on the account in Luke-Acts, but John's version shows Pentecost occurring on Easter Day (John 20:22). In both cases, it is clear that the gift of the Spirit is the making-present of the power of the death and resurrection, and therefore in a real sense is an inseparable part of that total event. The passages on baptism in Rom. 8 and Eph. 1-2 (among others) also make this point. Although this is not the place to plead for greater liturgical and homiletical attention to Ascension and Pentecost, the argument of this book would naturally tend in that direction.

taken together, however, is that Jesus' work was only provisional until his crucifixion. It is the cross, and the cross alone, that seals his mission and, in retrospect, illuminates and explains all that preceded it. That is why all four Gospels include three solemn passion predictions. The Gospel of John adds its own distinctive note when Jesus speaks of his "hour" of crucifixion as definitive, saying, as he breathes his last, "It is consummated [*tetelestai*, 'finished, completed']" (John 19:30).

The cross, incomparably vindicated by the resurrection, is the *novum*, the new factor in human experience, the definitive and world-changing act of God that makes the New Testament proclamation unique in all the world. The claim of the early church was that the historical death of Jesus "under Pontius Pilate," followed by the metahistorical event of the resurrection, had changed everything for all time.

Incarnation and Crucifixion

Much of what is taught and celebrated in church life today — creation, incarnation, spirituality — is not always anchored in the preaching of Christ crucified (I Cor. 1:23). We have noted that this can result in a triumphalist form of congregational life that is disconnected from pain, deprivation, and the dehumanization that Jesus suffered.[50] This is not just a challenge for ethics; it is a theological challenge as well. What is the effective antidote to gnostic otherworldliness? Incarnation without crucifixion will not do the job by itself. The cross can never be merely assumed but must always be interpreted and re-placed at the center. There is a centrifugal force at work in human nature; we want to spin out and away from the offense of the cross. A current tendency is to interpret the incarnation to mean embracing the world *just as it is,* because the Son of God hallowed the world by becoming flesh — *incarnatus est.* This, however, can easily become a sentimental evasion of the tension between the world as it is and the world as it ought to be — the

---

50. Emphasis on the resurrection is characteristic of Eastern Orthodox Christianity, a tradition that, for all its beauty, richness, and staying power, has not exhibited much ethical or political dynamism in our time — unlike Roman Catholicism and Protestantism in certain countries and situations (Orthodoxy in Russia has been largely hand in glove with the Putin regime). However, the mystery and transcendence of the Eastern liturgy do have the great virtue of preserving a sense of the resurrection as *an event powered from beyond the realm known to us* — an insight missing from most Easter preaching in America today. And even in the resurrection-centered Orthodox Church, there are some countervailing influences; the writings of Dostoevsky reveal a deep kinship with the crucified Christ.

life of the world to come, the world that God is going to bring into being. A single-minded focus on the incarnation produces a tendency, often shared with the environmental movement, to regard the creation as unfallen.[51]

It is only a *single-minded* focus on the incarnation that presents problems. In no way do we seek to minimize the incarnation; the meaning of the cross depends upon it. Christmas has been described as "the feast of Nicene dogma"; the infant is "God of God, Light of Light, Very God of Very God / begotten, not created."[52] If the crucified One is not "begotten by the Father before all worlds," the message of the cross loses all its power.[53] An almost exclusive emphasis on the incarnation diminishes the cross as though it were a minor theme. On the contrary, the two stand or fall together. No Anglican has written more eloquently about this than Kenneth Leech, a radical incarnationalist. In his book *The Eye of the Storm,* Leech tells how he learned that "creation-centered, incarnational, sacramental religion" in and of itself was not only insufficient but downright dangerous, because it left no room for judgment, prophecy, struggle, or redemption. It was precisely such a religion that provided the spiritual soil for Mussolini, Franco, and Stalin, and provides it for the oppressive regimes of today.[54] Another book by Leech, *We Preach Christ Crucified,* has a section aptly called "The Scandal of Incarnation and Passion," in which he writes, "Bethlehem and Calvary, crib and cross, stand together."[55]

In one of his Good Friday sermons, Theodore Parker Ferris, for many years the powerful preacher in the pulpit of Trinity Church in Boston, drew out the link between the completeness of Jesus' humanity and his suffering on the cross — between the incarnation and the crucifixion. Musing on Jesus' cry of dereliction (Matt. 27:46; Mark 15:34), Ferris says, "It seems almost inevitable to me that Jesus should go through this kind of darkness. . . . If you think of Jesus as God disguised as a man, then this will have no meaning

51. This effect has been multiplied by uncritical enthusiasm for romanticized versions of Celtic and Native American practices.

52. These words from the hymn *Adeste fideles* are sung widely throughout the Western Church. John Francis Wade (1711-1786), a learned specialist in early church music, is credited with the Latin words and the arrangement of an earlier tune. Charles Wesley's equally celebrated Christmas hymn, "Hark! the Herald Angels Sing," includes the words, "Veiled in flesh the Godhead see / Hail th'incarnate deity."

53. In the celebrated Merode Altarpiece (Robert Campin and workshop, South Netherlands, c. 1427-1432) depicting the annunciation at the Cloisters in New York, the embryonic Christ child *is already carrying his cross.* (The reproduction online at Art Resource points out virtually every little detail in the painting except that one.)

54. Kenneth Leech, *The Eye of the Storm: Spiritual Resources for the Pursuit of Justice* (London: Darton, Longman, and Todd, 1992), 153.

55. Kenneth Leech, *We Preach Christ Crucified* (New York: Church Publishing, 1994), 13.

for you. But if you think of him as a real man who in the very depths of his manhood disclosed the very nature of the Godhead, then this [suffering] is inevitable . . . this is an intrinsic part of human existence."[56] The uttermost depth of human misery has been plumbed by the incarnate Lord.

Personal engagement with the cross is difficult and painful, but leaders of congregations will have a hole in the center of their ministry without it. Leech writes,

> [I]t is the task of the preacher to hold up Christ [crucified] as a symbol of folly and scandal, a sign of contradiction, and so to bring about the *krisis,* that turbulence and upheaval in the soul which opens it to the word which is the power of salvation. . . . The proclamation of Christ's death involves an engagement with the wounded Christ, the Christ who suffers, who "bears in his heart all wounds" [Edith Sitwell]. If this engagement does not take place, the preacher is in deep trouble, and there is real danger of a descent into glibness and into that false sense of conquest which insults the sufferer and trivializes suffering.[57]

Leech argues that the only way to confront the smugness and self-satisfaction that so often paralyze the nerve of Christian action is to preach *participation* in the cross, a theme of great importance to which we will return.

Eucharistic Liturgies: Good Friday or Easter?

A shift in theological emphasis within recent decades has resulted in the resurrection being set over against the crucifixion when eucharistic liturgies are being designed or interpreted. Whether this is owing largely to liturgical

56. Theodore Parker Ferris, *What Jesus Did* (Cincinnati: Forward Movement Miniature Book, 1969), 83. I heard Ferris preach on Good Friday only once, but it was unforgettable. He was an extraordinarily effective Three Hours preacher because he seemed to be participating in the suffering he was talking about.

57. Leech, *We Preach Christ Crucified,* 14, 21. Notice Leech's use of the word *krisis:* this is an important Greek term in the Gospel of John. It means "judgment" or "division," but the English word "crisis" gives a sense of it also. The point is that the arrival of Jesus on the scene precipitates a crisis. Sometimes John connects the crisis specifically with the approach of the passion: "Now is the judgment *(krisis)* of this world, now shall the ruler of this world be cast out" (John 12:31). Earlier in the Gospel it refers more generally to the incarnation: "And this is the judgment *(krisis),* that the light has come into the world, and men loved darkness rather than light, because their deeds were evil" (John 3:19). In any case, the point is that Jesus' mission calls every human being and every human arrangement into judgment.

reform or to our contemporary cultural mood is debatable, but the received wisdom at present seems to be that the Eucharist is an Easter liturgy, so it is unsuitable to place undue emphasis on sin, death, and atonement. This point of view played a large part in the revision of the Episcopal Book of Common Prayer. Cranmer's eucharistic prayer was deemed too penitential and insufficiently celebratory; it is retained in the Prayer Book as Rite I, but it has almost disappeared in practice.[58] In any study of the crucifixion of Christ, this development needs to be examined. Is there biblical warrant for it?

This setting of Easter over against the cross and its significance is in conflict with the apostolic preaching. There was no thought of separating cross and resurrection, or of elevating one over the other. If you're making a ham and cheese sandwich, you don't ask which is more important, the ham or the cheese. If you don't have both of them, it isn't a ham and cheese sandwich. Moving from the ridiculous to the sublime, you can't have the crucifixion without the resurrection — and vice versa. The resurrection is not just the reappearance of a dead person. It is the mighty act of God to vindicate the One whose very right to exist was thought to have been negated by the powers that nailed him to a cross. At the same time, however, the One who is gloriously risen is the same One who suffered crucifixion. It is not an insignificant detail that "doubting Thomas" asks to see the marks of the nails and the spear in the Lord's resurrected body (John 20:25). The book of Revelation is an extended hymn to the risen Christ, but he is nevertheless the "Lamb standing, as though it had been slain," the One whose wounds still show, the One by whose blood the robes of the redeemed have been cleansed for all eternity (Rev. 5:6-7).[59]

The reason Paul said to the Corinthians, "I decided to know nothing among you except Jesus Christ and him crucified" (I Cor. 2:2), is not that

---

58. It has become almost an article of faith throughout the Episcopal Church that the emphasis on Christ's death in Thomas Cranmer's eucharistic prayer (1549 and 1552) was misplaced, since the Lord's Supper is now presented as a liturgy of the resurrection. This angle on Cranmer and the English Reformation has had a sweeping effect, making it more difficult now to locate the worshiping congregation at the foot of the cross. I do not wish to be misunderstood here; the Episcopal Prayer Book needed revision. The result of the revision, however, was a more thoroughgoing excision of the "most precious death and sacrifice" and the theme of atonement "for the sins of the whole world" than many Episcopalians in the 1970s had bargained for. The new emphasis has carried the day to such a degree that only elderly Episcopalians now remember what the liturgical emphasis on "the remembrance of his blessed passion and precious death" was like. (At the same time, Cranmer included "his mighty resurrection and glorious ascension" in equal measure in that remembrance.)

59. Charles Wesley, in one of his greatest hymns, writes of the "glorious scars" that will evoke exultation from Christ's worshipers when he comes again ("Lo, He Comes with Clouds Descending").

he considered the resurrection to be of lesser importance. The reason Paul insisted on the centrality of the cross in polemical terms was that the Corinthian Christians wanted to pass over it altogether. This tendency persists in the American church today. H. Richard Niebuhr put it unforgettably in *The Kingdom of God in America:* "A God without wrath brought men without sin into a kingdom without judgment through the ministrations of a Christ without a cross."[60] When this happens, we may have religiosity, we may have uplift, we may have spirituality, but we do not have Christianity.

The passion and resurrection are bound together in one narrative. Robert Jenson reminds us of "the ancient single service of the *Triduum*," dating from the third century — the three-day observance beginning on Maundy (Holy) Thursday and extending through Good Friday to the Easter Vigil.[61] Present-day worshipers who have undergone total immersion in modern versions of the Triduum can testify that this way of observing the central Christian events does indeed draw the community into the whole of the drama in a way that simply cannot be equaled by any abbreviated or selective liturgy. The influence of the liturgical movement in the various Protestant denominations has introduced more American Christians to some form of the Triduum. Anything that can correct our current tendency to expect an easy, nonthreatening leap from Palm Sunday to Easter Day is welcome.[62]

The Lord's Supper under the Sign of the Cross

Is the Lord's Supper therefore a sacrament of Christ's death, or of his resurrection? Or both? One of the most emphatic New Testament teachings about

60. H. Richard Niebuhr, *The Kingdom of God in America* (New York: Harper Torchbooks, 1959), 193.

61. Robert Jenson, *Systematic Theology,* vol. 1, *The Triune God* (New York: Oxford University Press, 1997), 181.

62. A counterbalance to this trend away from the cross is the now-common dramatic reading of the passion narrative on Palm Sunday in some denominations. This has been a tremendous contribution to understanding and participation. But the way still lies uphill, since the Palm Sunday liturgy is so long that the sermon tends to get short shrift. Few Protestants now attend services during Holy Week. Clifton Black, professor of biblical theology at Princeton Seminary, writes, "The functional avoidance of Good Friday among many Christians is a heresy of long standing. Its tacit justification seems to be that Easter Sunday signals a victory so complete that God effectively annihilated Golgotha. Such confusion makes for a theology that is not merely bad, but heartless and even dangerous. It . . . dares to attempt what even God refused: obliterating the wounds of Christ Crucified" (Black, "The Persistence of the Wounds," in *Lament: Reclaiming Practices in Pulpit, Pew, and Public Square* [Louisville: Westminster John Knox, 2005], 57).

the Supper occurs in a discussion about the insensitivity shown by the affluent toward the poor in the church in Corinth.[63] There was serious abuse going on when the community came together for the *agape* meal and the Lord's Supper. In that congregation, the occasion apparently afforded an opportunity for the well-to-do to arrive early, bringing their own food and wine, so that those who came late from their work and had no worldly goods were humiliated. In I Corinthians 11, Paul addresses this situation directly and at some length. "When you come together it is not for the better but for the worse. . . . It is not the Lord's supper that you eat. . . . Do you despise the church of God and humiliate those who have nothing?" (11:17, 20, 22). Paul is upset because the rite in Corinth has deteriorated into a mockery of itself. Correcting them, he writes, "for as often as you eat this bread and drink this cup, you proclaim *the Lord's death* until he comes" (11:26).[64] It appears that for Paul, the Corinthians' overemphasis on an already accomplished spiritual immortality (15:50-56) has thrown the Supper out of balance, leading to a failure on their part to "discern the body" (11:29) of Christ in its newly reconstituted reality where, as in the sayings of the Lord, "the last will be first, and the first last" (Matt. 20:16).[65] Paul is calling attention to what he said in the first part of the letter: "Not many [of you] were powerful [or] of noble birth; . . . [but] God chose what is weak in the world to shame the strong, God chose what is low and despised in the world [this, too, is a double reference, not only to the 'low and despised' members of the congregation, *but also and especially* to a crucified man], even things that are not, to bring to nothing things that are" (I Cor. 1:26-28).[66]

It is important to understand the additional reasons for Paul's alarm. The key verse for present purposes is 11:26: "For as often as you eat this bread and drink this cup, you proclaim the Lord's death until he comes." In addition to the concern about stratification in the congregation, Paul is

63. "Lord's Supper" is the least divisive term, since it is the one used in the apostolic age (*kuriakon deipnon*, I Cor. 11:20). Many Lutherans still resist the term *eucharist* (thanksgiving) because it seems to make the congregation, rather than the Lord, the active party in the sacrament.

64. Rudolf Schnackenburg, *The Church in the New Testament* (New York: Herder and Herder, 1965), 42-45. See also Günther Bornkamm, *Early Christian Experience* (New York: Harper and Row, 1969), 123-30.

65. Matthew 20:16 locates this well-known saying in a particularly startling context, the parable of the workers who are all paid the same at the end of the day, out of the Lord's generosity, even though some of them hardly worked at all — to the indignation of those who worked all day in the heat. Its relevance to the Lord's Supper, with its all-embracing erasure of distinctions, is obvious.

66. This is one of the clearest references in Scripture to *creatio ex nihilo*, creation out of nothing.

addressing two underlying failures in Corinth, failures that remain common in the church even to the present day. As Gordon D. Fee writes, "[The Corinthians'] new spirituality seems to have caused them to miss both [Paul's] points . . . (1) *Christ's death,* and (2) *until he comes.*"[67] The Corinthians seem to have little understanding of the "not-yet" aspect of Christian life. They want only the "now." They think of themselves as living in the resurrection already, all the time. This, as Paul sees, has ramifications for the cruciform pattern of life among God's people.

The cross and resurrection form a single entity, as has already been stressed. But here Paul places the emphasis specifically on the Lord's *death,* because his purpose in the Corinthian letter is to recapture the cross, in all its scandal and paradox, as the indispensable cornerstone of Christian proclamation.[68] Thus "discerning the body" probably has a double meaning: (1) the body of Christ crucified, given "for you" (11:24) and received in the bread and cup; and (2) the body of Christ as the church itself, in this case the specific local Corinthian congregation and the organic connection linking its members to their Lord.[69] If the affluent members are neglectful of the working-class members, the body of Christ is not being discerned in *either* sense. For reasons such as this, we may conclude, Paul postpones his climactic chapter on the resurrection to the end of the letter, in order to fasten the cross into place first as the determining sign of Christian existence in the world "until he comes."[70] An exclusively celebratory Eucharist encourages

---

67. Gordon D. Fee, *The First Epistle to the Corinthians,* New International Commentary of the New Testament (Grand Rapids: Eerdmans, 1987), numerals added.

68. "Cornerstone" seems the right word, in view of the New Testament's striking references to Christ as the "stumbling stone" (*skandalon;* see also *proskomma:* Rom. 9:33; I Pet. 2:8).

69. This organic link is defined by John as vine and branches (John 15:5). It would be hard to defend Paul's reference as a comment upon "the body" as the literal bread, as in much later debates about the nature of the eucharistic Host. That would not have interested Paul. What he cares about is the radical leveling of everyone who partakes of the Supper. Wherever there is a celebration of the Supper in a multiethnic setting or a context of wide socioeconomic disparity, there should be general wonderment at the miracle of oneness that is occurring by the grace of God. As a eucharistic hymn from the very earliest days of the church (c. A.D. 110) puts it:

> As grain once scattered on the hillsides,
> Was in this broken bread made one,
> So from all lands thy Church be gathered
> Into thy kingdom by thy Son.
>
> "Father, We Thank Thee Who Hast Planted," Episcopal Church Hymnal,
> #302-303, translated from the Greek by F. Bland Tucker (1895-1984).

70. Beverly R. Gaventa, "You Proclaim the Lord's Death: I Corinthians 11:26 and Paul's Understanding of Worship," *Review and Expositor* 80 (1983): 380.

a notion of an already-achieved immortality of the faithful, the very thing that I Corinthians 15 was written to rebut.

As for the Gospels, the link of the Last Supper to the death on the cross is explicit. In each of the four Gospels, Jesus goes directly from the supper table to the Garden of Gethsemane knowing that he is to be betrayed and arrested. The dramatic foot-washing action of Jesus in the Gospel of John takes place very specifically in the context of the Last Supper "when Jesus knew that his hour had come to depart out of this world to the Father" (John 13:1). Thus the biblical testimony emphasizes in various ways the uninterrupted link between the Supper and the death. Notice, for instance, the way that Luke constructs chapter 22, beginning with (1) the chief priests and scribes conspiring to put him to death and (2) the entrance of Satan "into Judas called Iscariot" (Luke 22:2-6).[71] He then moves without interruption (the reference to the Passover in 22:1 and 22:7 providing the link) to Jesus' directions for finding the upper room, which has clearly been chosen already by God (22:9-13).

Continuing with the eucharistic theme, let us think further about Jesus himself. What did he want to communicate to his disciples, and thence to the church, about his life's work? The traditional prayer begins, "On the night he was betrayed . . ." These words are taken not only from the accounts of the Last Supper in the Gospels, but also and especially from Paul's recapitulation in I Corinthians 11:23-26.

> For I [Paul] received from the Lord what I also delivered to you, that the Lord Jesus on the night when he was betrayed took bread, and when he had given thanks, he broke it, and said, "This is my body which is for you. Do this in remembrance of me." In the same way also the cup, after supper, saying, "This cup is the new covenant in my blood. Do this, as often as you drink it, in remembrance of me." For as often as you eat this bread and drink the cup, you proclaim the Lord's death until he comes.

The overwhelming impression given by the four Gospels plus I Corinthians 11 is that the Lord, knowing he was soon to be betrayed, deliberately and solemnly spoke of *my body* and *my blood* given *for you* (Matthew adds,

---

71. Only Luke and John mention the devil in relation to Judas's decision; Matthew and Mark do not. Thus the two Gospels that are generally thought to be less apocalyptic than Matthew and Mark are nevertheless the ones that explicitly identify Satan (not Judas himself) as the agent in the betrayal of Jesus. The stance taken in this book is to respect the significant differences among the four Gospels and not try to conflate them, but at the same time, it is not always a good idea to cordon off one or two of them over against the others.

"poured out for many for the forgiveness of sins"). This very specific talk about a body given and blood poured out can only be interpreted in terms of Jesus' *death*.[72] The "new covenant in my blood" is established, not by an assumption into heaven nor even by a heroic martyr's death, but by the strangest death ever conceived for a divine figure.

Thus the apostle Paul admonished the fractious Corinthians: "Because there is one bread, we who are many are one body, for we all partake of the one bread" (I Cor. 10:17). As the Lord welcomed sinners at table, so the communion service lifts and binds together "all sorts and conditions" of human beings.[73]

Do we meet the risen Lord in the Lord's Supper? Absolutely. Is the sacrament of the Lord's Supper a liturgy of the resurrection? Absolutely. But the resurrection did not occur independently of the crucifixion. The people who come forward to receive the sacrament are not a shining band of perfected saints — *not yet*. It is therefore of great importance, ethically as well as theologically, to recognize that there is no secure place of permanent rest in this world for the pilgrim people of God whose calling is to "proclaim the Lord's *death until he comes*" (I Cor. 11:26).

Summing Up the Primacy of the Cross

The New Testament witnesses had to fight with all their strength to keep the Lord's death at the forefront of the preaching, worship, and ethics of the new faith. Paul's term *skandalon* ("stumbling block," "pitfall") well conveys the perverse nature of the cross. Forces within and without the early church exploited every opportunity to minimize or set aside the absurdly irreligious claim that a degrading, state-sponsored execution had secured the salvation of the entire cosmos. But all four Evangelists resisted these pressures to move in the direction of something more spiritually familiar, and instead made the long, continuous passion narrative the climax of their work.

Of all the enemies of the "word of the cross," it is gnosticism, in particular, that offers parallels to contemporary American religious life. Our stock-in-trade is "positive thinking," with its partner, avoidance — blocking

---

72. John's version of the bread-word and cup-word is idiosyncratic, as always: "He who eats my flesh and drinks my blood abides in me, and I in him" (John 6:56). It would be easy to misread this as though Jesus were speaking of a gnostic mystery-meal, but in fact the Johannine writings are vigorously anti-gnostic, and the Greek of John 6:56 is startlingly earthy and materialistic.

73. Book of Common Prayer (1979), 814.

out difficult and painful issues. Gnostic denial of Christ's physical life and extraordinarily gruesome death has always found willing adherents, but a consumerist culture is especially susceptible, because many have the leisure, the economic resources, and the inclination to experiment with ever newer and more exotic sensations, including "spiritual" ones. Over against this type of religion, the Christian gospel places the cross. Paul's Corinthian correspondence is especially notable in its insistence upon redemptive suffering in this material world as the truest way of participating in Christ. Paul contrasts his own ministry with that of the self-satisfied Corinthian congregation; his diagnosis of their symptoms is that they lack grounding in "the word of the cross."[74]

The New Testament witnesses, and especially the author of I John, are fighting on a related front to secure the human, fleshly actuality of Jesus at the center of the faith. Jesus is the reality "which we have heard, which we have seen with our eyes, which we have looked upon and touched with our hands, concerning the word of life" (I John 1:1). His life was a real human life and his death was a real human death; he was not a god in a covering of human skin and his death was not an assumption into spiritual glory. His existence in this physical realm is a hallmark of authentic Christian faith: "By this you know the Spirit of God: every spirit which confesses that Jesus Christ has come *in the flesh* is of God" (I John 4:2). The New Testament writers see no competition between the incarnation and the cross. Vigilance is required by the church, however, to see that the ready appeal of the incarnation is not allowed to take over from the wrenching difficulties of preaching and living the offense *(skandalon)* of the crucifixion.

This chapter has been about the primacy of the cross. We have not yet said enough about the *godless* nature of it; that is the subject of the next chapter. Episcopal bishop Philip Rhinelander, in *The Faith of the Cross,* summarizes for us the astonishing but insufficiently noted fact that the first Christians were determined to make the *godlessness* primary:

> If ever mortal men found a real hero on this earth, those men were the disciples. They, indeed, were hero-worshippers. Then think of the horrid shock and shame which overwhelmed them at the Cross. It was no splendid martyrdom for a great cause, no glorious conquest won at the cost of

---

74. Paul is very annoyed with the Corinthians when he writes sarcastically, "Already you are filled! Already you have become rich! Without us [apostles] you have become kings! And would that you did reign, so that we might share the rule with you! For I think that God has exhibited us apostles as last of all, like men sentenced to death" (I Cor. 4:8-9).

life; no epic to be sung and celebrated. No, the Cross was simply an utter overthrow, a speechless failure. It was all sordid, cruel, criminal, a gross injustice, an intolerable defeat of good by evil, of God by devils. . . . He their hero, their chosen leader, he was numbered with the transgressors. He was cast out with a curse upon him. Think how loyalty would burn to right this wrong, to clear his memory, to save his reputation, to prove that gross outrage had been done him, to magnify the life so that the death might be forgotten. . . . But nothing of the kind seems to have occurred to the Evangelists. They literally glory in the Cross. . . . They are clear, with an absolute conviction, that the best and most wonderful thing he ever did was . . . to die a felon's death, between two robbers. It was their hero's greatest heroism that he was executed as a common criminal.[75]

To summarize, then: *the crucifixion is the touchstone of Christian authenticity, the unique feature by which everything else, including the resurrection, is given its true significance.*

75. Rhinelander, *Faith of the Cross*, 81-82.

CHAPTER TWO

The Godlessness of the Cross

In order to speak of the crucified God we need a theology of abandonment, of dereliction, of an alienation so profound that it can only be expressed in language marked by paradox and by great daring and risk. The Crucifixion of the Son of God by one of the most advanced civilizations in the ancient world does not seem to be an acceptable or reasonable method of redeeming the world. There is something so outrageous and obscene about it that the agony in Gethsemane becomes the only comprehensible part of the whole saga.

KENNETH LEECH, *We Preach Christ Crucified*[1]

As we began to see in the introduction, it takes some effort of the imagination to understand the singular degree of public disgust caused by crucifixion as a method of execution. Yet we must make this effort in order to understand more fully the meaning of the Greek term *skandalon* ("stumbling block," "pitfall") that the apostle Paul uses, as in the phrase "the *skandalon* of the cross" (Gal. 5:11). Most of us are conditioned to think of Jesus' *death* as the scandal, when in fact it is not the *death in itself* but the *mode* of death that creates the offense.

The Method as the Message

In the summer of 1998, Westminster Abbey unveiled ten new statues over the door of its main entrance. Niches that had stood empty for more than

---

1. Kenneth Leech, *We Preach Christ Crucified* (New York: Church Publishing, 1994), 69-70.

five hundred years were filled, in one breathtaking stroke, with figures of twentieth-century Christian martyrs. Those most recognizable to Americans are Martin Luther King, Dietrich Bonhoeffer, Oscar Romero, and Janani Luwum, who was Anglican archbishop of Uganda under Idi Amin. The ten men and women memorialized lost their lives bearing witness to their Lord. There is no hint, however, of how they died. There are no guns, no hangman's nooses, no machetes. The point is not *how* they died, but *that* they died.[2]

The death of Jesus is different because the "how" is of unique importance. In chapter 1, we noted the primacy given to the suffering and death of Jesus in the passion narratives and Pauline letters. Even more noteworthy, however, is the way Christians characteristically speak not only of "the death" or "the execution" of Jesus but also quite specifically of "the crucifixion," as though the *manner* of his death has special significance. And so it does. Many scholars believe that Paul's distinctive signature is found in the addition he appears to have made to the early Christian confession in Philippians 2:8: "He humbled himself and became obedient unto death, *even death on a cross.*" The *manner* of Jesus' death has stamped the character of the faith for all time. He himself made it central when he said that anyone who would be his disciple would "take up his cross and follow me." Other leaders may have called their followers to die heroically, but they did not call attention to the *means* of their deaths in this deliberate manner.

Many great figures of history have died prematurely and violently as a result of their activities. Here again, however, Jesus' death is singular. He was not hanged by Nazis (Bonhoeffer), murdered by a crazed dictator (Luwum), assassinated by right-wing thugs (Romero), or shot by a small-time racist fanatic (King). These men's deaths were to varying degrees aberrant, unlawful, or clandestine, but as Paul says of Christ in the Acts of the Apostles, "This was not done in a corner" (Acts 26:26). Jesus was put to death publicly, deliberately, and *with impunity* (a word we will return to). His execution was carried out by all the best people, representatives of the highest religious and governmental authorities. We might think of other luminaries who have been put to death by their governments, but once again, the analogies fail; Socrates was permitted a death of extraordinary dignity, Joan of Arc was in

---

2. It is true that for many centuries, Christian martyrs were depicted holding the instruments of their torture — Bartholomew with a flaying knife, Catherine with a wheel, Lawrence with a grill, and so forth. I think it is fair to say that these symbols were *derivative from* the cross of Christ and were used to show how the martyrs had participated in the Lord's death. Even in those cases, the emphasis is not *how* they died but *that* they died.

the process of becoming a sainted embodiment of France even as she was burning, Thomas More was allowed an elegant witticism as he put his head on the block. Public impaling and the hanging-drawing-quartering of Tudor England probably offer the closest parallels, but they were administered to all classes of society, even the aristocracy — whereas crucifixion was almost entirely used for the dregs of humanity, and never for Roman citizens.

John the Baptist's execution at the behest of Herod's wife is portrayed in the Gospels of Matthew and Mark as a portent of Jesus' own destiny. John was innocent of any capital crime, or indeed of any crime except confronting the ruler with his own misconduct, but John met a cruel fate by order of that ruler and his wife. John's death was memorably horrible; who can forget the severed head on the platter? Yet even this gruesome image does not carry with it the same stigma as crucifixion. It is *the stigma itself* that needs to be emphasized if we are to grasp the extreme peculiarity of a cross as a symbol of faith.

The Unique Irreligiousness of the Cross as a Mode of Execution

In 1995, an article in the *New York Times* described an episode in a nation-wide civic dispute that is, if anything, even more heated twenty years later. Concerning the holiday display of religious symbols in American parks and other public areas, the Capitol Square Review Board in Columbus, Ohio, argued that the cross may not be so displayed because it is "the quintessential symbol of the Christian faith." The civic authorities permitted a Christmas tree and a Hanukkah menorah, but according to the article, when someone in Columbus tried to erect a cross on public property, the agency refused, on grounds that *"unlike the other [symbols],* the cross was an exclusively religious symbol."[3]

We may cheer the Columbus review board for making this distinction. The continuing debate about Christmas decorations is sometimes amusing and always challenging, since it involves all sorts of deep feelings and usually ends up pleasing no one. We mention this particular episode here for two reasons. First, it is noteworthy that even a secular agency recognizes the unique status of the cross and says so in no uncertain terms. Second, however, the review board's assessment offers us an opportunity to focus on the description of the cross as a "religious symbol." Most people would not think twice about such a definition. It would not even occur to most Christians to question it. Yet at the most fundamental level — and this can't

3. *New York Times,* January 14, 1995.

be emphasized too strongly — *the cross is in no way "religious."* The cross is by a very long way the most *irreligious* object ever to find its way into the heart of faith. J. Christiaan Beker refers to it as "this most nonreligious and horrendous feature of the Gospel."[4]

The crucifixion marks out the essential distinction between Christianity and "religion." Religion as defined in these pages is either an organized system of belief or, alternatively, a loose collection of ideas and practices, *projected out of humanity's needs and wishes.* The cross is "irreligious" because no human being individually or human beings collectively would have projected their hopes, wishes, longings, and needs onto a crucified man.[5] In a PBS television series, *The Christians* (1981), a studiously impartial narrator said this: "Christianity is the only major religion *to have as its central focus the suffering and degradation of its God.* The crucifixion is so familiar to us, and so moving, that it is hard to realize *how unusual it is as an image of God"* (emphasis added). The description of the cross as "moving" is noteworthy, but not the point.[6] We focus on the narrator's (or screenwriter's) perception of *the wrenching unsuitability of a crucifixion as an object of faith.* He has come closer than many Christians to understanding not only the abhorrent and irreligious nature of crucifixion as a method of execution but also the unlikelihood of it arising out of religious imagination.[7]

Churches sometimes offer Christian education classes under the title "Why Did Jesus Have to Die?" This is not really the right question. A better one is, "Why was Jesus *crucified?"* The emphasis needs to be, not just on the death, but on the *manner* of the death. To speak of a crucifixion is to speak

4. J. Christiaan Beker, *Paul the Apostle: The Triumph of God in Life and Thought* (Philadelphia: Fortress, 1980), 207.

5. "It is the Crucifixion that distinguishes the new message from the mythologies of all other peoples. . . . The heart of the Christian message, which Paul described as 'the word of the cross,' ran counter not only to Roman political thinking, but to the whole ethos of religion in ancient times and in particular to the ideas of God held by educated people. . . . A crucified Messiah, son of God, or god must have seemed a contradiction in terms to anyone, Jew, Greek, Roman, or barbarian, asked to believe such a claim, and it will certainly have been thought offensive and foolish." Martin Hengel, *Crucifixion* (Philadelphia: Fortress, 1977), 1, 5-6. This was originally part of a Festschrift for Ernst Käsemann.

6. The cross is never merely "moving," though many have put the emphasis there, as in popular borrowings from the exemplary or moral influence model associated with the name of Abelard.

7. Robert L. Wilken quotes the early-fourth-century Christian apologist Lactantius: "[Pagans] cast in our teeth" the suffering of Jesus because they say "we worship a man and one who was visited and tormented with remarkable punishment" (*The Christians as the Romans Saw Them,* 2nd ed. [New Haven: Yale University Press, 2003], 155).

of a slave's death.[8] We might think of all the slaves in the American colonies who were killed at the whim of an overseer or owner, not to mention those who died on the infamous Middle Passage across the Atlantic. No one remembers their names or individual histories; their stories were thrown away with their bodies. This was the destiny chosen by the Creator and Lord of the universe: *the death of a nobody.*

> He was despised and rejected by men. . . .
> As one from whom men hide their faces
>   he was despised, and we esteemed him not. (Isa. 53:3)

Thus the Son of God entered into solidarity with the lowest and least of all his creation, the nameless and forgotten, "the offscouring of all things" (I Cor. 4:13). There is nothing remotely "religious" about any of this.[9] Of particular interest in this context is Deuteronomy 21:23, a prohibition against the display of a body on a "tree," accursed by God, which seized the attention of a Pharisee named Saul of Tarsus. Neither impaling nor hanging nor any other method of doing away with a person was ever *specifically identified in its religious context as being godforsaken.* We must put the greatest possible emphasis on this fact. Jürgen Moltmann writes:

> From the very first, the Christian faith was distinguished from the religions which surrounded it by its worship of the crucified Christ. In Isra-

8. The distinguished scholar Peter Brown has cautioned me against referring to crucifixion this way since it was not reserved specifically for slaves but, rather, for non-Roman citizens. He is, of course, correct, but it is nevertheless legitimate to emphasize crucifixion as a method administered to the lowest classes. The upper classes certainly managed, for the most part, to avoid it. Electrocution in America is not strictly speaking a poor black man's death, but in practice it usually has worked out that way. In one of his speeches, Cicero referred to crucifixion as *servitutis extremo summoque supplicio,* the most extreme form of torture inflicted upon slaves. Several Roman writers refer to it as *servile supplicium,* the slaves' death. Plautus, the comic dramatist known for his sympathetic if raucous depiction of slaves, shows in several casual remarks made by his characters that crucifixion was taken for granted as the method that would await slaves if they caused trouble. Indeed, according to Hengel, crucifixion was used "above all as a deterrent against trouble among slaves" (Hengel, *Crucifixion,* 51-52, 54; see also Raymond E. Brown, *The Death of the Messiah: From Gethsemane to the Grave; A Commentary on the Passion Narratives in the Four Gospels,* 2 vols. [Garden City, N.Y.: Doubleday, 1994], 947).

9. Walter Benjamin, the influential Jewish philosopher, kept a copy of Grünewald's gruesome altarpiece of the crucifixion in his office (as also did Karl Barth). Benjamin said it represented the *Ausdrucklose,* "a thing beyond telling, out of the reach of words." (Told by Roy A. Harrisville, *Fracture: The Cross as Irreconcilable in the Language and Thought of the Biblical Writers* [Grand Rapids: Eerdmans, 2006], 279.)

elite understanding, someone executed in this way was rejected by his people, cursed amongst the people of God by the God of the law, and excluded from the covenant of life. "Cursed be everyone that hangs on a tree" (Galatians 3:13, Deuteronomy 21:23). Anyone who, condemned by the law as a blasphemer, suffers such a death is accursed and excluded from the circle of the living and from the fellowship of God.[10]

That is Moltmann's description of the way crucifixion would have been regarded among Jews. Here is an excerpt from his discussion of the way it would have been seen by the Gentile intelligentsia of the Hellenistic world: "To the humanism of antiquity, the crucified Christ [was] an embarrassment. Crucifixion . . . was regarded as the most degrading kind of punishment. Thus Roman humanism always felt 'the religion of the cross' to be unaesthetic, unrespectable, and perverse. . . . It was regarded as an offense against good manners to speak of this hideous death for slaves in the presence of respectable people."[11]

The death suffered by Jesus does not belong on the list of martyrs' deaths. It is unique, and it has a unique significance. The four Gospels have nothing whatever to say about the physical suffering of Jesus during his passion. This omission is extraordinary, being so different from what we would expect. The Evangelists want us to focus elsewhere.

Crucifixion as Degradation and Shame

We offspring of the high-tech, antibiotic era are very different from anyone who has gone before us. It is not necessary to look back to Roman times to recall a period when the sight of death was commonplace and universal. Every family in the late nineteenth and early twentieth century experienced it close at hand. It has often been said that, whereas sex was the great unmentionable topic for the Victorians, death is the great unmentionable topic today. The greeting card industry, a mirror of our culture, has decreed the word "death" taboo in sympathy cards. Such scruples about death did not afflict our ancestors; it was a daily, up-close business. Crucifixion, however, was something else. What would it have been like, in Palestine and in the wider Roman Empire, to see a crucifixion or to hear it being discussed? How

10. Jürgen Moltmann, *The Crucified God: The Cross of Christ as the Foundation and Criticism of Christian Theology* (New York: Harper and Row, 1973), 33.

11. Moltmann, *The Crucified God*, 33.

difficult it is for us to grasp this! There is nothing in America today to which we could compare it. We do not even see our family members die natural deaths at home; much less do we view tormented bodies on display around town. We know that in Tudor times the population went out to watch people being tortured to death — scarcely conceivable as public policy today — and we know that hangings and lynchings were at one time social occasions in America, but most of us have no connection to such things, and besides, none of these examples will quite serve as analogues to crucifixion.

In a remarkably searching article by Philip Gourevitch and Errol Morris about the atrocities committed by Americans in Iraq, these words appear: "Of course, the dominant symbol of Western civilization is the figure of a nearly naked man, tortured to death — or, more simply, the torture implement itself, the cross. But our pictures of the savage death of Jesus are the product of religious imagination and idealization. In reality, he must have been ghastly to behold. Had there been cameras at Calvary, would twenty centuries of believers have been moved to hang photographs of the scene on their altarpieces and in their homes?"[12] "Religious imagination and idealization" have indeed been at work in artistic depictions of the crucifixion, and that has been necessary. Not even the gruesome painting by Grünewald can give us the full horror. What we need to do for theological understanding is not to exercise "religious" imagination, but to suspend it.

Susan Sontag, who suffered for years from the cancer that eventually killed her, wrote this: "It is not suffering as such that is most deeply feared but *suffering that degrades.*"[13] Here in a few words is a fundamental insight with which to view the crucifixion. If Jesus' demise is construed merely as a death — even as a painful, tortured death — the crucial point will be lost. Crucifixion was specifically designed to be the ultimate insult to personal dignity, the last word in humiliating and dehumanizing treatment. *Degradation was the whole point.*[14] As Joel Green describes it, "Executed publicly, situated at a major crossroads or on a well-trafficked artery, devoid of clothing, left to be eaten by birds and beasts, victims of crucifixion were subject to optimal, unmitigated, vicious ridicule."[15]

---

12. Philip Gourevitch and Errol Morris, "Exposure: The Woman behind the Camera at Abu Ghraib," *New Yorker,* March 24, 2008.

13. Susan Sontag, *AIDS and Its Metaphors* (New York: Penguin Books, 1989), 37.

14. In Anselm's *Cur Deus Homo?* the cross is referred to as *tam indecentia,* and the question is, why would God die a death so indecent, so unbecoming (1.6.185)?

15. Joel Green, "Crucifixion," in *The Cambridge Companion to Jesus,* ed. Markus Bock-muehl (Cambridge: Cambridge University Press, 2001), 91. Morna Hooker gives a particularly acute account of the shame of public nakedness "as an integral part of crucifixion," especially

And so, as Dietrich Bonhoeffer wrote, the meaning of the cross lies not only in physical suffering, but especially in rejection and shame.[16] To understand what the crucifixion means, we must look unblinkingly at its appalling qualities. In the context of a faith that proclaims "amazing grace," the cross would seem to be the ultimately *dis-grace*-ful event, utterly lacking in anything appealing, winning, or redemptive. Contrast, for example, Deuteronomy 25:3, which says forty lashes may be dealt to an offender, "but not more; lest . . . your brother be degraded in your sight." This provision in the Torah shows that the mercy of God is reflected even in the harsh law of the desert. God's Word protects the malefactor by referring to him as "your brother," and even though he is guilty, he is not to be permanently shamed "in the sight" of the one administering the punishment; the relationship of common humanity between the offender and the one who administers punishment is to be maintained. There are ramifications upon ramifications here. God's own law forbids the degradation of a "brother" — a fellow Israelite — but God's own Son died by a method designed precisely to deny the condemned person any vestige of common humanity, let alone brotherhood.[17]

We have already noted Bonhoeffer's words, "God lets himself be pushed out of the world on to the cross." He wrote that passage eight months before his execution, so it has exceptional power. The prisoner of Adolf Hitler continues: "[Christ] is weak and powerless in the world, and that is precisely the way, the only way, in which he is with us and helps us. Matthew 8:17 makes

---

for a Jew. She quotes Melito of Sardis in the second century: "The Sovereign has been made unrecognizable by his naked body, and is not even allowed a garment to keep him from view. That is why the lights of heaven turned away, and the day was darkened" (*Not Ashamed of the Gospel: New Testament Interpretations of the Death of Christ* [Grand Rapids: Eerdmans, 1994], 9-10).

16. Dietrich Bonhoeffer, *The Cost of Discipleship* (New York: Macmillan, 1963), 98. As this book goes to press, a significant increase of interest in shame has added urgency to this as a theological topic. *Christianity Today*'s March 2015 cover story was "The Return of Shame" by Andy Crouch. The importance of "face" in Asian cultures is related to shame and therefore to evangelism in those countries.

17. Marilyn McCord Adams emphasizes "the honor code, with its calculus of honor and shame." She argues that the category of *shame* is more useful than categories of *morality* in understanding what God has done and will do to defeat evil (*Horrendous Evils and the Goodness of God* [Ithaca, N.Y.: Cornell University Press, 1999], 107, 124-28). The category of shame works in a way that even the category of wickedness or ungodliness does not, because — as has often been remarked — a certain perverse glamour persists around wickedness, but there is no glamour in shame. Shame sounds the depths of radical evil because its currency deals in debasement, degradation, and finally dehumanization. Shaming another person is part of a process of declaring him worthless, without even the dignity of a four-footed beast — more like an insect to be squashed. Crucifixion was a manner of execution that piled shame upon shame to show that the victim was not fit for human company at any level.

it quite clear that Christ helps us, not by virtue of his omnipotence, but by virtue of his weakness and suffering. . . . That is a reversal of what the religious man expects from God. Man is summoned to share in God's sufferings at the hands of a godless world."[18]

It is precisely this "reversal of what the religious man expects," this *godlessness,* that we will emphasize again and again.

Perhaps we can gain further understanding by examining a horrific incident that occurred in Laramie, Wyoming, in 1998 and soon became emblematic of the ongoing struggle against persecution of homosexuals. A young gay man, Matthew Shepard, was beaten within an inch of his life by two other men and was then tied to a fence and abandoned. Eighteen hours later, in near-freezing weather, a passerby discovered the comatose figure and for a moment mistook it for a scarecrow. Matthew Shepard died in the hospital five days later without recovering consciousness.

The particular cruelty of this death left people groping for words. He was tied up and left dangling "like an animal," said one spokesman, recalling the Old West practice of nailing a dead coyote to a ranch fence as a warning to intruders. The emphasis here is on the dehumanization of the victim; declaring another person less than human is the well-attested first step toward eliminating that person, or that group of people. The phrase "like an animal" is therefore apt.[19] The strongest of all the statements, however, was this: "There is incredible symbolism in being tied to a fence. People have likened it to a scarecrow. But it sounded more like a crucifixion."[20]

The speakers who compared Shepard's death to a crucifixion were stretching for the most powerful imagery they could possibly find. The runner-up would probably be "a lynching," and indeed, that term evokes very strong reactions because of its connotations of racial hatred. Note, however, that "crucifixion" stands by itself atop the list of "incredible symbolism." No other word in our vocabulary evokes such complex and resonant responses. "Execution," "assassination," "murder" — these terms do not come close to "crucifixion." In that one word, the peculiar horror of Matthew Shepard's torment is evoked, not only because he was assaulted simply for his sexual orientation but also because he did not deserve what was done to him. The term suggests other levels of significance as well: it is a single death that

18. Dietrich Bonhoeffer, *Letters and Papers from Prison,* ed. Eberhard Bethge, enlarged ed. (New York: Macmillan, 1972), 360. Matthew 8:17 reads, "This was to fulfil what was spoken by the prophet Isaiah, 'He took our infirmities and bore our diseases.'"

19. In the weeks prior to the 1994 genocide in Rwanda, the word used by the Hutu *génocidaires* in order to incite murderous hatred toward their Tutsi victims was *inyenzi,* "cockroaches."

20. James Brooke, "Gay Man Dies from Attack," *New York Times,* October 13, 1998.

stands for many deaths; it is an innocent death that results from the evildoing of others; it is an iconic death that takes on universal meaning. These are some of the implications in the use of the term "crucifixion," but perhaps the most important for our argument here is that it implies an extremity of dehumanization and, therefore, of godlessness.[21]

We have noted Susan Sontag's insight about "the suffering that degrades." In *AIDS and Its Metaphors,* she writes further about "the privileged status of the face." She notes that illnesses like heart attacks and influenza that do not damage or deform the face never arouse the deepest dread. There is an icon in Eastern Orthodoxy that, translated from the Greek, is called "Utmost Humiliation." It depicts the head of the suffering and dying Christ on the cross.[22] The emotional impact of this icon, which is considerable, is produced by the artist's rendering of the facial expression; Christ is "suffering in his face."[23] Sontag's suggestive observation can be joined to the passage from Isaiah that the church has always associated with its Lord:

His appearance was so marred, beyond human semblance,
and his form beyond that of the sons of men. . . .
He had no form or comeliness that we should look at him,
and no beauty that we should desire him. . . .
He was despised and rejected by men; . . .
as one from whom men hide their faces
he was despised, and we esteemed him not. (Isa. 52:14; 53:2-3)

21. Marilyn McCord Adams writes, "On the cross, Jesus takes our defilement to the third degree. For crucifixion is not (like the right slit to the throat) a *clean* death. The Isenheim altarpiece [by Grünewald] draws a vivid and realistic picture of how — in killing — crucifixion caricatures humanity, twists the body, wrecks psycho-spiritual balance, does its best not only to blemish but to degrade" (*Horrendous Evils,* 98).

22. This iconographic subject is an exception to the generally stated rule that in the early centuries, Christ was always pictured as victorious on the cross. The icon is remarkable because of its emphasis on the suffering and humiliation rather than the victory. However, not even this suffering face conveys anything even approaching what must have happened to Jesus' face in reality.

23. Separation between face and body, Sontag continues, is "a main point of one of European culture's principal iconographic traditions, the depiction of Christian martyrdom, with its astounding schism between what is inscribed on the face and what is happening to the body. Those innumerable images of Saint Sebastian, Saint Agatha, Saint Lawrence *(but not of Christ himself),* with the face demonstrating its effortless superiority to the atrocious things that are being inflicted down there. Below, the ruin of the body. Above, a person, incarnated in the face, who looks away, usually up, not registering pain or fear; already elsewhere. *Only Christ,* both Son of Man and Son of God, *suffers in his face:* has his Passion" (*AIDS and Its Metaphors,* 40, emphasis added).

We still "hide our faces" from the cross and "esteem it not." It has always been difficult for the church to hold on to the cross at its center.[24] For one thing, it was a serious insult to aesthetics. Martin Hengel writes that "the Roman world was largely unanimous that crucifixion was a horrific, disgusting business. . . . The relative scarcity of references to crucifixions in antiquity . . . are [*sic*] less a *historical* problem than an *aesthetic* one. . . . Crucifixion was widespread and frequent, above all in Roman times, but the cultured literary world wanted to have nothing to do with it, and as a rule kept quiet about it."[25]

More seriously, the early church was threatened by far worse consequences than the contempt of the fastidious. During the first three centuries, the cross was not the sign in which the emperor conquered. It did not adorn medals and honors. It was not bejeweled, enameled, or worked in precious metal. It was a sign of contradiction and scandal, which quite often meant exile or death for those who adhered to the way of the crucified One.[26] After the establishment of Christianity as the official religion of the empire under Constantine, it was a different matter altogether. One of the telling points made by Martin Hengel is that after Constantine, the word *crux* was sanctified. It fell out of use in ordinary discourse; the word *furca,* meaning "gallows," was substituted. This is revealing, because it shows how the movement is always away from the wretchedness of the cross to something that, however dreadful, is nevertheless not so much associated with the unspeakable as was crucifixion. It also illustrates the way shallow piety attaches itself to the cross and, precisely in the process of reverencing it, robs it of its shame.

Even art and music, often so honest in comparison to popular piety,

24. This was true from earliest times. Jewish Christianity seems to have underplayed the cross, concentrating on the reversal of the cross by the resurrection. This pattern is noticeable in the sermons in Acts and is a point of difference between the Paul of Acts and the Paul of the letters. Cf. Beker, *Paul the Apostle,* 202.

25. Hengel, *Crucifixion,* 38, emphasis added. Episcopalians, with our penchant for good taste in all things, will perhaps recognize this upper-crust style of aesthetic disdain. Who would want a crucified person as the center of worship?

26. Scholars of the classical era point out that much of the martyrology of the early church has been exaggerated so as to encourage Christians to embrace the courage and virtue of their forebears in faith. The persecutions of Christians in the Roman Empire during the first two hundred years after Christ were not as constant or as relentless as popular imagination suggests; there were periods when Christianity was tolerated. The scope of Nero's persecutions was inflated in later Christian tradition, though it is fairly well attested that he blamed the Christians for the great fire of 64 and that Peter and Paul were executed during his reign. Later persecutions, however, were real enough and severe enough. The emperors who engaged in the most intense persecutions were Decius (249-251) and Diocletian, whose Great Persecution began in 303 and ended with Constantine in 312.

cannot fully convey the full ghastliness of crucifixion. Neither paintings nor sculptures nor film can do so.[27] The *Passions* of J. S. Bach bring us closer to the cross than most artistic works, although the ravishing beauty of the music keeps the horror at a distance. Jaroslav Pelikan illustrates the defining importance of the cross in Bach's thinking by showing how the composer combines Christmas with Good Friday. "The centrality of the story of the crucifixion and resurrection implied that 'Lenten music' was always pertinent," even in cantatas full of rapturous response to the nativity.[28]

Shifting his attention to George Frideric Handel, Pelikan continues, "Modern audiences may find the Lenten portions of *Messiah* disturbing to their thoughts about the birth of the baby Jesus, and modern conductors may feel justified in pandering to that sentimentality by excising those portions [about the suffering and death of the Messiah], thus transforming the oratorio into a Christmas cantata, and 'Hallelujah' into a Christmas carol, when it is in fact a celebration of the victory of the resurrection of Christ."[29] Thus the dislike of the cross works its way into the concert hall. When *Messiah* is performed in its totality, however, it brings forward not only the verse from Isaiah 53, "He was despised and rejected of men," but also a more explicit verse from the Psalms, "He hid not his face from shame and spitting."[30]

There is nothing more extraordinary in the literature of the world than Primo Levi's voice from the depths of Auschwitz. "The just [the righteous] among us . . . felt remorse, shame, and pain for the misdeeds that others and not they had committed, and in which they felt involved."[31]

This is even more painful than first appears. The shame that Levi describes here is a shame beyond shame. From his own experience he is reflecting on the way that victims of shameful treatment are enveloped in shame

27. Mel Gibson tried and failed, in his movie *The Passion of the Christ*. He certainly made the scourging and crucifixion sensational, but we are accustomed to graphic violence now, and our sensibilities are dulled. Piling up filmic details and effects cannot do the job. The true horror of crucifixion was not its shock value but its gruesome and disgusting nature, involving far more in the way of smells and sounds than can ever be conveyed at second hand.

28. Jaroslav Pelikan, *Bach among the Theologians* (Philadelphia: Fortress, 1986), 11.

29. Pelikan, *Bach among the Theologians,* 11.

30. The music historian Michael Marissen has mounted an attack on *Messiah* as anti-Semitic (*Tainted Glory in Handel's* Messiah: *The Unsettling History of the World's Most Beloved Choral Work* [New Haven: Yale University Press, 2014]). It has met mostly with bemusement if not outright repudiation. Most critics think the imagery ("Why do the nations so furiously rage together?") is universal and would not have been understood by anyone in Handel's audience as a chorus triumphing over the fall of Jerusalem in A.D. 70. Marissen's work on the problem texts in Bach's *St. John Passion* has met with more acceptance.

31. Primo Levi, *The Drowned and the Saved* (New York: Vintage Books, 1988), 86.

even when they have done nothing to merit it. The hideousness of inhuman deeds is infectious. For Christians there is an echo here of the shame visited upon the crucified One. We must be very careful in thus linking the victims of the Holocaust and the cross, lest we appear oblivious to the fury this move engenders in many Jews. And yet we must continue to emphasize that the *shame* of crucifixion is more important for the determination of its meaning than the physical suffering.

The book of the prophet Nahum depicts the shame of Nineveh, upon whom the wrath of God is descending:

> Behold, I am against you,
>   says the Lord of hosts,
>   and will lift up your skirts over your face;
> and I will let nations look on your nakedness
>   and kingdoms on your shame.
> I will throw filth at you
>   and treat you with contempt,
>   and make you a gazingstock.
> And all who look on you will shrink from you. (Nah. 3:5-7)

When a passage such as this is read from the perspective of Christian faith, it is not impossible to see a veiled reference to the shame and obloquy endured by Jesus. God's judgment upon "Nineveh" becomes God's judgment on the shame of the entire world, assumed by his Son in all its details.[32] When we say that Jesus Christ took upon himself the sin of the world, it means quite specifically that he suffered the shame and the degradation that human beings have inflicted on one another and that he above all others had done nothing to merit.

Paul's Struggle with the Corinthians: Religion and Secularity

We may think that it was easier for the early Christians to understand the cross than it is for us, and perhaps that is so, but at the same time they had even more reason to hide their faces from it than we do, because they knew

---

32. Nahum, with its implacable judgment upon Nineveh, can be read canonically in tandem with Jonah, the most universalist book in the Old Testament except for Isa. 40–55. God's compassion upon pagan Nineveh in Jonah is in a dialectical relationship with God's judgment on the Assyrian city in Nahum.

what it entailed. They had to face, as we today do not, the contempt of their contemporaries who knew only too well what an object of disgust a crucifixion was. The logical thing for the early Christians would have been to glide past the passion as quickly as possible, portraying it as an unfortunate but incidental episode on the way to the resurrection. That is what the Christians in Corinth wanted to do, but Paul would not let them.

First Corinthians 1:18-25 draws us into the heart of the difficulty that third-millennium Christians share with those of the first century. It helps us remember that the Corinthian church was not unlike many burgeoning American congregations today. The church parking lot is always full, new services have been added, signs and wonders abound, testimonies are given about changed lives, and there seems to be no limit to the enthusiasm of the congregation. Paul, however, sees grave danger ahead, because the Corinthians' life is oriented to the wrong center. He therefore writes:

> The word of the cross is folly to those who are perishing, but to us who are being saved it is the power of God. For it is written,
>
> > "I will destroy the wisdom of the wise,
> > and the cleverness of the clever I will thwart."
>
> Where is the wise man? Where is the scribe? Where is the debater of this age? Has not God made foolish the wisdom of the world? For since, in the wisdom of God, the world did not know God through wisdom, it pleased God through the folly of what we preach to save those who believe.... To those who are called, both Jews and Greeks, Christ the power of God and the wisdom of God. For the foolishness of God is wiser than men, and the weakness of God is stronger than men. (1:18-25)

Here, Paul is defending his preaching of the cross. He is contending against two factors: the rampaging religiosity of the Corinthian Christians and the urbane sophistication of their surrounding city. "Jews demand signs," he says, "and Greeks seek wisdom." This can be interpreted — with caveats — in modern terms if we recast "Jews" simply to mean religious people and "Greeks" to denote secular people.[33] The crucifixion is a "scandal" to religious people in general, not specifically the Jews of Paul's time, because it is offensively irreligious; it is "foolishness" to secular people not only because of its intrinsic nature but also because of its affront to the educated, sophis-

---

33. This move was made with great sophistication by Karl Barth in his commentary on Romans: *The Epistle to the Romans,* 6th ed. (Oxford: Oxford University Press, 1968), 382-407.

ticated mind.[34] Most churchgoing people are "Jews" on Sunday morning and "Greeks" the rest of the time. Religious people want visionary experiences and spiritual uplift; secular people want proofs, arguments, demonstrations, philosophy, science. The striking fact is that *neither one* of these groups wants to hear about the cross. It is "a stumbling block to Jews and folly to Gentiles" (1:23). The cross is not a suitable object of devotion for religious people, and the claims made for it are too extreme to be acceptable to secular people. It is the paradox of present-day American culture to be both religious and irreligious. We are secular and materialistic most of the time, but also so pious that candidates for president must stage photo ops of themselves coming out of church. Paul opposes all of this, at both ends of the spectrum, with the stumbling block *(skandalon)* and the foolishness that is the cross.

Paul further develops his argument by reminding the Corinthian congregation that most of them were down a few notches on the ladder when they were first called to Christian faith: "For consider your call, brethren; not many of you were wise according to worldly standards, not many were powerful, not many were of noble birth" (1:26). Then, in his most vivid and characteristic style, he summons up a series of paradoxes:

> *But God* chose what is foolish in the world to shame the wise, God chose what is weak in the world to shame the strong, God chose what is low and despised in the world, even things that are not, to bring to nothing things that are, so that no human being might boast in the presence of God. He is the source of your life in Christ Jesus, whom God made our wisdom, our righteousness and sanctification and redemption; therefore, as it is written, "Let him who boasts, boast of the Lord." (1:27-31)

Paul picks up the word "boast" from the Corinthians' own attitudes. Apparently they had been complaining of Paul's insufficient spiritual glamour. Paul accepts this charge and turns it to advantage as he pleads the cause of the gospel of the crucified One:

> When I came to you, brethren, I did not come proclaiming to you the testimony of God in lofty words or wisdom. For I decided to know nothing

---

34. Here, the contrast between "religious" and "secular" is meant impressionistically, not historically. There was plenty of religion among the Romans and throughout the Hellenistic world (Wilken, *The Christians as the Romans Saw Them*, 48-62; Neil Elliott, *The Arrogance of Nations: Reading Romans in the Shadow of Empire* [Minneapolis: Fortress, 2008], 121-28). The point is to expound and update Paul's use of the terms "Jews" and "Greeks."

among you except Jesus Christ and him crucified. And I was with you in weakness and in much fear and trembling; and my speech and my message were not in plausible words of wisdom, but in demonstration of the Spirit and of power, that your faith might not rest in the wisdom of men but in the power of God. (2:1-5)

Paul is willing to embrace his opponents' accusations of personal weaknesses and rhetorical dullness in order to make his point. One can see analogous situations in the church today. Preachers and teachers who are courageous and faithful in expounding the cross of Christ but lack the flashy, ostentatious style so much favored in this age of the sound bite find it difficult to gain a hearing, They are likely to be advised to improve their image and cultivate a more popular, even commercial, appeal. The criticisms brought by the Corinthians against Paul must have been along this line. The Corinthians wanted to hear "wisdom" — meaning, in this case, inspired speech that would dazzle their senses.

Paul is adamant. Razzle-dazzle does not serve the *kerygma* of the cross. He declares that he has determined to set aside everything except *Jesus Christ and him crucified* (2:2). The Corinthian Christians were heavily into an individualistic, self-involved notion of the Christian life, which had pernicious effects on their community as a whole. Paul sets the cross in opposition to these tendencies. His letter addresses the problem of aggressive, self-promoting "spirituality" in the congregation. As in today's environment, religion and spirituality are "in"; the cross, however, remains forever "out." As we read in the Epistle to the Hebrews, "Jesus also suffered *outside* the gate in order to sanctify the people through his own blood. Therefore let us go forth to him *outside* the camp, and *bear the abuse he endured*" (Heb. 13:12-13).[35]

The Role of the Spirit

Paul is seriously worried, indeed pushed to the edge (as portions of II Corinthians attest), by the abuses in the Corinthian church. Although he himself has been given an abundance of charismata (I Cor. 14:18; II Cor. 12:1-4), the congregation that came into being through his Spirit-filled preaching is now misusing its own gifts. We still see this when pentecostal evange-

---

35. The call to "bear abuse" is never to be interpreted as submitting to an abusive spouse, parent, employer, etc. Bearing abuse *for Christ* comes as a result of bearing witness to him against the powers and principalities, a subject we shall examine in chapter 10.

lists concentrate on flamboyant, flashy manifestations like tongues and instantaneous healings.[36] Paul warns specifically against this in I Corinthians 12–14. Throughout this volume we will refer to a "Corinthian" mentality in the church. Wherever there is emphasis on spiritual virtuosity with a corresponding de-emphasis on atonement for sin and self-sacrificing service, there we meet the Corinthians once again.

Thomas A. Smail, who has written much about the Holy Spirit from a Pentecostal perspective, is admirably clear about the relationship of the Spirit to the cross: "A Spirit who could derogate from the glory of Christ crucified in order to promote a more dazzling glory of his own, who passes by the sufferings of Christ in order to offer us a share in a painless and costless triumph, is certainly not the Holy Spirit of the New Testament [who] glorifies, not himself, but Christ, and therefore his mission is to reveal the full glory of Calvary, and to bring us into possession of all the blessings that by his death Christ has won for us."[37]

Smail tells a moving story about his first experience of speaking in tongues at a worship service. As he spoke, scarcely aware of what he was doing, a young woman whom he did not know, and never saw again, gave the interpretation of the strange syllables to the assembled congregation: "There is no way to Pentecost except by Calvary; the Spirit is given from

36. "Pentecostal" with a capital P refers to those Christians who designate themselves more or less officially by that name. Small-p "pentecostal" is used generically to denote any emphasis on the work of the Spirit, often including the more visible and dramatic manifestations. The quasi-pentecostal "charismatic movement" in some of the United States mainline churches — a largely middle- and upper-middle-class phenomenon — has lost most of its strength since the 1970s. The emphasis now in those circles tends toward eclectic spirituality. Some quasi-pentecostal ministries among middle-class people today present versions of the "prosperity gospel." More authentic Pentecostalism, especially among some African Americans, Latino immigrants, and in the developing world where it is notably ascendant, has some similarities to the charismatic movement but is not identical. Though Pentecostalism characteristically places great emphasis on glossolalia, trances, miracles of healing, and other such manifestations, it does not necessarily evince the spiritual elitism that Paul rebukes in Corinth, and has great appeal to the poor — unlike the situation in Corinth and the affluent American congregations. For a literary memoir of Pentecostalism at its best, see Mark Richard's widely praised *House of Prayer No. 2: A Writer's Journey Home* (New York: Nan A. Talese, 2011). "If you ask Pastor Ricks [the African American pastor of the Pentecostal congregation in the book] what happens when he lays hands on someone and he or she is slain in the Spirit, he says it's when the natural is overshattered by the supernatural, the person's overpowered by something greater than him- or herself and enters a sleep like Adam slept when God removed his rib. In that state there is a spiritual impartation, something changes in the person, letting him or her know the reality of God" (187).

37. Thomas A. Smail, *Reflected Glory: The Spirit in Christ and Christians* (Grand Rapids: Eerdmans, 1975), 105.

the cross."[38] Smail, convicted, made that a keystone of all his subsequent teaching.[39]

Smail's pastoral concern is for readers who have been tempted by their leaders into a triumphalist version of Christianity without sacrifice or suffering. This is precisely what Paul finds in the Corinthian congregation, as we can see from the first two chapters of I Corinthians. He is almost certainly referring to the cross when he emphasizes that which is "low and despised" (I Cor. 1:28). To Jews and Greeks alike, crucifixion was about as "low and despised" as one could get. It sent an unmistakable signal, "Not fit to live; not even human" (*damnatio ad bestias,* as the Romans put it — condemned to the death of a beast). This is very difficult for any congregation, first-century or twenty-first-century, to assimilate. It was so in Paul's time, and it remains so today. Yet the apostle insists that this assumption of lowliness and ungodliness by the incarnate Son — this and this alone — is "the power of God." Without this, there is no gospel. Without this, there is only a diffuse religiosity. Without the cross, we are just "Greeks" and "Jews" with nothing new or revolutionary to offer the world. The pentecostal dimension is clear throughout the New Testament; as Paul and John teach and as Luke illustrates throughout Acts, it is the eternal Spirit, the third person, in whom the crucified and risen Christ is a forever living presence and power.

The Paradox of Crucifixion

Moltmann shows how "Jesus' uncomplaining suffering and his powerless death were a visible demonstration to everyone of the power and the might of the law and its guardians. Consequently the disciples left him in the hour of his betrayal and 'all fled' (Mark 14:50)."[40] Moltmann points out, further, that the flight of the disciples is historically incontrovertible, because an authentic hero is not deserted by all his followers. For Mark, this is a further indication that Jesus' death was of the most godforsaken nature. The disciples could not have seen his humiliating and inglorious death as obedience to God, a vindication of his mission, or a heroic martyrdom. On the contrary, precisely *because it was a crucifixion,* they could have seen it only as the utter

38. Paul explicitly forbids tongues without interpretation in I Cor. 14:13-18.

39. Smail, *Reflected Glory,* 105. He says further, "The Holy Spirit's function is to reflect in us the likeness of Christ — of his truth and love and power — but how could he do that with any authenticity or completeness, if he did not also lead us into the likeness of his suffering? There could be no real reflection of Christ that did not consist of bearing his cross" (112).

40. Moltmann, *The Crucified God,* 132.

discrediting of his claims before man and God. He had been judged a threat to the state by the secular authorities, but far worse in the disciples' eyes, he had been condemned by the religious authorities, the guardians of faith and morals, as a blasphemer deserving of a godless death. It would be difficult to exaggerate the horror of such an unedifying and irreligious outcome to a ministry in the name of God.

The most radical of all perspectives on the cross will become clear to us if we reflect on the relation between the Old and New Testaments in this regard. To put it in the bluntest possible terms, *no one* expected a crucified Messiah. Isaiah 53 provided a clue of a suggestion of a hint of a prediction ("He was despised and rejected by men. . . . The Lord has laid on him the iniquity of us all," 53:3, 6), but virtually no one understood this to refer to the Messiah of Israel until after the resurrection. The "new thing" prophesied by Isaiah was — and still is — interpreted in a number of ways, but the one truly new thing is what Paul calls "the word of the cross."[41] Who could have known what God was announcing through Isaiah?

> "Behold, I am doing a new thing;
>   now it springs forth, do you not perceive it?
> I will make a way in the wilderness." (Isa. 43:19)

Who could have known that the way through the wilderness to redemption would be the path of humiliation trodden by the Son of God? What religious or secular insight would have led anyone at all to foresee a ghastly, exposed, reviled death for God-made-flesh? The unknown prophet of the exile rhapsodized from his far country, "Sing to the Lord a new song" (Isa. 42:10), but who knew that the content of that song would be praise for a man condemned? The last thing anyone would ever have imagined, *even with Isaiah 53 right in front of them,* was a crucified Son of God.

The Cross and the Electric Chair

Jürgen Moltmann has a phrase, "the resistance of the cross against its interpretations."[42] It is formidably difficult to understand the cross today in its

---

41. I take it for granted that Isa. 40–55 was written by an unknown prophet during the exile, but for convenience I am saying "Isaiah." More important, I follow Brevard Childs in believing that the book of Isaiah forms a canonical whole for theological purposes; see his *The Struggle to Understand Isaiah as Christian Scripture* (Grand Rapids: Eerdmans, 2004).

42. This is the title of the second chapter of *The Crucified God.*

original context, after two thousand years in which it has been domesticated, romanticized, idealized, and misappropriated. Occasionally a modern interpreter, struggling to find some correspondence that can be grasped by people today, will compare the cross of Roman times to the American electric chair. This is an inadequate analogy for a number of reasons, as we shall see, but we can learn a few things from it. Imagine revering an electric chair. Imagine using it as the focal point in our churches, hanging small replicas around our necks, carrying it aloft in procession and bowing our heads as it passes. The absurdity of this scenario can readily be grasped.

But other features in the comparison might help us. For instance, the electric chair, when it was still used, was almost always used for executing the lowest class of criminal, a majority of them black, with no powerful connections or other resources.[43] Similarly, the Romans virtually never used the cross for executing people who had occupied high positions, and never for Roman citizens.[44] Another point of contact is the contradictory response of revulsion and attraction familiar to anyone who has ever slowed to look at a wreck on the highway. Even the most fastidious person, when confronted by a photograph of an electric chair (let alone the real thing), will experience a disturbing fascination.[45] There have always been people who specialized in coming to cheer and applaud executions when they took place, whether lynchings, hangings, or electrocutions. That is what undoubtedly happened on Calvary when Jesus was nailed to the cross and left there to die. Crowds of people, then as now, took pleasure in reviling the one who was being put to death. When they became bored with this pastime, they went safely home to their comforts and gave the victim no further thought. "Is it nothing to you, all you who pass by?" (Lam. 1:12).

But there are very important differences. Electrocutions were at least theoretically supposed to be humane and quick, but crucifixion as a method of execution was specifically designed to intensify and prolong agony. In this sense the cross was infinitely more dreadful than the electric chair, odious though the chair was. Another difference is that the person to be electro-

---

43. It was widely noted at the time of the O. J. Simpson trial in 1995 that even if he were to be convicted, he would never be executed. His fame, his fans, and his powerful connections would have made it impossible.

44. Martin Hengel examines the few exceptions that prove the rule (*Crucifixion*, 39-40).

45. The nickname "Old Sparky" served to mask both the unease and the attraction. People are drawn to exhibits of instruments of torture in the same way; the iron maiden and other devices elicit shudders of lurid fascination. The electric chair is largely disused now, with the rise of lethal injection as the preferred and allegedly more "humane" method, but there was an electrocution in Virginia in 2010.

cuted is permitted the dignity of a mask or hood, presumably so that "the privilege of the face" noted by Susan Sontag would be protected. Most important of all, electrocutions took place indoors, out of public view, with only a few select people permitted to watch. Crucifixion, on the other hand, was supposed to be seen by as many people as possible. Debasement resulting from public display was a chief feature of the method, along with the prolonging of agony. It was a form of advertisement, or public announcement — this person is the scum of the earth, not fit to live, more an insect than a human being. The crucified wretch was pinned up like a specimen. Crosses were not placed out in the open for convenience or sanitation, but for maximum public exposure.[46]

The Psychological Torture of Crucifixion

In 1996, Georgetown University commissioned twenty-five artists to execute crucifixes to be displayed on campus in place of the older, more traditional ones. Sculptor Charles McCullough, an ordained United Church of Christ minister, fashioned one from a gnarled piece of wood that represented Christ in extreme agony. He spoke eloquently of the challenge of making such a work. "To draw, paint, or sculpt the crucifixion is a terrifying experience, for the artist must feel some bit of the horrible pain *and humiliation* of being hung up to die. It is hard to overemphasize the true brutality of this death by torture. It is important, I believe, to represent the crucifixion as state murder, not an abstract notion of death in general."[47]

Crucifixion as a means of execution in the Roman Empire had *as its express purpose* the elimination of victims from consideration as members of the human race. It cannot be said too strongly: that was its function. It was meant to indicate to all who might be toying with subversive ideas that crucified persons were *not of the same species* as either the executioners or the spectators and were therefore not only expendable but also deserving of ritualized extermination.

Therefore, the mocking and jeering that accompanied crucifixion were not only allowed, they were part of the spectacle and were programmed into

46. And, of course, deterrence was a motive too. To all who might be contemplating sedition, it was a warning: "This could happen to you." This would have been especially important in preventing slave revolts. Ironically, "law and order" is being defined here.

47. Quoted in Peter Steinfels's "Beliefs" column, *New York Times,* March 1999, emphasis added.

it. In a sense, crucifixion was a form of entertainment. Everyone understood that the specific role of the passersby was to exacerbate the dehumanization and degradation of the person who had been thus designated to be a spectacle. Crucifixion was cleverly designed — we might say diabolically designed — to be an almost theatrical enactment of the sadistic and inhumane impulses that lie within human beings. According to the Christian gospel, the Son of God voluntarily and purposefully absorbed all of that, drawing it into himself.

Mors Turpissima Crucis

Anyone seeking to interpret Jesus' crucifixion must decide whether or not to include a clinical description. Since the New Testament writers are conspicuously silent about the physical details, it is legitimate to ask whether it is suitable or helpful to introduce them.[48] On the other hand, people in New Testament times had all seen crucifixions, and did not need a description. The Evangelists and other New Testament writers were able to assume a familiarity with the method that is unthinkable for us today; most of us have never even come close to seeing anyone tortured to death. For this reason, as Martin Hengel writes, "Reflection on the harsh reality of crucifixion in antiquity may help us to overcome the acute loss of reality which is to be found so often in present theology and preaching."[49] The early theologian Origen called Jesus' death the *mors turpissima crucis,* the utterly vile death of the cross. Cicero, the great Roman statesman and writer, referred to crucifixion as the *summum supplicium,* the supreme penalty, exceeding *crematio* (burning) and *decollatio* (decapitation) in gruesomeness.[50] Some rudimentary knowledge of what was taking place will help us to understand these terms.[51]

48. I have wrestled a long time with this question. I have personally seen groups of normally fidgety teenagers rapt at attention as a Young Life speaker gave what used to be described as "the cross talk." The gruesome details of crucifixion seemed to evoke the same fascination in them as a horror movie, and in that sense was an inspired technique. It presented a marked contrast, however, to the reticence of the Evangelists, and I have wondered if it wasn't manipulative.

49. Hengel, *Crucifixion,* 90.

50. Hengel, *Crucifixion,* 33, 51. Cicero himself was decapitated, a relatively merciful method compared to crucifixion. The gruesome aspect of decapitation was the display of the severed head (and hands, in Cicero's case). A crucified victim was displayed *while alive.*

51. Some of these details are taken from a widely distributed article by William D. Edwards et al., "On the Physical Death of Jesus Christ," *Journal of the American Medical Association* 255, no. 1 (March 21, 1986). This *JAMA* article has been criticized and even ridiculed, with

The first phase of a Roman execution was scourging. The lictors (Roman legionnaires assigned to this duty) used a whip made of leather cords to which small pieces of metal or bone had been fastened. Paintings of the scourging of Jesus always show him with a loincloth, but in fact the victim would have been naked, tied to a post in a position to expose the back and buttocks to maximum effect. With the first strokes of the scourge, skin would be pulled away and subcutaneous tissue exposed. As the process continued, the lacerations would begin to tear into the underlying skeletal muscles. This would result not only in great pain but also in appreciable blood loss. The idea was to weaken the victim to a state just short of collapse or death. It was common for taunting and ridicule to accompany the procedure. In the case of Jesus, the New Testament tells us that a crown of thorns, a purple robe, and a mock scepter were added to intensify the mockery.

The condition of a prisoner after scourging, just prior to crucifixion, would depend upon several things: previous physical condition, the enthusiasm of the lictors, and the extent of blood loss. In the case of Jesus, these things cannot be known, but the fact that he was apparently unable to carry the *patibulum* (crossbar) himself would indicate that he was probably in a severely weakened state, and he may have been close to hypovolemia (circulatory shock).

Those being crucified were then paraded through the streets, exposing them to the full scorn of the population. When the procession reached the site of crucifixion, the victims would see before them the heavy upright wooden posts *(stipes)* permanently in place, to which the *patibulum* was to be attached by a mortise-and-tenon joint. The person to be crucified would be thrown down on his back, exacerbating the pain of the wounds from the scourging, and introducing dirt into them. His hands would be tied or nailed to the crossbar; nailing seems to have been preferred by the Romans. Ossuary finds have given us a clearer idea of how this was done; two thousand years of Christian iconography notwithstanding, the nails were not driven into the palms, which could not support the weight of a man's body, but into the wrists. The *patibulum* was then hoisted on to the *stipes* with the victim

---

some justification, because it wanders away from strict medical considerations to reliance upon biblical details that are theological, not scientific — and even refers to the Shroud of Turin! The particular, limited value of the *JAMA* article for us is that it gives a persuasive account of *the mechanics of the method.* Raymond E. Brown prefers a more recent article that proposes shock as the cause of death of a crucified person. See Brown, *Death of the Messiah,* 1088-92, for a summary of the debate. (In a 2012 interview with Terry Gross on NPR, Colm Toibín, author of *The Testament of Mary,* declared in an authoritative tone that crucified victims died of sunstroke. Where he got that, I don't know.)

dependent from it, and the feet were tied or nailed. At this point the process of crucifixion proper began.

Victims of crucifixion lived on their crosses for periods varying from three or four hours to three or four days. It has often been remarked that Jesus' ordeal was relatively brief. Perhaps he was weakened by the scourging, or had lost more blood than usual, or suffered cardiac rupture. We cannot know. In any case, it has been surmised that "the major pathophysiological effect of crucifixion, beyond the excruciating (Latin *excruciatus,* out of the cross) pain, was a marked interference with normal respiration, particularly exhalation."[52] Passive exhalation, which we all do thousands of times a day without thinking about it, becomes impossible for a person hanging on a cross. The weight of a body hanging by its wrists would depress the muscles required for breathing out. Therefore, each exhaled breath could only be achieved by a tremendous effort. The only way to gain a breath at all would be by pushing oneself up from the legs and feet, or pulling oneself up by the arms, either of which would cause intense agony.[53] Add to this primary factor the following secondary ones: bodily functions uncontrolled, insects feasting on wounds and orifices, unspeakable thirst, muscle cramps, bolts of pain from the severed median nerves in the wrists, scourged back scraping against the wooden *stipes.* It is more than any of us are capable of fully imagining. The verbal abuse and other actions such as spitting and throwing refuse by the spectators, Roman soldiers, and passersby added the final touch.

The New Testament shows us life lived between two worlds, the Roman and the Near (Middle) Eastern. Crucifixion was noxious enough in Roman eyes; Palestinian attitudes would have found it perhaps even more so. Middle Eastern cultures still have, to this day, "an acute sense of personal honor lodged in the body."[54] An amputation administered as punishment, for instance, would be seen as much more than just physical cruelty or permanent handicap; it would mean that the amputee would carry the visible marks of dishonor and shame for the rest of his or her life. Anything done to the body would have been understood as exceptionally cruel, not just because it inflicted pain, but even more because it caused dishonor. Furthermore,

52. From the *JAMA* article.

53. It would be even more difficult to say anything because speech is possible only during exhalation.

54. Historian Peter Brown and his wife Betsy have close personal as well as academic ties to eastern Mediterranean cultures, past and present. They have several distinctive observations concerning crucifixion, including the one about the victim being his own executioner. Most of this paragraph, and the first half of the next, including the four verbal quotations, is taken from an interview with Peter and Betsy Brown, February 3, 1999.

the passion accounts reflect, in part, "a very ancient ritual of humiliation."[55] The mocking of Jesus, the spitting and scorn, the "inversion of his kingship," and the "studious dethronement" with the crown of thorns and purple robe would have been understood as a central part of a total rite of infamy, of which the crucifixion itself is the culmination.[56]

Another aspect of crucifixion, not widely noted, is that a crucified person, gasping and heaving on his cross, is forced to be his own executioner. He is not even allowed the perverse dignity of having a human being corresponding to himself who hangs or decapitates him. He dies truly and completely alone, with the weight of his own body killing him as it hangs, causing his own diaphragm to suffocate him. Alexsandr Solzhenitsyn described how, in Stalin's gulag, the prisoners were forced to sleep with their hands outside their blankets, so that the simple gestures that are universally used by human beings to comfort their own bodies by stroking, massaging, or holding were impossible.[57] There really is something particularly horrible about causing one's own body to turn against one, and, in the case of crucifixion, actually becoming the *instrument* of one's exquisite suffering and asphyxiation.

Nevertheless, having said all this, we must to some degree set it all aside. We cannot know all the reasons for the reticence of the New Testament writers concerning the details of crucifixion, but a chief reason must have been that they wanted us to focus on something else.

55. We need to exercise our imaginations to understand how nakedness, in particular, shamed the victim. Thomas Cahill, in his little book about Jesus, *Desire of the Everlasting Hills,* makes the incontrovertible point that sexual humiliation and shaming would certainly have been part of the ritual leading up to crucifixion, as surely as it was in the Abu Ghraib prison scandals of the Iraq War. A naked victim of scourging and mockery would not be able to cover his genitals with his hands but would be utterly exposed to scrutiny, derision, and any obscenity that the spectators cared to hurl in his direction — and as Cahill points out, sexual taunts of the crudest sort would surely have been part of this "entertainment." Cahill's vivid descriptions of a crucified person are to the point: "a pitiable, shuddering worm of a man," a "comic gargoyle." He makes a particularly insightful comment on Jesus' identity precisely *as a Jew* in his death. He evokes the specifically Jewish aspect of Jesus' shame, with his "silly little circumcised penis" on show for mockery by the uncircumcised Roman soldiers and passersby. Thomas Cahill, *Desire of the Everlasting Hills* (New York: Nan A. Talese, 1999), 107-8.

56. In his commentary on Isa. 40-66, Claus Westermann writes, "As we see from the Psalms, in ancient Israel suffering and shame went together beyond possibility of separation in a way which we today fail to understand" (Westermann, *Isaiah 40-66* [Philadelphia: Westminster, 1977; 1st Ger. ed. 1966], 214).

57. Alexandr I. Solzhenitsyn, *The Gulag Archipelago* (New York: Harper and Row, 1973), 184 n. 5.

Rejection and Dereliction

Jesus took upon himself the role of the ultimate Other. He allowed himself to become less-than-human scum. All the evil impulses of the human race came to focus in him.[58] Now to be sure, in one sense the crucifixion is only one barbarous scene among many scenes of human atrocity. However, there is one feature of the crucifixion that sets it aside from the rest. Many have believed that the ultimate criterion for the interpretation of the cross of Christ is the "cry of dereliction": "My God, my God, why have you forsaken me?" There can be no honest interpretation of the event without an account of this uniquely terrible saying from the cross, *the only saying* to be reported by not just one, but *two* Evangelists.[59]

This cry haunts our collective imagination in revealing ways and turns up in unexpected places. The English scholar and literary critic John Weightman, examining the theme of the absurd, writes, "There are direct or indirect expressions of the Absurd in the Old Testament, in Greek and Latin literature, and in the works of many writers of later centuries, some of whom may have thought themselves to be predominantly believers of one kind or another. One might even claim that the cry *Eli, Eli, lama sabachthani* proves that, for a brief moment, Jesus himself was a near-Absurdist."[60]

This is a remarkable statement, because it brings the *irreligiousness* of the cross into sharp focus and shows how important the cry of dereliction is in demonstrating the complete identification of Jesus with our compromised, indeed absurd, human condition passing "from the stink of the didie to the stench of the shroud."[61] Jesus, in this moment on the cross, embodies in his own tormented struggle all the fruitlessness of human attempts to befriend the indifferent mocking silence of space[62] — *especially religious attempts.*

---

58. Morna Hooker reminds us, in a chilling sentence, that after Luke describes the denial of Peter, "then we are told about the mockery by Jesus' guards; *this occupies the rest of the night*" (*Not Ashamed,* 87, emphasis added). Ponder our Lord's experience, enduring sadistic brutality for many hours throughout the darkness of the night, until the sunrise of the next day brings his death by public torture. Assuming that, in addition to the scourging, he was subjected to an unusual amount of these personal attentions as the Gospel accounts suggest, it is no wonder that he died relatively quickly.

59. Only Matthew and Mark have the cry of dereliction. As will be noted later, Luke and John have different emphases.

60. John Weightman, "The Outsider," *New York Review of Books,* January 15, 1998. The quotation is from an essay-review of a revisionist biography of Albert Camus.

61. Robert Penn Warren, *All the King's Men.*

62. "The eternal silence of these infinite spaces terrifies me." Blaise Pascal, *Pensées* III, 206 (XIV, 201).

A feature of Bach's *St. Matthew Passion* that is apparently Bach's own invention is not only musically arresting but also of great theological importance. Jaroslav Pelikan describes it thus:

> [Bach uses] the "halo," the string quartet that plays various chords to accompany each of the sayings of Jesus and, it has been said, "floats round the utterances of Christ like a glory" [quoting music historian and Bach biographer Philipp Spitta]. . . . Bach was apparently the only one [among composers of his time] to see that the absolutely appropriate place to suspend the "halo" leitmotiv was at the cry of dereliction, *Eli, Eli, lama sabachthani.* . . . The glory of the Father was withdrawn from the solitary figure on the cross . . . *now he is all alone and forsaken.*[63]

Galatians 3:10-14 — the Accursed Death of Christ

As a climax to this chapter, we return to the extraordinary passage from Galatians 3.[64] It is somewhat difficult to understand because it refers to four different Old Testament texts; it also contains some of Paul's most taxing thought patterns. J. Louis Martyn's translation of Galatians 3:10-14 helps the reader to follow the thread:

---

63. Pelikan, *Bach among the Theologians,* 79-80, emphasis added. Was Jesus truly forsaken by God on the cross? It may be that Luke omits the cry of dereliction because he does not want to leave the impression that God was actually absent. On this point, Raymond E. Brown offers a striking insight. He suggests that, in the cry of dereliction, Jesus is experiencing the silence of God even though God is present and "speaking" in the sign of the darkness at noonday, "but *Jesus does not hear him*" (from my notes of a lecture by Brown at Fordham, March 8, 1994, emphasis added). I have found no better commentary than that of Clifton Black: "It seems to me suspect to rush to the Almighty's defense in Matthew and in Mark, protesting that the apocalyptic ambience of their crucifixion accounts demonstrates that God's beloved Son was truly not abandoned at three o'clock that afternoon . . . *sub specie aeternitatis,* under the appearance of eternity (Spinoza), that is true. *Sub specie cruciatus,* under the aspect of torturous execution, it is no less true — from the evangelists' point of view — that *Jesus ultimately, faithfully prayed to a God whose presence he could no longer perceive*" ("The Persistence of the Wounds," in *Lament: Reclaiming Practices in Pulpit, Pew, and Public Square,* ed. Sally A. Brown and Patrick D. Miller [Louisville: Westminster John Knox, 2005], 51, emphasis added). Both of these quotations suggest that it was Jesus' own perception that the Father had withdrawn from him.

64. The scene in Gethsemane is pertinent to the discussion of the cry of dereliction, but the major commentary on that scene will follow in chapter 9.

Those whose identity is derived from observance of the Law are under the power of a curse, because it stands written, "Cursed is everyone who is not steadfast in observing all of the things written in the book of the Law, so as to do them" [Deut. 27:26]. That before God no one is being rectified by the *Law* is clear from the fact that "The one who is rectified by *faith* will live" [Hab. 2:4]. Moreover, the Law does not have its origin in faith; if it did have its origin there, it would not say, "The one who does the commandments will live by them" [Lev. 18:5].

Christ redeemed us from the Law's curse, becoming a curse in our behalf; for it stands written, "Cursed is everyone who is hanged on a tree" [Deut. 21:23b]. He did this in order that the blessing of Abraham might come to the Gentiles in Jesus Christ; in order, that is, that we might receive the promise, which is the Spirit, through faith. (Gal. 3:10-14)[65]

This crucial passage is often overlooked in the church. Incomprehensibly, it is not found in the Revised Common Lectionary, not even as a choice for Good Friday.[66] It is an intricate passage even by Paul's standards, but that is not a sufficient reason for its neglect. It is almost as though the message were just too intense for public consumption. Paul has always been a strong dose for the church, yet it is he who, among the New Testament writers, was granted the most profound insight into the cosmos-shaking, universal nature of the Messiah's work.[67]

Reducing Paul's argument to its simplest components, we learn that:

- *Everyone* is living under the power of God's curse, because the Law (or Torah) pronounces a curse upon all who do not fulfill its demands (Deut. 27:26).[68]
- Rectification (*dikaiosis,* traditionally translated "justification")[69] —

---

65. Translation by J. Louis Martyn, *Galatians,* Anchor Bible 33A (New York: Doubleday, 1997), 307, emphasis added. Martyn capitalizes "Law" for two reasons. Its first meaning is, essentially, Torah. For Paul, it has a second meaning; like Sin and Death, the Law has become one of the Powers — not intrinsically, but because it has been bent into a weapon by Sin (as in Rom. 7:11).

66. In a lifetime of attending Good Friday services in mainline churches, I have never once heard it preached, except when I have done so myself.

67. Galatians 3:10-14 will be examined in more detail in chapter 10.

68. "If one wants to live out of the works of the law, it is the utterances of the law itself that prove the impossibility of it." Herman N. Ridderbos, *The Epistle of Paul to the Churches of Galatia* (Grand Rapids: Eerdmans, 1953), 125.

69. The contrast is between righteousness by the Law and righteousness by faith — Rom. 9:30-31; 10:5-6 (or, put another way, righteousness of our own versus the righteousness that is from God — Rom. 10:3).

meaning "to set right" — by the Law is impossible because the Law does not originate in faith. Faith, unlike the Law, is able to give life (Lev. 18:5; Hab. 2:4).

- God must therefore do the rectifying himself. He has done so through Jesus Christ, who actually took the full force of the curse of the Law into himself on the cross (Deut. 21:23).
- Our identity is now derived not from observance of the Law but from the gift of the Spirit through faith in Christ.

The important thing for our discussion here is Paul's announcement *(kerygma)* that God, in the person of his sinless Son, put himself voluntarily and deliberately into the condition of greatest accursedness — on our behalf and in our place. This mind-crunching paradox lies at the heart of the Christian message.

The closest link to Galatians 3:10-14 in the Gospels is the cry of dereliction. At this crucial point there is a split in the tradition of Good Friday preaching. It is common practice in some evangelical circles to connect the cry of dereliction with Galatians 3:13 ("having become a curse for us"), and yet many another preacher has struggled with *Eli, Eli, lama sabachthani* without ever taking note of that link. To be sure, there is much opportunity for misunderstanding. Sometimes it is objected that a father who would allow his own son to be cursed and abandoned must be monstrous. Trinitarian thinking is of the essence here, however. The Son and the Father are doing this in concert, by the power of the Spirit. This interposition of the Son between human beings and the curse of God upon Sin is a project of the three persons. The sentence of accursedness has fallen upon Jesus on our behalf and in our place, *by his own decree* as the second person.[70]

Closely related is a striking passage in II Corinthians that begins: "*All this is from God,* who *through Christ* reconciled us to himself," thereby nailing down the indispensable affirmation that the Father is acting, not *over against* the Son, but *through and in* the Son, whose will is the same as the Father's. The awesome transaction is taking place *within God.*[71] The passage ends with

70. *Opera trinitatis ad extra indivisa sunt* — "the works of the Trinity are indivisible." Quoted by Christopher Morse from Augustine, *On the Trinity* 1.5. See Morse, *Not Every Spirit: A Dogmatics of Christian Disbelief* (New York: Trinity, 1994), 207.

71. "This triune relationship between the Father, the Son, and the Holy Spirit applies to all their activity, not least in the movement of atoning propitiation and expiation whereby all who come to the Father through the Son and in the Holy Spirit are redeemed and saved from sin and death and judgment. Thus belief in the Holy Trinity does not have to do simply with our knowledge of God as he is in his inner life and being, but with the very substance of the

another of Paul's syntactically complicated but theologically mind-boggling sentences: "For our sake he [God] made him [Christ] to be sin who knew no sin, so that in him we might become the righteousness [*dikaiosyne*] of God" (II Cor. 5:18, 21).

No one understands exactly what is meant by "he made him to be sin." How could the Son of God "be sin"? Since Paul understands Sin not as an accumulation of misdeeds, but as a Power with a death grip on the whole human race, it certainly sounds as though Jesus somehow was overtaken by the dread Power of Sin, or was assimilated to it, or was held by it *in extremis* — imprisoned by it in some way that was commensurate with its annihilating intentions. Paul sets Jesus' sin*lessness* ("he knew no sin") over against "he made him to be sin" and brings the two phrases into closest proximity in order to heighten the shock of what is being said. He knew no sin; he was made sin. Note that Paul does not say "Jesus never sinned" or "Jesus did not commit sin." That is because Sin in Paul is not something that one commits; it is a Power by which one is held helplessly in thrall. The connection here with Galatians is indeed complex, and cannot be fully grasped unless we also have Romans 7:5-25 in view. In this passage, Paul shows that Sin and the Law are partners in a conspiracy involving a third partner, Death: "Sin, finding opportunity in the commandment [Torah or Law], wrought in me all kinds of covetousness. Apart from the law sin lies dead. [But] . . . sin, finding opportunity in the commandment, deceived me and by it killed me."[72] Sin is personalized here by the apostle, because it is not just "missing the mark," as has been so often taught; it is an active Power hostile to human beings.[73] In Romans 7:11, Paul depicts Sin using the Law as an instrument to deal Death to humanity, almost as though Sin were using the Law as a lethal club. And indeed, that is more or less what Paul is saying.

Richard A. Norris explains further the role of the Law: "Death, after all, was the penalty assigned in the Law of Moses for 'the prophet who presumes to speak a word in my name which I have not commanded him to speak, or who speaks in the name of other gods' (Deuteronomy 18:20). Such, apparently, was Jesus. Consequently, he was treated automatically as

---

Gospel of salvation. . . . It is indeed God's threefold giving of himself to us as Father, Son, and Holy Spirit that is our salvation." T. F. Torrance, *The Mediation of Christ,* rev. ed. (Colorado Springs: Helmers and Howard, 1992; orig. 1983), 126.

72. The idea that the Torah could be an agent of Sin would be deeply offensive and shocking to Jews. This is one of the points at which Christianity and Judaism part ways.

73. *Hamartia* does indeed mean "missing the mark," but fastening biblical theology to etymology has serious limitations. Words take on expansive meanings in the Scriptures that cannot be grasped through basic definitions.

one accursed. . . . For it stood written: 'a hanged man is accursed by God' (Deuteronomy 21:23)."[74]

Paul makes a typically audacious move in quoting Deuteronomy 21:23. Significantly, he omits the words "by God."[75] For Paul, it is not God, but the curse *of the Law* that condemned Jesus.[76] In his death, Paul declares, Jesus was giving himself over to the Enemy — to Sin, to its ally the Law, and to its wage, Death (Rom. 6:23; 7:8-11). This was his warfare. That is one of the most important reasons — perhaps the most important — that Jesus was crucified, for *no other mode of execution would have been commensurate with the extremity of humanity's condition under Sin.*

Jesus' situation under the harsh judgment of Rome was analogous to our situation under Sin. He was condemned; he was rendered helpless and powerless; he was stripped of his humanity; he was reduced to the status of a beast *(damnatio ad bestias),* declared unfit to live and deserving of a death proper to slaves — and what, according to Paul, were we if not slaves? The key passage here is Romans 6:16-18: "You are slaves of the one whom you obey, either of

---

74. Richard A. Norris, *Understanding the Faith of the Church* (New York: Seabury Press, 1979), 133-34.

75. As Martyn argues in *Galatians,* the "curse" is not precisely God's curse, but the curse of the Law. This solves some problems but presents others. Exegetically, in the context of Galatians, the Law is clearly meant. In particular, this reading has the great merit of guaranteeing the priority (both chronologically and theologically) of the gospel over the Law, blessing over curse, mercy over condemnation. Certainly in Galatians Paul is putting as much distance between God and the Law as possible. (Martinus C. de Boer stresses this in *Galatians: A Commentary* [Louisville: Westminster John Knox, 2011], 213.) Without Galatians, we would not know how truly radical the gospel is. On the other hand, even if God is not the *direct* author of the curse of the Law, God, being God, can hardly be absolved from responsibility for whatever occurs in relation to it. We cannot altogether eliminate God from the equation. The link between "the curse" and the cry of dereliction cannot be proven exegetically. It is the sort of theological-homiletical-poetic leap from the gut that preachers make (and Paul was above all a preacher).

At the end of World War II, as the Nuremberg trials were starting, E. B. White wrote something in the *New Yorker* that is astonishingly relevant to the death of Christ under the Law: "These so-called war trials . . . will be extremely valuable as precedents if they are presented as *a preview of the justice that may some day exist,* not as an example of the justice that we have on hand. . . . Nobody, not even victors, should forget that when a man hangs from a tree it doesn't spell justice *unless he helped write the law that hanged him*" (quoted in Max Frankel, "The War and the Law," *New York Times Magazine,* May 7, 1995, emphasis added).

76. As Calvin puts it, it was by "rigid and austere exaction, which remits not one iota of the demand," that the Son was born under the Law, condemned by the Law, and crucified under the curse of the Law — thereby redeeming us from it: "as the Apostle declares, 'Christ redeemed us from the curse of the Law, having become a curse for us'" (Gal. 3:13). Calvin, *Institutes of the Christian Religion,* ed. John T. McNeill, trans. Ford Lewis Battles, Library of Christian Classics (Philadelphia: Westminster, 1960), 2.7.15 and 2.16.6.

sin, which leads to death, or of obedience, which leads to righteousness[.] But thanks be to God, that you . . . having been set free from sin, have become slaves of righteousness."[77] This is what happened on the cross. The Son of God gave himself up to be enslaved by Sin, condemned by the Law, and subject to Death.

Linking all these passages, then, we see that Jesus exchanged God for Godlessness. He was in the form of God; he took the form of a slave (Phil. 2:7). He emptied himself of every prerogative, including that of sinlessness. He took the form of a slave, literally, on the cross, but we must say more. The slave's death undergone by Jesus that occurred on the *literal* level becomes something else entirely on the *apocalyptic battlefield* where the Lord of Hosts goes to war with the forces of the Enemy. On that battlefield, as we shall see in chapter 9, Christ is the victor, though for the present it is a victory hidden to all but the eyes of faith. What we see happening on the cross is that Jesus, who dies the death of a slave, "was made to be sin." Does this mean that Jesus became his own Enemy? It would seem so.[78] Just as his own human body turned against him on the cross, smothering and killing him, so his human nature absorbed the curse of the Law, the sentence that deals death to the human being (Rom. 7:11).[79] By making himself "to be sin," he allied himself with us in our farthest extremity, perfectly described in Ephesians: "Remember that you were at that time . . . alienated from the commonwealth of Israel, and strangers to the covenants of promise, having no hope and without God in the world" (Eph. 2:12). Thus he entered into our desperate condition. No wonder he cried on the cross, "My God, my God, why hast thou forsaken me?"[80] The

77. See also the important, related passage in John 8:31-36: "Jesus then said to the Jews who had believed in him, 'If you continue in my word, you are truly my disciples, and you will know the truth, and the truth will make you free.' They answered him, 'We are descendants of Abraham, and have never been in bondage to any one. How is it that you say, "You will be made free"?' Jesus answered them, 'Truly, truly, I say to you, every one who commits sin is a slave to sin. The slave does not continue in the house for ever; the son continues for ever. So if the Son makes you free, you will be free indeed.'"

78. If my readers protest that this is not making logical sense, then I must admit that is probably true. The imagery does not always fit harmoniously together. How can Jesus become, on the cross, a *slave to* Sin and also *be Sin* at the same time? But in the Gospel of John, in the space of a very few verses Jesus describes himself both as "the door [gate] of the sheep[fold]" and as "the good shepherd." How can he be both a shepherd and a gate at the same time? Our wish for order and logic does not necessarily serve the wide-ranging nature of the biblical texts.

79. Note this, however: a Catholic scholar well makes the point that "a law that can curse Jesus, the Son of God, in his very act of dying for us, cannot be absolute. Indeed, in cursing Jesus, the law has brought about its own downfall" (Peter F. Ellis, *Seven Pauline Letters* (Collegeville, Minn.: Liturgical Press, 1982]).

80. Some have said that the cry of dereliction is not a despairing cry at all, but simply the first verse of a psalm that ends in victory. In his commentary on this utterance of the Lord's,

important thing here is Paul's breathtaking announcement *(kerygma)* in Galatians 3:13 that God, in the person of his Son, put himself voluntarily and deliberately into the place of greatest accursedness and Godlessness — for us.[81]

The Significance of Godlessness

The purpose of this chapter has been to show that God's purpose is revealed, not only in the *fact* of his Messiah's death, but also in the *mode* of his death. We have attempted to say something about the depth of shame and ungodliness attached to crucifixion as a method, and to explain how much audacity and courage were required of the early Christians to proclaim a crucified Messiah to a world that could have been expected, then as now, to find such a message insupportable. Martin Hengel describes his research into "the constantly varying forms of abhorrence at the new religious teaching." He shows us why such a highly educated, well-born person as Paul would feel constrained to say, "I am not ashamed of the gospel":

Calvin offers a beautifully balanced interpretation: "He takes God as his God, and so with the shield of faith bravely repulses the sort of dereliction that shot at him from the other side" (*Harmony of the Gospels*, on Matt. 27:46). Similarly Martyn writes that "as one crucified, Jesus did stand under the curse of the Law. Now, however, Paul [in Gal. 3:13] sees that in that event God stood on the side of his Christ, not on the side of the cursing voice of the Law" (*Galatians,* 320).

There is considerable disagreement among theologians as to whether God actually forsook Jesus or not. Moltmann says yes, God forsook God — though he goes to great lengths to avoid splitting the Trinity or implying that God denies his own nature. Barth says a vigorous *Nein* to "God against God," insisting that God cannot deny his own nature; yet he affirms that it is in God's nature to forsake his prerogatives (*Church Dogmatics* IV/1 [Edinburgh: T. & T. Clark, 1956], 184-85). Moltmann's argument is subtle and seeks to avoid the obvious pitfalls. Both of these major theologians of the cross want to say that in the Godforsakenness of Jesus, *God was involved.*

81. Some readers may object to a strong emphasis on the cry of dereliction in view of the contrasting serenity of Luke's words from the cross (the Fourth Gospel, being in a class by itself, will be discussed in other contexts). In this particular book, a compelling reason is that we are inquiring about *crucifixion* instead of some other form of death. On this particular issue, Luke, who apparently omitted the cry of dereliction deliberately (though he has his own tradition of sayings from the cross), does not shed as much light as do Mark, Matthew, Paul, and even Hebrews, because he wishes to present Jesus meeting his destiny in faithful submission to the Father ("Father, into thy hands I commit my spirit" — Luke 23:46).

We will find our way most surely by following an *aperçu* of Paul Lehmann. After the tragic death of his son and only child Peter, Lehmann continued as he had always done to wrestle openly with the deepest questions, with yet more anguish of soul. When asked about how to seek guidance after a grievous loss, he said, "It is found in the dialectical tension between 'My God, my God, why hast thou forsaken me?' [in Mark/Matthew] and 'Father, into thy hands I commit my spirit'" (Luke 23:46).

The heart of the Christian message, which Paul described as "the word of the cross," ran counter not only to Roman political thinking, but to the whole ethos of religion in ancient times and in particular to the ideas of God held by educated people. . . . To believe that the one pre-existent son of the one true God, the mediator of creation and the redeemer of the world had appeared in very recent times in out-of-the-way Galilee as a member of the obscure people of the Jews, and even worse, had died the death of a common criminal on the cross, could only be regarded as a sign of madness. The real gods of Greece and Rome could be distinguished from mortal men by the very fact that they were *immortal* — they had absolutely nothing in common with the cross as a sign of shame.[82]

We have looked at passages from Paul's Corinthian letters to show what happens to a church when it loses sight of the cross. Paul's insistence on the "word of the cross," then as now, causes offense, because a "Corinthian" church is self-congratulatory, certain of its own spiritual attainments, whereas the cross of Christ displays God's leveling of all distinctions in his godless death.[83]

Crucifixion itself, as an "utterly vile" method, was worse than any of us are presently capable of fully imagining. Reflecting upon it may help us, however, under the guidance of the Spirit, to draw closer to this unimaginable act of God's love for all humanity by means of the *mors turpissima crucis.* The cross is offensive to *everyone,* religious people ("Jews") and secular people ("Greeks") alike. It is this radical undercutting of who is in and who is out that makes the cross so deeply threatening to many. All human achievement, especially religious achievement, is called into question by the godlessness of Jesus' death. If God in three persons is most fully revealed to us by the Son's accursed death *outside* the community of the godly, this means a complete rethinking of what is usually called religion. As we continue with this project, looking ahead to chapter 3, we can speak not only of "Corinthians" but also of "Galatians," since the cross calls us into question on more than one front.

---

82. Hengel, *Crucifixion,* 5.

83. The Corinthians were self-congratulatory about their *spiritual* (so-called) accomplishments, and tended to be antinomian (*nomos,* "law"). As we shall see, the Galatian church was the opposite, being led in the direction of a new legalism.

CHAPTER THREE

The Question of Justice

Oh villain! Thou art condemned into everlasting redemption.
SHAKESPEARE, *Much Ado about Nothing*

Why crucifixion? That is the question we are asking. Why was this singularly horrific mode of death chosen by the triune God to demonstrate his love for his human creatures? Could it not have been some other sort of death?

In this chapter we will investigate the link between justice and righteousness, suggested by the epigraph above. The constable Dogberry's ignorant slip of the tongue in Shakespeare's play is meant to bring a laugh, but in fact it makes the point precisely.[1] The *condemnation* of Jesus means *redemption* for the world, and by extension God's condemnation of the sin of his people is part of his redemptive purpose. Isaiah says this clearly: "destruction is decreed, overflowing with righteousness" (Isa. 10:22). The cross of Christ is the place where we see most clearly the relationship between judgment (condemnation, destruction) and the righteousness of God (experienced *both* as judgment *and* as redemption). The Greek word for God's righteousness is *dikaiosyne,* also translated "justice." Therefore we are devoting a chapter to the matter of justice.

The all-important connection between the *method* used to execute Jesus and the *meaning* of his death cannot be grasped unless we plumb the depths

---

1. Those who believe that Shakespeare was a Christian and brought numerous Christian themes into his plays are smaller in number today than they used to be. It is my view nevertheless that the underlying meaning of this joke is meant quite seriously by the playwright and that he knows exactly what is being suggested by the juxtaposition of the two words "condemned" and "redemption."

of what is meant by *injustice*. There is much irony here, for injustice is a threatening subject for the ruling classes who have the time and inclination for reading books like this one. Those who suffer most from injustice are the poorly educated, the impoverished, the invisible. Justice is involved with law and judges; the people most likely to suffer injustice cannot afford good lawyers, do not even know any lawyers, whereas lawyers and judges are the ones who have the money to buy books. In other words, those most likely to be affected by the issues raised in this chapter are least likely to be reading about them. This puts an extra burden on the privileged reader, but such challenges are not unrelated to Jesus' teaching that the one who does not take up his cross and follow him is not worthy of him (Matt. 10:38). Trying to understand someone else's predicament lies at the very heart of what it means to be a Christian.

Justice in the Old Testament

A preacher on the radio observed that the New Testament tells us almost nothing about what went on in Jesus' mind; then he said, "If you want to know what went on in Jesus' mind, read the Old Testament."[2] That is a dazzlingly simple way of stating what every biblical scholar knows but seldom says. We tend to forget that what we call the Old Testament was the only Bible that Jesus, Paul, and the earliest Christians had. Not only so, but the Torah, the Prophets, and the Psalms were known to them by heart in a fashion that we today can scarcely imagine. There are many things that we do not know about Jesus, but of this we can be sure: his mind and heart were shaped by intimate, continuous interaction with the Scriptures.[3] If we are to have "the mind of Christ" (I Cor. 2:16), we need to know the Old Testament.

If the average churchgoing American is asked to describe God, he or she will almost certainly call God "loving." God is also commonly described as compassionate, merciful, welcoming, accepting, and inclusive. Very few white Americans will volunteer that God is just. Yet the revelation of God as just, or righteous (the same word is used in both Hebrew and Greek), forms such a huge part of the Old Testament prophetic literature that ancient Israel would have counted it a keystone of the faith. Even when the word "justice" is not specifically used, the idea is palpably present. Much of the Torah is

2. Unfortunately, I have forgotten the preacher's name.

3. It is not too far-fetched to compare Jesus' total immersion in the Scriptures to the young person of today who is continually plugged in to electronic media.

suffused with it. To give just one rather mundane example, in Deuteronomy we read that the Lord told Moses,

> You have been going about this mountain country long enough; turn northward. And command the people, You are about to pass through the territory of your brethren the sons of Esau, who live in Seir; and they will be afraid of you. So take good heed; do not contend with them; for I will not give you any of their land . . . because I have given Mount Seir to Esau as a possession. You shall purchase food from them for money, that you may eat; and you shall also buy water of them for money, that you may drink. (Deut. 2:3-6)

This is a very small illustration, hardly worth mentioning in the grand scale of God's justice, but it shows how even in the small details God is looking out *not only* for the "godly" and "chosen" children of Israel (Jacob), *but also* for the interests of the "ungodly" and "rejected" children of Esau.[4]

The "Holy One of Israel" (Isaiah's favorite term) is continually described in the Old Testament as a God of justice. "Righteous," "just," "holy": these words are virtually synonymous with the name of God.

> The Lord of hosts is exalted in justice,
>   and the Holy God shows himself holy in righteousness. (Isa. 5:16)

Wherever justice is administered, the Lord himself is present: "Jehoshaphat . . . appointed judges in the land . . . and said to the judges, 'Consider what you do, for you judge not for man but for the Lord; *he is with you in giving judgment.* Now then, let the fear of the Lord be upon you; take heed what you do, for there is no perversion of justice with the Lord our God, or partiality, or taking bribes'" (II Chron. 19:4-7).

What is the content of God's justice? A passage from Isaiah 1:11-27 is representative of many other passages from the eighth-century prophets and states the issues clearly.[5] The Lord, speaking through his prophet, declares in very strong terms that he is no longer pleased with the religious

---

4. As it is written, "Jacob I loved, but Esau I hated" (Rom. 9:13). This will become a mighty theme in the hands of the apostle Paul. We will return to Jacob and Esau in the final chapter of this volume.

5. It is generally considered indisputable that the greater portion of the book of Isaiah can be divided between the prophet Isaiah of the eighth century and the unnamed prophet of the exile in the fifth century (Isa. 40–55). (There is postexilic material as well, which some have called "third Isaiah.") In this study we will largely be regarding the book of Isaiah as a whole.

observance of the people, even though it is apparently both meticulous and lavish:

> "What to me is the multitude of your sacrifices?
>   says the Lord;
> I have had enough of burnt offerings. . . .
> Bring no more vain offerings;
>   incense is an abomination to me. . . .
>   I cannot endure iniquity and solemn assembly." (vv. 11-13)

As in communities today, the good churchgoing middle classes were not themselves murderers, and did not have blood on their hands in any direct or literal sense, but the indictment is relentless nonetheless, and the call to repentance and reform unequivocal:

> "Wash yourselves; make yourselves clean;
>   remove the evil of your doings
>   from before my eyes;
> cease to do evil,
>   learn to do good;
> seek justice,
>   correct oppression;
> defend the fatherless,
>   plead for the widow." (vv. 16-17)

God's justice is not vague or amorphous. It is not general or indeterminate. It is specific and particular, showing that God is attentive to the material details of human need. Notice these examples, which could apply to monetary practices of today:

> "You shall not pervert the justice due to your poor in his suit." (Exod. 23:6)

> "You shall not . . . take a widow's garment in pledge." (Deut. 24:17).

> "Thus says the Lord God: Enough, O princes of Israel! . . . cease your evictions of my people." (Ezek. 45:9)

"Perversion of justice" is hated by God. Justice for the defenseless is God's own work; it testifies to who he is: "For the Lord your God is God of gods and Lord of lords . . . who is not partial and takes no bribe. He executes justice for the fatherless and the widow, and loves the sojourner, giving him food and clothing. Love the sojourner therefore; for you were sojourners in the land of Egypt" (Deut. 10:17-19).

This last verse contains a key idea: the care given by the community to its weakest members, and even to those who are not members at all, is to be a mirror of God's own care for the Israelites when they were enslaved. The activities of the community are not undertaken on general principles; they arise out of the lively remembrance of God's just and merciful initiatives with them ("A wandering Aramean was my father" — Deut. 26:5).

Because justice is such a central part of God's nature, he has declared enmity against every form of injustice. His wrath will come upon those who have exploited the poor and weak; he will not permit his purpose to be subverted.

> Woe to those who devise wickedness
>> and work evil upon their beds! . . .
> They covet fields, and seize them;
>> and houses, and take them away;
> they oppress a man and his house,
>> a man and his inheritance. . . .
> Hear this, you heads of the house of Jacob
>> and rulers of the house of Israel, . . .
> because of you
>> Zion shall be plowed as a field;
> Jerusalem shall become a heap of ruins. (Mic. 2:1-3; 3:9-12)

In the Day of the Lord, when God's righteous judgments are put into effect, those most certain to be judged are the privileged, the rich, the heedless:

> They have become great and rich,
>> they have grown fat and sleek.
> They know no bounds in deeds of wickedness;
>> they judge not with justice
> the cause of the fatherless, to make it prosper,
>> and they do not defend the rights of the needy.
> Shall I not punish them for these things? says the Lord. (Jer. 5:27-29)

As we saw in the Isaiah passage, worship is hateful to God when it is not linked to justice. In one of the most striking passages in the prophetic literature, God declares his opposition not only toward the rich but also toward good churchgoing people who are oblivious to inequity. This was a favorite passage of Martin Luther King's: "I hate, I despise your feast days, and I will not smell in your solemn assemblies. . . . Take thou away from me the noise of thy songs; for I will not hear the melody of thy viols. But let justice [roll] down as waters, and righteousness as a mighty stream" (Amos 5:21-24 KJV).

Whenever justice rolls down like waters, it is a sign that God is on the move.[6] Furthermore, provisional victories of justice in this present world, whether large or small, are a foretaste of the Day of Yahweh. The advent of a Day of God when all injustice will be rectified forever is a central theme in the prophetic and apocalyptic literature of the Old Testament. The promise of a coming realm of perfect justice brings joy even now in the anticipation of it, as evidenced in this psalm of praise:

> Happy is the one whose help is the God of Jacob,
> whose hope is in the Lord his God . . .
>> who executes justice for the oppressed;
>> who gives food to the hungry. . . .
> The Lord watches over the sojourners,
> he upholds the widow and the fatherless;
> but the way of the wicked he brings to ruin.
> The Lord will reign for ever,
> thy God, O Zion, to all generations.
> Praise the Lord! (Ps. 146:5, 7, 9-10)

And so a major theme of the messianic passages in the Old Testament is the coming of God's kingdom of perfect justice.[7]

---

6. Maya Lin's memorial to the civil rights movement in Montgomery, Alabama, features a waterfall cascading over an upright stone slab. Amos 5:24b is inscribed on the stone under the waterfall. All around the overflowing pool of water in front of the cascade are the names of the martyrs of the civil rights movement who died unjustly: Jonathan Daniel, Andrew Goodman, Michael Schwerner, James Chaney, Medgar Evers, Viola Liuzzo, and many others. Their self-sacrificing deaths testify to the coming Day of the Lord when perfect justice will reign forever.

7. The kingdom to come includes judgment upon "the wicked." This will be radically reinterpreted in the New Testament gospel (see concluding chapter).

The Messiah Comes Bringing Justice

When Jesus comes announcing the kingdom of God, this Old Testament background forms an inalienable part of his proclamation. The expectation of this kingdom is the context for his preaching ("The time is fulfilled, and the kingdom of God is at hand; repent, and believe in the gospel" — Mark 1:15). According to the witness of the Hebrew prophets over hundreds of years, the Messiah's arrival would be the sign that the rule of God was near:

> Behold, the days are coming, says the Lord, when I will raise up for David a righteous Branch, and he shall reign as king and deal wisely, and shall execute justice and righteousness in the land. (Jer. 23:5)

> For to us a child is born,
>   to us a son is given;
> and the government will be upon his shoulder. . . .
> Of the increase of his government and of peace
>   there will be no end,
> upon the throne of David, and over his kingdom,
>   to establish it and uphold it
> with justice and with righteousness
>   from this time forth and for evermore.
> The zeal of the Lord of hosts will do this. (Isa. 9:6-7)

Jesus takes this messianic role upon himself in a very deliberate way when he gives his inaugural sermon in the synagogue in Nazareth:

> And he came to Nazareth, where he had been brought up; and he went to the synagogue, as his custom was, on the sabbath day. And he stood up to read; and there was given to him the book of the prophet Isaiah. He opened the book and found the place where it was written,

> > "The Spirit of the Lord is upon me,
> > because he has anointed me to preach good news to the poor.
> > He has sent me to proclaim release to the captives
> > and recovering of sight to the blind,
> > to set at liberty those who are oppressed,
> > to proclaim the acceptable year of the Lord."

> And he closed the book . . . and he began to say to them, "Today this scripture has been fulfilled in your hearing." (Luke 4:16-21)

When Jesus speaks in this way about the fulfillment of prophecy, it is tantamount to announcing himself as Messiah. The signs of the kingdom are already present in his ministry, with special emphasis on God's intervention on behalf of those who cannot help themselves. This is the picture of God's justice that we recognize from the prophets.

Another place where the prophetic Old Testament message most obviously penetrates the story of Jesus is in his mother's song, the Magnificat. We will understand it better if we remember that Mary is from the bottom rung of her society, one of the least and lowest, a member of the group called the *Anawim* that longs for justice:[8]

> "My soul magnifies the Lord,
> and my spirit rejoices in God my Savior,
> for he has regarded the low estate of his handmaiden . . .
> he has scattered the proud in the imagination of their hearts,
> he has put down the mighty from their thrones,
> and exalted those of low degree;
> he has filled the hungry with good things,
> and the rich he has sent empty away." (Luke 1:46-48a, 51b-53)

Overfamiliarity has caused the Magnificat to lose much of its edge, but when it is put next to its prototype, the song of Hannah in I Samuel 2:1-10, the theme of justice for those on the bottom of the socioeconomic scale jumps out at us. Both of these canticles are rapturous in their expression; they are outbursts of joy. God's justice will involve a dramatic reversal, however, which will not necessarily be received as good news by those presently on top of the heap (reader, that means us). Hannah rejoices in the same terms as Mary:

> "My heart exults in the Lord. . . .
> He raises up the poor from the dust;
>   he lifts the needy from the ash heap,
> to make them sit with princes
>   and inherit a seat of honor." (I Sam. 2:1, 8)

We can see from all this that the coming of the Lord was not projected as an altogether comfortable event. Those who thought they were secure were going to find that they had built on the wrong foundation. Those who

---

8. *Anawim* is Hebrew for the poor who depend on the Lord for deliverance.

counted on their accomplishments were going to find disreputable people taking up their space. Those who had been religiously observant all their lives were going to discover that God may have been looking for something else. The coming of the Messiah might, indeed, bring not peace, "but a sword" (Matt. 10:34).

Forgive and Forget?

The well-known passage in Micah 6:8 ("What does the Lord require of you . . . ?") declares that justice and mercy are two foundational aspects of God's character. Working out the relation between the two is an essential task of Christian theology, preaching, and pastoral care. In our own time this has become a particularly pressing question. There is a widespread impression that Christian forgiveness can be construed separately from the question of justice — that, in fact, forgiveness can be offered without reference to justice. However, forgiveness is by no means as simple or expeditious as is often suggested; it is a complex and demanding matter. The question of forgiveness and compensation really should not be discussed apart from the question of justice. When a terrible wrong has been committed and an apology is offered, the person or persons wronged may be justified in feeling that too much is being asked of them. If the impression is given that the wronged parties are simply supposed to "forgive and forget," the wrong will linger under the surface and cause further harm.

In recent U.S. history, various mass shootings in American schools and other public places continue to transfix the nation and set off a cataract of soul-searching. A significant related debate about forgiveness has also been taking place. Many of the shootings occurred in parts of the country where Christianity is strong. In case after case, from Jonesboro to Paducah to Columbine High School — three scenes of shootings of children *by children* — the call for forgiveness went out almost before the bodies were cold. Young people still trembling and weeping were asked by well-meaning Christian youth leaders, "Do you forgive Eric and Dylan?"[9] Many thoughtful people, Christians and Jews among them, raised serious questions about this.[10]

9. Eric Harris and Dylan Klebold, the killers at Columbine High School.

10. For example, in a December 15, 1997, *Wall Street Journal* column about the Paducah school shootings entitled "The Sin of Forgiveness," radio host Dennis Prager registers his objection to the "feel-good doctrine of automatic forgiveness." "Automatic" is the key word here. Forgiveness is costly and should be seen to be such. Another column, called "What Is Missing at Jonesboro," by Paul Greenberg, said, "Yes, there were words of comfort Tuesday night [at

A psychologist wrote: "Forgiving is hard work. It takes time, and involves pain. It's not just a simple declaration or automatic, reflexive action. False forgiveness is going through the motions without anything changing on the inside. It's lip service, and it actually interferes with authentic resolution and estranges people from their real feelings."[11]

This is a strong argument, related to the subject of this chapter. Even more pertinent, however, is a theological point. *Forgiveness in and of itself is not the essence of Christianity, though many believe it to be so. Forgiveness must be understood in its relationship to justice if the Christian gospel is to be allowed its full scope.* As Archbishop Desmond Tutu of South Africa has said, "Forgiveness is not cheap, is not facile. It is costly. Reconciliation is not an easy option. It cost God the death of his Son."[12]

During the Kosovo War, a journalist filed a report about ethnic Albanian deportees in Macedonia. He described the rage experienced by Kosovar professors, writers, and other intellectuals who were robbed not only of their homes but also of their books, papers, files — their irreplaceable life's work. "Can such a deep hurt ever heal?" asked a reporter. An ethnic Albanian newspaper editor, Ardian Arifaj, told him a story that he had heard as a child:

> Ardian Arifaj began, "There was a naughty boy whose father would hammer a nail into a piece of wood every time his son did something wrong. One day, the boy asked why, and when it was explained, the boy decided he would behave better. Each time he did something good, his father would remove a nail from the board. Eventually, all the nails came out." Mr. Arifaj let a few seconds pass, allowing suspense to precede the story's moral. "Yes, the nails were gone," he said. "But the holes always remained."[13]

---

the memorial service for the slain young people — March 24, 1998], words of mercy and grace and forgiveness, but I don't recall hearing anything about justice. And *what meaning can mercy and grace and forgiveness have if they are separated from justice?*" (*Greenville [S.C.] News,* April 6, 1998, emphasis added).

11. Jeanne Safer, "Must You Forgive?" *Psychology Today,* July/August 1999.

12. Desmond Tutu, 1998 Mollegen Lecture, *Virginia Seminary Journal,* January 1999. As this book goes to press, the American nation has been riveted by the grace and mercy offered to a young man who shot and killed nine leading members of the Emanuel A.M.E. Church in Charleston, South Carolina, while they were gathered for Bible study. This was a striking example in our midst of forgiveness that is neither cheap nor facile. It arose spontaneously out of the deep, long-nurtured Christian faith of the members of "Mother Emanuel" church.

13. *New York Times,* April 26, 1999.

Turning now to the "holes remaining" in Rwanda, where an estimated 800,000[14] were murdered in a few weeks of 1994 in one of the worst genocidal actions in a century of genocide, here is the voice of David Birney, an Episcopal bishop who traveled to Rwanda two years after the horror and spent four weeks listening to the people. On return he was interviewed by a journalist.

"To be in a country where a Christian would take up arms against a brother and sister and bludgeon them to death," he said, shaking his head, "when day after day for one month you look into the eyes of hundreds and hundreds and hundreds of widows — who's going to take care of them? I taught [as a teacher in Uganda years before] a lot of their clergy who have been murdered. It was difficult to wrap my heart and my mind around what happened. I don't have any answers; I don't have many recommendations. The hatred, the anger, the grief there are so great. If there is one thing that I believe with all my being must happen, it is that *before any effort at reconciliation can be made, there has got to be a means of getting a system of justice in place.*"[15]

This is as clear a statement as one could find of the issue we are discussing. "No justice, no peace," goes the familiar street chant, but Bishop Birney's lament crystallizes for us in a very personal way the necessity for justice at the very heart of the human problem.

In these stories, one senses the power and pull of evasion, of denial, of avoidance — the very same things that cause us to turn away from the cross. The "forgive and forget" syndrome looms very large on both fronts — personal and political. "The steady substitution of political argument in public life with the soothing rhetoric of healing is disturbing," writes Ian Buruma.[16] The painfully incomplete nature of investigations and the lack of justice around the world from El Salvador to Cambodia continue to be analyzed and deplored to the present day.

---

14. The exact number will never be known. Responsible estimates range between 500,000 and 1,000,000. It is reliably believed that seven out of ten Tutsis were killed. More than a decade later, the details of this genocide are little understood by the American public, who know of it only in the most general terms, if at all. Few have heard about the widespread use, during the genocide, of violent, repeated, sadistic rape and genital mutilation as a weapon against Tutsi women, often with the cooperation of Hutu women.

15. David Birney, interview with James H. Thrall, *Episcopal Life,* July/August 1996, emphasis added.

16. "The Joys and Perils of Victimhood," *New York Review of Books,* April 8, 1999.

The South African Example

In our time, the hardest work of coming to terms with a history of terrible atrocities was undertaken by the South African Truth and Reconciliation Commission (TRC). When the postapartheid constitution was being negotiated in 1993, the outgoing white regime wanted blanket amnesty, in the manner of Latin American juntas. Nelson Mandela and the African National Congress (ANC) would have none of it. A compromise was reached, with the goals of averting civil war and making a peaceful transition possible. The agreement was that amnesty would be granted only on a case-by-case basis, in return for full disclosure.[17] As a result of this compromise, the TRC was appointed by Mandela in 1995 with Anglican Archbishop Desmond Tutu as chairman. In November 1998, after three years of intense public hearings, the commission released the report of its investigations to a barrage of criticism from both ends of the political spectrum, as well as a cool reception from Mandela, whose own ANC was angered by damaging testimony about some of its activities during the worst days of the struggle. However, it is now largely recognized that the evenhandedness of the TRC was one of the most striking aspects of its work, for it detailed not only the extensive crimes of the white government, but also the misdeeds of the Inkatha Freedom Party, the ANC, and President Mandela's own ex-wife, Winnie. The moral courage and tenacity required to hold a steady course under such pressures were extraordinary, especially since it had never been done before.

The model of a truth commission was first developed in Latin America, but no previous commission prior to South Africa's had probed so deeply or required so much. Chilean human rights specialist José Zalaquett stated that such commissions should be created so that as much truth about atrocities as possible could be discovered, but also that this truth be "officially proclaimed and publicly exposed." Acknowledgment, he said, is the goal.[18] The Commission for Historical Clarification in Guatemala, to give one example, failed to do this because it lacked an adequate mandate. Because it was hamstrung by the military, it continued the same policies of cover-up and denial at the highest levels that had given the Guatemalan civil war its

17. Michael Ignatieff, "Digging Up the Dead," *New Yorker,* November 10, 1997. Ignatieff explained further that anti-apartheid veterans, not to mention the victims' families, didn't much like amnesty, "but it has proved the only bait capable of luring perpetrators onto the hook."

18. Timothy Garton Ash, "The Truth about Dictatorship," *New York Review of Books,* February 19, 1998.

sinister character in the first place. No names were named and no perpetrators had to face any victims.[19] Truth and acknowledgment, it seems, are not necessarily the same thing. Without acknowledgment, even an imperfect justice remains elusive.

The South African procedures, by contrast, were notable for their insistence on full acknowledgment. The 3,000-page report was called "the most comprehensive and unsparing examination of a nation's past that any such commission has yet produced."[20] The hearings themselves were often harrowing in the extreme. White officials testified, sometimes in gruesome detail, often defiantly and without remorse, about the tortures and deaths they had caused. During the testimony, the families of the victims were frequently present. Survivors testified about their sufferings in the presence of their tormentors. In return for full disclosure, the perpetrators received amnesty — meaning that they were declared free from prosecution.[21] Imperfect though this method clearly was, it was a reminder to everyone in the country that while South Africa was determined to seek reconciliation and move into the future, *justice had not been abandoned.*[22]

The TRC had to struggle intensely over a long period to cope with all the pressure from competing interests, not to mention the pain of listening to the harrowing testimony of many victims and their families. Nevertheless, the process gained strength as time went by, and the watching world saw the wisdom of the commission. No one argued that the procedure was not seriously flawed, because so many torturers and murderers would never have to pay for their crimes. But the cathartic nature of the hearings has been widely, if sometimes begrudgingly, acknowledged. In spite of the obvious gaps in the procedure, most analysts concluded that the whole thing had been conducted in an atmosphere of dignity, fairness, and respectfulness

19. Larry Rohter, "Guatemala Digs Up Its Army's Secret Cemeteries," *New York Times,* June 7, 1999. Buried in this long, detailed article about exhumations of victims in the civil war is this information: "At locations in the Péton jungle, they [the excavators] have found skeletons with hands and feet bound together behind their backs, the rope also stretched tightly around the necks — evidence of a form of death by torture that the scientists call 'forced self-strangulation.'" Reading this, my mind went immediately to the description of crucifixion by Peter Brown quoted in chapter 2 — "forced to be one's own executioner." Thus, when we come alongside those who have suffered the most ghastly torments, we find that the Son of God has been there.

20. Editorial, *New York Times,* November 1, 1998.

21. Not everyone was given amnesty. It was refused to the four men involved in the death of anti-apartheid hero Stephen Biko because the TRC did not believe their testimony.

22. Bill Keller, "A Glimpse of Apartheid's Dying Sting," *New York Times,* February 19, 1993, emphasis added.

toward all, including those who had committed crimes. In this respect, if in no other, it was an adumbration of justice in the kingdom of God.[23]

This extraordinary evenhandedness came down from the top. Desmond Tutu is distinguished for many things, but perhaps most of all for his vigilance over many decades to prevent his own oppressed people from turning into oppressors themselves. This explains the willingness of the commission to include criticism of the ANC in its findings.[24] Even as Tutu has himself been engaged in political affairs, he has steadfastly maintained the need for the church to be independent of any political party so as to be in a position to challenge any possible human rights abuses in the democratic future. In his own words, "We want to be bold politically to the hilt, but not determined in a partisan way by our membership in a party." As archbishop, he positioned the church to be "able to address every group. We don't belong to a church that is any party at prayer, and we can say to all and sundry, 'Thus says the Lord.' Today's oppressed [might] become tomorrow's oppressors. We sometimes see that — we see people who have had horrendous experiences, so that you never thought they would treat others as they had been treated, and lo and behold, they do."[25]

Many leading writers and political analysts have been impressed by the South African Truth and Reconciliation Commission. Timothy Garton Ash admiringly wrote, "The hearings are a sort of political theater; they are a kind of public morality play. Bishop Tutu has shown himself well aware of this. He leads others in weeping as the survivors tell their tales of suffering and the secret policemen confess their brutality."[26]

Christians will readily see that there is more than theater here. In Tutu's capacity to identify totally with those who underwent such torment, it is possible to see the image of the crucified One. The archbishop's unyield-

---

23. Observers will admit, however, that although the Truth and Reconciliation Commission *addressed* the problem of justice as best it could, it could not *provide* justice. That fact underlines the inadequacy of human justice.

24. Tutu told his old friend Mandela that he would resign as chairman of the TRC unless the ANC owned up to their own atrocities (reported in the *New York Times*, May 13, 1997).

25. Interview with Desmond Tutu, *The Living Church*, April 12, 1992. I have made very slight changes in word order and punctuation for the sake of clarity. Tutu's full account of the Truth and Reconciliation Commission can be found in his book *No Future without Forgiveness* (New York: Image Books, 1999).

26. Ash, "The Truth about Dictatorship." Tutu himself might distance himself from this assessment, however, because in his book about the TRC he says that he begged God not to let him break down crying again because "the media then concentrated on me and took their attention away from those who should have had it, the witnesses" (*No Future without Forgiveness*, 144).

ing commitment to political justice, refined throughout many trials during the long anti-apartheid travail, was rooted in the greater justice and radical mercy of God.[27]

In January 1998, Tutu was in New York to receive treatment for prostate cancer. He gave just one interview during that time.[28] He sought to explain the work of the TRC: "It is not enough to say let bygones be bygones. . . . Reconciliation does not come easy. Believing that it does will ensure that it will never be. We have to look the beast firmly in the eyes." At the same time, he said, "We seek to do justice to the suffering without perpetuating the hatred aroused." He continued,

> We recognize the past can't be remade through punishment. Instead — since we know memories will persist for a long time — we aim to acknowledge those memories. This is critical if we are to build a democracy of self-respecting citizens. As a victim of injustice and oppression, you lose your sense of worth as a person, your dignity. Restorative justice is focused on restoring the personhood that is damaged or lost. But restoring that sense of self means restoring memory — a recognition that what happened to you *happened.* You are not crazy. Something seriously evil happened to you. And the nation believes you.[29]

Michael Ignatieff is a secular writer, not a religious thinker, but his analysis of the TRC touches Tutu's at certain points, thereby illuminating the theological context, whether Ignatieff knows it or not.

---

27. Miroslav Volf could be describing Tutu in the following passage: "The cross of Christ should teach us that the only alternative to violence is . . . willingness to absorb violence in order to embrace the other in the knowledge that truth and justice have been, and will be upheld by God" (*Exclusion and Embrace: A Theological Exploration of Identity, Otherness, and Reconciliation* [Nashville: Abingdon, 1996], 295).

28. Bishop Tutu performed heroically, not only in the hearings themselves, but also in his personal battle against cancer, with trips to the United States for treatment alternating with sessions of listening to emotionally exhausting testimony back in South Africa. Most of the members of the TRC showed signs of physical or emotional trauma during or after their long ordeal.

29. Interview with Desmond Tutu, *Parade* magazine, January 11, 1998. In this same vein, a white South African, Albie Sachs, who is now a judge in the new South Africa, has said, "The TRC has made a huge contribution. . . . Very deep emotions have come out, and no one can deny the horrors of the past. *Maybe one of the worst things about horrors is denial, that they didn't even happen . . .* [now] no one can say that it never happened" (quoted by L. Gregory Jones, "Truth and Consequences in South Africa," *Christianity Today,* April 5, 1999, emphasis added).

Watching a society struggle with the dilemma of amnesty changes what one thinks about *justice. It is associated with punishment,* with putting people behind bars. *But* it can also mean something else: truth and moral reparation, *the restitching together of a moral world,* where sons and daughters do not disappear in the night. . . . The hearings in Centenary Hall make one aware of how much human beings need to believe that they belong to a moral order. What propels [the families of the victims] both black and white, to come before the Truth and Reconciliation Commission is the impulse to create a public *realm* where truth is truth and lies are lies, where actions are held accountable, where the state is held to certain standards. In South Africa, that is perhaps the deepest yearning of all, after decades of infamy.[30]

In this passage Ignatieff has contrasted two types of justice, one that simply *punishes* and another that is inseparable from a *realm,* that is, in biblical terms, a kingdom — a new creation from God. This is what Bishop Tutu has incarnated among us.[31] Day in and day out for more than forty years, under pressures that white Americans cannot even imagine, he has been the consistent embodiment of one who lives in this world according to the true reality ultimately to be determined by the realm of God. First as a leader in the church, and then as chairman of the TRC, he has shown in word and deed that he is not interested in punishment. He is interested in new creation.

The purpose of this lengthy examination has been twofold: (1) to begin an attempt to show just how deep-seated the human resistance to truth and justice can be; and (2) to illustrate a key thought that we have already met and will meet again, namely, *the impossibility of administering human justice that is proportionate to the offense.* Examples of corporate, rather than individual, injustice have been emphasized because it is so easy to ignore large-scale involvement or complicity in every conceivable kind of ill at home and around the world — the exploitative abuse of low-level workers

30. Ignatieff, "Digging Up the Dead," emphasis added.

31. Bishop Tutu's great gifts do not necessarily lie in the areas of systematic theology or biblical exegesis. He wanders off into strange doctrine occasionally. We do well to remember that it is not given to any one person to do or be everything. Tutu's gift to us is his unique combination of exuberance, humor, and joy together with a truly astonishing — especially in view of his irrepressible personality — political realism, lack of sentimentality, and capacity for suffering, all in the context of unconquerable biblical faith. Again, he is a living illustration of Miroslav Volf's words, "Only those who are forgiven and who are willing to forgive will be capable of relentlessly pursuing justice without falling into the temptations to pervert it into injustice" (*Exclusion and Embrace,* 123).

and illegal aliens, the rule of warlords, the deaths of innocent civilians, the endemic abuse of women, the terrible conditions in our prisons, "rendition" and "enhanced interrogation," mass rape and famine as public policy, private contractors who write their own rules in war zones, and so forth in an endless stream of malefaction.

Overcoming Denial

We have used up a good deal of space examining examples of large-scale injustice and some human responses — or nonresponses — to it. It takes effort to care when one is not directly involved. Tabloids feast on local homicides and scandals because that is where the readership is; only the most serious consumers of in-depth news hear the cries of the victims of mass injustice.[32] Yet in the Bible, the idolatry and negligence of groups *en masse* receive most of the attention, from Amos's withering depiction of rich suburban housewives (Amos 4:1) to Jesus' lament over Jerusalem (Luke 13:34) to James's rebuke of an insensitive local congregation (James 2:2-8). Juan Luis Segundo, the Uruguayan Jesuit, has been frequently quoted reminding us that "the world that is satisfying to us [the affluent] is utterly devastating to them [the poor and powerless]."[33] This is precisely the discovery that transformed the once-conservative Salvadoran archbishop Oscar Romero, costing him his life.

Gross injustice demonstrates a basic premise: *in our world, something is terribly wrong and cries out to be put right.* Perhaps this seems so obvious to the reader as not to be worth stating, but such is not the case. The wrongness of things is not as readily acknowledged as one might think. "In spite of all evidence," wrote one observer, "modern-day Americans keep trying to convince ourselves that happiness is the natural state of our species."[34] We are unusually naïve about the dark side of human life, and are known as

32. A political cartoon depicted a woman sitting in front of her TV set weeping over the fate of a mother and baby murdered in an affluent American suburb (it was the sensational case of the moment) while, on the floor beside her, lay a discarded newspaper with headlines about genocide in Darfur.

33. Juan Luis Segundo, *The Liberation of Theology,* paraphrased by Robert McAfee Brown, *Making Peace in the Global Village* (Philadelphia: Westminster, 1981), 12; also the widely respected physician Paul Farmer, *Pathologies of Power: Health, Human Rights, and the New War on the Poor* (Berkeley and Los Angeles: University of California Press, 2005), 157.

34. Jeffery Smith, quoted in a *Wall Street Journal* review of his book about depression, *Where the Roots Reach for Water,* September 13, 1999, emphasis added.

Pollyannas throughout the world.[35] Our boundless optimism, our "chipper avoidance of the tragic," is part of who we are; it is a central component of the engine that drives our energy and success.[36] We do not want anything to interfere with the smooth functioning of the engine. There is a downside, however; this tendency contributes to a distorted and sentimental view of reality. Walker Percy, in his novels, protests against this by creating a whole gallery of characters who stand out from everyone else around them because they cannot accommodate things as they are. They are not "adjusted." One of them says, "I cannot tolerate this age."[37] Such people often tend to operate alone, because not enough of us are willing to share their burden.

We cannot, it seems, come to terms with these thoughts. Our escapist mentality is constantly at work, readjusting reality to block out the unendurable aspects of life. It is very important for us Americans to believe that, in spite of the evidence, the world and human nature are essentially benign.[38] The American way of denial is a good match for the message of

35. It is hard to remember now, but when the Oklahoma City bombing occurred, it was widely seen overseas as a watershed in American life, a loss of supposed innocence. A note of derision was even expressed in some European newspapers, as though citizens of other countries who endured World War II and frequent terrorist attacks on their soil were saying, it's about time Americans had a dose of reality. The attacks of 9/11 were another matter; they were so extravagantly terrible that even the most cynical overseas observers were temporarily silenced. Twelve years later, however, the reaction to the Boston Marathon bombing of 2013 showed that our can-do spirit had not been dampened in the least. This is not to criticize our American culture of optimism *per se*. The problem is that it is not balanced by a sober grasp of the tragic aspects of human life.

36. Peter Steinfels of the Fordham Center on Religion and Culture, *New York Times*, September 10, 2005.

37. Walker Percy, *Lancelot* (New York: Farrer, Straus and Giroux, 1977), 157.

38. Many people know Anne Frank's diary largely from one famous sentence, "In spite of everything, I still believe that people are really good at heart." This line was lifted years ago from its original context (where it has a more ambivalent sound) and burnished into an inspirational slogan whereby, as Cynthia Ozick has argued, it has done great damage by encouraging a sentimental view of humanity that many people have mistaken for fundamental religious truth. In recent years there has been much criticism of this domesticated, sanitized version of Anne Frank. Ozick, in an influential essay, notes that the international success of the original play about Anne has permanently influenced the way that the diary is read — and not for the better. Ozick quotes Alvin Rosenfeld of Indiana University, who wrote that "Anne Frank has become a ready-at-hand formula for easy forgiveness." Ozick's article is a strenuous protest against the hijacking of Anne's image by those who insist on seeing her as a "merry innocent and steadfast idealist," a "funny, hopeful, happy Anne" when the outcome was so harrowing — the nature of which has been validated by testimony from those who knew Anne in the camp where she died (Ozick, "Who Owns Anne Frank?" *New Yorker*, October 6, 1997). In 2013, the Anne Frank museum in Amsterdam unveiled a revised presentation of the story. Discerning observers ob-

the Dalai Lama, which explains a lot of his astonishing popularity in our country. Richard Gere, the actor who is also a practicing Buddhist, knows the Dalai Lama well, and he said this about him: "In his presence, one feels that this man wants nothing except for you to be happy. . . . He reduces us to the simplicity of a child who just wants things to be right in the universe."[39] Although people feel blessed in the presence of a holy man who wants the world to be right and people to be happy, *the holy man cannot make that happen.*[40]

The message of the cross of Jesus Christ is that only the Creator of the universe can make perfect justice come about in the world that he created, and that he has done so in the body of his own Son, and that he will do so in the future Day of the Lord. "Shall not the Judge of all the earth do right?" (Gen. 18:25).

The Relation of Justice and Mercy

The challenge for American Christians is thus a dual one. *First,* how, in the midst of a feel-good culture, do we grapple responsibly with the biblical assessment of fallen human nature?

> The hearts of men are full of evil, and madness is in their hearts while they live, and after that they go to the dead. (Eccles. 9:3)

---

jected that the new displays simply continued the sanitizing tendency (e.g., Edward Rothstein, in "Playing Cat and Mouse with Searing History," *New York Times,* October 13, 2013).

39. Quoted in Orville Schell's *Virtual Tibet: Searching for Shangri-La from the Himalayas to Hollywood* (New York: Metropolitan Books, 2000), 56.

40. The Dalai Lama has been an admirable symbol of courage around the world and continues to trouble the Chinese Communist regime with his steadfast presence and his hold on his people and their aspirations. His inability or unwillingness to integrate injustice and suffering with his worldview, however, limits him. It is interesting to contrast him with his friend Desmond Tutu. Both of them have famous laughs. As has been noted by several observers, however, the Dalai Lama often uses his laugh to deflect attention from unpleasant subjects. He and Tutu are friends, but Tutu never laughs in that way. His laugh is an eschatological sign of God's triumph over evil. He has felt the intensity of the struggle in his bones in a way that does not appear either in the demeanor or in the writings of the Dalai Lama. For him, suffering is the way to compassion, which is the way to happiness and the cessation of suffering. His teaching often sounds as if suffering and compassion were not connected to actual suffering human beings at all, but are stages along the way to personal happiness and even "achieving one's goals." Dalai Lama, with Howard C. Cutler, *The Art of Happiness: A Handbook for Living* (New York: Riverhead Books, 1998), 128-30, 228, 310, and various other passages throughout.

"[My people] are skilled in doing evil [says the Lord],
    but how to do good they know not." (Jer. 4:22)

The heart is deceitful above all things,
    and desperately corrupt;
    who can understand it? (Jer. 17:9)

These blunt statements can be dismissed as relics from the "wrathful God of the Old Testament," or disdained as sources of the fire-and-brimstone preaching of previous centuries, or rejected as a threat to our "self-esteem"; yet if one takes the twentieth century as a whole — not to mention the mounting atrocities of the twenty-first — they seem quite realistic.

The *second* challenge is to help Christians understand that even secular justice should be and can be administered out of a deep sense of solidarity among all human beings, so that we never cease to remember that "there but for the grace of God go I."[41] It is paradoxical, but if we think of *all* human beings as equally in need of both justice and mercy, we will be much better able to support a legal system that can be severe without sentimentality, yet is unfailingly opposed to inhumanity of every kind — including inhumanity perpetrated by guards in maximum-security prisons.

Yet there can be no denying the extreme difficulty of determining what a Christian response should be in particular cases of barbarism. The relation of justice to mercy is not always clear. We have all heard of moving and dramatic cases of parents or spouses who forgave the murderer of their loved one, often motivated in part by a certainty that this is what the victim would have wanted also. Tutu spoke often of the Biehl family from California, whose daughter Amy, a young white anti-apartheid activist, was cruelly murdered in 1993 by militant blacks in Cape Town. Her parents have traveled repeatedly to South Africa to offer forgiveness and to work with their Amy Biehl Foundation for helping black youths. On the other hand, however, the bishop also holds up the example of Stephen Biko's family, who say they cannot and will not forgive the murderers of the black leader. Their stance, Tutu

---

41. According to *Bartlett's Familiar Quotations,* this familiar saying was first uttered by one of the English Protestant Reformers, John Bradford (1510-1555), who was watching some prisoners being taken off to be executed. Bradford was later imprisoned in the Tower of London during the persecutions of Mary Tudor's reign, along with Thomas Cranmer, Nicholas Ridley, and Hugh Latimer, with whom he studied the New Testament in their common cell. He was burned at the stake in 1555. The saying attributed to him was in character, whether he actually said it or not. He died asking forgiveness for himself and offering forgiveness to others. www
.britannia.com/bios.

says, demonstrates that forgiveness is a "long and demanding process" and must never be cheapened.[42] These are two opposing examples that illustrate the dialectic between justice and mercy.

Beyond Forgiveness

The New Testament scholar Reginald Fuller wrote that "forgiveness is too weak a word" to embrace the full scope of what Christ has done and what he calls us to.[43] How can we begin to speak even of forgiveness, let alone transformation, in the worst of the worst situations? The extermination of millions does not cry out for forgiveness. Never mind millions; what about just one baby burned up in a microwave oven by its own father? "After such knowledge, what forgiveness?"[44] Forgiveness is not enough. There must be justice too.

Vince Gilligan, creator and executive producer of the celebrated AMC drama *Breaking Bad,* was interviewed on NPR's *Fresh Air* program concerning his character Walter White, a high school chemistry teacher turned drug dealer and remorseless killer.[45] The interviewer asked Gilligan about a statement he had made: "Atheism is just as hard to get your mind around as fundamentalist Christianity." Gilligan, a self-identified lapsed Catholic agnostic, still wants to believe "there is more than just us out there." If there is no "cosmic justice," he muses, then what is the meaning of it all? This intelligent man, who has given much thought to people "breaking bad," reaches out in hope of "cosmic justice." Forgiveness is not enough. *Something is wrong and must be made right.* Miroslav Volf concurs: "The cross is not forgiveness pure and simple, but *God's setting aright* the world of injustice and deception."[46] This setting-right is called rectification (*dikaiosis* in Greek, also translated as "justification") by the apostle Paul, a word and concept that we will be examining at some length.

---

42. 1998 Mollegen lecture.

43. Reginald Fuller, *Interpreting the Miracles* (London: SCM, 1963), 51 n. I have heard Professor Fuller say the same thing in person.

44. T. S. Eliot, "Gerontion."

45. The interview can be found at http://www.npr.org/player/v2/mediaPlayer.html? action=1&t=1&islist=false&id=140111200&m=140593722.

46. Volf, *Exclusion and Embrace,* 298, emphasis added. This is not always understood in the church. The continuing exposés about clergy sexual abuse reveal a profound failure to understand the way in which the righteousness of God *(dikaiosyne)* works to make right what is wrong at the same time that forgiveness is unconditionally offered.

When we speak of setting-right, we are not talking about a little rearrangement here and a little improvement there. From the perspective of the Old and New Testaments, the whole creation has gone drastically awry. The incarnation of the Son of God should not be understood as the divine benediction on all that is. It was *an incarnation unto the cross,* and therefore an incarnation that sets a question mark *over against* the way things are. Walker Percy is not the only novelist who can't stand the world as it is. Novelists like Flannery O'Connor, Graham Greene, Cormac McCarthy, and others give us characters who cannot fit into this "present evil age" (Gal. 1:4). The Messiah came, not to a purified and enlightened world spiritually prepared for his arrival, but rather to a humanity no nearer to its original goodness than on the day Cain murdered his brother Abel. Indeed, the barbarity of crucifixion reveals precisely that diagnosis. From beginning to end, the Holy Scriptures testify that the predicament of fallen humanity is so serious, so grave, so irremediable from within, that nothing short of divine intervention can rectify it.[47]

Proportion and Its Relation to Justice

In April 1994, two U.S. Air Force fighter jets, in a terrible "friendly fire" misfortune, shot down two U.S. Army helicopters in a no-fly zone in northern Iraq, killing twenty-six people. Only one Air Force officer, Jim Wang, was court-martialed, out of six originally charged. In June 1995, a military jury found Wang innocent. It is not our purpose here to debate the correctness of the verdict. What is of interest for this chapter on justice is that the suffering of the victims' families was greatly exacerbated by what they saw as a failure of justice. The parents of one of the Army pilots bitterly described the affair as a "massive whitewash" by the Air Force.

The distressed families did not seem to be especially vengeful; they were not calling for extreme penalties. They just wanted to know that someone took their pain seriously. The reprimands and admonishments issued by the Air Force did not seem to be commensurate with the losses. "I am still baffled," said young widow Kaye Mounsey, "how 26 people could be brutally killed and yet *not one person* held accountable."[48] There is much here to re-

---

47. In Cormac McCarthy's *No Country for Old Men,* Sheriff Bell says, "I wake up sometimes way in the night and I know as certain as death that there aint nothin short of the second comin [*sic*] of Christ that can slow this train."

48. Bob Pool, "Military Briefing Fails to Ease Widow's Mind," *Los Angeles Times,* July 14, 1994.

flect upon in relation to the death of Christ. Notice how readily the concept of *accountability* and the language of *owing* come into play when there are serious issues at stake. Something is owed to the victims of such atrocity. No one needs to have it explained to them what is meant by this language. It is common human expectation that there should be justice, and that justice should be in some way related to the magnitude of the loss.

Note also the intimation that even one person, truly accepting a penalty, would have been a consolation for the twenty-six — the one for the many. This notion is dramatized in the Gospel of John: "Caiaphas, who was high priest that year, said, '. . . it is expedient for you that one man should die for the people.' . . . Being high priest that year he prophesied that Jesus should die for the nation, and not for the nation only, but to gather into one the children of God" (John 11:49-52).

Two ideas, then, are in play in this section. The one just mentioned is the notion of one person being accountable for many. The second is that a just or "expedient" resolution of a great offense should have some relationship to its enormity. This is the notion of proportionate justice: something of value is required to indicate the magnitude of the transgression. If the offering is the Son of God, does that not suggest a supreme order of magnitude?

Where's the Outrage?

In a *Newsweek* article about heaven, Kenneth L. Woodward noted, "Missing from most contemporary considerations of heaven is the notion of divine justice."[49] When affluent white Americans think of heaven, we tend to think of celestial serenity, natural beauty, and family reunions. Black Americans and other disadvantaged groups would be much more likely to think of God's promise that there will be ultimate justice. For anyone who has suffered great wrong, it is important to know, as the book of Revelation promises so wondrously, that all wrongs will be righted (Rev. 21:3-4).

To be sure, most people, of whatever color, tend to be intensely interested in justice when it is *for themselves*. It is the notion of justice *for all* that is missing from much of our public discourse. People turn out for justice when the issue is something that affects them directly, but it is difficult to generate public enthusiasm to support justice for somebody else, or some group other than one's own. The civil rights movement was an authentic miracle of God's justice because it managed to mobilize significant numbers

49. Kenneth L. Woodward, "Heaven," *Newsweek,* March 27, 1989.

of people from various constituencies. Unfortunately, this is rare. Apathy and lack of caring for others have something to do with this; determination not to lose one's own privileges may be a larger motivator. There is a theological dimension here. Justice for everyone is an alarming thought because it raises the possibility that *it might come upon oneself after all.* As the author of Ephesians puts it, "by nature" we are *all* "children of wrath, like the rest of mankind" (Eph. 2:3).

It makes many people queasy nowadays to talk about the wrath of God, but there can be no turning away from this prominent biblical theme. Oppressed peoples around the world have been empowered by the scriptural picture of a God who is angered by injustice and unrighteousness. The humor and exuberance of a freedom fighter like Desmond Tutu are evoked, fueled, and sustained by the conviction that God is on the side of those who are defenseless and voiceless, who have no powerful friends, who are abused and oppressed by the system. A slogan of our times is "Where's the outrage?" It has been applied to everything from Big Pharma's market manipulation to CEOs' astronomical wealth to police officers' stonewalling. "Where's the outrage?" inquire many commentators, wondering why congressmen, officials, and ordinary voters seem so indifferent. Why has the gap between rich and poor become so huge? Why are so many mentally ill people slipping through the cracks? Why does gun violence continue to be a hallmark of American culture? Why are there so many innocent people on death row? Why are our prisons filled with such a preponderance of black and Hispanic men? *Where's the outrage?* The public is outraged all over cyberspace about all kinds of things that annoy us personally — the NIMBY (not in my back yard) syndrome — but outrages in the heart of God go unnoticed and unaddressed.

The biblical message is that the outrage is first of all in the heart of God.[50] If we are resistant to the idea of the wrath of God, we might pause to reflect

---

50. Lesslie Newbigin, who expounds these matters with exceptional clarity, writes concerning the wrath of God: "We have seen that the whole world is in the power of sin, and is therefore in a state of enmity against God. And yet God loved the world and still loves it. That is the reason why He has put forth His power to save it. This is a fact which we must never forget. Sometimes Christians in trying to explain the cross of Christ have suggested that it was the love and self-sacrifice of Christ which turned away the Wrath of God and so secured our salvation. It is true that . . . the Wrath of God is revealed against the sin of the world. The Wrath of God is a reality. In order to understand the cross we must understand that. But the love which secured our salvation also comes from God. In Him there is both wrath and love. The wrath is the reverse side of His love. *But God's wrath is not turned away by anything from outside of God.* It was because God loved the world that He gave His Son to be its Saviour" (*Sin and Salvation* [London: SCM, 1956], 56, emphasis added).

the next time we are outraged about something — about our property values being threatened, or our children's educational opportunities being limited, or our tax breaks being eliminated. All of us are capable of anger about something. God's anger, however, is pure. It does not have the maintenance of privilege as its object, but goes out on behalf of those who have no privileges. The wrath of God is not an emotion that flares up from time to time, as though God had temper tantrums; it is a way of describing his absolute enmity against all wrong and his coming to set matters right.[51]

On September 2, 1990, a murder occurred in New York City that horrified the nation. The Watkins family from Provo, Utah, a father and mother with their two barely-grown sons, had come joyfully to the city for a long-anticipated trip to attend the U.S. Open tennis matches. While waiting on the subway platform for the train to Flushing Meadows, the family was assaulted by a band of four youths. The older of the two sons went to his mother's rescue as she was being kicked in the face, and he was killed in the attempt. The judge, Edwin Torres, sentenced all four attackers to life without parole, the toughest sentence possible in New York at that time, and in doing so issued a striking statement expressing grave alarm for a society in which "a band of marauders can surround, pounce upon, and kill a boy in front of his parents [and then] stride up the block to Roseland and dance until 4 AM as if they had stepped on an insect. For a mother to hold a dying child in her arms, murdered before her very eyes, is a visitation that the devil himself would hesitate to conjure up. *That cannot go unpunished.*"[52]

Surely this judge's words about *impunity,* a concept we will develop at some length, must call forth a sympathetic response even from people who ordinarily dislike the concept of judgment.

In 1989, Sister Dianna Ortiz, a young, politically unsophisticated American nun, was abducted and tortured by members of the Guatemalan security forces who were under the command of an American they called Alejandro. In her detailed, exceptionally harrowing testimony she said:

> I was asked questions. I was asked by others, friends as well as strangers, *not whether I was receiving any justice from my government but whether I had forgiven my torturers.* I wanted the truth. I wanted justice. They

51. C. F. D. Moule sums up the position that I favor: God's wrath (Greek *orge*) is not a feeling (Latin *affectus*) that God has; it is his action *(effectus)* against wrong. "Punishment and Retribution: Delimiting Their Scope in New Testament Interpretation," in *Stricken by God? Nonviolent Identification and the Victory of Christ,* ed. Brad Jersak and Michael Hardin (Grand Rapids, Eerdmans, 2007), 256.

52. *New York Times,* January 4, 1992, emphasis added.

wanted me to forgive, so that they could move on. I suppose, once I forgave, all would be well — for them. Christianity, it seemed, was concerned with individual forgiveness, not social justice.

Let me introduce a word into the discussion of whether the United States should torture, or engage in cruel, inhumane, or degrading treatment. The word is *impunity*. It is a word of considerable importance to survivors. Survivors . . . seek justice, that is, accountability for its practice. We get neither from our government or any other. Therefore, this is one of the objectives of our organizing.[53]

These examples illustrate (1) the complex relationship of justice to mercy and (2) the disastrous consequences of impunity. We have ranged across a wide territory to show that forgiveness is not a simple matter. If we think of Christian theology and ethics purely in terms of forgiveness, we will have neglected a central aspect of God's own character and will be in no position to understand the cross in its fullest dimension. God's new creation must be a just one, or the promises of God will seem like mockery to those whose defenselessness has been exploited by the powerful. Furthermore, if we fail to take account of God's justice, we will miss the extraordinary way in which it is recast in the New Testament *kerygma*.

John the Baptist stormed out of the desert with a fiery message, "You brood of vipers! Who warned you to flee from the wrath of God?" In our own day, in our haste to flee from the wrath of God, we might ask whether we have thought through the consequences of belief in a god who is not set against evil in all its forms. Miroslav Volf writes, "A non-indignant God would be an accomplice in injustice, deception, and violence."[54] Perhaps the reason we have trouble with this is that we are ourselves accomplices. Yet most people will say at some point that their "blood boils"; the question

---

53. Sr. Dianna Ortiz, O.S.U., "Theology, International Law, and Torture: A Survivor's View," *Theology Today* 63, no. 3 (October 2006): 344-48 (emphasis on word "impunity" original, other emphasis added). The young, virginal nun's account of her torture, rape, and its aftermath was investigated and largely corroborated. The details are exceptionally dreadful. Sister Dianna's story can be found in her book, *The Blindfold's Eyes: A Journey from Torture to Truth* (Maryknoll, N.Y.: Orbis, 2002). A compelling account is available online at http://www.salon.com/2002/11/19/ortiz/. She received no recognition from Presidents Bill Clinton and George H. W. Bush in spite of years of protest and, in 1996, a five-week fast and vigil in front of the White House. President Clinton finally ordered the release of documents related to the United States and Guatemala. She helped to found the Torture Abolition and Survivors Support Coalition International (TASSC).

54. Volf, *Exclusion and Embrace*, 297.

then becomes, what is the boiling temperature?[55] If our blood does not boil at injustice, how can we be serving the God who said the following through his prophet Isaiah?

> Woe to those who make unjust laws,
>   to those who issue oppressive decrees,
> to deprive the poor of their rights
>   and withhold justice from the oppressed of my people.
>
> (Isa. 10:1-2 NIV)

Where is the outrage? It is God's own; it is the wrath of God against all that stands against his redemptive purpose. It is not an *emotion;* it is God's righteous *activity* in setting right what is wrong. It is God's intervention on behalf of those who cannot help themselves.

No one could have imagined, however, that he would ultimately intervene by interposing *himself.* By becoming one of the poor who was deprived of his rights, by dying as one of those robbed of justice, God's Son submitted to the utmost extremity of humiliation, entering into total solidarity with those who are without help. He, the King of kings and Lord of lords, voluntarily underwent the mockery of the multitudes, and, in the time of greatest extremity, he could do nothing to help himself (Mark 15:31).[56]

Even more astonishingly, however, he underwent helplessness and humiliation *not only for the victimized but also for the perpetrators.* This version of the Lord's double indemnity will be a major theme of this study and will be built up throughout the book. Who would have thought that the same God who passed judgment, calling down woe upon the religious establishment (Matt. 23; Luke 11), would come under his own judgment and woe? This is a shockingly immoral and unreligious idea; as we shall see over and over again, however, the crucifixion reveals God placing himself under his own sentence. The wrath of God has lodged in God's own self.[57] Perfect justice is wrought in the self-offering of the Son, who alone of all human beings was perfectly righteous. Therefore no one, *neither victim nor victimizer,* can claim any exemption from judgment on one's own merits, but only on the merits of the Son.

---

55. I had a conversation in the 1970s with a representative of a conservative evangelical missionary organization at the height of the repression by South American military governments. I asked him about his group's stance in view of the political conditions. His exact words were, "We don't recruit any workers whose blood is going to boil at injustice."

56. Martin Hengel, *Crucifixion* (Philadelphia: Fortress, 1977), 31.

57. We cannot emphasize strongly enough or often enough that this action is not Father against Son. It is undertaken within the three persons of the Trinity.

Dikaiosyne: Justice and the Righteousness of God

In 2012 Charles Taylor, former president of Liberia and warlord, was sentenced by an international tribunal to fifty years in prison (the first conviction of a head of state since the Nuremberg trials just after World War II). He was found guilty of "aiding and abetting, as well as planning, some of the most heinous and brutal crimes recorded in human history," and there was a sense that justice had been served. However, the chief prosecutor said, in a press conference afterward, "The sentence today does not replace amputated limbs; it does not bring back those who were murdered. It does not heal the wounds of those who were raped or forced to become sexual slaves."[58]

Human systems of justice are crucial to the functioning of society, but they can only do so much. Human justice cannot make right what was wrong. Therefore, we need to stretch our definition of justice. We are about to attempt a great leap forward in biblical understanding. The crucial notion of love as *agape* is well known, even in congregations that are entirely ignorant of biblical languages; the equally vital word *dikaiosyne,* however, is hardly known at all. When the Hebrew Scriptures were translated into Greek in the second century B.C. (the translation known as the Septuagint, also called the LXX), the Hebrew word-group *(tsedaqa)* usually translated "righteousness" but closely allied and almost synonymous with *mishpat* (justice) was carried over into the single Greek word-group *dikaios, dikaiosyne, dikaiosis, dikaioo.* So here is the problem for English-speakers: our Bible translations use *several* English words — "righteous," "righteousness," "just," "justice," "justification," "justify" — to translate *one* Greek word-group. If we can make the effort to understand the semantic and theological connections between the several English words and the single Greek word-group, we will possess a crucial tool. This is not easy for us, since the English words "righteousness" and "justice" sound nothing like one other. However, *these two words, "justice" and "righteousness," not semantically connected in English, are the same word-group in the Hebrew of the Old Testament and in the Greek of the New.*[59] Indeed, if one looks up "justice" in a dictionary of the Bible, one will be referred to "righteousness." Great strides can be made both in

---

58. Brenda Hollis, chief prosecutor at the international criminal court in Leidschendam, the Netherlands, quoted in the *New York Times,* May 31, 2012.

59. I could be accused of imprecision in using *tsedaqa* (righteousness) and *mishpat* (justice) as though they were precisely the same word-group. However, as Jacqueline Lapsley has pointed out to me, the phrase "righteousness and justice" appears so often in the Psalms and Prophets that the principle of *hendiadys* (a single idea expressed by two words linked together by "and") permits us to speak of them as though they were the same word.

theological comprehension and in ethical motivation when this connection comes into play.[60]

Working at the most fundamental level, then, we first need to know that God's *justice* and God's *righteousness* are essentially the same thing. This won't help us, however, until we make some further leaps. Righteousness, as in "the righteousness of God," does not mean what we typically think it means, and it is a bit of a struggle to get past our misconceptions. To our contemporary ears, "righteousness" is a stuffy word connoting adherence to a set of moral codes or strictures. We are not likely to be attracted to a "righteous" God (unless we are looking for justice!). The meaning of the word "righteousness" in Hebrew, however, is a world away from our idea of legalism or moralism. When we read in the Old Testament that God is just and righteous, this doesn't refer to a threatening abstract quality that God has over against us. It is much more like a verb than a noun, because it refers *to the power of God to make right what has been wrong.*[61] That in itself sounds inoffensive enough, but the radical message underlying it, and the one we resist, is that God does this right-making in spite of our resistance. This is the real meaning of Paul's use of *dikaiosis,* traditionally translated "justification," but better translated "rectification" ("rectify," from Latin *rectus* [right] + *ficare* [to make]).[62] "Rectification" is the only English word that covers the bases. It is better than "justification" because the verb "rectify" — to make right — is closer to the English word "righteousness" than is the verb "justify." Because it is relatively uncommon in daily usage, it is not ideal,

60. A more thorough discussion of this central concept will be found in chapters 8 and 12.

61. Gerhard von Rad won wide acquiescence in the twentieth century with an emphasis on righteousness as "right relationship" within the covenant made by God with Israel; the righteousness of God is his *chesed,* his covenant faithfulness. This has carried over into the twenty-first century; many clergy and Bible teachers still speak of righteousness as "right relationship." However, this has been challenged by scholars who have (rightly in my judgment) expanded the concept of righteousness beyond the context of the covenant with Israel to the entire cosmic order. Clearly, this is what the apostle Paul intends, and Second Isaiah (Isa. 40-55) as well — perhaps also Revelation (21:24-26). Perhaps the most succinct thing we can say against "right relationship" as an adequate definition of righteousness is that it is not a verb! The most important thing to remember about the righteousness of God is that it is the *powerful action* of God in making right. "Righteousness in the Old Testament is not some ontological state of cosmic harmony, but an event inaugurated by God's intervention in the world for the sake of humanity and rendered according to the divine will" (Brevard Childs, *Biblical Theology of the Old and New Testaments: Theological Reflection on the Christian Bible* [Minneapolis: Fortress, 1993], 490).

62. J. Louis Martyn was apparently the first biblical scholar to persuade a significant number of others to use "rectification" (noun) and "rectify" (verb) as a translation for the *dikaios* word-group. (See *Galatians,* Anchor Bible 33A [New York: Doubleday, 1997], 239-50.)

but it is the best equivalent we have. "Rectification" will be used hereafter throughout this book.

Dikaiosyne as Pursuit, *Dikaiosyne* as Aggression

The movement of God toward us even when our backs are turned away from him is described in a number of ways in Scripture. Some of these descriptions are more congenial for our contemporary sensibility than others. Hosea, for instance, speaks of God's moves in terms of a parent and child. The righteousness of God is an aspect of his parental love. He pursues his covenant people in spite of their determination to turn their backs on him:

> When Israel was a child, I loved him. . . .
> The more I called them,
>   the more they went from me;
> they kept sacrificing to the Ba'als,
>   and burning incense to idols.
> Yet it was I who taught Ephraim [the children of Israel] to walk,
>   I took them up in my arms;
>   but they did not know that I healed them.
> I led them with cords of compassion,
>   with the bands of love. . . .
> My people are bent on turning away from me;
>   so they are appointed to the yoke,
>   and none shall remove it.
> How can I give you up, O Ephraim!
>   How can I hand you over, O Israel! . . .
> My heart recoils within me,
>   my compassion grows warm and tender.
> I will not execute my fierce anger,
>   I will not again destroy Ephraim;
> for I am God and not man,
>   the Holy One in your midst,
>   and I will not come to destroy. (Hos. 11:1-9)[63]

63. Jeremiah also makes use of this motif:
> Is Ephraim my dear son?
>   Is he my darling child?
> For as often as I speak against him,

Hosea's image of parent and child includes the parent's "fierce anger." It is taken for granted that God would be within his rights to hand over his people to their just deserts. But the righteousness of God is not like that of a remote judge handing down severe pronouncements. It is in the very nature of God, "the Holy One in your midst," to step down from the bench and pour himself out in unquenchable compassion.

At the same time, Hosea does not say everything that needs to be said. Searching and pursuing, forgiving and restoring are not the only things that God does to redeem his creation. God's righteousness leads him to all lengths to oppose what will destroy what he loves, and that means declaring enmity against everything that resists his redemptive purpose. This is the aggressive principle in God's justice.

God does not possess his justice (righteousness, same word) far off in a remote empyrean. The righteousness of God is not a static, remorseless attribute against which vulnerable human beings fling themselves in vain. Nor is it like that of a judge who dispenses impersonal justice according to some legal norm. God's justice, as Desmond Tutu insisted, is not retributive but restorative.[64] It is natural that many do not understand this, because "God's love, resisted, is felt as wrath."[65] That is why there must be a different sort of language to expound this in all its dimensions. Everything that threatens the community (called "Ephraim" by Hosea) must be exposed, rejected, eliminated.[66] This is where we find it necessary to speak, not only of God's loving pursuit, but also of God's aggressive action. The message of Hosea about the love that will not let the object go needs to be complemented by the tough language of (for example) Isaiah:

> Therefore the Lord says,
>> the Lord of hosts,
>> the Mighty One of Israel: . . .
> *"I will turn my hand against you*
>> *and will smelt away your dross as with lye*
>> *and remove all your alloy.*

I do remember him still.
Therefore my heart yearns for him;
I will surely have mercy on him, says the Lord. (Jer. 31:20)

64. Tutu, *No Future without Forgiveness,* 54.

65. James D. Smart, *Doorway to a New Age* (Philadelphia: Westminster, 1972), 50.

66. Christopher Morse writes, "In electing to have a world and love it into freedom God rejects all that stands in the way of this destiny" (*Not Every Spirit: A Dogmatics of Christian Disbelief* [New York: Trinity, 1994], 248).

And I will restore your judges as at the first,
   and your counselors as at the beginning.
Afterward you shall be called the city of *righteousness,*
   the faithful city."
Zion shall be redeemed by *justice,*
   and those in her who repent, by *righteousness.* (Isa. 1:24-27)

Note how, in the last sentence, "righteousness" clearly refers, not to human virtue or correct behavior, but to the *action of God* in restoring justice and righteousness to Israel. Again, "righteousness" has the character of a verb rather than a noun; it is not so much that God *is* righteous but that he *does* righteousness.[67] It is true that God will turn his hand against Israel in judgment, but (remember that the word "judge" is part of the same word-group as "righteousness") the judgment is not for destruction; it is for smelting away impurities and removal of alloy. It is clear that this will happen *in spite of Israel's resistance;* it will be God's action throughout. The goal is restoration and renewal. In the fullness of time, the covenant people will become a mirror of God's own covenant faithfulness; however, this will not happen from the side of human competence. It must and will happen as a movement from God's side to our side.

The Appearance of Apocalyptic Theology

With Jesus, the whole idea of justice undergoes a radical reframing, implicitly in his ministry and explicitly in Paul's letters. The preparation for this shift was already there, however, in some of the later writings of the Old Testament, because the exile, which seemed to signal the end of the covenant as it had been understood, caused a "theological emergency" for the children of Israel.[68] It

67. Käsemann calls the righteousness of God an "active, salvation-creating power." Richard Hays, quoting this, offers a helpful extension of this central conception by a careful reading of Ps. 143, quoted by Paul in Rom. 3. The word *dikaiosyne* (LXX) is used in the psalm in a way that "unambiguously means God's own righteousness" (as opposed to "imputed" righteousness). "God's righteousness is conceived as a power that will reach out and save the Psalmist" (Hays, *The Conversion of the Imagination: Paul as Interpreter of Israel's Scripture* [Grand Rapids: Eerdmans, 2005], 58-60).

68. John Bright uses this striking phrase when he describes how the fall of Jerusalem to the Babylonians plunged the nation into "a theological emergency." When the end came, "The official theology was helpless to explain it" (*A History of Israel* [Philadelphia: Westminster, 1972], 331-32).

was no longer possible to think of righteousness in terms of the Psalms' familiar distinction between "the righteous" and "the wicked" (e.g., Ps. 34:21). Whereas Israel had thought herself safe, she no longer had any firm ground to stand on. If the covenant had come to be largely understood as a cooperative affair between God and the community, it could be understood that way no longer. If the distinction between being blessed by God and being cursed (Deut. 12:26-28) had come to its appointed end in the exile, then the whole setup would appear to be a message of terminal hopelessness. The righteousness of God had come down upon Israel with full force. The throne of David had toppled; Jerusalem was not Zion after all. God, it seemed, had canceled the covenant. "Our bones are dried up, and our hope is lost; we are clean cut off" (Ezek. 37:11).

The late books of Ezekiel, Zechariah, and Daniel express this in different ways, as do some of the later psalms and the Wisdom literature.[69] Even before the Babylonian conquest, it was becoming obvious that things were not working out as had been expected. To all appearances, God's purposes were not immutable after all. By the time of Habakkuk, the Babylonians were about to sweep away the foundations of Israel, literally and figuratively:

> O Lord, how long shall I cry for help,
>   and thou wilt not hear? . . .
> Why dost thou make me see wrongs
>   and look upon trouble? . . .
> The law is slacked
>   and justice never goes forth.
> For the wicked surround the righteous,
>   so justice goes forth perverted. (Hab. 1:2-4)

Habakkuk poses not only the problem of God's apparent absence, but also the conundrum of evil rewarded and faithfulness persecuted — "justice goes forth perverted." These dilemmas did not arise in their fullest dimensions until after the exile. The old formulas had served well enough in their time ("The Lord loves justice / . . . the wicked shall be cut off. / The righteous shall possess the land, / and dwell upon it for ever" — Ps. 37:28-29), but they had been overtaken by events and were not working anymore. By the time of Daniel, chronologically the last book in the Old Testament, Israel was

---

69. The Wisdom literature famously does not refer to the covenant at all. Ecclesiastes is a view from the world of the exile in which there seems to be "nothing new under the sun" (Eccles. 1:9). This is important for understanding the apostle Paul's relatively few references to the covenant, which will be discussed later.

thoroughly familiar with the strain begun in Deutero-Isaiah that prophesied another type of intervention altogether. The new apocalyptic theology set the stage for the preaching of John the Baptist; it established the framework for the ministry of Jesus and the *kerygma* of Paul the apostle, who recast the whole concept of righteousness and justice in light of the cross.

It was in the atmosphere of theological extremity during the exile that a new message appeared as if from the gates of heaven itself, and indeed, that is exactly what the Isaianic prophet of the exile claims for it: "Comfort ye, comfort ye my people, saith your God. Speak ye comfortably to Jerusalem, and cry unto her, that her warfare is accomplished, that her iniquity is pardoned. . . . Hast thou not known? hast thou not heard, that the everlasting God, the Lord, the Creator of the ends of the earth, fainteth not, neither is weary?" (Isa. 40:1-2, 28 KJV). Ernst Käsemann launched a new movement in the world of biblical theology with this much-quoted announcement: "Apocalyptic was the mother of all Christian theology."[70] Strong currents are rising up from the theological riverbed that are once again being channeled into the mainstream where they belong. A powerful argument can be made that the most important movement in twentieth-century New Testament theology was what Klaus Koch called "the recovery of apocalyptic."[71] This rediscovery of apocalyptic theology in our time is in the process of reshaping our understanding of the cross.

Apokalypsis in Greek means "revelation" or "disclosure." Taking that a step further, it will become clear that the only way we can receive this hope is if *the message itself* comes from beyond our sphere: hence, "apocalypse" or "revelation." The new *kerygma,* or announcement, is an electrifying bulletin from somewhere else, over against and independent of anything, religious or otherwise, that we human beings could ever have dreamed up or projected out of our own wishes.[72] The irreligious and unimaginable humiliation and crucifixion of the Son of God is therefore an apocalyptic event; indeed, it is *the* apocalyptic event. As such, it could only have been inaugurated by God. The essential, foundational idea undergirding

70. Ernst Käsemann, *New Testament Questions of Today,* trans. W. J. Montague (London: SCM, 1969), 102. Käsemann, of Tübingen, is the scholar whose groundbreaking 1960 essay, "The Beginnings of Christian Theology," caused a ferment in New Testament studies that is still being absorbed to this day.

71. "Käsemann had suddenly declared the tributary was the main stream." Klaus Koch, *The Rediscovery of Apocalyptic: A Polemical Work on a Neglected Area of Biblical Studies and Its Damaging Effects on Theology and Philosophy* (London: SCM, 1972), 14.

72. This is meant to be a sidelong rejoinder to Freud's great argument in *The Future of an Illusion.*

apocalyptic theology is that of the primary role of *the divine agency*. After the exile, any illusion of some form of give-and-take cooperation between humanity and God in the building of a just and righteous realm had to be abandoned. The note sounded by Deutero-Isaiah from the depths of the exile is truly a *novum:*

> From this time forth I make you hear new things,
>   hidden things which you have not known.
> They are created now, not long ago;
>   before today you have never heard of them. (Isa. 48:6-7)

There is no way to exaggerate the revolutionary quality of Isaiah 40–55.[73] For sheer sustained exaltation there is nothing to equal it in all of Scripture. To read it is to feel oneself transported into a different universe; and, indeed, that is exactly what is happening. The prophet himself is caught up into the heavenly council chamber where he hears the divine announcement: God himself will descend from his sphere of transcendent power to deliver his people from their servitude and restore them to a transfigured homeland. The central theme is not "justice" in the older sense of the reward of the righteous and the punishment of the wicked; it is the coming triumph of God *independent of* anything human beings can do "either good or bad" (Rom. 9:11).[74] Postexilic Isaiah delivers an astonishing rebuke to the traditional distinction between the righteous and the wicked with these words: "all our righteousnesses are as filthy rags" (Isa. 64:6 KJV).

Summing up this brief overview, "apocalyptic" theology can be defined on the simplest level as the thought-world that emerged among the Hebrew people after the exile, in which the human situation is seen as so tragic and insoluble that the only hope for deliverance is from outside this sphere altogether.

---

73. It is widely accepted today that Isa. 40–55 was written from Babylon two hundred years after the original Isaiah by a prophet whose name we do not know. His work was taken up into that of his great predecessor for compelling canonical reasons. See especially Christopher Seitz, "How Is the Prophet Isaiah Present in the Latter Half of the Book?" in Seitz, *Word without End: The Old Testament as Abiding Theological Witness* (Grand Rapids: Eerdmans, 1998), 168-93.

74. This is part of the most cosmic-universal passage in Paul, Rom. 9–11, where he quotes Mal. 1:2-3: "Jacob I loved, but Esau I hated" (Rom. 9:13). This is to underscore "God's purpose of election . . . not because of works but because of his call" (Rom. 9:11). No abbreviated formula like "faith versus works" comes anywhere close to the radicality of Paul's vision in these chapters. This will be further discussed in the concluding chapter.

"Condemned into Redemption"

The point of introducing apocalyptic theology in this chapter on justice is to begin to build up a picture of the New Testament *kosmos* that will show how radically it challenges our usual understanding of justice and righteousness as *human possibilities*. The New Testament writings all presuppose that the fallen human race and the equally fallen created order are sick unto death beyond human resourcefulness.[75] The crucial factor here is precisely identified in Jesus' parable of the wheat and the tares (Matt. 13:24-30). The parable tells how noxious weeds are sown in a farmer's fields, and when the laborers inquire of their master, he tells them, "An enemy has done this." The interpretation that will be followed in this book is not that some individual people are tares to be burned and others are wheat to be gathered in, but that each of us is, in Shakespeare's words, "a mingled yarn, good and ill together."[76] The weed-sowing Enemy, presented in the Gospels as Satan and in Paul's letters as Powers, holds all humanity and the entire created order in bondage, a theme to be further developed in chapter 10.

This reign of Sin and Death over the *kosmos* is inseparable from the question we are asking in this book: Why did God in three persons agree on such a peculiarly gruesome *manner* of death for the second person? What does *the method itself* tell us about the meaning of the death? There is no quick and easy answer to that question. The biblical account offers hints and suggestions rather than worked-out solutions.

Pushing this train of thought to its most radical application, however, we arrive at a point that is all too rarely acknowledged. In the final analysis, the crucifixion of Christ for the sin of the world reveals that it is not only the *victims* of oppression and injustice who are in need of God's deliverance, but also the *victimizers*. Each of us is capable, under certain circumstances, of being a victimizer.[77] Václav Havel, president first of Czechoslovakia and then of the Czech Republic, was imprisoned several times for his dissident activ-

---

75. This is not meant to say that the created order, any more than the race of humanity, retains no trace of the Creator. The creation, though disturbed to its foundations by the Fall, still praises God. Many Christian thinkers during the Enlightenment held this view. The stars and planets, "as they shine," proclaim that "the hand that made us is divine" (Joseph Addison [1672-1719], paraphrase of Ps. 19:1-6). Christopher Smart, writing while imprisoned for alleged mental instability, has portrayed the creation praising God as well as anyone has, in his beloved poem about his cat Jeoffry (*Jubilate Agno*, fragment B).

76. William Shakespeare, *All's Well That Ends Well*, 4.3.84.

77. The perspective of René Girard and his interpreter James Alison fails precisely at this point. This will be discussed further as we go on.

ities under the Communist regime, the longest stretch being from 1979 to 1983. He wrote extensively about life in the Stalinist galaxy. Here is one of his reflections: "The line [between good and evil] did not run clearly between 'them' and 'us,' but *through each person. No one was simply a victim;* everyone was in some measure co-responsible. . . . Many people were on both sides."[78]

Those of us who have never lived under such a regime should take care about denying the truth that *all* are under the Power of Sin. In the sight of God, *everyone* is in need of deliverance from the forces that are capable of sucking every person into an orbit of antihuman actions. This was the extremity well illustrated by Havel in his extended observations about living in circumstances where no one was able to escape the daily necessity for small betrayals.[79]

The pervasive and monstrous nature of injustice around the world forces us to acknowledge that forgiveness alone does not give a true picture of God's purpose. The reaction of many who have thought deeply about horrendous evils underscores the sense that although many believe that forgiveness *in and of itself* is the essence of Christianity, this is not so. A policy of

78. Quoted by Ash in "The Truth about Dictatorship," 36-37, emphasis added. Many other writers who have known cruel regimes at their worst have said much the same thing. Adam Michnik wrote in the same vein in his 1985 letter from the Gdansk prison. Primo Levi wrote, "Compassion and brutality can coexist in the same individual and in the same moment, despite all logic" (*The Drowned and the Saved* [New York: Vintage Books, 1988], 56). A passage on this subject from Alexsandr Solzhenitsyn's *Gulag Archipelago* is so frequently quoted that it even found its way onto a cable TV legal drama, *The Divide* (2014). Here is a less well known quotation from him: "If only it were all so simple! If only there were evil people somewhere insidiously committing evil deeds, and it were necessary only to separate them from the rest of us and destroy them. But the line dividing good and evil cuts through the heart of every human being. And who is willing to destroy a piece of his own heart?" (*The Gulag Archipelago* [New York: Harper and Row, 1976], part I, 168). This line occurs early in the book; Solzhenitsyn writes immediately preceding it that anyone not willing to understand it should "slam the covers" of his book immediately.

79. Nowhere are these circumstances more unforgettably and terrifyingly illustrated than in Heda Margolius Kovály's account of life in Prague under Stalin, *Under a Cruel Star: A Life in Prague, 1941-1968* (New York: Holmes and Meier, 1997). Her son's memoir is almost equally gut-wrenching (Ivan Margolius, *Reflections of Prague: Journeys through the 20th Century* [Chichester: John Wiley and Sons, 2006]). The Academy Award–winning German-language film about the Stalinist era in East Germany, *The Lives of Others,* greatly impressed its audience in 2006, but the daily details can only be understood from memoirs like these. In a certain way, the Stalinist era was worse than the Nazi era: the lines between good and evil were sometimes difficult to discern, and there was no obvious enemy — no uniforms and jackboots, no swastika armbands, no yellow stars, no identifying emblems. Every person was swept up into the web of deceit and lies. In such a case, it is easier to understand how no one could remain untainted.

"forgive and forget" can produce lasting harm on the political level as well as the personal. Peace without justice is an illusory peace that sets the stage for vengeful behavior later on. The strength to persevere in the struggle is found in knowing that the wounds remaining in human society after great atrocities are the wounds of Christ himself, now risen and reigning but still the Lamb *standing yet slain* (Rev. 5:6).

The wrath of God, which plays such a large role in both the Old and New Testaments, can be embraced because it comes wrapped in God's mercy.[80] To appropriate the inspired misstatement of Shakespeare's Dogberry, the cross shows how we, in Christ, are "condemned into redemption."[81] As we in baptism are incorporated into his godforsaken death (condemnation), so we are raised into his resurrection (redemption). As Paul writes, "If we have been united with him in a death like his, we shall certainly be united with him in a resurrection like his" (Rom. 6:5). We may be sure that when Paul says "a death like his," he means crucifixion with all its accursedness and godlessness. The wrath of God falls upon God himself, by God's own choice, out of God's own love. The "justice connection" may not be clear to those who are accustomed to privilege, but to oppressed and suffering Christians in the troubled places of the earth, there is no need to spell it out. God in Christ on the cross has become one with those who are despised and outcast in the world. *No other method of execution that the world has ever known could have established this so conclusively.*

Summing Up

To repeat: lying behind everything in this chapter is a basic premise: *in our world, something is terribly wrong and must be put right.* If, when we see an injustice, our blood does not boil at some point, we have not yet understood the depths of God. It depends, though, on what outrages us. To be outraged on behalf of oneself or one's own group alone is to be human, but it is not to participate in Christ. To be outraged and to take action on behalf of the voiceless and oppressed, however, is to do the work of God.

There is a great challenge here. Whenever we take up the cause of jus-

---

80. Colin Gunton puts this another way: "Salvation is bound up with judgment." This leads into his point that ignoring judgment leads into "Christian talk of reconciliation," which collapses "into a sentimentality that ignores moral right and wrong" (*The Actuality of Atonement: A Study of Metaphor, Rationality, and the Christian Tradition* [Grand Rapids: Eerdmans, 1989], 108). We will return to this point when we speak further of reconciliation.

81. *Much Ado about Nothing*, 4.2.50.

tice, we can easily be drawn into an inflated idea of ourselves and our work. To understand the radicality of the gospel, it is necessary to realize that God is on the side of the defenseless, *whoever they are.* If a victorious revolutionary turns on the oppressor, then the former oppressor has suddenly become the defenseless one toward whom God declares his partisanship. Although some will always understand biblical passages about division and judgment as referring only to righteous and unrighteous *individuals,* this human tendency to divide "we" from "they" is not on the deepest level of interpretation. Rather, "the line runs through each person." Therefore, so long as we live in this fallen world, we are *simul iustus et peccator* (saint and sinner simultaneously), until the destruction of the "old Adam" is completed as God makes all things new (Rev. 21:5; Isa. 42:9; 43:19; Gal. 6:15).[82]

We have seen how, in the biblical languages, "justice," "righteousness," and "justification" are all part of the same word-group in Greek — *dikaiosyne.* When we read of the righteousness of God, it also means the justice of God, and, most important, it means *the action of God in making conditions and relationships right.* "Righteousness" has the force of a verb rather than a noun; it is not a static quality but a continual going-out in power to effect what it requires. Nor is it an abstraction; it can only be understood in the context of the community called into being by God, which is itself the image, however flawed, of the new humanity. This understanding of the righteousness of God affords a greatly enlarged perspective on the cross and resurrection.

When Israel was still in the Promised Land and was ruled by a king, much of the population — like that of America today — took their covenant privileges for granted as a sign of God's blessing. When Jerusalem fell to the Babylonians, however, it was no longer possible to be complacent. Human options had run out. Apocalyptic hope began to replace confidence in the progressive march of history. In the postexilic prophets, the announcement of divine intervention — the key to apocalyptic thought — accompanied the growing expectation of a Messiah who would inaugurate the realm of God in justice and righteousness. The great originality of Paul the apostle was to show how this apocalyptic, messianic event was located precisely *in the cross,* so that the triumph of God was hidden in the suffering of Jesus.

Earthly suffering on the part of the church, rather than the trappings of victory, continues to be the sign of authentic life in Christ until he comes again, taking upon itself the judgment of God (I Pet. 4:12-19). This suffering is not simply for the purification and preservation of the church, but for

---

82. The "old Adam," a central aspect of the recapitulation theme, will be discussed in chapter 12.

the sake of the whole world (Matt. 28:18-19). Lest there be any mistake, the cosmic-universal note was sounded by Paul in no uncertain language: "For God has consigned all [human beings] to disobedience, that he may have mercy upon all" (Rom. 11:32). Thus the whole arena of God's justice and righteousness has been relocated from the usual tit-for-tat scheme of crime and punishment into a completely new sphere where the righteousness of God *(dikaiosyne),* understood as *power to grant what it requires,* has dismantled the old system of righteousness-by-the-law and incorporated us into the new-world-creating righteousness of God. When this is enacted in our world by faith, however imperfectly — as in the South African Truth and Reconciliation Commission — we know that God is on the move.

Anselm Reconsidered for Our Time

Of all those who have written about God's justice, none is more renowned or more controversial than Anselm, abbot of the monastery at Bec and archbishop of Canterbury at the turn of the first millennium. He gets a chapter to himself as a bridge between "the question of justice" and "the gravity of sin," because these two issues lie at the heart of what Anselm is up to. The influence and impact of Anselm upon the interpretation of Jesus' death would be hard to overstate, for two contradictory reasons:

1. Anselm's momentous work, *Cur Deus Homo? (Why the God-Man?),* has been so influential that it is impossible to study the history of Christian doctrine without it.[1]
2. The fame and influence of this work have been matched by the degree of scorn that has been heaped upon it. Anselm has been blamed for everything from the Crusades to the Iraq War. His "theory" of "satisfaction" has been reviled as juridical, feudal, rigid, absolutist, vengeful, sadistic, immoral, and violent.

The argument of this chapter is that these points of view arise out of overly literal, unimaginative, tendentious, and unsympathetic readings of Anselm. In an important sense, the Bible is art rather than science or philosophy, and theology is a sort of art too, since it is largely based upon the

---

1. Sometimes Anselm is depicted as having single-handedly introduced an illegitimate perspective into Christianity (at the portentous and suspiciously precise date of the turn of the second millennium). This is inaccurate. Anselm's insights are anticipated by Ambrose, Hilary of Poitiers, and Victorinus, among others (see J. N. D. Kelly, *Early Christian Doctrines* [New York: Harper and Row, 1959], 388 — not to mention Isa. 53:4-6; Rom. 5:12-21; 8:3-4; II Cor 5:21; Gal. 3:10-14; I Pet. 2:24; 3:18; etc.).

narrative form of the Scriptures. We should read Anselm first as an artist, even as a storyteller, and only then as a thinker.[2] Theology, for him, is not primarily an intellectual exercise. He did not coin the phrase *fides quaerens intellectum* (faith seeking understanding) for nothing. Faith precedes understanding, and faith is grounded in the story of Christ.

To many at the turn of the third millennium, Anselm seems more remote than Jeremiah or Paul. Some would like to see him consigned to oblivion.[3] This "bridge section" (to use a musical term) is designed to show that certain features of Anselm's teaching about the deliverance wrought for us by Christ are still of pivotal importance for us today, particularly with regard to justice. This is a case for the modern relevance of Anselm in thinking about the human predicament and the remedy that God has put forward in the cross. The current backlash against the word "closure" suggests that Anselm is relevant still in his protest against shallow ideas of recovery shown in such phrases as "forgiving and forgetting," "moving on," and "putting it behind you."[4] Perhaps some readers, clearing their heads of

2. To be sure, Anselm's scholastic training works against the story form. The schematic form of his arguments has understandably cost him support in the postmodern milieu.

3. Three anti-Anselmian perspectives are set forth by, respectively, Anthony W. Bartlett (*Cross Purposes: The Violent Grammar of Christian Atonement* [Harrisburg, Pa.: Trinity, 2001]), Douglas Campbell (*The Deliverance of God: An Apocalyptic Rereading of Justification in Paul* [Grand Rapids: Eerdmans, 2009]), and James Carroll, in his widely read "popular" history, *Constantine's Sword: The Church and the Jews* (New York: Houghton Mifflin, 2001). Bartlett calls *Cur Deus Homo?* "the master-text of divine violence" and says "violence is its beating heart" (76, 84). This is really very strange, since the only violence evidenced in the life and death of Jesus was that visited upon him by human beings. Campbell, with some justification, regards Anselm's argument as too literal-minded, not sufficiently attuned to the fluid dynamic of the New Testament, especially Paul (50-55). As for Carroll's assessment of Anselm, Eamon Duffy, professor of the history of Christianity at Cambridge University, calls it "breathtakingly crass. . . . In Anselm's account there is no question, as Carroll seems to think, of a sadist Father torturing an innocent Son, but the joyful cooperation of the whole Trinity to rectify human disaster" ("A Deadly Misunderstanding," *New York Review of Books,* July 5, 2001). Note the use of "rectify," which we will argue throughout, best translates *dikaiosyne* (justification).

4. The term "closure" has become deeply offensive to many, for precisely the reasons we are discussing. Many people who have suffered loss have protested against the pressure put upon them by others who expect them to achieve "closure" too soon and without sufficient appreciation of what it costs. Television commentator Cokie Roberts, nine years after her beloved sister's death from cancer, said, "I detest the word 'closure,' and I hate the idea of 'moving on' " (quoted in *Good Housekeeping,* October 1999). A piece of dialogue in *The Whites,* by acclaimed crime novelist Richard Price (writing under the name of Harry Brandt), takes place between two cops on homicide detail, one of whom says to the other, "What's the most bullshit word in the English language?" Answer: "Closure" ([New York: Henry Holt, 2015], 24).

inherited disdain, will want to take a new look at Anselm's *Cur Deus Homo?* *(Why the God-Man?).*[5]

Justice Must Be Seen to Be Done

Something is terribly wrong and needs to be set right. As we saw in the previous chapter with the story of the young killers on the subway, there are some things that cannot go unpunished. This is not an abstract philosophical proposition. If there is to be a moral order, justice must be done and must be seen to be done. In the cross of Christ, justice is indeed seen to be done, but it is such a strange justice that interpretation has frequently tied itself into knots trying to explain how it works. We can begin by saying this much: contrary to the teaching of some over the years, in the crucifixion God has not declared a general amnesty. The Christian emphasis on forgiveness and redemption has to be given its proper context, for God is not in favor of impunity. No one except a criminal is going to be satisfied with a general amnesty. Even without reference to God's justice, our own human sense of justice demands that reparations be made, that sentences be served, that restitution be offered when there is great offense.

Many of the attempts made over the years to explain the cross have arisen out of the intuition that on the cross we see some sort of justice being done. If you or I were God, we would have arranged for the perpetrators of injustice to suffer that sentence, someone we figured was deserving of condemnation, but God did not do what you or I would have done. God arranged for God's own self to step into that place. Jesus, the one person who did not deserve condemnation, stood forward under an unjust sentence and submitted to an unjust penalty. "For Christ also died for sins once for all, *the righteous for the unrighteous,* that he might bring us to God" (I Pet. 3:18).

In the cross we see the response of God to the world's injustices. Do we also hear the voice of the judge quoted earlier who said that some things "cannot go unpunished"? In the crucifixion, do we see someone not only paying a penalty but also suffering punishment? In recent years, numerous voices have been raised against the idea of a "punitive" interpretation of the cross. Yet if we accept the idea that some things "cannot go unpunished," do we not have to entertain the possibility that the event on Golgotha has

---

5. Even Anselm's title, *Why the God-Man?* has greatly annoyed some. He has been accused of smuggling in the sacrificial, "juridical" death of Jesus under the rubric of the incarnation. But, as we saw in the introduction, the incarnation was an incarnation into the death.

something to do with God's ultimate sentence upon all the evil in the world? We will examine this further as we go along, always insisting that these concepts must be held in a Trinitarian perspective, never splitting the Father from the Son or the Spirit.

If we read Anselm solely as a dry scholastic thinker, we will never understand him. There is considerable warmth and tenderness in his work, which is not often recognized. Those who read and pray his prayers will recognize him as a man of compassionate concern for Christ's flock.[6] For all his emphasis on *ratio,* he is essentially a believer whose passion for explanation is given shape and meaning by his love of God. A little statement put into the mouth of Anselm's interlocutor, Boso, will give the idea: "I come not for this purpose, to have you remove doubts from my faith, but to have you show me the reasons for my confidence" (1.15).[7]

Boso is already a believer; his faith is seeking understanding. His statement could stand, today, as an affirmation for third-millennium Christians who know that they will continue to have many doubts but that the tradition offers ample intellectual support for their faith.[8]

The Universal Human Predicament

First, Anselm introduces us to the dimensions of the human predicament and the need for an act of deliverance by God from beyond our sphere of command and control.[9] "Consider that the human race, that work of God's so very precious, was wholly ruined, and it was not seemly that the purpose which God had made concerning man should fall to the ground, and moreover, that this purpose could not be carried into effect unless the human race were delivered by their Creator himself" (1.4).

How is our "wholly ruined" relationship to God restored in Christ? This

6. *The Prayers and Meditations of Saint Anselm with the Proslogion* (London: Penguin Books, 1973).

7. All Anselm quotations are from *St. Anselm, Basic Writings,* trans. S. N. Deane (La Salle, Ill.: Open Court, 1974). In a few instances I have changed the wording of the translation very slightly for the sole reason of simplifying the syntax.

8. Stanley Hauerwas delights in telling the story about Barth, who, when asked by "an immature student" what role reason played in his theology, replied "I use it!" Hauerwas, *With the Grain of the Universe: The Church's Witness and Natural Theology* (Grand Rapids: Brazos, 2001), 167 n. 58.

9. As we proceed, we will see that such an action of deliverance is properly called "apocalyptic." I am not suggesting that Anselm, at the turn of the first millennium A.D., moves in the apocalyptic thought-world of the New Testament. However, in a few instances we can see points of contact between Anselm and the apocalyptic viewpoint.

is the question Anselm discusses with his interlocutor Boso. Anselm makes two points: first, if a man wishes to restore what he owes to God on account of sin but is *unable* to, he is *needy;* and second, if he does not *wish* to do so, he is *unjust.*

> *Boso.* Nothing could be plainer.
> *Anselm.* But whether needy or unjust, he will not be happy.
> *Boso.* This also is plain.
> *Anselm.* So long, then, as he does not restore [what he owes to God], he
>   will not be happy. (1.24)

This little colloquy seems quaint today, but in fact, it describes the contemporary human dilemma as accurately as it does Anselm's concerns of a thousand years ago. We are still longing for happiness, though its meaning for us is elusive. It is defined by Jesus himself as the highest human good, if one accepts the use of "happiness" for *makarios* in the Beatitudes: "Happy are the peacemakers . . ." (Matt. 5:9). In our present culture of consumerism, the American obsession with the "pursuit of happiness" derives more from advertising copy than it does from the Declaration of Independence.[10] For Anselm, however, happiness is defined as "enjoying the supreme good, which is God" (2.1).

Anselm's description of the human being as being either *needy* or *unjust* should also strike a chord with us. We would typically appropriate such terms by dividing up humanity into those who are needy and those who are not, thus delimiting a group on the bottom and a group on the top. The needy on the bottom have no opportunity to be unjust on the macrosocial level; instead, they are the recipients of injustice from those who are on the top. The unjust on the top cannot imagine themselves as needy; they pride themselves on their supposed self-sufficiency — "God helps those who help themselves." From the standpoint of the gospel, however, every single one of us, rich or poor, is a complex mixture; we are all capable of injustice and we are all living on the edge of neediness at any time. "The line runs through each person."[11] Allowing for shadings of difference between Anselm's time and ours, we can read him to say that it is this universal human person, *both*

---

10. The ever-more-frenetic chase after happiness — status? riches? sexual fulfillment? — throws into relief the vast gap between the extremely wealthy and everyone else in the United States, since the goods and services marketed as bringing happiness are available only to the very affluent.

11. This quotation from Václav Havel is fully footnoted in chapter 3 and will reappear many times throughout this book.

needy *and* unjust, that Christ died to save, for "in order that man may attain happiness [blessedness], remission of sin is necessary" (1.10).[12]

Anselm's argument proceeds as he continues to reflect on what is required for true happiness: "Happiness ought not to be bestowed upon anyone whose sins have not been wholly put away, and . . . this remission ought not to take place save by the payment of the debt incurred by sin, according to the extent of sin" (1.24).

Many people today will not make the effort to grapple with this way of thinking. For one thing — a point to be elaborated later — there is no use talking about sin to anyone who does not already understand himself or herself to be upheld by grace. Since Anselm clearly knows this, his talk of sin, which sounds to us like dry reasoning, is actually grounded in faith. However, the assumptions in the passage just noted also illustrate the difficulty of giving Anselm the benefit of the doubt, since we do not think the way he does. We see no reason why sinners should not be happy — as long as they are *our kind* of sinners, that is; it's all right if they are stylish libertines and charming cads. However, we move closer to Anselm if we think of those who are sinners in ways that we cannot approve — neo-Nazi terrorists, say, or child rapists. We certainly don't want *them* to be happy. In such cases we are quite ready to agree with Anselm that there needs to be some sort of payment: God's justice must be satisfied. The crunch comes when we realize that Anselm means *all* types of human beings mired in sin, including himself, and you, and me.

Debt and Payment of Damages

Returning to Anselm's point about "payment of the debt incurred by sin, according to the extent of sin," it seems strange that we would resist Anselm on this point, provided that we don't force it into abstraction. We are familiar with demands for reparations "according to the extent of sin" in our world. Jews have sought repayment of what is owed to them as a result of the wholesale theft of their property in the 1930s and 1940s. Korean "comfort women" of World War II who were forced into prostitution by the Japanese finally received reparations of a sort in 1997. Workers from the World Trade Center site have brought suit for the harm done to their lungs. Every day of

12. The word "necessary" is tricky. The concept is more rationalistic and philosophical than it is biblical. The Bible is essentially a narrative and does not trade in logical necessity, for God is under no necessity. This is discussed later in the chapter.

the week in our litigious society, Americans seek restitution for damages. We should therefore be able to appreciate what Anselm says.[13] He continues in a vein reminiscent of today's litigation for "pain and suffering":

> So long as he [the offender, or sinner] does not restore what is taken away, he remains in fault; and it will not suffice merely to restore what has been taken away, but, considering the contempt offered, he ought to restore *more* than he took away. For as one who imperils another's safety does not enough by merely restoring his safety, without making some compensation for the anguish incurred; so he who violates another's honor does not do enough by merely rendering honor again, but must, according to the extent of the injury done, make restoration in some way *satisfactory* to the person whom he has dishonored [hence Anselm's term "satisfaction"].[14] (1.11)

Who does not understand this? Anselm is our contemporary in this respect and should be read afresh. Continuing in this vein, Anselm asks whether it is right to "let bygones be bygones." "Let us return and consider whether it is proper for God to put away sins by compassion alone, without any payment of the honor taken from him . . . to remit sin in this manner is nothing else than not to punish; and since it is not right to cancel sin without compensation or punishment, if it be not punished, then it is passed by undischarged" (1.12).

We might protest that "proper" is not a suitable word for God's activity, nor is it up to us to determine what is "proper" for God! Again, we simply do not think in this schematic way, nor does the narrative style of the Bible seem to support it. However, the point that Anselm is making, however forced it may seem to us, is the same that we will have occasion to note again and again in these pages: a society of impunity is intolerable.[15] If sin

---

13. In the 1970s at Union Seminary in New York, where I was a student, some of the African American students particularly appreciated this part of Anselm's argument. Reparations meant something more to them than to the rest of us.

14. When the word "satisfaction" is understood in this way, it does not sound so schematic. Hugo Grotius (1583-1645) anticipated liberal criticism of Anselm, but affirmed the concept of "satisfaction," despite its nonbiblical origin, because it could lay claim to being a "suggestive expression" of biblical language (see Jaroslav Pelikan, *The Christian Tradition: A History of the Development of Doctrine*, vol. 4, *Reformation of Church and Dogma [1300-1700]* [Chicago: University of Chicago Press, 1984], 360).

15. In 2011, the year of the "Arab Spring," the word "impunity" recurred again and again in accounts of the repressive regimes in Tunisia, Egypt, Libya, Syria, Bahrain.

is not exposed, named, and renounced, then there has been no justice and God is dishonored. We saw this in chapter 3 in Bishop Tutu's commentary on the South African Truth and Reconciliation Commission. The crimes investigated will go unpunished in the usual sense, he has noted, but they were laid bare for the world to see and named for what they were. They were unmasked. They were not passed by undischarged. The South African example, as Tutu and others have pointed out, was very different from that of Chile. General Pinochet was allowed to slip off to England to enjoy his cocktails with Baroness Thatcher.[16] Well might the families of Chile's *desaparecidos* wonder if there is any justice, divine or otherwise. Anselm again:

> And so, though man . . . refuses to submit to the Divine will and appointment, yet he cannot escape it; for if he wishes to fly from a will that commands, he falls into the power of a will that punishes. (1.15)

> *Compassion* [without atonement or "satisfaction"] *on the part of God is wholly contrary to the divine justice,* which allows nothing but punishment as the recompense of sin. Therefore, as God cannot be inconsistent with himself, his compassion cannot be of this nature. (1.24)

Compassion alone will not make right what is wrong. It will not rectify (from the Latin *rectitudo,* meaning "right") the horrors perpetrated over the ages. This emphasis on *rectification* is a central concern in this volume. Anselm's language of punishment, however, causes problems for many liberal-minded Christians and must be examined.

Punishment as "Inconsolable Need"

What did Anselm mean by punishment? A careful reading yields no references to hellfire; Anselm is not so crude as that. It is possible his use of the word "punishment" is something like Paul's conception in Romans 1:24-28 where three times he says "God gave them over" to the consequences of their own actions. The true "punishment" for sin, Paul is suggesting here

16. This was not allowed in South Africa. Bishop Tutu explains that the unmasking of the crimes of the apartheid regime was in itself a kind of punishment, as the atrocities committed by good family men, husbands and fathers, were brought into the light and exposed for all to see. "Thus it is not entirely the case that the perpetrator is being allowed to get off scot-free" (Tutu, *No Future without Forgiveness* [New York: Image Books, 1999], 51). This, too, is an illustration of Anselm's central concern.

(and Paul conspicuously never uses the word "punish"), is Sin itself. The consequence of the Fall (Gen. 2–3) has been the enslavement of the human race to Sin (and its allies, Death and the Law), separation from God with no hope of restitution from the human side. The question then becomes, does God intend to allow this enslavement to persist? Anselm, we suggest, is at one with Paul here, not only in his understanding of the whole world shut up under the power of Sin and in need of a deliverer, but also in his depiction of God's determination to unstring that old world.[17]

The will in Anselm's phrase "a will that punishes" is *constructive* and *restorative*.[18] The righteousness of God, we have seen, is a righteousness of love that must resist and finally eliminate all that is destructive of his divine purpose for the redemption of the world. An observation by Paul Ricoeur is relevant here: "The very idea of [*divine, not human*] vengeance conceals something else; to avenge is not only to destroy, but by destroying to re-establish. . . . By negation, order reaffirms itself. Thus, in the negative moment of punishment, the sovereign affirmation of primordial integrity is anticipated."[19]

If this were not enough to show that Anselm's idea of punishment is not what his detractors think, in his *Monologium* (71) Anselm defines "eternal punishment" as "inconsolable need."[20] It can't be emphasized strongly enough: Anselm understands punishment with a pastor's heart. He is saddened by our predicament. He is not in love with the idea of punishment; rather, like Paul the apostle, he simply observes that we reap what we sow ("God gave them over" to the power of Sin — repeated three times, in Rom. 1:24, 26, 28). The ultimate "punishment" would be exile from the *enjoyment* of the blessings of God. Here again we see Anselm's pastoral concern bubbling up from under the logic. In the following passage he is "thinking God's thoughts after him":

17. "So when the last and dreadful hour / This crumbling pageant shall devour, / The trumpet shall be heard on high, / the dead shall live, the living die, / and Music shall untune the sky." John Dryden, "A Song for St. Cecilia's Day," 1687.

18. A psychoanalyst once explained to me that "the negative moment [in therapy] is in the service of the positive moment." This conviction underlies a great deal of what appears in these pages concerning the justice and mercy of God. God's justice is always in the service of his mercy.

19. Paul Ricoeur, *The Symbolism of Evil* (Boston: Beacon Press, 1967), 43. We need to stress that Ricoeur's words hold true only for *God's* vengeance, not ours (Rom. 12:19).

20. Adam Linton has pointed out to me that this is strikingly in line with the musings on hell in Dostoevsky's *The Brothers Karamazov,* which in turn were taken from Saint Isaac the Syrian, whose thinking is important for the novel as a whole.

Anselm. God has made nothing more valuable than rational existence [for Anselm this means simply *human* existence] capable of enjoying him; it is altogether foreign from his character to suppose that he will suffer [permit] that rational existence utterly to perish.

Boso. No reasonable being can think otherwise.

Anselm. Therefore it is necessary for him to perfect in human nature what he has begun; but this, as we have already said, cannot be accomplished save by a complete expiation of sin, *which no sinner can effect for himself.* (2.4, emphasis added)

This exchange shows that Anselm's thought is not incompatible with an apocalyptic interpretation that reveals God's grace to be an *irresistible invasion* (a subject to be greatly expanded in chapters 8 and 9). God will not allow his will for the creation to be frustrated by our resistance; "it is altogether foreign from his character to suppose that he will suffer that rational existence utterly to perish." As we hope to show, this point has more in common with the patristic *Christus Victor* theme than it does with the forensic/juridical arena where unsympathetic interpreters want to imprison Anselm in perpetuity.

Is "Necessity" the Right Word?

For those wondering whether Anselm has created Boso to act the part of a prodigious nitwit, the monk's next objection to the abbot's argument may come as a welcome surprise:

Boso. But if it be so, then God seems as it were *compelled,* for the sake of avoiding what is unbecoming [foreign to God's nature], to secure the salvation of man. How, then, can it be denied that he does it more on his own account than on ours? But if it be so, what thanks do we owe him for what he does for himself? How shall we attribute our salvation to his grace, if he saves us from *necessity?* (2.5, emphasis added)

Anselm himself (speaking through Boso) anticipates two accusations that many bring against Anselm even today, not without cause: first, it sounds as though God is concerned only for his own honor; second, the whole thing is presented as a rational necessity, so that any element of love or graciousness seems to be absent. Anselm, to his credit, does not allow these objections to go unanswered.

Anselm. When one does benefit from a necessity to which he is unwillingly subjected, less thanks are due him, or none at all. But when he freely *places himself under* the necessity of benefiting another, and sustains that necessity without reluctance, then he certainly deserves greater thanks for the favor. *For this should not be called necessity but grace.* (2.5, emphasis added)

Anselm is not speaking of necessity in the way we might think. Nothing is "necessary" for God in the sense of logical steps that he is bound by some external force to follow. Rather, it is *ontological* necessity — it arises out of God's own gracious nature, which he cannot deny. In this respect Anselm's writing is as much doxology as it is logic; he is glorifying God in each step of his argument. "Necessity," for Anselm, means nothing mechanical; it means, rather, that the story of our deliverance has an inner logic that brings joy to the believer.

Honor Means Righteousness

What does Anselm mean by God's "honor"? Anselm's use of this term is often caricatured, as though God were a petty despot with no thought for anything except his own prerogatives. He has been accused of casting God in the role of feudal lord.[21] To be sure, it might have been more understandable and certainly more biblical if Anselm had spoken of God's "righteousness" instead of his "honor." We may substitute the word "righteousness" for "honor" and do no violence to Anselm's argument.[22] We will continue to emphasize

21. The context of feudalism has often been held against Anselm, and those who are unsympathetic to his approach fault him for his emphasis on God's "honor." Anselm's concern, however, is quite different from that ascribed to him by these critics. For Anselm, the whole conception revolves around our need to honor God, not God's need to be honored.

22. Eamon Duffy, continuing his criticism of James Carroll's account of Anselm in *Constantine's Sword,* writes, "*Cur Deus Homo* was in fact addressed to specifically Jewish criticisms of Christianity, made by learned Jews from Mainz recently arrived in London. For these Jewish intellectuals, Christianity was repellent because it dishonored God, claiming that the impassible and eternal had descended into time in a woman's womb, and had undergone the diminishment of hunger and thirst, suffering and death. Anselm's purpose therefore was to show that the Incarnation, far from dishonoring God, revealed the depths of his loving will to save suffering humanity. Anselm's insistence on 'honor,' therefore, is not the product of fixation with feudal hierarchy, but an *argumentum ad hominem* addressed to intelligent Jews who felt that the Christian story debased God. 'Honor' in Anselm's thought stands not for some imagined hypersensitivity by the Creator to his own dignity, but is a metaphor for the

that God's righteousness is best understood as a verb, not a noun, and that it is God's own self graciously acting to make right what is wrong. As Anselm wrote, "There is nothing more just than supreme justice [righteousness], which maintains God's honor [righteousness] in the arrangement of things, and which is nothing else but God himself" (1.13).

In that last phrase, Anselm affirms the point made in chapter 3, that the righteousness of God is an integral part of who he is; in manifesting his righteousness he manifests himself. Furthermore, "No one can . . . dishonor God *as he is in himself;* but the creature, *as far as he is concerned,* appears to do this when he . . . opposes his will to the will of God" (1.15, emphasis added).

This sentence is of first importance in understanding Anselm and, by extension, the righteousness of God. Not only Anselm but also the Old Testament can be mistakenly read as though a "jealous" God were preoccupied with defending his own honor. In the sentence just quoted, Anselm is saying that God does not need to defend his own honor. It is *for the creature* that he is concerned — for the hapless human being who has neither the will nor the capacity to straighten out his relationship to God.

Anselm means something very different by "honor" than we are readily equipped to understand without effort. God is not a tin-pot dictator obsessed with his privileges. On the contrary, the Trinitarian movement that Anselm always has in mind is described in Philippians 2:5-7: "Christ Jesus, who, though he was in the form of God, did not count equality with God a thing to be grasped, but emptied (Greek root *kenosis*) himself, taking the form of a servant, being born in the likeness of men." God's honor is God's righteousness, his holiness, his perfection — but it is also his love and freedom, which show themselves in the kenotic self-emptying of the Son.

Only God Can Save from a Weight of Sin So Great

We can identify the center of Anselm's logic in 2.6. Here, he urges that the weight of sin is so great *(nondum considerasti quanti ponderis peccatum sit)* that there is no possibility of atonement or satisfaction unless the price paid is "greater than all the universe besides God."

---

deep logic of reality, in which the balance of a universe is disrupted by the fact of death and by human alienation from others and from God, a situation which could only be rectified by divine action" (Duffy, "A Deadly Misunderstanding").

> *Boso.* So it appears. . . .
>
> *Anselm.* Therefore none but God *is able to* make this satisfaction.
>
> *Boso.* I cannot deny it.
>
> *Anselm.* But none but a man *ought* to do this [he has already established that it is the guilty party, and no one else, who *ought* to make the restitution].
>
> *Boso.* Nothing could be more just.
>
> *Anselm.* If it be necessary, therefore . . . that [salvation] cannot be effected unless the aforesaid satisfaction be made, which *none but God can make* and *none but man ought to make,* it is necessary for the God-man to make it.
>
> *Boso.* Now blessed be God! We have made a great discovery.[23]

Anselm has been disparaged in some circles for so long that the simple elegance of this series of steps does not always receive its due. Granted, Anselm's arguments in *Cur Deus Homo?* are sometimes so earnestly rational that they sound unintentionally funny to us, so they require some getting used to. His reliance on "infallible reason," as he calls it (2.21), seems naïve today. How methodically he takes us through each logical step! From a purely biblical standpoint, such a procedure must be deemed suspect, for there is nothing remotely like it in Scripture. However, when at the end of the long exposition about the necessity for a God-man, Boso breaks out, "Blessed be God!" we smile for a different reason, for in Anselm's fine phrase, we are "gladdened by understanding" (1.1).[24]

Anselm from an Eastern Orthodox Perspective

David Bentley Hart has recently offered an appreciation of Anselm from his own Eastern Orthodox perspective.[25] He faults the Eastern Orthodox tradition for oversimplifying and misunderstanding Anselm. Many Orthodox theologians, he explains, believe that "Western narratives of salvation have all too often reduced the atonement worked by Christ to the status of

---

23. *Cur Deus Homo?* 2.6, emphasis added.

24. Ellen Charry has noted that Anselm's pastoral concerns override the rationalism at several points, and that Anselm "wanted his readers to believe that they really can trust in divine mercy" (*By the Renewing of Your Minds: The Pastoral Function of Christian Doctrine* [New York: Oxford University Press, 1997], 168).

25. David Bentley Hart, "A Gift Exceeding Every Debt: An Eastern Orthodox Appreciation of Anselm's *Cur Deus Homo,*" *Pro Ecclesia* 7, no. 3 (Summer 1998): 330-49.

a simple transaction . . . intended solely as an appeasement of the Father's wrath against sin,"[26] charging Anselm with blame for this supposed state of affairs. Hart notes further that Anselm is misread in various other ways; for instance, many have thought of him as an enthusiastic representative of "penal suffering" when the actual text of *Cur Deus Homo?* has gotten lost in "the welter of adverse judgments."[27] That is precisely the point being made in this chapter.[28]

Hart admits that Anselm's style of presentation lends itself to "a simple economic model of atonement."[29] However, he continues, "Anselm's argument, thus denuded of every nuance . . . is susceptible of every casual misconstrual the theological mind can devise; it becomes indeed a theological 'theory,' removed from any larger theological narrative." This puts very neatly the concern of the present volume, which is to eschew theory in favor of thematic richness and narrative power.

Hart cites Orthodox theologian Vladimir Lossky as a representative of the anti-Anselm position:[30]

> Everything that Eastern theologians imagine to be constitutive of Western soteriology — the legalism of its "juridical" categories, the ruthlessness of the God it depicts, the mechanical simplicity of its model of atonement — Lossky finds exemplarily expressed in the *Cur Deus Homo?* . . . Lossky takes special offense . . . at Anselm's apparent reduction of the Resurrection and Ascension to a simple happy ending and of salvation to a change not in human nature, but only in the divine attitude towards humanity.

26. Hart, "Gift Exceeding Every Debt," 334.

27. Hart, "Gift Exceeding Every Debt," 340.

28. Robert Dean tells me that many of his evangelical students want to read "penal suffering" back into Anselm. He notes that, on the contrary, Anselm himself says, "It is necessary, therefore, that either the honor taken away should be repaid, or punishment should be inflicted." In other words, God chose satisfaction over punishment (*Cur Deus Homo?* 1.13).

29. Daniel Bell, the noted Harvard sociologist, has noted how we cannot help misreading Anselm when we bring our modern capitalist presumptions to bear upon his text. "In particular," Bell writes, "Anselm discloses how Christ's work on the cross cannot be correlated with a capitalist logic that revolves around scarcity, with its calculi of debt, equity, and death, but instead illuminates a divine economy of charity, an economic order characterized by plenitude and generosity that exceeds the strictures of capitalism as surely as Christ burst the bonds of death" (*The Economy of Desire: Christianity and Capitalism in a Postmodern World* [Grand Rapids: Baker Academic, 2012], 149). I am grateful to Robert Dean for this striking quotation.

30. See Vladimir Lossky, "Redemption and Dedication," in *In the Image and Likeness of God,* ed. John H. Erickson and Thomas E. Bird (Crestwood, N.Y.: St. Vladimir's Seminary Press, 1974), 97-110.

Salvation, so conceived, is little more than a drama enacted between an infinitely offended God and a humanity unable to satisfy the demands of his vindictive wrath.[31]

This is a skillful summary of the objections to Anselm that one hears continually, and not just from Eastern Orthodoxy.[32] Hart argues that Anselm's "theory" is deeply rooted in faith and prayer (and, we might add, in a kinship with the Bible far greater than he has been given credit for) as well as pastoral concern for believers, and is therefore unfairly characterized as purely rationalistic and schematic. More important still, Anselm's view of God's action on our behalf is actually quite close to the patristic narrative that he is accused of leaving behind. Hart explains:

> Sin having disrupted the order of God's good creation, and humanity having been handed over to death and the devil, God enters into a condition of estrangement and slavery to set humanity free. . . . Formidable linguistic shifts aside, Anselm's is not a new narrative of salvation. In truth, this facile distinction between a patristic soteriology concerned exclusively with *the rescue of humanity from death* and a later theory of atonement concerned just as exclusively with *remission from guilt . . .* is perhaps supportable, but only in regard to emphasis and imagery; Athanasius, Gregory of Nyssa, and John of Damascus (to name a few) were no less conscious than Anselm that *the guilt which places humanity in bondage to death* is overcome on the cross, nor is he any less concerned than they with *the Son's campaign against death's dominion* over those [all human beings] who have turned from God in disobedience. Indeed, in *Cur Deus Homo,* the matter of guilt is somewhat recused; it is guilt that is set aside, made of no account by Christ's grace, so that death should be overcome without violence to divine justice. (emphasis added)[33]

This remarkable summary not only brings Anselm into proper focus, it also lays out the program for much of this book. We will make some adjust-

---

31. Hart, "Gift Exceeding Every Debt," 340.

32. Anthony W. Bartlett's book-length critique of Anselm from a Girardian perspective *(Cross Purposes)* is of this sort. There is something odd about Bartlett's reading of Anselm. He seems tone-deaf to the echoes of the biblical narrative found in *Cur Deus Homo?* because he is so focused on "mimetic anthropology" — a "theory" if ever there was one. We could almost accuse Bartlett of a lack of poetic imagination, a complaint that can be made of a great many readings of Scripture in academic circles in our time.

33. Hart, "Gift Exceeding Every Debt," 342.

ments to Hart's description, notably by bringing Sin and the Law into the picture in a much more vivid way (following Rom. 7:7-25), but his argument that Anselm and the patristic theologians share a common understanding of the human predicament as *both **guilt requiring remission** and **captivity requiring deliverance*** is fundamental to the argument in these pages.

Hart makes another point that places Anselm even more firmly within the scheme of this book:

> Anselm is already situated in the Christian theological tradition, he already knows that Christ has recapitulated human nature in himself and conquered evil on our behalf; it is from this narrative that Anselm has undertaken a (by no means final or exclusive) reduction of the tale, in order better to grasp the inner necessity of its sacrificial logic. . . . If Anselm's account appears to leave the resurrection and ascension as a mere coda . . . it also corrects a certain occasional *aporia* in patristic thought, insofar as the latter often fails to say how the resurrection vindicates — rather than merely reverses — Christ's self-oblation.[34]

Hart is thus saying, from a quite different perspective, almost exactly the same thing as J. L. Martyn: the resurrection is God's *validation of* his Son's redemptive death, not the *replacement* of it. "The resurrection of the Son does not eclipse the Son's cross."[35]

Feminist Criticisms of Anselm

In recent years Anselm has come under particular attack from some feminist theologians, who view his argument in *Cur Deus Homo?* as a prime example of deplorable models of atonement that seem to set the Father against the Son so that the cross appears as a form of child abuse, with the innocent Son suffering from the wrath of a vindictive Father.[36] Anselm, however, has anticipated these criticisms. He has Boso say:

> How will it ever be made out a just or reasonable thing that God should treat . . . in such a manner . . . his beloved Son in whom he was well

---

34. Hart, "Gift Exceeding Every Debt," 344.

35. J. Louis Martyn, *Galatians,* Anchor Bible 33A (New York: Doubleday, 1997), 166.

36. Leanne Van Dyk tackles this perspective in "Do Theories of Atonement Foster Abuse?" *Dialog* 35, no. 1 (Winter 1996): 22-25.

pleased . . . ? For what justice is there in his suffering death for the sinner, who was the most just of all men? What man, if he condemned the innocent to free the guilty, would not himself be judged worthy of condemnation? (1.8)

It is a strange thing if God so delights in, or requires, the blood of the innocent, that he neither chooses, nor is able, to spare the guilty without the sacrifice of the innocent. (1.10)

Anselm has not failed to note these important objections that, a thousand years later, are presently being reconsidered in the church. Anselm emphasizes that the "God-man" goes to his death *in full knowledge* of what he is doing. The crucifixion "is an event in God's triune life."[37] It should never be interpreted as a deed done to an unsuspecting Son by his Father.[38]

Anselm is at pains to show that the Son laid down his life of his own accord (John 10:18). "The Father did not compel him to suffer death, or even allow him to be slain against his will, but of his own accord he endured death for the salvation of men" (1.8).

To the objection that the Son had no choice since the Father commanded him to obey, Anselm replies that this was not at all the way it unfolded:

[S]o precious a life . . . given with such willingness . . . the Son freely gave himself to the Father. For thus we plainly affirm that *in speaking of one Person we affirm the whole deity,* to whom as man he offered himself. And, by the names of Father and Son, a wondrous depth of devotion is excited in the hearts of the hearers when it is said that the Son supplicates the Father on our behalf. (2.18, emphasis added)

The Son had agreed with the Father and the Holy Spirit that there was no other way to reveal to the world the height of his omnipotence than by his death. (1.9)

---

37. Robert Jenson, *Systematic Theology,* vol. 1, *The Triune God* (New York: Oxford University Press, 1997), 189. Jenson notes that one of the most important criticisms of Anselm is that the work of atonement is done by Christ's human nature, whereas we should attribute reconciliation to Christ according to neither nature but only according to both, jointly and simultaneously. This accusation that Anselm splits the human nature from the divine would indeed be a count against him, if true, but many theologians think this is an unfair reading.

38. Anselm's prayers are distinguished by, among other things, a truly exceptional (especially for his time) interest in *maternal* imagery for God. This is all the more impressive because he was not forced into it by ideological or political considerations.

In that last, deceptively simple sentence there is a world of glad tidings and Nicene truth. It would be hard to imagine how Anselm could be more explicit: the self-oblation of the Son on the cross proceeded out of God's eternal, triune inner being. In our preaching, teaching, and learning we must emphatically reject any interpretation that divides the will of the Father from that of the Son, or suggests that anything is going on that does not proceed out of love. As we shall see again and again, God's justice and God's mercy both issue forth from his single will of eternal love.

Who Gets Reconciled, God or Us?

One of the objections brought against Anselm is that he makes it sound as if a change has to take place within God — as though the crucifixion altered God's attitude toward his rebellious creatures.[39] The New Testament, however, never mentions God being reconciled to us. It speaks only of our being reconciled to him. This factor has become a key to most present-day discussions of reconciliation. How can we talk about the wrath of God unless we conclude that somehow the sacrifice of Jesus caused the Father to change his mind? This indeed would cast the Father in a bad light. This is not, however, what Anselm says; it is a distortion that has unfortunately taken on a life of its own. Hart briskly corrects this distortion: "Christ's death does not . . . effect a change in God's attitude towards humanity; God's attitude never alters; he desires the salvation of his creatures, and will not abandon them even to their own cruelties."[40]

If we are to appreciate — if not entirely adopt — Anselm's language of satisfaction, we need therefore to be clear that *the change effected* by Christ's self-oblation *does not occur within God.* This is of primary importance. If we do not emphasize this, we end up with a dangerously capricious God who is indeed open to the critiques brought by those who think of the wrath of God as an emotion that must be appeased. In all our discussions of reconciliation, this underlying point is fundamental. It is not God that is changed. It is the relationship of human beings and the creation *to* God that is changed. As with so much in Christian doctrine, there is an already–not yet quality about

39. These objections were influential in shaping "subjective" theories of atonement that concentrate upon the effect of the crucifixion upon human affections. Associated originally with Abelard (1079-1142), the subjective, or "exemplary," view is advocated today in a revised version by René Girard and his disciples.

40. Hart, "Gift Exceeding Every Debt," 348.

this. Our relation to God is changed *already* by our baptismal incorporation into Christ's death (Rom. 6:3-4), yet we "groan" together with the whole cosmos as we *wait* for our full redemption at the second coming (Rom. 8:22) when "we *shall be* changed" into the glorious body of his resurrection (I Cor. 15:52). This should clarify for all time the vexed discussion about the wrath of God, sweeping away the misunderstandings that occur when God's judgment is not understood as the servant of his love. We find the same idea throughout the Bible; for instance, Isaiah says,

> "In overflowing wrath for a moment
>   I hid my face from you,
> but with everlasting love I will have compassion on you,
>   says the Lord, your Redeemer." (Isa. 54:8)

God's judgment is enclosed in his love.

Having nailed this point into place, we can conclude our discussion of Anselm. In chapter 3 we examined the intertwined relationship of justice and mercy. Indeed, we can say more, as Hart does; he shows that the cross does not effect a "mere posterior reconciliation of justice and mercy" but is — in a lovely phrase — the "filial intonation" of the preexistent divine love. He sums up: "In the God-man [*Deus Homo*], within human history, God's justice and mercy are shown to be one thing, one action, life, and being . . . the righteousness that condemns is also the love that restores."[41]

And here is Anselm himself, speaking through Boso, giving a summary of the achievement of Christ that could hardly be bettered: "He freed us from our sins, and from his own wrath, and from hell, and from the power of the devil, whom he came to vanquish for us, because we were unable to do it, and he purchased for us the kingdom of heaven; and by doing all these things, he manifested the greatness of his love toward us" (1.5).

This little summation by Anselm is in many ways congruent with what this book intends. It is astonishingly comprehensive. It has the essential form of a *narrative,* and of *kerygma,* rather than scholastic formulation. Many central biblical and doctrinal themes are identified here, either explicitly or implicitly.

It is quite true, as many have noted, that in the final analysis Anselm's method — his way of working through Boso to produce a rationalistic conclusion — is not congruent with the narrative mode of the Scriptures. Not only so, but his "if this, then that" way of demonstrating truth seems foreign

---

41. Hart, "Gift Exceeding Every Debt," 344.

to biblical (and contemporary) modes of thought. And yet Anselm's genius for incorporating the biblical narrative into his argument is not noticed by many, if not most, of his readers today, nor is the essential sweetness of his faith. In every facet of God's action on the cross, Anselm teaches, divine love is at work. The various images and motifs found in Scripture guide us in our understanding.

Another motif in Anselm will be evoked at the conclusion of this volume. To anticipate: those who are so certain of what they judge to be Anselm's narrow and punitive impulses might take note of his hints of a universal meaning for the Lord's death. Colin Gunton puts it this way: "It has frequently been claimed, for instance by Anselm, that the salvation won by Christ is of such moment as to serve for those who are outside the temporal and spatial limits of the institution [the church], and nothing prevents us from seeking and finding the work of the Spirit in other forms of life than the consciously Christian."[42]

Summary

This "bridge" chapter is a commentary on the contribution of Anselm to our understanding of justice, which was the subject of the previous chapter, and it leads into the next chapter, which takes up Anselm's emphasis on the gravity of Sin. In these pages devoted to Anselm's presentation of Christ's self-offering, we have tried to demonstrate that aspects of his much-misunderstood teaching remain uniquely valuable and deserve a much wider hearing than is customary today.[43] We have decisively rejected the popular understanding of Anselm as a proponent of penal suffering. We have highlighted his prayerful faith, his pastoral concerns, and his sensitivity to the biblical narrative in spite of his rationalistic approach. We emphasized his Trinitarian theology and the indispensable role of "faith seeking understanding" *(fides quaerens intellectum),* but focused especially on his insistence that the disrupted relation between God and his creatures cannot simply be "passed by undischarged." Anselm's word for what Christ has done is "satis-

---

42. Colin Gunton, *The Actuality of Atonement: A Study of Metaphor, Rationality, and the Christian Tradition* (Grand Rapids: Eerdmans, 1989), 171.

43. There is one point where Anselm's assumptions should be decisively repudiated, and that is where he rhetorically asks Boso, "Why did the Jews persecute him even unto death?" (1.9). Here he shows himself to be a man of his time, making no distinction between ethnic Jews and the religious enemies of Christ in the New Testament. At other points, however, Anselm shows that he knows that *all* human beings "persecuted him even unto death."

faction"; we might think of "reparation," "restitution" — or "rectification," the word preferred throughout these pages.

The tragedy of human existence, in fact, calls out for *rectification*. We end this chapter therefore as we began: ***Something is wrong and must be put right***.[44] When we feel that in our bones, when we admit that something is wrong not only with the whole human situation in general but also with one's own self in particular, then God is at work bringing us closer to the cross of Christ.

44. African American Christians have frequently, if implicitly, affirmed Anselm in their insistent concern that there can be no reconciliation without justice. The 1987 Howard Beach trials in New York City were a demonstration of this. When the prison sentences were handed down for those convicted of blatantly racial attacks on a small group of black youths who had innocently strayed into a white neighborhood, the courtroom rang with the calls of the black community ("Thank you, Judge," "Praise the Lord"), and it was clear that the gravity of sin is a vital consideration in the administration of justice.

CHAPTER FOUR

The Gravity of Sin

Who would know Sin, let him repair
Unto Mount Olivet; there shall he see
A man so wrung with pains, that all his hair,
  His skin, his garments bloody be.
Sin is that press and vice, which forceth pain
To hunt his cruel food through every vein.
GEORGE HERBERT, "THE AGONIE"[1]

Nondum considerasti quanti ponderis peccatum sit.
ANSELM OF CANTERBURY

Who is going to read a whole chapter about sin? Surely this is a most un-congenial topic. The category of sin has been displaced in our time by other categories such as disease, maladjustment, neurosis, deficiency, addiction. There was a time in America, fifty years ago, when the influence of Reinhold Niebuhr made it possible to take sin seriously as a corporate affliction, but the culture has shifted further and faster toward self-regard and self-affirmation than even Niebuhr imagined.[2] It is very difficult to talk about sin today with-

---

1. George Herbert, "The Agonie," in George Herbert, *The Complete English Poems,* ed. John Tobin (New York: Penguin Books, 1991), 33.

2. Niebuhr, in *The Nature and Destiny of Man* (1941), wished to disturb "the easy conscience of modern man" who "continues to regard himself as essentially harmless and virtuous" in spite of the historical evidence (1:93-96). In his 1964 preface to the second edition of the book, Niebuhr writes ruefully, "I used the traditional religious symbols of the 'Fall' and of 'original sin.' . . . My only regret is that I did not realize that the legendary character of the one

out losing one's audience. More to the point, however, it may be that sin has always been misunderstood by most Christians. Douglas John Hall proposes this in striking terms: "Whether the biblical concept of sin has ever been grasped by most Christians is a good question. Anyone who moves from the Gospels and Epistles of the New Testament into the Christian writings of the 2nd and 3rd centuries will realize that the process of sin's reduction has begun. Already sin (singular) has become sins (plural)." The Reformers, Hall continues, reclaimed a radical sense of sin: "They saw that sin meant disobedience, rebellion, refusal, turning away. In short, they saw it as a relational term . . . the foundational relationship of human life — our relation with God — is broken; and this brokenness shows up in all our other relations. . . . Whether we should even speak of 'sins' (plural) is questionable; but if we do, we should understand that they are *consequences* of what is wrong, not its *causes*."[3]

There is no way of taking the Bible seriously unless we are willing to entertain its presuppositions about sin, especially Sin in the singular. This is a catch-22 of sorts, because it is not possible to have a grasp of one's own involvement in sin without a prior or simultaneous awareness of God's prevenient love (Latin *pre-venere,* "going-before"). We need to recover that word "prevenient" because no other word or phrase captures so well the essential fact about grace: it *prevenes* (goes before), or *precedes,* recognition of sin, *precedes* confession of sin, *precedes* repentance for sin, and *precedes* forsaking of sin. Readers of this book are already held by God's gracious intention toward them, whether they know themselves as sinners or not.

For this reason, the chapter on justice has been placed ahead of this chapter on sin, with Anselm between as a bridge. God's justice is not in competition with his mercy; *both* are manifestations of his redemptive purpose.[4]

---

and the dubious connotations of the other would prove so offensive to the modern mind." At the end of the preface he seems to doubt whether the "historic symbols will contribute much to the understanding by modern man of his tragic and ironic history." He was certainly right about the resistance of the "modern mind" to the biblical perspective, but he did not foresee the persistence of the power of the "historic symbols" of the Fall and original sin, "modern man" notwithstanding. Reinhold Niebuhr, *The Nature and Destiny of Man: A Christian Interpretation,* 2nd ed., 2 vols. (New York: Scribner, 1964).

3. Douglas John Hall, "The Political Consequences of Misconceiving Sin," *Witness,* March 1995, emphasis added.

4. In some Mennonite works, it is argued that justice and mercy are at war within the being of God — "the violence of two natures vying for supremacy" — which suggests that violence originates in God, a position that is unconditionally rejected in these pages (e.g., David Eagle, "Anthony Bartlett's Concept of Abyssal Compassion and the Possibility of a Truly Nonviolent Atonement," *Conrad Grebel Review* 24 [2006]: 67). Walter Brueggemann seems to espouse this quasi-Jungian view of God in a review of Jerome F. D. Creach's *Violence in Scrip-*

If we can understand that God's righteousness (*dikaiosyne,* the same Greek word translated as "justice") is liberating and restorative, not crippling and retributive, then we can discuss sin with a more open mind and heart.

Paradox: The Knowledge of Sin as Joyful Good News

A curious phenomenon exists in Christianity. Many people in the past have rejoiced to confess their sins, even to call themselves "miserable offenders." This phrase was removed from the Episcopal Church's 1979 Book of Common Prayer because it was thought to be off-putting, and it is undoubtedly true that many of today's churchgoers, not having grown up with the phrase, would be baffled, even repelled, by such language if they walked in off the street. The underlying dynamic here is that we cannot rejoice to think of ourselves as sinful, let alone "miserable offenders," unless we are *already* claimed by the divine light of the gospel. There is no way to help people to the knowledge of sin except to offer the news of God's "prevenient" purpose in overcoming sin through the cross of Christ. It is with a sense of light-heartedness that one comes before the mercy seat of God, but none can understand this until the light of grace dawns upon them. The light of Christ reveals sin by the brightness of the redemption already accomplished. The South African novelist and Nobel Prize winner J. M. Coetzee writes: "There is always something unmotivated about conversion experiences: it is of their essence that the sinner should be so blinded by lust or greed or pride that the psychic logic leading to the turning point in his life becomes visible to him *only in retrospect, when his eyes have been opened.*"[5]

---

ture. Brueggemann is "disquieted" by Creach's support for a figurative reading of the violence in the Old Testament. He asks, "What if this God has a propensity toward violence with which God struggles, as in Hosea 11:1-9? What if God's own life is unsettled and in contestation?" ("Warrior God," *Christian Century,* December 11, 2013). This seems a strange reading of the beautiful passage in Hosea (quoted in chap. 3). It is one of numerous anthropomorphic pictures of God in the Old Testament, clearly not meant to be read literally as if God were actually a father trying to make up his mind whether to destroy his child or not! In I Sam. 15:11, God says, "I repent that I have made Saul king," and in *the same chapter* (15:29) Samuel says that God "is not a man, that he should repent." Clearly the reader of Scripture is expected to hold two things in mind at the same time regarding God in a *literary,* not a *doctrinal,* sense. The tradition rejects any sort of doctrinal definition of God as "unsettled" within God's own life. "This is the message we have heard from him and proclaim to you, that God is light and in him is no darkness at all" (I John 1:5).

5. J. M. Coetzee, review of *Memories of My Melancholy Whores,* by Gabriel Garcia Márquez, *New York Review of Books,* February 23, 2006, emphasis added.

Only those whose "eyes have been opened" to the light of Christ rejoice to have their deeds exposed. It is baffling that our whole society knows and apparently loves the hymn "Amazing Grace." What are people thinking of when they sing, "Amazing grace, how sweet the sound / that saved a wretch like me"? The man who wrote the hymn was a slave trader who came to see the wickedness of his activities. Most of those who sing the hymn today know nothing of this background. It is startling to hear it robustly sung by people who are so imbued with today's talk of self-esteem that one can't imagine them identifying themselves as wretches.[6] A chasm of incomprehension has opened up between the awe of the old slave trader who knew that he had been redeemed by Christ in spite of himself and the contemporary notion of a generalized sort of spiritual self-improvement. The joy of the hymn writer is specifically that of being released from the burden of sin. His gratitude is "for the means of grace and for the hope of glory."[7] The link between the confession of sin and a *prevenient* state of blessedness, however poorly understood today, remains indissoluble.

Bach Celebrates the Lord of the Dance

For the sake of unpersuaded readers who are willing to undertake this chapter in spite of misgivings, here are a few encouraging thoughts based on the music of J. S. Bach and its capacity for inspiring joy. In Bach's music, the knowledge of sin is encompassed by rapturous gladness. Bach's unique contribution to the church's worship is the way he frequently combines passages of the deepest anguish with dance forms and their capacity for inspiring delight. Jaroslav Pelikan, in his writing about Bach as theologian, calls this "confession and celebration."[8] Part of the effectiveness of the music at these points is Bach's affinity for Martin Luther's experience of *Anfechtung* — a soul-threatening attack. This will help us to understand how a knowledge of sin, a sense of estrangement, and all other manifestations of *Anfechtung*, when understood *from within the context of saving grace*, bring an unburdened happiness to the human heart. No great artist, writer, or composer has exceeded Bach in this insight, or in the capacity for bringing it to joyous

---

6. An example of how completely the original meaning of the words "amazing grace" has been lost to us is Senator Edward M. Kennedy's use of it to describe John F. Kennedy Jr. in a eulogy at his nephew's memorial Mass — "He had amazing grace."

7. The Book of Common Prayer, The General Thanksgiving, 58.

8. Jaroslav Pelikan, *Bach among the Theologians* (Philadelphia: Fortress, 1986), 21-22.

life. Bach ecstatically celebrates the victory won in the cross while at the same time insisting, as Paul does, upon the cross's shame and degradation and therefore its corresponding appeal to those who suffer today.[9]

The experience of listening to a Bach cantata or passion, with its movement back and forth between deepest, heart-wrenching lamentation and exuberant, life-affirming dance forms, suggests the experience in life of having one's deepest fear and shame understood by someone else in a context of promise and hope. Bach conveys the joy of the believer who comes to understand that we are not left to our own devices for all eternity: God "is able . . . to present you without blemish before the presence of his glory with rejoicing" (Jude 24).

The analogy to the cantatas of Bach, with their combination of grief-stricken laments and ecstatic dance forms, is this: participation in Christ means abandoning our pretenses, openly acknowledging our identities as sinners in bondage, and *in the same moment* realizing with a stab of piercing joy that the victory is already ours in Christ, won by him who died to save us. The action of God's grace *precedes* our consciousness of sin, so that we perceive the depth of our own participation in sin's bondage simultaneously with the recognition of the unconditional love of Christ, which is perfect freedom. We recognize that love, moreover, not from the depths of the hell we were bent on creating for ourselves, but from the perspective of the heaven that God is preparing for us. In the victorious presence of the crucified and risen One, the whole company of the redeemed will throw off every bond and join in a celebration of mutual love and joy where no one will be a wallflower and everyone will be able to dance like Fred Astaire and Michael Jackson combined. Thus "Lord of the Dance" is truly an apt title for the risen Christ and for the kingdom of God: "The Great Dance . . . has begun from before always. . . . The dance which we dance is at the center and for the dance all things were made. Blessed be He!"[10]

Before Guilt, Grace

The church has always been tempted to recast the Christian story in terms of individual fault and guilt that can be overcome by a decision to repent. This undermines the gospel at its heart. The liturgy for the Jewish high

---

9. Victor Austin has recently written on the authority of Bach: "Authority in Bach's Passion and Anglican-Catholic Dialogue," *Living Church*, October 17, 2010.

10. C. S. Lewis, *Perelandra* (New York: Macmillan, 1965), 214.

holiday, Yom Kippur, contains these words: "Repentance will turn aside the severe decree." No disrespect is intended in pointing out that this is perhaps the major difference between Christianity and Judaism.[11] The germ of the Christian proclamation is already present in the apocalyptic late sections of the Old Testament, when the biblical writers have begun to realize that human repentance is not powerful enough or thorough enough or dependable enough to deliver the human race from wrong. Only the incursion of God's irresistible grace will suffice to prevent us from self-destructing. As Austin Farrer wrote, "Christ . . . took us, and associated us with his divine life, *even while we struggled against him. He has wrought all our repenting in us.*"[12]

Karl Barth preached regularly to the inmates of the prison in his home-town of Basel, Switzerland. Knowledge of the context adds poignancy to the sermons. Here was an audience of people who had been officially judged and condemned as guilty. One of the sermons is based on Ephesians 2:8, "For by grace you have been saved through faith; and this is not your own doing, it is the gift of God." He illustrated by retelling a Swiss legend:

> You probably all know the legend of the rider who crossed the frozen Lake of Constance by night without knowing it. When he reached the opposite shore and was told whence he came, he broke down horrified. This is the human situation when the sky opens and the earth is bright, when we may hear: By grace you have been saved! In such a moment we are like that terrified rider. When we hear this word we involuntarily look back, do we not, asking ourselves: Where have I been? Over an abyss, in mortal danger! What did I do? The most foolish thing I ever attempted! What happened? I was doomed and miraculously escaped and now I am safe! You ask, Do we really live in such danger? Yes, we live on the brink of death. But we have been saved. Look at our Savior, and at our salvation! Look at Jesus Christ on the cross. . . . Do you know for whose sake he is hanging there? For *our* sake — because of *our* sin — sharing *our* captivity — burdened with *our* suffering! He nails *our* life to the cross. This is how

11. This is affirmed, in somewhat different terms, by Ephraim Radner, not incidentally a Jewish convert to Christianity, in his Leviticus commentary: "Jewish and Christian exegesis part ways decisively at this point. The Day of Atonement becomes infused with a radically penitential spirit within Judaism after the temple's destruction, demanding repentance as the effective basis for the Day of Atonement's usefulness. . . . But Jesus, through his flesh's own afflictions, becomes the true or perfect penitent" (*Leviticus,* Brazos Theological Commentary on the Bible [Grand Rapids: Brazos, 2008], 169).

12. Austin Farrer, *Saving Belief* (New York: Morehouse-Barlow, 1965), 105.

God had to deal with *us*. From this darkness he has saved *us*. He who is not shattered after hearing this news may not yet have grasped the word of God: "By grace you have been saved!"[13]

The story of the rider well illustrates a central phenomenon in the Christian life: "Not the man who is lost, but the man who is saved can understand that he is a sinner."[14] Gary Anderson writes, "The notion of human sin and fallenness is nothing other than a considered reflection on the unmerited and unfathomable moment of salvation."[15] Properly understood, the knowledge of one's sinful condition comes as good, even joyful, knowledge.[16]

The familiar caricature of the evangelistic tent revival depicts the preacher attempting to whip up a sense of sinfulness in the audience so that it will "come to Jesus" for mercy and forgiveness. The discussion here makes precisely the opposite point. If a congregation is led to an understanding of salvation, the sense of sin will come as a *consequence* — and then the knowledge that the danger is *already past* will result in profound and sincere repentance. That is the proper time to start talking about sin.

The interpreter is at a crossroads here. There cannot be an adequate representation of the meaning of the crucifixion without a deep personal response to the problem of sin. The human response to the prevenient grace of God is the acknowledgment of one's sinful condition and trust in God's unfailing mercy. That is why we have Ash Wednesday, with its sobering list of "crimes and misdemeanors" and its solemn recitation of Psalm 51:

Wash me thoroughly from my iniquity,
and cleanse me from my sin!
For I know my transgressions,
and my sin is ever before me.

13. Karl Barth, *Deliverance to the Captives,* first paperback ed. (New York: Harper and Row, 1978), 38, emphasis in original. It is typical of Barth to use typographical emphasis.

14. Samuel Terrien, *The Psalms and Their Meaning for Today: Their Original Purpose, Contents, Religious Truth, Poetic Beauty, and Significance* (Indianapolis: Bobbs-Merrill, 1952), 170.

15. Gary A. Anderson, *"Necessarium Adae Peccatum:* The Problem of Original Sin," in *Sin, Death, and the Devil,* ed. Carl E. Braaten and Robert W. Jenson (Grand Rapids: Eerdmans, 2000), 39.

16. An interesting illustration of a secular person reaching for the word "sin" when he cannot think of another one that conveys a sufficiently strong judgment occurs in a documentary about Gilles Pontecorvo's famous film, *The Battle of Algiers.* An admirer observes, with some degree of emotion, that Pontecorvo's failure to make more masterpieces was "a sin" (Criterion Collection supplement, *The Battle of Algiers*).

Against thee, thee only, have I sinned,
    and done that which is evil in thy sight,
so that thou art justified in thy sentence
    and blameless in thy judgment. . . .
Hide thy face from my sins,
    and blot out all my iniquities.

(Ps. 51:2-4, 9)

This psalm, particularly hallowed by its use on Ash Wednesday, exemplifies the way that a "sense of sin" arises, not out of browbeaten guilt, but from a yearning for God and his goodness. God is moving upon a person's heart before the person even realizes what is happening. In presenting the gospel, then, we do not begin by attempting to convict people of sin. The movement of God's prevenient ("going-before") mercy comes first, in the disclosure of the presence of God, which then awakens the sense of sin by exposing the chasm between us and the holiness of God. When this recognition dawns on us, we are *already standing within* God's grace ("this grace in which we stand" — Rom. 5:2). This is another way of explaining why the confession of sin can come as such a blessed relief.

Sin, then, is an exclusively biblical concept. The word is used, of course, in various nonbiblical contexts by people who know nothing of the Bible, but outside its biblical matrix it simply comes to mean wrongdoing of some sort, defined by whoever happens to be using it — almost always with reference to someone other than themselves. To be in sin, biblically speaking, means something very much more consequential than wrongdoing; it means being catastrophically separated from the eternal love of God. It means to be on the other side of an impassable barrier of exclusion from God's heavenly banquet. It means to be helplessly trapped inside one's own worst self, miserably aware of the chasm between the way we are and the way God intends us to be. It means the continuation of the reign of greed, cruelty, rapacity, and violence throughout the world. In view of God's nature, it is impossible that this state of affairs would be allowed to continue forever. Once we come to know God in Jesus Christ, we can no longer imagine the Father's joyful banquet continuing into all eternity with the elder brother still standing outside looking in, imprisoned forever in his envy and resentment (Luke 15:25-32). This whole line of thinking exemplifies what we have been saying for several pages now, namely, that we cannot talk about sin for very long without being drawn into doxology. Were it not for the mercy of God surrounding us, we would have no perspective from which to view sin, for we would be entirely subject to it. That is the reason for affirming that wherever sin is unmasked and confessed, *God's redemptive power is already present and acting.*

A Central Proclamation: Christ Died for Sin

Here we begin to capitalize the word "Sin," for reasons first set out in the introduction. Whenever we are speaking from the perspective of the apostle Paul, "Sin" and "Death" are capitalized as Powers — a subject to be fully discussed in later chapters. Sin is not so much a collection of individual misdeeds as it is an active, malevolent agency bent upon despoiling, imprisonment, and death — the utter undoing of God's purposes. Misdeeds are signs of that agency at work; they are not the thing itself. It is "the thing itself" that is our cosmic Enemy.[17]

The New Testament repeatedly uses a formula to explain Christ's death that has become so familiar to churchgoers that we do not stop to think what it might signify: Christ died *for sin*.[18] The earliest and best-attested such statement is found in Paul's chapter about the resurrection in I Corinthians: "For I delivered to you as of first importance what I also received, that *Christ died for our sins in accordance with the scriptures,* that he was buried, that he was raised on the third day in accordance with the scriptures" (I Cor. 15:3-4).[19]

Here, Paul has staked out a piece of inviolate territory "according to the scriptures." Mainstream American churches have been mistaken in seeking to ignore, disparage, or dismiss *the clear statement of the New Testament that Jesus died for sin.*[20] The connection between the crucifixion and Sin is permanently and emphatically fixed in the biblical text. Having shown that the acknowledgment of sinfulness comes as good news to those who hear and receive the gospel, we now discuss the pervasive problem of Sin.

17. A full exposition of the Enemy will follow in chapter 9.

18. The arguments about the words *huper, peri,* and *anti,* each of which can be translated "for," will be taken up at length in chapter 11.

19. The fact that the plural ("sins") is used in this case is evidence of the very early date of this confession. When Paul is not quoting an earlier formula, he uses the singular ("sin").

20. There is strong resistance to this foundational scriptural proclamation in some circles. In particular we might note the work of some feminist/womanist theologians. Delores Williams believes that linking the conquest of sin to Jesus' *death* (as opposed to his *life*) glorifies death and suffering in a way that has been harmful to people of color. There may be some truth in this latter point, but rejecting the connection between the cross and the overcoming of sin is rejecting the entire Christian message. The antidote to misuse of the gospel is not renouncing it altogether, but presenting it afresh.

Sin: Individual or Corporate?

If acknowledgment of fault is difficult for individuals — perhaps especially for men, who have been conditioned not to show weakness — how much more so is it for groups. A nation, tribe, corporation, or other human collective will typically define itself as superior to its enemies, competitors, or antagonists. Think of how difficult it is for any country or national group, *including our own,* to admit that it has done anything wrong. The wars in Vietnam, Afghanistan, and Iraq will continue to haunt the United States. Even after all the pain and second-guessing, our tendency is still to hunt for exculpating factors. We continue to think almost entirely in terms of *American* casualties, as though the deaths of Vietnamese peasants and Arab civilians are of lesser consequence.[21]

To grasp the full dimensions of the biblical picture, we need to face up to our proclivities in this regard. The Bible is full of stories about individual transgression (all the patriarchs and matriarchs are shown in a bad light at one time or another), but even more, it contains sweeping indictments of whole societies — as we saw in the previous chapter. We are so accustomed to thinking of individuals that we unconsciously transpose the biblical "you" into the singular when the Bible means it to be plural. To illustrate, we can take a verse almost at random:

> "Though you wash yourself with lye
> > and use much soap,
> > > the stain of your guilt is still before me,
> > > > says the Lord God." (Jer. 2:22)

Americans reading this verse out of its context in our individualistic culture will think it refers to a single person, but it is directed to the whole people collectively. Thus Paul Ricoeur writes, "If guilt is defined only as a feeling of unworthiness, then obviously only a minority would qualify; but sin includes the real situation of all human beings before God whether they know it or not."[22]

Here we draw closer to the heart of the nature of Sin. The ineluctable connection of the individual to the whole can readily be illustrated. For example, the Reverend Niall O'Brien describes his transformation from

---

21. The Iraq Body Count (IBC) estimates 125,000–140,000 *civilian* dead as of June 2014, based on cross-checked morgue reports, hospital records, NGO and official figures.

22. Paul Ricoeur, *The Symbolism of Evil* (Boston: Beacon Press, 1967), 7.

conventional priest to activist in the Philippine Islands as a result of his encounter with the sufferings of the poor. He began to ponder "the mystery of the evil that good people do." As an example he writes of a woman "who ran the hacienda near San Ramon, worried to tears about not being able to go to Communion but unworried about the children who were dying on her farm."[23] This shows how easily an individual can focus on her own moral purity while ignoring larger claims on her conscience. This is an aspect of the gravity of Sin that *all* Christians need to ponder.[24] We do not have to go to the Philippines to see such contradictions, as affluent American society focuses on its own security and comfort yet coexists with abysmal conditions for migrant farm laborers, many immigrants, and prisoners. Corporations consider themselves benevolent if they provide funding for education or the arts, but at the same time they pollute wetlands, exploit workers, market harmful products, and lie about it.[25] This is corporate Sin on a massive scale. All over the globe, poor people and people of color find themselves without recourse when they are marginalized, ignored, discounted.

In the early years of the third millennium, the gap between the very rich and the rest of the American population increased exponentially, a situation that began to trouble many consciences. Such a chasm, and the suffering it causes, is the result of Sin in which our whole society participates. The prophet Amos, in a startlingly modern-sounding passage, scathingly addresses the affluent women in the fashionable sections of town who sit around their swimming pools — so to speak — having their nails done and sipping their cocktails high above the struggles of the poor:

23. Niall O'Brien, *Revolution from the Heart* (New York: Oxford University Press, 1987), 188.

24. "People don't want to see farm workers," said a spokesman for farm laborers. "They don't want to see these little brown men in their communities. They want them around at 6am to bid down each other's wages, and then they want them to disappear at 6pm." "As Economy Booms, Migrant Workers' Housing Worsens," *New York Times,* May 31, 1998.

25. A striking illustration is the McWane company in Birmingham, Alabama, one of the world's largest manufacturers of cast-iron pipes. "Dangerous Business," an exposé in the *New York Times,* partnered by PBS *Frontline* and the Canadian Broadcasting Company, stretched across many pages in three issues (January 9-11, 2003). The McWane family was noted for its quiet, civic-minded philanthropy, yet the record of conditions in their plants made McWane "one of the most dangerous businesses in America." The very long, intensively researched articles by David Barstow and Lowell Bergman (for which they won the 2004 Goldsmith Prize) detail horrific examples of neglect, bullying, intimidation, cover-up, and denial as workers suffered dreadful injuries and deaths over a period of years. The secretive and punitive attitude of the corporation toward those who tried to protest could not have been more at odds with the image that the McWane family sought to project.

> "Hear this word, you cows of Bashan,
>   who are in the mountain of Samaria,
> who oppress the poor, who crush the needy,
>   who say to their husbands, 'Bring, that we may drink!'" (Amos 4:1)

These women are almost certainly unaware that they personally are crushing the needy; they are not thinking of the needy at all. This is no excuse before a righteous God, who pronounces harsh judgment upon the gentry:

> "I will smite the winter house with the summer house;
>   and the houses of ivory shall perish,
> and the great houses shall come to an end,"
>   says the Lord. (Amos 3:15)

In a situation of intricate interconnectedness between individuals and their societies, we see the ubiquity and inevitability of sin.[26] We are preparing to speak of the motif of deliverance at the heart of the theology of the cross. Such a *theologia crucis* will be seriously diminished if the Christian community does not understand the corporate nature of sin, and if Christian individuals do not have a deep personal response to that problem. Paul Ricoeur reminds us that the concept of sin is "at once and primordially [both] personal *and* communal." He argues against understanding sin as purely individual, as though it were only a punch list of personal errors. The great Yahwistic narrative of Adam and Eve in Genesis 2–3 shows how corporate bondage to Sin is transmitted from generation to generation. Ricoeur explains that "original sin" is best understood not as a theological construct but as a *metaphor* depicting the "enigmatic bond which is acknowledged . . . in the 'we' of the [liturgical] confession of sins."[27] The "we" points toward our solidarity in the disobedience of Adam. The clearest exposition of this "enigmatic bond" is found in Romans 5:12-21. Paul gives all humankind the name of Adam. The fraternity of Adam is the most comprehensive community of all, for it is universal. "Sin came into the world through one man and death through sin, and so death spread to all men because all men sinned" (Rom. 5:12). This universal conception of "Adam" is used in I Corinthians also: "In Adam all die" (I Cor. 15:22). *Human solidarity*

---

26. It is not often remembered that the American Founders had a sense of original sin, though they did not refer to it that way. For example, James Madison: "The latent causes of faction are . . . sown in the nature of man" (*The Federalist Papers* [New York: Penguin, 1987], 124).

27. Ricoeur, *The Symbolism of Evil*, 83-84.

in bondage to the power of Sin is one of the most important concepts for Christians to grasp.[28]

But it is not enough to say that we are in bondage to Sin. A result of that bondage is that we have become *active, conscripted agents* of Sin. Philip Ziegler, in an astute analysis of Ernst Käsemann on this subject, writes,

> To be lorded over by Sin is to have been engaged to be its representative, "member, part, and tool." . . . In our very existence "we are exponents of a power which transforms the cosmos into chaos," our lives actually "making a case" for the power that possesses us and in whose service we are enrolled. This is why Paul characterized the guilt of Sin not in terms of ignorance, but rather in terms of "revolt against the known Lord."[29]

Thus the human condition is not only one of captivity, but also one of "active complicity."[30]

The Twofold Aspect of Sin: A Thesis of This Chapter

Sin is a category without meaning except in reference to God. A *Calvin and Hobbes* comic strip illustrates this in an endearing way. Calvin, a little boy, is hurtling down a snowy slope on a sled with his friend Hobbes, a tiger, conducting a discussion about sin (the wildly improbable nature of this scene is part of its charm). Here is the dialogue:

> *Calvin.* I'm getting nervous about Christmas.
> *Hobbes.* You're worried you haven't been good?
> *Calvin.* That's just the question. It's all relative. What's Santa's definition? How good do you have to be to qualify as good? I haven't killed any-

---

28. When the foreign service officer Moorhead (Mike) Kennedy — a churchgoing Episcopalian — was released from his long ordeal as a hostage in Tehran and was invited to give speeches in churches about the experience, he would begin by addressing his audiences not as "fellow Episcopalians" but as "fellow hostages." This was both amusing and pointed. Whether consciously or not, he was echoing Paul's declaration that all are held under the Power of Sin.

29. Philip Ziegler, "Christ Must Reign: Ernst Käsemann and Soteriology in an Apocalyptic Key," from *Apocalyptic and the Future of Theology: With and Beyond J. Louis Martyn*, ed. Joshua B. Davis and Douglas Harink (Eugene, Ore.: Cascade, 2012), 206. Quotations are from Käsemann.

30. Ziegler, "Christ Must Reign," 208.

body. That's good, right? I haven't committed any felonies. I didn't start any wars. . . . Wouldn't you say that's pretty good? Wouldn't you say I should get lots of presents?

Hobbes. But maybe good is more than the absence of bad.

Calvin. See, that's what worries me.[31]

Deftly and humorously, this little dialogue raises four important issues. (1) What's Santa's definition of good and bad? (What's *God's* definition?) (2) How good do you have to be to qualify as good? (And who makes that determination?) (3) Maybe good is more than the absence of bad (which raises the issue of evil as the absence of good — *privatio boni*).[32] And finally, we may conclude, (4) such conundrums understood *philosophically* lead to worry. Only a *theo*logical answer delivers from ultimate anxiety.

As the comic-strip tiger suggests, "bad" might be somehow more than just falling short of the mark. The story of Adam and Eve shows that there is something much more willful, something much more deliberate, something much more *active* than merely "missing the mark" (as *hamartia* is literally defined) or the "absence of bad." Before God, it just isn't enough to fall back on "Nobody's perfect," or "I misspoke," or "We all make mistakes." C. S. Lewis wrote, "Fallen man is not simply an imperfect creature who needs improvement; he is a rebel who must lay down his arms."[33]

Still less is sin defined by comparing ourselves favorably to others, like the Pharisee in Jesus' story: "God, I thank thee that I am not like other men, extortioners, unjust, adulterers, or even like this tax collector" (Luke 18:11). The Pharisee does not understand that sin is not defined by comparing one person to another, but by grasping how deeply he, as an individual, is enmeshed in a world mired in godlessness. Sin is the universal human condition, but this is not fully obvious unless one is *God*-directed, *God*-saturated, *God*-intoxicated. The concept of sin is not *anthropo*logical, but *theo*logical.[34] As God makes himself known to us, we recognize that we are "not merely insulated victims of the 'world of sin' but rather its settled

---

31. *Calvin and Hobbes* comic strip by Bill Watterson, December 23, 1990.

32. The definition of evil as the absence of good will be addressed in chapter 10.

33. C. S. Lewis, *Mere Christianity* (New York: Harper and Row, 1952), 59.

34. Northrop Frye's definition has merit: "Sin is . . . a matter of trying to block the activity of God, and it always results in some curtailing of human freedom, whether of oneself or of one's neighbor" (*The Great Code: The Bible and Literature* [New York: Harcourt Brace Jovanovich, 1982], 130). The special value of this definition lies in its identification of human freedom with the purposes — the "activity" — of God.

inhabitants, actively habituated to its ways and means as subjects in the service of its false gods."[35]

The well-known hymn "Rock of Ages" has a few lines of real theological significance. Here is the key verse:

> Should my tears for ever flow,
> Should my zeal no languor know,
> All for sin could not atone
> Thou must save, and thou alone;
> Be of sin the *double cure;*
> Save me from its *guilt and power.*[36]

Here, in the briefest possible compass, are two crucial affirmations:

- "All for sin could not atone." As Anselm of Canterbury was at such pains to demonstrate, *only God* can supply the remedy for sin. No amount of religious effort on our part can effect a significant change. Deliverance and atonement must come from outside our sphere of influence, for we are powerless to save ourselves from Sin's sphere of power.
- "Be of sin the *double cure;* save me from its *guilt and power.*" Sin has two components, of equal gravity. Sin is *both* a guilt and a power. Ricoeur denotes its two aspects as *"subjective weight"* and *"objective maleficence."*[37]

Sin has, then, a twofold aspect:

1. Sin is a **responsible guilt** for which atonement must be made. It follows that the crucifixion is understood as a sacrifice for sin.[38]
2. Sin is an **alien power** that must be driven from the field. All human beings are enslaved by this power (Rom. 3:9; John 8:34) and must be liberated by a greater power. The crucifixion is therefore understood to be Christ's victory over the Powers of Sin and Death, commonly called *Christus Victor.*[39]

---

35. Ziegler, "Christ Must Reign," 209.

36. Augustus Montague Toplady, 1773. There is some controversy about the quoted lines; the original has the more Wesleyan "Save from wrath and make me pure." However, Toplady's hymnal of 1776 has the lines as quoted here.

37. Ricoeur, *The Symbolism of Evil,* 95.

38. Anselm, using different thought-forms, offers the alternative term "satisfaction."

39. I am borrowing here not only from Ricoeur but also from J. Christiaan Beker, *Paul the Apostle: The Triumph of God in Life and Thought* (Philadelphia: Fortress, 1980), 209.

Many interpreters have chosen to emphasize either one or the other of these, but *both* categories were of utmost importance to the apostles and Evangelists, and therefore are to us.[40]

The Witness of Psalm 51

We do not come to a theological understanding of sin, or any other aspect of the Christian *kerygma,* as a consequence of being religiously insightful by nature. In fact, "religion" (defined anthropologically) can be an effective barrier to such understanding. The quickest way out of anthropology and into theology is to move straight to the Bible.

The Psalms are always a dependable source. Let us take another look at the great psalm appointed for Ash Wednesday, Psalm 51. This psalm has traditionally been attributed to King David at the time when his adultery with Bathsheba was exposed. Even if this is not its provenance, it is an inspired attribution. We can readily imagine it arising out of a particular situation where a human being is forced to face his sinfulness. The psalm begins,

> Have mercy on me, O God, according to thy steadfast love;
> according to thy abundant mercy blot out my transgressions.

Notice how the psalmist's plea for mercy is grounded in the knowledge of God. The words "steadfast love" and "abundant mercy" are not projections out of wishful human thinking ("religion" defined anthropologically); they are part of God's revelation of himself in the history of Israel. Israel's experience with God in the desert and in the Promised Land had proven God to be faithful and trustworthy. Therefore, though the psalmist's spirit is near to being crushed by the knowledge of his sinfulness, stronger still is his confidence in God — specifically, in two things *about* God: first, God *is able* to cleanse from sin, and second, God *provides for* the washing away of sin. Thus David beseeches the Lord, in great distress but also with unmistakable confidence:

> Wash me thoroughly from my iniquity,
> and cleanse me from my sin!

---

40. Likewise Nancy J. Duff: "Humanity not only needs to be *forgiven for guilt* incurred for sin, but *freed from the power of sin* which holds the human will captive and causes some people to be victimized at the hands of others" ("Atonement and the Christian Life: Reformed Doctrine from a Feminist Perspective," *Interpretation* 53, no. 1 [January 1999]).

He continues,

Against thee, thee only, have I sinned,
   and done that which is evil in thy sight,
so that thou art justified in thy sentence
   and blameless in thy judgment.

Here again is an illustration of how sin can be understood only from the vantage point provided by God. The verse is startling; surely sin harms other human beings, yet the assertion is, "Against thee, *thee only,* have I sinned." It could almost be dismissed as Levantine hyperbole, except for one thing: the passionate rhetoric is commensurate with the singer's profound understanding of God's righteousness — against which our failures, both witting and unwitting, show up like splotches of garbage on a landscape of pure snow.[41] So again, we see that the problem is not specific wrongdoing but a wrenching disruption of our relationship with God. The Dutch theologian G. C. Berkouwer writes,

> In all the multiformity of sin there is always a common trait: sin is always *against God.* Never can we get at the essence of sin as long as we ignore this relation of sin and God and regard our sin as a mere "phenomenon" in human living. This fact is apparent when sin is described as enmity and rebellion, disobedience and alienation from God. That kind of terminology is a far cry from the common view which leaves no room for the relational character of sin and implies that sin is a bothersome "deficiency."[42]

When the psalmist says, therefore, "against thee [God] only have I sinned," it is a striking acknowledgment of the relationship between *understanding sin* and *knowing God.* The confession of sin is even combined with thoughts of joy, in a surprising juxtaposition reminiscent of what we were saying earlier about Bach:

Fill me with joy and gladness;
   let the bones which thou hast broken rejoice.

---

41. Both Isaiah and Paul speak not only of sins as garbage, but far more shockingly, of "righteous deeds" as "a polluted garment" (Isa. 64:6) and "righteousness under the law" as excrement (Phil. 3:6-8).

42. G. C. Berkouwer, *Sin* (Grand Rapids: Eerdmans, 1971), 242.

Again, it is certainly not the modern sensibility to suggest that God has broken our bones. The "old Adam" in us does not want the pain of self-knowledge, even though it is the gracious God-given highway to our eternal inheritance of blamelessness (I Thess. 3:13). Given the cultural climate we live in today, this is very understandable. Not many messages reach us about the singleness of God's purpose in *both* condemnation *and* redemption. Perhaps recognizing this connection is simply a gift for which we can only be thankful. It is a recognition given by God's grace; only as he opens our lips can our mouths show forth his praise (Ps. 51:15). Throughout this penitential psalm, the note of joy is present: "Restore to me the joy of thy salvation," the psalmist prays,

> and uphold me with a willing spirit.
> Then I will teach transgressors thy ways,
> and sinners will return to thee.

Jesus' Death for Sin in the New Testament

Speaking of the Story, we must have certain presuppositions in place to understand the deliverance from sin wrought by Christ. There are three fundamental premises in the biblical picture of Sin:

1. The Fall — the story of Adam and Eve that tells, in mythological terms, of a primeval cataclysm that involves all human beings in a vast rebellion against our once and future destiny in God[43]
2. The subsequent solidarity of all humanity in bondage to the power of Sin
3. A cosmic struggle between the forces of Sin, evil, and Death ("the world,

---

43. Ronald Goetz misunderstands when he writes, "There never was a historical Adam and Eve. For all of mainstream theology's vaunted concern for contemporary relevance, when it speaks of sin . . . it refuses to face the implications of the collapse of the historicity of the Fall" (*Christian Century*, March 11, 1992, 275). But the truth of the Adam story isn't dependent on historicity; it can't even be shown that Paul believed the story to be "historical." Its power to tell us something crucial about God and ourselves is undiminished. Adam and Eve seem like real people in the story — that is part of the Yahwist's genius — but what is really going on is that they stand for us all. Thus Paul can refer to "Adam" and mean the entire dismal story of the whole human race. F. F. Bruce writes that in Rom. 7 Paul "is re-telling the Genesis Fall story in the first person singular" (*Paul: Apostle of the Heart Set Free* [Grand Rapids: Eerdmans, 1997], 194), which has been definitively reversed by our incorporation into the second Adam, Jesus Christ. This will be discussed at length in chapter 12.

the flesh, and the devil," as the baptismal service used to say) and the unconquerable purpose of God

We cannot understand the biblical picture of Sin without these basic building blocks.[44] The first one comes from Genesis, but we have seen how it has been given its place in the story of the crucified One by Paul in Romans 5:12-21. The second biblical picture is adumbrated in passages from the Psalms and Isaiah, quoted by Paul in Romans 3:10-18. The third biblical premise emerges out of the postexilic apocalyptic framework that forms the thought-world of large sections of the New Testament. We will refer to these foundational affirmations constantly as we proceed.

The New Testament states unequivocally in various places and in various ways that Jesus Christ came and died for the overcoming of sin(s).[45] Since the New Testament uses a great many images and motifs to interpret the cross, however, these motifs have sometimes been forced into overly schematic categories around which various ecclesiastical parties have clustered, with mutual suspicion. This tendency has been harmful to the church. Unless we are to abandon the New Testament witness altogether, we must acknowledge that *the overcoming of sin* lies at the very heart of the meaning of the crucifixion. Modern attempts to interpret the cross without reference to sin make no sense either from the standpoint of Scripture or from the overwhelming evidence in our own time that the entire human race is heir to what John Henry Newman called a "vast primordial catastrophe," and that only a stronger power from outside ourselves can repair the breach.[46] The mission of Jesus is understood in these terms to a greater or lesser degree by all the New Testament writers.

44. I am aware that not all portions of Scripture emphasize solidarity in sin equally, nor do they refer explicitly to the Fall. The authors of the Wisdom literature do not speak with the same voice as the Yahwist of Gen. 2–3. However, when Paul makes Adam the eponymous head of a development characterizing all human life, he clearly expects everyone in his congregations to know what he means (Rom. 5; I Cor. 15).

45. A partial list of references: Matt. 1:21; 26:28; Mark 2:10; Luke 1:77; 7:47-49; John 1:29; 8:24; Acts 2:38; 3:19; 5:31; 10:43; 13:38; 26:18; Rom. 4:25; 5:16; 6:1-10; 8:2-4; I Cor. 15:3; II Cor. 5:21; Gal. 1:4; Col. 1:14; 2:13-15; Heb. 1:3; 2:17; 9:26-28; 10:12; 13:11-12; I Pet. 2:24; 3:18; I John 1:7; 2:1-2; 3:5; 4:10; Rev. 1:5.

46. This phrase, "vast primordial catastrophe," is quoted by Brendan Gill in a review of a revival of Edward Albee's play *Who's Afraid of Virginia Woolf?* (fourteen years after the first production). The context is pertinent. Gill writes that, contrary to the opinion of some, the play isn't about marriage "or any other form of sexual relationship but, rather, that relationship of which Cardinal Newman was indirectly speaking when he said of the human race that it was implicated in some vast primordial catastrophe" (Gill, "In Vino Veritas," *New Yorker,* April 12, 1976).

Here are some examples from each of the four Gospels:

Matthew

The very first chapter of the first book in the New Testament begins with the angel saying, "Joseph, son of David, do not fear to take Mary your wife . . . she will bear a son, and you shall call his name Jesus, *for he will save his people from their sins*" (Matt. 1:20-21). The Evangelist does not explain why the people need to be saved; it is presupposed. Jesus' name, *Yeshua,* means *God saves;* Matthew's reference makes explicit the connection between the Messiah's name and salvation from sin.

Mark

Early in the Gospel, when a paralyzed man is let down through the roof at Jesus' feet, Jesus announces himself publicly (albeit obliquely) with great drama as "the Son of man [who] has *authority on earth to forgive sins*" (Mark 2:10). We are not told what the paralyzed man's sins were or why they needed to be forgiven; the general human condition of sinfulness is assumed. The focus of this Markan pericope is on Jesus' claim to forgive sins; it is immediately recognized as messianic, for "Who can forgive sins but God alone?"

Luke

The Third Evangelist is generally thought to have no interest in the crucifixion as an atoning sacrifice; however, the theme of the overcoming of sin is present from the very beginning in Luke's beautiful infancy narrative. Zechariah's song includes these words about his son John:

> "And you, child, will be called the prophet of the Most High;
> for you will go before the Lord to prepare his ways,
> to give knowledge of salvation to his people
> in *the forgiveness of their sins.*" (Luke 1:76-77)

The theme is brought forward also in the final words of the risen Jesus in Luke's Gospel, in which Jesus makes it a constituent part of the *kerygma:* "Thus it is written, that the Christ should suffer and on the third day rise from the dead, and that repentance and *forgiveness of sins* should be preached in his name to all nations, beginning from Jerusalem" (Luke 24:46-47). Nothing is said about why the nations need forgiveness; again, it is presupposed. Luke leads off the second book of his two-volume work, Acts, with the ascension of Jesus and the descent of the Holy Spirit, whereupon Peter promptly announces to the people,

"Repent, and be baptized every one of you in the name of Jesus Christ *for the forgiveness of your sins;* and you shall receive the gift of the Holy Spirit" (Acts 2:38). No one protests that he has no sin; it is assumed.

John

The passion narrative in the Gospel of John is not known for its emphasis on Jesus' death as atonement, but the Evangelist goes to some lengths to portray him as the Passover lamb, changing the chronology of his last earthly days to do so. Moreover, one of the first scenes in the Gospel has John the Baptist announcing, "Behold, the Lamb of God, who *takes away the sin* of the world!" (John 1:29). Jesus himself, speaking to the Pharisees in chapter 8, makes the closest possible connection between deliverance from sin and faith in his own person: "You will *die in your sins* unless you believe that I am he" (John 8:24).[47]

In none of these cases does the Evangelist indicate a need to explain what is meant. Sin, against the Old Testament background, is taken for granted as the basic human condition, which only God the Creator can restore to its original perfection.

Following are brief illustrations from other sections of the New Testament about the overcoming of sin as the central purpose of Christ's life and death:

Epistle to the Hebrews

Its theme is stated early in the letter: Christ "made purification *for sins*" (1:3). In chapter 6 we will show in more depth how he was "made like his brethren in every respect, so that he might become a merciful and faithful high priest in the service of God, to make expiation *for the sins* of the people" (2:17).

First Epistle of Peter

This apostolic letter states with piercing clarity that "he himself *bore our sins* in his body on the tree" (2:24).

---

47. Specialists may protest at this point that I am not allowing for the fact that Luke and John do not specifically associate the remission of sin with the crucifixion. However, I am speaking here of the foundational premise that runs through the New Testament, most certainly including Luke and John: sin afflicts the human condition unto death, and Jesus has come to redeem us from it. All the Gospels agree on that, and as explained in chapter 1, the dominance of the passion narrative in all four Gospels attests to its central importance.

First Epistle of John

This letter is particularly forceful in making the connection: "The blood of Jesus his [God's] Son cleanses us *from all sin*" (1:7); "he is the expiation for our sins, and not for ours only but also *for the sins* of the whole world" (2:2); "God . . . loved us and sent his Son to be the expiation *for our sins*" (4:10).

Revelation

The opening greeting to the seven churches defines Jesus Christ in arresting phrases, and is followed by an ascription that seems to presuppose universal assent among Christians. It names "Jesus Christ the faithful witness, the first-born of the dead, and the ruler of kings on earth" and then ascribes glory to him in these words: "To him who loves us and has freed us *from our sins* by his blood and made us a kingdom, priests to his God and Father, to him be glory and dominion for ever and ever. Amen" (1:5-6).

Sin as a Power in the Letters of the Apostle Paul

Paul, more than any other apostolic writer, makes *explicit* what is *implicit* in the Gospels about the nature and ubiquity of Sin. In Romans he spells out the way in which all humankind not only fell into bondage to Sin but also collaborated with it. As already mentioned, he draws upon the story of the Fall in Genesis, referring to Adam as the first, representative man (human being) and to Christ as the determinative final man. Here is a portion of that crucially important section of Romans:

> Sin came into the world through one man and death through sin, and so death spread to all men because all men sinned. . . . Death reigned from Adam to Moses, even over those whose sins were not like the transgression of Adam, who was a type of the one who was to come. . . . If many died through one man's trespass, much more [has] the grace of . . . that one man Jesus Christ abounded for many. . . . As one man's trespass led to condemnation for all men, so one man's act of righteousness leads to acquittal and life for all men. For as by one man's disobedience many were made sinners, so by one man's obedience many will be made righteous. (Rom. 5:12-19)

We will be referring to this key passage more than once — particularly in the final chapters — but the striking central point for now is this: Death and Sin alike rule over the human condition, a consequence of what John Milton memorably calls the "first disobedience" of Adam.[48] Only through the "first obedience" of the Son of God can this situation be set right. Adam is "a type of the one who was to come"; in the history of Jesus Christ, the entire history of "Adam" (the human race) is retold in the right way. In that *recapitulation,* the powers of sin and death are routed.[49]

Here we introduce explicitly the primary teaching of Paul that Sin is a Power. It is a malign force over which the unaided human being has no control. Charles Cousar shows how, in Romans 3, Paul is able to hold two conceptions of sin at the same time, though the second predominates:

- Sin is a *verb,* something people perform or engage in (Rom. 3:23).
- Sin is a *dominion* under which humanity exists (Rom. 3:9).[50]

This is another way of defining the twofold aspect of sin described a few pages back, following Ricoeur. The *verb* suggests the "responsible guilt for which atonement must be made," and the idea of *dominion* implies "an alien power which must be overcome." Paul is aware of both, but his emphasis in Romans falls largely on the latter. In Romans 1–3, Sin is so all-inclusive that there is "no one righteous, no, not one," and therefore there is nowhere to look within this world order for deliverance. This is very much against the grain of the Jewish conception of people as righteous and unrighteous that Paul the Pharisee grew up with, and it is very much against the grain of our own common tendency to assign people into groups of "bad guys" and "good guys." Paul personifies Sin in his writings as though it were a reigning monarch; "sin won dominion," he says in Romans 5:21.[51] He depicts Sin with its favorite and characteristic weapons, Death and the Law (Rom. 7:10-11), forcefully advancing through the world like an annihilating army: "Sin came into the world . . . and death through sin, and so death spread to all men because all men sinned" (Rom. 5:12). Sin and Death thus "have the character of universal forces which no one escapes."[52]

This is poorly understood in the churches, but sometimes unlikely

---

48. Milton, *Paradise Lost,* 1.1.

49. "Recapitulation" is a word associated with Irenaeus in the second century. This will be examined at length in chapter 12.

50. Charles B. Cousar, *A Theology of the Cross: The Death of Jesus in the Pauline Letters,* Overtures to Biblical Theology (Minneapolis: Augsburg Fortress, 1990), 57.

51. Translation by Ernst Käsemann, *Commentary on Romans* (Grand Rapids: Eerdmans, 1980).

52. Käsemann, *Commentary on Romans,* 149.

sources will shed light upon the matter. A reader of *New York* magazine wrote an arresting letter in response to an article about cosmetic surgery: "While reading your cover article I began to wonder what our society would be like if kind hearts and strong minds were respected, revered, and a turn-on. Obsessing about beauty and thinness is a luxury that only wealthy countries can afford. We worship the media and the false idols they provide us while in our own cities and elsewhere in the world people are starving. Yet we are the slaves. Vanity is a disease, and we Americans are infected."[53]

This letter writer instinctively understands what many church people no longer know: namely, that sin is not so much naughty actions or even egregious wrongdoing; it is an infectious disease.[54] Even more to Paul's point, it is an enslaving power that has us all in its grip.[55] Note the language used in the letter: "worship," "false idols," "slaves." These are categories that Paul would recognize, whether the writer knows it or not. Indeed, the parallels to Romans 6:16-18 are striking: "Do you not know that if you yield yourselves to any one as obedient slaves *(douloi),* you are slaves of the one whom you obey, either of sin, which leads to death, or of obedience, which leads to righteousness? But thanks be to God, that you who were once slaves of sin have become obedient from the heart to the standard of teaching to which you were committed, and, having been set free from sin, have become slaves of righteousness."

Americans are *slaves* of marketing and surfaces, which we *obey* by investing in them both literally and figuratively *(worship).* This leads to *death* (people go hungry as the wealthy pursue luxury). Though we fancy ourselves

---

53. *New York,* August 5, 1996. Since this was written, our enslavement to Botox and other cosmetic procedures has increased exponentially.

54. This can easily be linked to the concept of sin as impurity. Much of Leviticus is concerned with purification. This is not a negligible theme, but will not be central to the purposes of this book because it plays little role in the New Testament.

55. William Stringfellow is especially good on this. He generally prefers to speak of Death rather than Sin, but the point is the same: "Sin . . . does not mean that men are bad, or that men have a proclivity for wickedness, or that they are proud and selfish, but, instead, sin is the possession of men by the power of death, the bondage and servitude of men to death, the usurpation of God's office by the arrogance of death" (*Count It All Joy: Reflections on Faith, Doubt, and Temptation* [Grand Rapids: Eerdmans, 1967], 90-91). In his final collection of writings, when he knew he was dying, Christopher Hitchens, who famously and flamboyantly advertised his atheism, refers continually to death as "the alien" (*Mortality* [New York: Twelve, 2012], passim). The writer, commentator, and television personality Andrew A. (Andy) Rooney loathed death and its depredations, and this was clear in his conversation. In this respect the two atheists were closer to the New Testament than they thought. In I Cor. 15:26, Paul refers significantly to death as "the last enemy" to be conquered by Christ.

blessed with an array of personal choices, we are not free people, but *slaves to sin*. The letter writer wistfully wishes that "kind hearts and strong minds" were revered instead, but she senses that we are in *bondage* to cultural obsessions. Paul's gospel tells us that only the movement of the righteousness of God upon human hearts will reorient us to God's will and produce the *obedience that leads to righteousness* (a society in which kind hearts and strong minds are respected). We will then be *slaves of righteousness*. This rather shocking phrase is illustrative of Paul's conviction that, in Bob Dylan's often-quoted line, "You gotta serve somebody." We will live under one dominion or another, the penultimate dominion of Sin or the ultimate dominion of Christ.[56]

Repositioning Repentance

We referred earlier to the distinction between Judaism and Christianity illustrated by the affirmation in the Yom Kippur liturgy: "Repentance will turn aside the severe decree."[57] Psychoanalyst Dorothy Martyn writes that Sin is "a powerful force that grips us *beyond the sovereignty of our wills*" and is therefore not a simple matter of "bad actions" (let alone "bad choices," in the current parlance).[58] The Fourth Gospel understands this also: "Jesus answered them, 'Truly, truly, I say to you, every one who commits sin is *a slave to sin*'" (John 8:34).[59] This means that *not even repentance* can overcome sin and restore us to God. We note two points:

1. **There *is* a severe decree.** This is analogous to Anselm's *ponderis peccatum*. The entire Old Testament tradition testifies to the great weight *(ponderis)* of sin *(peccatum)* in human life, and Christian attempts to moderate or minimize it are anti-Hebraic.

56. In the Johannine writings, the metaphors for the two dominions are darkness and light (John 11:9-10; I John 1:5-7). It can't be emphasized too strongly that the two domains are not equal, either in present potency or in ultimate existence.

57. I am indebted to the late Dr. Dana Charry, the son of a rabbi, for his insights on this point. He told me that he would not have converted from Judaism to Christianity if he had not detected an insufficiency in the Yom Kippur liturgy. Conversation in Princeton, autumn 1997.

58. Dorothy Martyn, "Compulsion and Liberation: A Theological View," *Union Seminary Quarterly Review* 36, nos. 2-3 (Winter/Spring 1981): 128, emphasis added. Martyn has elaborated this biblical perspective in her book *Beyond Deserving: Children, Parents, and Responsibility Revisited* (Grand Rapids: Eerdmans, 2007).

59. The story of the healing of the paralytic in Mark 2:1-12, Matt. 9:1-8, and Luke 5:17-26 dramatically makes the point that the release from physical disability is secondary to the overcoming of sin.

2. But *second,* and this is where Christianity really does differ from rabbinic Judaism, **repentance is not enough.**[60] Something has to happen from God's side *first* to remedy the situation. The entire sphere of power has to be invaded from outside, from another sphere where Sin and Death have no sway.

It is surely no accident that Paul the Pharisee eschews all talk of repentance in his letters. He distances himself from any concept of repentance preceding, or being necessary for, the setting-aside (or "weakening," in some versions) of God's "severe decree."[61] At the risk of oversimplifying, for Paul the sequence is not sin-repentance-grace-forgiveness, but grace-sin-deliverance-repentance-grace. Grace drives the sequence from first to last.[62]

The victory of God's domain (or kingdom, in the terminology of the Gospels) is certain. That is what Paul is getting at when he says, "Christ being raised from the dead dieth no more; *death hath no more dominion over him. . . .* Reckon ye also yourselves to be *dead indeed unto sin, and alive unto God* through Jesus Christ our Lord" (Rom. 6:9-11 KJV). The cross-resurrection event marks the decisive turn in the *kosmos.* Repentance does not make this possible; God engenders the whole thing, including our repentance. There is a "new creation" (II Cor. 5). The fix we were in has been dramatically and decisively reversed. We are already in a new situation, as the deutero-Pauline baptismal text of Colossians 1:13 wonderfully affirms: "He has delivered us from the dominion of darkness and transferred us to the kingdom of his beloved Son." Equally significant, however, is the not-yet aspect of this reversal, for we await the redemption of the *kosmos* yet to come, when "the creation itself will be set free from its bondage to decay and obtain the glorious liberty of the children of God" (Rom. 8:21).

60. The Old Testament contains this truth first and foremost in the *unconditional* election and call of Abraham, as seen by Paul in Rom. 4:1-25.

61. Ellen Charry has cautioned me against speaking of "rabbinical" Judaism in Paul's time. Pharisaic Judaism is a proto-rabbinism, but the prayer book containing the Yom Kippur liturgy did not exist in Paul's day. Paul rejects the idea of repentance as a precedent human work that was not only present in Second Temple Judaism but is also suggested in parts of Luke-Acts. From Paul's perspective, Luke was not as careful as he might have been to show that repentance was evoked by the gracious justification of God, not the other way around.

62. In one of only two mentions of repentance in all his letters, Paul is explicit about the origin of repentance: "Do you not know that God's kindness is meant to lead you to repentance?" (Rom. 2:4). The only other mention is in the highly personal and atypical context of the Corinthians' antagonistic attitude to Paul himself (II Cor. 7:10). The absence of any other mentions of repentance is remarkable in view of Paul's background in pharisaic Judaism, and cannot be accidental.

This brief overview of biblical material is intended to drive home the breadth and depth of the New Testament witness to Jesus' death *for sin*. "The Lamb of God who takes away the sin of the world" has given himself in order to deliver us from the whole spectrum of individual failure and systemic evil.

Not Just Bad Deeds and Bad Choices

Douglas John Hall has written about the gravity of sin. He begins by quoting the prophet Isaiah, who says that even our *righteous* deeds — not to mention our unrighteous ones — are "like a polluted garment" (Isa. 64:6).[63] Hall continues,

> Even the association of sin with humanity's reputedly "greatest" achievements and successes, and with what individuals are prone to consider their best and most honorable deeds — even such an association, though it is as old as the prophets of Israel, seems difficult for our contemporaries to grasp. When it comes to this profound category of biblical faith, most of us seem to have advanced little beyond the mental estate of that fictitious but representative character, Boso, the dialogue partner of St. Anselm in *Cur Deus Homo?* who, evidently incapable of getting beyond the idea that sins are bad deeds, proposed that a mere declaration of forgiveness on the deity's part could remedy the situation. In response, Anselm uttered what may be the most penetrating insight ever stated [concerning the doctrine of sin]: "You have not yet considered the weight *(ponderis)* of sin."[64]

This "profound category of biblical faith" is indeed widely misunderstood. We think that sins are "bad deeds." *People* magazine once undertook a part-serious, part-tongue-in-cheek survey of its readers on the subject of sin. The results were published as a "Sindex," with each sin rated by a sin coefficient. The outcome is both amusing and instructive. Murder, rape, incest, child abuse, and spying against one's country were rated the worst

---

63. The translation of the Hebrew here has always been a challenge. Origen and the Syrian Martyrius Sahdona hewed close to the Hebrew in referring to a "menstrual rag" (quoted in Robert L. Wilken, *Isaiah: Interpreted by Early Christian and Medieval Commentators,* Church's Bible Series [Grand Rapids: Eerdmans, 2007], 505-6). More euphemistic translations offer "filthy rags" (KJV), "polluted garment" (RSV), "filthy cloth" (NRSV). Whatever the translation, it's an extreme image.

64. Douglas John Hall, *God and Human Suffering: An Exercise in the Theology of the Cross* (Minneapolis: Augsburg, 1989), 78.

sins, in ascending order, with smoking, swearing, masturbation, and illegal videotaping far down the list. Parking in a handicapped spot was rated surprisingly high, whereas unmarried live-togethers got off lightly. Cutting in front of someone in line was deemed worse than divorce or capital punishment. Predictably, corporate sin was not mentioned, though it is at the top of the Hebrew prophets' list. Most telling for our purposes here, "Overall, readers said they commit about 4.64 sins a month."[65] We may laugh at this, but clearly, our sense of sin as specific actions is deeply ingrained. There used to be liturgical and catechetical opportunities for correcting this mistaken view, but they have been largely expunged. For instance, Episcopalians used to say, "There is no health in us," in the General Confession. The questions inevitably raised by this phrase opened the way for the church to teach that sin is not individual transgressions, but a universal malady. As Dorothy Sayers wrote, it is "a deep interior dislocation at the very center of human personality."[66] W. H. Auden called it "The error bred in the bone."[67]

Poets and novelists often understand what good churchgoers do not. "The wages of living are sin," as poet Rita Dove wrote, paraphrasing Paul's "The wages of sin is death" (Rom. 6:23).[68] Particularly apt is the insight of Haze Motes in Flannery O'Connor's novel *Wise Blood*. Haze is apprehended by a crazed blind man who adjures him to repent of his sins. He is asked to renounce them by name, beginning with fornication and blasphemy. "They ain't nothing but words," says Haze. *"If I was in sin I was in it before I ever committed any"* (emphasis added).

In these last three paragraphs we have appeared to move away from our main theme, Sin as a Power, in order to show that sin can also be understood as a contagion or "deep interior dislocation."[69] All these metaphorical

65. *People,* February 10, 1986.

66. Dorothy L. Sayers, *Letters to a Diminished Church: Passionate Arguments for the Relevance of Christian Doctrine* (Nashville: Nelson, W Publishing Group, 2004), 59. In this entertaining but very serious collection, Sayers concocts a list of "sins" (p. 18) similar to the one in *People.*

67. Auden, "September 1939."

68. Rita Dove, "Black on a Saturday Night," in *On the Bus with Rosa Parks: Poems* (New York: Norton, 1999). It is rather sad that a major study of Dove's work does not even bother to identify the quotation from Romans (Therese Steffen in *Crossing Color* [New York: Oxford University Press, 2001], 148-49). This poem has been set to music by John Williams.

69. I will not say much in this book about the theme of contamination, infection, or defilement. This concern is linked to the rites of purification, which played a part in the worship of Israel (Num. 8:21; 19:12; Lev. 15; etc.). Purification from ritual uncleanness plays little part in the New Testament except as a foil for the teaching of Jesus, who in his struggles with the Pharisees taught that "what comes out of the mouth, this defiles a man" (Matt. 15:11) and did

ways of saying we are "in sin" are useful because they contradict the notion of sin as individual misdeeds. Paul is not unaware of these various modes of defining sin. For instance, when he says, "death spread to all men because all men sinned" (Rom. 5:12), he suggests contagion as well as conquest by a Power.[70] Following this line, Sin is not something *we commit;* it is something we, like Haze Motes, *are in.* However, Paul's overriding concern is to show that Sin is a Power holding our lives in thrall. Sin, theologically understood, is analogous to the unconscious impulses and drives that shape our personalities in harmful ways, making us perfectionists, procrastinators, deceivers, abusers, addicts, schemers, bullies, fanatics, adulterers, and all the other manifestations that afflict the human species from sources beyond our control. We do not understand Sin in terms of specific, discrete actions willfully committed, but as compulsions over which we have little or no control. This is not at all the same thing as excusing Sin by calling it neurosis. It should be apparent by now that the last thing we are recommending is any euphemistic downgrade in the status of Sin. What we want to emphasize is Sin's *power to enslave.*

Sentimentality: The Sacrifice of Fools

Even with the conspicuous coarsening of our public life and the greatly increased fear of dangers that requires us to lock our doors, get burglar alarms, and keep our children out of the streets, we Americans remain a sentimental people. Flannery O'Connor defines sentimentality as "a distortion . . . in the direction of an overemphasis on innocence." After discussing the fall of Adam and Eve, she writes, "Sentimentality is a skipping of this process [fall and redemption] in its concrete reality and an early arrival at a mock state of

---

not hesitate to touch lepers (Matt. 8:3). Likewise, Peter in Acts says, "What God has cleansed, you must not call common" (Acts 10:15). In his comprehensive study of what went wrong with the creation, Paul Ricoeur considers the theme of defilement within the whole biblical picture. His analysis of defilement or impurity is in some ways congruent with the concept of Sin as a Power (my capitalization); he writes that a "more archaic conception of fault is the notion of defilement . . . [a] stain or blemish that infects *from without.*" Note the "from without," which corroborates the notion of an Enemy that operates like a contaminant from beyond the sphere of human willpower. Ricoeur, *The Symbolism of Evil,* 8 (emphasis added), 12, 50.

70. The elderly, wise preacher in Marilynne Robinson's *Gilead* often reflects upon the ubiquity of the reign of Sin. He does not like the word "transgression." He muses, "There is never just one transgression. There is *a wound in the flesh of human life* that scars when it heals and often enough never seems to heal at all" (*Gilead* [New York: Farrar, Straus and Giroux, Picador, 2004], 122, emphasis added).

innocence."[71] This "early arrival" is the key to understanding sentimentality. It is the lazy person's way of receiving data about life, without struggle. It is apparently very important to us to believe in innocence. Such a belief is a stratagem for keeping unpleasant truth at bay; it is a form of denial.

In light of these tendencies, we do well to remember how utterly untouched the Bible is by sentimental manipulation of any kind; this has been universally acknowledged by a wide spectrum of unbelieving critics who read it as literature. Beginning with the murder of Abel by his brother Cain, we are given a full picture of human noninnocence. We have seen so many Sunday school pictures of dutiful children in biblical garb that we forget how utterly unblinking the Scriptures are about human nature. Far from being a collection of inspirational stories, the Old Testament is replete with unedifying R-rated tales of every conceivable kind of crime and villainy, much of it committed by men and women of God's own choosing.

Israeli writer Avishai Margalit took his country severely to task a few years ago for what he viewed as its sentimentality. He defines it thus: "Sentimentality distorts reality by way of turning the object (or event) represented into an object of complete innocence." It is closely linked to self-righteousness, he believes; it is "accompanied by total blindness to one's own defects."[72] If one can believe in innocence at all, it is only a short step from there to believing in *one's own* innocence; that is the point.[73] Anyone who believes in his own innocence is offering "the sacrifice of fools; for they do not know that they are doing evil" (Eccles. 5:1). A believer in innocence is going to be impervious to the biblical message about Sin. This is a strange thing about us. The more cynical and unshockable our culture becomes in a superficial sense, the more sentimentality it seems to pour forth; the more raw the sex and violence on TV and in film, the greater the demand, it seems, for nostalgic kitsch encouraging the pretense that we can escape to a Norman Rockwell world that never was.

---

71. O'Connor, "The Church and the Fiction Writer," from *Mystery and Manners* (New York: Farrar, Straus and Giroux, 1969).

72. Avishai Margalit, "The Kitsch of Israel," *New York Review of Books,* November 24, 1988.

73. During the civil rights movement, Will Campbell wrote, "There were no innocent [in the civil rights movement]. All were guilty, all were sinners and stood in desperate need of the message of judgment and redemption. . . . The new and dramatic protest movements . . . must [also] hear the gospel of the Lord who burns and heals. . . . We have moved into Christian social action from the wrong point of departure [he means the suffering of the victims, which is no different from the secular view of social action] and with a superficial understanding of the depth of man's involvement in sin" (*Race and the Renewal of the Church* [Philadelphia: Westminster, 1962], 48).

In some ways, however, it is becoming more difficult to close our eyes to reality. We are beginning to see more clearly now that children who rape and murder seem to be getting younger and younger, that no school or church seems to be safe from gunfire, that the Internet has greatly increased our capacity to share lethal information. Too many clergy have been arrested for child molestation, too many teachers have been caught sexually abusing students, too many supposedly upstanding citizens have downloaded too much child pornography. There is something sickening in human nature, and it corresponds precisely to the sickening aspects of crucifixion. The hideousness of crucifixion summons us to put away sentimentality and face up to the ugliness that lies just under the surface. The scandal, the outrage of the cross, is commensurate with the offense and the ubiquity of sin. Views of atonement wrought by Christ that do not acknowledge the gravity of Sin are untruthful in two respects: they are untruthful about the human condition, and they are untruthful about the witness of Holy Scripture, Old and New Testament alike. Sin is the colossal X-factor in human life. It is not something we do so much as it is something done to us by our mortal foe, the alien Power that has lured us into becoming its agents. There is no room for sentiment here; the stakes are too high. The cross rears up over all human life because it is the scene of God's climactic battle against the power of a malignant and implacable Enemy.

"The Discarded Notion of Man's Inherent Depravity"

Optimistic American Christianity resists the notion that the human race, left to itself, will self-destruct. Although the can-do American spirit has taken some hard hits in the twenty-first century, and the future for our nation is not as bright as it was, our politics continue to exhibit a self-righteousness that partners well with religious self-righteousness on both the right and the left. There is little of the tragic sense that Abraham Lincoln brought to his office and embodied so well in his leadership.[74] Understanding Sin requires us to recognize its power lodged in ourselves. The novelist William Golding has written of these matters as effectively as anyone. The *dénouement* of *Lord of the Flies* comes in the form of an oracle uttered by a slaughtered pig's head: "Fancy thinking the Beast was something you could hunt and kill! You

---

74. The Second Inaugural is the high point, but he exhibits this in a great many of his letters.

knew, didn't you? I'm part of you!"[75] After the climax in which terrible deeds are done by the "innocent" marooned boys, the novel ends on the explicit note of "the darkness of man's heart."[76] In comments made later about his devastating conclusion, Golding observed that the adult naval personnel who come to the rescue of the children appear trim and dignified, but will soon be off on their mission of man-hunting. "And who," Golding asks in his postscript, "will rescue the adult and his cruiser?"

Novelist Harry Crews writes of the community of fallen humanity in his memoirs. Desperately poor and deprived in rural Bacon County, Georgia, he and his black friend Willalee daydream about the models in the Sears catalogue as a form of escape. "Nearly everybody I knew had something missing, a finger cut off, a toe split, an ear half chewed away, an eye clouded with blindness from a glancing fence staple. . . . But the people in the catalogue had no such hurts. They were not only whole, . . . they were also beautiful." Even at an early age, however, Mr. Crews knew that the pictures were lying: "Under those fancy clothes there had to be scars, there had to be swellings and boils of one kind or another *because there was no other way to live in the world.* And . . . I had decided that all the people in the catalogue were related, not necessarily blood kin, but knew one another, and because they knew one another there had to be hard feelings, trouble between them off and on, violence, and hate between them as well as love."[77]

That is a good description of the human predicament under the rule of Sin. *There is no other way to live in the world.*

The relentlessly optimistic Scottish American tycoon Andrew Carnegie (1835-1919) wrote, in his memoirs, of a point in his development that he considered crucial:

> When I [was in a] state of doubt about theology, including the supernatu-
> ral element, and indeed the whole scheme of salvation through vicarious
> atonement and all the fabric built upon it, I came, fortunately, upon Dar-
> win's and Spencer's works "The Data of Ethics," "First Principles," "The
> Descent of Man." Reaching the pages which explain how man has absorbed
> such mental foods as were favorable to him, retaining what was salutary,

---

75. In an admittedly lighter vein, the immortal Pogo observed, "Yep, son, we have met the enemy and he is us." Comic strip by Walt Kelly. For an appreciation of the Pogo comic strip, see Brad Leithauser, "Lyrics in the Swamp," *New York Review of Books,* April 25, 2002.

76. What does it mean that this book has been assigned to American high school students ever since it first appeared in 1955, yet we are more sentimental than ever?

77. Harry Crews, *Childhood: The Biography of a Place* (Athens: University of Georgia Press, 1995), 58, emphasis added.

rejecting what was deleterious, I remember that light came as in a flood and all was clear. Not only had I got rid of theology and the supernatural, but I had found the truth of evolution. "All is well since all grows better," became my motto, my true source of comfort. Man was not created with an instinct for his own degradation, but from the lower he has risen to the higher forms. Nor is there any conceivable end to his march to perfection.

Can anyone read this with a straight face today? But this is not the last word from Carnegie, as it turns out. The last paragraph of the autobiography, which was never finished, reads in part as follows:

As I read this [what he had previously written] today what a change! The world convulsed by war as never before! Men slaying each other like wild beasts! I dare not relinquish all hope.

The manuscript breaks off abruptly.[78]

The horrors of the Great War, which shook Carnegie's optimism to its foundations, have since been half-forgotten as the Holocaust and the genocides of the later twentieth century have come to dominate our attention.[79] A great many people nevertheless remain deluded about human potential, in spite of so much evidence to the contrary. No human being has proven capable of breaking the grip of Sin and Death on the human race. Only God can do that. Evidence of God's doing is largely hidden from us, however. Christian hope is known to us *only in the mode of promise;* there is no way to prove empirically that the promise of God is trustworthy.[80] It can be grasped

---

78. Excerpts from Carnegie's memoirs quoted in "The Talk of the Town," *New Yorker,* November 22, 1982.

79. Notably, however, the 100th anniversary of the beginning of World War I in 2014 occasioned a significant number of articles and essays that cited that war as a colossal turning point in Western civilization and its view of itself (a particularly good example is A. O. Scott, "A War to End All Innocence: The Enduring Impact of World War I," *New York Times,* June 20, 2014).

80. I am grateful for conversations with David Tracy. Citing Simone Weil and Walter Benjamin, he suggests that the existence of radical evil, in his words, "blasts away" optimism and clears the way for hope. He is more drawn to "hints and guesses" — (T. S. Eliot: "the hint half guessed, the gift half understood") — than to apologetics grounded in rational attempts to convince. "In Christian theological terms this can be read as a preference for Mark's fragmentary, discontinuous apocalyptic gospel, expressed in fragments of the memory of suffering, over the Luke/Acts view of history as a fundamentally structured, continuous, realistic narrative." I would put this in more *theo*centric terms, but Tracy's insights about Mark and Luke/Acts, and his affinity for the apocalyptic milieu, is striking. (From my notes, conversations with David Tracy, Princeton, 1998.)

only by faith. It is therefore a betrayal of the gospel to succumb to sentimentality — the "sacrifice of fools" — as though God's saving work could be manifest in pure and untainted ways by "innocent" human beings. Events have shown that human progress is an illusion and that we live on the brink of the precipice all the time. Terrorist attacks since September 11, particularly the Boston Marathon bombing of 2013, have shaken our American tendency to think of ourselves as relatively immune to convulsions elsewhere.

Carnegie was right about one thing: "Man was not *created* with an instinct for his own degradation." On the contrary, humanity was created in the image of God and was pronounced good (Gen. 1:31). Catastrophically, however, the image of God was fractured in human nature as a result of "Adam's" disobedience, and the result has been the enslavement of human impulses, chillingly described in Genesis 4–11. The Adam-Christ story as the apostle Paul recovers and reworks it in Romans 5 is of central importance for a full understanding of Christ's work on the cross, and we will be referring to it many times. Indeed, in many ways it will be the capstone of this volume.

"Irredeemable Darkness" and the Price of Atonement

In the introduction we asked: What sort of predicament are you and I in that we should require the crucifixion of the Son of God? The magnitude of what God in Christ undertook on the cross requires a corresponding magnitude of interpretation. The degrading death of the Son of God demands a more-than-ordinary explanation. We have referred twice already to Anselm's thunderous warning to Boso, so much more impressive in the original Latin: *Nondum considerasti quanti ponderis peccatum sit* (you have not yet considered the gravity of sin).

Stephen Westerholm writes concerning the crucifixion, "So catastrophic a remedy demands a catastrophic predicament."[81] The crucifixion of Jesus is of such magnitude that it must call forth a concept of sin that is large enough to match it. In Leviticus, the instructions given for making sin and guilt offerings indicate that a *value* was assigned to the offerings (Lev. 5:14–6:7). It is only implied, but there is a hint of a suggestion that there should be some sort of equivalence between the value of the offering and the magnitude of the offense. Looking at Jesus on the cross, we see

---

81. Stephen Westerholm, "Righteousness, Cosmic and Microcosmic," in *Apocalyptic Paul: Cosmos and Anthropos in Romans,* ed. Beverly R. Gaventa (Waco: Baylor University Press, 2013), 33.

the degradation and Godforsakenness of it, and we see the corresponding gravity, the weight, of sin. This cluster of ideas is related to the conception of the crucifixion as *satisfaction.* Not to push the hint in Leviticus too far, it suggests a correspondence between the value of the sacrifice and the weight of the guilt, or sin. If we transfer this notion of value to the cross, noting the extreme dehumanization and humiliation of it, we may conclude that the gravity of sin was so great that no correspondence in heaven or earth was weighty enough except the self-offering of the Son of God — not by the swift guillotine blade, but by submitting to the degradation of crucifixion.

The editor of the *New Yorker,* David Remnick, wrote of Aharon Appelfeld's novels, "In all Appelfeld's books the subject is invariably the apocalyptic fall from innocence the Holocaust represents both to the Jewish people and to mankind — the sense of relative innocence before and the terrible, *irredeemable* darkness after."[82] This is the conclusion David Remnick, no less than Anselm, has come to; the situation is "irredeemable." "All for sin could not atone."

The concept of irredeemable evil shows up in surprising places. Here is an excerpt from *The Autobiography of Malcolm X:*

> I believe that God now is giving the world's so-called "Christian" white society its last opportunity to repent and atone for the crimes of exploiting and enslaving the world's non-white peoples. . . . Does white America have the capacity to repent — and to atone?
>
> Many black men, the victims — in fact most black men — would like to be able to forgive, to forget, the crimes. But most American white people seem not to have it in them to make any serious atonement. . . . Indeed, how *can* white society atone for enslaving, for raping, for unmanning, for otherwise brutalizing millions of human beings, for centuries? What atonement would the God of Justice demand for the robbery of the black people's labor, their lives, their true identities, their culture, their history — and even their human dignity? A desegregated cup of coffee, a theater, public toilets — the whole range of hypocritical "integration" — these are not atonement.[83]

82. David Remnick, in "Book Currents," *New Yorker,* June 22-29, 1998.

83. Alex Haley and Malcolm X, *The Autobiography of Malcolm X* (New York: Grove Press, 1965), 376. We will never know what the loss of Malcolm X cost America. This excerpt is an example of his angry anti-Christian rhetoric, yet embedded in it is a suggestion that forgiveness is possible, even desirable.

There has been a trend in the mainline churches to steer away from the concept of atonement, but Malcolm simply assumes its necessity and uses the word unapologetically, as if it had a plain meaning. Most especially we should note his hint that atonement is *not possible*. "How *can* white society atone?" "What atonement would the God of Justice demand?" His use of the word "atonement" highlights both the gravity of the offense and the impossibility of a human attempt at rectification.

This accumulating testimony should suggest to us that nothing short of a world-overturning transformation will suffice to reverse the effects of Sin.[84]

Summary and Conclusion: The Reign of Sin and Death

Sin cannot be overcome by human determination, human capacity, or human moral resolve. It is false and misleading, and untrue to human nature, to continue to think of Sin in terms of individual, avoidable acts or failures to act. Sin and its cohort, Death, rule over the *kosmos* as semi-autonomous Powers. This, however, is not the way we Americans ordinarily think. We believe that we can resist Sin (not that we call it that!) by "making good choices," and Death we keep at bay simply by not thinking about it, or by domesticating it. The biblical story places us correctly within a completely different worldview.

No novelist in our time has conveyed this worldview with more authority than Cormac McCarthy. In *The Crossing,* we meet one of his enigmatic sages: "The old man [said that] the wolf . . . knows what men do not: *that there is no order in the world save that which death has put there.*"[85] Most of McCarthy's novels set out this picture of Death as a Power ranging throughout the world claiming its victims through violence. In his masterpiece, *Blood Meridian,* he illustrates Paul's description of "the whole creation . . . groaning in travail" in its "bondage to decay" (Rom. 8:21-22). McCarthy describes the hostile landscape through which the murdering raiders ride, in which even its relentless blowing dust, "the very sediment of things," is animated with Death: "As if in the transit of those riders were a thing so profoundly terrible as to register even to the uttermost granulation of reality." Shortly after, he invokes the crucifixion in this universe of terror: "On a rise at the western edge of the

---

84. Paul Minear reaches for this in his book titled *The Golgotha Earthquake: Three Witnesses* (Cleveland: Pilgrim Press, 1995). See especially 89, 122-25.

85. Cormac McCarthy, *The Border Trilogy: The Crossing* (New York: Knopf, Everyman's Library, 1999), 45, emphasis added.

playa they passed a crude wooden cross where Maricopas had crucified an Apache. . . . They rode on."[86] The juxtaposition of utmost horror and cruciform imagery is clearly intentional, and the passing of the riders evokes the biblical picture: "Is it nothing to you, all you who pass by?" (Lam. 1:12).[87]

McCarthy invokes Death rather than Sin, but we can't emphasize strongly enough that ever since Adam, the two Powers have been hand in hand. Romans 7 lays it out, and in verses 23-24 Paul explicitly links "the law of sin" with the "body of death." Thus the murdering Glanton gang in *Blood Meridian* "rode like men invested with a purpose whose origins were antecedent to them, like blood legatees of an order both imperative and remote."[88] His terrifying central character, Judge Holden, asks,

"What do you think death is, man? . . . What is death if not an agency?" He picks out a man from the crowd in the cantina to use as an example: Can he say, such a man, that there is no malign power set against him? That there is no power and no force and no cause? What manner of heretic could doubt agency and claimant alike? . . . To whom is he talking, man? Can't you see him?[89]

In this way McCarthy builds up a comprehensive picture of Death as an annihilating *agency* capable of commandeering human *agents* to do its work

86. Cormac McCarthy, *Blood Meridian* (New York: Vintage International, 1992), 247. McCarthy's often-repeated refrain, "They rode on," gives an impression of an ineluctable destiny, as though the "profoundly terrible . . . transit of those riders" were a forced march driven by Death itself. Which, indeed, it was and is. (McCarthy constructed his masterpiece as a symphonic expansion of, and a protracted meditation upon, the historical career of the Glanton gang, a notorious band of scalp hunters in the Mexican borderland in 1849-1850.)

87. The text from the book of Lamentations continues, in words long associated with the crucifixion of Christ:

> "Look and see
> if there is any sorrow like my sorrow
>   which was brought upon me,
> which the Lord inflicted
>   on the day of his fierce anger.
> From on high he sent fire;
>   into my bones he made it descend;
> he spread a net for my feet." (Lam. 1:12-13)

The link of God's judgment with the cross is a time-honored one, as we have already discussed, although we should always understand this from a Trinitarian perspective (not taking the imagery so far as to separate the Father from the Son in any essential way).

88. McCarthy, *Blood Meridian*, 152.

89. McCarthy, *Blood Meridian*, 329-30.

(the judge being an archetypal, bone-chilling example of such an agent). If it is difficult for us to think of ourselves as agents of Sin and Death on the scale of McCarthy's judge, we need to develop our biblical antennae so we can see how the agencies of Sin and Death infect entire structures that then become malign Powers of their own — perhaps most readily understood by us in concrete terms like Dwight D. Eisenhower's famous warning about a "military-industrial complex." This has been illustrated in our own day by the pernicious interconnection of the Pentagon with the Blackwater company of independent contractors during the Iraq War.[90] There is no escape, humanly speaking, from the hermetically sealed orb of these Powers. We can only look for deliverance from another sphere of power altogether. "How long, O Lord?"[91]

And yet this chapter about Sin concludes as it began, on a note of joy. God's grace comes unsuspected, invading our circumscribed sphere in which we contrive fruitlessly to exonerate ourselves. The knowledge that we are imprisoned by Sin is not a *prior condition* for restoration. Such knowledge *arises out of,* and is therefore *overcome by,* the joyful tidings of redemption and release. In this glad certainty of new life, the people of God go to their knees to acknowledge their need for a deliverance from Sin *that they have already received.*

And so we end this chapter in the same key that we began. The grace of God *prepares the way for* the confession of sin, *is present in* the confession, and even before the confession is made has already worked the restoration of which the confession is *not the cause, but the sign.*

90. Blackwater operated within a culture of impunity, which always unleashes the worst in human nature.

91. This anguished cry is found in numerous places, e.g., Pss. 13:1; 35:17; 79:5; 94:3; Isa. 6:11; Jer. 12:4; Hab. 1:2; Rev. 6:10.

PART 2

The Biblical Motifs

Motifs of the Crucifixion

Will It Preach?

Having laid the groundwork in part 1, we look in part 2 at major images and themes used in Scripture to interpret the cross of Christ. There are some problems with separating out the motifs in this way. This book, however, is written with only half an eye cocked toward the academy of professional scholars. Its major concern is with the classic challenge: "Will it preach?" and, by extension, will it teach? Will it offer illumination and encouragement to Christians who are not necessarily theologically trained but seek to deepen their understanding? The hope is that readers who have been intimidated by the scholarly disputes might find some encouragement here for their own preaching, teaching, Bible study, social action, and personal faith.

Discerning what exactly is meant by "Jesus Christ and him crucified," however, is a considerable challenge. If the universe of self-identified believers were asked the question, "What happened when Jesus was crucified?" there is a good chance that, even in this era of high suspicion about sin, many respondents would automatically fall back on the traditional biblical language, saying, "Jesus died for our sins." Another answer, representing the influences discussed in the introduction, would likely be, "To show us how much God loves us." Many evangelicals would typically say, "Jesus took my place on the cross." If asked for more detail, however, even lifelong churchgoers might be hard pressed to say more. Everyone recognizes the cross as a symbol of Christianity, but there is widespread bafflement about its interpretation. Here in part 2, we will focus on various ways in which the Bible proclaims and interprets the crucifixion.

How to Group the Motifs

The purpose of part 2 is indeed the concern of this entire volume: to identify the various themes and motifs used by the New Testament to expound
the crucifixion of Christ *and to locate them within the biblical narrative so as
to avoid forcing that narrative into one narrow theoretical tunnel.*[1] Physicists
use the term "unitary" to denote an underlying consistency in a seemingly
contradictory collection of data; the proposal here is that there is a unitary
reality underlying the varying biblical accounts of Christ's crucifixion (and
resurrection, for that matter), and that the multiplicity of motifs attests to
the same truth.[2]

   The biblical images and concepts have been divided into eight chapters.
There are difficulties inherent in this structure. For one thing, eight chapters
does not mean there are only eight images. For another, the division of biblical themes into separate chapters might undermine the central concern of
this book to show how the images often overlap and interpret one another.
A third problem is that the chapter headings themselves may seem arbitrary.
In the past, scholars have often grouped the themes into three convenient
categories.[3] The division into eight is more than is usual in such projects.
This is because *the actual biblical imagery* is being invoked rather than certain
theological positions or even what Stephen Sykes calls "idea-complexes."[4]
There are actually more than eight motifs, and it is impossible to add them
up, or even agree on what they are. No such grouping will ever be definitive, and of course this study, like all others, will be open to criticism that
the actual biblical images are indeed being defined here as theological idea-

---

   1. It is a bit disappointing that the penal substitution model is still being defended as the
only one to have, as recently as 2014 (Donald MacLeod, *Christ Crucified: Understanding the
Atonement* [Downers Grove, Ill.: InterVarsity, 2014]).

   2. Stuart Crampton, professor of physics and provost (retired) at Williams College, introduced me to the unitary concept.

   3. Various scholars have proposed different groupings of three. Gustav Aulén's grouping
was familiar to generations of theological students: (1) "Objective" or Latin view (Anselm);
(2) "Subjective" view (Abelard); (3) "Classic" view: *Christus Victor* (the Fathers, Martin Luther). Aulén's classification of three is based on the history of interpretation. In my own teaching over the years I have used a grouping based on the biblical images themselves: (1) *Christus
Victor:* Jesus identified as the conqueror of the demonic powers; (2) *Sacrifice:* Jesus identified
as the unblemished offering for sin; (3) *Substitution:* Jesus identified as the judge judged in our
place. I eventually became dissatisfied with this division into three and now prefer the twofold
emphasis set out in the following section.

   4. Stephen W. Sykes, *The Story of Atonement,* Trinity and Truth Series (London: Darton,
Longman, and Todd, 1997), 88.

complexes. Nevertheless, part 2 should give readers some idea of the depths and riches of the biblical witness.

Wherever controversial decisions have been made, they will be explained at the place they occur. Continuing controversies about cross-interpretation suggest that a dynamic, flexible *combination* of the various themes and motifs in the Old and New Testaments is the best way to proceed.

A Proposed Two-Part Approach: Atonement and Deliverance

As a preliminary exercise, let us think in terms of *two* overall categories, rather than three (let alone eight). These two are more or less applicable to each of the motifs examined, and have already been anticipated in the preceding chapters. The two categories, taken together, encompass, in one way or another, the multifarious biblical imagery as fairly as any categories could. Taking the Scriptures as a whole, considering the Old Testament and the four Gospels together with the Epistles and Revelation, we see two things happening in the cross of Christ:

> **God's definitive action in making vicarious atonement for sin:** the cross is understood as sacrifice, sin offering, guilt offering, expiation, and substitution. Related motifs are the scapegoat, the Lamb of God, and the Suffering Servant of Isaiah 53.
>
> **God's decisive victory over the alien Powers of Sin and Death:** the cross is understood as victory over the Powers and deliverance from bondage, slavery, and oppression. Related themes are the new exodus, the harrowing of hell, and *Christus Victor.* This category is particularly linked to the kingdom of God and as such is strongly future-oriented.

These two categories are parallels to the two crucial points laid out in chapter 4: *atonement for* sin as a responsible guilt and *deliverance from* it as an alien power. We should of course be wary of being held strictly to these two categories. There is overlapping and blending. However, there are good reasons for highlighting and differentiating them, and for insisting on the importance of each. As we proceed, we will refer sometimes to sin as guilt and sometimes to Sin as a Power, for *both* are true to the biblical witness. Following Paul, however, our chief emphasis will be on Sin as a Power.

Since the Reformation, the sad divisions in the church have often been marked by bitter disputes about the nature of the atonement, with some parties insisting that only one explanation of it is correct and others are erroneous. This has been a difficult stance to maintain, since there was never a Council of Nicaea or Chalcedon to determine an orthodox position regarding the crucifixion, as there was about the nature of Christ and the Holy Trinity. The strong reaction in recent decades against "theories" of the atonement has actually been useful. "Theories" are spun out of human mental capacity, and we are dealing here with an event far beyond human mental capacity.

Leanne Van Dyke puts it well, from a Reformed perspective:

> Atonement theories do not claim to define or explicate the inner mechanics of salvation. They seek to express in limited, analogical language the reality of God's decisive act on behalf of a broken world. There was some kind of victory that took place, some kind of power shift in the universe, some kind of ransom paid, some kind of healing initiated, some ultimate kind of love displayed, some kind of dramatic rescue effected. Of course, the terrible paradox of the Christian faith is that this rescue, this victory, this healing happened because of a death — a notorious public execution. This is the dark mystery of the Atonement. No theory of the atonement can effectively account for that central paradox. Rather, the range of atonement theories attempt to focus our attention, illuminate the truth and point beyond themselves to God.[5]

The Role of Imagination and the Role of History

Biblical interpretation today is plagued by literal-mindedness. This is by no means a problem restricted to "fundamentalists" (a more accurate and useful term is "inerrantists"). Literal-mindedness is widespread in the mainline churches and in secular settings as well. A person who considers himself an enlightened Bible reader will complain about the naïve conception of "up" and "down" in the story of Christ's ascension, and in the next breath will say he is going "up" in the elevator or that a friend is "moving up" in her company.[6]

---

5. Leanne Van Dyk, "Do Theories of Atonement Foster Abuse?" *Dialog* 35, no. 1 (Winter 1996).

6. Raymond Brown gives an amusing illustration of literal-mindedness in one of his footnotes: "Every year before Christmas I am contacted by newspaper reporters who have hit on the bright idea of writing a Christmas column on the stories of Jesus' birth and have learned that I wrote a long commentary on them. Almost unfailingly they [state] that the only focus of the article will be 'What actually happened?' . . . With little success I try to

Much of today's literal-mindedness is doubtless owing to the fact that fewer and fewer people read novels and poetry.[7] Much of the complaining that we hear about atonement language, for example, is owing to a misunderstanding about the way that language works. Sallie McFague is very good on this point: "The poet mounts many metaphors, many ways of seeing 'this' as 'that,' many attempts to 'say' what cannot be said directly. The poet sets one metaphor against another, and hopes that the sparks set off by the juxtaposition will ignite something in the mind as well."[8]

This is particularly valuable for its description of the way that one image interacts with another, setting off "sparks"; this is a goal of the presentation in these pages.

Overly rationalistic "theories" force the pictorial, poetic, and narrative structures of the Bible into restrictive categories. Even the writings of Paul, often construed as dry doctrine over against the more accessible stories of the Gospels, are for the most part urgently contextual. Paul is a man on a battlefield. He is a man seized by the gospel story, or, more accurately, by the Lord of the story. The fact that Paul has made the story into a sword of the Word to be wielded against the enemies of the gospel in specific situations, rather than retelling stories about Jesus' life, does not make his preaching any less firmly grounded in The Story.[9] For that matter, even Anselm, whose rationalism is so much excoriated, will be seen by a sympathetic reader as anything but indifferent to the biblical tapestry. He wrote, "Many other things

---

convince them that they could promote understanding of the birth stories by concentrating on the message of those stories instead of on an issue that was very far from primary in the detectable mind of the evangelists. That effort usually leaves the reporters convinced that they have been misdirected to a pious preacher who knows nothing about the important issues" (Raymond E. Brown, *The Death of the Messiah: From Gethsemane to the Grave; A Commentary on the Passion Narratives in the Four Gospels,* 2 vols. [Garden City, N.Y.: Doubleday, 1994], 1:24 n).

7. Eugene Peterson has said that he would like to assign a whole year of reading literature to seminary students.

8. Sallie McFague, *Speaking in Parables: A Study in Metaphor and Theology* (Philadelphia: Fortress, 1975), 39. Cousar quotes this passage from McFague also, in a section dealing with Paul's allusive language (Charles B. Cousar, *A Theology of the Cross: The Death of Jesus in the Pauline Letters,* Overtures to Biblical Theology [Minneapolis: Augsburg Fortress, 1990], 86).

9. "Although the crucifixion of Christ was indeed an event in history, it punctures other times and other stories not just as a past event recalled but as a present event that, in an important sense, happens anew for its hearers [as it did for Paul] . . . in 'a revelation of Jesus Christ' [Galatians 1:12]." John M. G. Barclay, "Paul's Story: Theology as Testimony," in *Narrative Dynamics in Paul: A Critical Assessment,* ed. Bruce Longenecker (Louisville: Westminster John Knox, 2002).

also, if we carefully examine them, give a certain indescribable beauty to our redemption as thus procured."[10]

We are not suggesting, however, that feeling is more important than understanding. Paul Ricoeur wrote, "The symbol gives rise to *thought*," not to emotion.[11] Gustav Aulén wrote that the biblical images were only "popular helps" to aid the reader in understanding the idea, but Charles Cousar rightly faults Aulén on this, accusing Aulén of not recognizing "the generative power of the metaphor."[12] It is precisely this *generative power* that will be sought as we look at the various images the New Testament uses in speaking of the crucifixion.

We can never lose sight of the fact, however, that *the cross itself is not a metaphor.* The purpose of the metaphors and images used in the New Testament is to help us to understand, and above all to respond to, the *historical event.* Here, above all, is where we part company with those who read the Bible exclusively as literature. In the literary journal the *New York Review of Books,* the English scholar J. M. Cameron wields a scalpel to divide metaphor from history, referring to the Bible's message concerning

> what lies *outside* the poetic myth or the literary aspect. . . . There are many instances of this. I choose only one: Paul's insistence on *the non-mythical, historical, brutally factual character of the crucifixion.* When he writes that "we preach Christ crucified, a stumbling block to Jews and folly to Gentiles," we may gloss what he says as follows. To the Gentiles, the preaching is foolish, for the Greek world is full of stories about dying, suffering, and resurrected gods, but these things happen *in illo tempore* ["in that time," used to mean an indeterminate past time] . . . not "under Pontius Pilate." As to the Jews, here is the Messiah of promise, this scarecrow figure on a gibbet; and for this to be a stumbling block it has to be as historical as the Roman procurator under whom the crucifixion happened.[13]

Cameron's boldness in pushing this point to the fore in a determinedly secular intellectual journal is a cause for thanksgiving. This is the crux (lit-

---

10. *Cur Deus Homo?* 1.3. Anselm's prayers have a beauty of their own. This is not to deny that *Cur Deus Homo?* suffers from an overly schematic scholasticism.

11. Paul Ricoeur, *The Symbolism of Evil* (Boston: Beacon Press, 1967), 19, 237.

12. Cousar, *Theology of the Cross,* 86.

13. J. M. (James Monro) Cameron, "A Good Read," *New York Review of Books,* April 15, 1982, emphasis added. Cameron, an Oxford graduate in philosophy, was a respected lecturer in the UK and a professor in the University of Toronto. He was the Terry Lecturer at Yale in 1964-1965. A Roman Catholic, he wrote with great sensitivity about theological matters.

erally) where "religion" and the gospel of Jesus Christ split off from one another. The "speech-event" that came into being when the Christian message burst upon the scene was not evoked by literary imagination.[14] It was called forth by the resurrection of the dead.

Looking Ahead

The aim of part 2 is to present in some detail the multiplicity of motifs used in the New Testament to convey the epochal significance of the cross of Christ. The goal is to allow each motif to speak in both literary/metaphorical and literal/historical ways, as the context requires, and to support a deepened commitment to preaching, teaching, praying, and working in the total context of this rich tapestry, not selecting some threads to the exclusion of others, but allowing them all to interact with one another.

---

14. "Speech-event" is Amos Wilder's phrase. Amos Wilder, *Early Christian Rhetoric* (Cambridge: Harvard University Press, 1971), 18.

CHAPTER FIVE

The Passover and the Exodus

Old and New Testaments

What should we learn from the Old Testament about the cross of Christ? The relation of the New Testament to the Old is a topic of vast scope that continues to generate much discussion. However that may be, the Old Testament is the living Word of God for the Christian community.[1] The current state of neglect of the Old Testament in the churches is cause for great concern. In attempting to understand what the Bible is saying to us about the crucifixion of the Son of God, it is essential that we listen carefully, with understanding, to the many voices that come to us from the history of Israel.[2]

The importance of what Christians know as the Old Testament can hardly be overstated. The Hebrew Scriptures were mined by the apostolic authors as they proclaimed the gospel of the cross and resurrection. The Old

1. It has become the vogue in many mainline churches to refer to the Old Testament as the "Hebrew Scriptures." One's intentions in doing so are generally of the best, for they arise out of a wish to honor the primacy of the Jews in God's plan of salvation. However, as a number of Old Testament specialists have recently pointed out, the Old Testament is not the same thing as the Hebrew Scriptures; the books are arranged in a different order and give a quite different impression for that reason. It is verging on presumption for Christians to appropriate the Tanakh (Hebrew Bible) by calling the Old Testament the Hebrew Scriptures, even with the best of intentions. It might be more respectful to acknowledge the differences and allow for the distinction. The real challenge for the church is not terminology. It is recovering — in preaching, teaching, and worship — the place of honor that the Old Testament should have. If it is not intentionally and consistently preached and taught, the current practice of reading selections from it in worship along with two New Testament readings will not take us very far.

2. The relationship between the Testaments is discussed at greater length in the introduction to my collection of Old Testament sermons, *And God Spoke to Abraham* (Grand Rapids: Eerdmans, 2011).

Testament is not just a source of further information for the New Testament, or an interesting sideshow attached to it, or even the indispensable prelude to it. The New Testament *will not work* without the Old Testament. Jesus of Nazareth knew no other Scriptures than the Law and the Prophets. The apostles knew no other Scriptures. The New Testament is inconceivable without the First Testament. It was not simply a history book. It was the living lode from which to discover the meaning of what the God of Israel had done among them.[3]

In emphasizing the necessary character of the Old Testament and its relation to the story of Jesus Christ, however, we should understand that there is also a certain discontinuity between the old covenant and the new. Just how much discontinuity there is, and exactly how it manifests itself, is a matter of lively debate, and the subject will be further developed later in these pages. For the present, we affirm with Roy A. Harrisville that the *novum* (new thing) of the gospel is "eschatologically" new. That is, the New Testament gospel "possesses a dynamic that renders continuity with the old possible only on condition that the old retain its status as servant of the new."[4] The discussion about discontinuity will continue throughout these pages; the essential point here is that anyone seeking to understand the cross or anything else about God in Jesus Christ in its fullness must know the First Testament well. Throughout the New Testament, a thorough knowledge of the Hebrew Scriptures, particularly the Law and the Prophets, and a commitment to their authority as Word of God are simply presupposed.

The Theme of Deliverance

In the introduction to part 2, *two broad categories* were proposed for understanding the themes and motifs concerning the crucifixion:

3. Three books from different perspectives are helpful in reflecting upon the two Testaments: *The Character of Christian Scripture: The Significance of a Two-Testament Bible* by Christopher R. Seitz (Grand Rapids: Baker Academic, 2011), *The God of Israel and Christian Theology* by Kendall Soulen (Minneapolis: Augsburg Fortress, 1996), and *The Conversion of the Imagination: Paul as Interpreter of Israel's Scripture* by Richard Hays (Grand Rapids: Eerdmans, 2005).

4. Roy A. Harrisville, *Fracture: The Cross as Irreconcilable in the Language and Thought of the Biblical Writers* (Grand Rapids: Eerdmans, 2006), 60. Harrisville gives his book about the "word of the cross" the title *Fracture* in order to throw the strongest possible spotlight on the turn of the ages that comes with the Christ event. At stake is the radicality of the gospel. In the cross and resurrection of Jesus Christ, do we see something entirely new? This question will confront us at every stage of this book.

1. There is *sin and guilt* for which *atonement* needs to be made.
2. There is *slavery, bondage, and oppression* from which humankind needs *to be delivered.*

Both categories will function in mutual interrelatedness throughout these pages. In this chapter, the second category, *deliverance from bondage,* comes to the fore. The original narrative of deliverance is the Ur-story of the Israelites, the fundamental event of the exodus from Egypt that forever after defined the identity of the Hebrew people, as shown by the ancient credo embedded in the book of Deuteronomy:

> "A wandering Aramean was my father; and he went down into Egypt and sojourned there, few in number; and there he became a nation, great, mighty, and populous. And the Egyptians treated us harshly, and afflicted us, and laid upon us hard bondage. Then we cried to the Lord the God of our fathers, and the Lord heard our voice, and saw our affliction, our toil, and our oppression; and the Lord brought us out of Egypt with a mighty hand and an outstretched arm, with great terror, with signs and wonders; and he brought us into this place and gave us this land, a land flowing with milk and honey. And behold, now I bring the first of the fruit of the ground, which thou, O Lord, hast given me." (Deut. 26:5-10)

Patrick Miller writes that the Great Credo is "the paradigm of God's way with God's people . . . a way that is attested from the first outcry of human pain when Abel's blood cried out from the ground, through the cries of the victims of Sodom and Gomorrah, the people under oppression in the time of the Judges, an exiled people in Babylon, and the suffering ones whose voice is heard in the psalms of lament, to the cry of abandonment of God's righteous sufferer on the cross."[5]

Passover and Lord's Supper

To this day, Jews continue to say "we" instead of "they" when they tell the story of the exodus during the Passover Seder. This is of the greatest significance, deriving from the way the Bible itself consistently understands the

---

5. Patrick D. Miller, *Deuteronomy,* Interpretation Series (Louisville: John Knox, 1990), 182.

exodus as a living event. For instance, hundreds of years after the events at the Red Sea, the prophet Amos writes:

> Thus says the Lord: . . .
> "I brought *you* up out of the land of Egypt,
> and led *you* forty years in the wilderness,
> to possess the land of the Amorite." (Amos 2:6, 10)

The old story about the fathers and mothers becomes the new story for the generation just emerging, who become actors in the story as their parents and grandparents did before them. If the tale remains simply a stirring narrative about a past episode, however "inspirational," then it is not the life-transforming story that ancient Israel knew it to be. To quote a Jewish source, "tradition properly understood enables us to tell our communal story . . . in each of our own individual life stories, such that in the process, we become transformed. For then we no longer simply study or recite the story; instead, *we become* the story."[6] Gratitude for the saving acts of God results, as in the ancient Deuteronomic credo, in living out the story through the presentation of the firstfruits, an essentially *theological* idea that has made a lasting imprint even upon secular, assimilated Jews whose philanthropic instincts and concern for strangers and sojourners have remained notable into the present day.[7]

The Passover Seder is ordained in the Torah: "This day shall be for you a memorial day, and you shall keep it as a feast to the Lord. . . . You shall observe the feast of unleavened bread, for on this very day I brought your hosts out of the land of Egypt: therefore you shall observe this day, throughout your generations, as an ordinance for ever" (Exod. 12:14, 17). The Passover is to be observed as a "memorial day." Biblically understood, this is a world removed from what we usually mean by "memorial." Memory (remembrance) in biblical thought does not mean "calling to mind." "Remembering" means *present and active*. That is the reason for the statement in the Passover Haggadah that it was not our ancestors who were brought by God out of bondage into freedom,

6. Michael Goldberg, *Jews and Christians: Getting Our Stories Straight* (Philadelphia: Trinity, 1991), 99, comma and emphasis added.

7. Frederick P. Rose, New York philanthropist, was approached (two months before his death) by a friend proposing that they raise a million dollars for Kosovar Muslim refugees during the "ethnic cleansing" of 1999. Rose readily agreed but stipulated that the money be collected through the American Jewish Committee, "because we want to show the world that Jewish people are helping Muslims." Two days later they had $1.4 million in hand (obituary of Frederick P. Rose, *New York Times*, September 16, 1999).

but we ourselves. The Seder supper is not a memorial of God's saving action in the past, but an appropriation of that same saving power in the present.[8]

This whole matter of remembrance is very important for biblical understanding. The exodus story begins this way: "The people of Israel groaned under their bondage, and cried out for help, and their cry under bondage came up to God. And God heard their groaning, and God remembered his covenant with Abraham, with Isaac, and with Jacob. And God saw the people of Israel, and God knew their condition" (Exod. 2:23-25).[9]

This passage has sometimes been made to seem ridiculous, as though it meant that God had forgotten — the Israelites had just slipped his mind somehow — and now he has suddenly recalled them. Similarly, prayers asking God to "remember" have been misunderstood — as though God needed us to remind him of something that he might otherwise forget! That was never the meaning of *remembering* in the prayers of the church. Remembering in Scripture refers to present action. If a woman prays to God to *remember* her mother, that does not mean "please think about my mother from time to time." It means, "Take action on behalf of my mother." Similarly, if we say that the Lord's Supper is a "memorial," we do not mean that we are simply *thinking about* Jesus' last supper. When we repeat Jesus' words, "do this in remembrance of me," in the communion service, we do not simply call Jesus to mind. Jesus is *actively present with power* in the communion of the people. Disputes about the Lord's Supper have divided the Christian church, but understanding the biblical concept of remembrance can help us. We are not just *thinking about* Jesus' actions in the upper room; we acknowledge that *he is present and acting* with the community gathered at the table in the present time. The doctrine of the real presence of Jesus in the

---

8. Imitations of the Passover Seder during Holy Week in Christian churches were popular for a while as well-meaning Christians attempted to get in touch with their Jewish roots, but this experiment is now falling out of favor. The real Jewish Seder is held in the home, in the bosom of family and friends. This can't be duplicated in a church hall. Imitation Seders do not really work either as liturgical rites or as familial gatherings.

9. One frequently reads or hears in the popular media that modern archaeology has proven that the events described in Genesis and Exodus never happened. This sort of thing is very disturbing to believers who have no context for understanding such pronouncements. F. W. Dillistone is helpful on this point: "Whatever conclusions may be reached about the patriarchal stories — how far they contain reliable accounts of what actually happened in the period before the Exodus — there can be little doubt that a group of Hebrews who had been enslaved in Egypt were brought out into a new kind of freedom under the leadership of Moses and that the general pattern of this redemption has never been erased from the national memory. Though Moses was the human agent, the true Saviour and Redeemer had been Yahweh Himself" (*The Christian Understanding of Atonement* [Philadelphia: Westminster, 1968], 81).

Lord's Supper can be understood in this way by everyone, from the most sophisticated person to the simplest.

The Passover and the exodus are reflected in the Lord's Supper in a number of ways, all of which underscore the active presence of God doing something completely new, even as the ancient saving event is recalled as the prototype. The *something-completely-new* is that this time, instead of intervening from on high as in the exodus, the intervention has taken place *from within God's own life, in the form of the Son's self-offering.* That sacrifice is described in terms based on the crossing of the Red Sea; as the eucharistic prayer in the Episcopal liturgy puts it: "He has brought us from bondage into freedom, from sin into righteousness, from death into life." The passage of God's Son from death to life is recapitulated in the prayer and, with that "us," becomes our story just as in the Passover Haggadah. The exodus imagery is right there for those who have learned to look for it.

Jesus' death has been construed from the very earliest moments of the Christian church as the new Passover, and his resurrection as the new exodus. Chronologically within the New Testament, the earliest explicit connection is made in I Corinthians 5:7-8, widely dated no more than twenty-five years after the resurrection — "Christ, our paschal lamb [*pascha,* meaning Passover in Greek], has been sacrificed. Let us, therefore, celebrate the festival, not with the old leaven, the leaven of malice and evil, but with the unleavened bread of sincerity and truth." All four Gospels — with John, as usual, offering a somewhat different picture within the same framework — place the passion narrative specifically within a Passover setting. The emphasis is upon two main themes:

1. *Rescue from death,* as on the night when the dark angel "passed over" the homes of the Israelites.
2. *Deliverance from slavery,* as in the climactic passage through the Red Sea.[10]

The blood of the "Passover lamb" was not, in this context, an offering for sin, but God's own ordained means of preserving his people from death. Moving the Last Supper forward one night to make Jesus' actual death coincide with the slaughter of the Passover lambs, however, as the Fourth Evan-

10. Many commentaries today refer to the "sea of reeds" or Reed Sea. No doubt the original body of water crossed — assuming that there was one — was considerably less prepossessing than the actual Red Sea. However, it seems to me that when a phrase from the Bible has been honored in song and story for so long, and has meant so much to so many, it should remain in the traditional form.

gelist does, is extremely audacious, combining as it does within one Gospel the concrete identification of Jesus not only as a sin offering ("Behold, the Lamb of God, who takes away the sin of the world" — John 1:29) but also as the Passover lamb whose blood saves from death. Yet another breathtaking step is taken by I Peter when the Passover lamb (1:19) is put in proximity to the Suffering Servant of Isaiah 53 in I Peter 2:23-24. These are examples of the imaginative leaps that make the biblical witness so inexhaustible.

The Exodus from an Eschatological Perspective

Viewed from a New Testament perspective, we see the impetus for projecting the exodus into the future as an eschatological event already present in the Old Testament. *Eschaton* in Greek means "last." To speak of the eschaton, therefore, means to speak of the Last Judgment, the second coming, the new heaven and new earth — traditionally grouped under the heading of the last things. However, eschatology is not so much a cluster of topics as it is a thought-world. A good basic definition is that of C. K. Barrett: "In characteristically eschatological thinking, the significance of a series of events in time is defined in terms of the last of their number. The last event is not merely one member of the series; it is the determinative member, which reveals the meaning of the whole."[11]

There are foreshadowings of an eschatological new exodus in some of the postexilic portions of the Old Testament: "As I live, says the Lord God, surely with a mighty hand and an outstretched arm, and with wrath poured out, I will . . . bring you out from the peoples and gather you out of the countries where you are scattered. . . . As I entered into judgment with your fathers in the wilderness of the land of Egypt, so I will enter into judgment with you, says the Lord God" (Ezek. 20:33-36).

We need not be thrown off the track by this prophecy of wrath and judgment, for in other portions of Ezekiel the prophet shows how this eschatological *judgment* is a component of God's *salvation*. The unknown prophet of the exile also uses the imagery of the exodus to depict the *future* actions of God to redeem his people:

11. C. K. Barrett, "New Testament Eschatology," *Scottish Journal of Theology* 6 (1953): 136-55, 225-43. In chapter 9 we will look beyond Barrett's definition of eschatology, because as he himself seems to recognize, it does not go far enough in identifying the radical quality of *apocalyptic* eschatology.

Was it not thou that didst . . . make the depths of the sea a way
　　for the redeemed to pass over?
And the ransomed of the Lord shall return,
　　and come to Zion with singing;
everlasting joy shall be upon their heads;
　　they shall obtain joy and gladness,
　　and sorrow and sighing shall flee away. (Isa. 51:10-11)[12]

The idea of a future exodus is not foreign to the Old Testament in its late period. The experience of the exile, in this as in other respects, caused the Hebrew thinkers to look toward the time yet to come *not just as an extension of the saving event of the past,* but as a *new* exodus, *a new creation.* The great Isaianic prophet of the exile sounded this note in other passages as well:

"Behold, I am doing a new thing;
　　now it springs forth, do you not perceive it?
I will make a way in the wilderness
　　and rivers in the desert." (Isa. 43:19)

There evolved among the Hebrew people a greatly increased emphasis on God's future intervention, not on the ground of the people's righteousness but on the ground of his great mercy. Righteousness itself became more clearly an eschatological concept, since events had shown that there was not going to be any true and lasting righteousness on earth unless God brought it.[13]

---

12. Note the use of the terms "ransomed" and "redeemed" here. We will return to Isaiah's use of this concept in chapter 7. Rarely do we see motifs presented singly, without reference to other motifs. In Isa. 40–55, deliverance (a new exodus) is combined with creation and redemption in a breathtaking way.

13. Markus Barth writes, "The Old Testament shows that long before Paul's time even the best and strongest instruments of the covenant (e.g. God's appearance and promise; the gift of the law, the land, the temple; the institutions of sacrifice, priestly dynasties, holy times and holy wars) offer no assurance by themselves that Israel will have peace and will live. There must be a true servant of God, 'a . . . covenant mediator' on duty and at work" (*Justification* [Grand Rapids: Eerdmans, 1971], 35-36 n). This last sentence would be one good way, among others, of reading Isa. 52:13–53:12. Parenthetically, I once spent the better part of a year exploring the manifold interpretations of this famous text — arguably the most disputed major passage in the Bible — from various Jewish and Christian perspectives. In the end I was not satisfied with any of them. It means very different things to Jews and Christians. I concluded that the passage is meant to be a mysterious divine disclosure of a singular nature,

There was a consequential shift among Israel's thinkers after the catastrophe of the destruction of the temple and the collapse of the throne of David. In a certain sense, many of these thinkers gave up on history. The postexilic Wisdom literature (Ecclesiastes, Song of Songs, Proverbs, Job) never mentions history at all, and the apocalyptic writings (Zechariah, Daniel) look for the divine deliverance from beyond history. This does not mean that history has no direction or goal, or that human beings play no part in it. On the contrary, history remains the arena of God's activity, and remains the plane on which the people of God live out their witness. The difference is in the way of seeing historical events. Apocalyptic is just that: *a way of seeing*. It is a way of discerning God's invading power *now*, in human events, as signs of what is to come. Jewish scholar Nahum Sarna hints at this when he writes, "The Exodus . . . becomes the paradigm of future redemption; it offers *a pattern for God's intervention* in history in times to come."[14]

Whether Sarna intends to or not, he is here touching upon the apocalyptic theme of God's intervening power. The words "eschatology" and "apocalyptic," though future-oriented, are not interchangeable. The key apocalyptic idea, to be developed further in later chapters, is *the sovereign intervention of God,* with a corresponding displacement of the capacity of human beings to bring that intervention about. It must be said in the strongest possible terms: in no way does this emphasis on the divine agency mean that there is nothing for us to do, or that our activity is meaningless. What it means, rather, is that human activity *points to* the future reign of God and *participates in it* proleptically (*prolepsis,* "to anticipate"). It does not, however, make it come to fruition; only God can complete his purpose. At no time does the Bible suggest that we are, in the currently popular phrase, "co-creators with God"; rather, we are graciously called and moved to be *participants* in what God alone is able to create.[15] The word "eschatology" does not necessarily make this distinction clear; it is possible to refer to the "last things" and thus speak eschatologically, without being careful to show that *God alone* will cause those last things to come to pass — the emphasis that is the hallmark of apocalyptic. The role of the people of God is *participation in what God is already doing.*

---

to be apprehended in the Spirit, by faith, until Jews and Christians are fully reconciled in the eschaton (Rom. 11).

14. Nahum Sarna, *Exploring Exodus: The Origins of Biblical Israel* (New York: Schocken Books, 1986), 3, emphasis added.

15. The word *bara,* "create," is used exclusively with God as its subject throughout the Old Testament.

Christians and Jews Interpreting the Exodus

Rabbi Michael Goldberg shows his understanding of the relationship between the two stories — the exodus and the passion/resurrection — in his imaginative and empathetic book *Jews and Christians: Getting Our Stories Straight*.[16] His term for the two narratives is "master stories." He writes, powerfully, that both of them function as fundamental sources "through which we are to get our bearings for the rest of Scripture, and hence, for the rest of history itself." He continues,

> Thus, for Christians, the narration of the events surrounding Jesus' crucifixion is the biblical account that most plainly illuminates the Bible's other portions — including the saga of Israel's deliverance from Egypt. The church takes that part of Christ's story as its formative Christian master story and sees it as following from the Exodus by being its natural follow-up, decisive climax, and ultimate fulfilment. And what do Jews say for their part? "No! That's not the way at all to take the Exodus, our Jewish master story." What the Christian story represents, say Jews, is not a true interpretation or working out of the Exodus narrative, but instead a serious misreading and profound distortion of it.[17]

A Christian understanding of the exodus as an anticipatory event fulfilled by the cross and resurrection is more offensive to Jews than the Jewish appropriation of the story is to Christians, particularly in view of the persistence of anti-Semitism around the world. Just as Rabbi Goldberg has taken the Christian viewpoint seriously and respectfully even though he does not share it, Christians may seek to engage the Jewish viewpoint with similar empathy. In fact, the Christian perspective on the exodus can accommodate the Jewish perspective more readily than vice versa. Brevard Childs identifies the problem from the Jewish viewpoint: "The death, resurrection and Messianic kingdom of Jesus Christ was soon understood as the bringing of the *true content* of the Old Testament Passover which was consequently set *over against* the Jewish Passover."[18]

Rabbi Goldberg makes a great contribution by throwing a spotlight on

16. Indeed, Rabbi Goldberg retells the Matthean passion narrative so sympathetically that it is hard to imagine how he could remain unconvinced of its truth.

17. Goldberg, *Jews and Christians*, 14. The painfully disputed question of the theological reality to the actual nation of Israel is a separate issue.

18. Brevard Childs, *The Book of Exodus: A Critical, Theological Commentary*, Old Testament Library (Philadelphia: Westminster, 1974), 209, emphasis added.

this difficulty without calling for either side to jettison its understanding.[19] From the standpoint of the New Testament gospel, the exodus is not only a historical event defining the elect people (and that, in itself, stands as truth both for Christians and Jews) but also a proleptic (meaning "anticipatory") incursion of God's saving power that points forward to the definitive, apocalyptic event of the cross where the Powers are engaged in the first and decisive stage of God's final battle.[20] Surely the danger here is that Christians may be, and often have been, tempted to think that the constituting of Israel by God as "a peculiar people" (see Exod. 19:5; Deut. 14:2 KJV) has been invalidated by the Christ event. This notion should be decisively repudiated (Rom. 9:4). It is of utmost importance that Christians recognize the historical exodus as a completed event in relation not only to the theological reality of God's chosen people Israel but also to its material preservation. Brevard Childs writes, "The book of Esther provides the strongest canonical warrant in the whole Old Testament for the religious significance of the Jewish people *in an ethnic sense.*"[21]

The Exodus as an Easter Liturgy

The mainline churches in America have been bending over backward not to offend, but at the same time we are in danger of allowing the Old Testament to slip away from us. If we really want to combat anti-Semitism, what better way to do it than to foster love of the Hebrew Scriptures? There is a gap in the mental furnishings of white Christians in America today. The thrilling story of the exodus of the children of Israel from Egypt ought to make our collective hairs stand on end, but the mention of it is likely to be met with blank stares. We need more sermons on this central shaping story. We Christians need to be able to recount the basic outlines of the central event of the Old Testament and of the Jewish people, need to understand why the exodus passage is always read at the climax of the Easter Vigil, need to hear these central texts taught in our congregations. This story of surpassing power ought to be an indispensable part of every Christian's operating system.[22]

19. The most compelling part of Goldberg's book is at the very end when he calls upon Christians and Jews to show forth the deepest meanings of their "master stories" *in their lives.*

20. This will be spelled out in much more detail in chapter 10.

21. Brevard Childs, *Introduction to the Old Testament as Scripture* (Philadelphia: Fortress, 1979), 606-7, emphasis added.

22. Octogenarians will have some recollection of Charlton Heston as Moses in the blockbuster Cecil B. DeMille movie *The Ten Commandments,* but a commercial product hardly has the power to function as a formative story for a worshiping community!

The Hebrew story of deliverance is the source of much of the Easter imagery of the church. Nowhere is it more apparent that the exodus narrative is the prototype of the cross and resurrection than in the victory-shout of these two Easter hymns:

Come, ye faithful, raise the strain
Of triumphant gladness;
God has brought his Israel
Into joy from sadness.
Loosed from Pharaoh's bitter yoke,
Jacob's sons and daughters,
Led them with unmoistened foot
Through the Red Sea waters.[23]

At the Lamb's high feast we sing
Praise to our victorious King . . .
. . . Where the Paschal blood is poured
Death's dark angel sheathes his sword.
Israel's hosts triumphant go
Through the wave that drowns the foe.[24]

These hymns bring us to the very shores of the sea where Miriam and her women are jubilant with tambourines and dancing:

And Miriam sang to them:
"Sing to the Lord, for he has triumphed gloriously;
the horse and his rider he has thrown into the sea." (Exod. 15:21)[25]

23. Hymn text by John of Damascus, eighth century, trans. John Mason Neale. Episcopal Hymnal #199.

24. Latin hymn, 1632, trans. Robert Campbell, Episcopal Hymnal #174.

25. Speaking of literal-mindedness, there have been many complaints over the centuries about the celebration on the shore when the Egyptians are drowned. A number of attempts have been made, even in the Talmud itself, to improve upon the exodus story. With all due respect, this is not the place for worrying about the dead enemy. On the figurative Red Sea shore, we are supposed to be giving ourselves up to the immediacy of the story, not focusing on our own tender-minded afterthoughts. Would the troops coming ashore on Omaha Beach on D-Day have stopped en route to their inland positions to worry about the dead Germans? This sort of thing blunts the impact of the story. It displaces the raw power of the miracle and substitutes our own supposedly finer feelings. The rabbinical gloss on the Red Sea story is not biblical. It distracts us from the main message of triumph and deliverance. Clearly, Miriam and her women weren't worrying about the drowning Egyptians. The right time for paying

This verse should give us goose bumps, for even the most skeptical scholars agree that it goes back to the very event itself, whatever it was. This is therefore one of the oldest fragments of writing in the Bible. It is a direct link to the imagery of the New Testament, for as Stephen Sykes writes, "Slavery is a metaphor for the consequence of sin. . . . Those who are in bondage need to be freed. We are enslaved by Satan, which covers all the bases — systemic evil as well as individual sin and error."[26] That reference to "systemic evil" remains vital; it is important not to spiritualize, de-historicize, or individualize the exodus too much, or it will lose its edge. Affluent communities need to understand that they are enslaved by the pursuit of wealth, comfort, and status, often achieved at the expense of the poor.[27]

Some communities reenact the exodus story liturgically by observing the full Easter Vigil. Only the full-dress version in the profound darkness of night can adequately suggest the earthshaking, sea-splitting, grave-opening power of the resurrection precisely in terms of the exodus from Egypt, the parting of the waters, and the deliverance on the seashore.[28] The ancient canticle *Exsultet* ("Rejoice now!") is sung at the Easter Vigil.[29] Notice how several motifs — the sin offering, the payment of debt (satisfaction), the blood sacrifice, and *Christus Victor* — are combined in the thrilling recital of the deliverance wrought for us by Christ in the new exodus:

---

attention to the enemy is later in the story of Israel when they are taught to show mercy to the sojourner "because you were sojourners in the land of Egypt" — and ultimately in the second Passover when Jesus says, "Father, forgive them, for they know not what they do," and when Paul says, "Christ died for the *ungodly*."

26. Sykes, *The Story of Atonement*, 16.

27. Several articles regarding the attitudes of the rich to the poor were published in 2013. The theme, based on recent studies, was that the rich lack empathy for the poor and powerless, even for those who are not poor but are in some way lower on the socioeconomic scale (e.g., Daniel Goldman, "Rich People Just Care Less," *New York Times,* October 25, 2013).

28. The Paschal Vigil, with baptism as its centerpiece, can be reliably dated as far back as the second century. The observance of an abbreviated vigil in the daylight cannot be entirely blamed on our present day, for such a service was in use in the Sarum rite as early as the twelfth century. Nevertheless, one may agree with liturgist Marion Hatchett: "Because of its content, the rite should begin in the darkness, as it did in the first centuries. . . . For the most dramatic effect, it may be so scheduled that the congregation gathers before dawn and the light of the sun would stream into the church at the beginning of the Eucharist" (*Commentary on the American Prayer Book* [New York: Seabury Press, 1981], 243). The earliest (titular) churches of Rome are still celebrated for their ancient liturgies of the lighting of the Easter fire in the middle of the night.

29. In the Roman Catholic Church the *Exsultet* is called the *Praeconium*. It is impossible to date it exactly, but it seems to have originated in Rome as early as Pope Zosimus (d. A.D. 418).

It is truly right and good, always and everywhere, with our whole heart and mind and voice, to praise you, the invisible, almighty and eternal God, and your only begotten Son, Jesus Christ our Lord; for he is the true Paschal Lamb, who at the feast of the Passover paid for us the debt of Adam's sin, and by his blood delivered your faithful people.

This is the night, when you brought our fathers, the children of Israel, out of bondage in Egypt, and led them through the Red Sea on dry land.

This is the night, when all who believe in Christ are delivered from the gloom of sin, and are restored to grace and holiness of life.

This is the night, when Christ broke the bonds of death and hell, and rose victorious from the grave.

In the full-length service, nine lessons are traditionally read following this canticle, *all from the Old Testament.* If the service must be shortened, one lesson is *always required,* and that is the exodus passage (14:10–15:1) that tells the story of the deliverance at the Red Sea. It depicts the band of cruelly oppressed slaves gathering in the middle of the night, their few worldly goods packed up and their traveling clothes on, eating their final anticipatory meal in haste, preparing to venture out into the unknown with only the Word of God through Moses their leader to trust, ready to follow the Word of this God out of the house of bondage into the way of freedom. This is the atmosphere that is duplicated in the Easter Vigil when it is done the way it should be — in the middle of the night, the church dark, the story of the exodus read as the worshipers tremble on the brink of the final and conclusive deliverance — the resurrection of the dead.

The Exodus in Life

This story can and should have the same power for us today as it did for the very earliest Christians. They saw it as the Old Testament event *par excellence* from which to understand the death and resurrection of Jesus the Messiah. In their worship, it was not necessary to explain that the Lord's Supper is the new Passover and the resurrection is the new exodus. The worshiping community already understood, without being told, that the passing of Jesus through death into life unfolds the eschatological *significance* of the passage of the Israelites from bondage into freedom. The Easter liturgy of the Eastern Orthodox Church is particularly rich in these associations. The exodus narrative has been central for the African American community as they, too, experienced deliverance from slavery.[30] In Negro spirituals such as "Go Down, Moses," the singers identify themselves with the Hebrew slaves of old. They have no need of interpretation. They know the story is their own story.[31]

The exodus narrative has functioned powerfully in the Christian community under siege. Robert Spike, a white man, was head of the Commission on Religion and Race for the National Council of Churches at the height of the civil rights movement. In the summer of 1963, he made a journey to Savannah, Georgia, where the young black leaders Hosea Williams and Andrew Young were leading mass meetings to prepare for dangerous night marches to win the vote. More than five hundred Savannah blacks had already gone to jail. Few white people had ever witnessed anything like those so-called mass meetings, which in many ways were really services of Christian worship. The preaching was impassioned and the singing thunderous. Spike — who had a theological education — wrote back to his colleagues, "I had the strongest feeling that I was in Egypt on the night of the Passover . . . or in the Warsaw ghetto twenty-five years ago, or in Sharpeville, South Africa, not so very long ago."[32] Thus the old

30. In his valuable book *The Preacher King,* about Martin Luther King's actual *preaching* (as opposed to the published written works), Richard Lischer shows how King powerfully and consistently interwove the two key themes of the exodus and the suffering love of Jesus. The motif of the substitutionary death of Jesus as atonement for sin, Lischer reminds us, plays little part in the African American pulpit, yet the cross is central because in it the black church sees its Lord bearing their suffering and overcoming it in the victory that they too would share. King worried that a seminary-taught *theologia crucis* was "Germanic and otherworldly" instead of calling the church to action. Despite these reservations, Lischer continues, "King's public character increasingly came to be shaped by resonances to the Crucified One. . . . The crucified Savior [was] the organizing principle for his own depression, failures, rejections, and impending death" (*The Preacher King: Martin Luther King, Jr., and the Word That Moved America* [Oxford: Oxford University Press, 1995], 188-89). This is a powerful example of the way in which the cross works in one way in one community at a given time, another way in another at a different time.

31. A play in New York in the early '90s, called *Beau Jest,* contained a controversial scene. It showed a Passover Seder in the home of a secular, assimilated Jewish family. Following the old custom, they have invited a Gentile, in this case a black man who, like many African Americans who grew up in church, knows the Bible well. The members of the host family go through all the time-honored motions accompanying the reading of the Passover Haggadah, performing the traditional actions and asking the traditional questions (e.g., "Why is this night different from all other nights?"), but after a while it becomes obvious that the family doesn't really understand or care very much about what it all means. The black visitor takes the copy of the Haggadah and reads the story of the exodus in a way that reveals to the family for the first time the power of their own tradition. (We should note, however, that some Jews in real life are becoming resentful, perhaps with some justification, at this universalizing of the exodus narrative.)

32. Taylor Branch, *Pillar of Fire: America in the King Years, 1963-65* (New York: Simon and Schuster, 1998), 127. I was almost tempted to elide the reference to the Warsaw ghetto,

story comes alive again as the power of the once and future Spirit moves among the people:

> Over my head, I see freedom in the air,
> Over my head, Oh Lord, I see freedom in the air,
> There must be a God somewhere.[33]

In his book about the civil rights movement, Andrew Young recalls the parting of the waters in Birmingham, Alabama, in 1964. "Easter Sunday dawned with Martin [Luther King] in jail. . . . We planned a march from New Pilgrim Baptist Church to the city jail for the afternoon of Easter Sunday. . . . By the time church ended some five thousand people had gathered . . . dressed in their best Sunday clothes."

The marchers set out in a festive mood. Suddenly they saw police, fire engines, and firemen with hoses in front of them, blocking their path. "Bull" Connor bellowed, "Turn this group around!" Five thousand people stopped and waited for instruction from their leaders.

> Wyatt Walker and I were leading the march. I can't say we knew what to do. I know I didn't want to turn the march around. . . . I asked the people to get down on their knees and offer a prayer. . . . Suddenly Rev. Charles Billups, one of the most faithful and fearless leaders of the old Alabama Christian Movement for Human Rights, jumped up and hollered, *"The Lord is with this movement! Off your knees! We're going on!"* . . . Stunned at first, Bull Connor yelled, "Stop 'em, stop 'em!" But none of the police moved a muscle. . . . Even the police dogs that had been growling and straining at their leashes . . . were now perfectly calm. . . . I saw one fireman, tears in his eyes, just let the hose drop at his feet. Our people marched right between the red fire trucks, singing, "I want Jesus to walk with me."

---

thinking it not quite apt since all those in the Jewish ghetto uprising perished; but I think I know what Spike meant. The Warsaw ghetto uprising of April-May 1943 (not to be confused with the Warsaw uprising of the Polish Home Army of August-September 1944, the largest single military effort taken by any European resistance movement in World War II, but equally futile) took place at Passover. If it is viewed from the perspective of the end-time, it was not a failure because it was a sign planted in history that the stirrings of freedom cannot be repressed forever. The struggle for freedom must operate under a shadow in "this present evil age," but it is nevertheless a sign that God is present even when he is hidden. The ghetto uprising (as well as the heartbreaking 1944 uprising) will be honored in memory as a sign that God was present even in those extremities. An action that appears to be futile in the eyes of the unbelieving world can nevertheless be part of God's mysterious plan.

33. http://ctl.du.edu/spirituals/freedom/civil.cfm.

... [Bull Connor's] policemen had refused to arrest us, his firemen had refused to hose us, and his dogs had refused to bite us. It was quite a moment to witness. I'll never forget one old woman who became ecstatic when she marched through the barricades. As she passed through, she shouted, "Great God Almighty done parted the Red Sea one mo' time!"[34]

No one has more powerfully recast the stories of the exodus and the civil rights movement in apocalyptic language than Paul L. Lehmann. Here is his summation in *The Transfiguration of Politics:*

Reading the "Dream Speech" now is to relive the day of its utterance for all who heard it, on the Washington Mall or through the media. And in so doing one can affirm again Mrs. King's report that "it seemed to all of us there that his words flowed from some higher place, through Martin, to the weary people before him. Yes — heaven itself opened up and we all seemed transformed." "Transfigured" is perhaps the truer word. And this, not only because another Exodus was in the making, but also because a moment of truth had broken in from which there could be no turning back. Moses and Elijah were in the wings. Righteousness and resurrection were on the move. And there was yet great suffering to be endured.[35]

This capsule includes almost all the elements that we have been stressing. God is on the move. His activity takes the form of an in-breaking from another sphere of power. It is his initiative from first to last. He gives his Word from a higher place to his weary people. Another exodus is in the making. Our engagement in what God is already doing is "transfiguring"; it is the discovery that one belongs to an altogether different order of existence from which there can be no turning back. And yet there is great suffering still to be endured. In *The Preacher King,* Richard Lischer shows how King powerfully and consistently interwove the two key themes of the exodus and the suffering love of Jesus.

The exodus story functions in one way in one community at one time, and in another way in another community at a different time. During the suppression of the East Timorese people in 1999, the Roman Catholic bishop Belo put himself in danger for his flock, later winning a Nobel Peace Prize.

34. Andrew Young, *An Easy Burden: The Civil Rights Movement and the Transformation of America* (New York: HarperCollins, 1996), 223.

35. Paul L. Lehmann, *The Transfiguration of Politics* (New York: Harper and Row, 1975), 182-83.

During the conflict, reporter Seth Mydans wrote from Dili, East Timor: "Here at the broken heart of this small city, [a Roman Catholic priest] tried to persuade his threadbare listeners that suffering is rewarded and that there is such a thing, even for them, as resurrection. 'You are like the people of Israel who suffered for peace, suffered for freedom, suffered so that they could have their own land,' said the priest, the Rev. Joao Feligueras . . . who has worked in East Timor since long before the Indonesians invaded in 1975."[36]

Thus the exodus narrative continues to hold out the promise of life around the world over the centuries as people who have been oppressed cling to the promise that God is acting among them. The struggling priest in the ruins makes the connection between the story of the enslaved Israelites and redemptive suffering in the present. He has portrayed both cross and resurrection in terms of the sacred story.

> When Pharaoh drew near, the people of Israel lifted up their eyes, and behold, the Egyptians were marching after them; and they were in great fear. And the people of Israel cried out to the Lord; and they said to Moses, "Is it because there are no graves in Egypt that you have taken us away to die in the wilderness?" . . . And Moses said to the people, "Fear not, stand firm, and see the salvation of the Lord, which he will work for you today; for the Egyptians whom you see today, you shall never see again. The Lord will fight for you, and you have only to be still." (Exod. 14:10-14)

36. Seth Mydans, "At Last, Timorese Can Pray and Count the Costs," *New York Times*, October 4, 1999.

CHAPTER SIX

The Blood Sacrifice

Who knows not Love, let him assay
And taste that juice, which on the cross a pike
Did set abroad; then let him say
If ever he did taste the like.
Love is that liquor sweet and most divine,
Which my God feels as blood; but I as wine.

GEORGE HERBERT, "THE AGONIE"[1]

In the modern period there has been a negative reaction in the mainline churches to the concept of the cross of Christ as a sacrifice. Disdain for the "blood" imagery of the New Testament has become widespread, even though it has been prominent in hymnody and piety throughout Christian history.[2] This chapter will argue for its enduring importance. Theologian George Hunsinger has written, "The motif of Christ's blood, as derived from

1. George Herbert, "The Agonie," in George Herbert, *The Complete English Poems*, ed. John Tobin (New York: Penguin Books, 1991), 33.
2. Early in my ministry, I was invited to be the preacher at the Good Friday service in a prominent parish. The rector was a good friend and fine leader, but when I arrived for the occasion he instructed me that I was not to preach about "the blood." This injunction was echoed a couple of years later when I was further told by a respected professor from a leading Episcopal seminary that it was unacceptable to do so. I accepted this at the time, since I wanted to be on the cutting edge of academic fashion, but looking back, I now realize how deeply baffled and distressed I was by these strictures. The idea of Jesus sacrificing himself for me and for the whole human race had been my mainstay during my whole life. Had I misunderstood? More to the point, was I really not to preach it anymore?

the New Testament, is unsurpassed in its metaphorical range, complexity, and richness," and he quotes the poem of George Herbert that serves as the epigraph for this chapter.[3]

The motif of sacrifice, and specifically *blood* sacrifice, is central to the story of our salvation through Jesus Christ, and without this theme the Christian proclamation loses much of its power, becoming both theologically *and ethically* undernourished.

Here are just a few of many New Testament references to the blood of Christ:

Be shepherds of the church of God, which he bought *with his own blood.* (Acts 20:28 NIV)[4]

For in [Christ] all the fulness of God was pleased to dwell, and through him to reconcile to himself all things . . . making peace by *the blood of his cross.* (Col. 1:19-20)

You know that you were ransomed . . . not with perishable things such as silver or gold, but *with the precious blood* of Christ, like that of a lamb without blemish or spot. (I Pet. 1:18-19)

For the bodies of those animals whose blood is brought into the sanctuary by the high priest as a sacrifice for sin are burned outside the camp. So Jesus also suffered outside the gate in order to sanctify the people *through his own blood.* (Heb. 13:11-12)

Looking at these four passages as representative of many others, one can readily see that the motif is not expendable. If we were to go through the Bible and the eucharistic liturgy and remove all the references to blood and sacrifice,

---

3. George Hunsinger, *Disruptive Grace: Studies in the Theology of Karl Barth* (Grand Rapids: Eerdmans, 2000), 361.

4. Some translations render this as "the blood of his own Son," but the Greek simply says "the blood of his own" *(dia tou haimatos tou idiou),* which is theologically more suggestive of the total participation of the Father. Fitzmyer helpfully comments that "Luke may be thinking of the action of God the Father and the Son as so closely related that his mode of speaking slips from one into the other; if so, it resembles the speech patterns of the Johannine Gospel" (*The Acts of the Apostles,* Anchor Bible 31 [New York: Doubleday, 1998], 680). The phrase "blood of his own Son" is very untypical of Luke. This suggests that the phraseology is part of an earlier church confession taken over by Luke, much like the language in Rom. 3:24b-25a, which is not typical of Paul either. Paul may very well have been quoting a formula already in circulation in Rome.

we would be tearing out much of the heart. Yet it is not so easy to gain a hearing for the motif of "the blood of Christ" in the mainline churches today. There are many reasons for this, some of them superficial (snobbery about "primitive" faith) and some serious; we will address the more serious ones in this chapter.

"The Blood of Christ" as Metaphor

One reason for the reaction against the sacrificial motif is surely the literal-mindedness of a culture unaccustomed to reading poetry. It is one of the peculiarities of our time that we support a vast entertainment industry specializing in ever more explicitly gory movies and video games while at the same time covering ourselves with a "politically correct" cloak of fastidious high-mindedness. In an earlier and perhaps in some ways more sophisticated time, Christians actually sang the words of poet William Cowper, "There is a fountain filled with blood, drawn from Emmanuel's veins," with no sense of disgust. They were accustomed to extravagant literary images. It would not have occurred to them to take such a trope literally, any more than evangelical congregations do today when they sing "Power in the Blood." Looking at the matter from another angle, most Protestants are turned off by baroque sculptures of a bloody Jesus, but it is not always possible to tell whether this is because of theological scruples or just a northern European concept of Mediterranean bad taste.[5]

Literal-mindedness is the enemy of vital biblical interpretation (a similar point was made previously with regard to Anselm). Anyone who focuses on the "blood" in an exclusively literal sense will completely miss the point. When John Donne told his congregation that God "wrote your name in the blood of that Lamb which was slain for you," he spoke as a poet and a preacher. Even the boldest illustrator might hesitate to picture this actually

---

5. These are not always easy discernments to make. When artist Barry Moser unveiled his ambitious project to illustrate the entire Bible, the *New York Times* featured it (May 26, 1999). The editors reproduced only one picture from a great many in the collection. It was startling, to say the least. Displayed on the front page of one of the *Times'* popular inside sections was an illustration showing the feet of the crucified Christ as he hung on the cross, being kissed by an unidentified woman (probably Mary Magdalene). Blood is running down from the feet onto the face of the woman, who appears to be drinking it. The effect is revolting and erotic, fascinating and shocking all at once. It is tempting to suspect the *Times* of having chosen this particular picture in order to make the Christian faith look ridiculous. On the other hand, one would not want to reject the picture out of mere squeamishness or prudery. The one thing we can say with certainty is that whatever "the blood of Christ" refers to, it is not what is going on in Moser's illustration.

happening, with an inkwell full of Jesus' blood! The poetry of George Herbert is full of imagery beckoning us to respond to the gospel imaginatively. Unfortunately, many today are so accustomed to hearing only the language of the social sciences that they are unable to recognize and be gripped by the power of metaphorical language.[6]

British theologian Kenneth Leech, hardly a reactionary, speaks of "our need to trust in the blood, in the achievement of Jesus."[7] Doesn't the simplicity of this statement undo all the objections constantly being made about "the blood" — its barbarity, its vulgarity, its crudeness? Can't we learn to speak metaphorically? There is nothing whatsoever in the New Testament about the hideous mess and horror of blood. The passion narratives are notable for their reticence about physical matters. This is significant on a number of counts. Instead of being evoked in visual or olfactory terms, "the blood" of Jesus is understood by way of its effects, its inner significance — "the achievement of Jesus." In classical rhetoric, this is called *metonymy,* now more commonly called *metaphor.*[8]

The Epistle to the Hebrews is a particularly good example. The author, known for his thorough treatment of the theme of sacrifice, was not at all concerned about getting the minute details of the Old Testament sacrifices right.[9] A comprehensive and fluid imagination is at work here. In this letter (more properly called a treatise), the Old Testament motifs are combined in a completely new way, with no more than a glance at the historical details of how the Israelites actually performed their sacrifices in the desert. The

6. A prominent professor from a major seminary tossed off a remark at the Presbyterian "Re-imagining" Conference in November 1993 that was widely quoted in reports of the event. She said the church needed to get away from focusing on the cross "with blood dripping and all kinds of weird stuff." Indeed, this is precisely what the New Testament does not mention. There is no "weird stuff" anywhere to be found. No doubt the remark was made casually and was not intended to be a fair representation of what the speaker really thought; nevertheless, it betrayed either a deliberately reductive or an alarmingly unsophisticated view of biblical imagery. I forbear to mention her name here because I feel sure she would not want to be remembered by this off-the-cuff statement.

7. Kenneth Leech, *We Preach Christ Crucified* (New York: Church Publishing, 1994), 29.

8. I am concerned about being misunderstood here. I do not mean to suggest, like many scholars of "text," that metaphor is all there is. I am not saying that it does not matter if anything lies behind the text. I have been instructed by Joel Marcus that a principle of Jewish exegesis is that in many cases "the literal meaning leads further than the metaphor." I am saying, however, that when the biblical writers have chosen to speak in images, pictures, and "figures," we should let our imaginations follow without forcing the passages into a narrow channel where they cannot function.

9. It has been proposed that Hebrews was written by a woman. Unless further evidence turns up, this tendentious conjecture must remain suspect.

general idea was sufficient. The salient point was that God, knowing that the Israelites could not come near to him as they were in their guilt, provided the means for them to live in his presence. Another life, unblemished and blameless, was offered instead. The spilled blood of the animal, offered by the priest, was the means of obtaining remission from sin.

We think of the apostle Paul with some justification as the most purely intellectual thinker of the New Testament, but figures of speech came easily to him. In Romans 5:9-10 he uses the phrase "by his blood" as a synonym for Jesus' death.[10] In I Corinthians 5:7 he says, "Christ, our paschal lamb, has been sacrificed." First Corinthians 10:16 speaks of "participation in the blood of Christ." In the New Testament as a whole, references to the "blood" of Christ are three times more frequent than those to the "death" of Christ — a compelling statistic. For centuries, the sacrificial system of Israel prepared God's people to understand that "without the shedding of blood there is no forgiveness of sins" (Heb. 9:22). Jesus' own "words of institution" at the Last Supper clearly refer to sacrifice: "This is my blood of the covenant, which is poured out for many" (Mark 14:24). The biblical testimony, we repeat, consists of many themes and many variations; there can be no doubt, however, that Jesus' death interpreted as a sacrifice, and specifically a sacrifice *for sin,* is one of the dominant ideas in the New Testament.[11]

To be sure, there are problems here. Some have wondered if imagery associated with blood hasn't become dead to middle-class American Christians, living as we do in a high-tech society far removed from real blood and real death, let alone sacrificial death.[12] We may question, however, whether the power of shed blood is lost to us. Certainly Jacqueline Kennedy — master manipulator of symbols that she was — was aware of it when she fiercely refused to allow her husband's blood to be cleaned from her stockings, or to change her pink suit, saying, "I want them to see what they have done." The New Testament passion narratives, on the other hand, are not concerned

10. Cousar points out the parallelism in "by his blood" and "by the death of his son" (Charles B. Cousar, *A Theology of the Cross: The Death of Jesus in the Pauline Letters,* Overtures to Biblical Theology [Minneapolis: Augsburg Fortress, 1990], 63).

11. I was told a story by a reliable source, concerning a Ph.D. candidate whose dissertation was on the subject of forgiveness in process theology. A Jewish scholar was among the members of the committee who heard the oral defense. After the candidate had made his presentation and the discussion had proceeded for a time, the Jewish professor spoke up and said that he was puzzled. He as a Jew knew that there was no forgiveness without sacrifice; how could the candidate write a whole dissertation on the subject and never mention sacrifice? The answer is unrecorded; the question makes the point.

12. See, for example, David L. Wheeler, "The Cross and the Blood: Living or Dead Images?" *Dialog* 35, no. 1 (Winter 1996): 7-13.

with arousing this sort of reaction in us at all. They do not want us to "see" the blood. When John's Gospel tells us that "blood and water" came forth from the side of Jesus, the significance is clearly theological, not literal. Indeed, in the portrayal of the crucifixion considered by many to be the greatest of all (and certainly the most gruesome), the Isenheim altarpiece by Matthias Grünewald, we do not notice any blood. The "blood of Christ" in the New Testament is not a description of a physical happening on Golgotha. Again, it is *metonymy* or *synecdoche* — the use of one idea for another, or the part for the whole, in order to enlarge or heighten its meaning. Why do so many insist on a literal interpretation of the term? It seems almost willful, as though the objectors simply refuse to see that "the blood of Jesus" is an image, and an extremely powerful one at that. When an African American congregation sings the gospel chorus "There to my heart was the blood applied / Glory to his Name!" they are not thinking literally, and it seems almost perverse to imply that they are. They are thinking of the power of the crucified Jesus in their own lives. We are once again in the realm of poetry.[13]

The Blood: Life or Death?

There has been a great deal of discussion on whether "the blood" represents life or death. A number of heavy hitters have drawn on Leviticus 17:11 — "For the life of the flesh is in the blood; and I have given it for you upon the altar to make atonement for your souls; for it is the blood that makes atonement, by reason of the life" — or other passages that maintain that the life of every creature is the blood of it (see Gen. 9:4 and Deut. 12:23). The argument is that the "blood" means the pouring out of the life.[14] This has become almost an article of faith for many scholars of

---

13. Having established all this, however, we must say that if *bloody* sacrifice was all there was to it, God would have arranged a bloodier death than crucifixion for his Messiah. The scourging and the nails drew blood, but the only blood that is *specifically* mentioned in the Gospels is the blood from the spear wound, and that took place after Jesus was dead. A beheading or a disemboweling would have been much bloodier. For an even deeper meaning of crucifixion we must look elsewhere.

14. This is an influential view associated especially with Vincent Taylor and B. F. Westcott of earlier generations, still widely held by many today. Nahum Sarna, for example, writes, "The blood is the life essence, a point made explicit in the Bible several times" (*Exploring Exodus: The Origins of Biblical Israel* [New York: Schocken Books, 1986], 92-93). The view that blood in the context of Christ's self-offering *always* means life rather than death is an article of faith for scholars who consider themselves progressive and recommend its exclusive use for those who "have no stomach for violence in any form" (James Rowe Adams, ed., *The Essential Reference*

comparative religion and ritual in Old Testament times. In this view, the essential element in sacrificial death is the pouring out of life. Death is almost incidental to this process, as though it were simply an unpleasant necessity in order to get at the blood. The issue here is of the greatest importance. If all the emphasis is on the giving of Jesus' *life*, then we are left with no explanation of his being Godforsaken or under any kind of a curse, which — as we argued in chapter 2 — is one of the most profound aspects of Christ's crucifixion. It is surely right to say that the essence of Christ's sacrifice is the giving of his life, but the insistence of these scholars in detaching the life from the death means that we cannot speak of representation, substitution, propitiation, vicarious suffering, or even exchange happening on the cross because the whole idea of God coming under God's own judgment is eliminated. Such an interpretation would leave us still in the dark as to the wherefore of the barbarity of the cross, for if it is simply a matter of obtaining the life-essence in the blood, it surely could have been given in a cleaner, more aesthetic way.

In the final analysis, this dispute between the blood as life and the blood as death is unnecessary. The forthright teaching on this subject by the nineteenth-century interpreter James Denney is valuable. With an indignation on behalf of the gospel worthy of Paul, Denney assails B. F. Westcott for his "strange caprice" in dividing the life from the death, the blood offered from the blood shed, the life liberated so as to be made available to us and the life laid down in death.

> I venture to say that a more groundless fancy never haunted and troubled the interpretation of any part of Scripture than that which is introduced by this distinction into the Epistle to the Hebrews ... there is no meaning in saying that by his death his life, as something other than his death, is "liberated" and "made available" for men. One the contrary, what makes his risen life significant and a saving power for sinners is neither more nor less than this, *that his death was in it.*[15]

Stephen Sykes has stressed the idea of sacrifice as life-giving in the sense of total commitment, the offering of one's entire being. Imagine a person totally committed to your best interests, devoted to seeing you flourish, fight-

---

Book for Biblical Metaphors: From Literal to Literary, 2nd ed. [Dallas, Word, 2008], 255-57). This robs the death by crucifixion of its unique significance.

15. James Denney, *The Death of Christ,* ed. R. V. Tasker (London: Tyndale Press, 1951; orig. 1902), 149.

ing for you against all enemies, determined to eliminate everything destructive from your life, attentive to every detail of who you are, never thinking of himself at all but only of you. That is Jesus in relation to us all — sacrificial in his life, sacrificial in his death. It is hard to discern any useful reason for being forced to choose between the offering of life and the acceptance of a godless death in our understanding of what Jesus accomplished in giving *himself.*

The Concept of Sacrifice

There are several basic ideas present in the concept of sacrifice. Think, for instance, of the sacrifice bunt in baseball, whereby one gives up his own chance for a hit in order to advance another. A very common use of the word continues in references to soldiers who have "made the supreme sacrifice" of their lives. Chess players "sacrifice" pawns in order to gain advantage later on. A professional woman might say that she won't marry or have children because she doesn't want to "sacrifice" her career. From the other end of that issue, we are certainly familiar with the frequent use of the word "sacrifice" to describe what parents give up in order to see their children succeed. The seriousness of the idea depends upon the context. Martin Luther King talked about sacrifice a great deal: "Everyone in the movement must lead a sacrificial life."[16]

In all these examples, at least two ideas are present:

- Something of value is relinquished.
- The purpose is to gain a greater good.

The word "sacrifice" can be either a verb or a noun. Important layers of meaning can be discerned from looking at both ways the word is used. Where it is a verb, we generally see a person *making a sacrifice,* that is, giving up something. Where it is a noun, the *act* of giving up may be in view (the "sacrifice" in baseball) or — note this — the thing relinquished or offered *is itself* the sacrifice, as in the case, say, of the pawn in chess or the slaughtered rooster in the voodoo ritual.

When we see Jesus, we see all these meanings coming together. Jesus takes on his priestly role, offering sacrifice by *going* (an active verb) deliberately to Jerusalem where he knows death awaits him; he then allows himself

---

16. Quoted in Taylor Branch, *Parting the Waters: America in the King Years, 1954-63* (New York: Simon and Schuster, 1988), 727.

to be sacrificed (the passive form of the verb) by refusing to resist; and in giving himself up, he himself *becomes the sacrifice* (the noun). Jesus is not altogether unique in combining all these meanings in one person, but the claim made by the apostolic preaching stands alone in the history of the world, let alone the history of religion, in this one regard: it proclaims this one sacrifice as *efficacious for the whole human race and the entire cosmos for all time.*[17]

This brings us to the purpose of sacrifices, biblically understood.

The Sin Offering in Leviticus

The biblical motif of sacrifice offered to God is a major one in the Old and New Testaments. This volume cannot attempt a survey in depth. Of all the themes we are examining, this one is the most intimidating for those not versed in the history of religion. Trying to unravel the complexities of the sacrificial systems of ancient cultures in general and of Old Testament religion in particular can drive the ordinary Christian inquirer to distraction. Pity the poor preacher trained in the historical-critical method who is trying to preach about the sacrifice of Christ. How is she to deal with the distinctions between sin offerings, guilt offerings, thank offerings, alimentary offerings, scapegoats, surrogates, holocausts, expiatory sacrifices, propitiatory sacrifices, covenant sacrifices, and so forth?[18] But seminary education has changed so much in the last forty years that there is now a danger of preachers making *too little* effort to study background. Still, a reminder may be in order. The preacher or teacher seeking to say something theological need not be held hostage to the significance of every last thing that has been dug up in the ancient Near East. Sooner or later, the interpreter must arrive at *a theology of Christ's atoning sacrifice* that takes into account the findings of historical research without being tyrannized by them. The concept of sacrifice has a universal meaning that is more to the point.

Leviticus, with its elaborate proscriptions and rituals, is considered foreign and is even presented as laughable in some circles today, but it contains a remarkable amount of fertile soil if one knows where and how to look

17. *Ephapax,* "once for all," is unique to Hebrews and is repeated four times in relation to Jesus' self-offering: "He has appeared *ephapax* at the end of the age to put away sin by the sacrifice of himself" (Heb. 9:26; also 7:27; 9:12; 10:10).

18. When I first began to learn the technical refinements of modern critical research into these practices, I was afraid to utter a word about Jesus' sacrifice lest some expert on the ancient Near East leap out at me from beneath the pulpit. Fortunately, we are no longer captive to this sort of thing; theological students today need not experience the same fright that I did.

for it.[19] The first thing to remember is that these codes were given to God's people living in alien territory. This was true of the Israelites throughout most of their biblical history; they were "sojourning" in either Canaan or Babylon or the Roman Empire. The period when they were truly at home was all too brief. This is still true for Christians, or should be, because the people of God are always going to be uneasily situated. We live as exiles in territory that is either besieged or occupied by alien gods.[20] The church should always have a sense of being in a strange land, and if we are not feeling this tension, we are not really being the church: "Woe to those who are at ease in Zion" (Amos 6:1).

The Holiness Code in Leviticus begins in chapter 18 and casts a retrospective light on the whole book. Generally dated from the early exilic period, the code is designed to *differentiate* the people of God from the people of Babylon and, later, of the other lands of the Diaspora. This differentiation, this set-apartness, has a high purpose: the holy community is to be a perpetual witness to the God who is altogether different from and other than the so-called gods of the nations. *"I am your God"* is no small thing to say, since there were and are "gods many, and lords many" (I Cor. 8:5 KJV). The pertinence of this for today should be obvious. The Canaanite and Babylonian gods were honored with names, statues, and altars, but the Baals of today are idols no less.[21] Celebrities today are called "icons," a term once reserved for objects of religious veneration. We now refer to "building wealth" as though

19. Ephraim Radner's theological commentary on Leviticus argues for "world-historical," global, indeed "cosmic" significance of this much-disdained book, for both Christians and Jews. Radner cautions against focusing exclusively on the motif of sacrifice when reading the book christologically, because sacrifice is a "reflective element . . . within [Leviticus's] larger display of the character of *all* creation . . . as variously related to God through the reality of self-offering" (*Leviticus,* Brazos Theological Commentary on the Bible [Grand Rapids: Brazos, 2008], 174). One need not agree entirely with all of Radner's imaginative readings to appreciate his rethinking of Leviticus in conversation with such premodern interpreters as Origen, Rashi, and Pascal. Leviticus is by no means focused exclusively on atonement, ritual purification, blood sacrifice, and related issues. In the Jubilee chapter (chap. 25), the themes of economic justice and deliverance from bondage are powerfully present. See F. W. Dillistone, *The Christian Understanding of Atonement* (Philadelphia: Westminster, 1968), 183-84.

20. This theme of being an alien and a stranger has been superlatively developed in the novels of Walker Percy — hence the title of his collected essays, *Signposts in a Strange Land.* Likewise, William Stringfellow's excellent, if idiosyncratic, book about Revelation is called *An Ethic for Christians and Other Aliens in a Strange Land. Resident Aliens* is the title of a well-known collaboration of Stanley Hauerwas and Will Willimon.

21. Leviticus was not put together in its present form until after the fall of Jerusalem to the Babylonians, but it is based on much older material, hence my references to "Canaanites." I mean the Canaanites and the Baals to stand for idolatry in general from that day to this.

we were building a cathedral. Luxurious possessions, erotic sensation, self-seeking and self-aggrandizement of all kinds — these are some of our gods today, and we sacrifice staggering amounts of money, attention, time, and energy to them. Indeed, if truth be told, we sacrifice most of our lives to them. Strange though much of Leviticus seems to us today, the theological foundation of the Holiness Code has never sounded more relevant:

> The Lord said to Moses, "Say to the people of Israel, I am the Lord your God. You shall not do as they do in the land of Egypt, where you dwelt, and you shall not do as they do in the land of Canaan, to which I am bringing you. You shall not walk in their statutes. You shall do my ordinances and keep my statutes and walk in them. I am the Lord your God. You shall therefore keep my statutes and my ordinances, by doing which a man shall live: I am the Lord." (Lev. 18:1-5)

Note the solemn asseveration, repeated throughout the book, "I am the Lord." There is nothing prescribed in Leviticus that is not designed to point beyond itself to the one God. Most of the actual ordinances in Leviticus are inconceivable to us today, but with a little extra effort we can grasp the significance of the "holiness" to which God's people are called. "Holiness" is part of a foundational word-group in both Hebrew *(qadhosh, qodhesh)* and Greek *(hagios)* that, in translation, includes "sacred," "saint," "sanctification"; its root meaning is "to be set apart from, to be distinct from." The purpose of living "apart" is to glorify Israel's God in the midst of a rampaging pagan culture.[22] The only way this can be done is by a distinct way of life. God's people adhere to a different mode of existence in the world, one that proclaims the true God over against the "gods many and lords many" that Paul spoke of to the Corinthian church — for ultimately, looking far beyond Leviticus, the distinction is between the gods of the surrounding culture and the crucified Messiah, who is unique in all the world and unheard of in "religion."[23]

This distinction does not mean that Israel is allowed to disdain the people around her. In a particularly significant passage, Leviticus instructs, "The stranger who sojourns with you shall be to you as the native among you, and you shall love him as yourself; for you were strangers in the land of Egypt"

---

22. The narratives of Dan. 1–3 concerning the behavior of Shadrach, Meshach, Abednego, and Daniel in Babylon have great power to this day.

23. "For though there be that are called gods, whether in heaven or in earth, (as there be gods many, and lords many,) but to us there is but one God, the Father, of whom are all things, and we in him; and one Lord Jesus Christ, by whom are all things, and we by him" (I Cor. 8:5-6 KJV).

(Lev. 19:34). Ellen F. Davis calls this a "destabilizing factor within Leviticus," meaning that even within the strict Holiness Code, a future way is already opened up; "the Levitical vision contains the mustard seed that will grow to burst the limits of that vision . . . this is what happens with Jesus and his followers."[24] Set-apartness is not meant to encourage a sense of superiority on the part of God's people; it is *God* who is superior, not his servants.[25] The members of the community are not to look down their collective noses at the Canaanites floundering in their idolatry. If we take the whole grand sweep of the Old Testament into consideration, the ultimate design is for Israel to be a blessing to *all* the peoples of the earth. Looking ahead to Romans 4, concerning the promise made to Abraham, there is no one, however far gone in unrighteousness, who is beyond the reach of the crucified One who died for the *ungodly* (Rom. 5:6). Therefore, the people of God both do, and do not, hold themselves apart.

The early Christians had no New Testament. Their single source for discovering the meaning of the strange death of their Lord was the Scriptures they had always known. Imagine the attention with which early Christian leaders searched every syllable of the Hebrew Bible, seeking to understand how the terrible death of the Son of God had been in the mind and plan of God all along. It must have been a very exciting process. Anyone reading Leviticus and thinking of Jesus at the same time could hardly fail to notice a phrase like "a male without blemish" in the list of stipulations. This is the sort of detail that would jump off the page of the Hebrew Scriptures in those first years after the resurrection. If we make the effort to read the Old Testament in a similar way, looking for clues, we can come much closer to the mind of God in preparing his people for the coming of the Messiah.[26]

---

24. Ellen F. Davis, "Reading Leviticus in the Church," *Virginia Seminary Journal* (Winter 1996-1997).

25. Philip Hughes, in his commentary on Hebrews, makes a nice distinction between "separation from" and "separation to," which removes some of the problems associated with the idea of being "set apart." He makes this point with reference to Heb. 13:12-13, where Christians are called away from the sacred precincts to go "outside the camp," where Jesus "endured the cross, despising the shame" (12:2). "By suffering outside the gate, Jesus identifies himself with the world in its unholiness. . . . On our unholy ground he makes his holiness available to us in exchange for our sin which he bears and for which he atones on the cross. . . . This following of Christ inescapably involves going outside the camp where the cross, too shameful to be placed inside the camp, is located." He then quotes F. F. Bruce to great effect: "What was formerly sacred was now unhallowed, because Jesus had been expelled from it, and what was formerly unhallowed was now sacred ground because Jesus was there" (Philip Edgcumbe Hughes, *A Commentary on the Epistle to the Hebrews* [Grand Rapids: Eerdmans, 1977], 580-82).

26. We don't want to be imperialistic about reading the Old Testament; it is very im-

In Leviticus 1:3, we read that the petitioner is to make his offering "at the door of the tent of meeting, that he may be accepted before the Lord." The basic presupposition here is that we aren't acceptable before the Lord "just the way we are," as is glibly said so often today. Something has to transpire before we are counted as acceptable. Nor can we expect to be rendered acceptable this week and then be off the hook for the next month. In Leviticus, the gap between the holiness of God and the sinfulness of human beings is assumed to be so great that the sacrificial offering has to be made on a regular basis.

The provisions of the Hebrew sacrificial system are partly intended for purification from ritual uncleanness — in that regard they are not so different from sacrifices in other religious contexts — as an aspect of atonement for sin. Thus we learn that *God himself has provided the means* for the continual restoration of the people in view of their sinfulness. The Old Testament sacrificial system has a gentleness about it that is hard for us to see from our distance, but perhaps we can grasp the general idea of God's patience and kindness in giving his perpetually wayward people the means to stand before him. His righteousness is active in making his people righteous.

The instructions at the beginning of Leviticus are these: the worshiper "shall offer a male without blemish; he shall offer it at the door of the tent of meeting, that he may be accepted before the Lord; he shall lay his hand upon the head of the burnt offering, and it shall be accepted for him to make atonement for him" (Lev. 1:3-4). "For him" can mean "on behalf of," or it can mean "in the place of." The laying on of hands has the effect of declaring the animal to be a vicarious representative of the worshiper.[27] There is certainly a suggestion of substitution here. In some sense the sacrificial animal *takes the place of* the person who needs forgiveness and restitution. The blood of the substituted animal is thus received as an atonement or "cover" for sin (see also Exod. 29:35-37).

The provisions for the sin offering begin with chapter 4: "The Lord said to Moses, . . . if anyone sins unwittingly in any of the things which the Lord has commanded not to be done . . . if it is the anointed priest who sins . . . if the whole congregation of Israel commits a sin . . . when a ruler sins . . . if any one of the common people sins . . ." There are extensive arrangements

---

portant for Christians to remember that this is not exclusively our book. However, if we allow our fear of offending Jewish people to lessen our appreciation for the wonderful things that the early church saw in the Hebrew Scriptures about Jesus, the church will continue to suffer from malnutrition.

27. This is, in part, the idea that Joseph Mitchell was reaching for in the story about his dying sister's question (see introduction).

for every individual and every group. The outcome of the blood sacrifices is that the priest shall make atonement for them and their sins shall be forgiven. The fundamental presupposition here is that there must be *atonement* for sin, an idea that was stressed in chapter 3. Sin can't be just forgiven and then set aside as though nothing has happened. If someone commits a terrible wrong, Christians know that we are to forgive seventy times seven; but something in us nevertheless cries out for justice. The Old and New Testaments both speak profoundly to this problem. It is not enough to say, "Mistakes were made," or "I didn't mean to"; the whole system in Leviticus is set up to prevent anyone from thinking that "unwitting" sin doesn't count.[28]

Basic to the ritual is the idea that atonement for sin *costs something.* Something valuable has to be offered in restitution. The life of the sacrificed animal, together with the sense of awe associated with the shedding of blood, represents this payment. "Without the shedding of blood there is no forgiveness of sins" (Heb. 9:22). The blood represents the ultimate cost to the giver. There is something powerful here that grips us in spite of ourselves. The use of the phrase "blood of Christ" in the New Testament carries with it this sacrificial, atoning significance in a primordial sense; we cannot root out these connections even if we wanted to.

Leviticus 5:14 maintains that one who sins must bring a guilt offering to the Lord "valued . . . in shekels of silver." Note the emphasis on assigning *value* to the offering. The suggestion is that there should be some correlation of the value of the offering with the gravity of the offense. If the supposed sacrifice is just something we are getting rid of, like those old clothes in the back of our closet that we haven't worn for years, then restitution is not made. Anselm's word "satisfaction" seems right here, with its suggestion of comparable cost. We are familiar with this notion; we are infuriated when people who have committed great crimes get off with light sentences. The trouble is that there is no adequate punishment for a truly great crime. How could there be any offering valuable enough to compensate for the victims of just one bombing, let alone genocides of millions? Anselm's point is once again apposite: "You have not yet considered the weight of sin." The obvious conclusion, explicitly drawn in Hebrews, is that the sacrificing of animals just isn't enough. One of the simplest ways of understanding the death of Jesus

---

28. Significantly, there is no provision made in the priestly code for deliberate sin. See the rather shocking passage in Num. 15:30-31: "The person who does anything with a high hand . . . that person shall be utterly cut off; his iniquity shall be upon him." There are many possibilities for reinterpretation around the declaration that *Christ died for the ungodly,* a central theme that will be prominent in the final chapters of this volume.

is to say that when we look at the cross, we see what it cost God to secure our release from sin.

None of this will be persuasive to anyone who does not already know himself to be within the sphere of God's grace. In view of the widespread notion that the Old Testament is all about sin and judgment, there is an urgent need in the church for more intentional teaching of the enveloping grace in the First Testament. God's redemptive purpose in electing a people (Gen. 12:1-3; 17:1-27) was put into effect *long before* the giving of commandments and ordinances.[29] This covenant security is the foundation that allows us to come before God in full knowledge of our sinful condition. We cannot remain before him "just as we are." The sacrificial system of the Old Testament, however forbidding it may appear to us today, shows that the people of God *already* stand in grace, *even before* the sacrifices are offered. God has already told them, *You are my people*.[30] God himself has ordained the means whereby we may draw near to him. The ordinances in the Torah are not a catalogue of tribal customs. They are gifts from the living God.

The rise of apocalyptic in the years just before the birth of Christ influences our reading of Leviticus. This postexilic way of seeing, with its emphasis on God's intervention from beyond human capacity, was not simply a religious adaptation to a calamitous series of events.[31] The calamitous series was itself an aspect of the unfolding of God's purpose. The point came when it was time to declare the old sacrifices ineffective. This doesn't mean that God tried the sacrificial system for a while and then abandoned it when he saw it wasn't working. The inadequacies in the system were not a flaw in its design, but part of God's purpose from the beginning: "Now if perfection had been attainable through the Levitical priesthood . . . what further need

29. We can see how this works in everyday life. If a child is rebuked, the rebuke must be done by an unconditionally loving person, so that the child can receive the message in safety. That is the way grace works. As we said in chapter 4, it is the knowledge that we are *already secure* that allows us to receive the word of reproach with gratitude.

30. Even toward the end of Leviticus, where there are a number of stern warnings, there are these words: "Yet for all that, when they are in the land of their enemies, I will not spurn them, neither will I abhor them so as to destroy them utterly and break my covenant with them; for I am the Lord their God; but I will for their sake remember the covenant with their forefathers, whom I brought forth out of the land of Egypt in the sight of the nations, that I might be their God" (Lev. 26:44-45).

31. This can never be demonstrated to the satisfaction of historians of religion, anthropologists, sociologists, literary critics, etc. It is a faith claim, based on the Bible's own claims for itself. There will always be counterclaims that apocalyptic is a move of desperation; see, for instance, Jasper Griffin, "New Heaven, New Earth," *New York Review of Books,* December 22, 1994.

would there have been for another priest . . . ?" (Heb. 7:11). The perceived inefficacy of the sacrifices for keeping Israel on the straight and narrow was part of God's preparation of his people for *the sacrifice that would not fail,* namely, the self-offering of the Son. This is a crucial theological point, namely, that the sacrifice of Christ was not God's reaction to human sin, but an inherent, original movement within God's very being. It is in the very nature of God to offer God's self sacrificially.

The Scapegoat and the Day of Atonement in Leviticus

Leviticus 16 has two descriptions of the Day of Atonement. There is a short version (16:6-10) and a long version (16:11-28); the long one has more interesting detail. There are two goats in view here; one is to be killed and one is to be sent away.

> Then [Aaron] shall kill the goat of the sin offering which is for the people, and bring its blood within the veil . . . sprinkling it upon the mercy seat and before the mercy seat; thus he shall make atonement for the holy place, because of the uncleannesses of the people of Israel, and because of their transgressions, all their sins. (vv. 15-16)

> And when he has made an end of atoning for the holy place and the tent of meeting and the altar, he shall present the live goat; and Aaron shall lay both his hands upon the head of the live goat, and confess over him all the iniquities of the people of Israel, and all their transgressions, all their sins; and he shall put them upon the head of the goat, and send him away into the wilderness by the hand of a man who is in readiness. The goat shall bear all their iniquities upon him to a solitary land; and he shall let the goat go in the wilderness. (vv. 20-22)

> The sin offering and the goat for the sin offering, whose blood was brought in to make atonement in the holy place, shall be carried forth outside the camp; their skin and their flesh and their dung shall be burned with fire. (v. 27)

There are two types of animals here in Leviticus 16, the sin offering and the scapegoat. We will have all sorts of problems if we try too hard to make literal connections between Jesus and these two animals. For one thing, neither one is a lamb; Jesus was never called "the goat of God"! Even the author of Hebrews, who was by no means expert about the details of the sacrifices, knew that it was the "blood of bulls and goats" rather than lambs that was generally used for the sin offering. So there is considerable conflation of symbols in the New Testament, and we may be thankful for the freedom that this allows us today.

As it happens, the scapegoat image makes little direct imprint in the New Testament.[32] Morna Hooker and E. G. Selwyn suggest that it is present in I Peter 2:24 ("he himself bore our sins in his body on the tree"), but this is far from certain.[33] We cannot make an explicit case for Jesus as a scapegoat from the New Testament. Theologians, however, have seen that since the phenomenon of scapegoating is virtually universal in human nature, it makes sense to think that Jesus' taking our sin upon himself would involve his being a scapegoat as well as a sin offering. T. F. Torrance certainly thinks so: "That piece of ritual [the sending out of the scapegoat], which has ever since haunted the memory of Israel throughout its generations, made it clear that *both kinds* of sacrifice were needed to help people understand what God was about in making atonement for sin."[34] Miroslav Volf has also developed this theme; he writes that "the cross lays bare the mechanism of scapegoating."[35] In saying that Jesus was an antitype of the scapegoat, we recognize that he was the innocent person onto whom we projected all our anxieties and fears. Jesus really entered into our sin, as various New Testament passages affirm; surely we can agree that he functioned as a scapegoat, "driven into the wilderness" or "outside the camp" carrying the burden of our sin, to be assaulted by the demonic powers in full strength.

The phenomenon of the scapegoat has gained a good deal of traction lately because of the work of the literary critic and cultural anthropologist René Girard, and his disciple, James Alison, who has interpreted his work for

32. I have not been able to find anyone other than myself who sees a glancing reference to the scapegoat imagery in Mark 1:12 ("The Spirit immediately drove [Jesus] out into the wilderness," where he contended with Satan) or in Heb. 13:13 ("Let us go forth to him outside the camp, and bear the abuse he endured").

33. E. G. Selwyn, *The First Epistle of St. Peter* (London: Macmillan, 1964), 94; Morna Hooker, *Not Ashamed of the Gospel: New Testament Interpretations of the Death of Christ* (Grand Rapids: Eerdmans, 1994), 127.

34. Thomas F. Torrance, *The Mediation of Christ,* rev. ed. (Colorado Springs: Helmers and Howard, 1992; orig. 1983), 36.

35. Miroslav Volf, *Exclusion and Embrace: A Theological Exploration of Identity, Otherness, and Reconciliation* (Nashville: Abingdon, 1996), 292. The scapegoat motif seems to be the province of the theologians rather than the biblical scholars, which suggests that there needs to be more cross-conversation between the two.

the church.[36] There is a good deal in Girard that we can endorse. Scapegoating, the transferal of one's own sin to an innocent victim (the term is derived from Lev. 16:20-22), is a universal human phenomenon, one of the most virulent manifestations of the Enemy's effectiveness (not that Girard would put it that way). In particular, we can emphatically affirm Girard's and Alison's emphasis on Jesus' identification with the lowly, the victimized, the oppressed — with the *abandonados,* as Latin Americans call them. Certainly this identification helps us understand why Jesus was *crucified* instead of being put to death by some other, more seemly method. However, the relentless Girardian emphasis on victims leaves us with nothing to say for or about victimizers, and that will be one of our central concerns as we continue to examine the meaning of the righteousness of God *(dikaiosyne theou)*. Another failing of the Girard-Alison presentation is its lack of any sense of the Powers that have all human beings in their grip.[37] Indeed, a sense of sin is lacking altogether. The emphasis on victims therefore threatens to tip over into sentimental "victimology."[38]

We cannot find any more support for the scapegoat concept in the New Testament. The Epistle to the Hebrews says a great deal about the other animal, however, the slaughtered sin-offering whose remains are burned "outside the camp." We turn now to that unique New Testament book.

36. Girard's work is difficult for the nonacademic reader. James Alison has written numerous books interpreting Girard's ideas for religious seekers and for the reading public in general. A significant number of Christians have taken up Girard's ideas through Alison, and there are some correlations with the theology of the cross that cause people to conflate Girard/Alison with the ideas in this book. For this reason, I myself have read Alison (though not Girard) and find myself in general agreement with the assessments of Miroslav Volf and William Placher, academic theologians who are familiar with the work of Girard himself. Placher, like many others, complains that Girard seems to think that if people will only see the universal myth of the scapegoat through his eyes, the problem of scapegoating will go away (Placher, "Christ Takes Our Place: Rethinking Atonement," *Interpretation* 53, no. 1 [January 1999]: 7-9). George Hunsinger has examined Girard in detail and has retrieved some of his insights — with important reservations — for Christian theology in *Disruptive Grace* (21-41).

37. Miroslav Volf affirms Girard in his emphasis on God's concern for victims, but goes much further to address the problem. He notes (1) Girard's inability to envision the rectification *(dikaiosyne)* of the perpetrators, and (2) his naïveté about the persistence of scapegoating even after it has been "unmasked" *(Exclusion and Embrace,* 93, 118, 292-93). For further critiques of Girard, see Placher, "Christ Takes Our Place."

38. The reader is referred back to the section on sentimentality in chapter 4. Gerhard Forde begins his treatment of Luther's *theologia crucis* with a critique of sentimentality and its emphasis on victims. We should not "rush into some sort of cozy identification with" Christ as crucified victim. "God and his Christ . . . are the *operators* in the matter, not the ones operated upon" *(On Being a Theologian of the Cross: Reflections on Luther's Heidelberg Disputation, 1518* [Grand Rapids: Eerdmans, 1997], viii-ix).

The Theme of Sacrifice in the Epistle to the Hebrews

The Epistle to the Hebrews is distinctive among New Testament writings for several reasons, including the mystery of its provenance. The most important thing about this book for us is that it is the only New Testament writing that focuses almost exclusively on Christ's death as a sacrifice for sin. In contrast, Paul does not emphasize this theme, though he certainly uses it from time to time, as in Romans 3:25 and 5:9 and I Corinthians 5:7. Paul takes in more territory in his vision of the cross than any other New Testament writer, which explains why we are paying so much attention to his letters. In the interest of presenting the most comprehensive view possible, however, we must examine the special, idiosyncratic genius of Hebrews as one part of the total picture.[39]

In the nineteenth century, Hebrews was one of the most popular books among Protestant preachers. In our time, however, Hebrews has received much less attention.[40] This is unfortunate, because Hebrews combines some of the highest Christology in the New Testament with some of the most wrenching descriptions of Jesus' suffering humanity. For this alone it should

39. One of many decisions that we must make in understanding the cross is how we treat the various books of the Bible and various voices within those books. For instance, we will be right to make a distinction between the way Paul speaks of the blood and the way Hebrews does. Pauline specialists point out that Paul is not much interested in the cult of sacrifice; "by his blood" is "not a pointed allusion to the sacrificial system" (Cousar, *Theology of the Cross,* 63). To be sure, no book of the New Testament compares with Hebrews for emphasis on the Old Testament sacrificial cult, but the preacher/exegete working from a canonical context will not feel slavishly bound to leave the insights of Hebrews out of the picture. It isn't a good idea to conflate Paul and Hebrews unthinkingly, because it will blunt Paul's radicality; but the fact that Paul doesn't generally use "blood" with a conspicuously cultic connotation doesn't mean that those who especially value Paul can't preach from Hebrews with conviction and gratitude. In Rom. 3:25, Paul combines the images by referring to "Christ Jesus, whom God put forward as an expiation *(hilasterion)* by his blood," which is cultic language. Paul is comfortable appropriating such language, which was probably the common property of the New Testament church, but it is not typical of him.

40. Indeed, it is sometimes said that Hebrews is so uncongenial for modern sensibilities that it cannot be taught in parishes today. Having taught it myself many times, I take vigorous exception to this. It takes some effort to learn the special language and outlook of Hebrews in order to understand it, but it is by no means as difficult as catching on to Paul's worldview. In fact, many people, I have discovered to my bemusement, love hearing about the wilderness tabernacle and the Aaronic priesthood; they even like Melchizedek, because it is all "historical" and therefore less challenging than Paul's radical message. The teaching about angels in Heb. 1 has become newly relevant because of the sudden upsurge of interest in angels in popular culture. All in all, therefore, Hebrews is by no means unteachable.

be prized. The letter begins with this proclamation about Jesus Christ: he is the Son "whom [God] appointed the heir of all things, through whom also he created the world. He reflects the glory of God and bears the very stamp of his nature, upholding the universe by his word of power. When he had made purification for sins, he sat down at the right hand of the Majesty on high" (Heb. 1:2-3).

Astonishingly, it is this uniquely divine being who "had to be made like his brethren in every respect, so that he might become a merciful and faithful high priest in the service of God, to make expiation for the sins of the people. For because he himself has suffered and been tempted, he is able to help those who are tempted" (2:17-18).

How was this expiation *(hilasterion)* accomplished? Hebrews works this out in fascinating detail, which should not be dismissed as esoteric and inaccessible.

The role assigned to Christ by the unknown author of Hebrews is that of high priest; no other portion of Scripture does so with such elaborate emphasis. The death of Christ is identified as a sacrifice squarely in the line of the Old Testament sacrifices, but with differences so great as to make the two virtually incomparable. The author begins by contrasting Jesus' high priesthood to that of the priests in Levitical times, and then makes numerous other comparisons to teach the surpassing superiority of the Lord's sacrifice; this is, according to one noted scholar, "the longest sustained argument of any book in the Bible."[41] It is too lengthy to quote here in full, but here is an outline. Note especially the *contrasts:*

- Christ, *unlike the former priests,* has been tempted, and sympathizes with our weakness yet remains *without sin* (4:15).
- Christ has become High Priest, not according to earthly ancestry but — in a beautiful phrase — "by the power of an indestructible life" (7:16).
- The former priests died, but Christ holds his priesthood *permanently* and "always lives to make intercession" for us (7:23-25).
- Christ's work and the covenant he mediates are superior, since they are founded on *better promises* than those of the old priesthood (8:6-7). The author illustrates the "better promise" by quoting the celebrated "new covenant" passage from the Old Testament (Jer. 31:31-34).
- "Christ has entered, not into a sanctuary made with hands, *a copy* of *the true one,* but into heaven itself" (9:24). He is "a minister in the . . . true

41. Bruce Metzger, introduction to Hebrews, in *New Oxford Annotated Bible* (Oxford: Oxford University Press, 1973).

tent which is set up *not by men* but *by the Lord*" (8:2). "The [Levitical law] has *but a shadow* of the good things to come instead of the *true form* of these realities" (10:1).[42]

- Christ "has no need . . . to offer sacrifices daily . . . ; he did this *once for all* when he offered up himself" (7:27; cf. 9:25-26). "In these [Levitical] sacrifices there is a reminder of sin *year after year*. . . . [But Christ] offered *for all time a single sacrifice* for sins" (10:3-4, 12).

- "Every [Levitical] priest *stands* daily at his service, offering repeatedly the same sacrifices, which can never take away sins. But [Christ] *sat down* [the sign of power] at the right hand of God" (10:11-12); this image conveyed the efficacy and finality of his sacrifice.

- "He did not enter by means of *the blood of goats and calves;* but he entered the Most Holy Place once for all by *his own blood,* having obtained eternal redemption" (9:12-14).[43]

These carefully drawn contrasts are not as technical or abstruse as they may sound. If we approach them with a receptive spirit, we will see that the author's purpose is deeply pastoral. The message is addressed to our fears and insecurities, as the following verses show; the author stresses that before Christ, there was no access to the mercy seat behind the curtain (the "veil of the temple") except through the high priest, and that only once a year. The word *ephapax,* meaning "once for all," was very important to the author of Hebrews and should be very important to us. It is repeated four times (Heb. 7:27; 9:12; 9:26; 10:10). The unique event of the crucifixion is fully sufficient. Nothing further can be or need be done. Everything has changed now that Christ has made the once-for-all sacrifice of his own blood, replacing the blood of the sacrificed animals that could never have taken away sin. Unlike the dumb beasts who had no choice in the matter, Jesus was a fully sentient human being who gave himself up for us in the fullest and most intentional way. This action taken by the Son of God has dramatically altered our situation before God; there is now no barrier (curtain) between us and him, since Jesus himself is our High Priest forever. Notice the kindly pastoral assurances:

42. B. F. Westcott writes beautifully about this: "The difference between the 'shadow' and the 'image' is well illustrated by the difference between a 'type' and a 'sacrament,' in which the characteristic differences of the Old and New Covenants are gathered up. The one *witnesses to* grace and truth beyond and outside itself; the other is *the pledge and the means* through which grace and truth are brought home to us" (*The Epistle to the Hebrews* [1889; reprint, Grand Rapids: Eerdmans, 1967], 304, emphasis added).

43. NIV, to correct errors of RSV.

We have this as a sure and steadfast anchor of the soul, a hope that enters into the inner shrine behind the curtain, where Jesus has gone as a forerunner on our behalf, having become a high priest for ever. (6:19-20)

Therefore, brethren, since we have confidence to enter the sanctuary by the blood of Jesus . . . let us draw near with a true heart in full assurance of faith, with our hearts sprinkled clean from an evil conscience and our bodies washed with pure water. (10:19-22)

These are wonderful passages, full of confidence in the achievement of Christ and replete with promise for sinners. Hebrews offers a picture of the human Jesus as rich in some ways as any in the Gospels.[44] The author means to stir the affections with love and gratitude for the Savior who has offered himself for the eternal salvation of us all, the "pioneer and perfecter of our faith, who for the joy that was set before him endured the cross, despising the shame, and is seated at the right hand of the throne of God" (12:2). This last verse is especially pertinent to our subject, highlighting as it does the "shame" of the cross. In addition, Hebrews has its own version of the scene in the Garden of Gethsemane, one that brings us very close to the anguish of our Lord as he takes our sin upon himself:[45] "In the days of his flesh, Jesus offered up prayers and supplications, with loud cries and tears, to him who was able to save him from death, and he was heard for his godly fear. Although he was a Son, he learned obedience through what he suffered; and being made perfect he became the source of eternal salvation to all who obey him" (5:7-8).

In his obedience and self-sacrifice, Christ abolishes the first sin offerings, the ones in which God has "taken no pleasure" (10:6). This theme of God's displeasure in ritual sacrifices tainted by injustice and idolatry is conspicuous in the Hebrew prophets, from Isaiah 1 all the way through to Malachi 1. Christ has remedied this by substituting his own offering, which is himself. The old order is null and void; it has been superseded by the new order

44. We see him entering into our "lifelong bondage" (2:15), wrestling with temptation (2:18; 4:15), suffering throughout his life to be obedient (5:8), enduring hostility from us sinners (12:3), conforming his will to God's will in everything (10:6-10), perfecting his offering of himself through suffering (2:10) so that "by the grace of God he might taste death *for every one*" (2:9).

45. In saying that he takes our sin upon himself, I am illustrating the way in which I believe we can draw upon various meanings. As we shall see with regard to the Lamb of God image, we can understand the cross as removing ("taking away") sin, as bearing sin (II Cor. 5:21), as expiation for sin (Heb. 2:17), and as victory over sin. These are not mutually exclusive. Each has a part to play.

wrought in the *body that was prepared* for the Son at his incarnation. Thus we see once again that the purpose of the incarnation was the offering of his entire incarnate life on the cross. " 'I have come to do thy will' (Hebrews 10:6) is written over the whole record of our Lord's life; this was his attitude from first to last."[46]

The miracle of Christ's sacrificial death is that priest and victim have become one. Instead of an unthinking animal involuntarily slain, the Son of God knowingly offers himself. Instead of a sacrifice endlessly repeated by sinful human beings to no ultimate avail, Jesus' death is *once for all,* having been made by the one who *abides forever* (7:24). Instead of a mere animal physically unblemished, this Victim, though he becomes "lower than the angels" in order to offer himself as a sacrifice for us, is in fact the incarnate Son, whom God "appointed the heir of all things, through whom also he created the world. He reflects the glory of God and bears the very stamp of his nature, upholding the universe by his word of power" (1:2-3). No book of the Bible, not even Colossians or the Gospel of John, combines the two poles of Christ's exalted divinity and his suffering humanity as explicitly as does Hebrews. The *result* of this undertaking — the salvation of humanity — from out of the inner being of the Holy Trinity is, incredibly, that the hearts and minds of sinful human beings should be eternally perfected and at rest in the near presence of the heavenly Father. Therefore "we have confidence to enter the sanctuary by the blood of Jesus" (10:19), for he has brought many sons and daughters to glory (2:10).

In his chapter "The Atonement and the Holy Trinity," T. F. Torrance chooses the language of Hebrews to proclaim the unity of Christ's life and death. He warns against too sharp a distinction between the cross and the totality of Jesus' incarnate life, a characteristic of the Western Church that has always bothered the Eastern Orthodox. "We are not saved by the atoning death of Christ," he writes, "but *by Christ himself.*"[47] There are numerous borrowings from Hebrews in this excerpt from *The Mediation of Christ:*

> The oneness of God's being and act in the incarnation and the atonement once for all bridges the relation between man and God, history and eternity. Jesus Christ himself, God and man in his one person, is the way, the

---

46. F. F. Bruce, *The Epistle to the Hebrews,* 2nd ed., New International Commentary on the New Testament (Grand Rapids: Eerdmans, 1997), 236.

47. From an unpublished paper by Torrance, quoted by George Hunsinger, *Disruptive Grace,* 32 n. 33, emphasis added.

truth, and the life, and there is no other way to the Father. In him priest and sacrifice, offering and the offerer are one, so that he constitutes in himself the new and living way opened up for us into God's immediate presence. He is our Forerunner, our High Priest, in whom our hope is lodged as an anchor sure and steadfast. . . . In him God has drawn near to us, and we may draw near to God with complete confidence as those who are . . . included in his atoning self-presentation through the eternal Spirit to the Father. That is surely what it means for us sinners to have access to the Father through the blood of Christ.[48]

Hebrews is a curiosity among the New Testament books. It would be a mistake to gloss over its singularity and the problems it poses on account of its completely unknown provenance and unique approach. However, when an important theologian like Torrance (who was known for his interest in Jewish-Christian dialogue as well as current developments in the physical sciences) finds the language of Hebrews congenial for a cutting-edge update of his earlier book, we can be confident that there is life yet undiscovered in the image of the sacrifice of Christ. "He has appeared once for all at the end of the age to put away sin by the sacrifice of himself" (Heb. 9:26).

The Lamb of God

The image of the *Agnus Dei,* prominent in the iconography of the church from early times, has a suitable place in a chapter on blood sacrifice. However, it will only be possible to explore briefly the background of the Lamb of God prior to affirming the mystery and radiance of this symbol that has figured so powerfully in the imagination of the church. The phrase itself appears in Scripture only twice, early in John's Gospel: "The next day [John the Baptist] saw Jesus coming toward him, and said, 'Behold, the Lamb of God, who takes away the sin of the world!'" (1:29), and "The next day again John was standing with two of his disciples; and he looked at Jesus as he walked, and said, 'Behold, the Lamb of God!'" (1:35). We do not meet this "Lamb" again in this Gospel, but John makes a significant alteration in the passion narrative (already noted in chap. 5); he changes the chronology so that Jesus is put to death at the same time that the Passover lambs are being slaughtered. Thus two distinct lambs of the Old Tes-

---

48. Torrance, *The Mediation of Christ,* 114-15.

tament — (1) the sin offering, and (2) the paschal (Passover) lamb whose blood was a sign of deliverance from death — are combined into one; this imaginative move should free us from slavish adherence to consistency for its own sake.

It would be a loss, however, to omit the background entirely, for it is richly laden. The phrase "Lamb of God" carries with it at least four distinct traditions, each of which has complexity and richness of its own.[49]

The Apocalyptic Lamb

In Jewish apocalyptic literature, there appears — improbable as it may seem — a figure of a militant lamb who destroys evil. In *I Enoch* 90:38 a messianic figure is represented as a lamb, which then grows to become a ram. Its enemies "sought to lay low its horn, but they had no power over it," and a great victory was achieved. In the *Testament of Joseph* 19:8, a messianic lamb appears among twelve bulls with great horns, symbols of might and dominion, and treads his enemies underfoot. If indeed the actual historical person called John the Baptist referred to Jesus as the Lamb of God, this would almost certainly have been the lamb he had in mind. As far as we can tell, John the Baptist had no conception of a suffering, dying Messiah.[50] However, the modifying phrase "who takes away the sin of the world" does not fit with the destroying lamb, which raises the interesting question of what John the Evangelist had in mind. The conquering seven-horned Lamb in Revelation, a work of the Johannine school, clearly has links to the apocalyptic Lamb ("The Lamb will conquer them, for he is Lord of lords and King of kings" — Rev. 17:14), but since it "has been slain," it is also closely connected to the paschal lamb, and of course, to the crucified Christ. Therefore this aspect of the image should not be discounted.

49. In the cause of clarity, I am loosely following C. H. Dodd's *Interpretation of the Fourth Gospel* (Cambridge: Cambridge University Press, 1965) in this fourfold analysis, but am adding material from the commentaries of Raymond E. Brown, Rudolf Schnackenburg, and Rudolf Bultmann. For simplicity's sake I have glossed over their many disagreements in ways that I trust are not irresponsible.

50. There are several good reasons for thinking that the Evangelist had access to an authentic John the Baptist tradition, including the fact that the title "Lamb of God" is not used again in the Gospel. Even Bultmann thinks so (*The Gospel of John* [Philadelphia: Westminster, 1971], 95).

The Lamb as the Suffering Servant of Isaiah 53

In Isaiah 53:7, the innocent, vicariously suffering Servant is depicted as a lamb:

> He was oppressed, and he was afflicted,
>   yet he opened not his mouth;
> like a lamb that is led to the slaughter,
>   and like a sheep that before its shearers is dumb,
>   so he opened not his mouth.

This image almost certainly lies behind I Peter 2:23-24: "When he was reviled, he did not revile in return; when he suffered, he did not threaten; but he trusted to him who judges justly. He himself bore our sins in his body on the tree." We have no evidence that this particular connection was ever made prior to the early Christian era, so it is not likely to have been in the mind of the historical John the Baptist, but John the Evangelist may very well have been thinking of it. The portion of the Servant passage that resonates most deeply with Christians is verse 5:

> He was wounded for our transgressions,
>   he was bruised for our iniquities;
> upon him was the chastisement that made us whole,
>   and with his stripes we are healed.

This is not specifically linked with the lamb image, but in the imagination of those who love Jesus for his vicarious self-offering, the identification lies close at hand.[51]

The Paschal (Passover) Lamb

This image would have had a very high degree of recognition in any early Christian audience. Most people, including many Gentiles, knew about the slaughtered lamb that was a *central feature* of the Passover rite (whereas the

---

51. Thus Elisabeth Schüssler-Fiorenza: "the expiatory functions of the Lamb of God in the present context of the Gospel [of John] and its interpretation in the light of Isaiah 53 and the Paschal Lamb are accepted" (*The Book of Revelation: Justice and Judgment* [Philadelphia: Fortress, 1985], 96).

lamb in Isaiah 53 is not at all the center of the Suffering Servant passage). We know from I Corinthians 5:7 ("Christ, our paschal lamb, has been sacrificed [for us]") that the identification of Jesus with the paschal lamb must have been made very early — within twenty or thirty years, at most, of the resurrection. Furthermore, the Gospel of John is replete with Passover imagery, including the reference to "not a bone of him shall be broken" (John 19:36; cf. Exod. 12:46). Although taking away sin was not the function of the paschal lamb, as Raymond Brown writes, the early Christians would hardly have made a fine distinction between a lamb's blood on the doorpost as a sign of deliverance from slavery and a lamb's blood offered as a sign of deliverance from sin. In the I Corinthians 5:7 reference, the paschal lamb is called a sacrifice; "in such a Christian deepening of the concept of the Paschal lamb, the function of taking away the world's sin could easily be fitted."[52]

The Lamb as the Sin Offering of Leviticus 14

Although the sin offering was usually a bull or a goat, there were no hard-and-fast distinctions among the various motifs in the minds of the New Testament writers. Clearly they blended the sacrificed male lamb of Leviticus 14 and 23:12 with various other meanings. But we cannot insist too much on the references in Leviticus, since the lambs prescribed in that book are often female. The emphasis must lie elsewhere. As Brevard Childs has noted, in the New Testament "the slaughtered Lamb becomes a symbol of *the cost to God* of Israel's redemption, indeed the redemption of the whole world. I Peter [brings] together the Passover lamb with the suffering Servant, which becomes a model for later Christian theology."[53]

None of these four "lamb" categories, taken alone, is enough to carry the whole weight of John the Baptist's saying in John's Gospel, "Behold, the Lamb of God, who takes away the sin of the world!" It is the *combination* of all these traditions — the apocalyptic lamb, the *ebed Yahweh* (servant of the Lord) in Isaiah, the Passover lamb, and the sin offering of Leviticus — that made the image so fraught with implications. As C. H. Dodd writes in his excellent, if controversial, discussion of the subject: "The [apocalyptic] 'Lamb'

52. Raymond E. Brown, *The Gospel according to John* (New York: Doubleday, 1966), 62. This passage illustrates the way that Brown, a historical-critical scholar *par excellence* in his training, was able to work with imagery even in his early writing, before the turn in the academy to more consciously literary criticism.

53. Brevard Childs, *The Book of Exodus: A Critical, Theological Commentary,* Old Testament Library (Philadelphia: Westminster, 1974), 213.

is the Messiah, and primarily the militant and conquering Messiah; but in the Christian writing, which has in view the historical crucified Messiah, the [apocalyptic] bellwether of God's flock *is fused with* the lamb of sacrifice."[54]

Disputes about these important issues will continue to arise. All controversy aside, however, the numinous aura of the *Agnus Dei* will remain with us as long as the great settings of the Mass by Bach, Haydn, Mozart, Stravinsky, and others are sung.[55]

The Binding of Isaac: A Theological Interpretation

The story of the sacrifice of Isaac on Mount Moriah (Gen. 22:1-14), with the climactic intervention of God providing a ram as a substitute for Isaac, is one of the church's appointed readings for Good Friday.[56] Not incidentally, it is the most refined and polished of all the patriarchal narratives. It is placed to serve as the climax of the saga of Abraham, and it tells of his journey, at God's bidding, to offer his only legitimate son, Isaac, the inheritor of the promise, as a sacrifice. In the tradition, it has been seen as a link between the Old Testament and the death of the Son of God.

This has long been recognized as a uniquely challenging Old Testament story. Søren Kierkegaard, in his idiosyncratic but sometimes insightful meditation called *Fear and Trembling,* asks if this story does not reveal an ultimately capricious, arbitrary, and undependable God.[57] In the command that Abraham slaughter his own son, the promise of the salvation of the whole world that Abraham had followed so faithfully for so many decades seemed to be revealed as nothing more than a passing fancy of the deity. God had abandoned

---

54. Dodd, *Interpretation,* 232, emphasis added. Similarly, Schnackenburg writes, "As soon as Jesus was identified as the Paschal lamb . . . the thought of his expiatory death was necessarily involved . . . the triumphant Lamb in Revelation still bears the identifiable marks of slaughter upon him so that the same typology is at work." In other words, early Christianity did not hesitate to combine motifs. Schnackenburg, *The Gospel according to St. John,* 3 vols. (New York: Crossroad, 1982), 1:299-300.

55. The great hymn "Ah, Holy Jesus," sung during Holy Week, evokes Jesus as "the Lamb of God who takes away the sin of the world" by using the related imagery of shepherd and sheep from John 10:1-18: "Lo, the Good Shepherd for the sheep is offered; / The slave hath sinnéd and the son hath suffered; / For our atonement, while we nothing heeded, / God interceded." Johann Heerman, 1585-1647, trans. Robert Seymour Bridges. Episcopal Hymnal #158.

56. In Hebrew tradition, the story is called the *Akedah* ("binding" of Isaac).

57. At the time he wrote *Fear and Trembling,* Søren Kierkegaard was suffering from a major personal crisis concerning his former fiancée Regina, who was in the process of becoming engaged to another man.

his promise and with consummate cruelty had ordered Abraham to destroy what he (God) had been playing around with all along — casting both father and son aside as though they were of no account, as though all those years of obedience and trust had been nothing but a ghastly celestial joke. Kierkegaard satirizes the preacher who does not enter into the "fear and trembling" of the story: "He who is to deliver the discourse can very well sleep till a quarter of an hour before he has to preach, the auditor can very well take a nap during the discourse, for all goes smoothly. . . . It's an affair of a moment, this whole thing, if only you wait a minute, you see the ram, and the trial is over." Kierkegaard summons us rather to "either consign Abraham to oblivion . . . or learn to be dismayed by the tremendous paradox which constitutes the significance of Abraham's life." One of Kierkegaard's insights is particularly useful. He compares his hero Abraham with Agamemnon, who sacrificed his daughter Iphigenia for the recognizable greater good, thereby becoming a tragic hero, whereas Abraham is asked to commit child murder for no apparent purpose. It appears to be the ultimate absurdity. Kierkegaard says at this point, "The tragic hero has need of tears and claims them, and where is the envious eye which would be so barren that it could not weep with Agamemnon; but where is the man with a soul so bewildered that he would have the presumption to weep for Abraham? . . . One cannot weep for Abraham. One approaches him with a *horror religiosus,* as Israel approached Mount Sinai."[58]

Beyond this point in *Fear and Trembling,* Kierkegaard's treatment is not very helpful, but this particular point is exactly right. It is common today to hear impressionistic versions of the story that take Sarah's point of view. The feminist intention of these presentations is that we should weep for Sarah, who as it happens does not even receive the dignity of a mention in the narrative.[59] This, however, is to misappropriate the story for a nontheological purpose. Weeping for Sarah, or for that matter for Abraham and Isaac, is to

---

58. Søren Kierkegaard, *"Fear and Trembling" and "The Sickness unto Death"* (Garden City, N.Y.: Doubleday Anchor Book, 1941, 1954), 71. Kierkegaard's famous phrase describing the story's trajectory is "teleological suspension of the ethical," which certainly has a nice ring to it but does not really bring us to the heart of the matter — the trust placed in God even when there is no humanly discernible future. That is a thought not unrelated to the possibility that humanity might destroy itself in a man-made catastrophe.

59. I do not wish to distance myself from feminism, but from sentimental, tendentious readings. In my opinion, it does the feminist cause no good to wrench the story off its axis in this way. It directs the attention to the wrong subject. Sarah is interesting, and Sarah has her place in the saga, but her place is not here. If we insist on being literal-minded about it, we could say that Abraham most likely did not tell her why he and the boy were going away. (Though there is a late Jewish tradition that Sarah, when the two returned safely, uttered six cries and died on the spot.)

put a very modern psychological twist into the story that is not there. "The ancient grandeur of the passage . . . shows no trace of sentimental features."[60] Children, hearing this story without affect on the part of the teller, do not have sentimental reactions. They may ask hard questions, but they never ask the hard questions that adults *think* they are going to ask. They are apt to receive the story with something much more like the *horror religiosus* of Kierkegaard than with tears for Abraham and Sarah.[61] There is more than one way to absorb the terror of the story.[62]

Kierkegaard's likening of Abraham to Mount Sinai is not unlike Paul's evocation of Abraham in Romans, where the patriarch becomes infinitely more than a specific human person because he embodies the entire unconditional action of God in election and promise as received by faith: "That is why it depends on faith, in order that the promise may rest on grace and be guaranteed to all his descendants — not only to the adherents of the law but also to those who share the faith of Abraham, for he is the father of us all, as it is written, 'I have made you the father of many nations' — in the presence of the God in whom he believed, who gives life to the dead and calls into existence the things that do not exist" (Rom. 4:16-17).

It would be impossible to enlarge the figure of Abraham any more than it is already enlarged in Genesis, but Paul has brought Abraham into the foreground where Christ's death and resurrection have revealed his true apocalyptic significance as the "father of all who believe" (Rom. 4:20-25). This passage is connected by Paul to Abraham's faith as he waited for Sarah to conceive, but the apostle seems to be referring specifically to the *Akedah* when he writes, four chapters later, "What then shall we say to this? If God be for us, who is against us? He who did not spare his own Son but gave him up for us all, will he not also give us all things with him?" (Rom. 8:31-32).

That verse influenced the church in selecting Genesis 22:1-14 as a Good Friday reading. Another caveat is in order, however. The tendency today is

---

60. Old Testament scholar Otto Procksch, quoted by Gerhard von Rad, *Biblical Interpretations in Preaching,* trans. John E. Steely (Nashville: Abingdon, 1977), 38.

61. Milan Kundera's concept of "the second tear" can help us here. The second tear is the tear that we shed along with others who are already weeping, to show solidarity with them. It is vicarious, but does not come from direct emotional involvement and is therefore to some degree false. "What Kundera paid no attention to is the further twist in kitsch, when the second tear comes without the first one's ever occurring" (Avishai Margalit, "The Kitsch of Israel," *New York Review of Books,* November 24, 1988).

62. It is a moral imperative in our time to combat child abuse, marginalization of women, and cruel masculine gods, but these concerns have made it difficult to read the story with Abrahamic trust.

to take the *Akedah* story *too literally,* but that is not to suggest that we are to take it *lightly.* Taking it *not lightly,* though, might mean reading it in simpler trust than we are accustomed to in these complex, irony-laden times.[63]

With these caveats, then, we approach the story of the *Akedah.* First, we need to see it in its context. The saga of Abraham begins in chapter 12; its climax occurs with the command to sacrifice Isaac, ten chapters and several decades later. The last story is deliberately told in the same form as the first:

Leave your country,	Take your son,
your people,	your only son Isaac,
and your father's house	whom you love,
and go to the land	and go to a mountain
that I will show you. (12:1)	I will tell you about. (22:2)

In chapter 12 Abraham is asked to cut himself off from the past. In chapter 22 he is asked to cut himself off from the future.[64] This is the deeper meaning of the story. The path set before Abraham is not only one of child sacrifice, unspeakable as that is.[65] It is "the road out into Godforsakenness."[66] Abraham is asked to burn up the charter of salvation, "leaving for himself nothing but death and hell."[67]

We need to remember all that happened to Abraham and Sarah in the

63. Gretchen Wolff Pritchard has been for many years an advocate of telling stories straight to children, without adult comments. When my grandmother read the Abraham and Isaac story to me, she did not moralize or try to interpret it. She never really even commented on it. She just read it, in a way that conveyed safety and trust. An adult recovery of a childlike trust in *the story itself* is related to what Paul Ricoeur calls "the second naïveté" (*The Symbolism of Evil* [Boston: Beacon Press, 1967], 351).

64. Gerhard von Rad, *Genesis,* rev. ed., Old Testament Library (Philadelphia: Westminster, 1972), 239. Much of what follows is from his chapter on Gen. 22 in *Biblical Interpretations in Preaching,* as well as his *Old Testament Theology,* 2 vols. (New York: Harper and Row, 1962; Louisville: Westminster John Knox, 1965). I have also leaned on Nahum Sarna, *Understanding Genesis: The Heritage of Biblical Israel* (New York: Schocken Books, 1970), as well as Calvin's commentary on Genesis — another superlative resource for preachers.

65. I am not trying to dismiss the horror of the story. Martin Luther is especially good on this; he writes that he could not have been even a spectator, let alone a participant. He says that he and all the rest of us are no better than the beasts of burden that are left at the bottom of the mountain as the father and son ascend to the dread altar. Luther's response, however, is a good illustration of *horror religiosus* rather than the tears for Agamemnon.

66. Von Rad, *Genesis,* 244.

67. John Calvin, *Genesis,* 22.2, in *Calvin's Commentaries,* ed. David W. Torrance and Thomas F. Torrance, trans. William B. Johnston (Grand Rapids: Eerdmans, 1963).

years between Genesis 12:1 and 22:2, the first time and the last time that "God spoke to Abraham." For a great many years, this aging man with a barren wife lived on a promise. God appeared, withdrew, appeared again, withdrew again. Sarah could only laugh at the absurdity of it all, and no wonder.[68] But as Paul says, in spite of these trials Abraham went on hoping against hope *because of the God in whom he believed.* So we have before us a man who has been living with radical trust for a very long time. His response to God's appearance in chapter 22 speaks volumes: "After these things God tested Abraham, and said to him, 'Abraham!' And he said, 'Here am I.' He said, 'Take your son, your only son Isaac, whom you love, and . . . offer him . . . as a burnt offering upon one of the mountains of which I shall tell you.' So Abraham rose early in the morning" (22:1-3).

The narrative is extraordinarily economical, like all biblical narratives. We are told exactly what we need to know, and no more. Abraham has been following and trusting God for so long that it has become a habit. He doesn't storm the gates of heaven with his prayers as Job does. He is ready to submit even before he hears what the command is, *because of the God in whom he believed.* He seems to believe that God is within his rights. On the next day, instead of lying prostrate in bed, Abraham cannot get up too early to do the will of God.[69]

We are meant to see Abraham's seemingly incomprehensible acquiescence in an unthinkable action as a demonstration of the full range of faith, from the heights to a depth no other person but One has ever been asked by God to enter. The fact that Abraham has to do the deed himself is not *theologically* related to the barbarity of it. It is *theologically* related to something else: God asks for a demonstration of faith so extreme that Abraham must be the active participant in it, not just one who stands aside while God strikes Isaac dead. Abraham's trial is a once-for-all event showing us that God can be trusted even in unimaginable darkness. Many have drawn strength from this story, learning what it means to trust God even when he seems to have turned against his own works in "incomprehensible self-contradiction."[70]

The depth of Abraham's faith is suggested by the narrative in the subtlest terms. First, there is the steady repetition of

---

68. The report of Sarah's ribald, scoffing laughter (Gen. 18:9-15) has been much commented on in Christian and rabbinic literature. For years I have quoted this: "Sarah's laughter is faith's constant companion" (Ernst Käsemann, *Perspectives on Paul* [Philadelphia: Fortress, 1971], 69).

69. Calvin, *Genesis*, 22.3.

70. Von Rad, *Old Testament Theology*, 1:171.

your son,
your only son,
Isaac,
whom you love . . .

It is a drumbeat of pain. Then there is the twice-repeated statement, also a drumbeat:

The two of them
went on
together.

Many imaginations have been applied to the question of what they said to each other on the way, but the singular artistry of our storyteller preempts all such speculations:

As the two of them went on together,
Isaac spoke up and said to Abraham,
"Father?"

"Yes, my son?" Abraham replied.

"The fire and the wood are here,"
Isaac said,
"But where is the lamb for the burnt offering?"

Abraham answered,
"God himself will provide the lamb
for the burnt offering,
my son."

And the two of them
went on
together.

This is beyond commentary. It sinks in of its own weightiness. The pace of the narrative, so reticent, so controlled, now slows to an excruciating crawl:

Abraham built an altar there
    and arranged the wood on it.
He bound his son Isaac
    and laid him on the altar,
      on top of the wood.
Then he reached out his hand
    and took the knife
      to slay his son.

Isaac apparently does not resist, a factor that deeply impressed Jewish interpreters. It may not be too much to say that his trustfulness in this excruciating extremity mirrors his father's trust in God. But this does not mean the end of Abraham's personal hopes only, for Isaac is not just any son. He is the sole bearer of the promise for the future. The end of Isaac would mean the end of hope, blessing, and salvation for the whole world. The narrator holds the moment:

Abraham put forth his hand
    and took the knife
      to slay his son. . . .

And suddenly it is allegro:

But the angel of the Lord called to him from heaven and said,
"Abraham, Abraham! Do not lay your hand on the boy or do anything to
    him: for now I know that you fear God,
seeing you have not withheld your son, your only son, from me."
And Abraham lifted up his eyes and looked, and behold!
behind him was a ram, caught in a thicket by his horns,
and Abraham went and took the ram,
and offered it up as a burnt offering instead of his son.
So Abraham called the name of that place "The Lord will provide."

We pause here in silence for a moment, in homage to the gravity of what we have just read. Note that there is no outcry of gladness. The father and the son together have seen the face of something unspeakable. Perhaps they said nothing at all on their three days' journey home. Perhaps this event may be understood as encompassing all the incomprehensible silences of God from that day forward.

So Abraham received his son back again from the dead. He received him

265

at the outermost limit of human experience, and because of this we perceive that the gifts of God come from a realm far beyond our manipulation, our imagining, our expectation, our deserving. To have faith in God, to "fear" God as Abraham did, means to trust God totally and to put oneself and all one's life into God's hands totally, even when the fulfillment of the promises seems to have receded into impossibility.

In conclusion to this section, here is a Good Friday reading of the passage. We note two verses especially: "The Lord himself will provide the lamb for a burnt offering, my son," and "You have not withheld your son, your only son, whom you love." Abraham is for us the unparalleled example of steadfast trust in unimaginable circumstances. God never asked this of anyone else; it was a onetime event, never to be repeated. Never, that is, until the day of the ultimate "counter-attack" (Calvin), God seeming to be against God, when God's own Son cried out on the cross, "My God, my God, why hast thou forsaken me?"

For Isaac, a substitute was provided — Abraham saw a ram caught in the underbrush. "God himself will provide the lamb for an offering, my son." When Jesus came to the cross to bear the sin of the world in fathomless darkness, there was no substitute for him. He himself was the Lamb.[71] God did not withhold his son, his only son. The Son himself became the substitute — for us. But the crucial difference between the *Akedah* and the cross, finally, is that the Father is not sacrificing the Son. God the Father and God the Son *together, with a single will,* enacted the eternal purpose of God that the second person of the blessed Trinity would become "once for all" the perfect burnt offering, for us human beings and for our salvation.

The Temple Veil and the Mercy Seat

The Gospels of Mark, Matthew, and Luke each give "the veil of the temple" a prominent position at the climax of the passion narrative. Here is Mark's wording: "And Jesus uttered a loud cry, and breathed his last. And the curtain [or veil] of the temple [or sanctuary] was torn in two, from top to bottom" (Mark 15:37-38). Note the passive voice, "was torn," signifying that God is the agent. Matthew and Luke use remarkably similar wording, and

71. Here I am going against von Rad, among others who say that the ram is not a type of Christ. Nevertheless, I believe that the use of the word "lamb" in Gen. 22:7 provides us with this interpretive opening, and it is hallowed both by Christian usage and by the suggestion in Rom. 8:31-32.

all three associate the sign with the moment of Jesus' death, though Luke places it just before the death rather than at the very instant. Much homiletical and expository imagination has been brought to bear on the sign of the rent veil; R. E. Brown humorously refers to this interpretive profusion as "luxuriant overgrowth."[72] It results from a classic instance of fusion, because the singular discussion of the veil in Hebrews has often been homiletically combined with the quite different picture given by the Gospels.[73] On the veil in the Synoptic passion narratives, we cite several points. *First,* Jesus predicted the destruction of the Jerusalem temple, so the rending of the curtain vindicates Jesus by signaling the destruction of the sanctuary. *Second,* the Markan wording implies an act of the wrath of God against the corruption of the temple and its priests (as, for instance, in Mal. 1:6–3:4). *Third,* since the rending of garments signified mourning, there may be an element of that as well. *Fourth,* the rending of the veil is included by Matthew in his carefully worked-out list of four signs indicating that the apocalyptic turn of the ages is occurring with the death of the Messiah.[74]

The image of the veil and its corollary, the mercy seat, appears in Hebrews with a different meaning from that of the Synoptic Gospels. Here, the curtain appears as a supporting detail in the overall portrait, unique to Hebrews, of Christ as the High Priest who has offered himself as a sacrifice for sin. Now, to be sure, this angle on the curtain, being peculiar to Hebrews, cannot be described as a major New Testament theme. Furthermore, the whole matter of the veil lends itself to being nibbled to death by historians who have repeatedly pointed out that the author of Hebrews didn't understand the actual setup in the tent and the temple. Vexed though the veil motif may be from the standpoint of the scrupulous historian of religion, it is exceptionally useful as a means of conveying, even to young children, an aspect of the significance of Jesus' death. The two major interpretations

72. Raymond E. Brown, *The Death of the Messiah: From Gethsemane to the Grave; A Commentary on the Passion Narratives in the Four Gospels,* 2 vols. (Garden City, N.Y.: Doubleday, 1994), 2:1098. Brown discusses thoroughly the apocalyptic significance of the veil rending in the Synoptic Gospels in 2:1098-1118.

73. I for one am not disposed to clamp down on free-ranging interpretations of this richly suggestive sign — indeed, I have one to propose — *provided that* each individual New Testament voice is allowed to have its own distinctive parallel place. The layered meaning of the sign in the Gospels (compared with that of Hebrews) should not be allowed to slip out of sight, so I mention it here even though it does not specifically fit with the theme of sacrifice.

74. The power of Matthew's Christology is often overlooked because of a widespread tendency among preachers to emphasize excerpts from the teachings of Jesus while ignoring Matthew's overall narrative structure, which is clearly designed to reveal Jesus as Messiah and Son of God (as described by Jack Dean Kingsbury and Dale Allison, among others).

— the Gospels' use of the "rending" motif to indicate the destruction of the temple as an apocalyptic sign, and the picture of it in Hebrews as the opening of the way into God's presence — can be excitingly combined by preachers and teachers. Adults and children alike are fascinated by the accouterments of the temple and are therefore attracted to this approach.

There are three explicit references to the veil and the Holy of Holies in Hebrews. The author is drawing upon the wilderness tent, or tabernacle, rather than the Jerusalem temple, but this distinction need not be rigorously observed in nonacademic settings where the chief aim is to awaken faith in the benefits of Christ's once-for-all sacrifice. Here is the description in Hebrews: "For a tent was prepared, the outer one, in which were the lampstand and the table and the bread of the Presence; it is called the Holy Place. Behind *the second curtain* [the 'veil of the temple'] stood a tent called the Holy of Holies, having the golden altar of incense and the ark of the covenant. . . . Above it were the cherubim of glory overshadowing *the mercy seat* (Heb. *kapporet;* Gk. *hilasterion*)" (9:2-5).

The Jerusalem temple itself, where Jesus taught every day during the last week of his life, was arranged according to a hierarchy of religious privilege. A general idea of its arrangement seems relevant to our understanding of the veil rending, even though there are no explicit references in Hebrews. The temple was a series of courts within courts. The first court that one entered was the Court of the Gentiles, which was open to everyone. This was the only part of the temple accessible to tourists, sightseers, and pilgrims from other faiths. The "ungodly," no matter how well-placed in Hellenistic or Roman society, were not permitted to penetrate farther. The next court was the Women's Court, which was open to all Jews. That was as far as a Jewish woman could go, however; she could not climb the fifteen steps elevating the Men's Court above the Women's. Within the Men's Court were the sacred precincts. Only the priests could go beyond into the Priest's Court, and thence into the Holy Place. The inmost shrine of the Hebrew faith, the Holy of Holies itself (called the Most Holy Place in some translations), was entirely forbidden to all except the high priest, and even that worthy was permitted to enter only once a year, on the Day of Atonement described in Leviticus 16.

All these distinctions were taken seriously. A warning inscription from the temple of Jerusalem was discovered that read, "No foreigner is to enter within the forecourt and the enclosure around the Temple, and whoever is caught will have himself to blame that his death ensues." Philo of Alexandria reports that any Jew or priest lower than the high priest who entered the Holy of Holies would suffer death without appeal.[75] This ranking of people according to degrees of godliness is basic to religion in general, and remains relevant to all societies today. The whole setup was based on distinctions that separated groups from one another and restricted access to the mercy seat. This is no strange idea; every teenager can understand it. They know about the rope at the clubs that closes off the holy of holies.

Scholars point out that there were at least two curtains in the temple, probably more. One of them closed off the Holy Place from ordinary humans, but the veil in Hebrews is not that one. The final barrier was the hanging that separated the Holy of Holies from *everyone* except the high priest. In Hebrews, the significance of the mercy seat is heightened tremendously by the repeated contrasts, noted above, that the author makes between the old sacrifices and the sacrifice of Christ. The effect upon the reader, once the basic idea is understood, is one of great longing for direct access. Of all the many superiorities attributed to the sacrifice of Christ, the one that concerns us most here is *the opening of the way to all.* No priest of the old covenant had been able to do this. The Aaronic high priest went in to the mercy seat alone; he came out alone. Jesus, however, has performed a radically new act. Here are the two passages explaining the opening of the way:

> We have this as a sure and steadfast anchor of the soul, a hope that enters into the inner shrine behind the curtain, *where Jesus has gone as a forerunner on our behalf,* having become a high priest for ever. (Heb. 6:19-20)

> Therefore, brethren, since we have confidence to enter the sanctuary by the blood of Jesus, by *the new and living way which he opened for us through the curtain,* that is, through his flesh, and since we have a great priest over the house of God, let us draw near with a true heart in full assurance of faith, with our hearts sprinkled clean. (10:19-22)

In a striking and original act of imagination, the author of Hebrews reinterprets the temple veil as the human flesh of Jesus. Christ has gone ahead of us in his incarnate body as our forerunner, bringing our human nature along with him.[76] The curtain that was a constant reminder of the exclusion of sinful humanity from the presence of God is gone forever. The temple has been figuratively destroyed and "raised up again in three days"

---

75. Brown, *Death of the Messiah,* 1:366-67.

76. "Veiled in flesh the Godhead see," writes Charles Wesley in his great doctrinal hymn "Hark, the Herald Angels Sing."

in the body of Christ (John 2:19-21). No longer is the sanctuary forbidden, no longer is an intermediary required, no longer is there any restriction on access to the mercy seat and the remission of sin. Now — broadening the tent image to include the temple — there is no longer any hierarchy. The way is open for Gentiles, for women, for laypeople, for sinners of all sorts and conditions.

Now we may draw on the Gospels along with Hebrews. In Jesus' death on the cross, distinctions forbidding access to God came to an end, because the old earthly sanctuary had come to an end. God himself had destroyed it ("the veil *was rent*," says Matt. 27:51, again the passive voice indicating God's agency). As the Son of God died, Hebrews tells us that his blood was sprinkled, figuratively speaking, on the heavenly mercy seat once and for all, and as the curtain came down, that celestial benefit became ours without distinction or conditions. There was no longer any separation between the godly and the ungodly — a theme to which we will return many times. "The way that was formerly closed is now open. At the moment of his death on the cross, . . . the menacing and obstructing curtain was rent from top to bottom, indicating that God had acted and the way into his holy presence was open at last."[77]

Finally, to cast the whole thing in Paul's apocalyptic terms, the arrangement whereby repentance secured pardon, over and over again — the old *kosmos* of "dead works" — has been put to death *once and for all (ephapax)*. The rending of the veil signals the end of that old world-order. The sacrifices of old have been proven temporary, like the "schoolmaster" in Galatians 3:23-26. They existed to prepare the way for the new creation in the "blood of Christ." From now on, the self-offering of the Son of God, which *precedes* repentance and faith, shows forth its power to give birth to them both in a manner that belongs altogether to the new world-order that comes forth from God, in which there is no need for any further sacrifice. "And I saw no temple in the city, for its temple is the Lord God the Almighty and the Lamb" (Rev. 21:22).

The Unpopularity of Self-Sacrifice in Today's Culture

It is jarring to move from the vision of the new Jerusalem to the influence of advertising in today's culture, but that is the sort of shift that interpret-

---

77. Philip Edgcumbe Hughes, *A Commentary on the Epistle to the Hebrews* (Grand Rapids: Eerdmans, 1977), 407.

ers of the gospel must make in order to teach biblical faith today. One of the most far-reaching developments in the history of the advertising industry, perhaps even in global culture as a whole, was the move from simply pitching products to selling "lifestyles." In one sense, there is nothing really new about this; human beings have always been enthralled by fashion and novelty. In another sense, however, the consumer society that exists today is like nothing the world has ever seen before. The power of visual images, the lure of celebrity, the instantaneous delivery of services, the immediacy of virtual worlds, the demand for more and more stimuli — among many other factors — hold out false possibilities to young people, undermining their ability to postpone gratification in the service of higher goals. The weakening of family ties, school clubs, community associations, not to mention churches and other strong countervailing influences, has made it very difficult to convey any other set of values to young people. All this is well known and often lamented. We mention it here to underline the absence of any sense of *the value of sacrifice* in ordinary life.

At the same time, during the wars of the early twenty-first century in Iraq and Afghanistan, the word "sacrifice" was usually uttered in the solemn, quasi-religious tone reserved for those who have died in combat.[78] It seems that sacrifice is honored in this one area of life but disdained in others. Thoughtful analysts have been complaining for years that there has been no call for sacrifice in America as a whole during the period of these conflicts, especially compared to World War II when the entire society participated in privation. It has been repeatedly noted that the burden of sacrifice in war when there is no draft is borne almost entirely by very young, poorly educated soldiers with few economic prospects, mostly from rural areas and small towns, while other Americans are advised to go shopping — a dictum that gained still more traction during the Great Recession of 2008 and 2009. Objections to the young and underprivileged making all the sacrifices have been largely ignored. There is a good deal of sentimentality about military service, but little enthusiasm for honoring it in any way that would cost us more than displaying American flags and Support Our Troops bumper stickers.

---

78. An extreme example of sacrificial language gone berserk is Hitler's inflammatory use of the German phrase "sacrificial death" *(Obfer-tod),* which has rendered it unusable in German theology today. Stephen W. Sykes, *The Story of Atonement,* Trinity and Truth Series (London: Darton, Longman, and Todd, 1997), 123-24.

Rethinking Women's Objections: Sacrifice as Empowerment

There is presently an intense reaction, rooted in women's experience, against the whole concept of sacrifice. This is one of the most important challenges to the theology of sacrifice, and in some quarters it is now being taken with great seriousness. It is argued that women have traditionally been the ones to assume a disproportionate amount of sacrificing. Many women have been conditioned to think that they have no choices except to be ignored, patronized, exploited, and abused. This has been disabling for women, profoundly so in many cases, and it is part of the work of the church in our time to rethink this whole matter.

A celebrated seventy-five-year-old book, little read during recent decades, was back on must-read lists for geopolitical reasons at the turn of the third millennium. Rebecca West's massive *Black Lamb and Grey Falcon* is purportedly a travel book about the Balkans, but is actually about Rebecca West's views on a great many wide-ranging matters. Relevant to our theme, she has a good deal to say about the "repulsive pretence that pain is the proper price of any good thing."[79] Her almost obsessive loathing of the idea of sacrifice is enshrined in her brilliantly realized description of a Muslim fertility ritual that she saw carried out on a sacred rock in Macedonia, involving the slaughter of many animals, including a black lamb. Inveighing against the whole conception of sacrifice, she concludes that the crucifixion of Jesus could have in no way been God's plan, but was rather the supreme demonstration of man's vileness in opposition to the good. She is absolutely right on that second point. However, her objections to what she sees as our infatuation with the idea of sacrifice are, I think, more aesthetic than anything else. She is too literal-minded about sacrifice (understandably, perhaps, in view of the scene on the rock in the Sheep's Field that she describes in stomach-turning detail); she focuses almost exclusively on the relish with which the slaughterers went about their work.[80] Were you or I actually to see this, we might well have the same reaction. West's angle on this spectacle as a commentary on the entire notion of sacrifice, however, is an illustration of a failure of imagination, a strange thing to say about such a wondrously gifted writer. What is in fact at stake here is an authentic understanding of sacrifice. All her life West inveighed against "the sin of self-sacrifice," particularly as it was recommended to women who were

79. Rebecca West, *Black Lamb and Grey Falcon* (New York: Viking, 1941), 827.
80. This relish, as it happens, was indeed part of "man's vileness," which, in the crucifixion, was fully unleashed upon the Son of God.

supposed to be sheltered in their homes so that "the tranquil flame of [their] unspoiled soul[s] should radiate purity and nobility upon an indefinitely extended family."[81] The question is whether this passionately negative view of sacrifice is the only one possible.[82]

These sorts of feminist objections, made by West more than seventy years ago, have come into their own in our time as a number of female theologians and biblical scholars have provided critiques.[83] The central objection is that the concept of sacrifice has functioned, and has been valued, as a means of denying fulfillment to women. Whenever such a repressive use is made of the sacrificial motif, it should be resisted and opposed. There is nothing in Jesus' life or teachings to suggest that he ever made any distinction whatsoever between men and women in his call to a life of cross-bearing. The problem lies in the definition of sacrifice. The feminist objection has been that a sacrificial way of life has left many women in a weakened state, unable to bargain their way out of the subordinate, overburdened positions in which they have found themselves. This is impermissible by the light the Spirit has shown us today, and we can never go back from the advances it has been given us to make. At the same time, however, a new conception of sacrifice is needed. We will never get past this hurdle if sacrifice is thought to be a form of weakness and abject self-suppression. The way to rethink sacrifice is in terms of power.

Power comes in two kinds, bad and good. A life of sacrificial service as defined by the life and death of Jesus Christ is not weakness, but *an al-*

---

81. Quotation from Brian Hall, "Rebecca West's War," *New Yorker,* April 15, 1996.

82. West betrays some confusion (certainly some romanticism) when, within the narrative of the black lamb on the rock, she inserts a favorable assessment of another scene she had witnessed the night before, which seems to contradict her vehement antipathy toward the sacrifices on the rock. It is particularly notable in view of her fierce feminist stance. She recalls, in highly favorable terms, a rite for women in a Muslim shrine that called for the embracing of a stone thought to have spiritual properties. "The Moslem [*sic*] women . . . put out their arms to embrace the black stone and dropped their heads to kiss it. . . . Such a gesture is an imitation by the body of the gesture made by the soul in loving. It says, 'I will pour myself in devotion to you, I will empty myself without hoping for return . . .'" (*Black Lamb and Grey Falcon,* 825). But what is this if not sacrifice? It is not literal blood-letting, but it sounds mightily like the age-old reiteration of a female creed.

83. These critiques will be addressed in chapter 11, in the section on objections to the penal substitution model. The concept of sacrifice is by no means the only aspect of atonement to come in for feminist criticism. Not only the substitution theme but also Anselm's satisfaction idea has been deplored. Partly to blame has been carelessness in the church's teaching, especially in evangelical circles, dividing the Father from the Son so that the Father appears to be brutally sacrificing his helpless child — hence the trope of child abuse. This critique from feminist theologians has been helpful in correcting errors.

ternative mode of power.[84] This truth undergirds the whole New Testament message about self-giving. No one understood this better than the apostle Paul. We have seen that he did not, in his letters, show much interest in the cultic language that predominates in (for instance) Hebrews — let alone Leviticus. That is partly because Paul did not understand the crucifixion of Christ primarily as a sacrifice in the cultic sense; he understood it as the definitive apocalyptic engagement with the forces of the enemy, at the frontier of the ages where Jesus' self-abandonment was the ultimate weapon. It was the ultimate form of the "passive resistance" that overwhelms and routs the enemy — very much along the lines of "the War of the Lamb" envisioned by Yoder. This theme is by no means missing from Hebrews, by the way. Hebrews 2:14-15 beautifully combines in one sentence the incarnation, the life offering, the conquest of death, and the deliverance from slavery: "Since therefore the children share in flesh and blood, [Christ] himself likewise partook of the same nature, that through death he might destroy him who has the power of death, that is, the devil, and deliver all those who through fear of death were subject to lifelong bondage."

True power is best seen in a life willingly offered as sacrifice for the sake of others. There is unexcelled strength in such sacrifice when it is embraced — not simply imposed or inflicted — as a way of aligning oneself with the good kind of power. Who, looking at the example of Nelson Mandela, can doubt it? Another example is Daw Aung San Suu Kyi, Nobel Peace Prize laureate, a small-boned, pretty little lady who looks as delicate as baby's breath. The oppressive government of Burma was scared to death of her, keeping her under house arrest for decades. She knew the right use of sacrifice in the service of the Power that lies beyond tyranny. She was offered her freedom, not because she was oppressed and cowed, but because she was resolute and strong.[85]

The true charter of freedom for women lies in the old-world-destroying, new-world-creating power of the cross, not in some new version of the old world of religion with its gradations of legalism (the Galatian church) or spir-

---

84. "Revolutionary subordination," a phrase bearing the same implications, is the title of chapter 9 in John Howard Yoder's celebrated book *The Politics of Jesus.* Yoder's precipitous fall from grace as a result of unimpeachable accusations against him for reprehensible sexual abuse — which he unrepentantly sought to connect with his theological project — has permanently tarnished his reputation, yet the strength of the argument of the book, and the influence it has had, cannot be gainsaid.

85. As this book goes to publication, there is considerable disappointment in the way that Aung San Suu Kyi, since her release from house arrest, has embraced the Burmese military. The point, however, is the same.

ituality (the Corinthian church). Indeed, the real meaning of sacrifice in the Christian life is a dying to the old world; "all of us who have been baptized into Christ Jesus were baptized into his death" (Rom. 6:3); "the world has been crucified to me, and I to the world" (Gal. 6:14).

God's apocalyptic war is fought with weapons of self-giving love and total identification with those who suffer "outside the camp" (Heb. 13:13), whoever they are. The resistance of the demons to God's coming kingdom is intense and determined and must be continually opposed. The armor of God, however, is the opposite of that used in this present age:

> For not with sword's loud clashing, nor roll of stirring drums,
> But deeds of love and mercy the heavenly Kingdom comes.[86]

Dorothy Day wrote, "Patience, patience — which means suffering."[87] Her life of sacrificial service to the poor was one of great power that places her in the first rank of Christians who will be remembered. This sort of sacrificial witness is so different from that of the submissive battered wife that they can scarcely be said to have anything to do with each other. The important distinction is that Dorothy Day's commitment to a sacrificial life arose from a place of strength, not a place of weakness. Such a life, rightly understood, is uniquely empowering because it is aligned with the self-giving of God in Jesus Christ. Wherever there are gracious acts of un-selfishness, there are the signs of God's kingdom of remade relationships based on mutual self-offering. Even in this old world ruled by Sin and Death, who would want to live a life of utter selfishness? To show any sort of care for others at all, some sort of sacrifice is necessary every day — to be magnanimous instead of vindictive, to stand back and let someone else share the limelight, to absorb the anger of a teenager in order to show firm guidance, to be patient with a parent who has Alzheimer's, to refrain from undermining a colleague, to give away money one would like to spend on luxuries, to give up smoking, to bear with those who can't give up smoking — all such things, large and small, require sacrifice. What would life be without it?

---

86. Hymn, "Go Forward, Christian Soldier," by Ernest Warburton Shurtleff.

87. *The Duty of Delight: The Diaries of Dorothy Day,* ed. Robert Ellsberg (Milwaukee: Marquette University Press, 2008), 279.

Sacrifice on Behalf of the Ungodly

But the life of Christian sacrifice is even more radical than we thought. "For Christ also died for sins once for all, the righteous for the unrighteous" (I Pet. 3:18). *The righteous for the unrighteous?* Humanly speaking, this makes no sense. We aren't supposed to sacrifice ourselves for the *un*righteous. We might be ready to die for our families or our countrymen, our tribe or our group, but talking about the righteous dying for the unrighteous is like asking a refugee from Darfur to die for the *janjaweed* militia, like asking a South American peasant to die for a death-squad commander, like expecting a torture victim to die for her torturer. Paul puts it like this: "It's rare to see a person willing to die even for a *righteous* man, let alone an *un*righteous one — though occasionally perhaps for a *righteous* person one might dare even to die" (Rom. 5:6-8, my paraphrase).

In the cross of Christ, we see something revolutionary, something that undercuts not just conventional morality but also religious distinctions across the board. Christ has died for the *un*godly, the *un*righteous. You and I, Paul says, would not do that. We might conceivably die for a "good guy," but we would not die for someone designated as a "bad guy." Jesus, however, has "died for the ungodly" (Rom. 5:6). This radical pronouncement is frequently not well understood in its full sense. At the Last Supper, Jesus says, "Greater love has no man than this, that a man lay down his life for his friends" (John 15:13). This familiar saying has often been appropriated to honor soldiers killed in action. It is therefore easily misunderstood to mean that Christian sacrifice is for those who are on our side. It is difficult to get past this understanding, especially among men. War veterans speak with religious awe of the bonds they felt with their comrades in arms. This emphatically excludes the enemy, of course. If we think of Jesus' sacrifice in the same way that we think of soldiers in wartime, therefore, we will miss the entire point. Jesus is speaking to a group of people who are not going to be beside him on the battlefield. Quite the opposite. They have consistently misunderstood him and are about to deny and abandon him. The twelve disciples are very poor excuses for friends. Only in the sacrifice of Jesus are they transformed from enemies into friends.[88]

---

88. Scrupulous exegesis requires me to note that John's Gospel, unlike the other three, lays no particular emphasis on the failure of the disciples in general. The notable exception is Peter. In John's version of the Last Supper, Jesus says to the eleven (Judas has already left), "You are already made clean by the word which I have spoken to you" (John 15:3). It is typical of this Gospel to emphasize the *already* of Jesus' word. The betrayal of Jesus by Peter just a few hours after the Last Supper, however, plays a large part in the Fourth Gospel, and it is only

Paul preached the good news for the ungodly more unmistakably than any other apostolic figure. In so doing, he makes it clear that the death of Christ for the unrighteous means constant identification with that death on the part of his followers. He commends his apostolic way of life several times in the Corinthian correspondence, not to commend himself, but because that church was triumphalist rather than self-sacrificing in its outlook.

> We [apostles] are afflicted in every way, but not crushed; perplexed, but not driven to despair; persecuted, but not forsaken; struck down, but not destroyed; always carrying in the body the death of Jesus, so that the life of Jesus may also be manifested in our bodies. For while we live we are always being given up to death for Jesus' sake, so that the life of Jesus may be manifested in our mortal flesh. So death is at work in us [apostles], but life in you [the Christian community]. (II Cor. 4:8-12)

The important factor here is the **combination of sacrificial living with power**. Paul is not crushed, not despairing, not destroyed. He goes from strength to strength, knowing that his mission is imparting life. He knows he is not determined by death. "Henceforth let no man trouble me" (Gal. 6:17) might be a good verse for Christian feminists, and this is a suggestion not entirely made in jest. The context of that startlingly confident, almost insouciant Pauline sign-off is notable: "Far be it from me to glory except in the cross of our Lord Jesus Christ, by which the world has been crucified to me, and I to the world. For neither circumcision counts for anything, nor uncircumcision, but a new creation. . . . Henceforth let no man trouble me; for I bear on my body the marks of Jesus" (6:14-17).

Although Paul does not speak here of cultic sacrifice, Paul has spent himself sacrificially for the Galatian churches. Now he is ending his most combative letter in his strongest vein, with his most powerful weapon — the cross of Christ, in which the old world of distinctions, divisions, and hierarchies has been put to death. Remember, this is the letter that contains the verse, "There is no longer Jew or Greek, there is no longer slave nor free, there is no longer male nor female; for all of you are one in Christ Jesus" (Gal. 3:28).[89]

---

that Gospel that includes the "restitution scene" of Jesus restoring the disciple who had denied him three times (John 21:15-19). For further clarification of the relation between the Word (as in John's prologue), the "word which I have spoken to you," and the restoration of Peter, we may look to the great *logizomai* (translated "reckon" — the "wording" that evokes and makes real "already" what it describes) of Paul, to be discussed in chapter 8. In this way as in so many others, Paul continually elucidates what we read in the Gospels.

89. Translation by J. Louis Martyn. Note his use of "no longer," as in "there is no longer

Hilasterion: Propitiation or Expiation?

In Romans 3:25, at a high point in his argument, Paul proclaims, "Christ Jesus, whom God put forward as *hilasterion* by his blood."[90] How are we to understand this word?[91] The two English words used in translation are

---

male nor female . . . ," as opposed to the usual translation "There is neither male nor female." Martyn's rendering emphasizes Paul's point that an entire universe (Gk. *kosmos*) of distinctions and classifications, especially those between sacred (circumcised) and profane (uncircumcised), has ceased to exist and has been replaced by another. "There is neither . . ." lacks the urgent sense of an apocalyptic transfer of worlds.

90. The wording of Rom. 3:25 seems to come from a preexisting (hence very early) Jewish-Christian confession. There has been much debate about the role of such borrowings of "traditional" language in Paul's letters. When he quotes material that he has received from preexisting sources, how much does he agree with it and how much does he reinterpret it? Romans 3:25 is a crucial example, where Paul speaks of "faith in [Christ's] blood" and uses the word *hilasterion* — variously translated "expiation" (RSV), "propitiation" (KJV), and "atoning sacrifice" (NIV). These cultic expressions are not typical for Paul (*contra* James D. G. Dunn, *The Theology of Paul the Apostle* [Grand Rapids: Eerdmans, 1998]). Does he want to ride in to Rome on what the church there might already know? Does he want to show the Jewish Christians that he can speak their language? T. W. Manson well encapsulates the essential message of the passage: "Christ crucified, like the mercy-seat in the Holy of Holies . . . was the place where God's mercy was supremely manifested" ("Hilasterion," in *Theological Dictionary of the New Testament,* ed. G. Kittel and G. Friedrich, trans. G. W. Bromiley, 10 vols. [Grand Rapids: Eerdmans, 1964-1976], 3).

Reading the letter as a whole, one notices that the expressions do not seem to fit into the overall argument, and Paul does not use them again. Nevertheless, over the years, many evangelicals have taken Rom. 3:25 as a key to the idea of the atonement in the New Testament. At the other end of the spectrum is a group influenced by Käsemann that wants to separate Paul from such cultic language altogether. The position taken here is that Paul uses *hilasterion* in its context because he wishes to incorporate this sacrificial imagery from the Jewish cult into his overall plan, but it is not the lodestone of his theology of the cross. The ritual of the Jerusalem temple was not at the center of his thoughts as he turned west toward Rome. The imagery of deliverance from the Powers overwhelmingly predominates in Romans, as will be shown in the *Christus Victor* chapter.

91. The word-group appears in the New Testament as *hilasterion* in Rom. 3:25; as *hilasmos* in I John 2:2, 4:10; and as *hilaschomai* in Heb. 2:17. One of these verses was well known to all Episcopalians prior to the revision of the Book of Common Prayer. The "comfortable words" in the service of Holy Communion included this: "If any man sin, we have an advocate with the Father, Jesus Christ the righteous: And he is the *propitiation* for our sins." That is the King James Version used in the 1928 Prayer Book. The revised 1979 Prayer Book uses the Revised Standard Version, which renders *hilasmos* as "expiation" (and in addition, the Prayer Book revisers wisely added the last part of the verse in I John 2:2, "and not for ours only, but also for the sins of the whole world"). To make matters more interesting, *hilasterion* appears also in Heb. 9:5, where it is generally translated "mercy seat," with reference to the Holy of Holies where the high priest offered sacrifice for sin on the Day of Atonement.

"propitiation" and "expiation," and they have long been a battleground. The translation of *hilasterion* and its word-group has often seemed to depend upon the theological bias of the translators; this is true to some extent of all translations, but in this case the problem is more exposed than usual. A thorough discussion of the debate is beyond the scope of this volume.[92] Instead, in this section we will mull over some of the theological, homiletical, and pastoral implications of the translation of *hilasterion*.[93]

Both words presuppose a barrier that exists and must be removed for the overcoming of sin. The following contrast has often been made, though it is highly doubtful that there was any such sharp distinction in the biblical mind:[94]

- "Expiation" means that the barrier thrown up by sin lies outside God, within humankind; it is often interpreted as action aimed at removing sin.
- "Propitiation" means that the barrier lies within God himself; thus it is usually interpreted as action aimed at satisfying the divine wrath.

Reaction against the concept of propitiation has been intense in some quarters. Evangelical interpreters should be prepared to take some of the blame, because the insistence on propitiation has, perhaps unwittingly but nevertheless wrongly, divided the Father from the Son. Such teaching has made it sound as though God had to have his mind changed by a human sac-

92. Many articles in biblical dictionaries give an overview of the territory. A recent one that shows deep familiarity with works still untranslated from German is Judith Gundry-Volf, "Expiation, Propitiation, Mercy Seat," in *Dictionary of Paul and His Letters: A Compendium of Contemporary Biblical Scholarship,* ed. Gerald F. Hawthorne, Ralph P. Martin, and Daniel G. Reid (Downers Grove, Ill.: IVP, 1993), 279-84.

93. A case could be made for placing a discussion of propitiation in the chapter on substitution rather than here. I have chosen not to put it there because I am offering a critique of the propensity of English-speaking evangelicals to make every part of the New Testament serve the cause of the substitutionary atonement in a specific doctrinal form, calling on Rom. 3:25 to play a more controlling part than Paul probably intended. The propitiation/expiation discussion does not entirely fit this chapter either, but because *hilasterion* is so closely linked with the mercy seat and the motif of the temple sacrifices, I have retained it here.

94. Martin Hengel's exposition of *hilasterion* is helpful. He argues that the idea of an *expiatory, propitiatory* blood-sacrifice, offered voluntarily, was familiar to the whole Greco-Roman world, especially through the frequently performed plays of Euripides (*The Atonement: The Origins of the Doctrine in the New Testament* [Philadelphia: Fortress, 1981], 19-21). Hengel cites the classics scholar P. Roussel, who, in writing in French about Euripides, uses the words "expiatory" *(expiatoire)* and "propitiatory" *(propitiatoire)* together as though the link between them was obvious and incontrovertible.

rifice. It is crucial to maintain the agency of the three persons and to remind ourselves that the whole enterprise is a transaction undertaken among the persons of the Trinity.[95] The Son is not intervening to change the Father's disposition toward us. His disposition toward us remains the same as ever — unfailingly determined upon our redemption. T. F. Torrance, fully aware of the dangers of misunderstanding propitiation, writes, "It is precisely in this propitiating movement of reconciliation and justification through his Son that God the Father opens his innermost heart and mind to us in the self-revelation of his love."[96]

The move away from propitiation was a process that needed to happen. Even so thoroughgoing a "propitiationist" as Leon Morris, a leading evangelical scholar, admits that his predecessors should have taken more care to interpret the concept correctly.[97] He pays tribute to C. H. Dodd, the godfather of expiation, acknowledging that there can be no turning back from many of the points Dodd has made against propitiation. Morris admits that, wrongly understood, propitiation makes the death of Jesus sound like a primitive sacrifice of appeasement. "It is a relief to know," he acknowledges, "that the God of the Bible is not a Being who can be propitiated after the fashion of a pagan deity."[98] This misconception can, one hopes, be laid firmly to rest; it should now be generally agreed that any concept of *hilasterion* in the sense of placating, appeasing, deflecting the anger of, or satisfying the wrath of, is inadmissible.

The more important, and truly radical, reason for firmly rejecting this understanding of propitiation is that it envisions *God as the object,* whereas in the Scriptures, *God is the acting subject.*[99] This is especially noticeable in Romans 3, the context for Paul's single use of *hilasterion.* He writes:

---

95. Robert W. Jenson, *Systematic Theology,* vol. 1, *The Triune God* (New York: Oxford University Press, 1997), 135.

96. Torrance, *The Mediation of Christ,* 111.

97. And indeed, by today's standards Morris has not done so himself. He is nowhere near careful enough to show that God's wrath is preceded and enveloped by God's mercy, nor does he see any problem with the word "penal." Had he written his classic book, *The Apostolic Preaching of the Cross,* thirty years later, he would have been under pressure to rethink these matters. However, his 1955 study remains valuable for its careful exposition of the pervasiveness of the biblical theme of God's wrath against all that hurts and destroys his loving purposes.

98. Leon Morris, *The Apostolic Preaching of the Cross* (Grand Rapids: Eerdmans, 1955), 148.

99. "*Hilasmos* does not imply the propitiation of God. It refers to the purpose which God Himself has fulfilled by sending the Son." Friedrich Büchsel, in *Theological Dictionary of the New Testament,* 3:317.

For there is no distinction; since all have sinned and fall short of the glory of God, they are justified by his grace as a gift, through the redemption which is in Christ Jesus, whom God put forward as an *expiation/propitiation* by his blood, to be received by faith. This was to show God's righteousness, because in his divine forbearance he had passed over former sins; it was to prove at the present time that he himself is righteous and that he justifies him who has faith in Jesus. (Rom. 3:22-26)[100]

This is an intricate passage, but we can get some idea of what Paul is up to. "There is no distinction" refers to the death of the old *kosmos* where religious classifications dictated who was righteous and who was not, even though righteousness did not and could not rule on account of the Power of Sin. The new *kosmos,* a gift of God's righteousness by pure grace, has come about through the cross ("by his blood"). In *former times,* God "passed over" sins, *but now* he has revealed his righteousness in the Messiah Jesus, to be received not by external observances but by faith. What is crucial here, though often overlooked, is that Paul is making a sharp contrast between *"passing over sins"* in the past and *the revelation of God's righteousness* "at the present time," which (as Paul says in chapter 4) justifies — makes right — even hitherto unacceptably unrighteous persons.

This is one of the places where there is a notable discontinuity between the old and new covenants. We have already seen — and will continue to see — that "righteousness" and "justification" are the same word in Greek *(dikaiosyne)* and that both have the force of a verb. God's justifying, rectifying action in Christ is bringing a new world-order into being. Sin is no longer "passed over." It is this contrast between *passing over sins* and the *revelation of God's righteousness* that will help us with propitiation. God "*condemned* sin," Paul says in Romans 8:3; this is quite different from "passing over" it. A helpful translation of "the righteousness of God" is the New English Bible's "God's way of righting wrong."[101] God's justification of sinners is not a forgetting, nor is it simply forgiveness. It is a definitive, wholesale, final assault upon and defeat of Sin, understood as a Power, and the creation of a new humanity.

C. K. Barrett is a balanced and judicious interpreter who thinks that the idea of propitiation plays an important role because of its link to the

---

100. Notice how Paul uses the word "sins" in the plural in the phrase "passed over former sins," which is atypical for him. He is speaking of the old dispensation. This contrasts with the very Pauline "[God] condemned sin [singular]" in Rom. 8:3, where he is coming to one of his high points, the proclamation of the defeat of *sarx* (the "flesh") by the new life in the Spirit.

101. J. L. Martyn and Markus Barth both commend this translation.

wrath of God, even if (as he recommends) the word "expiation" is used in translations. In an often-quoted passage from his commentary on Romans, Barrett says, "We can hardly doubt that expiation rather than propitiation is in his [Paul's] mind," because there is no trace of a suggestion that God is the object rather than the subject. However, Barrett continues, "it would be wrong to neglect the fact that expiation has, as it were, *the effect of propitiation:* the sin that might justly have excited God's wrath is expiated (at God's will) and therefore no longer does so."[102] Cousar summarizes Barrett's argument: "The propitiation is a *secondary result* rather than a *primary cause* of the atonement."[103] That, in one sentence, tells us what we need to know at the conclusion of the debate.

God is not divided against himself. When we see Jesus, we see the Father (John 14:7). The Father did not look at Jesus on the cross and suddenly have a change of heart. The purpose of the atonement was not to bring about a change in God's attitude toward his rebellious creatures. God's attitude toward us has always and ever been the same. Judgment against sin is preceded, accompanied, and followed by God's mercy. There was never a time when God was against us. Even in his wrath he is for us. Yet at the same time he is not for us *without* wrath, because his will is to destroy all that is hostile to perfecting his world. The paradox of the cross demonstrates the victorious love of God for us at the same time that it shows forth his judgment upon sin.

Summary

The principal concept to keep in view for this chapter is that God *himself* ordained the way in which his justice and his mercy would be simultaneously enacted in the "*hilasmos* [expiation/propitiation] for the sins of the whole world" (I John 2:2). *God himself* would be the *hilasmos.* We saw earlier that the word "sacrifice" can be both verb and noun. Jesus the Son of God does not just *offer* a sacrifice; he himself *becomes* the sacrifice because he offers up himself — as is so clearly indicated in the "High Priestly prayer" of John 17 ("And for their sake I consecrate myself, that they also may be consecrated in truth").

A fitting conclusion to this chapter is this portion of George Hunsinger's "Meditation on the Blood of Christ":

---

102. C. K. Barrett, *A Commentary on the Epistle to the Romans,* Harper's New Testament Commentaries (New York: Harper and Row, 1957), 77-78, emphasis added.

103. Cousar, *Theology of the Cross,* 64, emphasis added.

The motif of Christ's blood actually embraces the entire sweep of Christian soteriology [theology of salvation]. It pertains to salvation in its overall basic structure of *extra nos* — *pro nobis* — *in nobis* [from beyond us, for us, and in us]. It extends, so to speak, all the way from the cross to the Eucharist. . . .

Christ's blood is a metaphor that stands primarily for the suffering love of God. It suggests that there is no sorrow God has not known, no grief he has not borne, no price he was unwilling to pay, in order to reconcile the world to himself in Christ . . . it is a love that has endured the bitterest realities of suffering and death in order that its purposes might prevail . . . the motif of Christ's blood signifies primarily the depth of the divine commitment to rescue, protect, and sustain those who would otherwise be lost.[104]

104. Hunsinger, *Disruptive Grace,* 361-62.

CHAPTER SEVEN

Ransom and Redemption

Truly no man can ransom himself,
    or give to God the price of his life,
for the ransom of his life is costly,
    and can never suffice,
that he should continue to live on for ever,
    and never see the Pit.

PSALM 49:7-8

"The LORD has ransomed Jacob . . . from hands too strong for him."

JEREMIAH 31:11

Redemption is not an unfamiliar concept even in our secular society. Books and films are not infrequently described as having "redemptive" themes.[1] The word is used with surprising frequency by secular writers, at least as often as "deliverance" or "liberation," and far more often than "salvation."[2] Redemption, in fact, is arguably one of the more popular topics in our culture, because it lends itself to sentimental resolutions that imply that it is readily available and not particularly costly. It is often argued that felons and miscreants, especially of the Wall Street, political, and corporate classes, should be allowed a chance at "redemption," even before they have demonstrated that they are remorseful and eager to pay their dues to society. When the

---

1. Even Clint Eastwood has directed films with themes now discerned as redemptive (most notably *Gran Torino*), unlikely as that might have seemed in the days of Dirty Harry.
    2. This, to be sure, is an informed hunch. I have not done an actual word search!

theme is applied to the work of Christ, however, all sentimentality falls away as we contemplate its cost.

The challenge for this chapter is interpreting the biblical references to redemption. As we have seen, many biblical terms used in interpreting the cross of Christ are energetically disputed. The link between "redemption" and "ransom" has complicated the matter considerably. In this chapter we will look at "redemption" by using the Greek word-group that includes *lutron* (ransom) as a handy focal point. It appears in a familiar sentence from Mark: "The Son of man also came not to be served but to serve, and to give his life as a ransom *(lutron)* for many" (Mark 10:45; also Matt. 20:28).

We immediately find ourselves faced with the same question we have met before: Are the ideas related to this theme to be taken literally or not? Perhaps that is overstating the case a bit, because not even fundamentalists are likely to imagine Jesus actually handing something over to a kidnapper. The question should rather be phrased this way: Do the ideas of ransom and redemption refer to some sort of price paid, or does redemption refer simply to deliverance in general?

During the first centuries of the church, the ransom motif was prominent in the writings of the Church Fathers.[3] It was proposed that the ransom was actually paid to the devil himself. The popularity of this notion persisted into the Middle Ages, but as consensus grew that Satan had no claim on or rights to anything, let alone the life of the Son of God, this semiliteral interpretation of the ransom motif fell permanently out of favor. There has been a continuing struggle, however, for the heart and soul of the image, a struggle to which we now turn.

Paying the Price: Dump the Metaphor?

When the Episcopal hymnal was being revised in the 1970s, an attempt was made to remove a verse from a well-known Holy Week hymn, "There Is a Green Hill Far Away":

> There was no other good enough to pay the price for sin.
> He only could unlock the gate of heaven and let us in.[4]

---

3. For a summary, see J. N. D. Kelly, *Early Christian Doctrines* (New York: Harper and Row, 1959), 382-83, 396.

4. Hymn text by Cecil Francis Alexander (1818-1895), Episcopal Hymnal #167.

Episcopalians who questioned this were told that the revision commission wanted to "de-emphasize" the motif of a "price." Few thought to cite the text "You were bought with a price," which is used twice in rapid succession by the apostle Paul (I Cor. 6:19-20 and 7:23). The offending lines in the hymn were eventually reinstated, under duress.[5] This struggle over the hymn is one example of widespread antipathy in our time toward interpreting the cross as the payment of a price, just as we saw earlier the antipathy toward "the blood" and will note, later, a similar antagonism toward the motif of substitution. It is clear that the words of hymns do have lasting resonance.

The objections about redemption within the church clearly revolve around the concept of *price.* The more general notion of redemption is often used in liturgy and hymnody, and has not been subjected to the same critique as have "price," "blood," and "substitution." Redemption is second nature to those in liturgical denominations because it appears in unimpeachable contexts such as the Benedictus, from Luke's infancy narrative: "Blessed be the Lord God of Israel, for he has visited and *redeemed* his people." Other references familiar to ordinary Christians include:

Let the words of my mouth and the meditation of my heart
  be acceptable in thy sight,
  O Lord, my strength and my *Redeemer* (Ps. 19:14),

and (from Handel's *Messiah*) "I know that my *Redeemer* liveth" (Job 19:25).[6] The service of Compline used by many Episcopalians includes Psalm 31:5, "For you have *redeemed* me, O God of truth."

Flannery O'Connor, in her stories, deals insistently with these unpopular topics. In her essay "The Grotesque in Southern Fiction," she writes that the "reader of today" is indeed looking for redemption, "and rightly so, but

---

5. The begrudging nature of the restoration is evidenced by the asterisk in the hymnal indicating that the offending verse "may be omitted." There was, and still is, a lack of sensitivity in regard to these issues. During the controversy in the '70s about the hymn and its image of "paying the price," when I was still a layperson, I asked a prominent professor of theology why he was opposed to these words. He said, rather loftily, "We're moving away from that idea of atonement." I was hurt; I did not understand who this "we" was, and he did not seem to care that "that idea of atonement" had been the word of life to many. This attitude toward Christians who cherish the idea that Christ paid the price for us is still common today.

6. In a stunning comment on Job 19:25, Otto Procksch reminds us that the God who enters the lists on Job's behalf is the same God that smites him. "As [Job's] blood avenger, He enters the lists against Himself when He enables Job to see him" (*Theological Dictionary of the New Testament,* ed. G. Kittel and G. Friedrich, trans. G. W. Bromiley, 10 vols. [Grand Rapids: Eerdmans, 1964-1976], 4:330).

what he has forgotten is *the cost of it.* His sense of evil is diluted or lacking altogether, and so *he has forgotten the price of restoration.*"[7]

She has identified the heart of the argument. The human predicament is so dire that it cannot be remedied in any ordinary way. If we fail to see this, then we "have not yet considered the great weight of sin."[8] Redemption (buying back), therefore, is not cheap. In the death of Jesus we see God himself suffering the consequences of Sin. That is the "price." When Christian teaching falls short of this proclamation, the work of Christ on the cross is diminished to the vanishing point, becoming nothing more than an exemplary death to admire, to venerate, perhaps even to emulate, but certainly not an event to shake the foundations of this world order.

The question arises: Is this our same bugaboo as before, namely, literal-mindedness? Austin Farrer has a particularly good way of describing the way that the biblical imagery functions. His term for biblical metaphors and motifs such as those of "ransom" and "price" is "parable." Farrer cites the same line in the "green hill" hymn: "There is no other good enough to pay the price of sin" (he also quotes the lines mentioned earlier from "Rock of Ages"), and then asks if the imagery in these lines is literally true. Here is his answer: "If you . . . require a Yes or No answer, you force me to vote for the negative; they are not true. But I shall vote with reluctance, because the parable of the hopeless debtor redeemed by Christ's infinite generosity is an excellent parable."[9] He explains that "parables" have "gleams of truth," and "the great merit of parable is *to convey passion or lay on moral colour; when we break it down to literal statement the colour fades, the passion evaporates.*" Yet we must do this breaking down, he says, if we are to do the work of systematic theology. The question then becomes whether the truth of the parable is accurately conveyed in the theological propositions being put forward. He shrewdly takes the reader through various steps, trying out first this objection to the imagery and then that, firmly concluding that, although God's action in Christ "is nothing so formal or so ineffective as the deletion of a ledger entry on account of payment received from a third party," nevertheless "God's act of universal forgiveness is the whole train of action he sets working through Christ. . . . And *of this great process Christ's blood was, once more, the cost.*"[10]

---

7. Flannery O'Connor, *Mystery and Manners* (New York: Farrar, Straus and Giroux, 1969), 48, emphasis added.

8. Anselm, *Cur Deus Homo?* 1.21.

9. Farrer prefers to interpret the "price" imagery in the sense of debt paid, rather than ransoming. The distinction is not important to the point being made here.

10. Austin Farrer, *Saving Belief* (New York: Morehouse-Barlow, 1964), 102-7, emphasis added.

Farrer thus shows how we may reflect systematically and theologically upon "parables" (metaphors) without forgoing the "passion" and "moral colour" they convey. In what follows, I will try to build a case for understanding redemption both in a general way as deliverance, and in a specific way as *deliverance at cost,* or, in a phrase used by Vincent Taylor and taken up by many other scholars, *deliverance by purchase.*[11]

Preaching the Imagery

Until recently, most graduates of mainline seminaries were conditioned to turn up their noses at conservative-evangelical commentary on passages related to the atoning death of Christ. However, some of this exposition has proven to be more deeply heartfelt *and preachable* than much of the work being done at the other end of the spectrum. When the Evangelist Mark tells us that Jesus said, "The Son of man came . . . to give his life as a ransom for many,"[12] there is no "theory of the atonement" in view; what we can say without doubt is that Mark wanted all hearers of the saying to be struck to the heart, *knowing themselves to be among those many.*

A passage that exemplifies this appeal to the congregation even more directly is I Peter 1:18-19: "You were ransomed . . . not with perishable things such as silver or gold, but with the precious blood of Christ, like that of a lamb without blemish or spot."[13]

Notice the direct address to "you." This is an evangelistic text if ever there was one. The apostolic author wants the gathered church to see that "with his own blood he bought her [the church], and for her life he died"[14]

---

11. Vincent Taylor, *The Gospel according to St. Mark* (London: Macmillan, 1952; reprint 1966), 444. See also Leon Morris, *The Apostolic Preaching of the Cross* (Grand Rapids: Eerdmans, 1955), 27, and William L. Lane, *The Gospel of Mark,* New International Commentary on the New Testament (Grand Rapids: Eerdmans, 1974), 383.

12. The question of whether the "historical" Jesus "really" said this is irrelevant. The apostles and Evangelists were led by the Spirit to understand things that Jesus said and did before the resurrection in the light of a "new epistemology" (J. L. Martyn's phrase). The risen Lord is active in the shaping of his words and in the reception of them by the church today. That is part of what it means to say he is risen and reigning.

13. We can tell in I Pet. 1:18-19 that the "ransom" is *metonymy* (one thing standing for another), since the figurative "blood" is contrasted with the literal "silver and gold." Terms like "ransom," "price," and "blood" are figures for the death of Christ.

14. Another hymn:
   The Church's one foundation
   is Jesus Christ her Lord. . . .

— in other words, the price was paid for those who were hearing the gospel proclaimed at that very moment, and for those who hear the "word of the cross" with faith in every time and place — including those who are now reading these very sentences.

What we dare not lose in the "ransom saying" is the sense conveyed to us that *Jesus himself* is the price of our redemption. The church needs to hear the apostolic truth that the death of Jesus was an offering of incomparable value. That is the basic idea in ransom and redemption: not just any deliverance, but *deliverance at cost.* We may retain the more general sense and the more literal one at the same time, as long as we keep them in balance. Redemption can mean "loosing" or "freeing" in a very broad sense; but if we are to account for the very particular horrors of crucifixion, we must retain the idea of cost.

The Gospel Message of *Lutron*

The point of the foregoing paragraph is to show that the debate about "ransom" and "redemption," as they come over from the Old Testament into the New, has to do with the concept of *price* or *payment.* The transaction known as "redemption" in Old Testament times took place in the arena of legal exchange. Israel captured the terminology for theology by using it to describe what God had done among them. When the Hebrew Bible was translated into Greek in the Septuagint (LXX), several Hebrew words and concepts having to do with redemption were translated by just one Greek word-group.[15] Most students of the Bible learn that the word *go'el,* though it originally meant simply a kinsman, evolved to mean a kinsman with an obligation, specifically an obligation to extend oneself in a significant way either financially or personally.[16] As an example of the way the concept evolved

---

> From heaven he came and sought her
> > to be his holy bride;
> with his own *blood* he *bought* her,
> and for her life he died. (Hymn by Samuel John Stone, Episcopal Hymnal, #525)

I know of no objection to this verse, in spite of its double reference to "blood" and purchase.

15. Various standard reference works describe the complexities in detail; suffice it to say here that variants of *lutron* (which for simplicity's sake, if somewhat inaccurately, I am using to denote the whole word-group *lutron, lutroo, lutrosis,* and *apolutrosis*) were used to translate *go'el, kopher,* and *padha* from Hebrew.

16. The best-known kinsman-redeemer figure in the Old Testament is Boaz in the book of Ruth; see Ruth 2:19-29; 3:12-13; 4:1-10.

theologically, God is called the *go'el* (translated "redeemer") thirteen times in postexilic Isaiah (40–66), and the return from Babylon is repeatedly identified as a *redemption*. Isaiah often uses *go'el* to emphasize God's familial relationship with Israel and the sense of personal obligation that God shows toward his elect people. *Kopher* meant "to cover" when used as a verb. When used as a noun, it denoted, specifically, a ransom price paid to buy back (redeem) a life that was forfeit for some reason. Some scholars emphasize that *kopher* in particular conveys the idea of substitution: one thing offered in exchange for another as a compensation or cover.[17] The root of *padha* also means a price paid in ransom, but when God is the subject of the verb form, the meaning seems to shift into the idea of loosing or freeing in general without necessarily implying a payment.

Does redemption *(apolutrosis)* involve a payment or ransom? Has it not rather become a figurative way of saying that God delivers his people? When Israel was brought out of Egypt, and then again out of Babylon in the return from the exile, that is called a redemption, but there is no clear idea of a price paid by God. Some interpreters have pointed out, however, that God is actively engaged in the deliverance of Israel in a way that involves exertion ("a mighty hand and an outstretched arm") and personal commitment. The psalms that rehearse the exodus narrative give a strong sense of God investing *God's very self* in the events.[18] Retroactively, after the first Easter, this came to seem very much like a price paid for the deliverance of a far larger and more diverse group of enslaved people than in the first instance. Jew *and* Greek, slave *and* free, male *and* female (Gal. 3:28) — this is the redeemed new creation in Christ. Thus once again we see fusion: redemption with exodus, exodus with baptism, baptism with Passover, Passover with sacrifice, sacrifice with payment of a price. Mirroring the fluidity of the Old Testament itself, pastors find that the more they

---

17. When *lutron* is translating *kopher,* it always implies a vicarious or substitute-gift that compensates for the debt; the debt is not simply canceled. Otto Procksch, "The *Lutron* Word-Group in the Old Testament," in *Theological Dictionary of the New Testament,* 4:329.

18. In Ps. 77:15, God redeemed his people with his arm; in Ps. 78:52-54, he guided them like a flock of sheep; he led them on safely; he brought them to his sanctuary that *his right hand had purchased* (note the combination of deliverance and purchase, as with a price). Particularly striking in this regard is Hos. 7:13-14, where God speaks about his beloved but disobedient people, saying,

> I would redeem them,
>> but they speak lies against me.
> They do not cry to me from the heart.

This expresses the pain of God in the redemption that is to come. The cost to God will be huge because it will be undertaken without the gratitude, cooperation, or recognition of his own.

preach from these texts and themes, the more the texts and themes blend and flow back and forth into one another. Pushing the idea of price out of the picture in the interests of one theological agenda or another is a grave mistake that deprives us of the very heart of the gospel message, namely, *that God is involved* in our deliverance. He has not stood back and pulled levers. He has stepped into the situation himself, personally. That is in large part what the trope *ransom* means in the biblical literature. The principal idea is that of *cost to God.*[19]

Turning now to the New Testament, we find the *lutron* word-group used to denote the redemptive work of Christ. Here again, we ask whether the concept of deliverance in general does not contain the idea of a price paid. The only appearance of *lutron* in the four Gospels is Mark 10:45 and its parallel Matthew 20:28 — "The Son of Man also came . . . to give his life as a ransom *(lutron)* for many." Books have been written about this complex title, "Son of Man" *(ho huios tou anthropou),* but we can say with some degree of certainty that in Jesus' time, it had become the designation for a heavenly figure yet to come, a hoped-for messianic personage who, like the Son of Man in Daniel 7:13-14, would be invested with the privileges and power of God himself. So when Jesus says, "The Son of Man came," it is equivalent to saying "The Messiah came." Obviously he does not mean that he came from Galilee, but *from God;* we are in the realm of the numinous. The Son of Man, as we confess in the Nicene Creed, "came down from heaven." There are two implied contrasts that lend power to the Markan saying. The first lies in the contradiction between the messianic figure from heaven and the coming ("down") to be a ransom. The second is between the implied "few" and the explicitly identified "many." The whole is a most startling statement, especially in its Markan context. The occasion for the saying is an embarrassing and childish display of jealousy among the disciples, two of whom (James and John) are seeking special privileges for themselves and, consequently, are the butt of the other disciples' understandable anger. It is highly ironic; here is Jesus preparing to go to Jerusalem to hand himself over, and the disciples — who will abandon him in short order — think it is going to be a coronation. Jesus says to James and John, with surpassing understatement, "You do not know what you are asking."

19. Thus B. F. Westcott: "It will be obvious from the language of the LXX that the idea of a ransom received by the power from which the captive is delivered is practically lost. . . . On the other hand, the idea of the exertion of a mighty force, *the idea that the 'redemption' costs much, is everywhere present*" (*The Epistle to the Hebrews* [1889; reprint, Grand Rapids: Eerdmans, 1967], 296, emphasis added).

> And when the ten heard it, they began to be indignant at James and John. And Jesus called them to him and said to them, "You know that those who are supposed to rule over the Gentiles lord it over them, and their great men exercise authority over them. But it shall not be so among you; but whoever would be great among you must be your servant, and whoever would be first among you must be slave of all. For the Son of man also came not to be served but to serve, and to give his life as a ransom *(lutron)* for many."

How much more impressive and penetrating the saying is in its context! It is called forth out of the intense struggle of Jesus of Nazareth, the incarnate Son of God, to absorb and to pursue his course of perfect obedience; it is called forth out of the effort to communicate with his callow and uncomprehending disciples about the style of life and death that will be theirs; and it is called forth out of the Master's boundless generosity and steadfastness in sharing with them the nature of his coming self-oblation for the community that they will some day lead. The simple description of his "calling them to himself" speaks volumes; his patient understanding of them and their weaknesses, his loving correction of their foolishness, his patient reorientation of their way to his way, his total commitment to their eternal future — all these and more are manifest in this scene.

Moving more deeply into the context, we see that the ransom saying occurs only in Mark and Matthew, the two Gospels that give the cry of dereliction as their only "word from the cross." This suggests that these two Evangelists see a connection between the ransom motif and the God-forsaken nature of Christ's death. We have referred several times to the link between the particular horrors of crucifixion and the idea of cost. Only the death of the Son at the outermost extreme of human depravity and divine self-abandonment is commensurate with the gravity and power of Sin. This is the price of the *redemption* that is being accomplished. The narrative skill of Mark brings the earthly struggle of "Jesus Christ, the Son of God" (Mark 1:1) before us in a characteristically rugged and uncompromising style, yet manages at the same time to evoke wonderment at the approaching immolation. The image of the Son of Man giving himself over to his enemies in the sight of those same disciples who were so full of braggadocio before but then "forsook him, and fled" (Mark 14:50) — thus becoming in essence his enemies themselves — moves our hearts in ways that have nothing to do with arguments about prices. All the richness and depth associated with the *lutron* in Mark, when it is allowed its full scope in the proclamation of the church, will have a profound effect on the "many" for whom he died. Jesus' use of the ransom motif opens up many paths to himself.

The word "redemption" *(apolutrosin)* appears in the undisputed Pauline letters three times. Each occurrence is important. We discussed in the previous chapter the Pauline use of an early cultic formula: "Since all have sinned . . . they are justified by his grace as a gift, through the *redemption* which is in Christ Jesus, whom God put forward as an expiation by his blood" (Rom. 3:23-35). The second and third usages are Paul's very own: "We wait for adoption as sons, the *redemption* of our bodies" (Rom. 8:23); and "Christ Jesus, whom God made our wisdom, our righteousness and sanctification and *redemption*" (I Cor. 1:30). The *lutron* equivalent also appears in Ephesians 1:7, 4:30, Colossians 1:14, and I Timothy 2:6.[20] It is somewhat surprising that these passages do not make specific use of the image of release from bondage by means of a ransom as one might expect, given the history of *lutron*. Cousar, however, in his treatment of Paul's *theologia crucis,* makes the compelling point that "Paul's understanding of Sin as a controlling Power (Romans 3:9) from which humanity must be delivered, and the combination of Sin with the word redemption [a few verses later] lends itself to the extended use of the ransom/redemption imagery without strain."[21] This case can be made with still more certainty in view of the "price" texts in I Corinthians. We have seen that Paul combines a strong emphasis on the cross in I Corinthians with the twice-repeated "You were bought with a price." Of the New Testament writers, Paul most of all emphasizes Christ's work as deliverance from bondage to Sin, Death, and the Law. Therefore, it stands to reason that if the deliverance was achieved "with a price," the price must have been the cross. In the context of I Corinthians, not to mention Romans 3:24-25 and Galatians 3:13, it could hardly mean anything else. Crucifixion was the price paid by God's Messiah.

And so the New Testament proclamation of redemption in and by Jesus Christ carries forward two major Old Testament themes. Redemption continues to mean liberation by a mighty power, as in some of the postexilic portions of the Old Testament; and second, it continues to bear its original Old Testament meaning of a price paid. Hence, again, the meaning is *deliverance by purchase at cost,* allowing for considerable movement between the two.[22]

20. I Timothy 2:5-6 uses *antilutron,* translated "ransom" — "For there is one God, and there is one mediator between God and men, the man Christ Jesus, who gave himself as a ransom for all, the testimony to which was borne at the proper time."

21. Charles B. Cousar, *A Theology of the Cross: The Death of Jesus in the Pauline Letters,* Overtures to Biblical Theology (Minneapolis: Augsburg Fortress, 1990), 62.

22. Cousar, *Theology of the Cross,* 61. Similarly C. K. Barrett: "The word *(apolutrosis)* can

This is the balance we are seeking, and in spite of Paul's relatively infrequent use of the actual word "redemption" *(apolutrosis),* it is in his letters that the two meanings most obviously come together. No preacher or Bible reader needs to be skittish about believing and proclaiming that "there was no other good enough to pay the price for sin," as long as the theme of deliverance from another sphere of power is also kept in view.

But now, what about this ransom? What is the purpose of a ransom? Clearly it is to set somebody free. In a modern analogy, we can think of hostages in a takeover. They are powerless to free themselves. They can only be liberated if some sort of SWAT team comes in. Sometimes, though, hostage-takers demand some kind of exchange — one of their prisoners for one of ours. This might be thought of as a ransom of equivalent value. Like many analogies, this one begins to break down rather quickly under scrutiny (it's too literal to be really helpful), but the central ideas remain: the loss of freedom, the outside intervention, and the equivalent exchange. Jesus says the Son of Man gives his life as a ransom for many. The contrast is between *one* and *many*. His one life is an equivalent for many lives. Moving away from the analogy, we may say much more; Jesus' ghastly death was in some ineffable way commensurate with the enormity of Sin and Death. By submitting to these Powers, he overcame them. In him, a power strong enough to deliver the entire human race has appeared, as the Epistle to the Hebrews repeatedly says, *once for all.* This is surely at the very heart of the gospel.

Who Is Paying? Some Trinitarian Considerations

The gift of a human life for some great cause is always heroic and moving. But the Christian message, properly understood, is something qualitatively different. It all depends on who we think Jesus is. If we think he is a human martyr along the lines of — for instance — the self-immolated Tunisian who touched off the "Arab Spring" of 2011, that is one thing. But the luminous suggestion made by Jesus in the ransom saying is quite another. *In Jesus,* it is *the triune God himself* who has intervened to reclaim — to buy back, if you will — his lost creation, and the price he pays is his own self in the person of the divine Son of Man. The price is unimaginably great precisely because the

---

mean simply 'deliverance,' 'liberation' . . . but the connection with blood and death suggests that it has not completely lost its original sense of 'ransoming,' *emancipation by the payment of a price*" (*A Commentary on the Epistle to the Romans,* Harper's New Testament Commentaries [New York: Harper and Row, 1957], 76, emphasis added).

Adversary is unimaginably great. The Adversary could be seen as a sort of diabolical trinity as well, for Sin, Death, and the Devil are all three named by the New Testament writers — an "unholy trinity."[23] The cost of deliverance is the life of the Son of God. Not to push the analogy of hostage-taking too far, we can still appreciate the notion of an exchange; Jesus has given himself up for us, taking our place.[24] Again, I Peter is pertinent: "Christ also died for sins once for all, the righteous for the unrighteous" (I Pet. 3:18).

We have noted the extreme weight and gravity of sin (*ponderis peccatum* — Anselm) that correspond to the extreme nature of crucifixion. Such extremities cry out for reparation all over the world, all the time. During the "Dirty War" in Argentina (1976-1983), thousands of political prisoners were thrown out of airplanes over the Atlantic. A young woman said, "The last time I saw my mother was when I was seven, and I will never see her again. Someone must pay for my pain."[25] This readily understandable protest shows that the need for reparations runs very deep in the psyche. Reparations sometimes take the form of literal payments, like money (such as those made to family members of mistakenly killed civilians in Iraq and Afghanistan — as if that were adequate compensation!), or figurative payments like prison sentences — or, as in South Africa, public confessions before a tribunal. The longing for some sort of payment when there has been a great crime is universal.

In view of these examples and many like them, it is part of the good news

---

23. Note the title of *Sin, Death, and the Devil,* ed. Carl E. Braaten and Robert W. Jenson (Grand Rapids: Eerdmans, 2000). The combination of death with the devil in Heb. 2:14-15 is also striking: "Since therefore the children share in flesh and blood, [Jesus] himself likewise partook of the same nature, that through death he might destroy him who has the power of *death,* that is, the *devil,* and deliver all those who through fear of death were subject to lifelong bondage." As for sin, it is central in many other Hebrews passages.

24. I recognize that this analogy can be reductive. In general, when speaking of the ransom/redemption motif, it is probably better to avoid words like "hostage," "kidnap," "extortion," and perhaps "payment" too, concentrating instead on "cost," "value," and "price."

25. "Argentines Are Reliving a Nightmare," *New York Times,* April 5, 1999. More context is needed for this illustration. In the 1990s, there was a concerted effort by the Argentine government to put the lid on the matter of the "disappearance" of thousands of political prisoners during the Dirty War. (As noted previously, one of *los desaparecidos* was Elisabeth Käsemann, daughter of the great New Testament scholar.) Much can be said about the church's role in Latin American human rights crises. There are persistent questions about the conduct of Jorge Mario Bergoglio — now Pope Francis — who, when he was the Jesuit superior during the early years of the war, failed to speak out publicly even when his own priests were targeted. For further information, see Jon Lee Anderson, "Pope Francis and the Dirty War," *The New Yorker,* March 14, 2013. In contrast, the Chilean archbishop during the Pinochet years, Raul Silva Henriquez, actively encouraged his priests to speak out against the atrocities and is today regarded as a great defender of human rights and of the Chilean people.

that God has offered God's own self as "payment." The word is in quotation marks here to show that it is a figure of speech, but that really should not be necessary.[26] If the ransom saying of Mark 10:45 is allowed full rein as a fluid, suggestive metaphor, rather than a rigidly schematic transaction, we are freed to see with the eyes of faith that somehow, on the cross, *God himself is doing the paying.* This is consistent with the point we are emphasizing throughout, that *something is wrong and must be put right.* The whole concept of redemption is another way of identifying God's way of setting right what is wrong. This is the meaning of Paul's word "rectification" — *dikaiosyne* in New Testament Greek.

But the ransom image has two serious problems. We alluded to the frequently heard criticism that a god who would sacrifice his own son is not worthy of worship. From this perspective the cross has been described as a form of child abuse.[27] We hear also that it is barbaric for God to "require" the death of his Son. It is important and necessary for critiques to be brought against *distortions* of doctrine, but distinctions should be made between the distortion and the doctrine itself. Fundamental to Trinitarian theology, as

26. An example of the unfortunate tangle that interpreters can get themselves into is this statement by I. Howard Marshall, referring to the "price" and "ransom" images: "If we are right in seeing the notion of 'price' here [in Gal. 3:13], there remains the problem of the recipient, and there can be no doubt that it is God, if anybody, who receives the ransom" ("The Development of the Concept of Revelation in the New Testament," in *Reconciliation and Hope: New Testament Essays on Atonement and Eschatology,* ed. Robert Banks [Grand Rapids: Eerdmans, 1974], 156; likewise Büchsel, "God is the recipient of the ransom," in *Theological Dictionary of the New Testament,* 4:344). Marshall and Büchsel cross over into this off-limits territory because they are both trying to separate themselves from the idea that the "ransom" is "paid" to the devil, an idea associated with Origen and other Greek Fathers that was laid to rest centuries ago by Anselm, among others. (See, however, the superb short recasting of the "ransom to the devil" notion in Christopher Morse, *Not Every Spirit: A Dogmatics of Christian Disbelief* [New York: Trinity, 1994], 246.) Many interpreters today agree that the best way to understand the ransom image is to think of it in terms of cost without pursuing the notion that it is literally to be paid to anyone. One of Irenaeus's editors, Edward Rochie Hardy, writes, "Irenaeus [unlike the Gnostics with their complex systems] sticks to the simplicity of the faith, but gives it some of the thrill that allows one to describe the Creed as an epic and the dogma as the drama. The Son of God worsted the ancient enemy in fair fight, thus redeeming mankind from its slavery" ("An Exposition of the Faith: Selections from the Work *Against Heresies* by Irenaeus, Bishop of Lyons," in *Early Christian Fathers,* ed. Cyril C. Richardson [New York: Simon and Schuster, Touchstone, 1995], 351). And Hardy adds that "it is most unfair to read into the one word 're-deemed' the idea of a ransom paid to the devil" as, for instance, Hastings Rashdall did in *The Idea of the Atonement in Christian Theology* (London: Macmillan, 1919), 233-48.

27. Essays from this perspective are collected in Joanna Carlson Brown and Carole R. Bohn, eds., *Christianity, Patriarchy, and Abuse: A Feminist Critique* (New York: Pilgrim Press, 1989).

we have already seen, is the conviction that *God was in Christ* (II Cor. 5). The language of "the crucified God" is not confined to Jürgen Moltmann; it is as old as Ignatius of Antioch ("the blood of God") and as new as Jon Sobrino ("God was on Jesus' cross").[28] The critics of the God-language are wrong on this point; the tradition taken as a whole is solidly behind the idea that the cross of Christ is an event undertaken by the Three Persons united.[29]

The second problem with the ransom image is more subtle and even more crucial. When we say, "Something is wrong and *must be* put right," it sounds as though God is being forced into acting as a result of our bondage to Sin. This in turn makes God's loving act in Christ dependent upon, reactive to, or even coerced by Sin. It is as though God failed to foresee what might happen in the Garden of Eden and, having been overtaken by events, had to come up with an alternative plan. If the incarnate life and sacrificial death of the Son was God's emergency reaction to an unexpected departure from his original plan, then we do not have the Creator God of the Bible, but a creature like the rest of us, vulnerable to surprise and, therefore, to some extent dependent upon events in the created order.[30]

This is difficult to discuss, because we are using ideas from the created order to express that which is uncreated, but this is the only language we have. The basic idea, which is closely related to the doctrine of the Trinity, is that it is God's very nature to go out from God's self in love. The love that comes forth from God is expressed first, from all eternity, within the Tri-Unity itself; God has no need of a creation to love.[31] The going-forth

---

28. Ignatius, *To the Ephesians* 1. Jon Sobrino, *Jesus in Latin America* (Maryknoll, N.Y.: Orbis, 1987), 153.

29. Could God suffer? Should we not separate the divinity from the humanity? Nestorius tried to do that and was roundly denounced by Cyril of Alexandria. This matter was especially central for the Reformers, who took up the patristic discussions with new zeal. Lutherans, in particular, have found it easier than Calvinists to speak of God suffering on the cross, thus Moltmann can say that God forsakes God, so to speak, at the moment of the cry of dereliction (*The Crucified God: The Cross of Christ as the Foundation and Criticism of Christian Theology* [New York: Harper and Row, 1973], 243-44). Moltmann's exposition pushes at the boundaries of Trinitarian theology, but it has a certain persuasiveness. The conundrum awaits further theological exploration.

30. John Duns Scotus (c. 1265-1308), the leading Franciscan theologian of the Middle Ages, asserted over against the Thomists that the incarnation would have taken place even if there had not been a Fall.

31. In the popular play by Marc Connelly, *Green Pastures,* taking off from the first chapter of Genesis, "de Lawd" says, "I'm lonely; I'll make me a world." This is endearing, but it is as far off base doctrinally as it can be. God cannot be lonely; he is Love among Three Persons from before and beyond time and eternity (Dante, *Paradiso,* canto 23).

and the self-giving of God were already happening before the beginning of time and are not dependent on anything external. The self-sacrificing love that we see in the cross is present within the Godhead from before the creation; it was not an innovation prompted by the fall of human-kind. Milton, in *Paradise Lost,* seems to get this particular point wrong; he shows the Father and the Son taking counsel together to determine what is to be done about the Fall. Dante, on the other hand, has written of the Trinity with more sublimity than anyone else ever has.[32] The *Paradiso* is a symphony, a wheeling dance of "burning love" (*Paradiso* 28.45) that has been going on within God from before space and time. Dante's vision of the uncreated love and light of the Godhead forms the climax of his mighty *Divine Comedy* (unfortunately, the translations are mere approximations).

> The uncreated Might [the Father] which passeth speech,
> Gazing on His Begotten [the Son] with the Love
> That breathes itself [the Spirit] eternally from each.
>
> (*Paradiso* 10.1-3, trans. Dorothy L. Sayers)

> ... In the deep and bright
>   essence of that exalted Light, three circles
> appeared to me; they had three different colors,
> but all of them were of the same dimension;
>   one circle [the Father] seemed reflected by the second [the Son],
> as rainbow is by rainbow, and the third [the Spirit]
> seemed fire breathed equally by those two circles.
> . . . .
>   Eternal Light, You only dwell within
> Yourself, and only You know You; Self-knowing,
> Self-known, You love and smile upon Yourself.
>
> (*Paradiso* 33.118-226, trans. Allen Mandelbaum)

Nothing can be added to these ineffable lines in praise of the Trinity; we quote them to reinforce the central point that God is already perfect love *within God's self,* and whatever has emerged from that Self is an aspect of God's original, inalienable nature. That nature is the foundation on which

---

32. T. S. Eliot, who could read Italian, wrote that the last canto of the *Paradiso* was "the highest point that poetry has ever reached or ever can reach" ("Dante," in *Selected Essays* [London: Faber and Faber, 1972], 251).

the world and its redemption are built. The love that is God from the beginning does not suddenly become something different because the unexpected emergence of Sin and Death calls for a new strategy. Quite the contrary: it is God's primal, immutable nature to expend God's self in love.[33] The image that best expresses this eternal self-giving is in Revelation: "the Lamb slain from the foundation of the world" (13:8 KJV).[34] Complementary verses are "A lamb without blemish or spot . . . destined before the foundation of the world" (I Pet. 1:19-20), and "delivered up according to the definite plan and foreknowledge of God" (Acts 2:23).

The Sweep of Biblical Images of Redemption

The idea of ransom and redemption is found throughout Scripture, often in suggestive and expansive forms. Proverbs contains an interesting verse that assumes several different connotations for the word *go'el:*

> Do not remove an ancient landmark
> or enter the fields of the fatherless;
> for their *Redeemer* is strong;
> he will plead their cause against you. (Prov. 23:10-11)

Here there is a suggestion of a forensic idea, that of *an advocate* who pleads a cause, as well as the more familiar notions of obligation to the common traditions (the *go'el* as the protector of property), and to the weakest members of the community (the *go'el* as the "redeemer" in personal or familial relationships). The various motifs interact with and enrich one another.

---

33. Thus the final canto of the *Paradiso* concludes with a climactic, ascending trio of images making up the Beatific Vision: first, the three lights within a single light (the Trinity); second, the vision of human nature taken up into the Trinity (the incarnate life and death of the Son); and finally, the entire cosmos embraced by "the love that moves the sun and the other stars," fusing human will and desire into the divine will in the great celestial dance.

34. The translation of Rev. 13:8 is disputed. G. B. Caird makes a forceful defense of the KJV in *A Commentary on the Revelation of St. John the Divine* (New York: Harper and Row, 1966), 168. See also Paul Minear, who translates "the Lamb who was slaughtered ever since the world began" (*I Saw a New Earth: An Introduction to the Visions of the Apocalypse* [Washington, D.C.: Corpus Publications, 1968], 335-36); also Robert H. Mounce, *The Book of Revelation*, New International Commentary on the New Testament (Grand Rapids: Eerdmans, 1977), 256. Mounce adds, "The death of Christ was a redemptive sacrifice *decreed in the counsels of eternity*" (my emphasis).

In a passage from Lamentations, the ideas are similarly blended together; the advocate who "takes up the cause" becomes the judge who will dispense justice and rectify a wrong:

> Thou hast taken up my cause, O Lord,
>   thou hast *redeemed* my life.
> Thou hast seen the wrong done to me, O Lord,
>   judge thou my cause. (Lam. 3:58-59)

Other ideas are associated with redemption. An example of its ethical content appears in, for example, Deuteronomy 24:17-18, where a connection is made between redemption from slavery by God and the quotidian transactions of community members: "You shall not . . . take a widow's garment in pledge; but you shall remember that you were a slave in Egypt and the Lord your God *redeemed* you from there; therefore I command you to do this."

This text, in yet another example of the imaginative range and scope of the idea of redemption, links God's personal involvement in the liberation of Israel with the financial straits of a widow who needs someone to pay her debt. This juxtaposition of great and small is characteristic of Israel's God, whose mighty deeds on the Red Sea shore are only a part of who he is. His concern for the powerless in every detail of their existence is part of what it means to call God "Redeemer."

A passage in Isaiah depicts God as the redeemer who brings precious gifts to reclaim Israel for his own. It certainly sounds like a "ransom," and a "king's ransom" at that — only it is not the king who is *being* ransomed; rather, in a true gospel reversal, it is the king who is *doing* the ransoming. The passage is so gorgeous that it is worth quoting at some length; it is part of a reading associated with the Epiphany, and in keeping with the meaning of that season, it is a particularly resplendent manifestation of the glory of the Lord. The postexilic prophet, rapt in the Spirit, envisions the divine arrival from a world order outside this one with power to remake the future. Notice especially the emphasis on the value set by the Redeemer for the reclaiming of Israel (in italics):

> Whereas you have been forsaken and hated,
>   with no one passing through,
> I will make you majestic for ever,
>   a joy from age to age. . . .
> And you shall know that I, the Lord, am your Savior
>   and your *Redeemer,* the Mighty One of Jacob.

Instead of bronze I will bring gold,
   and instead of iron I will bring silver;
   instead of wood, bronze,
   instead of stones, iron. . . .
Violence shall no more be heard in your land,
   devastation or destruction within your borders. . . .
The sun shall be no more
   your light by day,
nor for brightness shall the moon
   give light to you by night;
but the Lord will be your everlasting light,
   and your God will be your glory. (Isa. 60:15-19)[35]

It is no accident that this radiant passage is followed almost immediately in Isaiah by the reading offered by the Redeemer himself in Luke's account, when Jesus of Nazareth begins his public ministry in his hometown synagogue. In reading this passage, Jesus thereby announces himself as the eschatological Deliverer. There is a palpable sense that the decisive moment has arrived. The new creation is already being set in motion:

"The Spirit of the Lord is upon me,
because he has anointed me to preach good news to the poor.
He has sent me to proclaim release to the captives
and recovering of sight to the blind,
to set at liberty those who are oppressed,
to proclaim the acceptable year of the Lord."

(Luke 4:18-19; cf. Isa. 61:1-2)

This reading by Jesus, with its conclusion ("Today this scripture has been fulfilled in your hearing"), is as self-consciously messianic as any declaration he could possibly have made. In his appearance, the hour of the kingdom of God has struck.

And so we end this chapter on a note of high exaltation. The redemption wrought by God in Christ was indeed a mighty deliverance and points ahead to the glorious future of the reign of God. The ransom imagery reminds us

---

35. For full understanding here, it is important to realize that the postexilic community had to learn to read this prophecy eschatologically, that is, from the perspective of the End. The return to the land after the Babylonian exile was a bitter disappointment, not in the least resembling the transporting prophecies of Isaiah.

that this great liberation involved *not only* a loosing from bondage, *but also* an atonement for sin; *not only* a cosmic victory *but also* an ultimate price. The cost of our redemption was the crucifixion of the Son of God. Otherwise we cannot find a place within our understanding for the sheer horror and godlessness of such a death.

CHAPTER EIGHT

The Great Assize

Everyone knows the courtroom drama. No moment is more familiar to us through movies and television than that of the jury bringing its verdict. The results in real life can set off racial strife, widespread protest, and cultural disconnect, as in the trials of O. J. Simpson in 1994-1995 and George Zimmermann in 2013. The drama of the verdict, "Guilty!" has retained its immediacy in American culture, despite the view in certain quarters of academia that guilt is no longer a cultural preoccupation. In this chapter, as we open up the subject of the Day of Yahweh, so frequently prophesied in the Old Testament, and its New Testament counterpart, the Last Judgment, we should note this dissenting view among many cultural commentators as well as theologians. Paul Tillich famously proposed three stages in cultural development: whereas we were once haunted by the fear of death, and then by guilt, the principal form of existential anxiety in the twentieth century was the specter of meaninglessness.[1] More recent commentators argue that we are no longer suffering from the acute guilty conscience that supposedly played such a part in the preaching of the Reformation, and therefore images of Christ's death addressed to this concern are of little use to us today.

These strictures should be taken seriously. We live in an ironic "post-*Seinfeld*" culture that trades in anxiety but has little place for guilt. "Not that there's anything wrong with that" has become a universal watchword applicable to almost everything. This factor has often been put forward in the church to explain a widespread shift away from guilt and sin in liturgy and preaching. It may be that the guilty conscience has indeed gone the

---

1. Paul Tillich, *The Courage to Be,* 2nd ed. (New Haven: Yale University Press, Yale Nota Bene, 2000), 40 n.

way of all the other bourgeois baggage that has become so embarrassing to us since the late '60s. The tortured soul of Arthur Dimmesdale in
Hawthorne's *The Scarlet Letter* is incomprehensible to the millennial generation. However, it is remarkable how many references to guilt one still
finds. We can pile up examples: in an interview on the CBS broadcast *60
Minutes,* the bodyguard who was the sole survivor of the crash that killed
Diana, Princess of Wales, was asked by the interviewer if he had feelings of
guilt. The bodyguard, Trevor Rees-Jones, replied, "It's human nature."[2] A
particularly striking observation is made by a preeminent American moun-
taineer in his autobiography. Discussing the breakup of his marriage, he
wrote, "I missed her, and I felt *guilty . . .* my *sin* was cowardice."[3] These
examples may serve to illustrate that the category of guilt is by no means
dead to us.[4]

When we speak *theologically* of guilt, we are speaking of ourselves in
the sight of God. Guilt in the theological sense is related to sin, and sin in
the biblical sense is sin *against God.* This is true whether we speak of Sin
as a Power, or of sin(s) as transgression. Without knowledge of God, the
concept of sin has no meaning, making it difficult for us to understand
the exclusively *theological* orientation of the codes in Leviticus, where
— as we have seen — provisions are made for the restoration of guilty
persons who have committed sin as a result of negligence or carelessness rather than conscious intent. Lack of intent is no excuse; "when he
comes to know it he shall be guilty" (Lev. 5:2-4). Indeed, the remission
of "unwitting" sin is the principal purpose of the offerings prescribed in
the Levitical codes. Sin and guilt are real whether we acknowledge it or
not, because God is real. Thus Ricoeur observes about sin and guilt in
the prophets: "Real evil . . . [is] revealed and denounced by the prophetic
summons and is not measured by the sinner's consciousness of it. This is
why the 'reality' of sin — one might even say the ontological dimension
of sin — must be contrasted with the 'subjectivity' of the consciousness of
guilt. . . . The Seeing [of God] preserves the reality of my existence beyond
the consciousness that I have of it, and more particularly the reality of sin
beyond the feeling of guilt."[5]

2. *60 Minutes,* March 12, 2000.

3. David Brashears, *High Exposure: An Enduring Passion for Everest and Unforgiving Places*
(New York: Simon and Schuster, 1999), 223, emphasis added.

4. Not all cultures experience these phenomena in the same way. For instance, shame in
Japan is *corporate* in nature, while Americans emphasize *individual* guilt. A calculus of honor
and shame is more important in the Middle East.

5. Paul Ricoeur, *The Symbolism of Evil* (Boston: Beacon Press, 1967), 82, 86.

Our Ruling Tyrant: Anxiety

Guilt, then, remains a chief affliction in human life. In our own time, however, the greater emphasis has been anxiety (an insight made famous by W. H. Auden when he coined the phrase "Age of Anxiety"). But what form does this anxiety take?

For at least three decades now, the term most often used by the mainline churches to characterize themselves at their best is "inclusive." "No outcasts" was the promise chosen by the Episcopal presiding bishop as his own 1990s' watchword. This suggests that there are many who feel outcast, or worry that others feel outcast. This is surely a clue to the anxieties of our time. Either people are afraid that they won't "make the cut" or — here it gets more complicated — they worry that they will not be sufficiently inclusive of others. We may not be plagued by a guilty conscience as much as our forebears were, but we are nevertheless driven and riven by anxieties of various sorts, and one of them is the fear of not being on the right side of some invisible dividing line. Why else would newcomers to the ultra-affluent Hamptons of Long Island go to extraordinary, even absurd and hysterical, lengths to obtain an "established" area code as opposed to a "nouveau" one? — to give just one example out of a possible thousand from that much-lampooned seaside microcosm of our anxieties.

Insecurity is related to fear of judgment. The main character in Albert Camus's novel *The Fall (La Chute)* is a sophisticated man of the world, Jean-Baptiste. One fateful night, he sees a young woman preparing to commit suicide. He passes by, hearing the splash in the water, and reports the incident to no one.[6] After this, his life takes on a fugitive quality. "Above all," he says, "the question is to elude judgment." But eluding judgment, he discovers, leads to futility: "I'll tell you a big secret, *mon cher.* Don't wait for the Last Judgment. It takes place every day."

Jean-Baptiste further analyzes his situation in universal human terms: "We wish to be pitied and encouraged in the course we have chosen. In short, we should like, at the same time, to cease being guilty and yet not to

---

6. Albert Camus, *The Fall*, trans. Justin O'Brien (New York: Knopf, 1956). An essay-review about Camus in the *New York Review of Books* indicates that in *The Fall*, he is attempting to work out his own guilt with regard to the suicide of his second wife. All his life, Camus treated women in a cavalier and self-serving fashion. The writer makes the point, however, that unlike another famous cad, Jean-Paul Sartre, Camus was a committed humanist, which illustrates the moral difference between a person capable of insight and remorse, and one who continues to feel entitled to behave in reprehensible ways. Camus's star faded somewhat in the '70s and '80s, but more recent trends have shown a new appreciation of him. See, for instance, John Weightman, "The Outsider," *New York Review of Books,* January 15, 1998.

make the effort of cleansing ourselves." Speaking from the perspective of the theology of the cross, we know that we can neither "cease being guilty" nor "make the effort of cleansing ourselves." It can only be done by one who stands upon the Archimedean point *outside* this present world-order where we are imprisoned in our own natures.[7]

Our view of ourselves as innocent goes all the way back to the story of Adam and Eve, where the man says,

> "The woman whom thou gavest to be with me, she gave me the fruit of the tree, and I ate." Then the Lord God said to the woman, "What is this that you have done?" The woman said, "The serpent beguiled me, and I ate." (Gen. 3:12-13)

Whenever possible, blame someone else. The first consequence of the first disobedience by the first couple is that the human being habitually turns to implicate another person as a way of "dodging judgment." This is not just a matter of feeling guilty. It is profound existential dread. The courtroom scene that dwells in the collective Western unconscious still has the capacity to engage our emotions at a deep level. The prospect of a verdict looms like an ogre: Not good enough! Outcast! "Depart from me!" (Matt. 7:2; 25:41; Luke 5:8; 13:27).

Thus, in T. S. Eliot's profoundly Christian play *The Cocktail Party,* the main character, Sir Henry Harcourt-Reilly, a psychiatrist, comments:

> Half of the harm that is done in this world
> Is due to people who want to feel important.
> They don't mean to do harm — but the harm does not interest them.
> Or they do not see it, or they justify it
> Because they are absorbed in *the endless struggle*
> *To think well of themselves.*[8]

---

7. The ancient Greek mathematician and inventor Archimedes (d. 212 B.C.) reportedly said, with regard to his lever, that if he only had a place to stand, he could move the world. No one imprisoned in Satan's house has access to that Archimedean point outside the house; Satan's occupied territory can only be entered by a power from another domain altogether. That is what has happened in Christ. He alone has access to the Archimedean spot from which he is able to move the cosmos, because he comes from and belongs to another, supreme sphere of power. Therefore, he is able to say, "The ruler of this world . . . has no power over me" (John 14:30; see also 12:31 and 16:11). This is a useful metaphor to indicate the wholly other sphere of power from which God operates, and we will meet with it again. I first heard the figure used theologically by Paul Lehmann, but it may have originated with Karl Barth (*Church Dogmatics* IV/1 [Edinburgh: T. & T. Clark, 1956], 258).

8. T. S. Eliot, *The Cocktail Party,* in *The Complete Poems and Plays* (New York: Harcourt, Brace, 1952), 348, emphasis added.

Philip Roth, a determinedly secular Jew, has given us a complete catalogue of the struggles of his male characters. They are "bowed by blurred moral vision, real and imaginary culpability, conflicting allegiances, urgent desires, uncontrollable longings, unworkable love, the culprit passion, the erotic trance, rage, self-division, betrayal, drastic loss, vestiges of innocence, fits of bitterness, lunatic engagements, consequential misjudgment, understanding overwhelmed, protracted pain, false accusation, unremitting strife, illness, exhaustion, estrangement, derangement, aging, dying . . . men *stunned by the life one is defenseless against.*"[9] This is the condition Paul identifies: "The very commandment which promised life proved to be death to me. For sin, finding opportunity in the commandment, deceived me and by it killed me" (Rom. 7:10-11).

This is the realm of the Law in its role as the captive servant of Sin. It all adds up to universal anxiety about judgment of one sort or another.[10] The inexorability of it, the inevitability of it, the inescapability of it caused Paul to cry out as though speaking for us all: "Wretched man that I am! Who will deliver me from this body of death?" (Rom. 7:24). The "body of death" is the whole existence of the human being under the Powers: it encompasses fear of exclusion, dread of condemnation, threat of judgment, enslavement by Sin, and the knowledge that according to the Law one is on very shaky ground.

But some readers may not be convinced by the argument that we are all anxious about some form of "exclusion" or condemnation. All right, let us assume that it is not a universal human state of mind. Here is an alternative proposal: there is another trait that is absolutely universal across every culture and race on earth, and that is the human preoccupation with *condemning somebody else,* sometimes to the point of wishing to eliminate that person altogether. This is a form of original sin, precisely the opposite of innocence and inclusiveness. An article in the *New Yorker* about a remarkably precocious and unsentimental eight-year-old Upper West Sider named Sophie shows how naïve some of our currently popular "tolerance" programs are. The reporter elicits some piquant opinions from Sophie while they are both swinging on swings in the playground. Sophie complains that her school forbids assigning negative traits to any group, puts people together who

9. Interview with Philip Roth, *New York Times Book Review,* March 16, 2014. John Updike, in his Rabbit series, has given us a similar angle on a man in the grip of Sin and Death.

10. The phenomenon I am describing is not limited to WASPs and Jews with their (presumably) overactive consciences. The uneducated urban youth who thinks he is being "dissed" or "disrespected" may react with violence.

don't like each other, and proscribes the word "hate." Honest Sophie sees through all this: "If you hate that person, so what? Would you really mind if something happened? Like they moved to Alaska or to the far end of the earth, even?"[11] Writ large across our recent history, this translates into Palestinian militants and Sudanese *janjaweed* and Muslim extremists who want Israeli settlers and Darfur refugees and Coptic Christians to be "at the far end of the earth, even," or, better still, dead. An eight-year-old can see more clearly than some of the rest of us that well-meaning programs for improving the human species are not going to accomplish much besides making the designers of the programs feel good about themselves.[12] We don't need a *program;* we need *deliverance* from this whole cycle of violence and vengefulness. Humankind needs to be saved from itself.[13]

Class Action: Society under Judgment

During much of the twentieth century, the biblical notion of a second coming of Christ and a Last Judgment was held suspect in the mainstream denominations. And yet the idea of a final reckoning persists. In 1997, a number of men were held hostage by rebels for 126 days in Lima, Peru. During their long incarceration, they had no idea if they would ever get out alive. Many of them, a journalist reported, began to think of dodging judgment. They drew up "the balance sheets of their lives." Some of them, the article continued,

11. Rebecca Mead, "Sophie's World," *New Yorker,* October 18 and 25, 1999.

12. Andrew Sullivan, one of the most original, fearless, and iconoclastic bloggers of our time, always on the lookout for sentimentality, writes: "It is crazy to expect that hate, in all its variety, can be eradicated . . . hate will never disappear from human consciousness; in fact, it is probably, at some level, definitive of it" ("The Fight against Hate," *New York Times Magazine,* September 26, 1999).

13. Steven Pinker, in his 2011 book *The Better Angels of Our Nature: Why Violence Has Declined* (New York: Penguin Books, 2011), argues that civilization has made great strides. Using generally recognized figures, he shows that far more people died violently in previous centuries than now, in spite of Hitler, Stalin, and Mao. This may be true, but the view taken here is that although it is indeed possible to organize better *societies,* the project to create a better *human being* is beyond the capacity of humankind. The veneer of civilization is very thin, now as always. Wherever and whenever there is impunity, there will be no shortage of people willing to inflict the worst sort of treatment upon their fellow humans; witness the use of torture even of children by the regime of Bashar al-Assad of Syria in the mid-2010s. Moreover, the specter of nuclear catastrophe always remains, in which case all the statistics about improved civilization would become meaningless. For a review of Pinker, see Jeremy Waldron, "A Cheerful View of Mass Violence," *New York Review of Books,* January 12, 2012.

"turned to religion."[14] This raises questions: What is an adequate defense at the bar of judgment? How much do you have to have on the merit side of the balance sheet to cancel out the debits? What sort of religion would do the job?

The Old Testament is pervaded from end to end by the idea that God has a case against his people.[15] Both pre- and postexilic Hebrew prophets warned of the Day of the Lord, a decisive future moment when God's chosen people as well as the entire world would be called to account: "Behold, a day of the Lord is coming" (Zech. 14:1). God's right to judge is taken for granted:

> The Lord is coming forth out of his place
>   to punish the inhabitants of the earth for their iniquity. (Isa. 26:21)

His power to destroy evil is a central theme:

> The day of the Lord is great and very terrible;
>   who can endure it? (Joel 2:11)

Whenever the Israelites grew complacent about this coming crisis, the prophets lit into them with frightening images:

> Woe to you who desire the day of the Lord!
>   Why would you have the day of the Lord?
> It is darkness, and not light;
>   as if a man fled from a lion,
>   and a bear met him;
> or went into the house and leaned with his hand against the wall,
>   and a serpent bit him.
> Is not the day of the Lord darkness, and not light,
>   and gloom with no brightness in it? (Amos 5:18-20)

The Day of the Lord is envisaged as a trial scene, with special judgment upon those who have acted unjustly or neglected the poor:[16]

---

14. *New York Times,* April 26, 1997.

15. It is much less noticeable in the Wisdom literature, but even there the idea is present — though typically of this introspective literature, less as a trial of the people than as a measuring of individuals (Eccles. 12:14; Prov. 2:22; 3:33; etc.).

16. The Hebrew word *riv* or *rib* — meaning controversy, indictment, personal or legal contest (e.g., Mic. 6:2f.) — is used to convey the idea that God has a case against his people; hence, the bar of judgment.

The Lord has taken his place to contend,
    he stands to judge his people.
The Lord enters into judgment
    with the elders and princes of his people:
"It is you who have devoured the vineyard,
    the spoil of the poor is in your houses.
What do you mean by crushing my people,
    by grinding the face of the poor?" says the Lord God of hosts.

(Isa. 3:13-15)

The *whole people* is called before the bar of God's judgment.[17] It is typical of the way we think, however, that *individual* fear of judgment is easier to understand than *corporate* guilt. It is typical of American Christians to want to choose between these two as though they were mutually exclusive, with the so-called Christian Right focusing on individual misdeeds and the liberal left emphasizing social injustice. The idea of judgment upon the sinful individual and the godless society *both at once* is epitomized in the outburst of the prophet Isaiah when he is confronted with the presence of the Lord: "Woe is me! . . . for I am *a man of* unclean lips, and I dwell in the midst of *a people of* unclean lips" (Isa. 6:5).

The Old Testament prophets are well known for their indictments of whole groups of people. There will be a day of reckoning for the heedless rich, judges who take bribes, tradesmen who cheat the poor.[18] Most shocking of all, the chosen people who had assumed themselves excused from the judgment will actually be first in line.

---

17. When I was a young activist in Virginia in the '60s, my comrades and I loved the fierce passages from the Hebrew prophets. We envisioned them as God's judgment on all the Southern conservatives who were still laboring in outer darkness concerning civil rights and the Vietnam War. Like many young idealists, we thought of ourselves as bringers of light. Later I learned that we are all in this together. I also am implicated in "grinding the face of the poor."

18. The poor have an unobstructed view of this. A building in Cairo, nicknamed Tower of Power, contains apartments for sale at prices beginning at $2 million and rising to $15 million and more. A mechanic who lives in a slum nearby said to a reporter, "The only people making this kind of money in Egypt are merchants of powder [cocaine]." The average per capita income in overcrowded Cairo is $600, and housing is scarce. "This [apartment building] is not for our kind of people," said a thirty-eight-year-old taxi driver who lives with his wife and six children in the slum. "I think you have to steal to live in there. I am not envious, *but I believe these people will be accountable on Judgment Day.*" The taxi driver is doubtless a Muslim, but he is expressing something that Christians can embrace. Youssef M. Ibrahim, "Cairo Journal: The 'Tower of Power'; Something to Babble About," *New York Times,* August 17, 1995.

"You only have I known
  of all the families of the earth [saith the Lord];
therefore I will punish you
  for all your iniquities." (Amos 3:2)

The First Epistle of Peter puts it directly to the church: "The time has come for judgment to begin with the household of God" (I Pet. 4:17). In the early decades of the third millennium in America, with dramatic increases in the gap between the small percentage of exceptionally wealthy people at the top and the middle and working classes who are losing ground, it is hard to escape the conclusion that God's case against our whole society is at least as strong today as it was in the days of the prophets Isaiah and Amos.

The Old Testament prophets indict the whole people of God for protesting their innocence. After a recounting of all the apostasy of the Israelites, God (speaking through Jeremiah) says:

"Also on your skirts is found
  the lifeblood of guiltless poor. . . .
  Yet in spite of all these things
you say, 'I am innocent;
  surely his anger has turned from me.'
Behold, I will bring you to judgment
  for saying, 'I have not sinned.'" (Jer. 2:34-35)

In short, the judgment of God that falls on individuals falls equally on corporate entities. In modern life, individual and corporate responsibility blend into one another so that we can scarcely separate them. Surely that nice man in the nearby pew with the well-mannered children is not responsible for the policies of the tobacco company that seeks to hook teenagers overseas on his product? Large technological corporations are full of men and women making a good living and contributing to the American economy; how can they be blamed if their systems were used to keep files on suspected subversives?[19] Sneaker companies are doing their part for the GDP; if

19. The e-mail account of Shi Tao, a dissident Chinese journalist and poet, was turned over to the Beijing government by Yahoo in 2005, resulting in his cruel incarceration for more than eight years. A congressional hearing on the matter brought Jerry Yang, CEO of Yahoo, into the public glare. He seemed clueless about the harm his company had done. Congressman Thomas P. Lantos, Democrat of California, said that "while technologically and financially you [people at Yahoo] are giants, morally you are pygmies" (Neil Gough, "Chinese Democracy Advocate Is Freed after 8 Years in Prison," *New York Times,* September

the price of this is operating sweatshops in poor countries, well, that's what it takes.[20] So the thinking goes. The overwhelming witness of the Old and New Testaments combined, however, is that God's judgment will fall on groups as well as individuals, and that the rich and privileged, in particular, will be held accountable for their presumptions of immunity. As Mary sings when the angel announces the birth of Jesus,

> "He has put down the mighty from their thrones,
> and exalted those of low degree;
> he has filled the hungry with good things,
> and the rich he has sent away empty." (Luke 1:52-53)

And so it will help us if we understand that the Great Assize is not just an event that transpires on the level of the individual. For the most part, the Bible is thinking collectively, communally, and, ultimately — as the apocalyptic framework begins to take over in the late Old Testament — cosmologically. The Powers that will be unmasked and sentenced by the Judge who is to come are the powers and principalities of this world, and finally, Satan himself.

Judgment in Bible and Church

For all that is wrong in the world, a cosmic reckoning is required. The Scriptures envision what Markus Barth has called, in a powerful phrase, "the great and final litigation."[21] Yet many leaders in the churches have wanted — for greater or lesser reasons — to ignore or de-emphasize the law-court image in speaking about the death of Jesus. This trend has been consequential, for in the lectionaries now widely in use, passages about trial and judgment have largely been excised or omitted. Even theologically untrained laypeople have picked up the idea that "we don't believe that stuff anymore." The whole set of ideas associated with judgment has become anathema. In our present culture, "judgmental" has become one of the worst things that can be said

---

7, 2103). Lantos, a lifelong champion of human rights, was the only survivor of the Holocaust ever to serve in Congress.

20. In the 2000s, Nike strongly resisted independent investigation into the conditions of its overseas factories. The controversy lasted for several years and, in many respects, continues (the disastrous garment factory fire in Bangladesh in November 2012 ignited another storm of criticism of American and European companies, with few concrete results).

21. Markus Barth, *Justification* (Grand Rapids: Eerdmans, 1971), 18.

about a person. We seem to have lost the ability to understand "judgment" as having any positive connotation.[22]

Whatever our cultural biases may be, it is incontrovertible that the imagery of condemnation at the bar of judgment pervades the Bible. We have just looked briefly at a few representative examples from the Old Testament. Many people speak dismissively of "the Old Testament God," not recognizing how often Jesus draws upon the same imagery. Just one illustration of many will make the point: "*On that day* many will say to me, 'Lord, Lord . . .' And then will I declare to them, 'I never knew you; depart from me, you evildoers'" (Matt. 7:22-23).

Not only in the Synoptic parables of judgment but also in John's Gospel, Jesus speaks directly about a day of judgment on numerous occasions. There is no escaping it in the tradition without wholesale evisceration.[23] It is embedded in the creeds: "He shall come again, with glory, to judge both the living and the dead." In the Te Deum we sing, "We believe that thou shalt come to be our Judge." In the music of Henry Purcell and G. F. Handel, the prayer goes up: "Thou most worthy Judge eternal, suffer us not for any pains of death to fall from thee." Nor have the current moves to squash the theme of judgment in the lives of Christian people succeeded in banishing it. The same old fear of condemnation lurks just under the surface, ready to jump out at any moment — not to mention the aforementioned ubiquitous tendency to deflect judgment and condemnation upon others.[24]

In the churches of the present day that use the Revised Common Lectionary, there is one season where the theme of judgment has been retained to some extent. Beginning with All Saints and extending through Advent III, the New Testament readings have preserved some passages on the subject,

22. Perhaps we need some perspective on the matter, for this is a very recent development. The 1971 edition of the *Oxford English Dictionary* does not contain the word "judgmental" *at all;* the closest thing to it is the rare "judgmatical," with the largely positive meaning of "judicious, discerning." The next edition of the *OED* indicates that its first significant appearance with the negative connotation of today was in *1965!*

23. T. F. Torrance writes, for example, that we do not find anywhere in the Bible "any suggestion that God will pardon or redeem apart from judgment. . . . God will not pardon apart from judgment and sacrificial expiation." And yet "it is ultimately God himself and God alone who removes sin and saves." From an unpublished manuscript, quoted by George Hunsinger, *Disruptive Grace: Studies in the Theology of Karl Barth* (Grand Rapids: Eerdmans, 2000), 34.

24. A striking example occurred in the small hours of the morning on Christmas Day 2011, when a catastrophic fire in Stamford, Connecticut, took the lives of three young children and their grandparents, while the mother of the children and a man she was involved with escaped. Within hours, cyberspace filled with virulent messages of two sorts, those condemning the mother for escaping without her children and others condemning the condemners.

giving preachers an opportunity to expound on the wrath of God and the Last Judgment in a high-octane context of hope and promise.[25] On the Sundays immediately preceding Advent, the appointed biblical texts are especially laden with the theme of judgment: the wise and foolish virgins, the parable of the laborers in the vineyard, the parable of the talents, and most conspicuously — on Christ the King Sunday every third year — the Last Judgment in Matthew 25:31 and following: "When the Son of man comes in his glory, and all the angels with him, then he will sit on his glorious throne. Before him will be gathered all the nations, and he will separate them one from another as a shepherd separates the sheep from the goats, and he will place the sheep at his right hand, but the goats at the left. . . ."

Even though "all the nations" are said to be gathered before the Judge, our tendency is immediately to think of individuals. We imagine ourselves personally before the bar and feel some degree of unease. Indeed, there is no one who will not be there, and if we do not feel threatened by this on some level, it is a sign that we are dangerously desensitized. Again, however, if we think exclusively in terms of *individual* judgment, we will be misunderstanding the *corporate* nature of the biblical message.

The book of Revelation is invaluable on this point. Forgiveness of individual guilt is not a theme in Revelation; the concluding book of the New Testament depicts the last days in terms of *tribes, churches, peoples, cities,* and *nations* rather than individuals. We today, as inheritors of the world-scale wickedness wrought by totalitarian systems, are rediscovering the social and global meaning of this final book of the canon. All the best modern commentaries on Revelation — and there are a goodly number of them — emphasize its relevance to the political struggles of our time.[26] The biblical language of

---

25. The Synoptic Apocalypse is always read on Advent I, while the rest of the culture is roaring into the Christmas season. John the Baptist, with his uncompromising message, is the focus on Advent II and III. At Grace Church in New York City in the 1990s, the Advent tradition of the medieval church was revived, with well-attended sermons devoted to the four last things — death, judgment, heaven, and hell, *in their traditional order,* suggesting a willingness to look deeply into the most threatening places of all as a preparation for Christmas. This positive assessment of Advent in the lectionary and in the Episcopal Church may have to be revised, however. The Revised Common Lectionary has toned down the theme of judgment in two of the Old Testament readings for Advent, substituting passages with a more comfortable tone.

26. Excellent commentaries on Revelation include (in chronological order) those by G. B. Caird, Paul Minear, Elisabeth Schüssler-Fiorenza, Allan Boesak, William Stringfellow, Bruce Vawter, and Joseph Mangina. Boesak was personally discredited for a number of indiscretions and improprieties, but his commentary from inside the South African resistance is noteworthy nevertheless.

trial and judgment has just as much, if not more, to do with structures and systems (the principalities and Powers) as it does with individuals.[27]

The Forensic Imagery

Richard A. Norris has an imaginative way of looking at the motif of the "great and final litigation":

> It is entirely fitting . . . that the story of Jesus' suffering and death is pictured for us by the Gospels as an extended trial scene. A courtroom is at once *an arena of conflict,* in which divergent claims and causes struggle to assert their right; and it is *a place of judgment,* where a verdict is rendered which is intended to declare the truth of the matter in contest. Jesus' last days represent just such a situation: a struggle of conflicting interests and differing values, and one in which a verdict of some sort had to be rendered. The Gospels tell the story with a touch of solemn irony. The courtroom we are allowed to see is that of Pilate or the Sanhedrin. All the while, however, we are made aware that this human scene is mere foreground. The case being tried involves a question of ultimate truth — the question of who God is and where he stands; and for just that reason, it is *God who will inevitably do the judging.* The decision which is declared will be his, not Pilate's. By the way things come out, *God will give his verdict and so reveal and identify himself.* He will show whether he is or is not the God and Father whom Jesus announced.[28]

Norris depicts the earthly trial of Jesus as the Last Judgment taking place in advance. In the judgment upon Christ, all judgments converge. On the surface, it appears that human judges are at work in the passion narrative. Faith alone discerns the deeper meaning, that there is only one Judge. The true character and power of this Judge will be revealed in the cross. There

---

27. It is not difficult to discern the workings of the principalities and powers in the daily news. For instance, a longtime chief prison inspector in Australia, speaking of the multinational security companies frequently associated with abuse of human rights, said, "These big global companies . . . are more powerful than the governments they're dealing with" (Nina Bernstein, "Getting Tough on Immigrants to Turn a Profit," *New York Times,* February 29, 2011). One of the most notorious of these companies was Blackwater (later calling itself Xe), which operated with relative impunity throughout the Iraq War.

28. Richard A. Norris, *Understanding the Faith of the Church* (New York: Seabury Press, 1979), 132-33, emphasis added.

are many levels to consider in the theme of the Great Assize. A persuasive account of the psychological significance of forensic imagery is given by Stephen Sykes:

> The importance of justification by grace to be received through faith, as of the whole juridical set of ideas applied to the atonement, lies in *the finality of the verdict of acquittal. Something is finished.* However much we continue to struggle with sins, perplexities, and ambiguities, we know that in our dealings with God our redeemer, revenge, resentment and slavish obligations are not just around the corner. Thank God, in Christ there is a new creation [II Cor. 5:17].[29]

The question thus becomes, what is finished and how do we know it? How can we know that God's completed verdict of acquittal is definitive? And how can we know it without presumption? Heinrich Heine's famous last words were "Bien sûr, il me pardonnera; c'est son métier" (loosely rendered, "Of course God will forgive me; it's his thing").[30] One thinks of Bonhoeffer's controversial but challenging distinction between costly grace and cheap grace.[31] The problem he is addressing remains ever-fresh: How do we appropriate God's finished work in the cross of Christ without taking it for granted?

Trying to Get Rid of Judgment

If the language of trial, verdict, and sentencing is a deeply ingrained human theme, why has there been so much resistance to the law-court motif in interpreting the atonement? It is true that many preachers have dwelt upon perdition with unnecessary relish, but by no means all, and besides, that type

---

29. Stephen W. Sykes, *The Story of Atonement,* Trinity and Truth Series (London: Darton, Longman, and Todd, 1997), 62, emphasis added.

30. No existential anxiety here! Heine, a German Jew (who submitted to Christian baptism but never took it seriously), spent the last two decades of his life in Paris, hence the French.

31. Dietrich Bonhoeffer, *The Cost of Discipleship* (New York: Macmillan, 1963), 45-60. The cheap-costly distinction has been controversial because it might be interpreted as putting conditions on the grace of God, thereby moving in the direction of justification by works. In his *Letters and Papers from Prison,* ed. Eberhard Bethge, enlarged ed. (New York: Macmillan, 1972), Bonhoeffer noted that there was indeed such a problem, which he had not noticed when he was younger. "Today I see the dangers in that book, though I still stand by what I wrote." Letter to Eberhard Bethge, July 21, 1944.

of preaching has been out of favor for a very long time. In America, the reaction against this type of preaching coincided with the emerging sentimentality of popular late-nineteenth-century American culture, with interesting theological results: God was no longer expressing judgment upon sin in the sacrifice of his Son, but only love for sinners; no longer was God's activity portrayed as onslaught, but rather as infiltration. Instead of an apocalyptic invasion, we got "gentle persuasion." Thus the strenuous emphasis on God's righteousness and opposition to sin, typical of earlier Calvinistic preachers, mutated into something very much more like the therapeutic preaching we have today, with a consequently weakened doctrine of sin and atonement.[32]

This culturally inflected shift of priorities ignores the biblical theme of God's judgment upon sin as an *aspect of* his mercy, *not the opposite* of it.[33] An image from a nineteenth-century Calvinist theologian may be helpful here. He asks us to imagine the magnetic needle of a compass. The upper end of the needle *consistently seeks* the North Pole. At the same time, the same upper, magnetic end is *repelled from* the South Pole. There are not two separate magnetic forces at work, but one only; the same magnetism that causes the working end of the needle to point north causes it to point *away from* south.[34] Thus, to be "*for* us and for our salvation," God must be *against* all that would threaten or destroy that purpose.

So in the end it comes down to who we want our judge to be. We don't want to be judged by other people, and we don't want to be judged by God, so that leaves ourselves. Down where it really counts, we want to be our own judge. We want to be in charge of evaluating ourselves. We want to be able to sing with Frank Sinatra, "I did it my way." The explosion of self-help books with titles like *Self-Creation, Looking Out for Number One,* and *How to Take Charge of Your Life* has profoundly affected our way of thinking.[35] This sort of language has become commonplace, even among Christians.

32. See Ann Douglas, *The Feminization of American Culture* (New York: Knopf, 1977), 121-64.

33. Colin Gunton writes that the forensic motifs so much criticized are full of grace. "So much depends on a sensitive appreciation of the possibilities of the legal metaphor" (*The Actuality of Atonement: A Study of Metaphor, Rationality, and the Christian Tradition* [Grand Rapids: Eerdmans, 1989], 87).

34. Robert L. Dabney, *Christ Our Penal Substitute* (Richmond, Va.: Presbyterian Committee of Publication, 1898), 50.

35. Mary Calderone, honored for her work in "the new sexuality" (her term), stated in the '70s that she was proud of her organization, Sexuality Information and Education Council of the United States (SIECUS), for going in "the same direction the churches are going in," that of "self-chosen ethics." (Taken from my notes from mid-1970s, no exact date.) It would be hard to overstate the influence of such views.

Life and death "on my own terms" sounds good to a lot of people. We have been encouraged to believe that the way to enlightenment is through various forms of self-actualization, or self-realization, or any other combination of "self" with another word, some of these techniques being explicitly religious. Thus the deep unconscious conflicts and anxieties that rage within us all are papered over and made to seem manageable and even dispensable. The result is more anxiety and more insecurity.

The great freeing motion of the gospel delivers us out of this welter of self-centeredness. In the *Paradiso,* as Dante ascends higher in Paradise, closer to the Beatific Vision of the Trinity, he realizes that he has ceased to think about himself altogether. Anxiety dissolves into the great wheeling dance of "burning love." This is the experience of all Christians when we realize that, in the apt words of Paul Zahl, "the question of worth has been taken out of our hands" and decided in our favor.[36] This is the place at which the most fundamental matter of all is joined, namely, whether or not we yield the supremacy in every aspect of the divine work of redemption to God and to God alone. This is what it means to acknowledge God as the Judge. The gospel means being seized by the news that God in Jesus Christ, "having canceled the bond which stood against us with its legal demands . . . set [it] aside, nailing it to the cross" (Col. 2:14).

We cannot grasp this except by faith; it is neither common knowledge nor common sense. If every possible system of merit has been swept away by Christ and buried with him in his death (Rom. 6:4), then we have nothing of our own to rely on. If the "balance sheet" has been torn up and discarded forever, we are in the position of the laborers in the vineyard who are angry because someone who worked fewer hours was paid as well as they were. That's what we don't like about God being the Judge. If human nature were the judge in such a situation, we would pay according to hours and productivity. Not so God, who, like the landowner in the parable, says, "Do you begrudge my generosity?" (Matt. 20:15). So God being Judge is a two-edged sword; on the one hand it slices the way we like because God is for us; but on the other hand it slices in a way we don't like because he is also for everyone else without the usual distinctions, and that means no more A list and B list, and therefore no more building up of our own egos at someone else's expense.

We turn now from the subject of judgment in popular culture and the churches to look at a more scholarly set of objections that will shed light on the more general dislike of all things "judgmental."

36. Paul F. M. Zahl, *The Protestant Face of Anglicanism* (Grand Rapids: Eerdmans, 1998), 78.

Forensic or Cosmological? Some Pastoral Concerns

The New Testament scholars J. Louis Martyn and Martinus C. de Boer respectively represent a second and third generation of scholars influenced by Ernst Käsemann. They have drawn a sharp distinction between the cosmological apocalyptic of Paul, which they favor, and a forensic interpretation of the work of Christ.[37] Their objections deserve the widest possible hearing, for their point of departure is not only different from but far more radical than that of the more familiar voices heard around the church in opposition to the forensic motif. In their view, the law-court motif is insufficient, not because it involves *judgment* — that is not at issue — but because it does not depict a cosmic *war,* as the apostle does in his letters. We will examine the New Testament battle imagery in the next chapter, but for the present, we will argue that we need both the forensic and apocalyptic themes *because they are both prominent, indeed determinative, in the Scriptures.*[38]

The problem comes, as Martyn and de Boer indicate, when forensic imagery is given pride of place. If the courtroom motif is our chief controlling image, then there is no possibility of a thoroughgoing apocalyptic viewpoint. It is quite true that centuries of interpretation went forward with virtually no awareness of the apocalyptic foundation of New Testament theology at all, but now that it has been recovered and shown to be the predominant thought-world of the New Testament, we can no longer choose to ignore it.[39] If we do, the losses will be incalculable in this new millennium. The apocalyptic way of seeing transcends an individualistic, pietistic, inward-looking "spirituality" and opens up a horizon of political, social, and cosmic implica-

---

37. Martinus C. de Boer, "Paul and Jewish Apocalyptic Eschatology," in *Apocalyptic and the New Testament: Essays in Honor of J. Louis Martyn,* ed. Joel Marcus and M. L. Soards (Sheffield: JSOT, 1989), 169-90. Douglas Campbell represents an even more recent generation in this line (*The Deliverance of God: An Apocalyptic Rereading of Justification in Paul* [Grand Rapids: Eerdmans, 2009]). From my perspective, the most important critique of a forensic model (he calls it "justification theory") in Campbell's 900-page work is that it is "ethically anemic" (887). A further development of de Boer's thinking, which is closer to my own, appears in his commentary on Galatians, where he argues that the forensic motif needs to be retained in the apocalyptic scenario.

38. In the paragraph from Norris quoted earlier, though it largely depicts the forensic scenario, there is a suggestion of a battle, though he casts it in terms of *struggle.*

39. There is a persistent line of New Testament interpretation, currently represented by the work of Troels Engberg-Pedersen, among others, that admits the pervasive presence of apocalyptic but recommends setting it aside. For reasons that I hope will become clear in the following chapters, I am arguing that this is a disastrous move, theologically, ethically, politically.

tions that has everything to do with the state of our world today and our role as Christians in that world. Let us see if we can make the apocalyptic perspective the controlling one and then view the forensic imagery through that lens.

Allowing the law-court imagery to predominate places us in the realm of legal standards — right and wrong, guilt and innocence. This immediately causes almost everyone to start thinking that there are guilty people and innocent people, whereas we have been taking pains to show that "the line runs through each person." If we are faithful to the gospel as "the justification of the ungodly" (cf. Rom. 4:5), we will not talk about being *morally right* according to a set of legal commandments, but about being *delivered from* hostile, enslaving Powers that are waging war against God's purposes. If we *begin* by talking about being acquitted in the courtroom, we are working from a diminished perspective. If legal language is introduced from the outset, biblical interpreters will find themselves in trouble because they will be operating in the realm of morality, not cosmology — and that will render the church theologically impotent in our geopolitically interlocked world.

A pastoral and homiletical concern thus becomes apparent. If the preacher/pastor is stuck in the realm of the law court, the presentation of the gospel is likely to drift into a moralistic frame of reference. Thus Martyn, in his commentary on Galatians, explains that the Galatian teachers who were Paul's opponents had an essentially forensic idea of the human plight, meaning that they dealt in choices between right and wrong, whereas Paul, renouncing that realm altogether, proclaims through the cross of Christ the inauguration of the victorious rule of God.[40] J. C. Beker reinforces this point by calling the forensic metaphor "juristic-meritorious" in contrast to the trumpet call of divine deliverance from the realm of Sin, Death, and the Law.[41] Thus the issue of what to do with the law-court imagery becomes a matter not only of abstruse scholarly dispute, but also of pastoral concern.

An illustration can be drawn, as is so often the case in Christian theol-

---

40. J. Louis Martyn, *Galatians,* Anchor Bible 33A (New York: Doubleday, 1997), 597 and passim. It is striking that in the Synoptic Gospels, the preaching of Jesus that announces the reign, or kingdom, of God operates more in the realm of apocalyptic than in the forensic frame of reference. The kingdom of God, so important for understanding Jesus' mission, is essentially an apocalyptic conception, not a moralistic one. It is an *announcement,* not an *exhortation.* If we speak of human beings "building the kingdom," that is moralistic (as well as presumptuous), for God is the One who builds the kingdom. Therefore "participation" is the better word for our role as disciples.

41. J. Christiaan Beker, *Paul the Apostle: The Triumph of God in Life and Thought* (Philadelphia: Fortress, 1980), 209. Beker himself succeeds to some extent in combining the forensic and the apocalyptic motifs, which is the intent in this chapter also. So also Alexandra Brown, quoted in J. Louis Martyn, *Theological Issues in the Letters of Paul* (Nashville: Abingdon, 1997), 109 n. 56.

ogy, from an unlikely source. In an article entitled "Thirteen Ways of Looking at a Black Man," concerning the aftermath of the O. J. Simpson murder trial, the African American scholar Henry Louis Gates wrote these words:

> We remain captive to *a binary discourse* of accusation and counter-accusation, of grievance and counter-grievance, of victims and victimizers . . . a discourse in which everyone speaks of payback and no one is paid. The result is that race politics becomes a court of the imagination wherein blacks seek to punish whites for their misdeeds and whites seek to punish blacks for theirs, and an infinite regress of score-settling ensues. . . . No doubt it is a far easier thing to assign blame than to render justice. *But if the imagery of the court continues to confine the conversations, it really will be a crime.*[42]

In a quite breathtaking way Gates has shown us what can happen when the image of the law court is allowed to "confine the conversations" in political debate. Gates's objection to the predominant influence of forensic language parallels that of Martyn and de Boer. In a world of "binary discourse" and "score settling," the hapless body politic is held "captive." This is an amazing insight that very likely derives from Gates's familiarity with biblical literature, whether he acknowledges it or not. The message of the gospel is that we have been lifted altogether clear of this captivity by the cross of Christ in which "there is neither slave nor free . . ." (Gal. 3:28). To apply the "zebra" motif, it is a world in which there is no black or white.

Forensic imagery *if taken in isolation* is inimical to the gospel — but not for the reasons that many critics think. The problem is not that we should get rid of the concept of judgment, which is a major theme of both Old and New Testaments. The problem is understanding judgment exclusively in terms of the metaphor of trial, verdict, and sentencing in a court of law.[43]

42. "Thirteen Ways of Looking at a Black Man," *New Yorker,* October 23, 1995, emphasis added.

43. Psychoanalyst Dorothy Martyn has reported that she is never impaneled for juries because the lawyers discover that she does not believe in guilt and innocence. Perhaps we laugh, or groan; but this is neither a technique for getting out of jury duty nor another example of the decline in public morality. If her position were to be taken *literally* (as the lawyers no doubt do), we could not have a system of justice at all; from a *theological* frame of reference, however, we understand that God's "court" does not operate on the assumptions of a human court. Dr. Martyn's observation is therefore more oracular than analytical; no wonder it confounds the system, pointing as it does to a different order of reality. Conversation with Dorothy Martyn, Bethany, Connecticut, 2004.

Verses such as "There is therefore now no condemnation for those who are in Christ Jesus" (Rom. 8:1) have sometimes been interpreted as though the courtroom was the primary reference. For Paul in Romans, however, the apocalyptic drama is the controlling center of the gospel. A caveat regarding this chapter, therefore, is that the apocalyptic framework of deliverance from one aeon to another should be *the starting point* for thinking theologically about the message of the crucifixion and resurrection of Christ. Then the forensic imagery finds its invaluable place in the whole.

The Wrath of God Understood Pastorally

At this point we return to the wrath of God because it is related to the law-court imagery (the Lord has a case against his people) and is also an integral part of the apocalyptic framework that we began to introduce in previous chapters. Most preachers today try to stay as far away from this theme as possible, yet it is strongly embedded in Scripture. Here is a representative passage on the wrath of the Lord from Isaiah:

> I will punish the world for its evil,
>   and the wicked for their iniquity;
> I will put an end to the pride of the arrogant,
>   and lay low the haughtiness of the ruthless. . . .
> I will make the heavens tremble,
>   and the earth will be shaken out of its place,
> at the wrath of the Lord of hosts
>   in the day of his fierce anger. (Isa. 13:11-13)

This text and others like it are read and interpreted so seldom in the mainline churches today that many liberal-minded Christians are under the impression that we have discarded them. However, it is precisely the combination of wrath and promise that makes the gospel so astonishing. It takes effort and risk to sit with these verses in order to study or teach them, but if we do not, we are left with sentimentality instead of transformation. The "day of the Lord's fierce anger," also known to the Old Testament prophets as the Day of Yahweh, is the time when the creation is finally set to rights. This cannot take place unless there is a conclusive judgment upon and rejection of all that threatens God's eternal plan. To use an environmental analogy, if poisonous contamination has been released into the air and water, it must be permanently eliminated in order for God's new creatures to breathe and have eternal life.

The challenge for pastors and preachers is to show that, given the nature of God, it can be said without qualification that the wrath of God is always exercised in the service of God's good purposes. It is the unconditional love of God manifested against anything that would frustrate or destroy the designs of his love.

A passage in Romans holds the key to this idea: "Christ died for us. Since, therefore, we are now justified by his blood, much more shall we be saved by him from the wrath of God. For if while we were enemies we were reconciled to God by the death of his Son, much more, now that we are reconciled, shall we be saved by his life" (Rom. 5:8-10).

On first glance this sounds like a *chronological* account of the wrath of God. First we were God's enemies, Paul seems to say, needing to be saved from his wrath; then, "justified by his blood," we were reconciled, meaning that God's wrath had been lifted. But this is a misreading of the passage. God did not change his mind about us on account of the cross or on any other account. He did not need to have his mind changed. He was never opposed to us. It is not *his opposition to us* but *our opposition to him* that had to be overcome, and the only way it could be overcome was from God's side, by God's initiative, from inside human flesh — the human flesh of the Son.[44] The divine hostility, or wrath of God, has always been an aspect of his love. It is not separate from God's love, it is not opposite to God's love, it is not something in God that had to be overcome. Theologian Bruce L. McCormack puts it well:

> God will not allow anything to stand in the way of his love. The holiness of the divine love is its irresistibility. God's will to love the creature will not be stopped by the will of the creature to resist that love. God's love will reach its goal, even if the path to that end lies through condemning, excluding, and annihilating all resistance to it. God's love turns to wrath when it is resisted, but not for a minute does it cease to be love even when it expresses itself as wrath.[45]

There is a parallel to the wrath of God in the human sphere. A passage in

---

44. Ricoeur, characteristically, is able to elucidate the seeming inconsistency in the biblical narratives: "Pardon . . . often takes the figurative form of a 'repentance of God' (Exodus 32:14) as if God changed his own course, his own plan. . . . This imagined change in God is full of meaning; *it means that the new direction* imprinted on the relation of man to God has *its origin in God, is divinely initiated.* This origin, this initiative is represented as an event occurring in the divine sphere" (*The Symbolism of Evil,* 78, emphasis added).

45. Bruce L. McCormack, "For Us and Our Salvation," in *Studies in Reformed Theology and History* (Princeton: Princeton Theological Seminary, 1993), 28-29.

C. S. Lewis's *Perelandra* may help us to understand this. On the yet unfallen planet Venus, a man from Earth named Ransom has been chosen to confront Satan, the great antagonist who seeks the fall of that planet also:

> What was before him [Ransom] appeared no longer a person of corrupted will. It was corruption itself to which will was attached only as an instrument. Ages ago it had been a Person; but the ruins of personality now survived in it only as weapons at the disposal of a furious self-exiled negation. It is perhaps difficult to understand why this filled Ransom not with horror but with a kind of joy. *The joy came from finding at last what hatred was made for.*[46]

The brilliance of this insight lies not only in Lewis's imaginative prose. The point is that hatred of Satan is not hatred at all as we generally use that term, because it has found its proper object and therefore can accomplish only good. The wrath of God is like that. If the wrath of God is turned upon us, it can only result in pure good, like the refiner's fire in the book of the prophet Malachi:

> "The Lord whom you seek will suddenly come to his temple; the messenger of the covenant in whom you delight, behold, he is coming, says the Lord of hosts. But who can endure the day of his coming, and who can stand when he appears? For he is like a refiner's fire . . . and he will purify the sons of Levi and refine them like gold and silver, till they present right offerings to the Lord. Then the offering of Judah and Jerusalem will be pleasing to the Lord as in the days of old and as in former years." (Mal. 3:1-4)

This passage has a famous musical setting (Handel's *Messiah*), which has the effect of gospel proclamation. The wrath of God against his people's faithlessness, which is described at length in Malachi, is clearly an aspect of

---

46. C. S. Lewis, *Perelandra* (New York: Macmillan, 1956), 156, emphasis added. Similarly, when Gonville Ffrench-Beytagh, an Anglican priest and active supporter of the anti-apartheid movement in South Africa, was arrested and subjected to psychological abuse in prison, he felt that he had learned the use of hatred. "Hatred is a theological word; it is the antithesis and complement of love. If you love something or someone very much, you must hate that which destroys the beloved, and the Bible is very clear about the many things that God hates. (I think that Christians are far too apt to try and escape from the need truly to hate evil, so that their love is also wishy-washy and weak.)" Ffrench-Beytagh, *Encountering Darkness* (London: William Collins Sons and Co., 1973), 162.

God's powerful activity in making righteous. Active intervention is needed if anyone is to survive ("endure") the Lord's appearance. Without such action, there will be no one to "present right offerings" to the Lord. "Who can stand when he appears?" The cumulative effect of such verses evokes an admission of human incapacity and a hope-against-hope (Rom. 4:18) that the Lord will once again enable Israel to stand upright in accordance with what is remembered about God's actions in time past. The Malachi passage is therefore a powerful proclamation of this very thing, the Lord's coming arrival on the scene to make things right by exercising his remembered righteousness. "The Lord whom you seek will suddenly come to his temple." No one as yet could have guessed that he would come in order to present *his own self* as the "right offering," but Malachi is clear that the thoroughly unworthy sons of Levi will be cleansed by God's purifying activity, not by anything they themselves contribute. It will be God's achievement from beginning to end.

The Biblical Word *Dikaiosyne* and Its Secret

How exactly does God deal with the problem of sin? Or, more comprehensively, how does God "make righteous"? How does God set right what is wrong? C. F. D. Moule defines sin in two complementary ways:

1. Sin is a malign force that twists human nature.
2. Sin is a dead weight that has to be shouldered.[47]

So far, so good; we have indicated two threads that can be distinguished in the biblical witness, one emphasizing deliverance from Powers, the other emphasizing atonement or expiation. However, when Moule continues, "shouldered and lifted away *by forgiveness,*" we may sense that he has used too weak a word. We discussed this matter at considerable length in chapter 3 where we examined the problem of forgiveness when there has been no justice.

Forgiveness is a prominent theme in the Synoptic Gospels, though perhaps not quite as prominent as one might think. The word appears only once in the Fourth Gospel. What is really striking and suggestive is that the theme

---

47. C. F. D. Moule, "The Energy of God: Rethinking New Testament Atonement Doctrines" (Sprigg Lectures, Virginia Theological Seminary, Alexandria, Virginia, March 1-2, 1983). I have complete transcriptions of these lectures, typed from tapes in 1983, but have been unable to ascertain from any source whether they were ever officially published.

of forgiveness appears almost not at all in the undisputed letters of the apostle Paul. One rare reference is a quotation from a psalm (Rom. 4:7); in another letter he uses the concept sarcastically (II Cor. 12:13). Clearly this is intentional. Does this mean that Paul was unforgiving, or that he did not think forgiveness was important? Indeed not; it is significant that his one significant reference to forgiveness is a section of II Corinthians (2:4-11), his most pain-filled letter, in which he urges the Christian community in Corinth to forgive — note this — a person who has offended *against him, Paul.*[48] It is indeed remarkable that the only time he speaks at length about forgiveness is in a situation where he himself is the one who has been hurt. We may conclude from this scarcity of the term "forgiveness" that Paul de-emphasized forgiveness to concentrate on something even more radical, namely, a wholesale recasting of *the righteousness of God* in light of God's messianic intervention.

As we began to argue in the chapter on justice, forgiveness is part of the story, but not the whole story. There are many sayings of Jesus and stories about Jesus in which the forgiveness of sins plays a major role.[49] Forgiveness by itself, however, does not satisfy the human craving for justice; more important still, it does not fully express either the power or the love of God.[50] We cannot ignore the massive testimony of the Old Testament that Yahweh is a God of justice.

In the Psalms and the prophetic literature particularly, the righteousness of God is a major theme and is inseparable from the covenant faithfulness of

---

48. Indeed, in this particular section of II Corinthians, we learn something about Paul personally because he gives instructions that the offender should be not only forgiven but also comforted. "*You should rather turn to forgive and comfort him,* or he may be overwhelmed by excessive sorrow. So I beg you to reaffirm your love for him. . . . *Any one whom you forgive, I also forgive*" (II Cor. 2:7-8, 10). This is the truly saintly and loving Paul, ready to extend himself most especially to the one who has hurt him personally. It recalls Christ on the cross, though Paul does not presume to say so. How often this apostle has been misjudged by those who know of him only by reputation or selective reading!

49. The Synoptics (particularly Luke) say several times that Jesus came for the forgiveness of sins, and in one signal instance, that of the paralyzed man let down from the roof (Mark 2:5-12; Matt. 9:1-8; Luke 5:22-25), he uses the healing as a way of identifying himself as the One who has messianic authority to forgive sins.

50. In Luke-Acts, forgiveness is stressed, unlike Paul's more radical apocalyptic concept of rectification/justification *(dikaiosis)*. The default position, for most, is to prefer Luke and forgiveness to Paul and justification. This may be partly because of a widely accepted view that forgiveness is the central feature of Christianity. This privileging of forgiveness can be a way of avoiding the difficulty of acknowledging the necessity for a complete overhaul of *both* the forgiver *and* the recipient of forgiveness. John's Gospel, in its own way, presents the human predicament just as radically as does Paul (the word "forgive/forgiveness" appears only once in the entire Fourth Gospel). Giving forgiveness first place without a corresponding (or, indeed, overriding) emphasis on *dikaiosis* should therefore be challenged in New Testament theology.

YHWH. The Old Testament scholar James Luther Mays notes, significantly, that *tsedaqa* (usually translated "righteousness") is a "relational concept" based on the covenant, rather than an "absolute ethical norm." He also argues that *mishpat* (usually translated "justice") is the fruit of *tsedaqa;* in other words, human justice derives from God's righteousness.[51] Thus, righteousness is not a human virtue to be cultivated, but is always in relation to and derived from the character and activity of YHWH. This fundamental Old Testament idea comes through in the New Testament with explosive power in the preaching of Paul, where *tsedaqa* and *mishpat* become not just *dikaiosyne* as generic righteousness but, in four key verses, *dikaiosyne theou* — the righteousness *of God* (Rom. 1:17; 3:21-22 [twice]; II Cor. 5:21).

There are few words in any language that can equal *dikaiosis* for theological depth and resonance.[52] It has been at the center of scholarly debate for centuries. Known largely as "justification," it is still a key word in ecumenical discussion. Yet we have great difficulty in translating it into English. We need to absorb the teaching of Austin Farrer, who wrote, "God has no attitudes which are not actions; the two things are one."[53] That is why we are using "rectification" throughout to translate the *dikaios* word-group. It is this power of rectification (and not simply that of forgiveness) that constitutes the eschatological Christian hope.

---

51. James Luther Mays, *Amos: A Commentary,* Old Testament Library (Philadelphia: Westminster, 1969), 92.

52. We noted the challenge of translating the Hebrew word-group *tsedaqa* into English in chapter 3. In English translations of the Old Testament, the word "justice" has sometimes been used, but more often, "righteousness." Once we arrive at the Greek word-group *dikaios* as an equivalent for *tsedaqa* in the New Testament, we are confronted with an even more fraught difficulty in translation. In the famous text Amos 5:24, the two Hebrew words *mishpat* (justice) and *tsedaqa* (righteousness) are used as virtual synonyms or *hendiadys* (see above, chap. 3, n. 58), as elsewhere in portions of the Old Testament. Because of Martin Luther King's fondness for this verse in Amos, the most familiar English rendering today is "Let justice roll down like waters, and righteousness like a mighty stream," a combination of RSV and KJV. The Jerusalem Bible idiosyncratically translates *tsedaqa* as "justice" sometimes, and at other times with words such as "virtue," "goodness," and "integrity." Another Roman Catholic translation of the same verse, the New American Bible, renders it as "Let justice surge like water, and goodness like an unfailing stream." The Anchor Bible (Andersen and Freedman) uses the words "justice" and "equity." J. L. Mays (Westminster Old Testament Library), like the RSV and NRSV, offers "justice" and "righteousness," the most typical translations. The difficulties are apparent. Understanding *dikaiosyne* from the perspective of Paul would require that words like "virtue" and "goodness" not be used because they suggest human traits rather than powerful actions of God. Moreover, using two different English words ("justice," "righteousness") for one Greek word *(dikaiosyne)* gives the wrong impression.

53. Austin Farrer, *Saving Belief* (New York: Morehouse-Barlow, 1964), 106.

When a reader of the Bible discovers that the *verb* translated "justify" and the *nouns* "justification," "righteousness," and "justice" are *the same word,* the effect on that reader's understanding can be revolutionary.[54] Ernst Käsemann opened up a new understanding of the term *dikaiosis,* traditionally translated "justification," that continues to bear fruit into the twenty-first century.[55] In his groundbreaking essay "The Righteousness of God in Paul," he shows that God's *dikaiosyne* is not an attribute but a *power,* namely, "a power that brings salvation to pass."[56] Thus, "righteousness" does not mean moral perfection. It is not a distant, forbidding characteristic of God that humans are supposed to try to emulate or imitate; there is no good news in that. Instead, *the righteousness of God* is *God's powerful **activity** of making right what is wrong in the world.* When we read, in both Old and New Testaments, that God is righteous, we are to understand that God is at work in his creation doing right. He is overcoming evil, delivering the oppressed, raising the poor from the dust, vindicating the voiceless victims who have had no one to defend them.[57]

54. Strictly speaking, I should perhaps say that "justice" and "righteousness," in Greek, "have the same root" instead of "are the same word," but for nonspecialist readers in English, it is surely not wrong to say that they are the same word. In Greek, the word appears in several forms. *Dikaiosyne* is "righteousness," as in "the righteousness of God" *(dikaiosyne theou). Dikaiosis* is "justification," or (preferred) "rectification." *Dikaioo* is "justifies" (as in "God justifies" or "God rectifies"). *Dikaios* is "righteous" (as in "to be righteous" or "to make righteous"). Experts in the *koine* Greek of the New Testament may find the word-group used with less than total precise correctness in these pages. For general readers, however, the point is indubitable that the word-group carries with it a force that cannot be rendered into English unless the reader grasps the direct correspondence between the English *nouns* "righteousness" and "justice" (both used to translate *dikaiosyne*) and the English *verbal construction* "to make righteous," or to rectify.

55. A corresponding development in Old Testament studies is well described by Elizabeth Achtemeier, "Righteousness in the Old Testament," in *The Interpreter's Dictionary of the Bible* (New York: Abingdon, 1962).

56. Ernst Käsemann, *New Testament Questions of Today,* trans. W. J. Montague (London: SCM, 1969), 181.

57. Again, the Magnificat of Luke 1:46-55 is a striking testimony to the righteous action of God, which works proleptically to make real in the present what is promised for the eschatological future. Thus the mere announcement of the angel, *prior* to anything demonstrable actually happening to Mary, sets future things in motion as though they were already accomplished:

> "He has put down the mighty from their thrones,
> and exalted those of low degree;
> he has filled the hungry with good things,
> and the rich he has sent empty away."

(The canticle of Hannah in I Sam. 2:1-10, on which the Magnificat seems to be based, also displays this present-tense usage to some extent.)

What is even more remarkable, however, is that not only is God going to put down the mighty from their seats (Luke 1:52), he is also going to remake hearts, so that even the mighty, the arrogant, and the selfish will be conformed to Christ (Rom. 12:2), becoming humble, loving, and unselfish. In other words, God's righteousness involves not only a great reversal ("the first will be last") but also an actual transformation and re-creation. When radicalized in terms of Václav Havel's insight about the line that runs through each person, the *dikaiosyne* of God means that no human being whatsoever will be exempt from or immune to his justifying action. Taking this a step further, we begin to see that when we say God will "justify" rather than merely "acquit," the action has a reconstituting *force* — hence the insufficiency of the courtroom metaphor "to acquit." God's righteousness is the same thing as his justice, and his *justice* is powerfully at work *justifying*, which does not mean excusing, passing over, or even "forgiving and forgetting," but actively *making right that which is wrong.*[58]

The complaint is often made that justification/rectification sounds as though God's action in the crucifixion and its consequences are all taking place over our heads, so to speak, without our involvement. In the sense that our liberation from the Powers of Sin and Death is accomplished by God's gracious power throughout, then, yes, it was over our heads. Jesus did it alone. As soon as we start trying to insert ourselves into the picture, we start to encroach once again upon God's righteousness, attempting to appropriate it for our own. This is to fall back into the arms of the Galatian teachers, with their insistence that we must add our own observance of the Law to Christ's finished work on the cross. This is another form of the bad news. If there is something you and I have to contribute to the equation in order to be justified, then we are back in the "juristic-meritorious" thought-world that oppresses and enslaves. Questions proper to that world are: How much must I do? How often should I do it? How do I know if I have done enough?

---

58. One of the most striking examples of the compound ways that the word *dikaiosyne* works, and its importance for the gospel, can readily be seen in the Greek of Rom. 3, where *dikaiosyne* occurs nine times in ten verses — four times as a noun, five as a verb. Unfortunately, in English translations we can't see the full implications of this. Particularly illustrative is the way *dikaiosyne* is used in 3:25-26, where we see that God is two things at once: God is himself the just (righteous) One and, at the same time, the One who justifies (makes righteous). There really is no way fully to convey this in English. "To prove that he himself is righteous and that he justifies the one who has faith in Jesus" does not do the job, and there is no suitable noun form of "rectification" to put in the place of "righteous" or "just." The reason this is so important is that Paul wants us to understand that there is a powerful seamless movement proceeding out of God's own righteousness to make us righteous (rectification).

The challenge for interpretation in this matter is to maintain a firm focus on the primary agency of the righteousness of God without seeming to rob the human being of any incentive to do good. This is a central issue. It is common in the churches to hear this issue framed in terms of human response to God's invitation, to God's call. The problem with this is that speaking of human *response* implies that the agency shifts from God to the human being. To put it another way, the use of "response" encourages us to think that whereas God initiates, we are on our own as to our next move. On the contrary, as the Book of Common Prayer puts it, all our good works are "begun, continued, and ended in thee."[59] This is at the very center of the gospel. God's righteousness is active *not only* in the call *but also* in the response, even the response of faith. The key word here for us, then, is "participation." This gives the right balance between the relationship of God's agency and human activity.

Faith Is Not a Work

If the righteousness of God is the sole agent in the life of the community that God brings into being, then what about faith itself? If faith is not a "work" and, as we have said above, not even a response, what is it? Paul addresses this in a passage that describes the relation of the Law to faith: "Now before faith came, we were confined under the law, kept under restraint until faith should be revealed. So that the law was our custodian until Christ came, that we might be justified by faith. But now that faith has come, we are no longer under a custodian; for in Christ Jesus you are all sons of God, through faith" (Gal. 3:23-26).

Paul has used "faith" as the subject of the verb "to come." Clearly, it is synonymous with the coming of Christ himself. The name of Christ can be substituted for the word "faith" throughout, and the passage makes perfect sense.[60] This reveals that faith, for Paul, is the power of Christ himself making faith happen in us. "Faith is constituted by the fact that with the preaching of the gospel the Lord who is the basis of the gospel comes upon the scene and seizes dominion over us."[61] We may say therefore that Christ evokes faith, begets faith, gives birth to faith, elicits faith, with the understanding that it never becomes a possession of our own that we can take credit for, but is

59. Collect for Guidance, 1979 Book of Common Prayer, 832. I grew up hearing this prayer every Sunday morning. It is a blessing that it comes back to me now when I really need it.

60. The same substitution can be made for the word *agape* in I Cor. 13.

61. Ernst Käsemann, *Commentary on Romans* (Grand Rapids: Eerdmans, 1980), 108.

always a work of *his* own.[62] This is unforgettably illustrated in the story of the demon-possessed boy in Mark 9. As the boy writhed on the ground, "Jesus asked his father, 'How long has he had this?' And he said, 'From childhood. And it has often cast him into the fire and into the water, to destroy him; but if you can do anything, have pity on us and help us.' And Jesus said to him, 'If you can! All things are possible to him who believes.' Immediately the father of the child cried out and said, 'I believe; *help my unbelief!*'" (Mark 9:21-24).

In this exceptional story, we see the power of Jesus at work giving birth to faith. The father's cry, which has been called the greatest utterance of faith in the whole Bible, sets out the whole reality in explicit terms. *First,* faith is evoked by Jesus' enabling word, "all things are possible to him who has faith." This gives birth to "the awful daring of a moment's surrender"[63] — the sudden, all-risking cry, "I believe!" *Second,* the faith that is thus evoked forever remains a gift, not a human achievement. In this life, there will never be a time when we will not need to say to the Lord, "Help my unbelief."[64] We cannot "choose" to have faith; we can only receive it with joy and thanksgiving. The reason we can speak of justification/rectification by faith, not by works, is that faith is not a work. It is our one necessary companion at the bar of judgment only insofar as it is God's gracious gift, Christ himself being our Advocate.[65]

Logizomai: Spoken ("Worded") into Righteousness

How does this powerful gift of justification (perhaps better translated "rectification") by grace through faith come into being?[66] Another Greek word

---

62. In a widely influential monograph, Richard Hays has shown that "faith in Jesus Christ" (Gal. 3:22) is actually "the faith of Jesus Christ." This means that the faithfulness of Christ in giving his life is what constitutes Christian existence, not works of our own, even if they are works of belief and trust (*The Faith of Jesus Christ: The Narrative Substructure of Galatians 3:1–4:11*, 2nd ed. [Grand Rapids: Eerdmans, 2002]). Martyn quotes J. Haussleiter, "Christ accomplishes faith, in that he communicates himself. . . . And then he remains active behind our faith, so that the redeeming power of faith lies in the fact that the living Christ is both the one who originates it and the one who carries it along" (J. Louis Martyn, *Galatians*, 270 n).

63. T. S. Eliot, "The Waste Land," in *The Complete Poems and Plays*, 49.

64. Flannery O'Connor, "It [faith] comes and it goes." Letter to "A" upon her leaving the church, in *The Habit of Being* (New York: Farrar, Straus and Giroux, 1979), 452.

65. The word "advocate" (also "helper," "intercessor," or "counselor") is a translation of *parakletos,* referring to the Holy Spirit. It appears in the Johannine literature five times (as the Holy Spirit in John 14:16, 26; 15:26; 16:7; and as the second Person in I John 2:1).

66. Many today prefer to say, as here, "by grace through faith" rather than "by faith," to

related to this discussion, *logizomai,* comes from the domain of commerce and means "to credit as," "to calculate as." A secondary meaning is "to regard as," or "to look upon as." In his letters Paul uses the word many times with a range of meanings. But in Romans 4 he uses it with an audacious new meaning, appropriating the term with its commercial connotation ("to reckon as" or "to credit as") for his own theological purposes. In this section of Romans the word *logizomai* becomes not just mental activity but the very heart of the gospel, namely, the saving Word of God. We may translate it as "to word," or, somewhat less awkwardly, "to speak into" (as, for instance, God "speaks us into faith"). The point of these somewhat clumsy renderings is to make *logos* into the verb, *logizomai* — the same move we made with *dikaiosyne.* The key appearance of *logizomai* is at Romans 4:3-8, a central text by any measurement. Quoting Genesis 15:6 and Psalm 32:1-2 in a wholly new context, Paul writes,

> What does the scripture say? "Abraham believed God, and it was *reckoned* to him as *righteousness.*" Now to one who works, his wages are not *reckoned* as a gift but as his due. And to one who does not work but trusts him who *justifies* the ungodly, his faith is *reckoned* as *righteousness.* So also David pronounces a blessing upon the man to whom God *reckons righteousness* apart from works: "Blessed are those whose iniquities are forgiven, and whose sins are covered; blessed is the man against whom the Lord will not *reckon* his sin."[67]

The link between *logizomai* and *dikaiosyne,* and the two words' central importance, is obvious in these verses (3-8). The *logizomai* word-group appears five times (three times more in vv. 9-11), and *dikaiosyne* four times (three times more in vv. 9-11). Clearly this combination is at the heart of what Paul wants to tell us. The quotation from Psalm 32:1-2 is brought over as an exact translation from the Septuagint, but Paul is going to take all this in a radically new direction that, we are to understand, would not have been possible from the perspective of this age but only from the apocalyptic standpoint provided by the appearance of God's final deed in Christ.

Paul's argument is somewhat convoluted, but it goes like this: From the perspective of the age that is "passing away" (I Cor. 7:31), Abraham's faith

---

emphasize the point the faith is not a "work." Thus *sola gratia* and *sola fide* are combined, but with an emphasis on *gratia.*

67. This is one of Paul's very rare uses of the word "forgiveness." He virtually never uses it unless he is quoting — in this case, from Ps. 32.

would have been regarded as a meritorious work, so that justification/rectification would have been "his due." From the perspective of the new creation, however, justification is entirely a gift, since Abraham has not "worked," but has "trusted in him who justifies the ungodly." For the present, the point is that the "wording" *(logizomai)* or "reckoning" of the sinner as righteous *(dikaiosyne)* is not a "legal fiction" as it has sometimes been called. It is not simply a declaration of amnesty, which would be the "passing over" of sin — an unacceptable solution that we have been protesting against for several chapters. It is actually a speaking ("wording") into *(logizomai)* righteousness. That is what God's Word *(logos)* is able to do. In the Old Testament, God's Word is performative; it creates what it names. The very first verses of Scripture show God creating *ex nihilo* (out of nothing) by his utterance: "And God said, 'Let there be light'; and there was light" (Gen. 1:3). God's Word alone brings creation into being. In just the same new-world-creating way, God's *logizomai* brings transformed persons into being. This is called *dikaiosis,* rectification (justification).

Paul has thus linked the commercial term "to credit/reckon as" with the unique Hebrew concept of the creating *logos* of God. Classical Christian doctrine teaches us that Jesus Christ himself is the living Word in our midst: "Therefore, if any one is in Christ, he is a new creation; the old has passed away, behold, the new has come. All this is from God" (II Cor. 5:17-18). The line "all this is from God" relates to the argument Paul was having with the Corinthians, who tended to think that their own "spirituality" was effecting righteousness. No, Paul says, *all* this is from God.[68]

The way that "wording" works can easily be illustrated. We tend to become what we are "regarded as." Here, for example, are two scenes. One is a first-grade schoolroom in East Tennessee in the mid-1960s, recently integrated. Three small black boys, looking miserable, are separated from the others (all white) for special remedial attention from the white teacher. After working with them for a while, she rises from the table and says to an

---

68. For Protestants of the Lutheran and Reformed traditions, the translation "it was imputed to him" has tremendous resonance, with its implication that the righteousness "worded" to us is always an "alien righteousness" (Martin Luther's term) that never becomes our own possession but is always received gratefully from God as a gift. "Imputed righteousness" and "alien righteousness" are still concepts of tremendous importance because they protect the central theme of Paul in the Corinthian letters, *panta ek tou theou* ("all things [are] from God" — II Cor. 5:18) and they guard against works-righteousness — *provided that* the phrases are understood to refer to something that is truly happening, not just theoretically "counted as." The righteousness of God is a gift that is received anew daily from the Giver, but it really is a gift, whereby the receiver *participates* in righteousness through Christ.

observer, in a stage whisper that the children surely hear, "How does anyone think they can ever learn anything?" The phrase "self-fulfilling prophecy" was invented for a situation such as that. The second scene occurs two decades later, in a supermarket in a suburban New York town. A mother is bending over a stroller containing her child, no more than two years old. With great intensity she is saying, over and over, "You're bad! You're bad!" What can the child have done, at that age? What grave sin had he committed? Spilled his drink? Snatched candy off the shelf? Cried from frustration? Who can doubt that the child will grow up with those words ingrained in his psyche? "You're bad!" Words have great power. Imagine, then, the power of the Word of God saying *Shamed! Condemned! Rejected!*

But those words are not the Word spoken against us, for indeed the Word is not spoken against us but for us. "He has not *reckoned* our sins against us" (II Cor. 5:19). This has been translated "not counting" (RSV) our sins against us, which, if carelessly interpreted, could be taken to mean "pass over" sin. When we understand that the words "not reckoned" or "not counted" are from the root *logizomai,* however, we can fill in the rest of the picture. The "not reckoned" is the other face of "reckoned as righteousness." Again, God's Word is *performative;* it has the power to create what it requires. When God regards one as righteous, a true metamorphosis is occurring.[69]

The power and efficacy of God's "wording" can be illustrated by numerous examples from the Bible, as for instance the story of Gideon: "Now the angel of the Lord came and sat under the oak . . . [as] Gideon was beating out wheat in the wine press, to hide it from the Midianites. And the angel of the Lord appeared to him and said to him, 'The Lord is with you, you mighty man of valor'" (Judg. 6:11-12).

This is really quite amusing; Gideon is not even remotely a "mighty man of valor" at this point. Nor does he flex his muscles and step into his role as an "alpha male" would; indeed, his behavior immediately following the appearance of the angel is timid and cautious. The Lord, however, keeps on "wording" him: "The Lord turned to him and said, 'Go in this might of yours and deliver Israel from the hand of Midian; do not I send you?'" (v. 14). Again, this makes us smile; the Lord is even willing to suggest that it actually is Gideon's own might; but the reminder comes quickly enough: "Do I

69. Philippians 2:5-8 is important here. As Christ underwent an exchange of *morphe* (form), so also in Christ the one addressed by the Word is being *metamorphosed* into righteousness. This is what it means to "have this mind among yourselves, which is yours in Christ Jesus" (v. 5). Therefore Paul can say, as though it were already performed, "we have the mind of Christ" (I Cor. 2:16).

not send you?" Gideon continues to protest: "Pray, Lord, how can I deliver Israel? Behold, my clan is the weakest in Manasseh, and I am the least in my family" (v. 15). His protestations are swept aside by the empowering Word: "And the Lord said to him, *'But I will be with you,* and you shall smite the Midianites as [though they were] one man'" (v. 16). Thus God creates valor where there was no valor.

Perhaps the best-known illustration of "wording" in the New Testament is the scene of Christ's reconciliation of Peter after the resurrection. Three times Jesus asks Peter, "Do you love me?" The thrice-repeated question reflects Peter's three denials of the Lord as he was being arraigned. We read that "Peter was grieved because [Jesus] said to him the third time, 'Do you love me?' And he said to him, 'Lord, you know everything; you know that I love you.' Jesus said to him, 'Feed my sheep'" (John 21:17). Jesus is "reckoning" Peter to be chief shepherd; he is not simply "regarding" him as such, but actually "speaking him into" his apostleship. Thus, in the often-used but never-tired formulation, Jesus enables Peter to become what he already is, by the grace of God. That is *logizomai*.[70]

Another reference to the contributions of Käsemann will help to summarize these sections on *logizomai* and *dikaiosyne* ("reckoning" and "rectification"). Interpreters who use the phrase "God's way of righting wrongs" (NEB) are putting his insights into play. Käsemann's particular contribution is to show that the righteousness of God is not a *gift* so much as it is a *power*.[71] God does not "word" us by simply saying, "I am now going to treat you *as if* you were righteous" (hence the inadequacy of the translation "to credit as" or "to regard as"). Rather, Paul announces that the power of God is already apocalyptically present and reestablishing dominion over the human being, making him or her a new creation. Thus Käsemann writes:

> Interpretation along the lines of an "as if" has already been warded off [by God's powerful action]. . . . God makes the ungodly person a new creature; he *really makes him righteous.* . . . The creative power of the di-

---

70. In the 1970s, when FitzSimons Allison was rector of Grace Church in New York, his expositions of *logizomai* were so powerful and memorable that when he left to become bishop of South Carolina, the congregation gave him a pectoral cross with the Greek word inscribed upon it.

71. Ernst Käsemann, "The Righteousness of God in Paul," in Käsemann, *New Testament Questions of Today* (Philadelphia: Fortress, 1969), 174. The Reformers have been accused of making the justification of the ungodly sound like an untruth, whereby the guilty were pronounced innocent even though there was in fact no change in their condition (a "legal fiction"). Käsemann's work on *dikaiosyne* solves this problem.

vine Word is presupposed and the link between justification [*dikaiosyne*] and this Word [*logizomai*] is not snapped. The new creature comes into being through the Word and will be preserved only under the Word. . . . As eschatological address, then, justification is that acquittal by the Judge which sets us free for new creation and *alone makes us capable of it.*[72] . . . For the apostle, *salvation . . . is not primarily the setting aside of the past guilt but freedom from the power of sin.* A different theological horizon results in a different set of terms.[73]

This crucial passage deserves a second look. Justification (rectification) is "eschatological address." This is vital. The word "eschatological" indicates that we are talking about *the last things,* and about that which is derived from the end-time. Käsemann explains this further: *logizomai* and *dikaiosyne* ("reckoning" and "justification"), taken together, derive their force and effectiveness precisely *from God's future.* They are therefore inalienable, since only God is in charge of the future. We may therefore call this irresistible grace! Pronouncing righteous (justifying/rectifying) is "an eschatological act of the Judge at the last day which takes place proleptically in the present."[74] This explains how we are able to say that a person is "made righteous" even though we can see that it isn't so. But it is so; it is *eschatologically* true. The verdict of "righteous" that God pronounces at the last day is already made a fact in the present. Thus, again, we may say, "Become what you already are," which is the only use of the imperative that carries the full force of the gospel. This is directly related to the description of the Holy Spirit in Ephesians 1:14 as an *arrabon* — a first installment, down payment, or guarantee. The Spirit is the eschatological power *par excellence*, being the third person of the Trinity and therefore entirely independent of any created limitations, continually active in exercising the power that calls forth the new creation *ex nihilo*.

The Motif of Reconciliation: Where Does It Fit?

Reconciliation *(katallage)* is one of the most important concepts in the New Testament. The problem of where to put it in this book has been a vexing

---

72. This, in different words, repeats Augustine's great insight "O Lord, grant what you command; and then command what you will" *(Da quod jubes, et jube quod vis)*. Augustine, *Confessions* 10.29.

73. Käsemann, *Commentary on Romans*, 112-13, emphasis and brackets added.

74. Käsemann, *Commentary on Romans*, 112.

one. Should reconciliation have a category of its own?[75] Or should it be a subset under another category? This is indeed a major issue.

The argument here is that justification/rectification is a larger category that *includes* reconciliation. Reconciliation is the *result* of God's justifying, rectifying activity.[76] This major category is therefore to be treated in this book under several different headings in different chapters. We mentioned the reconciliation of Peter a few paragraphs back, and we have quoted several times from II Corinthians 5, the *locus classicus* for Paul's teaching about reconciliation.

Two American activist theologians known for their radical views, Will Campbell and James Y. Holloway, knew the power of reconciliation as rectification when they named their journal *Katallagete!* (Be reconciled!).[77] They drew this word from the passage already cited several times, but here reproduced for the first time in full:

Therefore, if any one is in Christ — new creation! the old has passed away, behold, the new has come.[78] All this is from God, who through Christ *reconciled* us to himself and gave us the ministry of *reconciliation;* that is, in Christ God was *reconciling* the world to himself, not counting their

75. The entire fourth volume of Karl Barth's massive *Church Dogmatics* is entitled *The Doctrine of Reconciliation.*

76. There is a connection between *reconciliation* and *rectification* that can be illustrated by an analogy. In electrical engineering, "rectification" means making alternating currents flow in the same direction. (Someone must have suggested this to me, but I have forgotten.) The story of Adam and Eve tells, in mythological terms, how the original harmony between God and his creation was lost, so that they became alternating currents going in opposite directions. Reconciliation, in this image, would be turning our human current back in the direction of God's current, so that our wills become congruent with his will. When this happens, we will also be in harmony with one another. Like all analogies, this one is imperfect, but the link that it suggests between reconciliation and rectification might be an indicator of how God's action in justification is at the same time both rectifying (because it turns us from the wrong direction into the right one) and reconciling (because we are now all going in the same direction).

77. *"Katallagete!"* is an imperative; doesn't this negate what we've been saying about the weakness of imperatives? This deserves a careful answer. The imperative does not simply cease to exist in the *kerygma.* It is still there, especially in Paul's paraenetic (hortatory, or instructive) passages. However, Paul's *paraenesis* is so firmly lodged in the indicative that it never ceases to be kerygmatic. Campbell and Holloway (whose essays are collected in *Up to Our Steeples in Politics*) are good examples of theological writers who, though erratic in certain other ways, virtually always understand the difference between proclamation and exhortation.

78. This is the translation favored by Richard Hays, and is closest to the Greek. An inscription in the entrance to the Duke Divinity School is not quite as good, but comes close: "If anyone is in Christ, there is a new creation."

trespasses against them, and entrusting to us the message of *reconciliation.* So we are ambassadors for Christ, God making his appeal through us. We beseech you on behalf of Christ, *be reconciled (katallagete)* to God. For our sake he made him to be sin who knew no sin, so that in him we might become the righteousness of God. (II Cor. 5:17-21)

The context of this passage is important. Much of II Corinthians is agonized, almost as painful to read as it must have been to write. There was precious little reconciliation going on in the Corinthian congregation. The members were in conflict with one another, and most particularly, in conflict with Paul. In almost every word of the letter (several letters, actually) the apostle is struggling to turn their allegiance back to the apostolic message. Humanly speaking, this task is impossible. When Paul speaks of reconciliation in Romans and II Corinthians, he is using the most sweeping terms at his command so as to evoke the coming age of God — the only possible source of present power to accomplish reconciliation in the Corinthian church: "The old has passed away, behold, the new has come" (II Cor. 5:17). Immediately following, Paul asserts, "All this is from God." The paradoxical nature of the passage is shown in the dialectic between *the present reality* (a fractured congregation) and *the eschatological gift* (reconciliation), which enables Paul to say, "Be reconciled!" Become what you already are!

Another central passage expounding reconciliation is found in Ephesians. It is justly celebrated, but like the rest of the letter, it lacks the paradoxical, or dialectical, quality of Paul's undisputed letters, which is one reason why most scholars consider it deutero-Pauline.[79] Ephesians 2:11-16 describes reconciliation as a completed reality, without qualification:

Therefore remember that at one time you Gentiles . . . were at that time separated from Christ, alienated from the commonwealth of Israel, and strangers to the covenants of promise, having no hope and without God in the world. But now in Christ Jesus you who once were far off have been *brought near in the blood of Christ.* For he is our peace, who has made us both one, and has broken down the dividing wall of hostility, by abolishing in his flesh the law of commandments and ordinances, that he might create in himself one new man in place of the two, so making peace, and might *reconcile us both to God in one body through the cross,* thereby bringing the hostility to an end.

79. Markus Barth is a conspicuous exception (*Ephesians: Introduction, Translation, and Commentary on Chapters 1–3,* Anchor Bible 34 [Garden City, N.Y.: Doubleday, 1974]).

The emphasis here on the finished deed is congruent with Paul even if it lacks the tension that we feel in the Corinthians passage. And in any case, we should not overemphasize the "realized" aspect of Ephesians, because this letter also contains the famous "put on the armor of God" passage; it is clear that the church is being called to do battle "against the principalities, against the powers, against the world rulers of this present darkness, against the spiritual hosts of wickedness in the heavenly places" (Eph. 6:12).

Both passages link reconciliation with the cross, Ephesians explicitly and II Corinthians implicitly ("God made him to be sin"). It is therefore obvious that reconciliation must play a significant part in any discussion about the crucifixion.[80] The challenge in discussing the theme of reconciliation is to avoid saying too much about it on the one hand and too little on the other. Käsemann, for polemical purposes, de-emphasized the theme to the vanishing point. On the other end of the spectrum, as Charles Cousar points out, reconciliation strikes such a responsive note in the fractured culture of today that it is perhaps overemphasized.[81] The trick is to find the right balance. Reconciliation will assuredly be the accomplished result of God's great rectifying project, but a world set right will include more than reconciliation.

Reconciliation as Struggle

Kenneth Leech, in an important passage from his book *We Preach Christ Crucified,* presses us to reflect more deeply upon the theme of reconciliation:

---

80. R. P. Martin and C. F. D. Moule are among the New Testament scholars who have argued for reconciliation as the most inclusive category. Moule objects to the law-court metaphor of justification in terms that are relevant to this chapter (see previous section on forensic versus apocalyptic interpretations). His view is that reconciliation is larger than justification and includes it, rather than the other way round, because the experience of reconciliation is one that we recognize and know from personal experience without needing to reach for a metaphor. This distinction between metaphorical and literal reality is important to Moule. He seems to feel that metaphors are "impersonal" (he is thinking specifically of *dikaiosyne*) and therefore "ancillary" to the personal and readily apprehended "reality" of reconciliation. In believing that the theme of reconciliation has wide appeal, he is surely right; it is unquestionably a far more popular way of talking about Christ's work today than almost any other. Questions to be raised, however, include, *first,* is metaphor really one step removed from reality? if so, what becomes of all the New Testament metaphors? And *second,* does the category of reconciliation, if it is made to be the theological center, take sufficient account of the reality of struggle and conflict in this life on the frontier between the old age and the age to come (Moule, "The Energy of God")?

81. Charles B. Cousar, *A Theology of the Cross: The Death of Jesus in the Pauline Letters,* Overtures to Biblical Theology (Minneapolis: Augsburg Fortress, 1990), 82.

One of the most widespread and persistent images of Jesus is that of the great reconciler, one who promotes tolerance and harmony wherever he goes. Non-Christians often pay respect to "the spirit of Jesus" as a spirit of goodwill, tolerance, and kindness. This is to ignore a great deal in the accounts which suggest that, far from producing harmony, Jesus produced division, bringing not peace but a sword, setting members of families against one another, and leading to anger and social unrest. Yet we too easily emphasize reconciliation without seeing these other aspects. In one study in the Methodist Church [of the UK], 42 percent of ministers said that reconciliation was the first task of the church. But what does this mean? Certainly there is no idea in the New Testament of reconciliation with the powers of darkness, hence the centrality of the exorcisms in Jesus' ministry. Evil forces are to be cast out, not reconciled. Reconciliation is the *result* of the struggle, and is brought about only through conflict and eventually through death itself.[82]

"Reconciliation is the *result* of the *struggle.*" There are times when a premature emphasis on reconciliation can be as sentimental as the insistence on innocence that we examined earlier. Reconciliation in this world can never be anything other than provisional. In South Africa, a white Dutch Reformed pastor, Jaco Coatzee, who, much against his inclinations, found himself leading his church into the fight against apartheid, was later called upon to preside over intensely emotional and difficult meetings intended to foster reconciliation between white and black church members. He spoke of the trials of coping with people who wanted what he called "cheap reconciliation." He gave as an example a white minister who "didn't understand that the moment was just the beginning . . . he wanted everything to be forgotten and gone. He made it too easy, he wanted us to be further along the road than we actually were," Coatzee said. Thoughtfully, he continued: "Reconciliation only happens though pain and the cross . . ." — long pause — "and death."[83]

Reconciliation as Eschatological Gift

In a passage well known for its difficulty, Jesus says to the Twelve that he has come not to bring peace, "but a sword" (Matt. 10:34). Here, rather star-

---

82. Kenneth Leech, *We Preach Christ Crucified* (New York: Church Publishing, 1994), 49-50, emphasis added.

83. Conversation with Jaco Coatzee, Princeton, New Jersey, July 31, 2002.

tlingly, the "taking up of the cross" means not reconciliation, but division. This illustrates the point made by Leech, that reconciliation is given only through struggle. Because it is an *eschatological* gift, it belongs to the promised future of God, but the victories given in this life are always provisional. That is why Alcoholics Anonymous members never refer to themselves as "recovered" alcoholics but always as "recovering." When they say, "one day at a time," they are testifying to the daily challenge of remaining sober, especially since there will always be people who have a stake in their continuing to drink.[84] Jesus, in his words to the disciples, warns them that the proclamation of the imminent kingdom will cause a division. Although the work of reconciliation is indeed an imperative for Christian disciples, we can never expect too much from reconciliation in this orb. Whenever it happens, we hail it with joy and praise as a sign of the age to come, but it remains a *sign,* not a completed work in itself.

A number of passages in the Old Testament depict reconciliation from the perspective of God's apocalyptic intervention in the end-time. Here are the striking words that bring the Old Testament to a close: "Lo, I will send you the prophet Elijah before the great and terrible day of the Lord comes. He will turn the hearts of parents to their children and the hearts of children to their parents, so that I will not come and strike the land with a curse" (Mal. 4:5-6 NRSV).

It is not always recognized how extraordinary this ending is.[85] The setting for these verses is the "great and terrible day of the Lord" when, in the words of the older Book of Common Prayer, "the secrets of all hearts shall be disclosed."[86] "For behold, the day comes, burning like an oven" (Mal. 4:1). This day of reckoning is usually imagined in flamboyant meteorological detail on a cosmic scale, but here, all of a sudden, the prophetic spotlight shrinks and comes to focus on the smallest possible human unit, the microcosm of the family, the estranged parent and child whose ruptured relationship represents an entire cosmos of separation from the Creator. Enmity between

---

84. Therefore, a rupture between the alcoholic and these "enablers" or "codependents" might become necessary. Every one of us is in some sense an enabler of the status quo, which means that the coming of the Messiah will be disruptive for *everyone.*

85. The Hebrew Scriptures (the Tanakh) end with the Writings, or Hagiography. The Tanakh therefore closes with Ezra, Nehemiah, and Chronicles. The Christian Old Testament, while containing the same material, is arranged quite differently, ending with the prophet Malachi. This placement gives a powerful eschatological and christological impetus to the entire Old Testament canon and serves as an introduction to the New Testament.

86. From Holy Matrimony, 1928 Book of Common Prayer, 300. There are a few people still living who are sorry to see this disappear from the marriage service.

child and parent is a heartbreaking phenomenon, an offense against all that is human, all that is godly, evoking deep anguish in anyone who actually experiences or empathetically imagines it. Here in these climactic verses, the reunion of estranged parents and children stands for a whole world of reconciliation at every level in human affairs. This wondrous détente, divinely caused, is seen here as the penultimate sign of the Lord's sovereign reordering of human relationships into the pattern of the kingdom of God.

Passive or Active? Now, or Not Yet?

Are we passive or active in God's work of reconciliation? A good deal depends on the way we reply to this question. Clearly we are passive recipients in the first instance, since *"God was in Christ* reconciling the world to himself." We could not do it; God had to do it. Nowhere in Scripture is this stated more clearly than in Ephesians; in just three short verses, the apostolic author nails into place the relationship between faith and works: "For by grace you have been saved through faith; and this is not your own doing, it is the gift of God — not because of works, lest any man should boast. For we are his workmanship, created in Christ Jesus for good works, which God prepared beforehand, that we should walk in them" (Eph. 2:8-10).

This eminently preachable passage sets out the two things that every Christian should understand about the life in Christ.[87] The bedrock of the gospel is that the whole matter of reconciliation (laid out in Eph. 1:7–2:7) is God's work from beginning to end; we receive God's justifying grace *passively,* as pure gift. We are *acted upon* by God. But this is only half of the picture. Even as we receive God's gracious action passively, we are in the same motion *activated* for a life of service. Verse 10 is an extraordinarily illuminating verse, splendid for teaching the relation of human activity to the divine activity. This exceptional passage should lay to rest all complaints that the emphasis on God's agency leaves us with nothing to do.[88]

We become "ambassadors for Christ" (II Cor. 5:20) through the divine reckoning *(logizomai)* that sets us in motion. In his undisputed letters, Paul

87. Note particularly Karl Barth's sermon "Saved by Grace!" on Eph. 2:5. Barth, *Deliverance to the Captives,* first paperback ed. (New York: Harper and Row, 1978), 36-42.

88. The postcommunion thanksgiving prayer in the Book of Common Prayer asks our "heavenly Father . . . so to assist us with thy grace, that we may . . . do all such good works as thou hast prepared for us to walk in" — almost exactly quoting Eph. 2:10. The same idea is recast in the newer rite with less rhetorical grandeur and less emphasis on the agency of God — "to do those things which you have given us to do" (Book of Common Prayer [1979], 339, 366).

stresses the unrealized, *future* hope that empowers the *diakonia tes katallages* (service, or ministry, of reconciliation) in the *present*. We are activated by the Spirit to "Be reconciled!" with our fellow human beings because we are already reconciled with God — the already–not yet pattern that characterizes the New Testament. Ephesians has placed all this explicitly within the sphere of the cross (2:13-16), indicating the nature of the Christian life that must be lived in tension, struggle, and suffering. Because the resurrection has validated this struggle, the tension between the now and the not-yet aspects of reconciliation galvanizes, rather than paralyzes, the company of believers.

The brilliant strategist of the Montgomery bus boycott and the March on Washington, Bayard Rustin, was an instinctive theologian if not a conscious one. He sheds much light on this present-future dynamic in an interview: "Dr. [Martin Luther] King had this tremendous facility for giving people the feeling that they could be bigger and stronger and more courageous than they thought they could be. . . . He had this ability to communicate victory, and to let everybody know he was prepared to pay for victory."[89]

Here, in this description of a real-life situation, we see three crucial dynamics at work: (1) *logizomai* (to be reckoned or counted as); (2) *dikaios* (rectification/justification); and (3) the dialectic of the now and the not-yet, all brought together in one package as the *diakonia tes katallages* (ministry of reconciliation). That's a mouthful, but a closer look will reward us.

First, in King's preaching, *logizomai* was taking place. King wasn't ignoring or "not counting" or "not reckoning" the various manifestations of Sin that continually threatened the movement, such as pettiness, rivalry, ego, vengefulness, and fear. King's ministry of "wording" was not one of ignoring these problems among his people, nor was he exhorting them to behave better. Insofar as God gifted him, he did something that was engendered from a different world-order altogether. He was a channel for the Word that has the power to create something that was not there before, and his followers felt that power at work among themselves.[90] Rustin, still wondering at it after the passage of some years, told how he watched the reaction of the Ku Klux Klan. "They could not comprehend the new thing," he said. "They were no longer able to engender fear."[91]

And so we see, *second*, that the reckoning *(logizomai)* that took place

89. Howell Raines, *My Soul Is Rested: Movement Days in the Deep South Remembered* (New York: Putnam, 1977), 56.

90. Richard Lischer's analysis of Dr. King's sermons shows this clearly: *The Preacher King: Martin Luther King, Jr., and the Word That Moved America* (Oxford: Oxford University Press, 1995), 212 and passim.

91. Raines, *My Soul Is Rested*, 56.

under Dr. King's leadership actually brought righteousness *(dikaiosyne)* to pass. People didn't just feel different; they were different. Anyone who reads the history of the civil rights movement will be amazed that so many deeply flawed human beings could still be used in such a transforming way. The temptations and failures, when soberly recounted, were so massive that one wonders how the movement lasted for weeks, let alone years; but over and over, righteousness kept happening. The justifying, rectifying action of God was going forward.

Third, Rustin gives us a glimpse into the present-future dynamic that we are recommending throughout this volume. In Martin Luther King's preaching, the victory is already a fact, as in the previously noted Magnificat ("He has put down the mighty from their seats"). But at the same time, Rustin in just one sentence combines the already-present victory with the not-yet-realized aspect that requires total self-giving: "He had this ability to communicate victory," *and at the same time* "to let everybody know he was prepared to pay."

Here is an example of the way the ministry of reconciliation works out in real life. Most people don't know this, but in a sense the civil rights movement was conceived in the forties, twenty years before the Montgomery bus boycott, when James Farmer was race-relations secretary with the Fellowship of Reconciliation in Chicago. FOR sponsored a precursor of the 1961 Freedom Rides. It was called the Journey of Reconciliation, and several people ended up spending thirty days on a chain gang in North Carolina simply for refusing to get off their bus.[92] Not many church people talking about reconciliation today are willing to pay a price like that. It is not uncommon, both in and out of the church, for the people who do the most talking about reconciliation to be the ones who find it easier to smooth things over than struggle through them. That is why Kenneth Leech insists, "Evil forces are to be cast out, not reconciled. Reconciliation is the result of that struggle, and is brought about only through conflict and eventually through death itself."[93]

Summing Up, Looking Ahead

The imagery of the law court is subordinate in the New Testament to the theme of apocalyptic victory in the cross and resurrection of Christ. Never-

92. Raines, *My Soul Is Rested,* 34.
93. Kenneth Leech, *We Preach Christ Crucified* (Cambridge, Mass.: Cowley, 1994), 50.

theless, it plays a very important role in the whole biblical picture. The prominence of a day of reckoning ("the Day of the Lord") in both Old and New Testaments cannot simply be ignored, especially in view of the tendency in today's liturgies and lectionaries to eliminate the theme of judgment. The Lord has a case against his people, as the Old Testament prophets tirelessly preached, and the New Testament does not back away from this theme; a time of reckoning before God is certain, as powerfully evoked — to give just one example — in Matthew 25 with its parables of the wise and foolish bridesmaids, the talents, and the Last Judgment.

Discernment of the *kerygma* in its most radical form, however, enables us to see that distinctions between the "innocent" and the "guilty," while provisionally necessary in this fallen world, lose their power when seen from the perspective of the end-time. Categories of more and less guilt, and declarations of amnesty, so inadequate in this age of Sin and Death, become meaningless in the light of God's new day as we come to understand that in the sight of the Lord "there is no one righteous" (Ps. 14:3; Rom. 3:10). This is the heart of biblical understanding concerning the entire human race. In the light of what was permitted to be done to the Son of God by the machinations, duplicity, and collaboration of all the "best people," we come to see ourselves in bondage to forces far stronger than we are.

The rise of apocalyptic in the late Old Testament and intertestamental periods is the setting not only for Jesus' preaching of the arrival of the kingdom of God in his own person, but also his announcement of the time to come when the Lord will finally and conclusively judge the world (Mark 13:26-27; Matt. 25; Luke 21:25-28; also John 12:47-48). In the light of this promised final consummation, the declaration of the psalmist that "the ordinances of the Lord are true, / and righteous altogether" (Ps. 19:9) will be seen to have been true all along, operating powerfully in our daily struggles.[94] Thus the imagery of the Day of the Lord finds its place in the conflicts of this present time, "for though we live in the world we are not carrying on a worldly war, for the weapons of our warfare are not worldly but have divine power to destroy strongholds" (II Cor. 10:3-4). It will be seen from this perspective that it is of utmost importance that the forensic analogy of the law court should not be allowed to crowd out the other motifs on the apocalyptic stage of the New Testament *kerygma*.[95] The declaration in the

94. It is very much to the point that Abraham Lincoln quoted Ps. 19:9 in the Second Inaugural just as the Civil War was ending.

95. Along the lines just sketched out, Dillistone writes concerning Rom. 3:25 that although it is "set against a background of law and trespass and condemnation," it is not to be interpreted

courtroom, "Not guilty!" is properly grasped only when we recognize that the categories of guilt and innocence simply do not exist as such in the new age of God, but are rendered meaningless by the apocalyptic gospel of *the justification of the ungodly* (Rom. 4:5; 5:6).

In the present time, God's "wording" *(logizomai)* of his new creation proceeds largely in a hidden way. The invincible transforming power of God's coming future is acting simultaneously in and through the deeply flawed realities of the present human situation. This means that in "the present evil age" (Gal. 1:4) the disciples of Christ are constantly aware of hanging on to what can often seem like a desperate position between the now and the not-yet. We are those "upon whom the end of the ages has come" (I Cor. 10:11), and we are strengthened by the Spirit to live accordingly, between the times. This is what Paul means when he writes, "The appointed time has grown very short; from now on, let those who . . . deal with the world [live] as though they had no dealings with it. For the form of this world is passing away" (I Cor. 7:29, 31).

In numerous places the Scriptures identify reconciliation as a primary sign of the end-time (for instance, in Mal. 4:5-6; II Cor. 5:18-19; and Eph. 2:13-16). In this chapter, as previously explained, the theme of reconciliation has been included under the overall category of *dikaiosis* (rectification/justification). Although signs of reconciliation in this life are always proleptic parables of what God will do and are therefore much to be sought, its fulfillment is a work of the end-time — the gift of the Judge who is to come in the Great Assize.

C. F. D. Moule cites the biblical terminology involving "the use of main force," as in conquest, rescue, liberation — "a great raid on an enemy camp." When forgiveness and reconciliation are described in these terms, they take on the coloring of the apocalyptic struggle: "If we were robbed of the victory language, we should be lacking in a very important tool. It says that God will not tolerate the alienation and disorder that sin brings, that he will ultimately

---

"in terms of a strict payment for acts of lawlessness" (*The Christian Understanding of Atonement* [Philadelphia: Westminster, 1968], 183). In a particularly apposite passage, Dillistone continues, "The atmosphere of Romans 5-8 is not that of a law court nor of an adjudication of penalties. Rather it is of an utterly new beginning in human affairs made possible by a refusal to be bound by the strict injunctions of any legal system. . . . The atmosphere is that of *a great deliverance, a dramatic reversal, a glorious vindication. It is not that of penalties being measured out*" (182). (Dillistone's work on the death of Christ is shot through with brilliant insights. However, his literary interests carry him far afield, resulting in a theologically inconsistent and often confusing picture. "The Unique Redemption," however — the chapter on *Christus Victor* — is superbly clear and reliable within itself and is the one quoted here.)

claim us for his own, that he is strong enough to snatch us from the jaws of the enemy."[96]

This, finally, is a powerful affirmation. The imagery of rescue and victory places the themes of reconciliation and forgiveness into another context altogether, where they are brought in under the heading of *God acting to make right what has been wrong* (rectification). Then, and only then, can the whole complex of ideas and images be located where it belongs, on the battlefield of Christ against the Powers. This is the overarching panorama against which to place the imagery of the Great Assize, or Last Judgment.

96. Moule, "The Energy of God." It is interesting, in view of Moule's stated objective of de-emphasizing pictorial language, or metaphor, in favor of actual, literal experience, that pictorial language reasserts itself powerfully at this point. My own reading of Moule's rethinking of atonement language is appreciative while being critical. I have quoted portions where he seems to argue against his own propositions about the individual, personal nature of repentance, forgiveness, and reconciliation.

CHAPTER NINE

The Apocalyptic War: *Christus Victor*

The style [of the Bible] is of the battlefield rather than the cloister.

NORTHROP FRYE, *The Great Code*[1]

Naming a chapter "The Apocalyptic War" poses immediate problems. There is widespread mystification about the strange word "apocalyptic," and on top of that, there is the military metaphor. Addressing the second difficulty first: it must forthrightly be admitted that if the Christian community is being its true self, it will be deeply suspicious of battle imagery. The history of Christian militarism has not been edifying. Across the centuries, "Christian" nations and groups have thought that God was on their side and have behaved accordingly. It is painful to hear, in the twenty-first century, that "Christians" and "Muslims" are murderously attacking each other in various African nations. This should make Christians everywhere profoundly ashamed. In a world that, by and large, glorifies military action, it is not often recalled that Christian battle imagery is paradoxical; the military terms — "swords," "shields," "chariots," "armies" — are used in a metaphorical sense to evoke a warfare that takes place in the unseen realm. In the Bible, the term "apocalyptic" *(apokalypsis)* encompasses a worldview in which the truly significant battle is the ongoing one between the Lord God of *Sabaoth*[2] (Hebrew, meaning armies) and the Enemy, who deploys the principalities and Powers (Eph. 2:2). This contest on the heavenly level is enacted on

---

1. Northrop Frye, *The Great Code: The Bible and Literature* (New York: Harcourt Brace Jovanovich, 1982), 213.

2. Greek form of Hebrew *tsebaoth,* "armies"; hence, "Lord of hosts" in the RSV (Rom. 9:29; James 5:4) and the Te Deum. The KJV retains *Sabaoth.*

the earthly level by struggles large and small in the realm of human affairs
— battles waged not with worldly weapons but with the spiritual armor of
God (Eph. 6:11-17).[3]

Apocalyptic: A Review

This chapter will recall and expand some of the main points concerning
apocalyptic interpretation already begun in previous chapters. In the chapter
on justice, we paid special attention to Isaiah 40–55, where the prophet's
sublime voice emerges from the pit of the exile to mark the transition to
apocalyptic in the theology of Israel. In the sustained vocal line of these six-
teen chapters, we hear the Holy One of Israel saying, "Behold, I am doing a
new thing." This announcement, arriving from another sphere of reality and
power, is in itself an "apocalypse" or "revelation." The proclamation from the
depths of Israel's shame carries within it the same new-world-creating capacity as did the very word of God in the original creation.[4] Isaiah announces
the coming triumph of God *independently of human cooperation*. The advent
of a re-created, redeemed world is announced and brought into being by the
irresistible power of the One who comes.[5] From this unknown prophet of

---

3. Many treasures are to be found in the "old" 1928 Book of Common Prayer of the
Episcopal Church, now largely disused and forgotten. Here, for example, in a prayer for, of
all things, the General Convention of the church, the apocalyptic framework is assumed in
the reference to the "breaking down" of the "kingdom" of Sin, Death, and Satan. "We beseech thee so to direct, sanctify, and govern us in our work, by the mighty power of the Holy
Ghost, that the comfortable Gospel of Christ may be truly preached, truly received, and truly
followed . . . to the breaking down [of] the kingdom of sin, Satan, and death; till at length
the whole of thy dispersed sheep, being gathered into one fold, shall become partakers of
everlasting life; through the merits and death of Jesus Christ our Saviour. Amen." This sense
of an opposing realm and an Enemy to be displaced is largely missing from many versions
of the gospel.

4. In the book of Isaiah, the word for the revelatory and performative Word of God is
semu'a. In the LXX (the Greek translation of Hebrew used by New Testament writers), the
word is rendered as *akoe*. This is important, because in Paul's epistles, Rom. 10 for example, the
word is often translated "hearing," with the emphasis on the human act of hearing. In Isaiah,
however, it clearly means *the message itself*. The NEB has it right in translating Rom. 10:16-17
(the KJV and RSV are wrong on this one): "Isaiah says, 'Lord, who has believed our message?'
We conclude [Paul continues] that *faith is awakened by the message.*" This is an important issue
in translation, because apocalyptic theology is based on the purposeful action of God's Word,
not the sin-distorted reception of that Word by human beings.

5. As noted in the introduction, the Greek of the book of Revelation gives "the One Who
Comes" an actual title: *ho erchomenos* (Rev. 1:8).

the exile we hear for the first time in unmistakable terms the universal, cosmic note that will be characteristic of full-blown apocalyptic. After this, the idea of a redemption from within history begins to fade from the prophetic writings. Instead, we begin to hear such oracles as those of Zechariah 9–14, depicting the day of the Lord's victory on the apocalyptic battlefield when "The Lord will become king over all the earth; on that day the Lord will be one . . . [and] there shall be no more curse" (14:9, 11).

The transitional section on Anselm might seem to have little or no connection to apocalyptic theology, but his insistence on the magnitude of the human predicament *(ponderis peccatum)* is not inconsistent with an apocalyptic perspective. His project hangs on the conviction that God in Christ, the God-man, has acted *from outside the human sphere* to topple Sin, Death, and the devil from their thrones. "Christ conquered the devil as man had been conquered by the devil."[6] Thus it is not altogether out of bounds to say that Anselm, even from within his scholastic world of discourse, grasped something of the basic idea of apocalyptic — God's irresistible invasion of this orb of Sin from his own orb of greater power. Anselm does not think exclusively of our being acquitted, or even made morally right, but above all of our being liberated from forces too strong for us. "This purpose could not be carried into effect unless the human race were delivered by their Creator himself."[7]

In chapter 6 ("The Blood Sacrifice") we saw that in the provisions in Leviticus for atonement, God taught Israel to place her hope in *repentance* as a solution to the problem of godlessness. This arrangement held until the theological crisis precipitated by the exile.[8] This extremity forced Israel into abandoning hope for a human solution. The apocalyptic literature that flowered in the postexilic period is therefore characterized by a certain discontinuity. The rending of the veil of the temple at the time of the crucifixion was understood by Mark and Matthew as an apocalyptic sign from God that the

---

6. Paraphrase of Anselm, *Cur Deus Homo?* 2.19.

7. Anselm, *Cur Deus Homo?* 1.4.

8. The role of repentance continues to be a point of difference between Christianity and Judaism, because the theological crisis of the exile did not get translated into rabbinic Judaism in the same way that it did in the New Testament. We noted in chapter 4 the words from the liturgy for Yom Kippur, "repentance will turn aside the severe decree." In the Christian gospel, and in the cross in particular, it is disclosed that *nothing human* can turn it aside. Repentance is the proper *response*, ignited by God himself, to the completed work of Christ on the cross, whose vicarious self-sacrifice has turned aside "the severe decree" once and for all (though *not,* as we cannot repeat often enough, in the sense of the Father over against the Son).

decisive stroke against the old order was occurring; "something greater than the temple is here" (Matt. 12:6). The visions of the apocalyptic prophets — Ezekiel's vision of dry bones, Zechariah's vindication of Jerusalem, Daniel's dream of the advent of the Son of Man — reveal *a God who acts independently of his people's response.* And again, we hear the cosmic-universal note: God's salvation will encompass *the entire created order.*

The Passover-exodus chapter introduced a discussion of the important similarities and dissimilarities between the terms "eschatology" and "apocalyptic." In chapter 7, we saw that the ransom metaphor suggests persons held in bondage against their will by captors too strong for them. Deliverance must therefore come from another sphere of power. Jesus announces himself as the eschatological deliverer in his inaugural sermon in Luke 4:18-19. In chapters 5 and 8 we stressed human activity not as that which *brings about* the purposes of God, but rather as that which *points to* the action of God that is already at work in the world. Seeing the world through the lens of biblical apocalyptic is *a transformative way of seeing.* It is a way of discerning and participating in God's actions in the world as guarantees of his promised future.

Chapter 8 emphasized the corporate and cosmological aspects of God's case, not only against his chosen people or even against "the nations," but most of all against the despoilers of his created order — the Powers identified in the New Testament. If the coming judgment is in part to be envisioned as the forensic weighing-in-the-balance of God's people, how much more will it be God's righteous sentence upon an entire *kosmos* of perverted structures and inhumane systems. All of this happens, we saw, because the righteousness of God *(dikaiosyne)* is not simply an attribute (noun) of God; it is able to grant (verb) what it requires. That is the central idea in the concept of justification *(dikaios).* The righteousness of God is the same as *his power to make righteous — to rectify what is wrong.*

In this chapter we introduced two kinds of apocalyptic, forensic and cosmological. Both are present in Scripture, but the courtroom image must not be made the controlling metaphor; it is too individualistic, and hence reductive; it deals too much in categories of guilt and innocence; it does not envision an Enemy against whom a war has to be fought. Now that the cosmic, universal perspective of apocalyptic has been rediscovered by New Testament interpreters, it is vital not to lose sight of it in our own era of global interdependence.

Having reviewed the argument thus far, we now move to a more extensive examination of the apocalyptic perspective and its relation to the New Testament proclamation that *Jesus is Lord (Kurios Iesous).*

Apocalyptic Misunderstood and Understood

The word "apocalypse" has became familiar to virtually everyone, but rarely in its biblical form. For most, it means, simply, an extreme event — a cataclysm — especially one accompanied by real or imagined signs of the end of one's world, or a world. In secular culture, the biblical meaning of the word "apocalyptic" is, barring a miracle, lost to us. That is all the more reason for the church to reclaim it, not for cultic or exclusive purposes, but for her own self-understanding. The apocalyptic orientation of postexilic Judaism, which led into the New Testament, is not a bizarre fixation on imagined catastrophic events. It is a comprehensive worldview with a specifically ethical dimension. It is, moreover, a theory of history.[9] Even though Israel's thinkers gave up on history in the usual sense after the exile, history remains the arena of God's activity. The difference is in *the way of seeing* historical events. Human affairs take on a different meaning when seen from the perspective of biblical apocalyptic theology.

The word *apokalypsis* at its root means "disclosure," "unveiling," or "revelation." It came to denote a type of literature that flourished in Judea in the period between the Testaments. The finest of the genre is known to us as the Old Testament book of Daniel. The book of Revelation stands in direct descent from it.[10] The way of seeing the world that grew out of this apocalyptic literature was so pervasive in Jesus' time that it is reasonable to assume that he shared it; earlier generations of modern scholars sought to separate him from it, but increased understanding of the apocalyptic worldview has caused many to find that position less tenable. It now seems likely that some portions, at least, of the "Synoptic apocalypse" go back to Jesus himself (Matt. 24; Mark 13; Luke 21).[11]

We need not be detained here with specialized analysis of specific "apocalypses," for instance, in the intertestamental period.[12] Instead, we will focus

9. Marxism is also a theory of history with its own "apocalyptic" dimensions. *Vive la différence.*

10. A distinction is maintained herein between the *genre* called "apocalyptic" and the apocalyptic *worldview.* The genre is of vital interest to the specialist, but that lies beyond the scope of this book. Here, we will concentrate on the *worldview* (actually, *kosmos*-view), which is found in its most thoroughgoing form in the letters of the apostle Paul.

11. Raymond E. Brown was one of the most prominent biblical scholars in the 1970s to assert, against the then-prevailing opinion, that apocalyptic must have been part of Jesus' own worldview. At Union Theological Seminary in 1973, he designed and taught a full course in the apocalyptic genre, going on to show how it appears in the Gospels, and invited Norman Perrin, who represented the then-dominant view, to discuss and debate the subject.

12. Interested readers are directed to the many studies of apocalyptic literature and bib-

more specifically on the ways that the cross itself is the definitive *apokalypsis* of God, and in what ways it does and does not reveal something that was already there, only hidden. What the nonspecialist reader needs to grasp is the place of the cross in the apocalyptic framework. Here is the vital center of the Christian gospel, and it is accessible to anyone seeking to know Christ. The purpose of this chapter is to set forth the New Testament picture of the crucified and risen Lord at the head of his heavenly host, and thereby to hint at the confidence and hope that this perspective affords.

Breakthrough in New Testament Studies

It is not possible to discuss the *Christus Victor* theme without taking a position on whether the apocalyptic perspective is or is not the key to the New Testament symbolic universe. The scholarship lying behind this chapter is still not well known in the churches, but it is becoming more prominent in academic circles, and this will begin to filter down to the pews. A grasp of what is involved in apocalyptic theology will greatly strengthen the foundation for a comprehensive understanding of the *Christus Victor* theme. Biblical theologians who were influenced by the work of Ernst Käsemann have defined the foundations of apocalyptic theology in the New Testament in varying but essentially unified ways.[13] We will draw on the work of two of the most important of them: J. Christiaan Beker and J. Louis Martyn.[14]

---

lical studies that are available; for example, John J. Collins, *The Apocalyptic Imagination: An Introduction to Jewish Apocalyptic Literature,* 2nd ed. (Grand Rapids: Eerdmans, 1998); P. D. Hanson, "Apocalypticism," in *Interpreter's Dictionary of the Bible: Supplementary Volume,* ed. K. Crim (Nashville: Abingdon, 1976); Joel Marcus and M. L. Soards, eds., *Apocalyptic and the New Testament: Essays in Honour of J. Louis Martyn* (Sheffield: JSOT Press, 1989).

13. There is much confusion in the popular media about the term "biblical theologian," which has a precise definition and differs from, though it includes, the term "biblical scholar." When an academic is identified in this book as a "biblical theologian," it means that she is a scholar of the text *qua* text, but, in addition, she is also conversant with systematic theologians and, even more important, has gifts and inclinations that allow her to put the biblical witness to work *as proclamation.* This is not to diminish the work of the scholars who are known for their elucidation of the texts. Most, though not all, of the scholars cited in this volume can be identified as biblical theologians, largely because of their interest in preaching, their care for the church, and their knowledge of Christian doctrine.

14. Charles Cousar is a third New Testament theologian in the line of descent from Käsemann. He writes, "The death of Jesus has an apocalyptic, world-transforming character because it effects a complete change in the situation between sinful humanity and God" (*A Theology of the Cross: The Death of Jesus in the Pauline Letters,* Overtures to Biblical Theology [Minneapolis: Augsburg Fortress, 1990]). Cousar is deeply influenced by Käsemann but seeks to go even

Beker gives us a sense of what is at stake: "The discontinuity between this age and the age to come points to a radical transformation of the present world order, because the world is presently ruled by Satan, death, and the forces of evil. This dialectic of negation and affirmation is accompanied by a sense of imminent expectation of God's universal reign."[15]

In his appraisal of Paul, Beker lets us know that he has a personal stake in this way of thinking. His striking emphasis on the ethical dimension of the gospel stands in sharp contrast to the popular conception of apocalyptic literature as being exclusively focused on escape from the troubles of the present in hope of the hereafter. On the contrary, says Beker, apocalyptic is a powerful antidote to "the therapeutic captivity of the gospel." Paul's message, he emphasizes, does not linger on individuals who will be healed case by case, as in so much of American Christianity. Rather, Beker thinks in terms of the apostle's vision of global enslavement to the Powers that threaten at every turn to undo God's purpose of liberation. Beker's abiding concern is for those who are in need of hope in the midst of extreme suffering. He concludes the preface to *Paul the Apostle* with these words: "In a time like ours, where 'apocalyptic' signifies nightmare and pervasive systemic evil, the gospel of Paul with its very different apocalyptic thrust and its unswerving faith in the God of faithfulness should inspire us to a new strength in the midst of trouble."[16]

---

further in emphasizing ethics. He stresses Paul's use of the "language of crucifixion" not only as polemic but also "to nurture in the readers an identification of themselves as people of the cross, people who bear in their bodies the death of Jesus" (18).

In addition to Beker, Martyn, and Cousar, there are other senior figures not only in biblical theology but also in systematic theology, such as Paul Lehmann, Paul Minear, Roy A. Harrisville, and others. After them, there are a number of important scholars in the *third* academic generation after Käsemann, some of them biblical scholars and some systematic theologians. Indeed, it is striking that the usually unbridgeable gap between systematics and biblical studies in academia has been to some extent bridged in this case. Among the companions-in-arms from both disciplines are Christopher Morse, Martinus C. de Boer, Douglas Harink, Philip Ziegler, Alexandra Brown, Beverly Gaventa, Joel Marcus, Douglas Campbell, Joseph Mangina, James F. Kay, Stephen Westerholm, and Susan Eastman. Unclassifiable but important for apocalyptic ethics are Will Campbell, James Holloway, William Stringfellow, Vernard Eller, Jacques Ellul, John Howard Yoder, and others. Desmond Tutu is neither a biblical scholar nor a theologian, but he has acted in tune with apocalyptic ethics throughout his long and very public life.

15. J. Christiaan Beker, *Paul the Apostle: The Triumph of God in Life and Thought* (Philadelphia: Fortress, 1980), 136-37.

16. Preface to first paperback edition of Beker, *Paul the Apostle*, xxi.

Readers may be interested to know something of Beker's life. In 1943, when he was a high-strung, emotionally vulnerable teenager in the Netherlands, he was wrenched away from his family by the Nazis and shipped, alone, to Berlin for slave labor in the German war machine.

Beker's work is kin to J. Louis Martyn's in its debt to Käsemann. Martyn is probably the most influential interpreter of Paul's apocalyptic theology in the generation after Käsemann.[17] It is possible to pull together some identifying marks of the apostle's message and worldview from Martyn's teaching and writing over many years, especially those related to the *Christus Victor* theme.[18]

First, a new thing has been *apocalypsed,* called into being by God. The cross/resurrection event is a genuine *novum,* a first-order reversal of all previous arrangements — an altogether new creation *ex nihilo,* out of nothing. We are speaking of the God who "calls into existence the things that do not exist" (Rom. 4:17). Paul speaks of faith in Christ not so much as a human response to God's activity but as God's direct creation, something that did not previously exist but has now been called into being.

Second, there is a break between the old *kosmos* and the new. God's *novum* was prefigured in the Old Testament, and the Old Testament has not been superseded. However, Paul guides us into reading the Hebrew Scriptures (which, after all, are the only Scriptures he knew) in a different way. The change of *kosmos* has radically remade the relationship between law and gospel, religion and faith, imperative and indicative: "In the cross of our Lord Jesus Christ . . . the world *(kosmos)* has been crucified to me, and I to the world. For neither circumcision counts for anything, nor uncircumcision, but a new creation" (Gal. 6:14-15).

The "apocalypse" of the cross and resurrection, therefore, was not an inevitable final stage in an orderly process, or an accumulation of progressive steps toward a goal; it was a dramatic rescue bid into which God has flung his entire self.[19] The human situation is so desperate that nothing else will

---

He contracted typhus in the labor camp and came close to dying. Beside him in the camp infirmary lay a Polish boy who had been beaten senseless. He lay beside Chris for three days and nights and then died. "It was then, while lying beside the wasted body of a Polish boy murdered for no reason at all, that Chris determined to become a theologian." He went to the window and beheld Berlin in flames from the Allied bombardment, and there, "sick with typhus and viewing the apocalypse, Chris confessed, 'Only God is real'" (Ben C. Ollenburger, "*Suffering and Hope:* The Story behind the Book," *Theology Today,* October 1987, 350-59). Ollenburger uses the word "apocalypse" here in a way that suggests its theological significance for Beker.

17. What follows is culled from Martyn's essays, from his commentary on Galatians, and from my lecture notes throughout the 1970s and '80s.

18. This was foreseen by Deutero-Isaiah. In Isa. 40–55, the announcement that God is doing a new thing pervades the prophecy. Throughout those chapters, the only acting subject is God, and he is acting without reference to human deserving, human preparation, or human response.

19. This is a more radical definition of apocalyptic than the one given in our chapter 5 ("The Passover and the Exodus") by C. K. Barrett, and it differs from a salvation-history per-

do. Repentance, so central in the traditional view, can no longer solve the problem. Nothing short of the crucifixion of the old *kosmos* (Gal. 6:14) will suffice.[20]

Third, God is acting upon the *kosmos* from outside it. The experience of the exile and of subsequent bitter disappointments and humiliations signaled an emergency in the theological perspective of Israel. As the Old Testament comes to a close, apocalyptic modes of thought reflect the new way of seeing: the human situation is so tragic that there is no answer from within history. The Christ event is therefore the invasion of this world by Another, who is retaking for himself the world he created.

Fourth, there are hostile forces on the scene. Words just used in the preceding paragraph, "invasion" and "retaking," are drawn from the battlefield. As Martyn puts it, there are not two actors in the drama, God and humanity, but three — God, humanity, and the Powers. When Christ was "apocalypsed" to the world, he did not arrive in neutral territory. The occupying forces — pictured as Satan and his hosts — had to be driven from the field; this will be the subject of the next chapter.

Fifth, apocalyptic theology has a universal dimension. In a sweeping vision distinctive to Paul (approached only by Deutero-Isaiah),[21] the apostle sees the whole *kosmos* — the entire created order — "groaning" as it awaits its redemption (Rom. 8:22).

Finally, the apocalyptic perspective is "bifocal." Apocalyptic theology is neither this-worldly nor otherworldly, but "both-worldly." It is not exclusively "now" or "not-yet." It holds in view two things at once: the "present

---

spective, which has a less thoroughgoing view both of the cosmic predicament and the extreme nature of God's decisive invasion of the old *kosmos* in the mission of Christ. N. T. Wright is a particularly notable example of a contemporary New Testament scholar whose perspective is more that of salvation history, leading him to be antagonistic toward apocalyptic theology (some would say unnecessarily so). I go a long way with Wright in his interpretation of the New Testament. He is very exciting in his emphasis on the political dimensions of the gospel and the indissolubility of the Old Testament covenant with Israel, among many other interpretive issues that he clarifies. The difficulty, from the perspective of the views expressed here, lies with his penchant for projecting irreconcilable disagreements onto other scholars instead of seeking constructive dialogue. It is particularly disappointing that he continues to emphasize forgiveness without entertaining the larger concept of rectification.

20. This discontinuity is a chief difference between Paul's perspective and that of Luke-Acts.

21. This theme is strongly present also in the books of Zephaniah, Haggai, and Daniel as well as Zech. 9–14 in the Old Testament, and in parts of the book of Revelation in the New Testament. The principal sources, however, are Deutero-Isaiah and the letters of Paul, where the universal, cosmic dimensions are most obvious.

evil age" of violence and cruelty, greed and avarice, disease and death; and the age to come, known to us in the mode of promise and guaranteed by the Holy Spirit.[22] Thus we interpret self-giving actions not so much as examples of individual human moral choices, but as signposts toward God's coming new world, known to us by revelation *(apokalypsis)* and promise.

When this perspective is put to work for biblical theology and ethics, it takes on immediate relevance. Lesslie Newbigin (1909-1998) has proven to be one of the most important postmodern Christian thinkers. He spent most of his life in India and is known largely for his contributions to missiology. He was not trained as an academic scholar and is not ordinarily listed among the apocalyptic theologians. Remarkably, however, without ever crossing orbits with Käsemann (they were contemporaries), he grasped the apocalyptic perspective through his study of the New Testament: "The cross is the place where the decisive battle between Christ and sin took place, where the powers of Satan brought all their strength to the attack, and where they were defeated. It is the place where the wages of sin were accepted on behalf of the whole human race."[23]

Newbigin is able to take Pauline imagery that is often called into the service of a forensic view of the atonement ("the wages of sin is death") and lift it into the cosmic realm of apocalyptic.

Systematic theologian Philip Ziegler also uses the imagery of apocalyptic invasion even as he summons the believer into the new life in Christ: "In Paul's gospel 'revelation' *(apokalypsis)* denotes God's redemptive invasion of the fallen order of things such that reality itself is decisively re-made in the event. God's advent in Christ utterly disrupts and displaces previous patterns of thought and action and gives rise to new ones that better comport with the reality of a world actively reconciled to God. This is particularly true of theology and ethics in their interconnection."[24]

To sum up: God is acting *in the present.* By the power of the Holy Spirit working through "the lowliest of men" (Dan. 4:17), God is continually pushing into the occupied territories with dynamic force: "The weapons of our warfare are not worldly but have divine power to destroy strongholds" (II Cor. 10:4). Resistance against the Powers, therefore, is a Christian imperative.

---

22. Martyn calls this "bifocal" vision. For reasons to be explained, I prefer "transvision."

23. This quotation is from *Sin and Salvation* (London: SCM, 1956), 58. In *The Gospel in a Pluralist Society,* he gives a fuller account of New Testament apocalyptic that is truly astonishing. Newbigin picked up some clues from Walter Wink's studies of the Powers, but goes beyond them, guided by his deep Presbyterian convictions about the agency of God.

24. Philip Zeigler, "Dietrich Bonhoeffer: An Ethics of God's Apocalypse?" *Modern Theology* 23, no. 4 (October 2007).

Eschatology versus Apocalyptic and the Issue of Discontinuity

Although they are close kin, the words "eschatology" and "apocalyptic" are not synonymous.[25] All apocalyptic is eschatological, but not all eschatology is apocalyptic. "Eschatology" is derived from the Greek word *eschaton*, meaning "last." Eschatology is often defined for seminary students as the study of the "last things," such as the Last Judgment, the second coming, and the final resurrection of the dead. But this is not a useful definition, because it reduces eschatology to a few items stuck on to the end of the theological syllabus. New Testament eschatology, properly speaking, is not a group of topics but an encompassing thought-world — therefore pointing beyond to apocalyptic.[26] We quoted C. K. Barrett's 1953 essay on New Testament eschatology in chapter 5. His exposition remains useful. We can summarize some of it as follows:

1. Eschatology is *a way of thinking,* rather than a list of subjects to be studied under the heading of "last things."
2. Biblical eschatology points to the hidden, "not-yet" quality of God's activity that throughout the Bible calls the believer into future-oriented faith.
3. *Apocalyptic* eschatology differs from existential eschatology in this way: the last term in the series is different from and *discontinuous with* what precedes it.

25. J. Christiaan Beker made a conscientious effort to distinguish between apocalyptic and eschatology in his preface to the paperback edition of *Paul the Apostle,* explaining in his own distinct, provocative idiom why the difference is so crucial: "Questions about my use of the term 'apocalyptic' could have been muted if I had frankly emphasized the polemical thrust of my usage. I thought that 'apocalyptic' did not allow the degree of multivalence . . . that in recent theology adheres to 'eschatology' — a concept that denotes everything from existential finality and transcendent reality to 'life after death.' I used 'apocalyptic' not only because it is true to Paul's theology but also because its future-temporal, cosmic-universal and dualistic components constitute a challenge for the Church and its theology in our time. In other words, I intended to highlight the offensive character of the term, especially because both biblical and theological scholarship perpetuate the anti-apocalyptic ethos of the theological tradition" (xiv).

26. Readers may still be confused about the meaning of "apocalyptic" in New Testament interpretation. It is helpful to recall that apocalyptic presupposes, not two "ways" (as in the Hellenistic religious environment) but two *ages:* the age of Sin and Death, and the reign of Christ the Lord. The concept of two ways emphasizes human choice. Apocalyptic theology emphasizes the choices of God: "Therefore, if any one is in Christ — new creation! the old has passed away, behold, the new has come. *All this is from God*" (II Cor. 5:17-18, trans. Richard Hays, emphasis added).

Barrett's phrase "last term" refers to the final proposition or happening in a series. In the apostolic preaching of the gospel, this is the cross-resurrection event — the turn of the aeons. Barrett continues:

> The last term . . . is not merely the end of the old but the beginning of a new series which belongs to *a different order of existence.* It marks God's breaking into the historical sequence in fresh, unrepeatable, supernatural terms. We see . . . an event which stands on the boundary between this world and another world, and *therefore cannot be deduced from a study of what precedes it.* . . . The basic principle upon which [the apocalyptic writers'] thought rests is that of the Two Ages, the present Age in which the Powers of wickedness are in revolt against God . . . and the Age to Come, in which God will assert his authority, judge and punish the wicked and reign over his saints in bliss.[27]

In these helpful words from Barrett, we see that *discontinuity* between the old age and the age to come is a principal characteristic of apocalyptic. This discontinuity is prefigured in Isaiah 40–55 and other late portions of the Old Testament.[28] At stake is the radicality of the gospel, a theme with ultimate consequences. In Jesus Christ, and particularly in his cross and resurrection, do we see something entirely new? In the early confession of the church, *Jesus is Lord,* does the *Christus Victor* theme appear not simply as an affirmation of Christ's superiority, but as a signal that the ages have turned? Does the new dispensation in Jesus of Nazareth follow in a direct line from the Sinai covenant, or is there some sort of break between the two? Is something completely new introduced with the gospel of Christ? This hotly debated question has significant ramifications for New Testament theology. Certainly there is fundamental continuity with the Old Testament in the form of the unconditional covenant made with the patriarch Abraham (Rom. 4:1-24; also, Acts 3:25; Gal. 3:14; Heb. 6:13-15), but there is discontinuity as well (in Luke 3:8 and John 8:56, the references to Abraham are more subversive). This contradiction will be addressed as we proceed.[29]

---

27. C. K. Barrett, "New Testament Eschatology," *Scottish Journal of Theology* 6, nos. 2-3 (1953): 135-55 and 225-43, emphasis added. Exactly who are "the wicked" and who are the saints will be considered in the concluding chapter.

28. See, for instance, Hag. 2:10-23, Zech. 9–14, and the whole of Zephaniah.

29. The name of Ernst Käsemann is associated with discontinuity, and that of N. T. Wright — for example — with continuity. The issue centers on the radical justification of the ungodly and the persistent (and persisting) religious idea of *possibility.* Simon Gathercole has helpfully

Paul, in particular, seems to emphasize discontinuity. In Romans 10:5-6, he contrasts "righteousness which is based on the law" with "righteousness based on faith." In II Corinthians 3:9, he draws a sharp distinction between the "dispensation of condemnation" and the "dispensation of righteousness." Yet at the same time, Paul quotes from the Hebrew Scriptures almost constantly, and the main character in his principal argument for the righteousness by faith is none other than Abraham. Abraham was chosen unconditionally, Paul emphasizes, *before* he was circumcised (Rom. 4:10-12) — the point being that the concept of election in Jesus Christ is traced from the opening chapter of God's dealings with his chosen people (Gen. 12:1) and exemplified by the choice of Jacob over Esau, "though they were not yet born and had done nothing either good or bad, in order that God's purpose of election might continue, not because of works but because of his call" (Rom. 9:11). Thus Paul's radical reworking of Old Testament passages raises the question of continuity and discontinuity acutely; this will be examined at various points throughout the coming pages.

Gustav Aulén's *Christus Victor*

Every theological student knows Gustav Aulén's book *Christus Victor,* which appeared in 1931 and has remained on reading lists ever since. Aulén, a Swedish Lutheran bishop and theologian, designed the book to be historical and descriptive, though it is polemical as well, since he clearly favors what he identifies as the *Christus Victor* motif. The Latin title of his book has entered the theological vocabulary everywhere; and the importance of the book's central argument is now generally accepted, though, like any other groundbreaking work, the book should be read in light of subsequent developments. Eighty-plus years later and all things considered, Aulén's treatment of the *Christus Victor* theme stands up remarkably well.

---

explained this in layman's terms, in an article about the "new perspective on Paul." He writes that the "new perspective" scholars (E. P. Sanders, J. D. G. Dunn, N. T. Wright, among others) are right to warn us against caricaturing the Second Temple Judaism of Jesus' time as though it were the medieval Roman Catholic Church of Luther's time. However, there is much testimony from the time of Paul to indicate that "many of Paul's contemporaries seem to have believed that obedience was possible without a radical inbreaking of God." For Paul, "salvation was impossible without the earth-shattering events of the Cross, Resurrection, and Pentecost." Obedience to the covenant was not possible without "mighty acts of God." The "flesh" is not only powerless to obey, it actually wars with God (Rom. 8:7). Gathercole, "What Did Paul Really Mean?" *Christianity Today,* August 2007.

Bishop Aulén's now-familiar thesis is that there are three principal accounts of the atonement wrought on the cross and in the resurrection:

1. The Latin, forensic, "objective" view, first spelled out by Anselm and carried forward by medieval scholasticism through the Reformation to Protestant orthodoxy
2. The "subjective," humanistic view associated with Abelard
3. The "classic," "dramatic," or *Christus Victor* view of the New Testament, held by the Church Fathers, revived by Martin Luther

These divisions and identifications have been much disputed, and Aulén's evaluation of Anselm, in particular, has met with considerable criticism.[30] Much of what he writes about the first and second views can be passed over. For our purposes, Aulén's great importance lies in the way he trains the spotlight on the *Christus Victor* theme. His definition of that theme is closely allied to the apocalyptic perspective we have been describing: "The work of Christ is first and foremost a victory over the Powers which hold mankind in bondage: sin, death, and the devil. . . . The victory of Christ creates a new situation, bringing their rule to an end, and setting men free from their dominion."[31]

Aulén argues that this perspective was in eclipse during the Middle Ages, and that after a brief resurgence in the Reformation, it was suppressed once again.[32] The key insight in this regard — and here, Aulén's contribution has been massive — was that Martin Luther, at the very center of his theology, had mounted a robust reaffirmation of the biblical and patristic *Christus Victor* account, based on Luther's reading of the New Testament. Aulén quotes at length from Luther's shorter commentary on Galatians:

> Christ, who is God's power, righteousness, blessing, grace and life, overcomes and carries away these monsters, sin, death and the curse. When therefore thou lookest upon this [redeemed] person thou seest sin, death, God's wrath, hell, the devil and all evil overcome and dead. . . .

---

30. Jaroslav Pelikan summarizes some of the critiques and offers one of his own in a helpful and eloquent foreword to the 1969 edition of *Christus Victor* (New York: Macmillan). In a more recent article, David B. Hart has argued that Anselm's view of God's action on our behalf is actually quite close to the patristic narrative that Aulén accuses him of abandoning. This point is stressed in our bridge chapter on Anselm.

31. Gustav Aulén, *Christus Victor: An Historical Study of the Three Main Types of the Idea of the Atonement,* foreword by Jaroslav Pelikan (New York: Macmillan, 1969; orig. 1931), 106.

32. John Howard Yoder's view that the apocalyptic perspective was lost after Constantine seems right (*The Politics of Jesus* [Grand Rapids: Eerdmans, 1972], 137 and passim).

... this is not the work of any created being, but of almighty God. Therefore He [Christ] who of Himself overcame these must actually in His nature be God. For against these so mighty Powers, sin, death, and the curse, which of themselves have dominion in the world and in all creation, another and a higher power must appear, which can be none other than God.[33]

Aulén's account of Luther's reading of the New Testament features a good many of the characteristics of apocalyptic theology:[34]

- God as the acting subject
- the cosmic and universal nature of the apocalyptic drama
- the presence of hostile Powers that must be defeated
- the conclusive defeat of the Enemy by God's messianic agent
- the arrival of something altogether new

Aulén did not make as much of the now/not-yet element in the drama as he might have, and the urgent looking-ahead to the parousia (second coming) is largely missing, but he was really on to something, even if his grasp of apocalyptic may have been incomplete. Take, for example, this passage:

We have seen how essential to Paul's thought is the triumph of Christ over the hostile Powers. It is not that they are as yet wholly annihilated; he looks to "the end," when all power shall be taken from "His enemies" (I Corinthians 15:24 *ff.*) at the advent of the new age. Yet the decisive victory has been won already; Christ has assumed His power and reigns till at last all His enemies are subjected to Him. His victory avails for all mankind; He is the Head of the new spiritual humanity.[35]

Most of the elements are present in that brief summary.

Aulén's concern was not to displace the other motifs of Scripture. He

---

33. Aulén, *Christus Victor,* 106-7. To my way of thinking, the quotations from Luther are the best part of Aulén's book.

34. Philip Ziegler, two generations removed from Aulén, writes appreciatively that Aulén, much like Käsemann, "recommends the apocalyptic discourse of *Christus victor* in part because of its power to demythologize our all-too-human sense that sees us, wrongly and desperately, as the only agents on the field of history" ("Christ Must Reign: Ernst Käsemann and Soteriology in an Apocalyptic Key," in *Apocalyptic and the Future of Theology,* ed. Joshua B. Davis and Douglas Harink [Eugene, Ore.: Cascade Books, 2012], 216).

35. Aulén, *Christus Victor,* 70-71.

says this concretely in an article written some twenty years after he published the book.[36] The *Christus Victor* motif is not a complete doctrine in itself over against others, he explains, but is above all "a drama, where the love of God in Christ fights and conquers the hostile Powers." This underscores the nature of the apocalyptic gospel as a *drama* encompassing all the other themes in various ways. F. W. Dillistone, with his literary flair, has a particular affinity for the *Christus Victor* drama and has written a superb chapter on it in his book *The Christian Understanding of Atonement*. As we turn to an exposition of Romans 5–6, these words from Dillistone are worth quoting:

> Nowhere else in the New Testament is the theme of deliverance through the saving work of Christ celebrated so lyrically and so comprehensively as in the Pauline writings. Deliverance from the past, the present and the future, deliverance from the sinister control of evil cosmic influences, deliverance from the burden of a law from whose injunctions there seemed no way of escape, deliverance from the unbreakable chain of evil habit, deliverance from the awful power of the final enemy, Death — all this, Paul believed, had been achieved by the death and resurrection of the Redeemer.[37]

The Lord *(Kurios)* as *Christus Victor* in Romans 5 and 6

In the context of the *Christus Victor* drama, the fifth and sixth chapters of Romans call for special emphasis. Romans 6 builds upon the foundation laid by Paul in previous chapters. It is vital to recognize that he begins his letter with the good news, not the bad. His opening statement (1:16) is a resounding proclamation of the gospel *(euanggelion)* of the righteousness *(dikaiosyne)* of God that has been "revealed ['*apocalypsed*'] from faith to faith" (1:16). Then follows a long section in which Paul shows how the human race was "given over" by God into the power of tyrants — Sin, Death, and the Law.[38] The phrases "under sin" (3:9) and "under the law" (3:19) are early clues to this conception, which will become ever more important as the letter develops. The piling up of judgment against both Jews and Gentiles in the

36. Aulén, "Chaos and Cosmos: The Drama of the Atonement," *Interpretation* 4, no. 2 (April 1950): 156-67.

37. F. W. Dillistone, *The Christian Understanding of Atonement* (Philadelphia: Westminster, 1968), 88. Note how effortlessly Dillistone incorporates the ransom/redeemer theme.

38. The relation of Sin and the Law is the subject of Paul Meyer's influential essay, "The Worm at the Core of the Apple," which we will examine further in the concluding chapter.

first three chapters has an overpowering effect when read straight through. Jews and Gentiles alike have been imprisoned under the Law, each in their own way (2:14-16; 3:19; see also Acts 13:39). Paul is preparing his hearers for the astounding impact of the announcement that the righteousness of God has been made known *apart from the law* (Rom. 3:21). There is simply no way to overstate the radicality of this proclamation; it is one aspect of the discontinuity discussed above. To say, as Paul proceeds to do, that there is *no distinction* (3:22) between godly and ungodly, religious and irreligious, "good" people and "bad," is to snatch away the very foundations of religious certainty. In place of human religious certainty Paul brings something incomparably better — the message of God's righteousness "reckoned" *(logizomai)* to us by grace through faith, not by human works (4:3-8).[39]

Moving into Romans 5, we see the entire human race personified as "Adam" by Paul in 5:14-19. Thornton Wilder, in his novel *The Bridge of San Luis Rey,* writes of his major character the Marquesa, "She saw that the people of this world moved about in an armor of egotism, drunk with self-gazing . . . in dread of all appeals that might interrupt their long communion with their own desires. These were the sons of Adam from Cathay to Peru."[40] This beautifully encapsulates the notion of "Adam" as the progenitor of the human race in bondage to its "own desires." Paul takes this further, however, knowing that "appeals" to sinful human nature are ultimately of no avail, since the Powers are too much for us without the intervention of God. The last portion of chapter 5 identifies all three of the Powers and shows how grace trumps them: "*Law* came in, to increase the trespass; but where *sin* increased, grace abounded all the more, so that, as sin reigned in *death,* grace also might reign through righteousness to eternal life through Jesus Christ our Lord" (5:20-21).

These verses set out the apocalyptic framework, with its two realms: the reign of Sin and Death (with Sin's captive weapon, the Law) and the reign of

---

39. Equally astonishing is Paul's declaration that the manifestation of the righteousness of God *without the Law* (Rom. 3:21) has been witnessed, or affirmed, *by the Law* (and the Prophets). Obviously the Law has a dual role in Paul — it tyrannizes, oppresses, and imprisons us, yet it is a partner in the revelation of God's truth, "holy and just and good" (Rom. 7:12). The Law in Paul is a subject requiring subtle discernment. J. Louis Martyn explains that for Paul the Law has a history: it was taken captive and forced by Sin into an unholy alliance (Rom. 7:9-11), but in the new dispensation it is no longer captive to Sin but under the benevolent rule of the Spirit of Christ (Rom. 8:2). Martyn, "*Nomos* Plus Genitive Noun in Paul," in *Early Christianity and Classical Culture: Comparative Studies in Honor of Abraham Malherbe,* ed. John T. Fitzgerald, Thomas H. Olbricht, and L. Michael White (Boston: Brill, 2003). The role of the Law will be more fully discussed in the main text in chapter 11.

40. Thornton Wilder, *The Bridge of San Luis Rey* (New York: HarperCollins, 1986), 17.

righteousness and life by grace through Christ. Paul clearly envisions hostile, active Powers that must be dethroned to make room for the new Adam and the sphere of power that is ruled by the Spirit of righteousness and life.

Paul develops some striking parallelisms in 5:16-21, as he sets the victorious new age over against the old age:

Judgment → one sin → condemnation
Gift → many sins → justification (v. 16)

Adam's trespass → death reigned
Christ's grace and righteousness → reign in life (v. 17)

One trespass → condemnation for all
One act of righteousness → justification and life for all (v. 18)

Disobedience of one [Adam] → many were made sinners
Obedience of one [Christ] → will make many righteous (v. 19)

Sin → dominion → Death
Grace → dominion → righteousness *(dikaiosyne)* → eternal life (v. 21)

These remarkable parallel phrases are grounded in the conception of two competing spheres of power. Both of these Powers exercise dominion *(basileia, basileuo),* a word meaning mastery, rule, control, sovereignty (usually translated "reign"). The dominion or reign of Sin leads to Death; the dominion of God's grace in Christ leads to righteousness and life. Here is a literal translation of verse 21:

As reigned [root word is *basileus*] sin by death [*thanatos*],
So also grace might reign [*basileus*] through righteousness [*dikaiosyne*]
    to life eternal by Jesus Christ the Lord [*Kurios*] of us.

By presenting these verses in this way, we show how Paul's oppositional sentences offer us a clear image of the two opposing dominions. These oppositions are often not obvious in English. Now let us look at a more conventional English translation of 5:20-21: "where sin increased, grace increased all the more, so that, just as sin reigned in death, so also grace might reign through righteousness *(dikaiosyne)* to bring eternal life through Jesus Christ our Lord *(Kurios)*" (NIV).

When we take into account the way Paul uses the word *dikaiosyne* throughout the letter, beginning with 1:16-17 where he links *dikaiosyne* with power *(dunamis),* we arrive at the conclusion that the passage just quoted doesn't really make sense unless you understand *dikaiosyne* as a *verb,* that is, as an active agent. Paul is contrasting two Powers here. One Power is stronger than the other, hence his customary use of the words "all the more" (alternatively, "how much more"). The message here is that Death is a great Power, but *dikaiosyne* (the righteousness of God) is an even greater Power — "all the more" so — and it is actively at work, in tandem with God's grace, to overturn the rule of Sin and Death, recapturing the creation and inaugurating a new rule of righteousness and eternal life. This is what has happened in the cross and resurrection.

This brings us to the word *kurios* in the last verse of chapter 5.[41] Paul habitually uses this word to describe and identify Jesus. It is overly familiar to us, and we scarcely notice it. We rattle off the words "through Jesus Christ our Lord" at the end of prayers without thinking about it; it seems like nothing more than saying "Jesus Christ" in a fancier way. For Paul, however, the word *kurios* carries prodigious weight. Paul demonstrates this in a striking way by his use of the word in chapter 6. The word translated "dominion" (RSV, KJV, NRSV) or "mastery" (NIV) is from the root *kurios,* meaning "lord." This presents another challenge for English translation. The link between the noun and the verbal construction does not appear in English unless we translate the verbal form as "lord it over." If we do that, Paul's train of thought leaps out at us. This is the way it works:

- In Romans 6:9, Paul says, "Death no longer lords it [*kurieuo*] over him [Christ]."
- Then he says, "Sin shall not lord it [*kurieuo*] over you" (6:14).
- Finally he concludes, "The wages of Sin is Death, but the free gift of God is eternal life in Christ Jesus our *Kurios*" (6:23).

With this threefold use of the root *kurios,* Paul displays before us his entire worldview — two dominions, or domains, each with its lord.[42] As we

41. Christians from liturgical traditions and lovers of classical music will recognize the Greek word *kurios* (in a slightly different transliteration) in the Kyrie Eleison ("Lord, have mercy") of the Mass.

42. It is easy to understand why many readers of Paul's letters have missed this. He talks about the two realms, or domains, in different terms in different places. In Gal. 1:4, where Paul speaks of Christ delivering us from "the present evil age," he is referring to the realm of Sin and Death. Indeed, in Galatians (as well as Rom. 8) Paul uses the terms "flesh" *(sarx)* and "Spirit" *(pneuma)* to identify the two realms.

saw in the oppositional phrases of Romans 5:17 above, he speaks of reigning Powers. Through Adam's trespass, Death reigned over the fallen creation; now, Paul exults, how "much more" does Christ reign through righteousness. If there were to be any doubt about this, Romans 14:9 would be the clincher: "To this end Christ died and lived again, that he might be *Kurios* both of the dead and of the living."[43]

Here, then, in the Epistle to the Romans we see Aulén's "dramatic" idea of the work of Christ spelled out in the way Paul deploys the word "Lord."[44]

Freedom from Slavery

Each of the domains envisioned by Paul has its slaves:

> Do you not know that if you yield yourselves to any one as obedient slaves, you are slaves of the one whom you obey, either of sin, which leads to death, or of obedience, which leads to righteousness? But thanks be to God, that you who were once slaves of sin have become obedient from

---

43. N. T. Wright is very good on the subject of the Lordship of the *Kurios* over the empires of this world, with its consequences for geopolitics and social action. Some readers may wonder why I have not made more use of his work on *dikaiosis*, since there is so much to support, admire, and celebrate in his position. In particular, he argues forcefully against the individualized, spiritualized, depoliticized presentation of Christ's work on the cross that carried the day in Protestant circles for hundreds of years, and often still does. Throughout these pages we have sought to correct this misdirected view of atonement and reconciliation. However, Wright de-radicalizes Paul by excluding the narrative of the captivity of *the entire created order* under the rule of Sin and Death. In his wish to recontexualize Jesus in the milieu of Second Temple Judaism (a subject opened up by E. P. Sanders), Wright underestimates the wholesale degree to which Paul proclaims the crucifixion of *all* existing worlds, including religious worlds (Gal. 6:14-15). I do not wish to devalue Wright's work and influence, much of which has been very helpful to the church. However, he does not work in the dimension of imagination that has enabled the apocalyptic theologians (whose work he greatly dislikes) to give us a vastly expanded understanding of the cosmic vision of Paul. Indeed, the vehemence with which Wright rejects apocalyptic weakens his position. For more on this subject, see Stephen Westerholm, *Justification Reconsidered* (Grand Rapids: Eerdmans, 2013), and the *Journal for the Study of Paul and His Letters* 4, no. 1 (Spring 2014), with contributions by Beverly Gaventa, Martinus C. de Boer, Michael Gorman, and others, together with a response by Wright.

44. C. Kavin Rowe has shown how Luke also strongly favors *Kurios* as a title for Christ. He argues against the prevailing portrait of Luke, urging a more revolutionary stance vis-à-vis the Roman Empire than is usually claimed for Luke-Acts (*World Upside Down: Reading Acts in the Graeco-Roman Age* [New York: Oxford University Press, 2010], 103-16 and passim).

the heart to the standard of teaching to which you were committed, and, having been set free from sin, have become slaves of righteousness *(dikaio-syne)*. (Rom. 6:16-18)

No one is capable of being captain of his own soul, master of her own fate.[45] Each of us is worked upon by unconscious impulses of which we are not even aware and over which we have little control.[46] Paul, unlike the typical American, does not think in terms of autonomous human beings. Paul proudly identifies himself as a "slave of Christ" (Gal. 1:10). If the apocalyptic scenario is a picture of true reality, then *no one* is "free" in the domain of this world as it is. Either we must live our lives in the clutches of soul-destroying Powers or we are delivered into "the obedience of faith" (Rom. 1:5; 16:26). Paradoxically, the new life in Christ can be called *both* slavery (the service of God) *and* freedom.[47] This seeming contradiction of slavery and true freedom, which lies at the heart of the gospel, is beautifully invoked in the Episcopal Book of Common Prayer in words addressed to Christ, "whose service is perfect freedom."[48] Finally, we note Romans 6:20. A literal translation would be, "When you were slaves to sin, you were free to righteousness." Syntactically, this seems to make no sense. However, if we remember the two domains, we understand that what Paul means is that we were "free *from the control of righteousness*" (NIV), or "free *in regard to righteousness*" (NRSV). What Paul means by this is that, since we were slaves to Sin, righteousness had no place in us, no dependable foothold.[49]

45. It is ironic that Timothy McVeigh, the Oklahoma City bomber, wanted the poem "Invictus" to be his last will and testimony. Can we agree that here was a man clearly *not* the "master of my soul" but a slave to Sin and Death? (Yet even he, as we will suggest later, is not beyond the reach of the righteousness of God.)

46. Whatever one may think of Sigmund Freud, whose star has dimmed considerably of late, his identification of the power of the unconscious will forever be one of the most important advances in human understanding. The great writers knew it by intuition long before, but Freud brought it to the surface. (Psychoanalyst Dorothy Martyn, reading *Middlemarch,* exclaimed, "How did she [George Eliot] do it without Freud to help her?" Marcel Proust is the most striking example; he and Freud were contemporaries but took no account of each other.)

47. "The freedom we have in Christ Jesus" is arguably the central theme of the letter to the church in Galatia (2:4), yet Paul proudly identifies himself as a slave *(doulos)* of Christ (1:10). The paradox is heightened in I Cor. 7:22 — "For he who was called in the Lord as a slave is a freedman of the Lord. Likewise he who was free when called is a slave of Christ."

48. Collect for Peace, Morning Prayer, Book of Common Prayer, 57 and 99. This is a paraphrase of Augustine, who wrote that to serve God was to reign as a king. Augustine, sermon on Ps. 43:1.

49. That is what was originally meant by the Calvinist doctrine of total depravity. It has proven to be an unfortunate choice of words in English, but the basic idea is Pauline. The

The clear implication here is that there is no way for the human being to move from the domain of Sin to the domain of God's righteousness unless there is an invasion of the kingdom of Sin from outside. The domain of Sin leads to Death; its goal and purpose *(telos)* is Death. There is no way out of this downward-moving spiral of dissolution. But here is the good news: "You have been set free from [the domain of] Sin and have become slaves to God; your fruit is holiness and the *telos* is eternal life" (cf. Rom. 6:22).[50]

Being a "slave of righteousness" and a "slave of obedience" will sound intolerable to most modern ears. It takes hard mental work to enter Paul's thought-world and understand that these phrases do not describe a bondage to a harsh puritanical code imposed upon us by a tyrannical outside force. He means the opposite. The gospel of Christ means precisely *deliverance from* tyrannical outside forces into a realm of light and life where "the obedience of faith" is the only natural and joyful way to be. When Paul says in Romans 6:16 that obedience leads to righteousness, he does not mean this in the usual way, as though righteousness were the reward for a long, arduous struggle on our part to be obedient. Rather, he means that *the righteousness of God is the active, re-creating power that enables the new life of obedience to take shape.* This is what the new life in Christ means.

This is such an important idea that we must seek for varying ways to express it. Many people have found the story of Jean Valjean in Victor Hugo's *Les Misérables* to be a potent illustration. The basic idea is that a man embarked upon a slippery slope toward a life of criminality is delivered into new life because of a bishop's Christlike act of unconditional restitution.[51] It is not enough to speak of the bishop's unconditional *forgiveness* of Jean Valjean. The bishop's act of *logizomai* — reckoning righteous the man who has just stolen his silver — surprises the policemen who bring him to the door with the goods, but the effect upon Valjean is transformative. Not only is Valjean delivered from bondage; he is actively remade. He is no longer a slave of Sin; he becomes a "slave of righteousness"; using New Testament imagery, he is "clothed in righteousness," he has "put on Christ." This is the way that the righteousness of God *(dikaiosyne theou)* works; it is not a quality to be imitated, but an *active, invading power.* The illustration from *Les*

Episcopal General Confession used to contain the phrase, "There is no health in us," which expresses the same idea — our situation without divine rescue is hopeless. We have no power of ourselves to help ourselves.

50. See also II Tim. 1:10; Heb. 2:15; Rom. 8:38-39; I Cor. 15:55-57 for the same proclamation.

51. I am speaking of the novel, not the musical. Few today read the entire novel, which is a pity. Its cumulative impact is far greater than any dramatized version because it unfolds with far more complexity.

Misérables is helpful, up to a point, because it depicts the bishop up against active Powers that must be driven out of the man in front of him. Equally important, the bishop is engaging in a little trick on the police, who, because they represent conventional justice, cannot understand the act of subversion that they are witnessing.[52] When forgiveness is understood this way, it finds its place in the apocalyptic drama.

The theme of deliverance from one sphere of power into another — illustrated memorably in the story of Jean Valjean — dominates this section of Romans and is continued into chapters 7 and 8 and beyond. Paul's cry, "Wretched man that I am! Who will deliver me from this body of death?" has been emblematic for Christians over the centuries who recognize their own predicament and rejoice to hear the answer: "Thanks be to God through Jesus Christ our *Kurios!*" (7:24-25). The famous ending of chapter 8 ("Neither death, nor life . . . nor powers, nor height, nor depth, nor anything else in all creation, will be able to separate us from the love of God in Christ Jesus our *Lord*") is not an all-purpose, generic piece of religious uplift. Paul can promise this only because he has a genuinely revelatory piece of news to declare. A new world has come into being through Christ the *Kurios.*

Concluding his letter to the Romans, Paul asserts with the confidence that only the gospel can give, "The God of peace will soon crush Satan under your feet" (16:20). The cross is the foundation of a new world in which evil, sin, and death shall have no dominion. Paul brings this home to the believer in Romans 6 when he speaks of baptism: "Do you not know that all of us who have been baptized into Christ Jesus were baptized into his death? We were buried therefore with him by baptism into death, so that as Christ was raised from the dead by the glory of the Father, we too might walk in newness of life" (Rom. 6:3-4). For those who have been baptized, there is an *apocalyptic transfer of aeons.*[53] The deliverance into the dominion of the victorious Christ is accomplished by God and by God alone. This proclamation is not one theme among many themes. For Paul, it is the ground of them all.

---

52. During the Vietnam War, a widely circulated photograph depicted Father Daniel Berrigan, the war resister, being led off in handcuffs by two police officers twice his size. Many people noticed the contrast between the two burly policemen, who are wearing grim expressions, and the face of Berrigan, which is lit from within by a mysterious joy. A caption read, "Which is the free man?"

53. If there were further evidence needed, the baptismal affirmation in Colossians (probably extra-Pauline) makes it plain: the Father "has delivered us from the dominion of darkness and transferred us to the kingdom of his beloved Son, in whom we have redemption, the forgiveness of sins" (Col. 1:13-14).

We turn now from the Epistles to a completely different biblical picture to show how God's apocalyptic war is depicted in a scene from the Synoptic Gospels — Matthew, Mark, and Luke.

The Gethsemane Scene as Archetypal Conflict

The atmosphere of apocalyptic struggle pervades many passages of the Synoptics, though this is not often perceived by readers. We will look at a particular example, the scene in the Garden of Gethsemane on the night Jesus was betrayed and arrested. After the last supper with his disciples, Jesus goes directly from the dinner table out to the Mount of Olives. The disciples follow him to "a place called Gethsemane" where Jesus asked them to watch with him while he withdrew to pray.

In his massive study *The Death of the Messiah*, Raymond E. Brown analyzes the passage and surveys the history of its interpretation ("the incredible diversity of scholarly opinions") in exhaustive detail.[54] He introduces the subject in an eloquent paragraph:

> The scene of Jesus' prayer in Gethsemane has had a special place in Christian piety. . . . [The] combination of human suffering, divine strengthening, and solitary self-giving has done much to make Jesus loved by those who believe in him. Most Christians, then, are surprised to discover that outsiders have found the scene scandalous and ridiculous. Believers are annoyed to be told that scholars have judged parts of it illogical and the whole awkwardly put together.[55]

Because of such concerns about the place of Gethsemane in the hearts of believers over the centuries, Brown faces down skeptical historical critics to argue that there was a living tradition from earliest times that "before he died Jesus struggled in prayer about his fate," and that this memory was already vitally alive in the Christian community long before the Evangelists set about

---

54. Raymond E. Brown, *The Death of the Messiah: From Gethsemane to the Grave; A Commentary on the Passion Narratives in the Four Gospels*, 2 vols. (Garden City, N.Y.: Doubleday, 1994), 1:305. Joel Marcus's treatment of Gethsemane in his commentary on Mark is particularly valuable for its theological depth (*Mark 8–16: A New Translation with Introduction and Commentary*, Anchor Yale Bible 27A [New Haven: Yale University Press, 2009], 974-1000).

55. Brown, *Death of the Messiah*, 1:216-17. This sensitivity to ordinary, nonacademic Christians became a hallmark of Raymond Brown's later work.

their work.[56] He writes, in his own italics for emphasis: *"In the last days of his life in Jerusalem as the leaders of his people showed unremitting hostility, [the tradition that] Jesus would have struggled in prayer with God about how his death fitted into the inbreaking of God's kingdom is, in my judgment, so extremely plausible as to warrant certainty."* This scene, he concludes, logically follows from "Jesus' view that the inbreaking of God's kingdom involved a massive struggle with diabolical opposition."[57]

The *fact* of the struggle, then, can be taken for granted. But what does it signify? Brown's reference to "a massive struggle with diabolical opposition" places us on the apocalyptic battlefield and points the way toward an interpretation. After reviewing all the various scholarly options, Brown focuses especially on the word *peirasmos* ("trial," or "test"). The word appears in the Gethsemane story at Matthew 26:41, Mark 14:38, and Luke 22:40.[58] Brown builds upon these usages and shows how other appearances of *peirasmos* in the New Testament refer to the final apocalyptic battle.[59] We might derive a further insight here; this is a place in the text where two motifs shade into one another. The motif of the cosmic conflict in the Synoptic account is linked to the forensic imagery. The entire Gethsemane scene, writes Brown, is suffused with "the atmosphere of the final trial."[60] In Brown's translation of Luke 22:40, Jesus tells his disciples, "Keep on praying not to enter into trial *(peirasmos)."* This word has been translated "temptation" in the older English versions of the Bible.[61] It is true that *peirasmos* sometimes means simply the ordinary temptations of life, but Brown, reviewing the literature, notes that in the view

56. Brown, *Death of the Messiah*, 1:225.

57. Brown, *Death of the Messiah*, 1:234.

58. Even though the Gethsemane scene appears only indirectly in John's Gospel, the Evangelist stresses this motif. As the betrayal and arrest are imminent, the Lord says, "Now is the judgment of this world, now shall the ruler of this world be cast out" (John 12:31). And later he says, "The ruler of this world is judged" (16:11). The Fourth Gospel is known for its depiction of Jesus as an imperial ruler throughout his entire ministry. John is consistent in his portrayal of Christ as Victor throughout, even — perhaps especially — on the cross. Brown agrees that in both Mark and John the context of the arrest in Gethsemane is that of "an eschatological struggle with evil" (*Death of the Messiah*, 1:224-25).

59. Brown, *Death of the Messiah*, 1:160. Note, for instance, Rev. 3:10, with its sweeping, universal implications — "the hour of *peirasmos* which is coming on the whole world, to try those who dwell upon the earth." This is not about the testing of each individual case by case. The Lord's Prayer also contains the word — "Lead us not into temptation *(peirasmos)"* — which has led to the modern rendering, "Save us from the time of trial." *"In* the time of trial" would be better, since we are repeatedly told in the NT that we will all stand before the judgment seat of God (e.g., Rom. 14:10).

60. Brown, *Death of the Messiah*, 1:157.

61. But note "the time of testing" in the NEB, and "the time of trial" in NRSV.

of the great majority of scholars, "something more dangerous must have been meant" when Jesus told the disciples to "keep praying not to enter into *peirasmos*."[62] He is referring to the great apocalyptic trial or struggle involving divine judgment upon the Powers (discussed in the previous chapter). Anything involving God's judgment should be seen in the context of a number of biblical images, including the celestial judgment seat, the summoning of the nations, the passing of a sentence or verdict, the invasion of one *kosmos* by another, and above all the conclusive defeat of the Powers upon whom the sentence finally falls after being absorbed by the crucified One.[63]

Taking off from Brown's insights, then, we may say that in Gethsemane, on the eve of the crucifixion, God is initiating the definitive apocalyptic confrontation. It is the opening scene of a trial in two different ways — it is a trial or test of the Messiah's commitment, somewhat like the ubiquitous trial of the hero in world mythology, but it is also a trial in the sense of the final, or last, judgment. There is a sense in which the Gethsemane scene is the opening episode of Christ's passion, and therefore the beginning of the first day of the age to come. The very deep idea that we are approaching here is that the judgment of the ruler of this world — and therefore the judgment of the *kosmos* itself — coincides with the judgment that Jesus takes upon himself, in our place.

The scene in Gethsemane is traditionally called the Agony in the Garden. The Greek word *agon* (combat, struggle, contest) is related to *agonia* (agony, anxiety), used by Luke (22:44) to describe Jesus in the garden.[64] This is of unexpected significance. Jesus is readying himself for the apocalypse; he is an *agonistikos,* a combatant. The Greek *agonizesthai* means to contend, to struggle.[65] The Gethsemane story shows how Jesus, facing the eschatological "hour," struggled with his fear of it. Here is another connection between the trial scene and the apocalyptic battleground, since it is reasonable to suppose that part of the extremity Jesus is experiencing has to do with the dread of the judgment of God. Why would God's sinless Son fear his Father's

---

62. Brown, *Death of the Messiah,* 1:159-60.

63. Episcopalians of a certain age will remember a reference to this in — of all places — the marriage service. In the 1928 Book of Common Prayer the bride and groom are charged concerning "the dreadful day of judgment when the secrets of all hearts shall be disclosed." Believe it or not, there are still some persons living who treasure the memory of those words at their weddings (and not just the author!). The charge shows how commitments made on earth have consequences in heaven, an apocalyptic idea if ever there was one.

64. Brown, *Death of the Messiah,* 1:189-90.

65. Paul uses *agon* also in a derivative sense, to refer to his own struggle; he writes to the Philippians that they are to suffer with Christ, having the same *agon* that they see Paul going through (Phil. 1:29-30).

judgment? From a Trinitarian perspective, the Son cannot fear the Father any more than he can fear himself. The only possible answer, it would seem, is that the Son is taking upon himself the judgment that would have been directed to someone else.

This brings us to a notorious problem of interpretation. Why should Jesus demonstrate such unbecoming anguish when other men and women — Socrates has often been invoked, and in the Jewish context, the Maccabean martyrs — went to their deaths with calm serenity and resolve? Many commentators over the centuries have wrestled with this perplexing question. Mark's Gospel, unflinching as usual, presents it in baldest form. The word Mark uses *(ekthambeisthai)* to describe Jesus' emotions is extremely strong. It is softened by Matthew and omitted by Luke, but there is a distinct echo of it in Hebrews 5:7 — "strong clamor and tears." Raymond Brown defines Mark's *ekthambeisthai* as "to be greatly distraught," and elaborates, "a profound disarray, expressed physically before a terrifying event: a shuddering horror."[66]

Brown passes lightly over the various interpretations of the Gethsemane struggle familiar in the Reformed tradition,[67] since he is focused on the *agonia* of Jesus as the opening scene of the final apocalyptic drama. He emphasizes Jesus as the combatant who, in Luke's account, rises to his feet "as a sign of vigor . . . reflective of the tenseness of an athlete now ready to enter the trial."[68] The Son of God is about to initiate the decisive battle against the Powers of darkness.[69] In the context of the *Christus Victor* theme,

66. Brown, *Death of the Messiah,* 1:153. Most depictions of Christ in the Garden of Gethsemane show him piously kneeling in prayer. In the stained-glass window in the church of my childhood, the Lord has an expression of peace and tranquility. I was struck recently by an oil sketch in an old art book, purporting to be by Delacroix (I have not been able to find it online). It shows Jesus flat on the ground (Mark 14:35), almost writhing, stretching out his arm and open hand in a gesture of desperate pleading. Jesus "is engaged not just in a personal confrontation with his own death but in eschatological warfare against cosmic forces of evil, and his anguish is part of an ongoing battle for the salvation of the world" (Marcus, *Mark 8–16,* 984).

67. Brown, *Death of the Messiah,* 1:154. Note, however, that Reformed theologian Karl Barth also emphasizes Gethsemane in specifically apocalyptic terms as a "world-occurrence," the collision of the aeons, the final and climactic confrontation with Satan (*Church Dogmatics* IV/1 [Edinburgh: T. & T. Clark, 1956], 266-67).

68. Brown, *Death of the Messiah,* 1:193. In the largely meretricious film by Mel Gibson, *The Passion of the Christ,* there is one very good scene near the beginning. Jesus rises from his knees in Gethsemane and moves off with a determined stride, grinding a snake under his foot as he does so. The reference is to Gen. 3:14-15, christologically interpreted.

69. One need not look far to find similar conclusions in numerous commentaries. For example, William L. Lane speaks of Mark's "cosmic language" (*Gospel of Mark,* New International Commentary on the New Testament [Grand Rapids: Eerdmans, 1974], 60). D. E. Nineham writes, "The great eschatological battle is joined" (*Saint Mark,* Pelican New Testament

Brown's interpretation can be embraced without reservation. As we move on, however, a synthesis will be proposed; Jesus is preparing to enter the lists *not only* as the utterly undefended commander of the Lord's hosts *but also* as the one who will stand alone on the front line *in our place,* absorbing the full onslaught of Sin, Death, and the devil.

Further Biblical Evidence

We have looked at both Romans 5 and the Gethsemane story in light of the *Christus Victor* theme because neither passage is associated in most Bible readers' minds with the apocalyptic battlefield. We examine these two seemingly nonapocalyptic portions of the New Testament now in order to demonstrate how prevalent the motif actually is. Were we to list all the more obvious passages, we would have no space for anything else. Here are just two passages among many from the non-Pauline material:[70]

> [Jesus said,] "They will lay their hands on you . . . and you will be brought before kings and governors for my name's sake. This will be a time for you to bear testimony. Settle it therefore in your minds, not to meditate beforehand how to answer; for I will give you a mouth and wisdom, which none of your adversaries will be able to withstand or contradict. You will be delivered up even by parents and brothers and kinsmen and friends, and some of you they will put to death; you will be hated by all for my name's sake. But not a hair of your head will perish. By your endurance you will gain your lives." (Luke 21:12-19)

> Beloved, do not be surprised at the fiery ordeal which comes upon you to prove you, as though something strange were happening to you. But

---

Commentary [Middlesex: Penguin Books, 1963], 63). Joel Marcus emphasizes "the apocalyptic framework that is so important in understanding the passion narrative" in Mark. He refers several times to the collision that is occurring between the old age of the satanic powers and the age to come. This apocalyptic battle is being fought in reverse, with the righteous man being "betrayed into the hands of sinners" (Mark 14:41) instead of the other way round. This inversion is "consistent with an ironic and paradoxical Gospel in which God's anointed king triumphs . . . by ignominiously dying on a cross" — yet another example of the unique character of the Christian gospel (*Mark 8–16,* 989, 997, 1000).

70. To be sure, there are some New Testament books with more apocalyptic language and others with much less. It is most prevalent in the Gospels, Paul's letters, Jude, I John, II Peter, and Revelation. Even in Acts, various references to Satan, Sin, and Death as active agents (Acts 2:24; 5:3; 10:38; 13:10; 26:18) reveal the apocalyptic matrix in which Luke was working.

rejoice in so far as you share Christ's sufferings, that you may also rejoice and be glad when his glory is revealed. . . . If one suffers as a Christian, let him not be ashamed, but under that name let him glorify God. For the time has come for judgment to begin with the household of God. (I Pet. 4:12-17)

Finally, here are two notable passages that combine the *Christus Victor* theme with other themes. The first, from Colossians, blends the forensic motif ("legal demands") with the metaphor of the conquering Christ disarming the Powers and leading them captive. The passage from Hebrews combines the image of Christ as the victor over Death with that of the priestly sacrifice.

And you, who were dead in trespasses and the uncircumcision of your flesh, God made alive together with him, having forgiven us all our trespasses, having canceled the bond which stood against us with its legal demands; this he set aside, nailing it to the cross. He disarmed the principalities and powers and made a public example of them, triumphing over them in him. (Col. 2:13-15)

Since therefore the children share in flesh and blood, he himself likewise partook of the same nature, that through death he might destroy him who has the power of death, that is, the devil, and deliver all those who through fear of death were subject to lifelong bondage. . . . He had to be made like his brethren in every respect, so that he might become a merciful and faithful high priest in the service of God, to make expiation for the sins of the people. (Heb. 2:14-17)[71]

The Powers

The mind that has conceived a plan of living must never lose sight of the chaos against which that pattern was conceived.

Ralph Ellison, *Invisible Man*[72]

71. Dillistone quotes Ragnar Lievestad, author of *Christ the Conqueror*, on Heb. 2:14 — "Along with Colossians 2:14 this verse represents the most dramatic interpretation of the death of Jesus in the New Testament" (Dillistone, *Christian Understanding of Atonement*, 88).
72. Ralph Ellison, *Invisible Man*, 2nd ed. (New York: Vintage, 1995), 580.

Our salvation is played out with the Devil, a Devil who is not simply generalized evil, but an evil intelligence determined on its own supremacy.

Flannery O'Connor, letter to a friend[73]

Ellison's nameless hero is the epitome of the individual who struggles heroically to assert himself in the face of overwhelming odds. O'Connor's horizon is more consciously cosmic. Both, however, state in no uncertain terms that human existence must be wrought in the midst of a lifelong struggle with cosmic enemies.[74] This links us to the presence of hostile Powers in the drama of Christ's victory. Most biblical interpretation in the modern age has been done as though there were only two *dramatis personae,* God and humanity — thereby demystifying the New Testament, which presents three. The Croatian-born theologian Miroslav Volf has written of these matters with arresting authority, out of his experience of the Balkan conflicts. He has emphasized the presence of the Powers and the creation as occupied territory: "Jesus' public ministry . . . was not a drama played out on an empty stage. . . . Especially in a creation infested with sin, the proclamation and enactment of the kingdom of truth and justice is never an act of pure positing, but *always already a transgression into spaces occupied by others.*"[75]

These occupying "others" are also called the principalities and powers, most notably in Ephesians 6:10-12, and also in Romans 8:38.[76] The "others"

---

73. Flannery O'Connor, *The Habit of Being* (New York: Farrar, Straus and Giroux, 1979), letter to John Hawkes, November 20, 1959.

74. Indeed, the Ellison quotation is almost certainly a conscious echo of Gen. 1: the creation itself was the rejection of chaos, God's original act of negation.

75. Miroslav Volf, *Exclusion and Embrace: A Theological Exploration of Identity, Otherness, and Reconciliation* (Nashville: Abingdon, 1996), 293, emphasis added. With regard to Volf's use of the word "transgression," though it is correct etymologically, it gives the wrong impression, as though there were something illicit about it. I would prefer "invasion," as in Normandy invasion — the opening campaign to recapture the territory held by the Enemy (an analogy first made by Oscar Cullmann).

76. A seminal examination of this subject is *Christ and the Powers* (1953) by Hendrikus Berkhof, translated into English by none other than John Howard Yoder in 1962. There has been much discussion about the nature of the Powers since the 1960s. A brief, eminently clear, accessible description of the Powers is in Lesslie Newbigin's *The Gospel in a Pluralist Society* (London: SPCK, 1989), 199-210. Two mid-twentieth-century lay theologians, Jacques Ellul and William Stringfellow, took the position that the "principalities and powers" are earthly institutions that have been corrupted by the demonic Powers. Two examples will make the point. In 2002, the devastating exposure of U.S. corporate greed and mendacity (Enron and WorldCom in particular) resulted in a worldwide loss of confidence in the American markets. Bernard J. Ebbers, CEO of WorldCom, was an active member and Sunday school teacher at his Baptist church. He is now serving twenty-five years in prison. Then, in 2008, reckless lend-

are also named as Satan and his legions (Mark 5:9). Although Paul refers to Satan by name no fewer than ten times (I Cor. 5:5; 7:5; II Cor. 12:7; etc.), he does not depict Christ the *Kurios* in direct combat with Satan, as do the Synoptics in the story of the temptation in the wilderness.[77] Paul's preferred way of identifying the occupying Enemy is in its various manifestations as Sin, Death, and the Law — or, alternatively, as principalities and powers, as *kurioi* (lords), thrones, authorities, and other designations. In one of Paul's most striking passages, these Powers are called "the rulers of this age": "Among the mature we do impart wisdom, although it is not a wisdom of this age or of the rulers of this age, who are doomed to pass away. But we impart a secret and hidden wisdom of God, which God decreed before the ages for our glorification. None of the rulers of this age understood this; for if they had, they would not have crucified the Lord of glory" (I Cor. 2:6-8).

Paul is not referring to Caiaphas or Pilate or "the Jews" when he speaks of "the rulers of this age." He is speaking of the cosmic Powers who preside over the "form of this world" that is "passing away" (I Cor. 7:31). We are deceived by them into thinking that we are making our own decisions, when in fact they are compelling us through deceit, according to the fell purposes of the Archenemy.[78]

In the final chapter of his widely discussed book *Exclusion and Em-*

---

ing and leveraging by several hugely powerful financial institutions led to the Great Recession. Ellul's and Stringfellow's analyses sound very fresh in this context. A related explanation of the Powers is offered by Bill Wylie-Kellerman, a writer and activist who was deeply influenced by Stringfellow. In a 1995 speech he said: "Powers are good, powers are fallen, powers must be redeemed. The vocation of principalities and powers in creation is to praise God and serve human life. But in the Fall, that vocation is turned upside down, and they believe they are God and thereby enslave human life. Powers give themselves over to a ruthless ethic of self-survival. That is true about every principality and power. They have a fear of death, and they become servants of death" (in *Living Church* magazine, November 26, 1995).

77. John Milton, in *Paradise Lost,* book 2, shows Sin personified, speaking to Satan as her father:

> . . . thou wilt bring me soon
> To that new world of light and bliss, among
> The Gods who live at ease, where I shall Reign
> At thy right hand voluptuous, as beseems
> Thy daughter and thy darling, without end.

Milton was heterodox in certain ways, but in this respect he has it right. This colloquy between Satan and Sin (depicted not as a multiplicity of "sins" but as a Power) is a hideous parody of the reign of God "without end."

78. *The Jewish Annotated New Testament,* interestingly, concurs in this; the "rulers" are "evil and demonic forces" that are "soon to be either destroyed or radically transformed. Christ's death rescues humanity from these forces" (333).

brace, Volf, in just a few striking pages, draws out a theology of the book of Revelation that advances these points.[79] One of his conversation partners is the French writer Gilles Deleuze. According to Volf, Deleuze has accused Christianity, and the book of Revelation in particular, of "cosmic terror"; he describes the new Jerusalem as "totalitarian" and writes that John of Patmos has changed the loving Jesus of the Gospels into a vengeful figure in a bloody robe (Rev. 19:15).[80] Volf respects this critique but rejects the dichotomy. He develops his own interpretation of the violent images in Revelation. His response to Deleuze's challenge is a nicely turned sentence: *"Can one have ultimate judgment against terror without the terror of judgment?"*[81]

Volf continues with a series of pointed observations. "The drama of salvation starts and ends with violence" (he is referring to the Slaughter of the Innocents and the battle of Armageddon). Moreover, the brutal execution of Jesus is "the central act of the New Testament drama."[82] Volf's repeated, almost insistent, use of the word "drama" is reminiscent of Aulén, but, more important, it reminds one of the New Testament atmosphere. He continues with an analysis of the agony of Jesus. If the crucifixion was simply the endurance of ghastly suffering, Volf explains, then it is essentially meaningless and we would never have heard of Jesus of Nazareth. It was not a scene of mere pathos. "Jesus' mission certainly did not consist merely in passively receiving violence." Reflecting upon the various ways of understanding nonviolence, he notes that a purely passive interpretation is "barren, because it shies away from *'transgressing' into* the territory of the system of terror." This insight leads to the insight that nonviolent resistance based in the power of the cross, far from being "passive" (i.e., ineffective), is a weapon in what John Howard Yoder calls "the war of the Lamb."[83] Indeed, Yoder introduces the term "revolutionary subordination," which is meant to have even more subversive implications than the more familiar phrase "nonviolent resistance."

Volf and Yoder, from differing perspectives, both understand that the

---

79. Volf, in a layered passage, alludes to the crucifixion of Jesus by "the rulers of this age" in a context suggesting that whereas Pilate, Caiaphas, etc., were the human perpetrators, the real action is the apocalyptic "drama of salvation" (*Exclusion and Embrace,* 291).

80. This summary of Deleuze's critique is grossly oversimplified; it is Volf's response that interests me.

81. Volf, *Exclusion and Embrace,* 290.

82. Volf, *Exclusion and Embrace,* 290-91.

83. This is the title of the final chapter in Yoder's *Politics of Jesus.* A posthumously published book by Yoder, edited by Glen Stassen and Mark Thiessen, is entitled *The War of the Lamb* (Grand Rapids: Brazos, 2009).

Powers are the real Enemy. Twentieth-century theology developed the New Testament conception of the principalities and powers to include institutions — governments, universities, corporations, newspapers, banks, labor unions, and so forth — that were ordained for our good but have fallen into the grip of Sin and Death.[84] That is what the New Testament means by the "principalities and powers." Satan seizes the principalities and powers and manipulates them so they become his servants.[85]

Volf allows that the rider on the white horse in Revelation 19 might be interpreted as the triumph of vindictiveness over love, violence over nonviolence. But, he argues, if there is no judgment upon systems of political violence and economic oppression — represented by the Roman Empire in Revelation — then "there can be no world of peace, of truth, and of justice; terror (the 'beast' that devours) and propaganda (the 'false prophet' that deceives) must be overcome, evil must be separated from good, and darkness from the light. These are the causes of violence that must be removed."[86] This argument that Volf makes throughout his book is congruent with the New Testament theology of the Powers. However, in the sight of God the causes of violence lie not only in systems but also within every person. No one can boast of being innocent, and each person — as well as every collective — will be judged according to the purpose of God. Volf seems to endorse this when he asserts that God wills to embrace "even the sons and daughters of hell" (see Matt. 23:15).[87] Indeed, reflecting on Romans 3:23, he is moved to refer to *all* of "us" as "children of hell," but nevertheless objects of God's love.

Volf is scathingly critical of "liberal" neglect of the wrath of God. It is

---

84. Joseph Mangina quotes an extraordinary passage in which Jonathan Edwards seems to foresee global electronic communications and the way they would be used by the demonic powers (Mangina, *Revelation* [Grand Rapids: Brazos, 2010], 230).

85. Here's an example. At a hearing on the harmful effects of tobacco, a tobacco company executive testified with a straight face, "To my knowledge, it's not been proven that cigarette smoking causes cancer." That infamous statement reappeared years later when the makers of e-cigarettes began to deny even the possibility that their candy-flavored products might be appealing to children. In support of his company's position, a spokesman cited a study that had been funded by the company itself. Richard J. Durbin, senator from Illinois, said in an interview, "Let me be as dismissive as possible: When they start talking about their own research, I say 'been there, done that.' We listened to those tobacco companies for decades while their so-called experts tried to deflect our attention from the obvious" (*New York Times,* July 16, 2014). Puncturing the pretensions of the Powers is a valuable weapon in the arsenal of the freedom fighter.

86. Volf, *Exclusion and Embrace,* 296.

87. He is correcting Elaine Pagels on this point (Volf, *Exclusion and Embrace,* 85).

true, he writes, that God's wrath can be partially understood as the working out of the consequences of sins within history (he is referring to a typical liberal interpretation of Rom. 1:16–3:18). Yet Volf argues that this is inadequate. *God himself is actively engaged* in warfare — as we have seen, he is not afraid to use the term "violence" — against the Powers. In a particularly pointed passage, he writes:

> Without an eschatological [apocalyptic] dimension, the talk of God's wrath degenerates into a naïve and woefully inadequate ideology. . . . Outside the world of wishful thinking, evildoers all too often thrive, and when they are overthrown, the victors are not much better than the defeated. God's eschatological anger is the obverse of the impotence of God's love. . . . A "nice" God is a figment of liberal imagination, a projection onto the sky of the inability to give up cherished illusions about goodness, freedom, and the rationality of social actors.[88]

The Anabaptist tradition, consistently the most pacifist tradition in the history of the Christian church, has traditionally had no hesitation about speaking of God's wrath and judgment — and with good reason. There is no trace of a nonindignant God in the biblical text, be it Old Testament or New Testament, be it from Jesus of Nazareth or from John of Patmos. The evildoers who "eat up my people as they eat bread," says the psalmist in God's name, will be put "in great terror" (Ps. 14:4-5). Why terror? Why not simply reproach? Even better, why not reason together with them? Or display suffering love to them? Because the evildoers "are corrupt" and "they do abominable deeds" (14:1).[89]

---

88. Volf does not always hold to this crucial insight about the winners being little better than the losers in a thoroughly consistent way. This inconsistency illustrates the difficulty of the struggle with this most intractable mystery and the challenge of coming to any definitive conclusion. Volf swings back and forth between contradictory positions; sometimes he indicates that all persons are capable of evil — as in the statement just cited — and other times he speaks as though there were good people and evil people, the latter distinguished by their "irredeemability." He seems to be convinced of the irrationality of "social actors," yet he also appears to believe that people are rationally responsible for acting irrationally. He does actually seem to think that there are people who, in the last analysis, are able to resist "the powerful lure of the open arms of the crucified Messiah" (*Exclusion and Embrace*, 298). Indeed, he writes that "*nothing* is potent enough to change those who insist on remaining beasts and false prophets" (297). Nothing? No One? Disarmingly, Volf refers to the aphorism "I am not a universalist, but God may be" (299 n. 8). We will continue this discussion in chapter 12, but for now it is a separate issue. I am focusing here on Volf's striking contributions to our understanding of the Powers and of the wrath of God.

89. Volf, *Exclusion and Embrace*, 298.

Volf, a theologian with personal experience of tragic conflict unimaginable to most Americans in our time, is uncompromising in his rejection of "a God without wrath" who brings "men without sin into a kingdom without judgment."[90] Because Volf himself is in demand as a witness for a nonviolent, pacific Christian position, his bold declarations about "the indignant God" and "the violence of God" are all the more striking. Volf explains himself this way: "I set out to work [on *Exclusion and Embrace*] in order to give an account to myself about how I, as a member of a people who in recent history has suffered brutal aggression, ought to react."[91] He works out his own commitment to nonviolence in terms of his faith in the promises of the biblical God, which includes the divine violence involved in the overthrow of the Powers. It would be impossible, he says, to pursue a course of nonviolence in the face of great evil if one did not believe that God would judge justly in the long run. Thus it is not wrong to speak of a God of violence. This is the thought behind the image of the destruction of Babylon in Revelation:

> "Hallelujah! Salvation and glory and power belong to our God,
> for his judgments are true and just. . . .
> Hallelujah! The smoke from her goes up for ever and ever." (Rev. 19:1-3)

Volf's grasp of the inner meaning of Revelation illuminates the way that its images of God's apocalyptic war function in times of terrible earthly conflict and suffering. He shows how its word pictures open up theologically into an all-encompassing vision of the new Jerusalem ruled solely by the One who gathered all suffering and violence into himself. The One who rides out to conquer on a white horse as "King of kings and Lord of lords" is the same One who died on the cross precisely for the "children of hell."

Battle Imagery as a Guide for Christian Living?

Volf's section on the "violent imagery of the rider's conquest" concludes:

> The most surprising thing about [Revelation] is that at the center of the throne, holding together both the throne and the whole cosmos that is ruled by the throne, we find the sacrificed *Lamb*. At the very heart of "the

90. The full quotation from H. Richard Niebuhr is in chapter 1.
91. Volf, *Exclusion and Embrace*, 100.

One who sits on the throne" is the cross. The world to come is ruled by the one who on the cross took violence upon himself in order to conquer and embrace the enemy. The Lamb's rule is legitimized not by the "sword" but by its "wounds"; the goal of its rule is not to subject but to make people "reign for ever and ever" (22:5). With the Lamb at the center of the throne, the distance between the "throne" and the "subjects" has collapsed in the embrace of the triune God.[92]

The book of Revelation makes an easy target. It has been grossly misappropriated by fanatics, a particularly appalling example being the mass suicide of the Heaven's Gate sect in California at the time of the Hale-Bopp comet (1997). The teaching of the sect was linked to some of the imagery in Revelation about falling stars. Complaints about Revelation and its apocalyptic visions are legion. Typical modern objections include the following: (1) its message tends to focus on "heaven" and to encourage passivity; (2) it appeals to megalomaniacal leaders and mentally unstable followers; (3) it encourages people to withdraw into sectarian enclaves, disengaged from the world and its struggles. These objections need to be addressed. The proper antidote, however, is not abandonment of apocalyptic theology, but a more vigorous defense of its true biblical nature.

Much work was done in the century just past to show the vital intersection of the apocalyptic perspective with Christian ethics. John Howard Yoder's influential book *The Politics of Jesus* draws on apocalyptic for its defense of "revolutionary subordination" — nonviolent resistance (emphasis on *revolution* and *resistance*) against the Powers. The churches in South Africa were inspired continually by the book of Revelation during the decades of struggle against apartheid. Here is an excerpt from the sort of sermon Archbishop Desmond Tutu was giving in the 1970s:

> I am a bishop in the Church of God, I am 51 years old, yet I don't have a vote; an 18-year-old, through a wonder of biological irrelevance — white skin — is able to vote. . . . They can remove Desmond Tutu. They can end the South African Council of Churches. But the Church of God goes on. The government must know that the Church is not frightened of any earthly power. . . . More are for us than can ever be against us. A vast throng no one could ever count, from every nation and every tribe, standing before the throne and before the Lamb, robed in white and bearing

---

92. Volf, *Exclusion and Embrace*, 300-301.

palms in their hands, shout together, "Victory to our God!" We join with angels and archangels and the whole company of heaven.[93]

The language of struggle and combat is not incompatible with a commitment to nonviolence. The nonviolent combatants are sustained by their trust in God, who has promised that "vengeance is mine, I will repay." Harsh and jarring though it may sound, the portrayal of the Lord as "a man of war" (Exod. 15:3; Isa. 42:13) is a powerful source of courage when the "war" is understood as the apocalyptic war against the Powers. The following vignettes, taken from the American civil rights struggle (1953-1964), will illustrate the way in which military imagery like that in the Bible is used in nonviolent struggle to inspire, to encourage, and to interpret. The imagery places the freedom fighters in a meaningful narrative, empowering them for their ordeal.

When Rosa Parks was arrested in Montgomery for refusing to move to the back of the bus, the civil-rights pioneers Clifford and Virginia Durr, both born to privilege in white Alabama society, came to the jail to bail her out. When Virginia Durr died in February 1999, Rosa Parks wrote a letter addressed to her posthumously and sent it to the large surviving Durr family. It included these words: "I will miss you, old soldier." This is an aged, physically frail old lady speaking! Mrs. Parks did not need any politically correct person to tell her that military imagery was not appropriate. Mrs. Parks and Mrs. Durr knew what it was like to be in battle.[94]

In June of 1964 Mrs. Fannie Lou Hamer went to Oxford, Ohio, to address the Freedom Summer volunteers assembled there for orientation. "Number one, I told 'em what had happened to me in 1963, and I told 'em the same thing could happen to them in 1964. We didn't tell 'em no lies. We prepared 'em for exactly what it was like, and it was like you going into combat. You know, I've heard of combat, but that's exactly what we was having here."[95] Howell Raines observes, "The metaphor of Mississippi as a war zone appears over and over again in these interviews."[96] In an inter-

93. Bishop Tutu delivered this impassioned address more than once, in slightly varying versions. An example is in the *Living Church* 185, no. 16 (October 17, 1982): 6.

94. Eric Pace, obituary of Virginia F. Durr, *New York Times*, February 25, 1999.

95. Mrs. Hamer was brutally beaten and degraded in the Winona, Mississippi, jail in 1963. The quotation comes from Howell Raines, *My Soul Is Rested: Movement Days in the Deep South Remembered* (New York: Putnam, 1977), 275.

96. Raines, *My Soul Is Rested*, 275. Raines's book is one of the best sources for stories of the movement. Its title comes from the Montgomery bus boycott. Asked if she wasn't tired from walking, an elderly woman said, with the eloquence so often found in semiliterate black South-

view conducted for PBS, John Seigenthaler, who covered the civil rights movement, had this to say: "It was like being a war correspondent. It was clear that there was a war on. We [journalists] could see that the weapons of non-violence were stronger than those of violence."[97] Over and over, stories from the civil rights movement relate how profoundly shaken the reporters were as they witnessed the almost superhuman courage, forbearance, and capacity for suffering shown by the volunteers as the dangers escalated.[98] After the glory days of the movement were over and the Vietnam War escalated, the civil rights forces split, the younger generation became more rebellious, and the battle lines became harder to discern. King's struggle became more intense. He saw that "the 'friendly universe' of his halcyon days at Ebenezer [Baptist Church]" had been overtaken by "a vision of a frightful battle at the center of reality — a tension at the heart of the universe between good and evil."[99]

As we see from these examples and recollections, the theme of apocalyptic judgment and victory in the nonviolent civil rights movement in the early 1960s was not just an illusion or wish, but was powered through fearful trials by the knowledge that God's liberating invasion could not be stopped. "Won't let nobody turn me round, turn me round," as the freedom song put it. Charles Marsh writes that Mrs. Hamer's leadership of her people through song "did not remove their suffering or the particularities of their humiliation; rather, it embraced the suffering, named it, and emplotted it in a cosmic story of hope and deliverance."[100] It is precisely that cosmic story that Paul and the other New Testament writers tell. Mrs.

---

erners brought up on the King James Version, "My feets is tired, but my soul is rested." Growing up in Virginia, I often heard this sort of biblical utterance from older African Americans.

97. *A Force More Powerful,* PBS series, September 2000, written and produced by Steve York, a coproduction of York Zimmerman Inc. and WETA, Washington. Narrated by Sir Ben Kingsley.

98. This story is well told in Gene Roberts and Hank Klibanoff, *The Race Beat: The Press, the Civil Rights Struggle, and the Awakening of a Nation* (New York: Knopf, 2006), 271-72, 390, and passim. David Halberstam tells his own story in this regard in *The Children* (New York: Fawcett, 1999).

99. Richard Lischer, *The Preacher King: Martin Luther King, Jr., and the Word That Moved America* (Oxford: Oxford University Press, 1995), 108. It is of utmost importance that in speaking of a battle between good and evil we do not speak — Martin Luther King most certainly did not speak — of good and evil *people*. He as much as anyone recognized that "the line between good and evil runs through each person" (Havel). It is the good and evil Powers that are being invoked.

100. Charles Marsh, *God's Long Summer: Stories of Faith and Civil Rights* (Princeton: Princeton University Press, 1997), 22.

Hamer found it in her Bible. *It is not a story to be found anywhere else.* In the unique event that is the crucifixion of Jesus Christ, it is revealed that God is acting. In the divine invasion of this world, the Powers that have been allowed to rule in "the present evil age" are disarmed by the Powers of the world to come, that is, by the weapons of the Spirit. Christ the Lord is Victor even in the midst of the suffering of his followers.

Strengths of the Apocalyptic Perspective

In general, Aulén's thesis about the centrality of the *Christus Victor* motif in the New Testament (especially in Paul's letters), in the patristic period, and in Martin Luther's writings is still useful, albeit with numerous modifications and corrections. As a result, there have been many gains and some losses. Let us look at these briefly.

The most important feature of the *Christus Victor* theme in its apocalyptic setting is that it dramatizes and guarantees the agency of God. As Aulén wrote on his final page, "the fundamental idea . . . is above all a movement of God to man, not in the first place a movement of man to God." We have argued, further, that the metaphor of an invasion of occupied territory is indispensable for several reasons, not least because it shows how we, the tyrannized inhabitants of a territory held by enemies (variously identified as Sin, Death, and the Devil), can only be liberated by a movement "from another quarter" (Esther 4:14). The liberating force must be powerful enough, in the words of Jesus' parable, to "[bind] the strong man" (Matt. 12:29; Mark 3:27; cf. Luke 11:21).[101] The incarnation itself was widely understood during most of the Christian era to be God's invasion of Satan's territory. This can

---

101. Matthew, Mark, and Luke all report a parable in which Jesus says to his disciples, "If it is by the Spirit of God that I cast out demons, then the kingdom of God has come upon you. How can one enter a strong man's house and plunder his goods, unless he first binds the strong man? Then indeed he may plunder his house." By "the strong man" Jesus means Satan, and the "house" of Satan is this world. Jesus calls Satan "the ruler of this world" (John 12:31). In Ephesians, he is called "the prince of the power of the air" who directs "the course of this world" and is at work in the children "of disobedience" (Eph. 2:2). In the parable of the strong man, Jesus is saying that if Satan is not met with a force superior to his own, he will never yield. He is in possession of his kingdom until the one stronger than he renders him helpless and robs him of his goods (John Calvin, *Harmony of the Gospels,* on Matt. 12:29 and parallels). About the cross specifically, we read in Colossians, "[God] disarmed the principalities and powers and made a public example of them, triumphing over them in [Christ]" (Col. 2:15).

easily be illustrated by various medieval poems set to music for the Christmas season:

Perdidit spolia princeps infernorum . . .[102]

This little babe, but two days old,
Is come to rifle Satan's fold.[103]

When time had run its course, the Father . . . sent from the heavenly throne his only begotten son . . . that in this fleshly abode he might vanquish the devil.[104]

And from the Reformation:

This child, this little helpless boy,
Shall be our confidence and joy,
The power of Satan breaking,
Our peace eternal making.[105]

The theme continues even into the eighteenth century:

Remember Christ our Saviour was born on Christmas Day
To save us all from Satan's power when we were gone astray.[106]

In today's culture, references to "transgressive" art and behavior are compliments, and irony continues to be the pervasive tone of our times. Yet it is a sign of the underlying sentimentality of our culture that Christmas carols with themes such as these would be unthinkable today. Despite the terror and suffering all around us, we demand soft-focus peace-and-joy images

---

102. The literal translation of the old text is "The Prince of Hell has lost his spoils." The text of *Personent hodie,* frequently sung at Christmas in the Anglican tradition, first appears in *Piae Cantiones* (1582) but seems to be a version of a much older (1360) Latin carol. This has been lost in the more sentimentalized English translations, one of which was made for the composer Gustav Holst, who arranged the tune in 1924.

103. This text, by Robert Southwell (1561?–1596), is familiar today as part of Benjamin Britten's *Ceremony of Carols.*

104. Latin motet, based on one of the traditional antiphons for Advent.

105. Hymn text by Johann Rist (1607-1667).

106. "God Rest You Merry, Gentlemen." London carol, eighteenth century.

for our Christmas cards.[107] By contrast, the apocalyptic gospel dramatizes a cosmic struggle between good and evil, light and darkness, day and night in a symbolic world that grants evil its due and girds itself ahead of time for the irruption of such events as terrorist attacks. "But take heed," says Jesus in the Synoptic apocalypse, "I have told you all things beforehand" (Mark 13:23). One of the strongest arguments in favor of the apocalyptic perspective in the New Testament is that it gives the devil his due. Radical evil — ranging from macro to micro, from the massacre of millions to the torture-murder of a child — is not denied or glossed over. It comes as no surprise; "this must take place," Jesus warns the disciples (Mark 13:7). Hence the Advent call to "watch" and "resist."

> Discipline yourselves, keep alert. Like a roaring lion your adversary the devil prowls around, looking for someone to devour. Resist him, steadfast in your faith, for you know that your brothers and sisters in all the world are undergoing the same kinds of suffering [a more literal translation is "knowing that the same afflictions *are to be accomplished* in your brothers in the world"]. And after you have suffered for a little while, the God of all grace, who has called you to his eternal glory in Christ, will himself restore, support, strengthen, and establish you. To him be the power forever and ever. Amen. (I Pet. 5:8-11 NRSV)

This is a passage of encouragement, like a speech given by a commander to his troops.[108] The New Testament imagery *places us on the field of battle.*[109]

107. The most unforgettable Christmas card my husband and I ever received was designed by the Catholic Interracial Council of the Twin Cities in the late 1960s. On the front was a text from the Benedictus on a red background: "The day shall dawn upon us from on high to give light to those who sit in darkness and in the shadow of death" (Luke 1:78-79). On the inside was a black-and-white photograph of a small, ragged African American boy sitting forlornly in the bleak, littered courtyard of a slum dwelling. The Interracial Council continued to produce cards in this vein a year or two more, and then unfortunately gave in to consumer reality, offering cards with smiling black and white children holding hands in a circle.

108. The extraordinary contributions of Fannie Lou Hamer — female and semiliterate — were not honored or even acknowledged by the leadership of the civil rights movement during her lifetime, but she was a particularly good example of such a commander on the front lines of the apocalyptic war. Charles Marsh has written an extraordinary tribute to her in *God's Long Summer.*

109. This is true both in the corporate and in the individual sense. The war that rages all the time has two aspects: (1) it is *around* us in the form of the war with the Powers and principalities; and (2) it is *within* us: as Dostoevsky wrote, "the devil is struggling with God, and the battlefield is the human heart" (*The Brothers Karamazov,* Pevear-Volokhonsky translation, 108).

Paradoxically (and this is where the cross has its central place), suffering and persecution are the signs that the church is effectively resisting. These afflictions are "to be accomplished" (epiteleisthai) in and among the members of the Christian family throughout the world, and this news is not strange to Christians in many countries today. Discipline ("be sober") and vigilance ("be watchful") are necessary, because the Enemy is untiring. Note that the predatory activity of the devil is not explained or commented upon in the passage, because it is assumed; it is part of the New Testament thought-world.

This symbolic structure is not expendable. It is not merely packaging. Neither in I Peter nor in today's preaching is it disposable; it is part of the gospel, because the gospel is *a message of deliverance* from the grip of evil and Death. Although it is true that in a certain sense the devil is a symbol, the symbol encompasses a reality. New Testament apocalyptic gives us a peerless account of reality. Reality is about evil, and suffering, and ultimately victory over suffering. The overfamiliar way of describing this victory in our culture is to call it "the triumph of the human spirit."[110] From the perspective of the gospel, however, that is putting the emphasis in the wrong place. The Petrine author proclaims that when the human spirit is triumphant, it is the mercy and power of God working through the human spirit: "The God of all grace, who has called you to his eternal glory in Christ, will himself restore, establish, and strengthen you" (I Pet. 5:10).

The apocalyptic emphasis on the triumph of God celebrates not only God's *initiative* in Christ but also God's *coming victory* in Christ. This is the already/not-yet perspective of the New Testament that must always be held in balance. In the stories of the exorcisms of Jesus, for instance, we see that the demons are *already* in flight before him; however, they are *not yet* destroyed, for they will be given free rein to assault him as he is crucified. In much the same way, we read in Revelation that Satan is allowed "to make war on the saints and to conquer them. And authority was given [him] over every . . . nation" (Rev. 13:7). In other words, being joined to Christ in his death and resurrection through baptism (Rom. 6:3-11) does not mean being lifted clear of the cosmic battle, as the Corinthians thought it did. The life of the church is lived in a balance between the first advent of Christ and the second. It is a life of affliction for the sake of the gospel, but if there is one word that sounds the apocalyptic note, it is "hope" —

---

110. The writer Sebastian Junger speaks of "the quiet dignity of the human struggle," which — whether he knows it or not — is far more faithful to the biblical view of humankind than "the triumph of the human spirit" (NPR interview, April 18, 2013).

the hope that is beyond human hope (Rom. 4:18) because it is grounded in the promise of the future of Jesus Christ. Abraham is the great model here; he was "fully persuaded that, *what [God] had promised, he was able also to perform*" (Rom. 4:21 KJV). This is the bedrock. Because "God is able" — as black church people often say — we are not prisoners of the Powers; rather, we are, as the prophet Zechariah proclaimed, "prisoners of hope" (Zech. 9:12).[111]

Criticisms of *Christus Victor* and the Case for Conjoining the Motifs

Many biblical scholars and theologians have resisted the movement to restore the apocalyptic perspective to its central place. There are a number of reasons for this.

One complaint about the *Christus Victor* motif is that it seems to show the battle taking place at a cosmic remove, over the head of humanity. We have tried to show, in a preliminary way, that the Christian *participates* in the cosmic struggle, that she stands with her Lord under the world's sentence of death, that she is equipped for the fray with the armor of light, that she is clothed with the righteousness of God, that she bears the sword of the Word into battle, that she must bear her cross, that "for him that overcometh the crown of life shall be."[112] Being a Christian means that we are *involved* in the battle with the demons. This is the dignity that God has granted to us, that we should be his resistance movement. We can illustrate with the magnificent baptismal acclamation that was said over countless babies of both genders for hundreds of years in the Episcopal Church: "We receive this child into the congregation of Christ's flock, and do sign *her* with the sign of the cross, in token that hereafter *she* shall not be ashamed to confess the faith of Christ crucified, and manfully [*sic*] to fight under his banner against sin, the world, and the devil, and to continue Christ's faithful soldier and servant until *her* life's end."[113]

A second important criticism of the *Christus Victor* theme is related to its ethical consequences. Douglas John Hall, for example, cautions against the tendency in liberation theology to place all the blame on evil outside agencies, while attributing "too much innocence and goodness"

---

111. It is no accident that one of Bishop Tutu's books is entitled *Prisoner of Hope*.

112. Hymn, "Stand Up, Stand Up for Jesus."

113. This was removed from the Book of Common Prayer in the 1979 revision, no doubt because of the battle imagery.

to the group that sees itself in need of liberation.[114] This is a wise and necessary insight. It strengthens the view that *if all the motifs are allowed to work their particular emphases under the apocalyptic arch of Romans 4:5 and 5:6 — the justification of the ungodly — there is a built-in biblical corrective for this error.* Paul would caution, however, that the flesh — *sarx,* human nature under the reign of Sin — being what it is, constant vigilance must be exercised against the ubiquitous tendency to draw a line between the deserving and the undeserving.[115] Modern presentations of the *Christus Victor* theme tend not to be as complex and profound as that of the apostle, who puts forward the motif of the victorious liberating Christ in the context of the rectification (justification) of the *ungodly.* This recurring theme is a guard against the ever present danger of liberation theology becoming detached from its christological and kerygmatic foundations, resulting in one group setting itself up over against another in the church, so that one group is envisioned as right with God and the other is not — or alternatively, as victims and victimizers, with the victims typically cast in the role of innocents.

A third criticism, related to the second, is that the *Christus Victor* theme gives Christians a pass. The Lutheran scholar Gerhard Forde has explained this in a lively way. To understand what Christ has done for us on the cross, he writes, we need to be "caught in the act." He explains: "Christ's work is and remains always an act in which we are *involved* and *implicated,* which cannot be translated into *convenient and quiescent ideas.*"[116] He is arguing against "theories" of all kinds, Anselm's and Aulén's included, because they "let us off the hook." The crucifixion of Jesus, he thinks, is attributed by "theories" either to a necessity in the being of God (Anselm) or to the enmity of demonic Powers (Aulén), thereby leaving us feeling that we have been exonerated. In the latter case, we can even say, "The devil made me do it."

---

114. This critique is pertinent to the work of René Girard as well.

115. Constant vigilance as a characteristic of the life of the Christian community is a central motif in the Synoptic apocalypse and parables such as that of the ten bridesmaids; it is also at the center of Paul's *paraenesis,* in Rom. 13:11 for example: "It is full time now for you to wake from sleep."

116. Gerhard O. Forde, "Caught in the Act: Reflections on the Work of Christ," *Word and World* 3, no. 1 (Winter 1983): 22-31, emphasis added. I am indebted to Mark Reasoner for this article, which introduced me not only to Forde as a theological thinker but also, delightfully, to his snappy familiarity with today's lingo. We need to identify the "smoking gun," he writes, which will prove our complicity in the crucifixion. I do not think he goes far enough, however, with the motif of exchange (substitution).

Forde's argument is pertinent and helpful, especially as we look ahead to the theme of substitution. He gives Anselm his due, reminding us that Anselm was well aware of the *Christus Victor* theme but found it wanting because *it did not explain why Jesus had to suffer such a brutal death to defeat the demonic forces.* Forde quotes Anselm, asking, "Why should God have to 'stoop to such lowly things,' or 'do anything with such great labor,' when he could . . . just blow the demons away?" That question lies at the heart of this book. Earlier, in chapters 2 and 4 and in the Anselm chapter, we urged the point that the crucifixion, in all its revolting detail, corresponds precisely to what Anselm so memorably called *ponderis peccatum* (the gravity/weight of sin). Here, in the *Christus Victor* chapter, we are proposing further that the gruesome barbarity of crucifixion *corresponds also* to the outer limits of the evil that the Powers are able to perpetrate. We might paraphrase Anselm this way: "You have not yet considered the enormity of the Powers."

These criticisms of the *Christus Victor* theme, then, bring out some vital points and guide us ahead to further reflection.

Summary and Looking Ahead: Balancing the "Idea-Complexes"[117]

The *Christus Victor* theme in the New Testament is one we cannot do without. It is deeply embedded in the Scripture and the tradition, and it speaks with new force and relevance for today because it grants evil its due. The theme emphasizes the infernal intelligence, the annihilating force, the lethal fury of demonic Powers. In the contemporary world we know too much of this kind of evil. Anyone following the news as the twenty-first century continues to unfold must know the feeling that our globe is inhabited by truly unbearable wickedness, and that this wickedness is out of our control; it is something "loose and knocking at the world's heart."[118] In this situation, Christians live and bear witness with two images before them; one is the crucifixion, a scene of utter horror and apparent defeat, and the other is the *Christus Rex,* crowned, victorious, triumphant, risen — *ho erchomenos* (the One who comes). They are not separate images, side by side; they morph into one another.

117. As noted earlier, this phrase is Stephen Sykes's, from *The Story of Atonement,* Trinity and Truth Series (London: Darton, Longman, and Todd, 1997).

118. This phrase is from the marvelous writing of Loren Eiseley, *The Firmament of Time,* quoted in Dick Tripp, *The Biblical Mandate for Caring for Creation* (Eugene, Ore.: Wipf and Stock, 2013), 34.

Any tendency to interpret the victory of Christ on the cross without reference to Sin as one of the Powers has an ill effect on ethics. It encourages an unhealthy separation of personal piety from social action. It permits groups within the church to stand over against other groups, those doing the work of liberation and those obstructing it. When there is no sense of mutual sinfulness in the church, a dangerous condition exists, with one party in the church considering itself to be the true believers, showing subtle or not-so-subtle contempt for those less enlightened.[119]

Above all, Paul is concerned to show that the Christian life does not go on as if the world had remained unchanged. The church is not a redeemed boat floating in an unredeemed sea. It is not as if the only thing that has changed is that our sins are forgiven and we, person by person, come to believe in Jesus. Rather, there has been a transfer of aeons, an exchange of one *kosmos* for another. The Powers and principalities may not know it, but their foundations have been undermined and cannot last. The *creation itself* has been and is being invaded by the new world, the age to come. "For the creation waits with eager longing for the revealing of the sons of God; for the creation was subjected to futility, not of its own will but by the will of him who subjected it in hope; because the creation itself will be set free from its bondage to decay and obtain the glorious liberty of the children of God" (Rom. 8:20-21).

We have identified some problems associated with the *Christus Victor* theory when it is held in strict isolation rather than being allowed to interact with other New Testament motifs. This book has been designed to highlight the *whole cluster* of images surrounding the death of Christ, within *the overarching apocalyptic drama* that consistently presents God as the acting subject while at the same time enlisting even the humblest Christian (*especially* the humblest Christian) in God's band of resistance fighters.[120] The *Christus Victor* theme, understood in this way, holds together *both* atonement for sin *and* the rectification of sinners.

119. This is a state of affairs against which Paul sternly warned in both Romans and I Corinthians with his calls to "the strong" to show love and consideration for "the weak" — after all, in the sight of God we are *all* "the weak." Significantly, this scenario with one group considering another to be weak is the context for the famous chapter 13 on love. The whole of I Corinthians is a call to the Corinthian church to return to the message of the cross.

120. This is precisely the drama that J. R. R. Tolkien develops at length in *The Lord of the Rings*. The hobbits Sam and Frodo are the "least of these," but they are the ones chosen to bear the brunt of the battle. Tolkien, by his own admission in his letters, makes God the unseen actor behind all the developments. See my *The Battle for Middle-earth: Tolkien's Divine Design in "The Lord of the Rings"* (Grand Rapids: Eerdmans, 2004).

Finally, then, and looking ahead to the next chapter, we can do no better than to quote from Jaroslav Pelikan's preface to the Macmillan paperback edition of *Christus Victor*. After reviewing the numerous revisions proposed by Aulén's critics and agreeing with many of them, he nevertheless concludes that as a book that continues to set the terms for discussion, it "looks better all the time." And then, in words that sound even more timely in the twenty-first century than they did in the twentieth, he concludes: "And if, in our own time, we have experienced with new depth and bitterness the nihilistic reality of defeat at the hands of impersonal forces over which none can dispose, we must also learn anew the power and the subtle dominion of One who exercises his lordship and wins his victory through death, even death on a Cross."[121]

---

121. Jaroslav Pelikan, preface to the paperback edition of *Christus Victor* (New York: Macmillan, 1968).

CHAPTER TEN

The Descent into Hell

I have provided an outline for this chapter, as well as the next, to help us unravel the complicated themes discussed in them.

1. Why this chapter? Four goals
2. What is "hell"?
   - The biblical background
     — *Sheol*
     — *Hades*
     — *Gehenna*
     — The rise of a cosmology
   - New Testament texts related to the descent into hell
     — I Peter 3:17-21
     — Ephesians 4:8-10
3. Biblical themes related to the descent
   - Confrontation with death, the partner of Hades
   - Deliverance from another sphere of power
   - The Godlessness of hell
   - Condemnation: Provisional and penultimate, or ultimate and final?
4. The descent in the creed and the tradition
   - A hint of liberation theology in an early commentary
   - The iconography of the descent
   - The Middle Ages: Thomas Aquinas and "violent necessity"
   - The Reformation: John Calvin
   - The twentieth century: Karl Barth
   Looking ahead: Interpreting the descent in the age of genocide
   Some preliminary conclusions

5. The origin of evil
   - The serpent in Genesis
   - The figure of Lucifer
6. The nature of evil
   - The classic definition: evil as the absence of good
   - What the tradition affirms and rejects
7. Does the "argument from evil" disprove or discredit God?
   - Various accounts and their inadequacy
   - Marilyn McCord Adams and "horrendous evils"
   - Theodicy: the impact of Lisbon, Auschwitz, and the great tsunami of 2004
8. Is evil part of God's purpose?
   - *O felix culpa!*
   - Theodicy: a conclusion
9. The will to negate: why "Satan" is necessary
   - The alien Power in postmodern discourse
   - The negation of being
   - Speaking of Satan
10. Evil unmasked
    - The falsehood of innocence
    - The hidden factor of complicity
    - The moral unintelligibility of evil
11. "Rage against explanation"
    - "I cry to thee and thou dost not answer me" (Job 30:20)
    - Out of the whirlwind
12. New Testament cosmology and the hell of the perpetrators
    - "God's monopoly on violence"
    - Who deserves what?
    - The hell of the perpetrators
    - The descent of the righteous for the unrighteous
    - The irresistible Word
    - The future of hell
13. Summary and transition

> *More than ever*
> *life-out-there is goodly, miraculous, loveable,*
> *but we shan't, not since Stalin and Hitler,*
> *trust ourselves ever again: we know that, subjectively,*
> *all is possible.*
>
> W. H. AUDEN, "THE CAVE OF MAKING"[1]

> *The reason the Son of God appeared was to destroy the works of the devil.*
>
> 1 JOHN 3:8

1. Why This Chapter? Four Goals

An informed reader might reasonably protest that Christ's descent into hell, or the "harrowing of hell," as it was called in the medieval church, is not a separate motif deserving a chapter of its own. It barely appears in Scripture — certainly not by either of those names — and the article in the Apostles' Creed, *descendit ad inferna* ("he descended into hell"), has long been a subject of dispute.[2] Assigning a major chapter of considerable length to this motif might therefore seem perverse. Just as the prominent theme of reconciliation has been discussed under the heading of *rectification,* the descent into hell could have been made a subheading under *Christus Victor.* This has not been done, however, for reasons that should become clear.

The goals of this chapter can be stated as follows:

1. To look without blinking at the presence and potency of radical evil in order to register the worst about human nature, to fortify ourselves to resist that worst, and to prepare for this resistance by acknowledging that there are submerged dark inclinations *in all of us* that under certain circumstances can come to the surface.

2. To ask if horrific evil does not call into question the entire human project and therefore undermine any faith in divine purpose. We who believe in God demand from God that, if he will not explain radical evil to us in

---

1. W. H. Auden, "The Cave of Making (In Memoriam Louis MacNiece)," in *Selected Poems,* ed. Edward Mendelson, expanded 2nd ed. (New York: Vintage Books, 2007), 267.

2. It does not appear in the Nicene Creed at all.

this life, he will at least give us some framework with which to address it.

3. To show that the clause *descendit ad inferna*[3] implies a cosmology, since one of the overarching purposes of this book is to show that the story of Jesus Christ has cosmic implications.

4. To point ahead, suggesting that the descent into hell powerfully combines and illuminates *not only* the *Christus Victor* motif *but also* several others, including the substitutionary one.

The creedal affirmation of the descent into hell points us to such a framework and helps us to prepare for such a resistance against the Evil One. These considerations are so central to the purpose of this volume that devoting a long chapter to them is justified. However, the reader who wishes to skip over the background material in the first half may go directly to section 6, "The Nature of Evil."

2. What Is "Hell"?

The Biblical Background

Because the motif of Christ's descent into hell is disputed and poorly understood, and because its provenance is so complicated, this chapter contains more background material than others in this volume. The "history of hell" is notoriously difficult to sort out, since there is such a multiplicity of overlapping concepts. We select those of particular consequence.

The English word "hell" is derived from the Anglo-Saxon language.[4] The word is used by the King James Version of the Old Testament to translate *Sheol*.[5] Modern versions of the Old Testament generally use "Sheol" without translation. In the New Testament, however, it is another story, and this is significant. The English word "hell" is used in the NRSV — mostly in Mark and Matthew — to translate *Hades* and *Gehenna* (and, in one case, *Tartaros*).

---

3. *Ad inferos* (from *inferus,* "the lower world") has sometimes been used instead of *ad inferna* (from *infernus,* "that which is below"). Thomas Aquinas, Calvin, and Barth used versions of the Apostles' Creed that employed *inferos*.

4. It appears as *hellae* is an Old English version of the Apostles' Creed circa 1125, translating from the Latin Creed that had became standard in the eighth century.

5. It would be instructive to investigate words used to translate *Sheol, Gehenna,* and *Hades* in other languages — *enfer* in French, *Hölle* in German, etc.; but that lies beyond the scope of this book.

Modern translations have generally retained "Hades" untranslated but, interestingly, use the English "hell" for *Gehenna.*[6]

Sheol

Sheol is the Hebrew word denoting the underworld where *all* the dead dwell — after a fashion — in a shadowy subexistent state. *There is no meaningful life after death in the Old Testament world.*[7] We need to pause to let this sink in. Few Christians today (or Jews either, for that matter) fully comprehend the Old Testament's thoroughgoing renunciation of all speculation about life after death. We are so accustomed to thinking in vague, generically religious, quasi-Hellenistic terms about the "immortality of the soul" that we can scarcely grasp the degree to which the ancient Israelite community was expected, in the name of Yahweh, *to relinquish any hope for meaningful individual survival after death.* Insubstantial nonexistence in Sheol was the destiny of all.[8] This uncompromising doctrine differentiates the faith of Israel — it can hardly be repeated too often — from surrounding Near Eastern religions.

In Sheol the individual's life with God comes to an end. Psalm 88 describes it in the grimmest of terms, but there are numerous other places to look as well. The shades in Sheol do not and cannot praise God, and God no longer remembers them (Pss. 6:5; 115:17; etc.). They have no knowledge of what happens on earth, and all connections are severed (Eccles. 9:5; Isa. 63:16; etc.). There is no return from Sheol (Job 7:9-10); all is silence and darkness (Pss. 94:17; 49:19; etc.). There is no comfort or hope in the prospect of an afterlife spent in this condition; rather, the opposite is true (Pss. 39:13; 49:20).[9] A passage from Sirach in the Apocrypha sums it up:

> Who will sing praises to the Most High in Sheol,
> as do those who are alive and give thanks?
> From the dead, as from one who does not exist, thanksgiving has
> ceased. (Sir. 17:27-28)

6. Translators have struggled with Greek phrases such as *pulai hadou* (literally, "gates of Hades") in Matt. 16:18. In the KJV it is "gates of hell," in the RSV and REB "powers of death," in the NRSV and NIV "gates of Hades," in the NAB "jaws of death."

7. The only exceptions to this are two very late passages, Isa. 26:19 and Dan. 11:2-3. Because they are so late, they are the exceptions that prove the rule.

8. In the Psalms this was frequently lamented but never challenged; it was the just disposition of a righteous God who has authority over all the living and the dead.

9. A particularly poignant portrait of Sheol is the psalm of Hezekiah in Isa. 38.

It is truly remarkable that Israel continued with this rigorous belief for so long. It is one of the most admirable aspects of the Hebrew faith. The eternal God was worthy in and of God's self. Individual reward beyond death had nothing to do with it. The community had the responsibility and privilege to continue to praise God for his marvelous acts on behalf of his people *in this life*.

Perhaps the most telling aspect of Sheol for this particular chapter is the conception of God as entirely absent from the realm of Death and indifferent to those who dwell in it. This carried over into a concept of death as a contaminant, as something utterly unclean. In Mark 5:1-20, we are told that the Gerasene demoniac "lived among the tombs" as one cast out from human society. Therefore Jesus' victory over the man's "unclean spirit" is not only a miraculous healing and a victory over Satan; equally significant, it is an inaugural advance into the dreadful realm of Death.

Hades

In classical Greek, **Hades** was either the name of the god of the underworld (as in Homer's *Iliad*) or, more commonly, the dwelling place of the insubstantial dead (as in Hesiod and the *Odyssey*).[10] Significantly, Hades and Sheol are conflated in the New Testament; the Greek translation of the Hebrew Scriptures (Septuagint) uses the word *hades* to translate the Hebrew word *Sheol*. Therefore the one word, *hades*, comes to denote *both* the realm of the dead *and* the ruler of that realm in the New Testament. Sometimes it is imagined as a fortress barred with gates (Matt. 16:18), locked with a key that Christ has captured (Rev. 1:18). In Revelation 20:14, however, Death and Hades are personified. *Both* uses — Hades as realm, Hades as ruler — are valid for theological interpretation.

A crucial transition occurred in the apocryphal period between the two Testaments. The idea of Hades was expanded to mean not just the domain of the dead but also a place of punishment for the ungodly, thus taking on the character more familiar to us (and more feared) as the realm not so much of the *dead* as of the *damned*. Thus in familiar paintings such as Michelangelo's *Last Judgment*, it is clear that those on their way to hell are suffering the tortures of the damned.

It is easy for modern people to dismiss altogether this concept of hell as damnation, since our sense of accountability to God as our Judge has been

---

10. In Greek mythology, Hades was not only the ruler of the dread kingdom of the dead but also Ploutōn, god of wealth. The spouse of Hades was Persephone, the gentle goddess of springtime, who in turn was also the leader of the Furies. This sort of ambivalence, often found in ancient Mediterranean and Near Eastern mythology, finds no foothold in the Hebrew Scriptures.

weakened to the point of invisibility. However, it is important to grapple with this idea, if only because the symbolism of "hell" as the destination of the damned (understood metaphorically rather than literally) is a prominent motif in the New Testament. If this is ignored, our concept of God will be a pale imitation because it will lack any dimension of judgment.

Gehenna

Gehenna is the word closest to our English "hell." It is the Greek form of an Aramaic word, *gêhinnâm*.[11] By the time of Jesus, this word had taken on portentous significance, for it designated the consuming fire that would follow the Last Judgment. This is important because it shows how the imagery has moved into the realm of the cosmic. In the New Testament, the Greek terms *gehenna* and *hades* became associated concepts, with "Gehenna" being more closely identified with the eschatological "hell of fire" that would follow the final judgment (Matt. 5:22). The frequent use of "Gehenna" in Matthew and Mark carries this connotation. Jesus himself refers to it several times in unsparing terms. Warning the scribes and Pharisees, he calls them "sons of Gehenna" and says, "You serpents, you brood of vipers, how are you to escape being sentenced to Gehenna [translated 'hell']?" (Matt. 23:15, 33).[12]

These three concepts, while shading into one another at various points in the New Testament, remain difficult to pin down — but some familiarity with the background is necessary to understand what is meant by "hell."[13]

---

11. The development of the term is interesting, for it originally denoted an actual geographical location. The Hebrew form of the word, *gêhinnōm*, appears in English Old Testament translations as "the valley of the sons of Hinnom." This valley, located south of Jerusalem, is referred to several times in the Old Testament as an accursed place where child sacrifice had once been practiced. King Josiah deconsecrated it, "that no one might burn his son or his daughter as an offering to Molech" (II Kings 23:10). In a vivid passage in the book of Jeremiah, the prophet is called by God to go out to Topheth in "the valley of the son(s) of Hinnom" to declare it to be the place of God's coming judgment (Jer. 19:1-9; see also 7:30-34). *Topheth,* a "high place" erected for child sacrifice within the "Gehenna" valley (Jer. 7:31-32), was used as another synonym for hell in postbiblical preaching and in later literature as well, to carry forward the idea of judgment.

12. This kind of language occurs more often in the teaching of Jesus than many today realize or admit.

13. The matter is further complicated, or deepened, by the fact that there are other designations as well:

> *Abyssos,* the Greek word for "abyss," is used several times in Sirach to denote the underworld or place of the dead, and appears in the New Testament with more or less the same meaning (Luke 8:31; Rom. 10:7; Rev. 9:11; also 20:1, 3).
>
> *Abaddon,* a Hebrew word, appears several times in Job and Proverbs where it is syn-

The Rise of a Cosmology

We have seen that two central ideas were present in the use of the three principal biblical words. In the Old Testament, the predominant concept was Sheol, a domain where *all* the dead, without distinction, dwell in shadow without meaning. After the exile, however, with the rise of apocalyptic literature, this undifferentiated notion was overtaken by the new concept of a judgment after death and a final separation into eternal blessedness with God for the righteous and perdition in Gehenna for the wicked. During this period the concept of a ruling Enemy developed, who could be personified as Hades, Death, Beelzebul (the "prince of demons" in Mark 3:22), or Satan, among other names.[14] *This was the conceptual world into which Jesus of Nazareth was born and in which he was raised.*[15]

We have already begun to discuss the way that the apostle Paul under-

---

onymous with "Sheol." In the just-mentioned Rev. 9:11, however, Abaddon has become the name of "the angel of the bottomless pit [*abyssos*]; his name in Hebrew is Abaddon, and in Greek he is called Apollyon [Destroyer]." Like the word "Hades," "Abaddon" came to mean not only the underworld but also the *ruler* of the underworld.

Tartaros (more familiarly, the Latin *Tartarus*) is used in II Pet. 2:4 where it is synonymous with "Gehenna." In the *Iliad,* Tartaros is described as far below Hades. Later, in the development we have seen to be typical, Tartaros becomes a place of punishment for the wicked. It is used in this sense by later Greek poets as synonymous with Hades.

Zophos, meaning "darkness" or "gloom," is used to identify the place of punishment in II Pet. 2:4, 2:17, and Jude 6.

14. In the New Testament we find various designations: Satan, the devil, Beelzebul or Beelzebub (the Synoptic Gospels), Sin and Death (Paul), "the ruler of this world" (John 14:30), "the father of lies" (John 8:44), "the prince of the power of the air" (Eph. 2:2), and Hades (Rev. 20:14). In the plural, the demonic powers are Legion (Mark 5:9), "the elemental spirits of the universe" (Col. 2:8), and "the world rulers of this present darkness" (Eph. 6:12). The point is that, whatever the Enemy is called, there is a malign Power set against God.

15. In the Gospels, Jesus uses "Gehenna" and "Hades" more or less interchangeably, though "Gehenna" is more frequent. In his well-known promise to Peter that the gates of Hades shall not prevail against the church (Matt. 16:18), the translations have sometimes been perplexing. The RSV freely translates "the powers of death," which certainly puts across part of the point but does not incorporate the idea of punishment. The translators have been at pains to separate Jesus' use of "Gehenna" from that of "Hades." The NRSV renders Matt. 16:18 as "the gates of Hades," even though that version translates Gehenna as "hell." This seems overly finicky. In the story of the rich man and Lazarus, "Hades" is used to denote the realm where the rich man is "in torment." It seems to me that the terms "Gehenna" and "Hades" overlap in the teaching of Jesus in the Synoptic Gospels, as a suggestion of damnation and punishment is always present — contradicting the popular notion of Jesus as a teacher of perpetual gentle-

stands the Lordship of Christ within this cosmic framework. The identification of Gehenna with the final punishment of the wicked will lie behind our later discussion of the question: Is it really *final* condemnation, or only semifinal? Is it ultimate or penultimate?

New Testament Texts Related to the Descent into Hell
(I Peter 3:17-21 and Ephesians 4:8-10)

The most prominent passage dealing with our theme is I Peter 3:17-21, part of which we quote here: "For Christ . . . [was] put to death in the flesh but made alive in the spirit; in which he went and preached to the spirits in prison, who formerly did not obey, when God's patience waited in the days of Noah."[16]

The attention this passage has attracted has greatly enlarged its footprint. There is nothing specific here about the "lower world," but as we will see shortly, the passage about Christ preaching to "the spirits in prison, who formerly did not obey" was identified quite early as a description of the *descensus*.[17] Chapter 4 of the same epistle has been thought to contain a second reference to the event: "They [the disobedient] will give account to him who is ready to judge the living and the dead. For this is why the gospel was preached even to the dead, that though judged in the flesh like men, they might live in the spirit like God" (I Pet. 4:5-6).

Another biblical passage that seems to suggest a victory of Christ over the powers of the underworld is Ephesians 4:8-10:

> Therefore it is said, "When he ascended on high he made captivity itself a captive [KJV 'led captivity captive']; he gave gifts to his people" [Ps. 68:18]. (When it says, "He ascended," what does it mean but that he had

---

ness. It is Paul, the supposed firebrand, who never mentions hell and specifically surrounds his references to condemnation with the promise of cosmic justification.

In any case, I would argue that the word "Hades" should be translated "hell" in English in order to convey the full spectrum of consequences incurred by opposition to, or separation from, the purposes of God.

16. Later on in this chapter, we will return to this passage and the portions omitted here.

17. E. G. Selwyn's commentary on I Peter, written in England during the dark days of World War II, makes pastoral and theological use of I Pet. 3:17-21. His interpretation is too long to quote here in full, but like the rest of this wonderful commentary, it brims with love of the gospel and the church. He emphasizes the "universal range of Christ's work" and "the universality of His redemptive mission" when he is analyzing these two passages. See Selwyn, *The First Epistle of St. Peter* (London: Macmillan, 1964), especially under "The Relevance of I Peter 3:18ff. to Modern Times," 359-60.

also descended into the lower [*katoteros*] parts of the earth? He who descended is the same one who ascended far above all the heavens, so that he might fill all things.) (NRSV)

This Ephesians passage is debated, since "descent" into the "lower parts of the earth" could refer to the incarnation itself.[18] Assuming, however, that it refers to something more, at the very least it may mean simply that Christ, in death, "descended" to the realm of the dead. But what then about the reference to leading Captivity (it seems to be personified) captive? What is the link among the descent into *katoteros,* the capture of Captivity, and the ascension and session that pull together the whole train of thought?[19] It does not seem too much of a stretch to think of this verse as part of the testimony to Christ's plundering of Hades.[20] The best way to make sense of all this is to seek a fluid interpretation of these passages in which we can use all the various images.

3. Biblical Themes Related to the Descent

Our survey of these biblical words "Sheol," "Hades," and "Gehenna" suggests a number of overlapping themes that will help us to understand the descent of Jesus Christ into hell. As we shall see, the *descensus* functions most significantly for us today when it is understood in a proleptic, or anticipatory, way, but we need first to build on the foundation laid in Scripture and tradition. Let us identify several threads running through the Bible:

Confrontation with Death, the Partner of Hades

All mentions of Hades in the New Testament link it, or him (Hades personified as the ruler of the underworld), with Death, whether explicitly or

18. On this reading, it would mean that the "capturing of captivity" was achieved through the *kenosis* (emptying) of the Son as he came "down" to be born in human likeness, and by his subsequent session to the right hand of power (Phil. 2:7-11). But is the earth *per se* what is meant by *katoteros?* In the LXX this Greek word translates the Hebrew *tahtōn,* which is used in the Psalms to denote the realm of the dead (63:9; 86:13; 139:8; etc.). I don't see how we can have it both ways.

19. Selwyn goes so far as to say that this text shows that the *descensus* was already a doctrine fully accepted in the early church (*First Epistle of St. Peter,* 321).

20. Interpreters of the historical-critical persuasion largely reject this reading. I am working with a more expansive canonical method, including the history of interpretation.

implicitly.[21] When Jesus wrestles with Satan, therefore, he is also wrestling with Death. Like Hades, Death is conceived as an autonomous Power capable of imprisoning human souls without any hope of release.[22]

Death in the New Testament does not refer solely to extinction at the end of natural life, which was taken for granted (though not welcomed, to be sure) by the Hebrews of the Old Testament. In the New Testament, Death has become a hostile Power; therefore, to die is not simply to pass into Sheol, and certainly not to inherit immortality — Paul is explicit about that[23] — but is experienced as *condemnation and defeat at the hands of God's Enemy.* This is an apocalyptic idea that appeared in full strength during the intertestamental period and was an indispensable part of the symbolic world of Jesus of Nazareth and of the Epistles.[24] This understanding of Death as defeat by the great Enemy lies behind the strong reaction of Jesus at the tomb of Lazarus (John 11:33, 35, 38). It has little in common with the tenacious concept of death as a gentle passing into immortality.

21. Matt. 4:6; 16:18; Acts 2:24; Rom. 5:14; 6:9; 6:13; 7:24; II Tim. 1:10; Heb. 2:14-15; Rev. 1:18; 20:13; etc.

22. It should not be thought that the Enemy is absent from the Old Testament. "Job shares with the Psalms the false premise that . . . the world as it is — nature and history, including the fate of the individual — directly constitutes the work and the will of God. This is not the innermost meaning of the Bible. To be sure, it knows God's creation . . . and recognizes it as 'very good,' but it also knows about the Fall and the destruction that flowed from it. It [the Bible] knows even more than Job did about *the opposing power.* It expects the solution of the problem of God's justice to come from redemption by Christ; it expects it from God's and man's deed, which, following the example of Christ, make manifest the works of God through the struggle with evil and the enigma inherent in it" (Leonhard Ragaz, "God Himself Is the Answer," in *The Dimensions of Job: A Study and Selected Readings,* ed. Nahum Glatzer [New York: Schocken Books, 1969], 130-31, emphasis added).

23. Paul addresses this sharply when he writes that "flesh and blood cannot inherit the kingdom of God, nor does the perishable inherit the imperishable" (I Cor. 15:50). When Paul says, in Rom. 6:9, that "death no longer has dominion over him [Christ]," he is clearly envisioning Death as a Power with a realm, or domain.

24. The apostle Paul is explicit about the link between Sin and Death, understood as Powers. He mentions Satan less frequently but in those mentions he clearly assumes his presence and power. The devil as a devouring lion on the prowl in I Pet. 5:8 is described by Selwyn during World War II as "a graphic simile depicting the strength, ubiquity, and destructiveness of evil" (*First Epistle of St. Peter,* 237), which expresses "the fell and deliberate purpose of the malignant power of evil" (238). He compares the lion to the Gestapo (237).

Deliverance from Another Sphere of Power

In the symbolic universe of the New Testament, "hell" is a prison from which escape is impossible unless there is active deliverance from without. Jesus' teaching about this, while contained in the indirect form of a parable, could hardly be more clear: "If Satan has risen up against himself and is divided, he cannot stand, but is coming to an end. But no one can enter a strong man's house and plunder his goods, unless he first binds the strong man; then indeed he may plunder his house" (Mark 3:26-27).

The exorcisms related in the Synoptic Gospels illustrate this "binding of the strong man." It is no accident that the first public act of Jesus in Mark is an exorcism:

> And immediately there was in their synagogue a man with an unclean spirit; and he [the demon, not the man] cried out, "What have you to do with us, Jesus of Nazareth? Have you come to destroy us? I know who you are, the Holy One of God." But Jesus rebuked him, saying, "Be silent, and come out of him!" And the unclean spirit, convulsing him and crying with a loud voice, came out of him. And they were all amazed, so that they questioned among themselves, saying, "What is this? A new teaching! With authority he commands even the unclean spirits, and they obey him." (Mark 1:23-27)

Mark's message depends on our understanding that the demon is *separate from* the man he is tormenting, and that Jesus' authority over such demons derives from another realm that has never before appeared in full strength in the sphere of the flesh until the incarnation of the Son.

The Godlessness of Hell

The two passages from I Peter (quoted above) apparently refer to persons who were *disobedient* unbelievers. Indeed, they were the ones drowned for their godlessness "in the days of Noah." This would certainly have meant that they had suffered the wrath of God and had gone to the underworld. Whether hell is understood as a place of shadows like Sheol, the realm of Death like Hades, a place of tormented punishment like Gehenna, or *all of them blended together* (as they are in the New Testament), it is an abysmal realm.[25] We have

---

25. "In Jewish theology, death is thought of as a monarch, or even as a kingdom itself. So it may be that our Lord's obedience unto death (Philippians 2:8) is like an entrance into this

already seen that in Old Testament thought, the dead "go down" to Sheol where they have no faculties at all; they are not able even to praise God. For a pious Hebrew, there could be nothing worse. The author of Ephesians identifies this condition from a New Testament perspective — "strangers to the covenants of promise, *having no hope and without God*" (Eph. 2:12), a condition than which nothing more grim could be imagined.

Therefore the image of a descent into hell by the crucified Christ would mean that he entered the realm where *God was not.* One thinks immediately of the cry of dereliction. If Christ entered into Godforsakenness, and if hell is the absence of God, then something happened to him that was unprecedented. God was separated from God — while still remaining God.[26] In his idiosyncratic treatment of Holy Saturday, Hans Urs von Balthasar powerfully argues for the completeness of Christ's solidarity with us in Sin and Death.[27] In particular, he argues that the dead Christ sank into a pit of blackness so profound that no light of hope could reach it. That is to say, in the symbolic space between cross and resurrection, Christ was utterly cut off from his powers, from his Father, from any hope of redemption or victory, and that precisely in this *kenosis* (emptying) his solidarity with us and with our lot was complete. He suffered therefore what the book of Revelation calls the "second death" (Rev. 2:11; 20:6; 20:14; 21:8), as our substitute. Balthasar's picture of what Christ suffered is surely the most devastating depiction of hell that could possibly be. It presents some conceptual problems,[28] but in

---

realm, a kind of *descensus ad inferos.* This thought of death, which is in places almost personified as a demon power which enslaves humanity, is firmly embedded in the New Testament." Ralph P. Martin, *An Early Christian Confession: Philippians 2:5-11 in Recent Interpretations* (London: Tyndale, 1960), 31.

26. The metaphysical aspects of this have been much debated, and I am not qualified to evaluate that particular discussion. In no way do I mean to devalue the work of philosophical and systematic theologians, but as a preacher and pastor, I am working with images and suggestions from Scripture and the tradition, perhaps not always rationalistically worked out.

27. Hans Urs von Balthasar, chapter entitled "Going to the Dead: Holy Saturday," in *Mysterium Paschale: The Mystery of Easter* (San Francisco: Ignatius, 2000; orig. German ed., *Theologie der Drei Tage,* 1970). Balthasar understands Sin and Death somewhat as we do in this book — Powers experienced not only in their effects on individual human beings or even corporate entities, but also in their "bare reality" — their status as independent forces in business for themselves (to use Lance Morrow's phrase).

28. The question we would want to ask Balthasar is centered on the traditional alternative understanding of the *descensus* as Christ's aggressive invasion of the realm of Satan. This does not coexist easily with a concept of a dead Christ entirely robbed of his powers. It will be clear to readers that I favor the invading/binding/plundering imagery; however, I would argue that Balthasar offers an important counterweight, since we must always guard against any idea that

its insistence on the solidarity of Christ with us to the uttermost frontier of condemnation and annihilation, it is unparalleled.[29]

Condemnation: Provisional and Penultimate, or Ultimate and Final?

We have seen that "Gehenna" incorporates the idea of condemnation into the notion of hell. The apostle Paul never mentions hell; instead, he speaks of condemnation and the wrath of God, which amounts to the same thing but is more specifically related to Paul's focus on the righteousness of God powerfully overcoming Sin and delivering God's elect from condemnation (Rom. 8:1-2, 33-34). We will keep Paul's conception in view alongside that of the other New Testament books as we proceed, especially with regard to the identity of the elect and the finality (or not) of hell.

At several significant places in the New Testament, "hell" is specifically described as the realm where the ungodly (whether angelic or human) are kept in bondage *until* the Last Judgment (II Pet. 2:4, 9; Jude 6; I Cor. 5:5).[30] In other words, it is sometimes understood to be a *penultimate* state, as opposed to the ultimate "second death" of Revelation, also referred to as the "hell of fire" or the "eternal fire" (Matt. 25:41), which appears to *follow* the judgment. Is this to be understood literally or metaphorically? The metaphorical sense certainly predominates in Paul's case, but it is clear that he intends the wrath of God to be understood in a "real" sense, though entirely stripped of its fire-and-brimstone imagery. Also, the passages already examined from I Peter suggest that not even the dead are beyond the reach of the re-creating, revivifying Word. In Romans 11, with its powerful evocation of "life from the dead" in verse 15, Paul strongly hints at the redemptive activity of God *among unbelievers* even beyond the grave.

Jesus was not truly and completely dead, or that his solidarity with us in our powerlessness was not total. As in so much of Christian theology, we may profitably hold two seemingly contradictory motifs in creative, dialectical tension.

29. James F. Kay notes that the "mythopoetic theology" of Balthasar lends itself to a reimagination of Holy Saturday as a time of "prolonging and intensifying" Good Friday as the journey of Christ into the realm of godlessness ("He Descended into Hell," *Word and World* 31, no. 1 [Winter 2011]: 17-21).

30. Also, possibly I Thess. 2:16, "God's wrath has come upon them at last," or "until the end" *(eis telos)*. In I Cor. 5:5, the excommunication of the incestuous man is clearly *pen*ultimate.

4. The Descent in the Creed and the Tradition

There is certainly a sense in which the clause *descendit ad inferna* is an interpretation and extension of the preceding words in the Apostles' Creed, "dead and buried." Thus we can understand the descent as a commentary on what it meant for the only-begotten Son of the Father to be dead and buried. In the earliest days of creedal formulation and struggle against Gnostic spirituality, the word "buried" served to underscore the fact that Jesus had truly suffered death, not a mere semblance of it (see specifically I Cor. 15:4ff., where Paul insists upon the resurrection *from the dead*). As the proclamation of the faith unfolded during the early centuries, there were depths upon depths to be discovered. It is these depths that we inherit in the creedal clause.

A Hint of Liberation Theology in an Early Commentary

The theme of the descent into hell illustrates the vital importance of the history of interpretation in the church. The phrase *descendit ad inferna* appears incontrovertibly for the first time in the late-fourth- or early-fifth-century commentary on the Apostles' Creed by Rufinus.[31] In this illuminating reference, Rufinus specifically connects the creedal affirmation with the passage from I Peter 3:18-19 quoted above, with significant emphasis: "Whence and because Peter says: Christ, made dead in the flesh, made alive however in the spirit, in himself departed to those spirits who had been *confined in prison* to proclaim [to those who] had been unbelieving [or incredulous] in the days of Noah" (emphasis added).

A careful reading of this passage shows that Rufinus, in calling attention to the Petrine text, subtly enlarged it by adding a word in Latin to the original Greek, "the spirits in prison." Rufinus writes, *in carcere inclusi erant spiritibus,* meaning "those spirits who *had been confined* (or *shut up*) in prison." James F. Kay thinks his addition of the Latin word *inclusi* shows that he sought to underscore the motif of deliverance, or liberation, in the passage.[32]

The concept of the descent developed in the subapostolic period, along

---

31. Rufinus (c. 345-410) was a monk from Aquileia in northern Italy who traveled to Rome, Egypt, and the Holy Land. Rufinus's commentary on the Apostles' Creed is of great value because it gives us the earliest continuous text of the creed as it was used in Rome in the fourth century.

32. James F. Kay, "He Descended into Hell," in *Exploring and Proclaiming the Apostles' Creed,* ed. Roger Van Harn (Grand Rapids: Eerdmans, 2004), 120.

with a number of legends about the life of Christ. Yet, as John Calvin writes, "there is no one of the fathers who does not mention in his writings Christ's descent into hell, though their interpretations vary."[33] This is an important point. To give just one example from Cyril of Alexandria (d. 444): "When He shed His blood for us, Jesus Christ destroyed death and corruptibility. . . . For if He had not died for us, we should not have been saved, and if He had not gone down among the dead, death's cruel empire would never have been shattered."[34] Note how, in the phrase "death's cruel empire," various important concepts shade easily into one another: death as cruel, not benign; death as a ruling tyrant; death as a dominion; Death as a Power. Cyril does not refer simply to "the dead." A cosmology is in view here.

The Iconography of the Descent

Our subject was of intense pictorial interest during the early centuries of the Christian era, especially in Byzantine art. Frescoes, murals, and mosaics throughout Eastern Christendom depict the Lord as he storms the gates of hell.[35] In medieval England the motif came to be called "The Harrowing of Hell." In Old English, *herian* means "to harry, to make a war raid."[36] There is something thrilling about the image of a rampant Christ treading the padlocks of hell underfoot as he hauls the Old Testament patriarchs and matriarchs bodily out of the inferno by the might of his arm.[37] It is striking that

33. Calvin treats the descent in *Institutes of the Christian Religion* 2.16.8-12.

34. Quoted in J. N. D. Kelly, *Early Christian Doctrines* (New York: Harper and Row, 1959), 397-98.

35. One of the very greatest of these is in Istanbul, in the Church of the Holy Savior in Chora (also known as the Kariye Müzesi, or museum). Christ is shown in blazing white, striding triumphantly over the shattered gates of hell. When I was there in 1965, the archaeologist-antiquarian Stewart Perowne was our guide. "Sheer majesty and dominion!" he exclaimed.

36. *Oxford English Dictionary,* Old English *herian* (Middle English *herweng*, etc.). "Harrow: To harry, rob, spoil; also harrowing, the plundering or sacking (of a country), used especially in the phrase, to harrow hell, said of Christ." Here is a lovely nineteenth-century definition: "The harrowing of hell was *the triumphant expedition of Christ*" (Hensleigh Wedgwood, *Dictionary of English Etymology* [1859], emphasis added). This, it seems to me, is precisely the way for Christians to understand the references to God as a "man of war" in Exod. 15:3 and Isa. 42:13.

37. The great Renaissance artist Mantegna painted the theme several times. His pictures are generally titled "Christ Entering Limbo." The Roman Catholic Church in 2006 jettisoned the concept of Limbo as a place where unbaptized infants have a shadowy, unredeemed existence. This, however, is not the only way to understand Limbo. I am using it here in the sense of the *limbus patrum* (Limbo of the Fathers and Mothers) — referring to those who died before

Adam and Eve are often depicted as the first of those rescued; thus is the original sin reversed.

Are we then supposed to take the *descensus* literally, as though it could be pictured? Indeed, did the artists who depicted the harrowing of hell thousands of times in the Byzantine and medieval periods think they were painting an actual scene in the same sense as the scenes of the historical event of the crucifixion? That is an open question, but surely these painters were not so naïve as it would appear. They sought to depict *an idea* as much as a literal reality.[38] The idea was to penetrate the senses of the viewer with the divine significance and inner truth of the event.[39] Scenes of Christ's descent into hell and victory over the demonic Powers, at their best, summon us to think in terms of a dominion of evil that must be overcome by God if it is to be overcome at all. More, these images summon us to put our trust in this Lord of heaven and hell.[40]

Christ, yet wait for him to come as their deliverer. This concept leaves room, it seems to me, for a vision of the victorious Messiah overcoming the gates of hell on behalf of many who lie beyond the bounds of Christian fellowship as it is ordinarily understood, an idea strongly suggested in this chapter and the concluding one.

38. For that matter, ikons and other images of the crucifixion took on a mythic quality as well, so that the emphasis was not so much on what the scene might have actually looked like as what the ikon-writer hoped to convey of its meaning. Certainly no one thought that the cross was surrounded by gold leaf!

39. In fact, the ikon in the Orthodox Church is thought to convey the reality itself. I note this essential belief of Orthodoxy only in passing, since it is not within the scope of this brief discussion to do it justice.

40. In the early centuries, the baptism of Jesus was interpreted mythologically as a descent into the realm of Death and Satan. By his immersion, the waters are purified and the demons conquered. Thus the baptismal story is powerfully linked to the descent into hell (see Aloys Grillmeier, *Christ in Christian Tradition* [New York: Sheed and Ward, 1965], 79-80). There is strong biblical warrant for this interpretation in Rom. 6:1-11 where Paul affirms that the Christian is baptized not only into Christ's literal death but also into a "death unto sin." Thus Augustine: "The very sacraments of the holy Church show plainly enough that infants, even when fresh from the womb, are delivered from the bondage of the devil through the grace of Christ" (*On Original Sin* 45). A powerful carving of Jesus' baptism on the doors of the church of St. Maria im Kapitol in Cologne (c. 1050) depicts Christ coming up out of the water, still half-submerged, with the dove of the Spirit alight on his head and a demon prostrate in the water under his feet. Vigen Guroian powerfully describes this theme in liturgical art and the Armenian Rite of Epiphany. He quotes John Chrysostom: "For [Christ] being baptized and immersed, and then emerging, is a symbol of the descent into hell, and the return thence" ("O Death, Where Is Your Sting?" in *Sin, Death, and the Devil*, ed. Carl E. Braaten and Robert W. Jenson [Grand Rapids: Eerdmans, 2000], 122). Baptism itself is an exorcism; through the rite, the new Christian participates in the victory of Christ over the demonic Powers. It is perhaps

The Middle Ages: Thomas Aquinas and "Violent Necessity"

In his sermons on the Apostles' Creed, Thomas Aquinas gives four reasons for Christ's descent.[41] Two of them concern the rescue of the faithful dead. More significant for our purposes here is the way that Thomas makes use of *both* these major biblical conceptions: (1) Hades (Sheol) as the domain of death, and (2) Gehenna as the place of punishment and damnation. Thomas does not separate the two notions neatly. In this he follows the Scripture. Just as the biblical motifs concerning the crucifixion shade into one another, so do the motifs of hell in the New Testament; they are not kept in separate compartments. However, Thomas can also conceptualize the two in discrete ways, though he does not use the Greek terms. On Hades, he writes that Christ captured the devil in his own domain and assumed possession of his realm.[42] On Gehenna, Thomas writes that Christ descended "to shoulder the full punishment of sin, and so expiate all of its guilt."

Thomas shows how Christ in his descent found the way to be *both* an expiation for sin as "subjective weight" *and* the conqueror of the devil as "objective maleficence." Thomas further emphasizes that Christ actually "wished" *(voluit)* to undergo full participation in the fate of sinners, and therefore *not only* to die *but also* to descend into the place of condemnation and punishment — once again bringing both motifs to the fore.

Thomas also stresses that Christ's descent into hell was *voluntary.* He went "as a free man," whereas sinners went to the underworld "from necessity, and as if violently."[43] This mention of *violent necessity* accords well with the biblical proclamation of the wrath of God and, for that matter, with various sayings of Jesus in which he speaks of sinners being cast into outer darkness where men will weep and gnash their teeth. We should not shrink from these passages of Scripture. The violence implied in the casting out of sinners underscores the place of divine judgment in the story of salvation. The God who consigns human beings to condemnation is the same God who

---

not too much of a stretch to see this as one way of understanding the saying of Jesus in Matthew that he comes for immersion by John the Baptist "to fulfil all righteousness" (Matt. 3:15).

41. Nicholas R. Ayo, C.S.C., ed. and trans., *The Sermon-Conferences of St. Thomas Aquinas on the Apostles' Creed* (Eugene, Ore.: Wipf and Stock, 1988; previously published by University of Notre Dame Press), 77-85.

42. Here Thomas cites Phil. 2:10, "that at the name of Jesus every knee should bow, in heaven and on earth and under the earth."

43. Thomas Aquinas, in Ayo, *The Sermon-Conferences,* 79. (In this passage, as frequently elsewhere, Thomas separates body and soul in the fashion typical of his time, not realizing that the Hebrew tradition does not do this.)

gives himself up to a violent death to save those same human beings, "for God has consigned all men to disobedience, that he may have mercy upon all" (Rom. 11:32). We will return to this profound text more than once.

There is an important sense in which we must understand the love of God as "violence." To overcome the violence of the devil, God himself acts "violently" in assaulting Satan. Jesus' earthly ministry was aggressive; it was a declaration of war. Flannery O'Connor designed her stories with violence specifically to illustrate the invading action of God in delivering his children. It is not for nothing that she named one of her novels *The Violent Bear It Away*.[44] This "violence," however, has nothing in common with what we usually mean by violence, because it is begun, carried out, and completed in the love of God.[45]

Jesus' own language in the Gospels supports Thomas's interpretation of the descent as an act of aggression against the occupying Enemy. In Thomas's vivid portrayal, drawing upon John 12:31 and Matthew 12:29 (as well as Col. 2:15), the cross is the battlefield and the descent is the plundering of the devil's lair as the Lord binds Satan in his own house: "Consider that someone perfectly triumphs over another when they not only conquer them in the open field but also snatch from them the heart of their own kingdom . . . therefore, in order to triumph completely, Christ wanted also to capture the heart of the devil's kingdom, and to bind him in his own house, which was hell."[46]

The Reformation: John Calvin

John Calvin in his *Institutes* puts great stress on the descent. He acknowledges that it was not always in the creed, but insists that it is "of no small

44. The theological point is not weakened by O'Connor's reliance on the English translation of Matt. 11:12 in the Latin Vulgate. *Et violenti rapiunt illud* is rendered "the violent bear it away." Calvin writes, "It is necessary that Satan be violently driven out, in order that God may establish his kingdom among men" (Calvin, *Commentary on a Harmony of the Gospels*, trans. William Pringle, vol. 1 [Grand Rapids: Baker, 1984], on Matt. 12:28-29 and parallels). No one understood the motif of *grace as invasive power* more graphically than O'Connor. It is her consistent theme, perhaps most conspicuously in her story "Revelation," where it takes a book wrathfully flung at the head of Ruby Turpin, accompanied by an invasive insult from an exceedingly homely and unattractive young woman (named, not incidentally, Mary Grace) to shock Ruby out of her hitherto impregnable fortress of self-satisfaction. These sorts of episodes are found throughout her work.

45. Unfortunately, many have argued that this language of violence carries over into human affairs to justify Christian aggression and war, both in the past and in the present.

46. Thomas Aquinas, in Ayo, *The Sermon-Conferences,* 80-81.

moment in bringing about redemption . . . if it is left out, much of the benefit of Christ's death will be lost." He acknowledges that for some interpreters "hell" has meant, simply, "the grave," but with characteristic passion he argues that this not only goes against the logic of the creed's structure, but also robs the article of its key affirmation: *Christ suffered "a harsher and more difficult struggle than with common death."*[47]

As so many Christian thinkers in all ages have done, Calvin calls on Isaiah 53 ("He was wounded for our transgressions; he was bruised for our iniquities") to undergird his central conviction that although our sin and wickedness are fully deserving of God's eternal condemnation, the Suffering Servant has stepped into our place and endured this on our behalf. Christ bowed his head under the ultimate sentence in order to save us from it. For Calvin, then, the descent into hell took place on the cross.

We can also link the descent with Gethsemane. Calvin insists that Christ would not have asked his Father to save him from death, or even from torture. When he asks that the cup be taken from him, he is not praying to escape death; rather, "he prays not to be swallowed up by [death] as a sinner because he there bore our nature."[48]

The motif of substitution, or exchange, is obvious in the famous verses from Isaiah 53 (e.g., "the Lord has laid upon him the iniquity of us all"). Calvin underscores the theme with words like these: "Christ was put in place of evildoers as surety and pledge — submitting himself even as the accused — to bear and suffer all the punishments that they ought to have sustained." It would be a mistake, however, to think of Calvin as a one-note interpreter. The *Christus Victor* theme is usually associated with Luther, but notice how effortlessly Calvin mingles that theme with substitution and satisfaction: "If Christ had died only a bodily death, it would have been ineffectual. No — it was expedient at the same time for him to undergo the severity of God's vengeance to appease his wrath and satisfy his just judgment. For this reason, he must also grapple hand to hand with the armies of hell and the dread of everlasting death."[49]

This passage displays the sort of interpenetration of one theme with another that this book seeks to recommend. However, we must always allow for the need to rethink and reinterpret. In passages like this, Calvin does not sufficiently clarify his use of terms like "vengeance" and "satisfaction" in a Trinitarian context, and this approach has caused problems because it

---

47. Calvin, *Institutes of the Christian Religion* 2.16.8, 11.
48. Calvin, *Institutes of the Christian Religion* 2.16.11.
49. Calvin, *Institutes of the Christian Religion* 2.16.10.

sounds as if an innocent Son is suffering from his Father's separate, vengeful intentions. Perhaps Calvin should have foreseen the difficulties that these categories would cause in later generations, but no theologian can think centuries ahead of himself.

Calvin focuses on the cry of dereliction as the sign of the Lord's figurative descent into a hell that is a matter not only of being separated from God (as in Sheol) but, even more significantly, of experiencing the full force of the annihilating malediction (a theological extension of Gehenna) that must be pronounced against Sin. Here II Corinthians 5:21 finds its place: "[God] made him [Christ] to be sin." We should indeed tremble at this picture. It is vital to remember, however, that Calvin's concern throughout his work is pastoral. He wishes us to live free from anxiety and fear, knowing that Christ in his own body has shielded us from all harm.

The Twentieth Century: Karl Barth

Karl Barth interprets the descent in the same way Calvin does, only more so. He does not frequently refer specifically to the phrase in the creed, but in various places in his many works he expounds with tremendous energy and forcefulness the extremity of Christ's ordeal in Gethsemane and on the cross, which — like Calvin — he identifies as the descent into hell (understood as Gehenna, the destination for all who are accursed). At the same time, he avoids any suspicion of separating Father and Son. "God has made himself liable, at the point at which we are accursed and guilty. . . . This crucified man bears on Golgotha all that ought to be laid on us. . . . God comes in our place and takes our punishment upon himself."[50]

What Christ endured in his dereliction was truly and conclusively hell, beyond even the accumulated atrocities that humanity has experienced. We will never know this hell, because he has taken it from us by putting himself in our place. Barth has a keen sense of hell as the domain, or realm, of the Enemy, and he speaks of it often, as for instance in his commentary on the Heidelberg Catechism: "Sinful man falls into the power of Satan, into the hands of a *foreign* power."[51] In a striking phrase, he writes, "Man cannot go forward. He stands

---

50. Karl Barth, *Dogmatics in Outline* (New York: Harper Torchbooks, 1959), 118-19. Notice how Barth uses "God" interchangeably with "this crucified man." This is not a father doing terrible things to a son. God and Jesus are one.

51. Karl Barth, *Learning Jesus Christ through the Heidelberg Catechism* (Grand Rapids: Eerdmans, 1964), 31. Barth's lengthy interpretation of Gethsemane in the *Church Dogmatics*

under a *historical power* and can do nothing about it."[52] This underscores the activity of Satan, not exclusively on a mythological level, not only in individual lives, but on the world-historical scene. The theme of deliverance is prominent in such declarations. Barth, like Calvin, works easily with the *Christus Victor* theme and seamlessly interleaves it with his other material. In his section on the substitution theme, "The Judge Judged in Our Place," he presupposes the nature of Sin and Death as Powers that must be vanquished. Note the imagery of the divine violence that accords well with so much of what we have already seen concerning the descent: "The passion of Jesus Christ . . . has at its heart and center the victory which has been won for us, in our place, in the battle against Sin . . . it is the radical divine action which attacks and destroys at its very root the primary evil in the world."[53]

Barth depicts the struggle in Gethsemane as a preparation for entrance into hell. He writes further about what happened that night: "What shook [Jesus] was the coming concealment of the lordship of God under the lordship of evil and evil men. This was the terrible thing which he saw breaking on himself, on . . . God's own work, destroying everything."[54]

In a passage that conveys a powerful sense of Christ as conqueror, Barth writes that the Lord rose from his knees "in what we might almost call a supreme pride. . . . What Jesus did [in Gethsemane] is at its open core a radiant Yes to the actual will of God. This is not a withdrawal on the part of Jesus, but *a great and irresistible advance.*"[55] Barth is known for his focus on the theme of substitution, but he explicitly acknowledges the importance of the *Christus Victor* theme, which, it hardly needs to be repeated, is closely linked to the descent.[56]

Looking Ahead: Interpreting the Descent in "The Age of Genocide"[57]

One of the arguments of this chapter is that the terrible history of the twentieth century has made it imperative for Christian theology to expand and develop

---

evokes the struggle against Satan with remarkable, almost personal intensity (*Church Dogmatics* IV/1 [Edinburgh: T. & T. Clark, 1956], 264-73).

52. Karl Barth, *Learning Jesus Christ,* 37, emphasis added.

53. Karl Barth, *Church Dogmatics* IV/1, 247, 254. I have taken one liberty with these quotations, that of capitalizing "Sin." (Of course, it would have been capitalized anyway in German! I wonder if Barth might not have wanted this word capitalized in English, had he thought about it.)

54. Karl Barth, *Church Dogmatics* IV/1, 269-70.

55. Karl Barth, *Church Dogmatics* IV/1, 271, emphasis added.

56. Karl Barth, *Church Dogmatics* IV/1, 274.

57. Samantha Power's phrase.

the concept of hell so that it will stand up to the challenges of our genocidal times. Calvin's and Barth's powerful interpretations of the descent as the dereliction of Christ in Gethsemane and on the cross are extraordinary, and we will examine them further in the next chapter, but we need to go further. Barth seems to foresee this need as he shows signs of moving toward an understanding of hell not only as a symbolic representation of the judgment of God but also as the actual world-historical domain, or sphere, of the devil.

Nevertheless, there is a missing dimension in Barth's picture, and in the joyously personal Heidelberg Catechism of the Reformed tradition (1562) as well.[58] In his little commentary on this catechism, Barth specifically delimits the descent by concluding that Christ endured the pangs of hell "both on the cross *and before*" — it is striking that *"and after"* is missing.[59] Perhaps the medieval image of the harrowing of hell seemed too literal to the Reformers, too much bound up with the extrabiblical mythology of Limbo and Purgatory. An argument of this chapter is that in the twenty-first century we need to reclaim some of that imagery. We need to understand hell, not as a *place*, to be sure, but as a *domain* where evil has become the reigning reality — an *empire* of death, as Cyril called it.[60] Certainly Barth, in the Barmen Declaration against the Third Reich, showed himself to be thoroughly capable of standing up to demonic usurpation. In our era it has become essential for Christians to appropriate an apocalyptic scenario that takes full account of Satan's realm, Christ's invasion of it, and the calling of God's people to resist it in his name. A sense of the principalities and powers is necessary for discerning what the Enemy is up to.[61]

Some Preliminary Conclusions

We have looked at the biblical texts and the biblical motifs that bear on the descent into hell, and briefly at the history of its interpretation. We must take great care lest we leave the impression that Christ's work was not finished

---

58. The Heidelberg Catechism should be better known. It arose out of the Calvinist wing of the Reformation but has been described as having the intimacy of Luther, the charity of Melanchthon, and the fire of Calvin.

59. Karl Barth, *Learning Jesus Christ,* 71. This quibble about Barth's commentary on the catechism should not deter anyone from reading this exquisite little book, one of Barth's most accessible writings, ideal for personal devotion.

60. Quoted in Kelly, *Early Christian Doctrines,* 397-98.

61. A sense of black humor helps, also. Luther famously said that the devil cannot bear to be laughed at. C. S. Lewis's *Screwtape Letters* is still without peer in its humorous, yet penetrating, depiction of the machinations of Satan.

(*tetelestai,* John 19:30) on the cross. In discussing the descent, we do not want to suggest that Jesus died with more work still ahead of him. Following the traditions, we may understand the descent in either of two ways, not necessarily exclusive of one another, recognizing that each of them affirms a work completed:

- The descent into hell is a symbolic narrative affirming what happened on the *cross.*
- Christ's overthrow of the Powers of hell is the inaugural event of the *resurrection,* the first act of the One who has conquered Death.

Kay points toward a combination of these two when he writes that "the descent into hell can also be read as an interpretation of what it means to confess that Jesus Christ rose from the dead."[62]

What was going on in the life of God between Good Friday and Easter? We are not permitted to look into this mystery. Our responses to it will be more in the realm of poetry than of science. We will find something of the truth by maneuvering between, on the one hand, Balthasar's Holy Saturday picture of Christ utterly given over to Death in solidarity with all humanity, as powerless in the tomb as though he were in Sheol, and on the other hand, the image of the rampant Conqueror invading the realm of the "strong man," destroying him utterly and plundering his goods. In either case, and in various combinations and permutations thereof, the creedal confession of Christ's descent will give us a foundation from which to approach the ever-recurring problem of evil. We are required to ask, at this point, what is meant by a reign of Death and a domain called hell. The next section addresses that painful question, which has often been identified as the most difficult in Christian theology.

5. The Origin of Evil

How many writers of fiction have dared to approach the terrible mystery of the origin of evil? They have had better sense than to try.[63] Philosophers and theologians, however, have debated it endlessly. We will take a brief look at

---

62. Kay, "He Descended into Hell," *Word and World,* 21 n. 10.

63. Take, for instance, two masterworks concerning monstrous evil, Herman Melville's *Moby Dick* and Cormac McCarthy's *Blood Meridian.* The mystery of evil dominates both, yet the writers attempt no explanation, leaving the question open, like the gaping wound of Amfortas in Wagner's *Parsifal.*

the debate shortly, but the position taken in this book at the outset is that *there has never been a satisfactory account of the origin of evil, and there will be none on this side of the consummation of the kingdom of God. Evil is a vast excrescence, a monstrous contradiction that cannot be explained but can only be denounced and resisted wherever it appears.*[64]

The Serpent in Genesis

The Bible, significantly, does not attempt an explanation. Scriptural metaphors, parables, narratives, and figures of speech give us hints, but no more. The story of the Fall in Genesis does not tell us how the serpent got into the Garden of Eden.[65] Though its meaning remains elusive, the narrative

64. This position is sharply to be distinguished from the view of process theologians and others that evil arises out of creation and "the risk of freedom." That concept is an attempt to make evil serve the good, a position that we emphatically reject in this chapter. Furthermore, it makes God the author of evil, which, as we will shortly see, the tradition rejects. Finally, it suggests that the "freedom" to choose evil is somehow an authentic freedom. It is precisely that view that the story of Adam and Eve rejects. It is that view that Augustine rejects. These, I suggest, are examples of what Christopher Morse calls "faithful disbeliefs."

65. It is here assumed that the story of the Fall is a myth — that is, it tells the truth in narrative terms, not propositional or literally historical terms. Thus Paul Ricoeur explains, "We must keep the idea of event as *a symbol of the break between two ontological regimes* and abandon the idea of *past fact.* . . . The story of the fall has the greatness of myth" (*The Symbolism of Evil* [New York: Harper and Row, 1967], 235 n. 1, and 236, emphasis added). This "break," surely, is what Paul has in mind in Rom. 5 when he draws upon the story of Adam to interpret what Christ has accomplished. No one has explained the way that the myth of the Fall works better than Ricoeur.

> The serpent represents the following situation: in the historical experience of man, every individual finds evil already there; nobody begins it absolutely. If Adam is not the first man, in the naïvely temporal sense of the word, but the typical man, he can symbolize both the experience of the "beginning" of humanity with each individual and the experience of the "succession" of men . . . [which is definitively drawn by Paul in Rom. 5].

> The serpent . . . represents the aspect of evil that could not be absorbed into the responsible freedom of man. . . . The Jews themselves, though they were well armed against demonology by their intransigent monotheism, were constrained by truth . . . to concede something . . . to the great dualisms which they were to discover after the Exile [hence the rise of apocalyptic]. . . . Of course, Satan will never be another god; the Jews will always remember that the serpent is a part of the creation; but at least the symbol of Satan allowed them to balance the movement toward the concentration of evil in man by a second movement which attributed its origin to a prehuman, demonic reality. (Ricoeur, 257-58)

with all its subtlety has commanded respect throughout the centuries. In shaping the story, the Yahwist[66] made use of certain elements in Canaanite mythology, where the snake represented all that was sinister and uncanny among the animals. The Yahwist retains this mythological character of the snake, but affirms that it was *a mere creature under the sovereignty of God.*[67] This revolutionary insight proved valuable later in the tradition.

Claus Westermann well sums up the contradictions in Genesis 2–3: "God himself has created the being which leads man to disobedience. *The force of this paradox must not be weakened.* 'The defection . . . remains something utterly inexplicable amidst all the good that God has created. *It must be left as a riddle.*' The narrator also wants to say that *it is not possible to come to terms with the origin of evil.*"[68]

The striking thing about the role of the serpent in Genesis — compared to the various demonologies of the Near East — is that in itself the serpent is "natural, insignificant, demythologized."[69] It is a creature; unlike God, it has no creative powers. It is not even described as evil, only as shrewd. Given the inexplicable presence of the serpent, the narrative nevertheless places the responsibility upon Adam and Eve as much as possible; the focus is not on the serpent, but on the revolt of humanity against God.[70]

However — and this is of first importance for understanding the apocalyptic framework of the New Testament — the serpent is uncanny, and its mysterious capacity for insinuation seems to suggest a nihilistic presence within the creation that eludes explanation and can only be resisted. A breathtaking insight into this is given by Derek Kidner in his commentary on Genesis when he writes that the New Testament "unmasks" the figure of Satan standing behind the serpent.[71]

---

66. The widely accepted name for the unknown author of Gen. 2–3.

67. Brevard Childs, *Myth and Reality in the Old Testament,* 2nd ed., Studies in Biblical Theology 27 (London: SCM, 1962), 49.

68. Claus Westermann, *Creation* (Philadelphia: Fortress, 1974), 92, emphasis added; the interior quotation is of Walther Zimmerli.

69. Nahum Sarna, *Understanding Genesis: The Heritage of Biblical Israel* (New York: Schocken Books, 1970), 26.

70. Gerhard von Rad, *Genesis,* rev. ed., Old Testament Library (Philadelphia: Westminster, 1972), 87, 92-93. Von Rad was an Old Testament scholar whose strong theological bent makes him still exciting and helpful today for preachers and teachers of the Bible. He argues that the serpent story is not there to explain anything about origins, but has a much more important purpose: it sets forth the basic struggle that we all have with evil. "The narrator is obviously anxious to shift the responsibility as little as possible from man. It is only a question of man and *his* guilt."

71. Derek Kidner, *Genesis: An Introduction and Commentary,* Tyndale Old Testament Commentaries, vol. 1 (Downers Grove, Ill.: InterVarsity, 1967), 71.

The Figure of Lucifer

Elrond, the wise Elf-lord in J. R. R. Tolkien's *Lord of the Rings,* says, "Nothing is evil in the beginning. Even Sauron [the satanic figure in the story] was not so." Tolkien's remarkably well-thought-through concept of evil in his saga is parallel to the idea that grew up in the Christian tradition of the devil as an angel who rebelled and was consequently thrown down from heaven. This entity later came to be called Lucifer, after the hint in Isaiah 14:12: "How art thou fallen from heaven, O Lucifer, son of the morning!" (KJV).[72]

In Elrond's saying, Tolkien has preserved the concept of the fallen angel.[73] In ancient biblical interpretation, the imagery of Lucifer was readily brought into conjunction with Luke 10:18, where Jesus says, "I saw Satan fall like lightning from heaven." This inspired conflation of Satan with Lucifer is very early, going back at least to Origen (c. 185–c. 254).[74] Like the imagery of the serpent, the tradition of Lucifer is useful because it strengthens the conviction that evil must be kept separate from God, while at the same time it affirms that the devil was originally created by God and therefore can never be entirely independent, let alone coequal.[75] This paradox must be

72. The Hebrew word is *helel ben-shahar,* "bright son of the morning" or "son of dawn." In the LXX it is *heosphoros,* "dawn-bringer." This became *lucifer* (light-bearer) in the Latin Vulgate. The King James Version followed the Vulgate in the translation quoted here, an English phrasing with its own history. This is a good example of the indispensability of the KJV in the history of the English language and of theological reflection in English. Note that Satan, in this rendering, becomes a hideous parody of the One who truly is the light of the eschatological dawn. Christ is so identified in one of the "Great O" antiphons of Advent: "O come, thou Dayspring from on high . . . ," following Luke 1:78 — "the dayspring from on high hath visited us" (KJV).

73. Tolkien's letters show that he spent a lifetime thinking through the problem of evil. His conception is remarkably knowledgeable and subtle. When Elrond says, "Nothing is evil in the beginning," this reflects the orthodox consensus that the creation was entirely good.

74. Origen also quite brilliantly adduced the prince of Tyre in Ezek. 28:12-19 to create a complete and satisfying picture of Satan as a fallen angel. Jeffrey Burton Russell, *Satan: The Early Christian Tradition* (Ithaca, N.Y.: Cornell University Press, 1981), 130.

75. Gregory of Nyssa (c. 334–c. 395) writes: "Now that angelic power who begot envy in himself by turning from the good developed an inclination toward evil. When this had once happened, he was like a rock breaking off from a mountain ridge and hurled headlong by its own weight. Divorced from his natural affinity with the good, he became prone to evil; and as if by a weight he was spontaneously impelled and carried to the final limit of iniquity. . . . Cunningly he cheats and deceives man by persuading him to become his own murderer and assassin" ("An Address on Religious Instruction," in *Christology of the Later Fathers,* ed. Edward Rochie Hardy and Cyril C. Richardson, Library of Christian Classics, vol. 3 [Philadelphia: Westminster, 1954], 280).

Calvin struggles with this challenging imagery by affirming that whereas God created the devil, his malice does not come from his *created* nature but from "his perversion" of it, his "revolt and fall. . . . By degeneration they [the fallen angels] ruined themselves and became the

maintained: we have an Enemy whose wickedness, while neither created nor intended by the Creator, is nevertheless under his ultimate, sovereign authority.[76]

Neither the serpent story nor the imagery of Lucifer explains how the emergence of such an evil could have been permitted by the Creator. Nevertheless, both teach — through imagery and narrative — that *evil was not part of the creation that was pronounced good by God.*[77]

Numerous internal contradictions within the Bible make it impossible to speak of any one biblical "answer" to these problems. We are not left with nothing to say, however. In classical Christianity, some affirmations have been made repeatedly throughout the history of tradition, so that they carry a certain authoritative weight. To these we now turn.

6. The Nature of Evil

The Classic Definition: Evil as the Absence of Good

Augustine is generally considered to be the seminal promoter of the idea that evil is nonbeing. Evil lacks existence. Evil is therefore the negation of being.[78]

---

instruments of ruin for others" (*Institutes* 1.14.16). None of this imaginative language stands up to strict analytical scrutiny. It is full of paradox and mystery.

76. Reinhold Niebuhr comments succinctly, "To believe that there is a devil is to believe that there is a principle or force of evil antecedent to any human action. Before man fell, the devil fell" (*The Nature and Destiny of Man: A Christian Interpretation,* 2nd ed., 2 vols. [New York: Scribner, 1964], 1:180).

77. Some biblical texts seem to contradict the fundamental affirmation that God did not create evil. A passage in Isaiah is sometimes quoted:

I am the Lord, and there is no other,
  besides me there is no God;
  I gird you, though you do not know me,
that men may know, from the rising of the sun
  and from the west, that there is none besides me;
  I am the Lord, and there is no other.
I form light and create darkness,
  I make weal and create woe,
  I am the Lord, who do all these things. (Isa. 45:5-7)

This passage seems to say that God "creates woe." The chief function of this text, however, is to declare the comprehensive singularity of the God of Israel. Many interpreters have agreed that it was a great mistake to wrench the rhetorical Hebraic contrasts into unyielding metaphysical principles.

78. Among the Greek Fathers, Gregory of Nyssa makes the point well: "All wickedness

This is where we begin. As David B. Hart writes, "High among Christian tradition's most venerable and most indispensable metaphysical commitments is the definition of evil as a *steresis agathou* [Greek] or *privatio boni* [Latin], a privation of the good, a purely parasitic corruption of created reality."[79] This concept of *privatio boni* is indispensable because, bluntly stated, it fences off any thought that God is somehow responsible for evil. God is perfect Being; therefore he cannot create Nonbeing.

It is difficult, however, to put this foundational dogma to work. Sometimes one hears Christians with superficial theological training tossing off airy statements like "Evil is the absence of good" without recognizing that this seems to deny the power and agency of evil.[80] How can an *absence* be *present and active* in the world? Augustine's intent was to hold these two concepts together. In the words of a secular literary critic who teaches the *Confessions* regularly in a major university, Augustine "comes closer than any writer in the Christian tradition to *expressing the subjective horror of evil while denying it objective reality.*"[81]

Paul Ricoeur is aware of the difficulty inherent in calling evil the absence of good. He addresses this by writing that "evil is not nothing; it is not a simple lack, a simple absence of order; it is the power of darkness; it is posited; in this sense it is something to be 'taken away': *I am the Lamb of God who takes away the sin of the world.*"[82] Evil lacks existence, but it is *not nothing.*[83] The theologian and ethicist Paul L. Lehmann, who was given to

---

is marked by the absence of good [*steresis agathou*]. It does not exist in its own right, nor is it observed to have subsistence. . . . Nonbeing has no subsistence; and the Creator of what exists is not the Creator of what has no subsistence. The God, therefore, of what exists is not responsible for evil, since he is not the author of what has no existence" ("Address on Religious Instruction," 282). Gregory compares evil to blindness, which is a privation of light.

79. David B. Hart, *The Doors of the Sea: Where Was God in the Tsunami?* (Grand Rapids: Eerdmans, 2005), 72-73.

80. Augustine's concept of *privatio boni* is, of course, much more subtle than it sounds on its face. His concern is not to minimize the harm done by evil, but to deny it true created existence. He contrasts *substance* and *accidents:* "A wound or disease is not a *substance,* but a *defect* in the fleshly substance — the flesh being a *substance,* and therefore something *good,* of which those *evils* — that is, privations of the good which we call health — are *accidents*" (*Enchiridion* 11, emphasis added).

81. Andrew Delbanco, *The Death of Satan: How Americans Have Lost the Sense of Evil* (New York: Farrar, Straus and Giroux, 1995), 48, emphasis added.

82. Ricoeur, *The Symbolism of Evil,* 155.

83. The extraordinary difficulty of speaking in this way is clearly described by the East German scholar Wolf Krötke, who knew a thing or two about evil, having been imprisoned capriciously by the fearsome Stasi during the Cold War for the "crime" of "circulating propaganda dangerous to the state." I find Krötke's observations very helpful, because I have had difficulty

idiomatic outbursts in the midst of the most abstruse conceptual lectures, once responded to a challenger, "I don't know what the ontological status of evil is, but it ain't peanuts." Lehmann knew more than any of his students attending that lecture what the tradition said concerning the ontological status of evil as nonbeing. What he wanted to register was the manifest imprint of its ferocity in human life.

Jeffrey Burton Russell makes a helpful distinction between *absolute* nonbeing and *limited* nonbeing.[84] If we take the classical definition of evil as *privatio boni* to mean absolute nonbeing, that would make evil into a coequal principle over against God: Ultimate Being versus Ultimate Nonbeing. Resistance to this notion separated the apostolic faith from systems like Manichaeism and some forms of Gnosticism. Consequently, it may be preferable to think of evil as having *limited* nonbeing — it does not and cannot participate in "real" Being (God), but its presence and power in the world are not illusory; it "ain't peanuts."[85] Another way of understanding *privatio boni* is offered by Russell as he comments upon the apocalyptic sections of the Bible:

---

finding a way out of this impasse. In his extended study of Karl Barth's colossal struggle with the concept of nothingness *(das Nichtige)* in the *Church Dogmatics* (III/3 [Edinburgh: T. & T. Clark, 1960], 289-368), Krötke writes that the appearance of *das Nichtige* in the creation "has nothing to do in any way whatsoever with the coming into being of creation. And yet Barth has no other categories at his disposal with which to describe the . . . state of affairs. He thus describes nothingness with creaturely categories even though it does not belong to creaturely reality and may not be understood in analogy to it" (*Sin and Nothingness in the Theology of Karl Barth*, trans. Philip G. Ziegler and Christina-Maria Bammel, Studies in Reformed Theology and History [Princeton: Princeton Theological Seminary, 2005], 29). In this matter of evil, we must work within this paradox of being and nonbeing. (I am grateful to Philip G. Ziegler for introducing me to Krötke.)

84. Russell, *Satan*, 187. He is following Josef Huhn (translating from the German).

85. Hannah Arendt's famous phrase "the banality of evil" has been much debated. In a letter to Gershom Scholem, she wrote: "Evil possesses neither depth nor any demonic dimension. It can overgrow and lay waste the whole world precisely because it spreads like a fungus on the surface" (quoted by Daphne Merkin, in the *New York Times Book Review*, October 21, 2007). This is partly right and partly not. She is quite right to say that evil is a parasite with no proper created existence of its own. But she is wrong, I believe, to indicate that there is no "demonic dimension." Perhaps Arendt wished to guard against a perverse glamorization of evil, a very real and recurring phenomenon (witness the popularity of mobsters in popular culture). Her concept of "the banality of evil" was defended by cultural critic Judith Shulevitz, who argued that Arendt did not mean that evil itself was banal; but rather, that "Eichmann had too shallow a soul to grasp the enormity of his evil" ("There's Something Wrong with Evil," *New York Times Magazine*, October 6, 2002). Does this mean that the very large number (the majority, it seems) of people who willfully refuse to look at or reflect upon the great evils of our time are shallow of soul in this way? If so, the Christian community needs to be more intentional about its calling to resist Satan (I Pet. 5:8-9).

The solution proposed by apocalyptic and Christian literature is dualist. At the end of the world, evil will be negated. Now, since no part of the divine can be negated, it follows that evil is not part of the divine nature. And as the divine nature is ultimately that which is, evil has no real being of its own. Evil exists in the cosmos like holes in a Swiss cheese; the holes are there, but they are there only as noncheese and have no existence apart from the cheese. As one cannot eat a cheese and discard the holes into a box, one cannot remove good and put evil into another category.... These later theological assumptions are not explicit in the apocalyptic literature, but they are implicitly present.[86]

The definition of evil as *privatio boni* does indeed have indispensable importance metaphysically and doctrinally, but rhetorically it sounds like an abstraction. It has no shock value. We may be helped in grasping the concept, not by thinking of Swiss cheese, but by imagining an earthly hell like that of the Nazi death camps. These places were *realms,* in a real sense; they were kingdoms of evil. The intent was deliberately, purposefully, and systematically to exclude goodness. The purpose was not only extermination but a most thorough and radical negation of the humanity of millions of people. Perhaps, if we can imagine this, we can sense the pure hellishness of *privatio boni* — the absence of good.[87]

The notion of absence is particularly difficult to envision when there is so much fascination with the demonic. Often the evil figure in books and films gets more respect than the leading characters. Popular culture puts out an endless stream of satanic characters; actors vie to play these parts and even win Oscars for them.[88] In high culture, there is no more glamorous, even sexy Satan than Milton's in *Paradise Lost.* An important counterweight to this sense of the devil as an alluring *presence* is the view of Simone Weil, who wrote, "Imaginary evil is romantic and varied; real evil is gloomy,

86. Jeffrey Burton Russell, *The Devil: Perceptions of Evil from Antiquity to Primitive Christianity* (Ithaca, N.Y.: Cornell University Press, 1977), 205.

87. Toward the end of *The Reader,* a film about postwar Germany, a Holocaust survivor in New York City takes the measure of Michael Berg, a visiting German lawyer in search of absolution. She instructs Berg never to ask the question, "What did you learn in the camps?" because, she says, the camps were neither a form of therapy nor a university of learning. She continues, with asperity, "If you want catharsis, go to the theatre. Nothing came out of the camps. *Nothing.*" (The screenwriter for *The Reader* was David Hare, the esteemed playwright. In my opinion this line was the best thing in the movie, which, taken as a whole, seemed to me ethically muddled, suggesting redemption where there was no source for it.)

88. E.g., Heath Ledger as the Joker in *The Dark Knight,* Christoph Waltz as the SS officer in *Inglourious Basterds.*

monotonous, barren, boring."[89] Russell, commenting upon Dante's *Divine Comedy,* offers this insight into the *privatio boni:*

> Some critics have suggested that Dante simply failed to produce as impressive a Devil as Milton later did, but this explanation misses his point. Dante specifically intended Lucifer to be empty, foolish, and contemptible, a futile contrast to God's energy. Dante viewed evil as negation and would have thought Milton's Devil much too active and effective. . . . [Dante agrees with] scholastic theology in limiting the Devil's role. . . . The lack of dramatic action on the part of Dante's Lucifer is a deliberate statement about his essential lack of being. Satan's true being is *his lack of being, his futility and nothingness.* There he is in the dark at the very dead center of the earth, where sins have sunk to their proper place.[90]

The idea of the demonic as an absence rather than a presence has ethical consequences. Primo Levi, an Italian Jew recognized as one of the most profound writers among Holocaust survivors, casts the idea of evil as nonbeing in a specifically ethical context when he writes: "What had happened [in the Shoah] was irrevocable. Never again could it be cleansed; it would prove that man, the human species — we, in short — had the potential to construct an infinite enormity of pain, and that pain is the only force *created from nothing,* without cost and without effort. It is enough not to see, not to listen, not to act."[91]

The critic Clive James, in a penetrating article about Primo Levi's work, wrote, "There are some episodes of history so evil that they aren't even of any use in defining the good; they are simply *a dead loss.*"[92] A dead loss: this suggests deeper implications for *privatio boni* and its related concept, evil as nonbeing. Evil is not "nothing" in the sense that we use that word in colloquial speech, as though someone commiserates with us about an injury and we say, "It's nothing." Jonathan Edwards caught something of the

89. Simone Weil, *Gravity and Grace* (Lincoln: University of Nebraska Press, 1952), 120.

90. Jeffrey Burton Russell, *Lucifer: The Devil in the Middle Ages* (Ithaca, N.Y.: Cornell University Press, 1984), 225, emphasis added. In *Perelandra,* the second novel in his space trilogy, C. S. Lewis comes close to success in portraying the obscene, vulgar stupidity of evil. There is nothing magnetic or attractive in his devil; indeed, the reader experiences magnetic repulsion. Lewis's descriptions of the devil are memorable in this regard.

91. Primo Levi, *The Drowned and the Saved* (New York: Vintage Books, 1988), 86, emphasis added.

92. Clive James, quoting Jacob Burckhardt, "Writing about Tamburlaine," *New Yorker,* May 23, 1988, emphasis added.

palpable force of "nonbeing" as "dead loss" when he said that to be without "the beauty of the Godhead" would be "an infinite evil: without which, we ourselves had better never have been; and without which there had better have been no being."[93]

What the Tradition Affirms and Rejects

When we consider the orthodox Christian tradition as a whole (differentiating it from the various forms of Gnosticism ancient and modern), we are able to list these statements, which form a consensus within the great tradition:

- God did not create and does not intend evil.[94]
- Evil is not a component of God's being.[95]
- Although evil made its appearance in the creation, it possesses no existence or being of its own, but is rather a negation, or corruption, of being.
- God is not powerless against evil, but for some reason inaccessible to us, he permits it to operate within appointed bounds.[96]
- God is actively at work through human agents to challenge and resist evil, so that any penultimate victory over evil in this world is a sign of God's ultimate victory.
- Evil will be conclusively and finally defeated and obliterated by God in the final judgment.

93. Jonathan Edwards, *Treatise on the Religious Affections,* quoted in Delbanco, *The Death of Satan,* 87.

94. "The etiological myth of Adam is the most extreme attempt to separate the origin of evil from the origin of the good; its intention is to set up a radical origin of evil distinct from the more primordial origin of the goodness of things . . . its function is to posit a 'beginning' of evil distinct from the 'beginning' of creation, to posit an event by which sin entered into the world. . . . The myth of the fall is thus the myth of the first appearance of evil in a creation already completed and good . . . the myth [thus] tends to satisfy the two-fold confession of the Jewish believer, who acknowledges, on the one hand, the absolute perfection of God and, on the other hand, the radical wickedness of man." Ricoeur, *The Symbolism of Evil,* 233, 243.

95. It will be readily apparent that this is a case requiring "faithful disbelief" (Christopher Morse). Neither Scripture nor tradition supports any proposals similar to that of Carl Jung, who conceived of God as a yin-yang composite of light and dark (contrast I John 1:5; James 1:17).

96. Here I take the position (*contra* Calvin) that we must distinguish between God's intentional will and God's permissive will.

Having said all this, we are still faced with the difficulty of describing evil as nonbeing; it seems to lack force and malignity. How are we to proceed?

7. Does the "Argument from Evil" Disprove or Discredit God?

Various Accounts and Their Inadequacy

A specific formulation called "the argument from evil" has occupied philosophers since the time of the great eighteenth-century Scottish philosopher David Hume. More recently, J. L. Mackie's celebrated 1955 essay, "Evil and the Problem of Omnipotence," has become so well known that many people who have no knowledge of philosophy have absorbed a simplified form of this argument. One hears versions of it on every hand.[97] Whenever there is a disaster, particularly a natural disaster killing thousands, such as the Indian Ocean tsunami of 2004, indignant voices are heard proclaiming that — at last! — the nonexistence of God has been conclusively demonstrated.

Most people know Mackie's argument in its simplest form: if there is a God, he would not permit evil.[98] But as David B. Hart writes, "there is no argument here to refute," because God is by definition beyond any categories that mere creatures can assign to him.[99] The more salient question is about the *goodness* of God. Thus Mackie's argument has taken another form in the popular imagination:

---

97. J. L. Mackie, "Evil and the Problem of Omnipotence," in *The Problem of Evil,* ed. Marilyn McCord Adams and Robert Merrihew Adams (Oxford: Oxford University Press, 1990), 25-37.

98. Mackie's argument follows these lines:

God is said to be omniscient, omnipotent, and omnibenevolent (all-knowing, all-powerful, and all-good).

He would therefore know what sort of world is best.

He would have the power to create this best of all possible worlds.

Being omnibenevolent, he would create such a world.

But he has not done so, as can be readily seen from the existence of evils.

Therefore God does not exist.

99. The entire passage, in Hart's typical take-no-prisoners style, reads: "There is no argument here to refute; the entire case is premised upon an inane anthropomorphism — abstracted from any living system of belief — that reduces God to a finite ethical agent . . . whose purposes are measurable upon the same scale as ours, and whose ultimate ends for his creatures do not transcend the cosmos as we perceive it. This is not to say that it is an argument without considerable emotional and even moral force; but of logical force there is none" (*Doors of the Sea,* 13).

- If God is both good and powerful, he would not permit evil.
- Therefore he is either powerful but not good, or good but not powerful.

A refinement of Mackie's "argument from evil" was proposed by Nelson Pike, who saw that a perfectly good God who was capable of eliminating evil might not do so if God had a "morally sufficient reason."[100] This proved difficult to defend because there has been no agreement as to what a morally sufficient reason for horrific evil might be. Theologian John R. Schneider, in his essay "Seeing God Where the Wild Things Are," argues that even philosophers such as Alvin Plantinga and John Hick, whose treatments of the problem of evil have become famous, contradict themselves by admitting, at least tacitly, that there are some evils — like the Holocaust — which admit of no explanation and for which there can be no morally sufficient reason. Plantinga and Hick put forth their proposals believing that they are epistemically defensible, but apparently not, in the last analysis, adequate to account for the worst horrors.[101] Many philosophers and theologians of various stripes have concluded that the attempts to construct convincing and adequate theodicies (explanations of evil) have all failed to stand up to rigorous analytical scrutiny.[102]

Evil is a philosophical problem chiefly for those whose calling is philosophy. This does not mean that philosophy is useless, for indeed the discussion in recent decades has greatly helped theologians to understand how better to address the problem.[103] Nor do I mean to imply that philosophers have no personal experience of suffering. However, the rarefied nature of their discussions puts them beyond reach for a general readership of preachers, pastors, and the sorts of laypeople who will read a book like this. In the end, the various philosophical approaches to the problem of evil offer little help

100. Pike, "Hume on Evil," quoted by Marilyn McCord Adams, *Horrendous Evils and the Goodness of God* (Ithaca, N.Y.: Cornell University Press, 1999), 10.

101. John R. Schneider, "Seeing God Where the Wild Things Are," in *Christian Faith and the Problem of Evil*, ed. Peter Van Inwagen (Grand Rapids: Eerdmans, 2004).

102. See, for instance, Alvin Plantinga's elaborate dismantling of Nelson Pike in Plantinga's *God, Freedom, and Evil* (Grand Rapids: Eerdmans, 1974). However, Plantinga's well-known "free-will defense" has not proven conclusive either. Indeed, insofar as I am able to judge, Plantinga's approach comes across as a failed attempt to soften the most rigorous Calvinist conclusions without coming to terms with horrific evils.

103. The problem of evil has preoccupied me for my entire adult life. I have paid close attention to several of the classic treatments, including the well-known books and essays by what one wag has referred to as "the firm of Mackie, McCloskey & Flew, Atheists at Large" (Stephen Griffith, "The Problem of Pomegranates," in *Christian Faith and the Problem of Evil*).

to those who are grappling with actual horrific evils, either in their own lives or in their concern for the lives of others.

Marilyn McCord Adams and "Horrendous Evils"

Marilyn McCord Adams is an exception. Her book *Horrendous Evils and the Goodness of God* opens up the territory for those seeking a more practically helpful discussion of the problem of evil.[104] She reviews the history of philosophical solutions and finds them all wanting.[105] Her use of the terms "horrendous evils" and "horrors" will be adopted for this chapter. Such terms reflect the intensity of her engagement with evil, not merely as a philosophical conundrum but, more urgently, as an existential challenge to reason, faith, and life.

This intensity of engagement is obvious in the numerous passages where she defines "horrendous evils." For example: "Horrendous evils overwhelm human meaning-making capacities, . . . furnishing strong reason to believe that lives marred by horrors can never again be unified and integrated into wholes with positive meaning." Horrendous evils are "ruinous to the person's life." They are horrendous because they have "power to degrade" so as to destroy "personal meaning." She explains, "What makes horrendous evils so pernicious is their life-ruining potential," their soul-destroying power as they devour "the possibility of positive personal meaning in one swift gulp."[106]

This cluster of definitions provides us with strong conceptual advantages. It advances our concept of evil and confronts our idea of a beneficent God. The idea that "horrendous evils" can actually destroy a person's *self,* whether the body is destroyed or not, presents a particularly acute challenge to belief in a God of mercy.

---

104. Adams, *Horrendous Evils and the Goodness of God* (Ithaca, N.Y.: Cornell University Press, 1999). Adams's writing is full of grammatically awkward and forced phrasings typical of much academic work today, but if one can find one's way through it, one finds humane values at work.

105. Of particular interest is her analysis of Alvin Plantinga, a rare world-class philosopher working today who is also a confessing Christian. She is critical of the overly abstract and generalized view of evil that he is forced into in order to engage in apologetics with "atheological" philosophers, hoping to persuade them that it is possible to hold the idea of God together with the presence of evil without abandoning the existence of God. As an exception to this assessment, she quotes a "moving passage" from his own profile of himself, noting that he is drawing from the warmly personal Heidelberg Catechism (Adams, *Horrendous Evils,* 22).

106. Adams, *Horrendous Evils,* 26-27, 107, 166.

Theodicy: The Impact of Lisbon, Auschwitz, and the Great Tsunami of 2004

On December 26, 2004, a series of colossal tsunamis devastated the coastal communities of the Indian Ocean in one of the greatest natural disasters ever recorded. Official estimates of the total number of dead ranged between 227,000 and 280,000. Following this event there appeared a perfect storm of essays and articles asking "Whence comes evil?" and "Where was God?" and "What kind of God would allow this?" All the "experts" on evil were called in, and there were numerous reviews of "the problem of theodicy."[107] The voice that rose above them all was that of David B. Hart, the Eastern Orthodox theologian whose extraordinary little piece, "Tremors of Doubt," in the *Wall Street Journal,* attracted a good deal of attention.[108] At the invitation of Eerdmans Publishing, Hart expanded his ideas into a book, *The Doors of the Sea: Where Was God in the Tsunami?* His project is a wholesale dismantling of the very notion of a "successful" theodicy. His influence will be apparent in what follows.

Before the massive Lisbon earthquake of 1755, it was widely believed that natural disasters could be ascribed to the providential working of God. After Lisbon, the view that nature is morally neutral arose and is still with us today. An even more significant development came with the Nazi death camps. Before the Holocaust, it was possible to argue that human nature was essentially improvable, if not actually good, and that progress could be expected. It is remarkable that many people — Americans especially, with our congenital optimism — still have not absorbed the message that this Enlightenment view is dead.[109]

---

107. Most invoked Gottfried Leibniz, the eighteenth-century German philosopher who coined the word "theodicy" to denote the attempt to reconcile the existence of evil with that of a good Creator. Leibniz is associated with the "best-of-all-possible-worlds" theodicy, so memorably skewered by Voltaire in *Candide* after the Lisbon earthquake in 1755. Voltaire's savage attack on Leibniz was repeatedly recycled at the time of the 2004 tsunami (and again after Hurricane Katrina in 2005). Susan Neiman, a Kantian philosopher and author of *Evil in Modern Thought,* was quoted often; she has identified the Lisbon quake as a major turning point in European intellectual history, arguing that the Holocaust has similarly redefined the question of evil since World War II ("The Moral Cataclysm," *New York Times Magazine,* January 16, 2005). *New York Times* culture critic Edward Rothstein brought up the theodicy issue in regard to the September 11, 2001, attacks and again after Hurricane Katrina (October 5, 2002, and September 8, 2005). Ron Rosenbaum of the *New York Observer* (January 10, 2005), known for his inquiries into Hitler, heaped scorn on Harold Kushner's *When Bad Things Happen to Good People* (the "Kushner cop-out").

108. Hart, "Tremors of Doubt," *Wall Street Journal,* December 31, 2004.

109. Lance Morrow writes: "After Auschwitz and Hiroshima, the idea of progress was

Serious efforts to create theodicies have been made in the centuries since Lisbon, and as more and more horrendous catastrophes occur, there are continual calls for more and better theodicies to replace the old ones. But we are arguing here for a concept alien to modern philosophy. The position taken in this chapter is that theodicies are, almost by definition, unsatisfactory because they are constructed out of *human notions* of God, thereby negating the *theo-* in *theo*dicy. If there is really a God such as the Hebrew Scriptures proclaim, then God cannot be discovered by human logic. "My thoughts are not your thoughts . . . says the Lord" (Isa. 55:8).

Theodicy requires us to ask if the "argument from evil" disproves or discredits God. The committed Christian will have little trouble with the disproving part, for the reasons cited by Hart: belief in the God who is revealed in the Bible entails trust in a God whose purposes cannot be weighed upon the same scale as ours, he being God and we being creatures. The question of the *existence* of God is not the "deepest question" raised by the problem of evil. It is the *goodness* of God that is at stake.

8. Is Evil Part of God's Purpose?

O Felix Culpa!

Embedded in the Christian tradition is the notion of *felix culpa* (happy or blessed fault).[110] The idea at its best is complex, but it requires us to ask whether sin and suffering can somehow be justified by a greater good that emerges from it.[111] The philosopher Alvin Plantinga defends the notion of *felix culpa,* suggesting that suffering can have "salvific meaning."[112] What is

---

never the same. Those events brought the snake into the garden of the Enlightenment. . . . Progress now implies the danger of a simultaneous Endarkenment" (*Evil: An Investigation* [New York: Basic Books, 2003], 213).

110. The Latin Paschal Vigil liturgy contains the words *O felix culpa, quae talem ac tantum meruit habere Redemptorem.* The English translation of the Roman Catholic Church renders this "O happy fault, that earned for us so great, so glorious a Redeemer."

111. A variation on this is the idea of "soul making," the argument that suffering allows persons to attain higher levels of spiritual development than would otherwise be possible. Paul seems to suggest this in Rom. 5:1-5 and elsewhere, but there is a world of difference. Paul is not an apologist. He is not offering explanations of suffering or justifications of it. He is showing how God's love and the outpouring of the Spirit sustains the Christian in the suffering.

112. Plantinga, "Supralapsarianism, or *O Felix Culpa!*" in *Christian Faith and the Problem of Evil,* 25. To be fair to Plantinga, he works very hard to avoid the suggestion that suffering is a good thing in the end. Still, his is a philosophical argument and therefore, I am contending,

missing in such familiar presentations is Ivan Karamazov's challenge. In Fyodor Dostoevsky's *The Brothers Karamazov* there is a justly celebrated section where Ivan challenges his devout younger brother Alyosha. That challenge is very much to the point here: "Imagine that you are creating a fabric of human destiny with the object of making men happy in the end . . . but that it was essential and inevitable to torture only one tiny creature [a baby or small child] . . . would you consent to be the architect on those conditions?" Alyosha must answer, "No, I wouldn't consent."

Many Christians today continue to swear by a simplified version of *felix culpa*.[113] "Everything happens for a reason," they say. This is more a statement of faith than it is a rationale, and one does not want to rob people of the comfort they find in this thought, but it is not sufficient to account for the horrors that we will be discussing here. Marilyn Adams writes that horrendous evils "constitute reason to doubt whether the participants' life can have been or can be in the future worth living."[114] This may sound extreme, but it is applicable to many who have experienced the demonic. It applies — for instance — to the refugee women who, after the Cambodian genocide, became blind although there was no physical cause.[115] Primo Levi took his own life four decades after Auschwitz was abandoned by the retreating Germans, a deed that shook his admirers to the foundations because it seemed to set the sign of nullity over against all that he accomplished in his writing.[116] Likewise,

---

theologically and pastorally useless and, indeed, positively harmful. Plantinga does manage to introduce Satan into his abstruse philosophical ruminations in favor of "the free-will defense," but to my mind the juxtaposition is very odd — as though, in the process, Satan had simply eaten the argument.

113. The *felix culpa* notion is charmingly expressed in a popular anthem heard at Christmastime, Benjamin Britten's "Adam lay ybounden," set to medieval words: "Ne'er had that apple taken been, that apple taken been, ne'er had our Lady been heavené queen." In other words, we are better off because of Adam's rebellion than we would have been otherwise. This is an exceptionally tricky territory to navigate. In Calvin's system, *felix culpa* serves as a guarantee of the absolute sovereignty of God over all contingencies — a very important affirmation. The difficulty, however, is that *felix culpa* seems to suggest that God's original plan lacked something that was then supplied by the occurrence of Sin.

114. Adams, *Horrendous Evils*, 26.

115. Alexandra Smith, "Long Beach Journal: Eyes That Saw Horrors Now See Only Shadows," *New York Times,* September 8, 1989. There are many detailed accounts of this phenomenon online.

116. "[Primo] Levi is trying to make us see something that didn't happen to us . . . not even Levi could fully succeed in this task. We can't live with his memories, and in the long run it turned out that not even he could." Clive James, review of *The Drowned and the Saved,* by Primo Levi, *New Yorker,* May 23, 1988. (A small minority of those who have studied Levi's fall from an upper stairwell argue that it was an accident, but most have accepted it as suicide.)

Iris Chang, the young woman who bravely faced the absolute worst in order to write *The Rape of Nanking,* committed suicide not long after her widely acclaimed book, unremittingly gruesome in its detail, was published.[117] The ordeal of Sister Dianna Ortiz, who was cited earlier, resulted in the loss of memory of her life before her torture; she had to be reintroduced to her own family. She testified later that something had been done to her inner core that could not be repaired.[118]

Evil is a "dead loss," and it is a form of deception to say otherwise. Throughout his little book, Hart displays a profound pastoral motive. He is always concerned about what one would actually say to a sufferer. He is angered by the insensitivity and lack of empathy shown by those who want to have an explanation: "It is obscene to seek to mitigate the scandal of suffering by allowing hope to degenerate into banal confidence in 'God's great plan' . . . such confidence all too easily blinds us to the spiritual universe of the New Testament . . . even if by economy God can bring good from evil; it can in no way supply any imagined deficiency in God's or creation's goodness; *it has no 'contribution' to make.*"[119]

Here, Hart contrasts genuine Christian hope (the "hope against hope" of which Paul speaks in Rom. 4:18) with "banal confidence" and shallow optimism, or "positive thinking." He believes that such attitudes prevent us from understanding the New Testament.

Theodicy: A Conclusion

The whole enterprise of theodicy is misbegotten. Philosophical "defenses" founder. Attempts at explanation distract us from the real-life predicament of sufferers and perpetrators alike. Evil is *in no way* part of God's good purpose, and cannot be, since it does not have existence as a created good. Evil is neither rationally nor morally intelligible and must simply be loathed and resisted. The beginning of resistance is not to *explain,* but *to see.* Seeing is itself a form of action — seeing evil for what it is, not a part of God's plan, but a colossal *x* factor in creation, a monstrous contradiction, a prodigious negation that must be identified, denounced, and opposed wherever it occurs.

117. Iris Chang, *The Rape of Nanking: The Forgotten Holocaust of World War II* (New York: Penguin Books, 1998). There have been some protests, perhaps justifiable, against the use of "holocaust" in the subtitle. It does not really seem suitable. There can be no denying the magnitude of the atrocities, however.

118. *Theology Today* 63 (October 2006): 344-48.

119. Hart, *Doors of the Sea,* 69-70, 74, emphasis added.

9. The Will to Negate: Why "Satan" Is Necessary

The Alien Power in Postmodern Discourse

David Hart's reference to the "spiritual universe of the New Testament" brings us back to the subject of a dark agency operating in the world. To understand the conceptual panorama of the New Testament — whether we believe in it or not — it is essential to acknowledge the presupposed presence of a third power, an Enemy, identified by his various names. To be sure, this picture presents many difficulties, but it has the great merit of being not only biblical but also deeply serious in assigning the greatest possible importance to the problem of radical evil and suffering in the world.

Jeffrey Burton Russell, in his magisterial five-volume work on the devil, puts forward this argument:

> The Devil of the New Testament is not tangential to the fundamental message, not a mere symbol. The saving mission of Christ can be fully understood only in terms of opposition to the Devil. That is the whole point of the New Testament: the world is full of grief and suffering, but beyond the power of Satan is a greater power. . . . [In the New Testament] there is complete consistency on the essential point, which is that the new age brought by Christ is at war with the old age ruled by Satan.[120]

Russell is not the only thinker talking about the devil. Andrew Delbanco, in his 1995 book *The Death of Satan,* argues that we need such imagery. The horrors of World War II forced many to reach back for a stronger symbolism. The attacks of September 11, 2001, had a similar effect in the United States. These phenomena seemed to push us beyond the familiar, manageable categories of right and wrong. The essayist Lance Morrow writes about the difference between "evil" and mere "wrong." He would have trouble, he says, calling the Nazi "Final Solution" or the torture-murder of a child "wrong."

> A crucial difference between wrong and evil is that people are implicitly in charge of the universe in which rights and wrongs are discussed; people have systems of laws to right wrongs. But *evil implies a different universe,* controlled by extra-human forces. Wrong is a human offense that suggests reparation is possible and deserved. Wrong is not mysterious. *Evil suggests*

---

120. Jeffrey Burton Russell, *The Prince of Darkness: Radical Evil and the Power of Good in History* (Ithaca, N.Y.: Cornell University Press, 1988), 51, 48.

a mysterious force that may be in business for itself and may exploit human agency as part of *a larger cosmic conflict* — between good and evil, God and Satan.[121]

That last sentence is so close to the New Testament apocalyptic perspective that it might well be a description of it in a work of biblical scholarship.

Other writers and culture critics have sounded this note. Robert Coles, for instance, reviewing Russell's comprehensive work on the devil, says, "This century [the twentieth] has not treated [eighteenth- and nineteenth-century optimism] kindly. The Devil, has, in a sense, returned — our struggle, these days, is to find a way of thinking about the radical evil that lives all too comfortably in our communities . . . our usual secular pieties don't quite work in the face of our recent dark past."[122]

When Russell's volumes and Coles's review were written in the 1980s, the presenting crisis that demanded diagnosis was the fact that the Nazis had nearly succeeded in exterminating the Jews of Europe in plain sight. Ernst Cassirer, a German-Jewish philosopher who had believed in "man's progressive self-liberation," acknowledged after the war that he had been utterly deceived about the Holocaust. "We could hardly be prevailed upon to take them seriously," he said about the Nazi racial myths. "By the end of the war, however, it had become clear to all of us that this [disbelief] was a great mistake. . . . *The mythical monsters were not entirely destroyed.* They were used for the creation of a new universe, and *they still survive in this universe.*"[123]

---

121. Morrow, *Evil,* 51, emphasis added.

122. Robert Coles, "Eternally Evil and Never Out of Work," review of *Mephistopheles: The Devil in the Modern World,* by Jeffrey Burton Russell, *New York Times Book Review,* March 8, 1987.

123. Quoted by Delbanco in *The Death of Satan,* 189, emphasis added. Delbanco continues, "I believe that our culture is now in crisis because evil remains an inescapable experience for all of us . . . while we no longer have a symbolic language for describing it." Delbanco is a self-proclaimed secular liberal. He does not understand Christian faith and at times shows contempt for it. Yet he recognizes that many people are "bereft" without the old verities (223). Mark Lilla, professor of humanities and historian of ideas at Columbia University, writes in a similar vein: "Modern philosophy has no reason to rely on religious myths, but it ignores study of these myths at the risk of narrowing its vision of certain fundamental issues. One reason why Augustine's message to the Roman Christians [following the devastating sack of Rome by the Goths] may have offered them more solace than modern Europeans received after the Lisbon earthquake, and certainly more than we received after Auschwitz, was that his biblical faith provided him with *answers to the deepest questions regarding the ultimate sources of evil, questions to which we may have grown inattentive*" ("The Big E," *New York Review of Books,* June 12, 2003).

The Negation of Being

In our time the term "Manichaean" has regained currency among those who have opposed the tendency to divide up the world into absolute evil and absolute good.[124] When Augustine of Hippo renounced the Manichaeism of his time, he turned to the concept of *privatio boni* as a way of denying evil (nonbeing) the same status as God (Being).[125] Yet, as we have already seen, if we speak of evil simply as *absence,* we are in danger of abstracting its malign effects, or distancing ourselves from them. A better way of defining it is the *negation* of being, or the *negation* of good. This expression has force. "Satan" is the personification of *the will to negate.* We are speaking metaphorically here, but the argument of this entire volume is that metaphor comes closer to expressing biblical truth than pure concepts or principles. The personification of evil as the devil — whatever we choose to call him — embodies the idea that evil is "in business for itself," actively seeking to undo God's purpose for the creation.

In 1899, the great writer Joseph Conrad anticipated the unparalleled wickedness of the next century. In *Heart of Darkness,* Conrad's narrator, Marlow, tells of going up the river Congo in search of the mysterious Mr. Kurtz, "the chief of the Inner Station," "at the very bottom of there." As the steamer penetrates ever deeper into the interior, he describes his sense of evil as "the stillness of an implacable force brooding over an inscrutable intention. It looked at you with a vengeful aspect." This captures something of the personal will to negate that invests the satanic symbols with their meaning.[126]

124. In the first decade of the twenty-first century, there was much talk of Manichaeism because certain cultural and political commentators, casting about for a term to define the neoconservatives who supported the American invasion of Iraq, recalled the Manichaeans from Augustine's *Confessions.* The Manichaean system was oversimplified for these purposes; what the political analysts found useful about it was the implication that the world and all the people in it could be divided up into good and evil. President George W. Bush in particular was frequently referred to as Manichaean because of the way he and his closest advisers spoke of their perceived adversaries as evil while refusing to acknowledge any potential for evil close at hand. (In contrast, Abraham Lincoln, as the Civil War drew to a close, by a mighty intellectual and theological effort, denied himself and the Northern states the luxury of demonizing the South [the Second Inaugural Address].)

125. The problem with Manichaeism was not only its belief in absolute good and absolute evil with a neat division between the two. The fourth-century Manichaeans were thoroughgoing dualists; they taught that evil had a status equal to that of God. The larger issue for Christian theology was that the Manichaean system ascribed *existence* to the power of darkness. Augustine saw that this was wrong. He writes that in his youthful Manichaean days, "I believed evil . . . to be some kind of substance, and to have its own foul and hideous bulk" (*Confessions* 5.10.20). Hence his insistence on *privatio boni,* which denies existence to evil.

126. Significantly, Marlow shapes his narrative by making a supremely ironical distinction

Speaking of Satan

So we find that there is considerable support in elite intellectual circles for speaking of Satan. And yet, when we speak of the devil, we are faced with a complex intellectual and moral challenge. We can identify three imperatives:

First, we must avoid speaking of Satan in order to shift blame away from ourselves ("the devil made me do it"). When we speak of the demonic, we must do so in tandem with an understanding of the universal *human* capacity for actively causing evil, or, at the very least, passively cooperating with it.

Second, we must avoid seizing upon the figure of Satan in order to project evil outside our own group onto others. This universal human propensity routinely fuels conflicts around the globe.[127]

Third, we must hold two seemingly contradictory concepts simultaneously:

- Satan is an active intelligence contending against God for world domination.
- Satan has no independent ontological status of his own; he "exists" only as the will to negate.

The argument here is that New Testament cosmology makes each of these three imperatives possible, indeed essential. We may not demonize other human groups, but it is sometimes necessary to demonize *something*. The worldwide scope and malignant power of evil, both on an individual level and on a corporate level, require us to speak of a power far more monstrous than the mere sum of individual transgressions. Here the figure of Satan finds its place.[128]

---

between the glamorous European-based colonial "devils," with their supposedly "high and just" motivations, and the "flabby, pretending, weak-eyed devil" of the interior. The further one goes into the interior, the less glamorous the devils, the more "insidious," the more "rapacious and pitiless." It is, of course, an account of the human condition. The further in, the more likely to find "the horror." (The distinguished Nigerian novelist Chinua Achebe, in a much-cited essay, has denounced Conrad as "a thoroughgoing racist" and the classic novella as "offensive and deplorable" ["An Image of Africa: Racism in Conrad's 'Heart of Darkness,'" *Massachusetts Review* 18 (1977)]. The essay is important and its perspective is instructive. Like all great works of art, however, *Heart of Darkness* has dimensions that elude and transcend *all* attempts to capture or reduce it.)

127. The Christian church is once again in danger of "demonizing the opposition" with regard to Muslims, as has happened already in Nigeria, among other places. This requires ceaseless vigilance against future repetitions.

128. Sheriff Bell in Cormac McCarthy's *No Country for Old Men* describes this (the lack

From the past century — the century of genocide — there are countless testimonies from personal experience. During the genocide in Rwanda, *Time* magazine went against its practice of decades, putting a quotation instead of a photograph on the front cover. It was a statement by a missionary serving in that country during those unspeakable months: "There are no devils left in Hell; they are all in Rwanda."[129] Another reference to Satan in the same context is found in the anguished memoir of Roméo Dallaire, the French-Canadian general who was in charge of the UN forces during the Rwandan genocide. He writes, "After one of my many presentations following my return from Rwanda, a Canadian Forces padre asked me how, after all I had seen and experienced, I could still believe in God. I answered that I know there is a God because in Rwanda I shook hands with the devil. I have seen him, I have smelled him and I have touched him. I know the devil exists, and therefore I know there is a God."[130]

This striking quotation illustrates one remarkable man's capacity for grasping the cosmology of the New Testament. This imagination needs nurturing in the church.

10. Evil Unmasked

The Falsehood of Innocence

Susan Sontag wrote about those who are perennially surprised or indifferent when horrors occur: "No one after a certain age has the right to this kind of innocence, of superficiality, to this degree of ignorance and amnesia."[131] To

---

of punctuation and quotation marks is a McCarthy peculiarity): "I think if you were Satan and you were settin around tryin to think up somethin that would just bring the human race to its knees what you would probably come up with is narcotics. Maybe he did. I told that to somebody at breakfast the other mornin and they asked me if I believed in Satan. I said Well that aint the point. And they said I know but do you? I had to think about that. I guess as a boy I did. Come the middle years my belief I reckon had waned somewhat. Now I'm startin to lean back the other way. He explains a lot of things that otherwise dont have no explanation. Or not to me they dont" (*No Country for Old Men* [New York: Knopf, 2005], 218).

129. *Time* cover, May 16, 1994.

130. Roméo Dallaire, *Shake Hands with the Devil: The Failure of Humanity in Rwanda* (Toronto: Random House Canada, 2003), xviii (preface).

131. Susan Sontag, *Regarding the Pain of Others* (New York: Farrar, Straus and Giroux, 2003). Sontag's work taken as a whole has much to teach us, although it should be noted parenthetically that her short piece in the *New Yorker* immediately after 9/11 was widely (and rightly) criticized for being politically naïve — precisely the fault she deplores elsewhere.

understand something of what is involved in Christ's descent into hell, we must make an attempt to look directly at horrific evil.

Why should we subject ourselves to this quest at all? Many people do not have the stomach for it; others rightly question the morbid, semi-pornographic fascination that we have for hearing about atrocities. And yet, we may wonder with Sontag if those who do not reflect upon horrors might be more likely to turn a blind eye to them. As John Updike has observed, "the essence of evil, perhaps, is not to know itself."[132] The fundamental necessity for Christian theology in this matter, and for any kind of moral existence in the world, is a renunciation of the idea of innocence. The South African novelist and Nobel Prize–winner J. M. Coetzee puts it this way: "There are certain cruelties . . . of so morally debased an order that we cannot close our eyes to them. There are things we must know so that we will know the worst about ourselves; so that we may forever be on guard against that worst."[133]

The Hidden Factor of Complicity

As the twentieth century drew to a close, it was becoming clear that the extermination of six million Jews and several million Slavs, Roma (gypsies), homosexuals, mentally retarded people, resistance leaders, and others at the hands of the Nazis was not to be the last genocide in our time, in spite of pious and defiant cries of "Never again." The demonstrable failure of the Christian church during the roundup of Europe's Jews was to be exceeded — if that were possible — in 1994 by the sometimes enthusiastic participation of Christian leaders and institutions during the Rwandan genocide. The insistent question that such events raise, over and over, is whether Christian faith really makes any difference when self-identified Christians participate in radical evil. Stephen R. Haynes, writing in the *Christian Century*, observes

132. John Updike, "Elusive Evil," *New Yorker,* July 22, 1996.

133. Quoted in a review of *Chile: Death in the South,* by Jacobo Timerman, *New York Times Book Review* (1987). Timerman is an important figure who should still be noticed. He was known for his outspoken opposition to the Argentine "Dirty War," which resulted in his being incarcerated and tortured at length by the Argentine junta. He wrote about these experiences in his awards-winning 1981 memoir, *Prisoner without a Name, Cell without a Number.* He was later to become one of the first Israeli citizens with an impeccable Zionist record to criticize Israel for invading Lebanon (*The Longest War: Israel's Invasion of Lebanon* [1982]) and for its treatment of the Palestinians, making him a target in Israel. In 2000, he was posthumously named one of the fifty World Press Freedom Heroes of the past half-century by the International Press Institute.

that Rwanda was the most Christianized country in Africa (90 percent), yet huge numbers of victims were killed in church buildings where they had sought refuge. "Like Nazi Germany, genocidal Rwanda is an exceedingly unattractive venue for Christian self-examination. Much of the evidence indicates that 'blood' proved thicker than baptismal water, that faith was powerless to overcome the interests of class or ethnicity. . . . *Christians must ask what this and other episodes of mass killing reveal about the essence and extent of our fallenness.*"[134]

The Rwandan atrocities force us to reexamine our understanding of human nature. The manner of the murders has caused especial notice, since hundreds of thousands were hacked with machetes, burned in churches, and shot point-blank and face-to-face. This was not an industrialized, anonymous operation carried out at remote locations by a few fanatical officials "just doing their jobs"; it was a person-to-person massacre by people who in many cases knew their victims, and were even colleagues with them on the staffs of the same hospitals and members of the same parish churches. Anyone who cares about Christian witness must be haunted by the question: What would I have done?

The Moral Unintelligibility of Evil

Many have identified Ivan Karamazov's attack on his brother Alyosha's piety in Dostoevsky's *The Brothers Karamazov* as the most profound and wrenching challenge ever penned on the subject of God and evil. The horrific examples Ivan gives of the torture of children were taken by Dostoevsky from newspaper articles. Ivan hurls these at Alyosha to show that there is no account of salvation that can possibly coexist with such horrors. David Hart's brilliant insight into Ivan Karamazov is that, whereas Voltaire sees only "the terrible truth that the history of suffering and death is not morally intelligible," Karamazov sees "that it would be far more terrible if it were." The *moral unintelligibility of evil* is Hart's great theme.[135] At the risk of overload, two more examples from more recent times are cited here, precisely to drive home this point of unintelligibility.

The first example is from Coeur d'Alene, Idaho. In 2005 Joseph E. Duncan III murdered three members of a family, including a thirteen-year-old

---

134. Stephen R. Haynes, "Never Again: Perpetrators and Bystanders in Rwanda," *Christian Century*, February 27–March 6, 2002, emphasis added.

135. Hart, *Doors of the Sea*, 44.

boy, then kidnapped the two younger children — a boy, nine, and his sister, eight. He tortured and sexually abused both children for seven weeks, eventually killing the boy (the girl was finally rescued). The judge stated that the crime "exceeds the bounds of human understanding."[136]

The second example of horrific evil is told in Samantha Power's book about genocide, *"A Problem from Hell."* She relates this story from the Bosnian conflict of the mid-1990s:

> [A young American intelligence analyst] had been taught to greet reports with skepticism. And the stories emerging from Bosnia certainly seemed to warrant disbelief. One cable described a nine-year-old Muslim girl who had been raped by Serbian [Orthodox Christian] militiamen and left lying in a pool of blood for two days while her parents watched, from behind a fence, as she died. He did not believe it. . . . But the refugees kept talking, making themselves heard. The very same report about the Muslim girl crossed his desk a second time when a separate group of witnesses confirmed it independently to US investigators.[137]

The second story is a bridge between two categories. It not only is a record of an unspeakable atrocity toward an individual child and her parents, but also is *an act driven by policy.* The actions of the Serbs in the Bosnian conflict, like those of the military regimes in Latin America, those taken during Saddam Hussein's Anfal campaign against the Kurds, the conduct of the *génocidaires* in Rwanda, the deliberate policies of gang-rape in the Congo, and numberless other examples, were *premeditated instruments of a specific program of repression or extermination.* The second illustration of horrific evil is even more profoundly threatening than the first, because it arises not out of individual psychopathic criminality but out of a deliberate governmental strategy or group design.[138]

In addition to two kinds of evil, we might also say there are two kinds of unfathomable evil*doers*. *First* is the psychopath, like the serial killer H. H. Howell, whose career is described in the phenomenally best-selling *Devil in the White City.* Such a person appears to be only a simulacrum of a human be-

---

136. *New York Times,* National Briefing: Associated Press, November 4, 2008.

137. Samantha Power, *"A Problem from Hell": America in the Age of Genocide* (New York: Basic Books, 2002), 265.

138. The calculated use of rape by the *janjaweed* militia in Darfur in the first decade of the new century would be an example of government strategy; the Ku Klux Klan reign of terror in the American South would be an example of group design.

ing.[139] It is relatively easy to distance ourselves from this person; we see him as "evil personified," an evil person doing evil deeds. Far more challenging to the imagination is the *second* kind, the "good" person who is drawn into evil. Understanding group atrocities requires more of us because we are forced to see how we all might be capable of such deeds under certain conditions.

Richard W. Sonnenfeldt, chief interpreter at the Nuremberg trials, was interviewed in his eighty-third year. His memories of the chief Nazis were still sharp. He remembered the terrifying normality of their personalities. "They were without a doubt the world's greatest living criminals, but their hands were clean, their expressions were normal, they could have been people you meet on the street. You think, what kind of a man can do this, can serve someone like Hitler, and you realize, it's very simple. A yes man. A toady. Someone doing it for rank or uniform or money or glory. . . . People have to realize that *power and evil run on the same track*."[140] Can we not see our own souls possibly at risk in such a situation?

None of this, however, helps us to understand where these tendencies came from. In *Explaining Hitler*, Ron Rosenbaum examines contradictory theories about how Hitler could have become the genocidal killer he was if he was not a madman. In the end, Rosenbaum writes, "Explanation, however meretricious, [is] a shield against having to face the horror of inexplicability, the inexplicability of horror."[141] His conclusion is the right one: *there is no explanation.*

---

139. The prominent psychiatrist Otto Kernberg used the label "malignant narcissism" to ascribe an extreme form of personality disorder to figures who were monstrous in their deeds but not insane — particularly Hitler and Stalin. Such persons are adept at charming and manipulating those around them, but they are entirely unable to feel the pain of others. The utter absence of empathy in their personality is matched by boundless grandiosity, confidence in themselves, and the assurance that they above all know what should be done. Kernberg did not study Saddam Hussein, but psychiatric researchers Jerrold M. Post (George Washington University) and Amatzia Baram (University of Haifa, Israel) conclude that it applies to him also (Erica Goode, "Stalin to Saddam: So Much for the Madman Theory," *New York Times*, May 4, 2003).

140. Peter Applebome, "Veteran of the Nuremberg Trials Can't Forget Dialogue with Infamy," *New York Times*, March 14, 2007, emphasis added.

141. Ron Rosenbaum, "Explaining Hitler," *New Yorker*, May 1, 1995. John Gross, reviewing Rosenbaum's book *Explaining Hitler: The Search for the Origins of His Evil* (New York: Macmillan, 1998), underscores the point: "Evil is a *theologically* charged concept. . . . Trying to account for Hitler, we sooner or later enter the realm of the unaccountable" (*New York Review of Books*, December 17, 1998, emphasis added).

11. "Rage against Explanation"

"I Cry to Thee and Thou Dost Not Answer Me" (Job 30:20)

At the beginning of this chapter on the motif of the descent into hell, we identified four goals for it. The first was to look unblinkingly at radical evil and its power in the lives even of the "good." The second was to importune God about the presence and power of evil and unjust suffering in the world, even to demand from God some response — as the psalmists often do, as Ivan Karamazov does, and, in the archetypal example, as Job does:

> "Oh, that I had one to hear me!
> Here is my signature! let the Almighty answer me!" (Job 31:35)

All the best theological interpreters of the book of Job agree that it is not a theodicy; indeed, it is the great antitheodicy. The question of punishment for sin and reward for righteousness is set aside. The question of the *existence* of God does not come up; as throughout the Old Testament, God is simply assumed — indeed, God is the chief actor. The "argument from evil" to disprove the existence of God is entirely missing from the book of Job.[142] The thing to notice about Ivan Karamazov's uniquely powerful case is that he does not question the existence of God any more than Job does. Dostoevsky's challenge is that the world God has created is *intolerable on moral grounds.*[143] That is Ivan's accusation against God, and it is the only one that really counts, since there is no logic in saying that the existence of evil proves the nonexistence of God. In fact, these attempts, though mounted over the years by some of the best Christian minds, are ultimately offensive, because they ask us to believe that there is some meaning or purpose in such suffering. *There can be no explanation for horrendous evils.*[144] Efforts to give an

---

142. As we saw earlier, the "argument from evil" against the existence of God is associated with David Hume in the eighteenth century, and with J. L. Mackie in the twentieth.

143. The reasoning behind this accusation is quite precisely duplicated in C. S. Lewis's *Perelandra.* When the Oxford don, Ransom, discovers that the scientist Weston (the demonic figure in the story) has been slitting frogs open with his fingernails and leaving them to die slowly out of pure sadism, Ransom realizes that evil is "an intolerable obscenity which afflicted him with shame. It would have been better, or so he thought at that moment, for the whole universe never to have existed than for this one thing to have happened" (109).

144. Adams writes, "I agree with Anselm that any reasons [for God permitting evil] that we may discover are only partial" (*Horrendous Evils,* 54).

intelligible account of the presence of evil are not only intellectually inadequate but also morally offensive.[145]

What sort of "explanation" can possibly be anything other than enraging in the face of such evils as we have been describing? And how can we speak of God as other than a monster if he permits such things as part of his grand design? We conclude that in the presence of the tortured child who calls out to God, there is no supportable "answer."[146]

What we seek, therefore, is what Job sought. "Let the Almighty reply to me!" We do not seek an "answer," for we will not get one in this life.[147] What we — like Job — cry out for is some kind of *response* to pain so that we can live by faith in a world where the moral order is under radical threat. We now address the matter of a response, the second purpose of this chapter.

Out of the Whirlwind

God responds to Job by appearing out of the whirlwind with a mighty address summoning Job to behold the creation.[148] Nothing whatever is said

---

145. A stunning example of "rage against explanation" was given in an op-ed article by Lea Evans Ash, who was kicked in the spine by three teenagers as she was bending over her baby's stroller on a New York City subway platform in 1973. She suffered extreme nerve damage and traumatic arthritis, from which she was not expected ever to recover. She went to "a priest at the seminary in Chelsea where my husband was a student," who "apparently claimed a moral right to tell me 'why it happened.'" He spoke of the teenagers' (whose identities had never been discovered) economic deprivation, social isolation, black rage, etc. Twelve years later, Ms. Ash was still infuriated by this attempt to give a "rational" explanation. In addition, and strikingly, she wrote about the "menacing evil" she saw in the faces of those who witnessed the attack, or who saw her struggling home, and offered no help. *New York Times,* December 14, 1985.

146. There is only one honorable alternative, in my view, to the Christian angle on evil as we have outlined it here. It is Stoicism, an intellectually rigorous, atheist position that not many people are willing to hold. The Stoic is resigned to an essentially random and meaningless world in which no evil will ever be adequately redressed. Intellectually, it seems to me, this is the only honorable alternative to faith in a God who will judge the earth. Pious, undifferentiated, generically religious hopes for a better life hereafter are not sufficient to compensate for the suffering that we are attempting to evoke in this chapter.

147. Dorothy Day wrote of visiting a sick person in terrible pain: "There is so little one can do, except just be there and do nothing. . . . I told her that . . . one could only keep silence in the face of suffering" (*The Duty of Delight: The Diaries of Dorothy Day,* ed. Robert Ellsberg [Milwaukee: Marquette University Press, 2008], 279).

148. When the word translated "behold" appears in the Old and New Testaments, it does not simply mean "see!" or "look!," *contra* recent translations. It denotes a powerful revelation leading to understanding, insight, and faith.

about Job's suffering. Father Zossima likewise responds to Ivan Karamazov with a speech, and Alyosha, Dostoevsky's "hero" if there is one, also delivers an impassioned address to his older brother in "answer" to his outcry. Many have thought that neither Alyosha's nor the book of Job's response is satisfactory. In fact, there has been a good deal of complaining about the inadequacy and irrelevance of both of them, and in view of our earlier comments about the importance of silence, there is something to be said for these objections.[149] What then shall we say about God's "response" (if one can call it that) to Job?

A significant link occurs between Job 25:6 ("man . . . is a maggot, / and the son of man . . . is a worm") and 38:1-3 ("Then the Lord answered Job out of the whirlwind / . . . 'Gird up your loins *like a man,* / I will question you, and you shall declare to me'"). It would appear that the stupefying address of God to Job, though it appears to be irrelevant in the extreme, confers great dignity upon Job. He is neither a maggot nor a worm, but is called forth by God and made to stand upon his feet, covered in boils as he is. He is also summoned to "declare," to speak back to God. To be sure, it would be easy to see this summons as bullying, since Job's only "declarations" range from "I lay my hand on my mouth" to "I melt away; I repent in dust and ashes," but in the conceptual universe of the Old Testament, such a conclusion would be a mistake. The wonder is that Job is addressed by God man to man, as it were; he is not a pitiable victim, but one who, being made in the image of God, actually corresponds to God and receives God's revelation — an honor that we are meant to recognize as remarkable. We may truly speak of a theophany, a showing-forth of *God himself.* Job appears to realize this, and it seems not only to satisfy him but also to reorient him altogether. Job's determination to justify himself (most clearly exhibited in 27:5 where Job says, "Till I die I will not put away my integrity from me. / I hold fast my righteousness, and will not let it go") simply falls away in the light of the revealed righteousness of God.

The book of Job will always be debated; we brought Job into this discussion to show how the speech from the whirlwind points *away* from "answers" and "explanations." Instead, it brings us into the very presence of God. The final speech of Job confirms this:

"I know that thou canst do all things,
   and that no purpose of thine can be thwarted. . . .

---

149. Alyosha Karamazov's response to his brother Ivan has never seemed satisfying to me. Ivan's protest is what registers. God's response to Job, however, cannot be set aside.

Therefore I have uttered what I did not understand,
>   things too wonderful for me, which I did not know. . . .
I had heard of thee by the hearing of the ear,
>   but now my eye sees thee;[150]
therefore I despise myself,[151]
>   and repent in dust and ashes." (Job 42:1-6)

It is a new epistemology, a new way of knowing. When God reveals himself, the old arrangements become obsolete. The distinctive characteristic of Job, in the last analysis, is his consuming desire to receive a response from God. He got one. It was not the response he could have expected, but in an utterly strange way God was gracious to Job. The clue that we need is the detachment of the question about suffering from the self-revelation of God. The question "Why?" is not the right question and will never yield the right "explanation."[152]

David Hart, writing about *The Brothers Karamazov,* describes Ivan's posture as "rage against explanation."[153] Hart argues that we must not be persuaded into a position that requires us to make sense of everything that happens. It is premature to say to a sufferer, "There must be some reason for this." The sufferer may (or may not) eventually come to this belief by himself, *in and through* the suffering; but it is a first rule of pastoral ministry

150. It should be noted here that the "eye" is actually the ear. Job does not "see" God in the usual sense; he hears him and believes, which is the meaning of sight (John 9:35-41). This is entirely consistent with the biblical doctrine of the Word of God. Revelations of God's self in Scripture are auditory, not visual. It is through his Word that God makes himself known (John 1:1-18).

151. The word translated "despise" in many English versions may actually mean something more like "melt into nothing" (Samuel Terrien, *Job,* The Interpreter's Bible, vol. 3 [New York and Nashville: Abingdon, 1957], 1193).

152. On Palm Sunday, March 27, 1994, a tornado struck the Goshen United Methodist Church in Piedmont, Alabama. Twenty people were killed, including the young daughter of the pastor. No one attending the service in the church that morning had heard the urgent tornado warning. The pastor, Kelly Clem, questioned by a reporter, said, "We do not know 'why.' I don't think 'why' is the question right now. We just have to help each other through it" (*Atlanta Constitution,* March 29, 1994). In an article by Rick Bragg about the child's funeral, the preacher at the service is quoted: "People have asked why it happened in a church. There is no reason. . . . Our faith is undergirded by belief, when there is no reason" (*New York Times,* April 3, 1994). Marilyn McCord Adams endorsed these ideas in an interview with Peter Steinfels ("Beliefs" column, *New York Times,* October 13, 2001). A moving account of the congregation twenty years later can be found at www.al.com/living/index.ssf/2014/03/goshen_tornado _memorial.html.

153. Hart, *Doors of the Sea,* 44.

that the would-be consoler must never put such words into the sufferer's mouth. In many situations the best rule for the "comforter" may very well be silence. Unfortunately, it is often the case that the "explanations" offered are consoling only to the "comforter," not the sufferer. There are only two possible responses to horrendous suffering. The first is to share the sufferer's pain at length, in silence.[154] The second, as Hart concludes, is to "hate these things with a perfect hatred."[155]

12. New Testament Cosmology and the Hell of the Perpetrators

"God's Monopoly on Violence"[156]

We now come to the third of our four objectives laid out in the beginning of this chapter: to argue that the confession *descendit ad inferna* implies a cosmology. No interpreter in our time understands what this means better than Miroslav Volf. The announcement that the kingdom of God is incarnate in Jesus' person — a central proclamation in all three Synoptic Gospels — is not simply the news, however epochal, of an entrance of a messianic figure into neutral territory. On the contrary, it is the Lord's invasion of a kingdom held by another: "*Active opposition to the kingdom of Satan . . . is therefore in-separable from the proclamation of the Kingdom of God. It is this opposition that brought Jesus Christ to the cross. . . . Redemption cannot therefore be an act of pure positing, but entails negation and struggle, even violence.*"[157]

The reader is urged not to jump to extreme conclusions here; the language is metaphorical. The point is that Paul does not proclaim a "persuasive" God, but rather a *disruptive* one. This is the intent of a verse like "Our old self was crucified with him so that the sinful body might be destroyed" (Rom. 6:6). The apostle's language is not the language of persuasion. In Galatians 6:14, he speaks of "the cross of our Lord Jesus Christ, by which the world has been crucified to me, and I to the world." Insofar as the out-

---

154. In the book of Job, when Job's friends first come to him, their behavior is exemplary. They sit with him on the ground for seven days without saying anything. This is the origin of the Jewish custom of *sitting shiva* ("sitting seven"). Job's pain is greatly increased when the friends break their silence and begin to talk — hence the ironic phrase "Job's comforters," meaning a person who is well-meaning but actually makes the sufferer feel worse.

155. Hart, *Doors of the Sea*, 101 (the phrase "perfect hatred" is found in Ps. 139:22).

156. Miroslav Volf, *Exclusion and Embrace: A Theological Exploration of Identity, Otherness, and Reconciliation* (Nashville: Abingdon, 1996), 302.

157. Volf, *Exclusion and Embrace*, 293, emphasis added.

working of Christ's crucifixion is "violent," it is the necessary violence of the overthrow of the world *(kosmos)* in which Sin and Death are hell-bent on maintaining their sovereignty.[158]

The second question to be raised concerns the contrast between violence and persuasion. Our reaction to it will depend on what we mean by violence. We might recall the story of Jacob, who was set upon in the dark and lamed for life (Gen. 32:22-32) — hardly a "persuasive" method of righting the course of a man who, up to that point, had been largely indifferent to the God of his father and grandfather. The most obvious example, however, is Paul himself. His conversion on the road to Damascus was in no sense an event of persuasion. He himself describes his conversion as something unnatural — "as to one untimely born" (I Cor. 15:8). Paul's frequent use of military metaphors reinforces the biblical theme of God's invasive power.

The subject of violence in the gospel story has been introduced in the section on Thomas Aquinas. Here it is extended through Volf's insight that *God* has the monopoly on violence. Christians can engage in *nonviolent* resistance precisely because the wrath of the living God is directed neither at us *per se* nor at our adversaries, but at the realm of the Evil One. If we are enraged by the injustice we see, is not that a sign of the righteous wrath of God? Yet we are incapable of conquering the dark Powers. Without the wrath of God, which is ultimately on our side, we have no victory.

Volf admits that the idea of violent invasion by God is "unpopular with many Christians." The idea that redemption can be achieved without God's violent mercy he slyly calls one of the "pleasant captivities of the liberal mind."[159] Stanley Hauerwas makes this same point. In his typical scorched-earth style, he writes that liberal Christianity has beguiled the church into believing that it should have no enemies. "Christianity is unintelligible without enemies . . . to be a Christian is to be made part of an army against

---

158. We will be learning from the great second-century theologian Irenaeus in the chapter on recapitulation. He did not get everything right, however. On the subject of "gentle persuasion," he writes that Christ "gave Himself as a redemption for those who had been led into captivity. And since the apostasy tyrannized over us unjustly . . . the Word of God, powerful in all things, and not defective with regard to His own justice, did righteously turn against that apostasy, and redeem from it His own property, not by *violent* means, as the [apostasy] had obtained dominion over us at the beginning, when it insatiably snatched away what was not its own, but by means of *persuasion,* as became a God of counsel, who does not use violent means to obtain what He desires; so that neither should justice be infringed upon, nor the ancient handiwork of God go to destruction" (*Adversus haereses* 5.1.1, emphasis added). From the perspective of Paul, Martin Luther, Miroslav Volf, and Flannery O'Connor, we would say that persuasion is far too weak a weapon to wield against the "captivity" and "tyranny" of the Enemy.

159. Volf, *Exclusion and Embrace,* 304.

armies." Christians are "embattled," and "had better be ready for a fierce counteroffensive as well as be prepared to take some casualties."[160]

The cosmology of the New Testament, as Volf and Hauerwas evoke it in their writings, is fundamental to the work of numerous New Testament scholars and biblical theologians who have been cited throughout these pages. When it begins to make an impression in the pews, the church will be better enabled to discern her role in the conflicts and challenges of our times. In that event, the language of resistance against evil will take its proper shape as good news, not only for every human being who has been victimized, *but also* for those who have victimized others. The *dikaiosyne* (righteousness) of God is able to rectify each of us and all of us.

Who Deserves What?

The fourth and last point concerning the creedal affirmation of Christ's descent into hell is that it powerfully illuminates *not only* the *Christus Victor* motif *but also* several others, including the substitutionary one that we will examine in the next chapter. How is this so?

We can make a distinction between *impersonal* or *random* evils like tsunamis and cancer, on the one hand, and *moral* evil on the other. The essential difference is that whereas moral evil involves both victims and perpetrators, catastrophes like floods, earthquakes, and epidemics result only in victims; there are no perpetrators.[161] It is *the problem of the perpetrators* that offers the greatest challenge to our thinking about hell. Most of our New Testament motifs do not seem to require us to think about perpetrators. Take, for instance, the imagery of ransom and sacrifice; we have little, if any, difficulty in approving the payment of ransom or the offering of a sacrifice on behalf of someone who is valued. If we imagine a Great Assize, we have no

160. Stanley Hauerwas, "No Enemy, No Christianity: Theology and Preaching between 'Worlds,'" in *The Future of Theology: Essays in Honor of Jürgen Moltmann,* ed. Miroslav Volf, Carmen Krieg, and Thomas Kucharz (Grand Rapids: Eerdmans, 1996), 26-34. Volf, not to be outdone, has continued to expound these themes in *The End of Memory: Remembering Rightly in a Violent World* (Grand Rapids: Eerdmans, 2006).

161. To be sure, there are many who would say that Hurricane Katrina, in emptying the city of New Orleans, had a lot of help from the Army Corps of Engineers, which failed to maintain the levees properly. Similarly, if there are naturally caused wildfires in the canyons of southern California, one could say that people should never have built houses there in the first place. Some cancers are caused by smoking. The human factor is not always so easily separated from the impersonal. Nor is the hand of Satan missing from the disorder in the natural world. Nevertheless, the point about perpetrators is largely valid.

trouble rejoicing to see the judgment of God against great evildoers. We find the Passover/exodus and *Christus Victor* themes easy to grasp when they are understood as expeditions to rescue the oppressed, the imprisoned, the enslaved.

But what about the oppressors themselves, the jailers, the slave masters?

At the time of the 2003 U.S. invasion of Iraq, the U.S. government embarked upon a program of secret detention centers overseas where forms of torture were practiced, though it will probably be a long time before the full truth emerges about this matter.[162] It was learned that after the terrorist attacks of September 11, 2001, a private plan was drawn up for the White House and kept secret from the Department of State. Dick Cheney said of this plan, "We think it guarantees that we'll have [available and ready] the kind of treatment of these individuals that we believe they deserve."[163] This raises in an acute fashion the issue of perpetrators and the question of *deserving*.

There is nothing more characteristic of humanity than the universal tendency of one portion of that humanity to justify itself as deserving and some other portion as undeserving. Nothing is more foundational in Christian faith than the recognition that we can never be justified in that way. To speak of "deserving" is to divide up the world in a fashion that is utterly alien to the gospel. Christ came to die expressly for sinners, for the *un*deserving, for the *un*godly (Rom. 5:6). Calvin, with his characteristic concern for pastoral consolation, writes, "The promise of salvation is willingly and freely offered to us by the Lord *in consideration of our misery rather than our deserving*."[164] The great Holy Week hymn "Ah, Holy Jesus" concludes with a prayer to the crucified Lord: "Think on thy pity and thy love unswerving, *not our deserving*."

Philip G. Zimbardo was the designer of the famous Stanford Prison Experiment.[165] He published a book several decades later called, of all things,

162. See Jane Mayer's exposé in the *New Yorker* ("The Black Sites," August 13, 2007). The president, George W. Bush, was still insisting as late as 2008 that "the United States does not torture." Bush seems to have believed this. The judicial report written by John Yoo (the so-called Torture Memos) was designed to expand the options of "enhanced interrogations" in the operations of the CIA by redefining the definition of torture. Bush's *éminence grise,* Vice President Richard Cheney, is known to have supported this. Some of the language used by Cheney and Defense Secretary Rumsfeld continues to be quoted: "The gloves are going to come off"; "Some hands are going to get dirty"; the United States was going to have to "go over to the dark side." See also Mark Danner's five-part essay about Cheney and Rumsfeld in the *New York Review of Books* (2013-2014).

163. "After Terror, a Secret Rewriting of Military Law," *New York Times,* October 24, 2004.

164. Calvin, *Institutes* 3.2.29.

165. The famous experiments by Stanley Milgram and Philip G. Zimbardo in the 1960s and 1970s continue to be cited to this day. Zimbardo's is so well known that social scientists

The Lucifer Effect: Understanding How Good People Turn Evil.[166] It was clear, as shown in an interview he gave at the time of its publication, that he was still deeply troubled by his own loss of moral perspective as the experiment progressed. As the volunteer "guards" descended further into brutal and inhumane behavior, Zimbardo and his team were so engrossed in their study that they, too, lost their bearings. Not until his girlfriend visited the simulated "prison" and threatened to break up with him did Zimbardo fully realize what he was doing.[167] His conclusions are sobering for the "best" of us.[168]

Marilyn McCord Adams consistently uses the phrase "*participants in* horrors" when she refers to monstrously evil actions.[169] Her choice of the word "participants" is striking. She means the word to include not only victims of horrors but also perpetrators, collaborators, and "innocent" bystanders. We are arguing here that drawing a line between those who participate in horrors and those who do not is a dubious enterprise; all of us in one way or another are either potential perpetrators, potential participants, or (most likely) passive enablers of horrors.[170] W. H. Auden embedded this conviction in his

---

refer to it simply as the SPE (Stanford Prison Experiment). Both these experiments showed that in cases of egregious abuse by peer groups, it is a rare individual who refuses to obey or go along (TV documentary, "The Human Behavior Experiments," Court TV and Sundance Channels, 2006). See also review by Alessandra Stanley, "The Darkest Behaviors, in the Name of Obedience," *New York Times*, June 1, 2006). A review of Milgram's findings by Steven Marcus, a fellow of the Center for Advanced Study in the Behavioral Sciences at Stanford, while critical of the method, acknowledged the importance of the experiments because "it remains important that we know, or that we do not forget, these things about ourselves" (review of *Obedience to Authority,* by Stanley Milgram, *New York Times Book Review,* January 13, 1974).

166. New York: Random House, 2007. The reader will notice the use of the fallen-angel symbolism in the title.

167. Claudia Dreifus, "Finding Hope in Knowing the Universal Capacity for Evil," *New York Times,* April 3, 2007. Zimbardo later testified that the conditions in the Abu Ghraib prison in Iraq, where American military guards were allowed to run amok with impunity, were such that even the most clean-cut young Americans would have been sucked into participating.

168. In an essay-review of a film, *City of Life and Death,* about the Nanjing massacre (rape of Nanking), the exceptional writer and public intellectual Ian Buruma observes that the director "shows how terrifying ordinary young men can be when they exercise their power over those who have none. . . . It is as if the helplessness of the victims only provokes greater aggression." That human trait, under the power of Sin, is what crucifixion, as a method, exploited. The title of Buruma's piece is "From Tenderness to Savagery in Seconds," *New York Review of Books,* October 13, 2011. (For his humane work, Ian Buruma was awarded the Abraham Kuyper Prize at Princeton Theological Seminary in 2012.)

169. Adams, *Horrendous Evils,* 105 and passim.

170. I wish to be understood here. It is morally reprehensible to conflate victims with perpetrators by saying "We are all victims" or anything of the sort. Clive James wrote of Primo Levi, "Levi . . . is ready to *understand* [the persecutors], as long as he is not asked to *exonerate*

poem: "We shan't, not since Stalin and Hitler, trust ourselves ever again." If this is true, then the gospel has to be good news *not only* for victims *but also* for perpetrators. If we say that Jesus Christ descended into hell, perhaps we mean most of all *the hell of the perpetrators* — not just those who are in Sheol because they died, not just those who are in Limbo awaiting the Conqueror, but those who are in Gehenna under a sentence of everlasting condemnation.

The Hell of the Perpetrators

Many people are able to conceive of the possibility of redemption for some types of evildoers, but not for all. This is a complex matter. It is not wrong, surely, to see the face of Satan in the faces of torturers.[171] Whose face do we see, then, in the case of CIA operatives who were turned loose on the "detainees" after 9/11?[172] Here is a testimony about one of them. A former CIA officer described what conducting a prolonged interrogation had done to one of his colleagues: "[He] has horrible nightmares. When you cross over that line of darkness, it's hard to come back. *You lose your soul.* You can do your best to justify it, but it's outside the norm. You can't go to that dark a place without it changing you. He's a good guy. It really haunts him. You are inflicting something really evil and horrible on somebody."[173]

It would seem that the victims of torture are not the only ones who lose their souls. Is this "good guy" a "perpetrator"? Under certain conditions, ordinary human beings will do "evil and horrible" things. At the time of the fiftieth anniversary of V-J Day, Richard J. Harwood, a retired *Washington Post* correspondent who served in the Pacific during World War II, wrote of

---

them. His patience runs out only when it comes to those who parade their compassion without realizing that they are trampling on the memory of the innocent dead." James quotes Levi: "To confuse the murderers with their victims, he says, 'is a moral disease or an aesthetic affectation or a sinister sign of complicity'" (Clive James, "Last Will and Testament," *New Yorker,* May 23, 1988, emphasis added; this was written shortly after Levi's death). As was suggested in chapter 3, such confusion should be met with the question, "Where's the outrage?"

171. Dietrich Bonhoeffer's brother Klaus, a few days before he was executed by the Nazis, wrote on a piece of paper, "I am not afraid of being hanged, but . . . I'd rather die than see those faces [his torturers] again. I have seen the Devil, and I can't forget it" (Eberhard Bethge, *Dietrich Bonhoeffer: Man of Vision, Man of Courage* [New York: Harper and Row, 1970], 803, 832).

172. The widespread use of the word "detainee," rather than "prisoner," after 9/11 suggested that the captives were not considered legitimate prisoners of war and therefore not deserving of the Geneva Conventions.

173. Quoted by Jane Mayer, "The Black Sites," emphasis added. The "somebody" was Khalid Sheik Mohammed, the mastermind of the 9/11 attacks.

having seen his comrades horribly mutilated by the Japanese. Later, on Iwo Jima, he and his fellow Marines came upon a Japanese soldier "charbroiled by a flame thrower. He wanted water. He got, instead, the lighted end of a cigarette in his mouth, courtesy of a boy from Brooklyn. One of our unit's favorite snapshots from Saipan was of a dozen or so smiling Marines holding aloft Japanese heads on bamboo poles."[174] Thus brutality elicits brutality and callousness calls forth callousness. The entire American people were set against the Japanese in those days.[175]

Who, exactly, is a perpetrator? Books about the Holocaust with titles like *Neighbors* and *Ordinary Men* document the way that entire communities of "ordinary" people can be seized by a murderous frenzy lasting weeks and months.[176] Were they perpetrators? At what point does a passive bystander, or even a horrified bystander who takes no action, become a participant or enabler? In many cases of atrocity, a roster of bystanders would include just about all of us. The enemy lines shift, depending on who is vulnerable and who is free to act with impunity. Primo Levi wrote, "Compassion and brutality can coexist in the same individual and in the same moment, despite all logic."[177]

The Descent of the Righteous for the Unrighteous

Our text from I Peter should be studied in its entirety (only part of it appeared above). Here it is in full:

> Christ also died for sins once for all, the righteous for the unrighteous, that he might bring us to God, being put to death in the flesh but made alive in the spirit; in which he went and preached to the spirits in prison, *who formerly did not obey.* (I Pet. 3:18-20)

174. Richard L. Harwood, "Americans and Japanese Haunted by Horrors of the Pacific War," *Washington Post* Service, *International Herald Tribune,* August 1, 1995. Mr. Harwood served in the Pacific with the Fifth Marine Amphibious Corps from 1943 to 1946 and took part in many battles.

175. One hundred ten thousand Japanese Americans having been interned during World War II in the interests of national security, it was a short distance from such policies to lethal propaganda depicting the "Japs" as subhuman, deserving of a fate worse than death. Thus very few voices were raised about the bombings of Hiroshima and Nagasaki until the publication of John Hersey's *Hiroshima,* named as the most important work of journalism of the twentieth century by a panel of judges. This monumental account gave a human face to the previously unseen and unknown victims of the atomic explosion of August 6, 1945.

176. Jan T. Gross's *Neighbors* and Christopher R. Browning's *Ordinary Men* both recount such extreme episodes.

177. Levi, *The Drowned and the Saved,* 56.

If this complete sentence is set in proximity with *the descent into the hell of the perpetrators,* its implications are profound. The connections here have not been sufficiently expounded. The reference to Christ's preaching to the *formerly disobedient* spirits in prison occurs in a very specific context: the death of the righteous Son of God "for the *un*righteous." Once again we can follow the writer's train of thought. Having declared that the righteous Christ died *in exchange for* the *un*righteous — a thought that is startling enough to begin with — the writer finds it logical to speak not only of the *living* unrighteous but also of those many unrighteous persons who have been long dead, thereby encompassing all who have ever lived.

This phrase "the righteous for the unrighteous" suggests the motif of substitution or exchange, the subject of our next chapter. But here we note that nothing in the Petrine text works unless we grant that God has gained absolute and ultimate mastery over the Powers — Sin, Death, Satan. The meaning is multilayered, certainly, but this much seems clear: Christ is the righteous One who "brings us to God" by dying "for sins once for all," on behalf of and in the place of the *unrighteous.*[178] The suggestion is that the exchange is made on behalf of all the unrighteous who have ever lived. He does this by "being put to death in the flesh but made alive in the Spirit" by the power of God. The power of God over Sin and Death for the purpose of bringing the *un*righteous to himself is dramatically pictured as the preaching of the victorious Christ to the *disobedient* spirits shut up in the netherworld.[179] I Peter 3:18-20 is one of those places in Scripture where the Word of God is shown to be able to raise the dead and call forth into existence that which does not exist (Rom. 4:17).

The Irresistible Word

In I Peter 4:3-6, we seem to be carried even farther along this radical road:

> Let the time that is past suffice for doing what the Gentiles like to do, living in licentiousness, passions, drunkenness, revels, carousing, and lawless idolatry. They are surprised that you do not now join them in

---

178. In the next chapter we will take the position that *huper* has both of these meanings.

179. Notice also the interesting qualifier, "*formerly* disobedient." Does this mean "formerly" in the sense of "before Christ"? Or does "formerly" float free of chronological time, so that it can mean "before meeting Christ" at any time? Is the power of Christ limited to a specific action during his entombment? Rather, is this not a symbolic way of saying that Christ can loose bonds wherever and whenever he appears as our Liberator? We can't be sure, but the suggestion is there.

the same wild profligacy, and they abuse you; but they will give account to him who is ready to judge the living and the dead. For this is why the gospel was preached *even to the dead, that though judged in the flesh like men, they might live in the spirit like God.*

Christ preached the gospel of life "even to the dead," who will indeed be judged "like men," but the ultimate outcome will be divine life in the Spirit (I Pet. 4:6). The full content of Christ's preaching to the dead is not explicitly spelled out here, but it could hardly be anything other than the resurrection of the dead by the life-giving Word. We saw that Rufinus, as early as the late fourth century, called attention to the helplessness of the "formerly disobedient" spirits by adding the word *inclusi,* "shut up" (*in carcere inclusi,* "shut up in prison"), to his Latin translation. Anyone shut up in a prison is powerless to escape without a deliverer; the door is locked from the outside and must be unlocked by someone independent of the prison warden — someone operating from that transcendent realm that is independent of warden, prison, and prisoner alike.[180] This is what I Peter declares: the advent of Christ has changed everything. The Word of God that comes to the *formerly disobedient* prisoners of Death from that realm of greater power makes them live "in the spirit like God."

The apostolic author writes out of the great Hebrew conception of the Word of God. The voice of the Son of God is able to call life into being where there was death, obedience where there was disobedience, faith where there was disbelief. The power of God *to call into existence the things that do not exist* is one of the foundational truths about God. This can readily be illustrated from Scripture by the story of creation in the first chapter of Genesis. The words "and God said . . . and it was so" are repeated in stately measure nine times in that one chapter, a repetition that produces a powerful impression on the attentive listener. The passage proclaims the instantaneous efficacy of the voice of God, who calls into existence the things that do not exist. This is the doctrine of creation *ex nihilo,* creation out of nothing by the Word of God.

Therefore the gospel preached to the "formerly disobedient" dead is not the imparting of information to them, or an exhortation to them, or even an invitation to them. Were it only an invitation, the "spirits in prison" would perforce remain where they are, lying impotent in the bonds of Death and

---

180. Tertullian originated the vivid image of Christ smashing the bolts and trampling down the gates of hell (*quae portas adamantinas mortis at aeneas seras infererorum infregit*). Tertullian, *De resurrectione carnis* 44, in Russell, *Satan,* 121 n. 39.

hell. When Peter says that Christ preached to the spirits in prison, this does not mean that the Lord gave them a speech or a sermon. The preaching of Christ to the "spirits in prison" is analogous to God saying, "Let there be light," *and there was light* as a direct result of the spoken Word.

The Word preached in the prison of hell is able effectively to destroy the *zophos* by bringing the light of Christ. Artists over the centuries have painted hundreds of images of Christ bringing the Old Testament faithful out of Hades, but our Petrine text goes further. These are not the *faithful;* these are the *unregenerate* who failed to repent "in the days of Noah." Did those "spirits shut up in prison" remain there after the Son of God preached to them? What about those "Gentiles" whom the Petrine author so roundly condemns? They too will "give account to him who is ready to judge the living and the dead." How can we mortals make a final distinction between ourselves and those others who will be judged along with us? I Peter continues: "For the time has come for judgment to begin with the household of God" (I Pet. 4:17).[181]

Everything depends upon the way that "judgment" is construed. In chapter 3 ("The Question of Justice"), we saw that the judgment of God is utterly unlike human attempts to administer justice, since it always proceeds out of his perfect mercy and can therefore be unconditionally trusted. If the "household of God" understands this, it will rush to the Last Judgment with the confidence that can only come from trust in the promise of God.

But what of that Word, that gospel, that Christ preached to the "formerly disobedient" dead? That question has been asked in the form of another question: Could Lazarus have refused the command of the Son of God at the tomb, "Lazarus, come forth"? The one who is himself the Word made flesh (John 1:1, 14) gives the mere command, "And God said . . . and it was so."

John Donne preached:

The dead hear not thunder, nor feel they an earthquake. If the Cannon batter the Church walls, in which they lie buried, it wakes not them,

---

181. The context admittedly presents a more complicated picture. The Christian community is called to stand first in judgment, but the hints given concerning the restitution of the "formerly disobedient" dead are counterbalanced by verses like 4:17-18: "and if [the judgment] begins with us, what will be the end of those who do not obey the gospel of God? And 'If the righteous man is scarcely saved, / where will the impious and sinner appear?'" Here, the apostle seems to say that the salvation of the "impious and sinners" is almost inconceivable. I am suggesting that *almost* inconceivable is not *totally* inconceivable in the vision of the New Testament.

nor does it shake or affect them . . . but yet there is a voice, which the dead shall hear; the dead shall hear the voice of the Son of God and they that hear shall live. It is a clamour, a vociferation, a shout. It carries a penetration and a power, a command. Since that voice at the Creation said, *Let there be a world,* was never heard such a voice as this, *Arise ye dead.*[182]

Only such a gospel of the resurrection of the dead can adequately address the problem of the perpetrators.

The Future of Hell

James Nachtwey and Sebastião Salgado are photographers who have depicted the horrors of war, poverty, famine, and disease. In a review of their work, the Pulitzer Prize–winning critic Henry Allen has this to say: "These photographs seem to ask *if the Holocaust was in fact the rule,* and if the discarded notion of *man's inherent depravity* goes further than liberal optimism in explaining the man-made madness of the last hundred years, and of however many centuries there are to come."[183] At stake in this chapter is a concept of hell that is adequate to the horrors of the twentieth century and the looming terrors of the twenty-first. The argument here is that it is necessary to posit the existence of a metaphorical hell in order to acknowledge the reality and power of radical evil — evil that does not yield to education, reason, or good intentions. Evil has an existence independent of the sum total of human misdeeds. The concept of hell takes seriously the nature and scale of evil. Without a concept of hell, Christian faith is sentimental and evasive, unable to stand up to reality in this world.[184] Without an unflinching grasp of the radical nature of evil, Christian faith would be little more than wishful thinking.

182. John Donne, sermon preached on Easter Day 1622, on I Thess. 4:17.

183. Henry Allen, "Seasons in Hell," *New Yorker,* June 12, 2000, emphasis added. Salgado had a type of breakdown after he photographed the aftermath of the Rwandan genocide. He lost any faith in the possibility of salvation for humanity — as we have already noted in the case of other observers in Rwanda. The 2014 film *The Salt of the Earth* tells how he was able to recover through a project, Instituto Terra, which he developed on his drought-destroyed farm in Brazil.

184. This concern is well illustrated by the observation of the woman quoted in chapter 3, who said she could stand it if there were no heaven, but there had to be a hell because if there weren't, "where would Hitler and Pol Pot go?" (She speaks as though hell were an actual *place,* but this is metonymy, suggesting a *telos,* or final disposition.)

Hell is a *dominion*. It is the dominion of evil, of Death, the sphere where wickedness rules. Radical evil has a purposefulness all its own, which explains why we personify its ruler as Satan.[185] It is the domain of wickedness, of stupidity, of despair. In his gripping book *Schindler's List* (not the screenplay), Thomas Keneally refers to Auschwitz variously as a "duchy," a "kingdom," and "Planet Auschwitz." He wants us to understand evil — almost literally — as a *realm* that creates its own reality out of lies that no one contradicts, practices no one questions, authority against whom no one rebels. If this is not hell, what is?

What then is the final destiny of this realm?

J. Christiaan Beker provocatively writes: "The final apocalyptic triumph of God does not permit a permanent pocket of evil or resistance to God in his creation."[186] If Beker is right about this, then neither the devil nor hell can be allowed to continue indefinitely as a parallel (or even a subordinate) domain. The reign of Satan will not be permitted to keep its territory as a permanent realm alongside the kingdom of God. It must be finally and completely obliterated, and will pass out of memory.[187] It is toward this conclusion that our study has been pointing all along.[188] Whether this means the *redemption* of

185. "The commander of the atmosphere described in [Eph.] 2:2 is a monarch, his realm an absolute monarchy." Markus Barth, *Ephesians: Introduction, Translation, and Commentary on Chapters 1–3*, Anchor Bible 34 (Garden City, N.Y.: Doubleday, 1974), 228. Importantly, M. Barth qualifies this with a footnote on the same page: "According to Luke 4:6 the ruler of this realm is aware that his power is not absolute but derived: 'it is given to me [by God].'"

186. J. Christiaan Beker, *Paul the Apostle: The Triumph of God in Life and Thought* (Philadelphia: Fortress, 1980), 194. This theological argument for "annihilationism" is stronger than simply wishing that the mass murderers of the age of genocide would not suffer forever. Such wishing is rather too tender-minded, not rigorous enough to compete against the imagery of an ongoing hell of "wailing and gnashing of teeth" that most of us, in unguarded moments, have wished on someone or other at some point in our lives. This imagery is so strong in much of the New Testament, including the teaching of Jesus himself, that we cannot simply ignore it. In Matt. 25:46, Jesus himself speaks of "eternal punishment." The question is, assuming that this is not to be taken literally, exactly how far do we go with it imagistically? We will continue to wrestle with this question leading up to the concluding chapter.

187. The importance of the erasure, not only of the wrong done, but of the *memory* of the wrong done is the theme of Miroslav Volf's book *The End of Memory*. He draws upon Dante's final cantos in *Purgatorio* and *Paradiso*: "Forgetting is not a flight from the defective or the unbearable.... The forgetting of evil is in the service of remembering the good, and remembering the good is the consequence of being engrossed in God, 'the end of all desires'" (*The End of Memory*, 141, quoting Canto 33.47).

188. It is beyond the scope of this book to do an extended study of the book of Revelation, but I argue that the vision of John ultimately supports this conclusion. "The smoke from her

the Hitlers and the Pol Pots or their *annihilation* we cannot say. What we can say for sure, proleptically, in faith, is that "the kingdom of the world has become the kingdom of our Lord and of his Christ, and he shall reign for ever and ever [*eis tous aionas ton aionon;* literally 'into the ages of the ages']."[189]

The descent into hell and the triumph of Christ were prefigured all along in the incarnation. We alluded earlier to the way that hell is brought into close proximity to Christmas in medieval music. Over and over again we find it: the meaning of Christmas is that God is invading the territory held by the Prince of Darkness. The definitive closure of this cosmic invasion, the V-Day to its D-Day, will be the final Day of God.[190] On that last day there will be only one Ruler, only one Lord. Scripture is quite clear and unambiguous about that. The Judge of all the cosmos will not be Satan. Radical evil will have no status in the day of judgment, or the day of final reconciliation, as Volf calls it.[191] "Death shall have no more dominion" (cf. Rom. 6:9). If evil is the absence of good, then the victory of our Lord and of his Christ will be the absence of evil, "for ever and ever."

13. Summary and Transition

The theme of Christ's descent into hell signifies the impossibility of any human response adequate to the power of evil. The horrors are too great, the suffering is too terrible, the "heart of darkness" too intractable for any

---

goes up for ever and ever" (19:3) could symbolically refer to the ultimate and final annihilation of Babylon, not just its continuing fires.

A serious challenge to this view is in 20:10. What is meant by the torment of the beast and the false prophet *eis tous aionas ton aionon,* "for ever and ever" (a phrase used many times in Revelation, including in 11:15)? Is it simply a rhetorical expression? There are only two places in Revelation where one could argue that the writer means to equate the "forever and ever" of the kingdom of God with the "forever and ever" of the torment of the beast and the false prophet in 20:10. The other is in 14:11 ("they have no rest, day or night"). We might read this as figurative language meaning that evil will meet a fate, unimaginable by us, commensurate with all the horrors of human history.

For further investigation, I recommend George Hunsinger's review of the theological and biblical landscape: "Hell and Damnation," in his *Disruptive Grace: Studies in the Theology of Karl Barth* (Grand Rapids: Eerdmans, 2000).

189. Rev. 11:15. And we can say for sure that "here is a call for the endurance and faith of the saints" (13:10).

190. The V-Day analogy from World War II was originated by Oscar Cullmann in *Christ and Time* (1964).

191. Volf, *The End of Memory*, 179.

"religious" answer to be of any avail. In all religion, it is only the story of the crucified God that can stand up to the challenge of the long history of human wickedness. Christianity is unique. This is the claim with which we began; this is the claim we now repeat as we approach the next two chapters and the climax of this volume.

The unalloyed proclamation of Scripture is that the death and resurrection of Christ is the hinge of history. It is the unique old-world-overturning and new-world-constituting event that calls *every* human project into question — including especially our religious projects. The concept of the descent into hell and the hints given in Deutero-Isaiah, Zechariah, I Peter 3:18-22, and Romans 11:32 lead us out into a vista of God's ultimate power and purpose that we could not have imagined from any perspective that divides people up into righteous and unrighteous, godly and ungodly, good and evil. The descent of Christ into hell means that there is no realm anywhere in the universe, including the domain of Death and the devil, where anyone can go to be cut off from the saving power of God.

This chapter closes with a passage taken from a discussion of the descent into hell by Karl Barth, words that will help us make the transition to the next chapter on the theme of substitution:

> God Himself in Jesus Christ His Son, at once true God and true man, takes the place of condemned man. God's judgment is executed, God's law takes its course, but in such a way that what man had to suffer is suffered by this One, who as God's Son stands for all others. Such is the Lordship of Jesus Christ, who stands for us before God, by taking upon Himself what belongs to us. In Him God makes Himself liable, at the point at which we are accursed and guilty and lost. He it is in His Son, who in the person of this crucified man bears on Golgotha all that ought to be laid on us. And in this way He makes an end of the curse.[192]

192. Karl Barth, *Dogmatics in Outline,* 119.

CHAPTER ELEVEN

The Substitution

Outline of Chapter

1. Sketching the history of the motif of substitution
   - Substitution in the New Testament
     — *For us* or *in our place?*
     — Paul's letter to the Romans
     — Galatians 3:10-14: the man hanged on a tree
     — Isaiah 53 in the New Testament
   - The patristic period
   - The Middle Ages
   - Preliminary conclusion
   - The motif of substitution since Anselm
     — Martin Luther
     — John Calvin
     — Penal substitution in late Reformed scholasticism
2. Objections to the penal substitution model
   - It is "crude"
   - It keeps bad company
   - It is culturally conditioned
   - It views the death as detached from the resurrection
   - It is incoherent: an innocent person cannot take on the guilt of another
   - It glorifies suffering and encourages masochistic behavior
   - It is too "theoretical," too scholastic and abstract
   - It depicts a vindictive God
   - It is essentially violent
   - It is morally objectionable

Introduction to the Theme

Rabbi Michael Goldberg is an exceptionally gifted interpreter of the biblical story. In his book *Jews and Christians: Getting Our Stories Straight*, his retelling of Matthew's version of Christ's passion and crucifixion excels that of many Christians in its sympathetic appreciation of what the First Evangelist wants us to see. Notice, for instance, this question: "Why doesn't Jesus come down off that cross and let God put up there *in his place* those who *truly deserve to die:* Jews, Romans, in sum, *all humanity* which has in one way or another taken part in committing such a heinous crime?"[1] Here, in one sentence, this Jewish commentator makes two crucial points easily and gracefully, as if the substitution motif and the guilt of all humankind were manifest and plain to anyone reading Matthew. "Jews" and "Romans" become much larger here than the actual first-century Jews and Romans, because they represent all types of people in every century.

Rabbi Goldberg is not aware of, or chooses to ignore, a controversy that has been roiling the church for some time. He sees no problem with the idea that Jesus is crucified in place of those who "truly deserve to die," namely, "all humanity." However, this concept of substitution (or exchange), applied to the cross of Christ, arouses discomfort and even hostility in many circles today. Indeed, this antagonism is widespread and growing; it has been filtering down from academia into the mainline churches for the better part of a century.[2] The fact that so much of it comes from highly placed scholars and church leaders adds to the unease, even distress, of those who have always believed without question in what has been called "the substitutionary atonement."[3] It is not an exaggeration to say that in some circles there has been something resembling a campaign of intimidation, so that those who cherish the idea that Jesus offered himself *in our place* have been made to feel that they are neo-Crusaders, prone to violence, oppressors of women, and enablers of child abuse.[4]

1. Michael Goldberg, *Jews and Christians: Getting Our Stories Straight* (Valley Forge, Pa.: Trinity, 1991), 193-94, emphasis added.

2. Hans Urs von Balthasar has written, "The idea that in his suffering Jesus bore the sins of the world is a motif that has been almost completely abandoned in the modern world" (quoted by George Hunsinger, *Disruptive Grace: Studies in the Theology of Karl Barth* [Grand Rapids: Eerdmans, 2000], 361).

3. The cumbersome term "substitutionary atonement" will not appear again in this book. It sounds academic, theoretical, and unattractive. It arouses suspicion among many. Instead, I will refer more simply to "the motif of substitution" or, alternatively, "the theme of exchange."

4. The most useful recent collection of essays designed to treat these accusations and correct the faults of "penal substitution" as it was developed in later Reformed scholasticism is Brad Jersak and Michael Hardin, eds., *Stricken by God? Nonviolent Identification and the Victory*

By the middle of the first decade of the new millennium, the attacks on the motif of substitution had gained so much ground that retreat was being sounded even in the most "Calvinistic" redoubts. Against this backdrop, some readers may suspect the present chapter of being retrograde. On the contrary, the theme of substitution need not, and indeed should not, result in overly rationalistic, schematic versions of penal substitution as found in Reformed scholasticism. This chapter, in conversation with *both* the attackers *and* the retreaters, is a defense of the central importance of the *motif* of substitution (not the "theory") as it appears in numerous scriptural contexts and in the tradition. The intent, however, is to make this case while maintaining the centrality of the other biblical images we have examined — particularly the ones that most obviously place us on the front lines of God's apocalyptic war: *Christus Victor* and the descent into hell.

In the first section of this chapter we will trace the history of the theme of substitution. In the second section we will try to identify the reasons for the widespread withdrawal of approval of, and indeed, outright attacks on, this motif. In the third section we will respond to the points made in the second, and in the fourth we will propose a more comprehensive way of understanding substitution, or exchange, together with all the other images that we have been examining.

The increased prestige of the *Christus Victor* theme in our day is partly related to its effectiveness as an alternative to the formerly widespread, now much-reviled, "penal substitution theory." More important for our argument here is that the strong preference today for the *Christus Victor* theme, often to the exclusion of the others, is related to the distaste in the mainline churches and in liberal theology for the gravity and power of Sin and God's judgment upon it — a chief feature of the models based on sacrifice, "satisfaction" (Anselm), and substitution. Because there has been a good deal of overlapping among biblical, postbiblical, and nonbiblical models of the atonement, many interpreters over the years have been misled into thinking that the

---

of Christ (Grand Rapids: Eerdmans, 2007). Particularly valuable are essays by Miroslav Volf, C. F. D. Moule, N. T. Wright, and Mark D. Baker. Taken as a whole, however, the collection (with those notable exceptions), having been assembled under Girardian and Anabaptist auspices, gives the impression of existing entirely to show that nonviolence equals the sum and substance of the gospel — a problem that one of the essayists (Andrew P. Klager), to his credit, acknowledges. Coeditor Brad Jersak, in his introductory essay, displays all the indiscriminate passion of the convert who has pruned away so much of the plant that he has killed it. Brought up with penal substitution in its most egregious form — which he rightly rejects — he now puts forth the arguments against the motif of substitution with the same unsubtle, formulaic zeal as its contemporary supporters often do in its defense.

theme of Jesus' death *for us and in our place,* repeatedly attested in the New Testament, is inextricably bound up with penal concepts, abstract schemes of compensation, diagrammatic systems of transferred merit, and so forth.

This confusion of the simple biblical statement that Christ died not only on our behalf but also *in our place* should not be mistaken for the various elaborations that have been attached to it. We will attempt to show that the motif of substitution, rightly understood, is present behind and in all the other motifs. Moreover, it has features that we cannot do without. There is something deep in the human psyche that responds to the idea of substitution — someone who dies in my place so that I may live — and the loss of it from the preaching and teaching of the church would be grievous.[5]

1. Sketching the History of the Motif of Substitution

There have been a few notable occasions in the history of Christian doctrine when something new has been added to what has been believed *quod semper, quod ubique, quod ab omnibus.*[6] Disputes continue about some of these additions. We have already argued in favor of a clause that was added late to the Apostles' Creed: "he descended into hell." Another classic example is the late (sixth century) *filioque* clause, which remains a bone of contention between East and West.[7] Moving to our own time, the thoroughgoing reinterpretation of the biblical testimony about slavery and the place of women in the church could not now be undone even if we should want to undo it.[8] As for Anselm

---

5. The universal appeal of the notion of substitution is illustrated by the immense popularity of the book and movie series *The Hunger Games.* When a very young girl is chosen by lot to fight to the death, her big sister steps forward and volunteers to take her place. It is the simplest and most recognizable plot element imaginable; who can fail to understand it?

6. The Vincentian canon: "Always, everywhere, and by all."

7. The noted patristics scholar Richard Norris acknowledged the problem of the late appearance (sixth century) of the *filioque* clause, but thought that once it had found its place, it could not be removed without serious doctrinal consequences, even if the removal was an attempt to heal a breach between the Eastern and Western Church (my lecture notes, General Theological Seminary, 1975).

8. It is not possible to say at this writing whether the attempts to reinterpret scriptural teaching about homosexuality will be similarly successful, carrying the day across virtually all Christian churches, as has been the case with regard to slavery. In the case of women's equality in the church, even the Vatican is feeling the pressure. Proponents on both sides of the discussion about homosexuality agree that a scriptural case for reinterpreting the tradition is more difficult to make than it has been in the debates about slavery and the role of women, because the passages in Scripture concerning homosexual behavior, though relatively few, appear so

at the turn of the first millennium, when he made the connection between incarnation and atonement central to his argument, it changed the landscape permanently. The idea was always there, but it was not highlighted in the Fathers; Anselm brought it to the fore.[9] The link has proven to be such a powerful motif for preaching and faith that it seems perverse to try to purge it from Christian thinking and devotion.

Opponents of substitution typically call attention to the fact that the Fathers did not work out an official doctrine of atonement for the church.[10] Even so comprehensive and catholic a thinker as Jaroslav Pelikan, however, suggests that the Fathers, including even Augustine, had not fully thought through "the doctrine of redemption and the plan of salvation," and implies that Anselm, for all the charges brought against him, succeeded in filling in the picture.[11]

As we have suggested in earlier chapters, opposition to the motif of substitution derives at least in part from the contemporary wish to avoid the themes of sin and judgment — a move that is typical of the atmosphere in the culture and the churches today. Sin forms no part of many contemporary accounts of the crucifixion. Instead, we hear an exchange like this:

Q. Why did Jesus die?
A. To show us how much God loves us.

Although this answer about God's love is indeed true, it will not serve as an adequate account of what happened on Golgotha. At least three factors are missing from this explanation:

---

unambiguous, and countervailing passages have been hard to find — which is not true in the other two cases. The argument about same-sex marriage must be made from a general view of the canon taken as a whole without reference to specific texts.

9. As we have seen, Anselm's central figure is that of satisfaction, but the idea of substitution is intrinsic to his argument and he is frequently cited as the one who introduced the motif.

10. In the opinion of T. F. Torrance, "The most astonishing feature [of the apostolic fathers] was the failure to grasp the significance of the death of Christ" (*The Doctrine of Grace in the Apostolic Fathers* [Edinburgh: Oliver and Boyd, 1948], 137).

11. Jaroslav Pelikan, *The Christian Tradition: A History of the Development of Doctrine*, 5 vols. (Chicago: University of Chicago Press, 1975-1991); here vol. 4, *Reformation of Church and Dogma (1300-1700)* (Chicago: University of Chicago Press, 1983), 22-23; and vol. 1, *The Emergence of the Catholic Tradition (100-600)* (Chicago: University of Chicago Press, 1975), 141-55. Significantly, Pelikan distinguishes "the *picture* of Christ" from "the *dogma* of Christ" in discussing the Lord's saving work (*Emergence*, 142, emphasis added). This is a good way to describe the *modus operandi* of the book in hand. I am emphasizing *pictures* — images, metaphors, motifs — rather than *doctrines*.

1. the horror, disgust, and shame of crucifixion
2. the repeated New Testament declaration that Christ died "for sin"
3. the condition of the world, the hellish suffering of many, and the predicament of humanity

Making the connections among these three factors is essential if we are to plumb the depths of the crucifixion of Christ. Much of what has preceded deals with these subjects, but we are only now arriving at the most challenging complex of ideas.

Substitution in the New Testament

Discussions of substitution in the New Testament often focus on familiar short texts like I Peter 3:18 and II Corinthians 5:21. These important verses are discussed elsewhere in this book. However, because they have so often been cited, sometimes tendentiously, in the context of substitution, we will not examine them further here. Instead, the next passages will demonstrate how the notion of substitution lies behind not only scattered individual verses but also large sections of Scripture.

For Us *or* In Our Place?

Discussion about the meaning of Christ's death always involves the Greek prepositions *huper* and *peri*. These are the words that are translated "for" in English, as in "Jesus Christ died *for* us" or "Jesus Christ died *for* sin." "The words *huper* and *peri* are often used by the New Testament writers to convey the meaning of the cross."[12] What does it mean to say that Jesus Christ died

---

12. The Greek word *anti* is also used many times to mean "in place of," or simply "for," but not in connection with the death of Christ. Here are some further examples of *huper* (and one of *peri*) from Paul's letters:

Christ died *for (huper)* the ungodly (Rom. 5:6).
Christ died *for (huper)* us (Rom. 5:8).
One *for (huper)* whom Christ died (Rom. 14:15).
[He] has died *for (huper)* all (II Cor. 5:14).
Lord Jesus Christ, who gave himself *for (huper)* our sins (Gal. 1:4).
The Son of God, who loved me and gave himself *for (huper)* me (Gal. 2:20).
Christ . . . having become a curse *for (huper)* us (Gal. 3:13).
Our Lord Jesus Christ, who died *for (peri)* us (I Thess. 5:9-10).

for us? The debate about these words has to do, not with their frequency, which is indisputable, but with their meaning and relevance.

Sometimes these words seem to mean "for our sake" and sometimes "for our benefit" and sometimes "in our place" as a representative or substitute. It stretches credibility and common sense to insist that the words *never* mean "in our place." Insisting that they can *never* have this meaning is even more tendentious than insisting that they *always* do, because taking such a fixed position betrays an unreasonable antipathy for the concept of substitution, just as much as does the opposite position of stubbornly maintaining that substitution is the *only* idea that counts.

Some biblical scholars who have written extensively about atonement — preeminently the redoubtable Vincent Taylor in a previous generation — have had so much unease or antipathy for the idea that Jesus was in some way substituting himself for us that they could not bring themselves even to use the word "substitution." Much more recently, however, Charles Cousar, while acknowledging the difficulty of assigning a precise meaning to a preposition *(huper)* that sometimes has one sense and sometimes another, nevertheless states that in some verses *huper* "clearly denotes 'in place of,' a replacement of one party for another (so Galatians 3:13, II Corinthians 5:21; probably II Corinthians 5:14, and others) and thus a vicarious death."[13]

Not limiting the citations to Paul, we would be quick to include not only I Peter 3:18 but also another text that clearly sets forth the idea of substitution or exchange (without using *huper*), I Peter 2:24: "He himself bore our sins in his body on the tree, that we might die to sin and live to righteousness. By his wounds you have been healed." This last sentence is a relatively rare but unmistakable quotation from Isaiah 53; it is the most unambiguous use of that chapter in the New Testament to support the idea of Christ as our substitute. Substitution is not, however, the only word that suits this context, as we will see.

Paul's Letter to the Romans

In the central narrative of deliverance given by Paul in Romans 5:12-21, the apostle traces the entire arc of human history from the creation (which is assumed — see Rom. 1:20) and the fall of "Adam" to redemption in Jesus Christ. There is nothing explicit here about a "substitutionary theory of atonement"; the lion's share of the emphasis in Romans is on *Christus Victor*.

---

13. Charles B. Cousar, *A Theology of the Cross: The Death of Jesus in the Pauline Letters*, Overtures to Biblical Theology (Minneapolis: Augsburg Fortress, 1990), 56.

However, there is a thread in verses 15-21 — carried through with repetitive force — that can be summarized in the following way.

- Jesus Christ, "that *one* man," has in his own history reversed the self-destroying course of the *"many,"* meaning the whole race.
- "Adam," the "man of sin," is the representative human being.
- No fewer than seven times in seven different wordings, Paul asserts that whereas "Adam's" act of disobedience led to *condemnation for all human beings,* Christ's act of righteousness leads to *acquittal and life for all human beings.*

If this is a fair summary of Paul's argument, then does it not follow that by reenacting "Adam," Christ put himself in Adam's place?[14] Even if, as we will see in chapter 12, representation and recapitulation are key ideas here, is it not also logical to think of this as substitution?[15] We are not arguing here for a particular *version* of the theme of substitution; we are just noting that the motif is there. Paul explicitly says that *condemnation* was the logical outcome of the disobedience of "Adam." We have shown in earlier chapters that Jesus, on the cross, died the death of a *condemned man.* Here Paul declares that instead of condemnation for all, acquittal and life are won for all. Does this not quite easily lead to the notion that Christ takes upon himself the condemnation that was properly ours? What is that if not substitution, or exchange? And the repetition of "all," with its universal implication, emphasizes Christ's standing in for the entire human race. It is hard to see why this reading would offend as long as it is not forced into a complicated abstract model that freezes out all other readings.

---

14. Again, "Adam" is to be understood as the representative human being. As a symbol, "Adam" stands for the line of development in the human story that begins with the willful departure from the good governance of the Creator (see Rom. 1:25) and the setting up of the creature as arbiter. It is not at all certain that Paul himself cared whether Adam was an actual historical person; in any case, such belief is not in the least required for the sense of the passage.

15. Irenaeus, in his characteristic doctrine of recapitulation (which we will examine further in the next chapter), focuses on Paul's account of Adam and Christ. He writes that Christ entered into the flesh in order to "overcome through Adam what had stricken us through Adam" (*Demonstration of the Apostolic Preaching* 31). This does not specifically emphasize substitution as a motif, but it does not exclude it, either. Karl Barth, in his discussion leading up to the chapter on the substitution motif (*Church Dogmatics* [hereafter *CD*] IV/1 [Edinburgh: T. & T. Clark, 1956], 192ff.), emphasizes the obedience of Christ "even [unto] death on a cross" (Phil. 2:8) in very much the same vein as Irenaeus, who wrote that the disobedience of the first Adam was overcome by the obedience of the second Adam, most especially in his passion and death (*Adversus haereses* 3.18.7; 5.16.3).

Romans 8:3-4 is even more central as a summary of the apostle's understanding of how our deliverance from the primordial catastrophe was effected: "For God has done what the law, weakened by the flesh *(sarx)*, could not do: sending his own Son in the likeness of sinful flesh and for sin, he condemned sin in the flesh, in order that the just requirement of the law might be fulfilled in us, who walk not according to the flesh but according to the Spirit."

The main idea here is that Sin *(hamartia* is three times repeated) had to be condemned in human *sarx* (four times repeated). *Sarx,* usually but misleadingly translated "flesh," is a central concept for Paul. In his letters, palpable, material flesh (including sexual activity) is very rarely meant. The primary meaning is the entire existence of the human being under the reign of Sin.[16] When Paul therefore says that in sending his Son "in the *sarx* and for *hamartia,* God condemned *hamartia* in the *sarx,*" he is packing the sentence densely with several layers of meaning. The emphatic repetition of the words "sin" and "flesh" has the effect of emphasizing the gravity of the human predicament, trapped as we are in the orbit of the Powers.

Our redemption does not take place on a "spiritual" plane. It is "fleshly," so that the psychosomatic unity of the human person is emphasized. No gnostic flight into the spiritual is considered here; the Holy Spirit's work is with the whole of humanity in its material existence — an existence where the Law has been spectacularly ineffective, owing to the weakness of human *sarx.*[17] The real shock is that the triune God, in the person of the Son, enters precisely this *sarx* in all its dimensions and dies the death of one who is condemned by Sin. Does this not contain the idea — among other ideas — that the *sarx* of the Savior, in which sin was condemned, was a substitute for our *sarx* — his exchanged for ours? And if he was condemned in the flesh as the representative man of sin, whose place was he taking? Whose but all humanity's?

Two verses in Romans 6 make the same point: "Do you not know that all of us who have been baptized into Christ Jesus were baptized into his death? . . . We know that our old self was crucified with him so that the sinful body might be destroyed, and we might no longer be enslaved to sin" (Rom. 6:3, 6).

---

16. The word "flesh" in English is misleading as a translation of *sarx* because it suggests carnality (as in "sins of the flesh"). The word *sarx* for Paul means the whole realm of Sin and Death operating in the human being. The first version of the NIV made a stab at a better translation with "sinful nature," which had its good points, but it has been abandoned in the revised NIV.

17. The central fact of the incarnation is certainly implied here. Paul does not say "the Word was made flesh *(sarx)*" precisely as John does (John 1:14) — he says that Jesus was sent "in the likeness of sinful flesh" and that God condemned Sin "in the flesh" — but there is an affinity between the two.

The principal theme here is that of assimilation to Christ in baptism, but if we are indeed "crucified with him," then isn't it obvious (since the only crucifixion that actually took place was his) that in some sense he substituted himself for us, so that he alone received the full impact of Sin and its deserts, protecting us from them?

These texts from Romans are not the typical texts cited by the proponents of substitution. They are particularly relevant to the motif of recapitulation, as we shall see in the next chapter. We bring them to the fore here to show that the concept of substitution is present even when it does not predominate. It emerges organically out of the whole picture of what was accomplished in the death of Christ.

Galatians 3:10-14: The Man Hanged on a Tree

A Pauline text often cited by the Fathers is Galatians 3:10-14. This is perhaps the clearest statement of the substitution motif in Paul. We treated the passage in chapter 2, but here we look at it from the standpoint of the "statutes and ordinances" in Deuteronomy 12–26. It is from this section that Paul takes his ideas about the cursed man on the tree. A good deal of the Deuteronomy section is notable for its generosity and humaneness — care for the poor, manumission of slaves, the sabbatical remission of debt, tithing, and hospitality — but some of it is quite shocking to us today. Interspersed with instructions about generosity and compassion are repeated injunctions that offenders are to be pitilessly stoned to death. Among those to be eliminated from the community by this or some other means of execution are rebellious offspring, false prophets, anyone who flouts a decision by a priest or judge, and especially idolaters — those who "go after other gods and worship them."

The verses cited by Paul in Galatians 3 ("cursed be every one that hangs on a tree") are taken from a section of Deuteronomy where we encounter such things as the commandment to massacre the inhabitants of idolatrous cities (Deut. 13:15), a stern passage about the execution of murderers (19:13), the *lex talionis* ("an eye for an eye" — 19:21), the permission to loot conquered cities and capture their inhabitants (20:14-17), and the stoning of a disobedient son (21:21). Immediately after the stoning we come upon Paul's verse. The passage in Deuteronomy reads this way:

> "If a man has a stubborn and rebellious son, who will not obey the voice of his father or the voice of his mother . . . all the men of the city shall stone him to death with stones; so you shall purge the evil from your midst; and

all Israel shall hear, and fear. And if a man has committed a crime punishable by death and he is put to death, and you hang him on a tree, his body shall not remain all night upon the tree, but you shall bury him the same day, for *a hanged man is accursed by God;* you shall not defile your land which the Lord your God gives you for an inheritance."

When the verse that Paul quotes in Galatians is read *in its Deuteronomic context* (and Paul would have known that context intimately), the impact is tremendous. Notice that the mention of defiling the land suits the circumstances of crucifixion, a method understood by Jews and Romans alike to be the utmost in defilement, so that the victims were executed outside the city walls (see chap. 2, "The Godlessness of the Cross"). Paul concludes, "Christ redeemed us from the curse of the law, *having become a curse for us* — for it is written, 'Cursed be every one who hangs on a tree'" (Gal. 3:13).

The overwhelming effect of the Deuteronomic verse about the hanged man *in this context* is that Christ is *taking the place of* all the stoned, massacred, enslaved, defiled, and beheaded idolaters, rebels, apostates, and murderers (and all others) who have suffered under the Law. He is suffering the curse and the defilement that would have fallen upon them — that is, upon *us.* Understanding the Galatians verse in any other way strains unconvincingly at the obvious meaning.

To be sure, Galatians 3:10-14 is a difficult passage to understand because no fewer than *four* Old Testament quotations (one verse from Habakkuk, one verse from Leviticus, and two verses from Deuteronomy) are strung together by a logic not always easily grasped. In the context of this chapter, we can imagine Paul the Pharisee pondering the text about the man hanged on a tree, turning it over in his mind. It baffles and offends him. How can a crucified Messiah "who hangs on a tree," cursed by God, be an acceptable object of worship? His conclusion — and there is an Aha! moment here — is that Christ became a curse *for us (huper hemon)* precisely in order to blow wide open every possible conditional version of the covenant. None of the categories of sinners cursed by the Law that are listed in Deuteronomy are beyond the reach of God's unique saving act. Paul's gospel is radically expansive, and clearly suggests that Christ substituted himself for us all, godly and ungodly, Jews and Gentiles alike (3:28), under the curse of Sin. Other meanings can be found in Galatians 3:10-14, but substitution is surely predominant.

Paul has been called to witness for an elaborately worked-out doctrine of penal substitution when in fact it can be found nowhere in his thought. We are arguing here, however, that the concept of Jesus "in our place" *as well as* "on our behalf" lies behind everything Paul says.

Isaiah 53 in the New Testament

The role of Isaiah 53 in relation to the New Testament picture of the death of Christ is much debated. The passage has long been associated with Good Friday in both the Byzantine and the Latin liturgies, for reasons that are obvious from even a cursory reading, and the Fathers quoted from it lavishly.[18] The mystery of its original meaning only adds to its power as a prophetic utterance. Its relevance to the circumstances of the death of Christ is so apparent that it astounds:

> He was despised and rejected by men;
>> a man of sorrows, and acquainted with grief;
> and as one from whom men hide their faces. . . .
> Surely he has borne our griefs
>> and carried our sorrows;
> yet we esteemed him stricken,
>> smitten by God, and afflicted.
> But he was wounded for our transgressions,
>> he was bruised for our iniquities;
> upon him was the chastisement that made us whole,
>> and with his stripes we are healed.
> All we like sheep have gone astray;
>> we have turned every one to his own way;
> and the Lord has laid on him
>> the iniquity of us all.
> He was oppressed, and he was afflicted,
>> yet he opened not his mouth;
> like a lamb that is led to the slaughter,
>> and like a sheep that before its shearers is dumb,
>> so he opened not his mouth. . . .
> He was cut off out of the land of the living,
>> stricken for the transgression of my people[.]
> And they made his grave with the wicked
>> and with a rich man in his death,
> although he had done no violence,
>> and there was no deceit in his mouth.

18. See below under Athanasius, Cyril of Alexandria, and John Chrysostom. Brevard Childs writes that Cyril "reads the entire chapter, as if by reflex, to be a reflection of the passion of Christ" (*The Struggle to Understand Isaiah as Christian Scripture* [Grand Rapids: Eerdmans, 2004], 124).

Yet it was the will of the Lord to bruise him; . . .
he makes himself an offering for sin.

In view of the role this passage has played in the tradition, and the powerful effect it has in hymnody, in preaching, in Handel's *Messiah,* and in popular piety, it seems extraordinary that it has left so small an imprint in the New Testament.[19] It is hard to know what the relative neglect of such a striking passage might mean. At the very least, we should probably agree that care should be taken in using the passage uncritically to interpret the meaning of the cross, for at least two reasons:

1. In view of the New Testament silence, we should not use Isaiah 53 to construct a thoroughgoing penal-substitution model of the atonement based on "chastisement."[20]
2. We should be diligent in guarding against any division between the persons of the Trinity, using a line like "stricken by God" to separate the Father from the Son.[21]

However, provided that we assiduously work to avoid these two traps, there is theological gold in Isaiah 53, certainly for personal devotion to the crucified One, and for theological understanding also. The position taken here is that the passage serves as a guide or partial substructure for the New Testament as a whole. Isaiah 53 gives strong support to the affirmation that the suffering of the Messiah is part of the plan of God for salvation revealed proleptically to ancient Israel. And let us note that in the last verse quoted above, there are two different acting subjects: "It was the will of the Lord to bruise him" and "He makes himself an offering for sin." In the space of just a few words, this one verse combines two narrative arcs: one with the Father as the active agent, and the other with the Son as acting agent.

19. There is another direct quotation of the chapter in the story of Philip and the eunuch in Acts 8:26-39, where the verse about the Servant's sheep-like silence is quoted, but in line with Luke's characteristic approach, no explicit connection is made to the crucifixion.

20. Even though many of the Fathers did so! See below under Athanasius and Cyril of Alexandria. Notably, Anselm did *not* use it to make punishment a part of his interpretation in *Cur Deus Homo?*, although it is popularly believed by many that he did.

21. A blessedly simple statement of this error is given by Arthur Lyttleton: "The truth of the wrath of God against sin and the love of Christ by which that wrath was removed, has been perverted into a belief in a divergence of will between God the Father and God the Son, as if it was the Father's will that sinners should perish, the Son's will that they should be saved" ("The Atonement," in *Lux Mundi,* ed. Charles Gore [London: John Murray, 1889], 307). That makes the point very well.

It is actually quite surprising that the only unambiguous New Testament use of Isaiah 53 to interpret the death of Christ is I Peter 2:21-24.[22] The context urges servants to be submissive to their masters, even the "overbearing" ones:

> If when you do right and suffer for it you take it patiently, you have God's approval. For to this you have been called, because Christ also suffered for you, leaving you an example. . . . When he was reviled, he did not revile in return; when he suffered, he did not threaten; but he trusted to him who judges justly. He himself bore our sins in his body on the tree, that we might die to sin and live to righteousness. By his wounds you have been healed. (I Pet. 2:20-24)

The last sentence, "By his wounds [also translated as in Isaiah as 'stripes' — marks of scourging] you have been healed," is a direct quotation from Isaiah 53:5. Yet it only glancingly offers an image by which to interpret the deep significance of the apocalyptic drama of the cross. The passage appears to recommend an "exemplary" or "moral influence" approach to the meaning of the cross, which is associated with Peter Abelard, a near contemporary of Anselm. The exemplary model taken by itself has a Pelagian tinge and an inadequate Christology.[23] When it is combined with other models, however, especially that of substitution as in I Peter 2:24, the exemplary model finds its true place. "For it is better to suffer for doing right, if that should be God's will, than for doing wrong. For Christ also died for sins once for all, *the righteous for the unrighteous,* that he might bring us to God" (I Pet. 3:17-18).[24]

---

22. The eunuch Philip encounters in Acts 8:26-39 is reading from Isa. 53, but Luke does not use this to interpret the cross. Philip uses it to proclaim "the good news of Jesus" generally.

23. Eamon Duffy nails Abelard's "cheery optimism," which reflects "a particular form of Christian liberalism, repudiated in W. H. Auden's lines: 'Nothing can save us that is possible; / We who must die demand a miracle'" (*New York Review of Books,* July 5, 2001). A good short summation of the problem with the "exemplary" or "moral influence" theory is that of Green and Baker: "Sin appears as a relative and surmountable barrier in contrast to an absolute and insurmountable barrier in the other explanations" (Joel B. Green and Mark D. Baker, *Recovering the Scandal of the Cross: Atonement in New Testament and Contemporary Contexts* [Downers Grove, Ill.: InterVarsity, 2000], 139).

24. It could be objected that this recommends masochistic suffering. But even if it were (wrongly) to be construed that way, it should be apparent to the disinterested reader that the text recommends suffering not in a generalized sense, but specifically as imitation of Christ's deportment during his passion. This suffering would arise from a place of inner strength, not masochistic weakness. I Peter 3:18 certainly suggests a sort of substitution in the phrase "the righteous for the unrighteous," but these words should not be wrenched into the service of an overdeveloped context of "substitutionary atonement" or Anselmian "satisfaction." Similarly,

The Patristic Period

It is often stated, and sometimes taken as axiomatic, that the motif of substitution, or exchange, is missing from the theology of the first thousand years — that is, before Anselm. But that is not true. To be sure, substitution does not predominate, and is not worked out doctrinally until after Anselm, but the theme is present in the patristic era, in both Greek and Latin Fathers. Indeed — and this is noteworthy — it appears without particular emphasis, as though it was simply taken for granted, just as we argued above in reference to Romans.[25]

Athanasius is rightly associated with the theme of incorporation into Christ through the incarnation, but the cross plays a large part in his treatise *On the Incarnation.* He explicitly asks why Jesus died, and why he died *in such a way.* His answer to these questions centers on the *public* nature of Christ's death, which he interprets as necessary to show forth the power of the resurrection.[26] Athanasius puts forward the idea of exchange ("in the stead of") as though it were obvious, using the phrase several times. He writes about the death of Christ in a fluid, interchangeable way that arises out of Scripture itself. Athanasius's *principal* theme is not substitution (or exchange), to be sure, but the concept is present and does not seem to cause any problem for him. "Taking a body like our own, because we all were liable to the corruption of death, he surrendered his body to death *instead of all,* and offered it to the Father. . . . Whence, as I said before, the Word, since it was not possible for him to die, took to himself a body such as could die, that he might offer it as his own *in the stead of all.*"[27]

---

the passage in Eph. 5:22-24 enjoining the subordination of wives to husbands — which has been misused in support of the subjugation of women — is meant to be understood in the context of Christ's headship of the church, not a programmatic notion of "substitutionary atonement." It is the command to the *husbands* that takes its cue from the cross: "Husbands, love your wives, as Christ loved the church and gave himself up for her" (Eph. 5:25).

25. J. N. D. Kelly in his classic work *Early Christian Doctrines* (New York: Harper and Row, 1959) shows that Eusebius of Caesarea, Cyril of Jerusalem, Basil, Gregory of Nazianzus, and John Chrysostom all speak of "substitution based on the Saviour's kinship with us; as the new Adam" (380-86). Note the nuance, however; this concept of substitution is not the same as the full-blown (overblown) doctrine that it became in nineteenth-century Protestant orthodoxy.

26. Athanasius's point suggests that the intensity of Paul's personal faith in the resurrection (I Cor. 15:1-9) corresponds to his emphasis on the cross as accursed (Gal. 3:10-13). In other words, the resurrection was all the more remarkable for being the destiny of a crucified man. The sermons of Peter in Acts also emphasize (in their Lukan way) the contrast between crucifixion and resurrection (Acts 2:23; 4:10).

27. *De incarnatione* 8, emphasis added. In 21 he says it a third time: "in the stead of all." Likewise, in the *Orations against the Arians* (3.31), Athanasius uses the imagery of substitution

Speaking of Athanasius should remind us that the theology of the cross *(theologia crucis)* should never be detached from the incarnation. Jesus' self-offering did not occur suddenly at the time of his arrest. His whole life was an offering, an assuming of our sinful human nature in order that we should be delivered from it into righteousness and life.[28] Whenever we speak in this way, the idea of exchange is present; "Adam" is dislodged from his place under the reign of Sin and Death because the second Adam has moved into that place in his stead as Victor.

Hilary of Poitiers, to give an example from the Latin Fathers, uses the language of recapitulation (see next chapter), which was common in the patristic period, but he combines it seamlessly with the language of substitution, borrowing from Galatians 3:13: "He offered Himself to the death of the accursed, in order to abolish the curse of the Law."[29] Hilary uses "satisfaction" as a synonym for "sacrifice" and has been seen as a precursor of Anselm.[30] Likewise, *Victorinus*, Hilary's contemporary, speaks of substitution rather than sacrifice.[31]

Ambrose strikingly echoes the theme from Galatians, combining it with an emphasis on the "fleshly" incarnation: "Jesus took flesh so as to abolish the curse of sinful flesh, and was made a curse *in our stead* so that the curse

---

and exchange easily and naturally, quoting Isa. 53, although his chief focus is on the *Logos-sarx* Christology. Athanasius is unusual among the Church Fathers for his emphasis on the "dreadful and ignominious" nature of crucifixion, linking it explicitly with Gal. 3:13, "It was well that the Lord suffered this for our sakes. For if he came himself to bear the curse laid upon us, how else could we have 'become a curse' unless he received the death set for a curse? For this is exactly what is written: 'Cursed be he that hangeth on a tree'" (*De Incarnatione* 24, 25).

28. The link between the incarnation and the crucifixion is attractively explained by Arthur Lyttleton. He cites the words of Paul, "[God] made him to be sin who knew no sin" (II Cor. 5:21), and asks how this can be. He then answers: "The solution of the difficulty can only be found in the truth of the Incarnation. In order that the sacrifice might be representative, He [Christ] took upon Him the whole of our human nature. . . . It was not only in His death that we contemplate Him as the sin-bearer, but throughout His life. . . . The Crucifixion does not come as the unexpectedly shameful end of a glorious and untroubled life, though it was undoubtedly in a special sense the manifestation of the 'curse' under which He laid Himself [note the reference to Gal. 3:11-13 and the active choice of the second person in the crucifixion]. We cannot say that at a given moment in His life . . . He began to bear iniquity, for the very nature which He took . . . was in itself, by its necessary human relations, sin-bearing." Lyttleton, like many Anglicans, emphasizes the cross as Jesus' vicarious sacrifice. Lyttleton, "The Atonement," 296.

29. Hilary, *Tractatus super Psalmos* 68, 23, in Kelly, *Early Christian Doctrines*, 388.

30. Pelikan, *Emergence of the Catholic Tradition*, 147; see also Kelly, *Early Christian Doctrines*, 388.

31. Kelly, *Early Christian Doctrines*, 388.

might be swallowed up in blessing. . . . He took death, too, upon Himself that the sentence might be carried out, so that He might satisfy the judgment that sinful flesh should be cursed even unto death."[32] Kelly observes that in Ambrose, the patristic motif of recapitulation is combined with that of substitution, even with a reference to a penalty suffered: "because he shares human nature, Christ can substitute himself for sinful men and endure their punishment in their place."[33]

Cyril of Alexandria is perhaps the most explicit of all; he wrote that Christ "was stricken because of our transgressions [Isa. 53] . . . this chastisement, which was due to fall on sinners . . . descended upon Him." Kelly goes so far (probably too far) as to say that Cyril's "guiding idea" is "penal substitution."[34]

Melito of Sardis combined at least five motifs in his breathtaking Easter homily:

> The Lord . . . suffered for the sake of him who suffered, and was bound for the sake of him who was imprisoned, and was judged for the sake of the condemned, and was buried for the sake of the buried. So come, all families of human beings who are defiled by sins, and receive remission of sins. For I am your remission, I am the Passover of salvation. I am the Lamb sacrificed for your sake. I am your ransom. I am your life. I am your Resurrection. I am your light. I am your salvation. I am your King. I lead you toward the heights of heaven. I will show you the eternal Father. I will raise you up with my right hand.[35]

Karl Barth found this testimony of Melito compelling evidence that "the Judge judged in our place" motif was present as early as the second century.[36]

32. Ambrose, *De fuga saeculi* 44, in Kelly, *Early Christian Doctrines*, 389, emphasis added. The list goes on and on. Jerome wrote that Christ "endured in our stead the penalty we ought to have suffered for our crimes" (quoted in Kelly, 390). Kelly shows that Ambrose proposes a proto-Anselmian explanation of Christ's death as a sacrifice that satisfies God's requirements of justice (389).

33. Kelly, *Early Christian Doctrines*, 389.

34. Quoted in Kelly, *Early Christian Doctrines*, 398.

35. Melito of Sardis, Paschal Homily (or Sermon on the Passover). Readily available on line at kerux.com. This astonishing piece of literary and rhetorical dazzlement was only discovered in the 1930s (Michigan-Beatty Papyrus) and published in 1940. Melito was bishop of Sardis and died circa 190.

36. Barth, *CD* IV/1, 211. A personal testimony: I first heard portions of Melito's homily when it was read aloud at an Easter service at St. Paul's Within the Walls in Rome, and was bowled over by it.

Gregory of Nazianzus could hardly be more specific: Christ saves us "because He releases us from the power of sin and offers Himself as a ransom *in our place* to cleanse the whole world."[37]

John Chrysostom is clearest of all. Kelly summarizes the relevant teaching: "Christ has saved us . . . by substituting Himself in our place. Though He was righteousness itself, God allowed Him to be condemned as a sinner and to die as one under a curse, transferring to Him not only the death which we owed but our guilt as well."[38]

These examples should show that the argument, so often heard, that the substitution motif was unknown in the first thousand years is untenable. The motif of substitution was present from the beginning. It was not simply an *idée fixe* of Protestant orthodoxy. In the Fathers, it arose organically from their immersion in Scripture and was interwoven by them with other themes in their writings.

The Middle Ages

In addition to these examples from the patristic period, we note the following from later centuries (Anselm having been treated earlier):

Richard of St. Victor (d. 1173), one generation after Anselm, wrote independently of Anselm: "They were being held by the debt of eternal condemnation, not because it was for them, but because it had been [*fuisset* — 'would have been'] for them unless the death of Christ absolved them."[39] This strongly echoes the theme of exchange, or substitution, in the same way that Galatians 3 and Romans 5 do; the sentence of "eternal condemnation" under the Law that properly belonged to "Adam" was taken away by the death of Christ. As also in the patristic period, the motif of substitution is not insisted upon; it is simply assumed.[40]

37. Gregory of Nazianzus, *Oratio in laudem Basilii* 30.20, in Kelly, *Early Christian Doctrines,* 384.

38. John Chrysostom, *Homiliae in epistulam ad Hebraeos* 15.2, in Kelly, *Early Christian Doctrines,* 386. (We should note, however, the atypical tendency in this passage to suggest a split between the Father and the Son, which is no more allowable in the Church Fathers than in popular Christian belief today.)

39. Quoted in Hans Urs von Balthasar, *Mysterium Paschale: The Mystery of Easter* (San Francisco: Ignatius, 2000), 166.

40. The incarnational explanation of the means of salvation shares prominence in the Greek Fathers with the *Christus Victor* theme. Indeed, incarnation could be invoked without explicit reference to the cross at all — a choice that many today would make, to the great detriment of the gospel. The Fathers must be read with subtlety and care. The dominance of the

Thomas Aquinas (c. 1225-1274) can also be cited in passages such as this: "In order to bear our guilt, as it was fitting that he should die in order to redeem us from death, so was it also fitting that he should go down into Hades, to redeem us from descent into Hades." Thomas then, like so many before him, quotes Isaiah 53: "[A]ccording to the word of Isaiah, 'Truly he has taken upon himself our malady, he has borne our pains.' "[41] In chapter 10 we saw that Thomas emphasizes Christ's full participation in the condition and fate of sinners. The theme of substitution is not explicit, but the idea is there in the background, especially when Isaiah 53 is quoted.

Preliminary Conclusion

It is not accurate to state that the theme of substitution emerged with Anselm, and it is not responsible to suggest that we can escape from it into the *Christus Victor* motif. In all its forms — New Testament, patristic, scholastic/medieval, and later with Luther — the *Christus Victor* imagery carries with it the profound conviction that humanity is in bondage to sin and in need of deliverance. These are the identical assumptions that undergird the substitution theme. These two ways of speaking about the cross coexist creatively in the Scriptures and interpret one another, as they did in the Fathers long before Anselm and the Reformers.

The Motif of Substitution Since Anselm

We have attempted to give Anselm his considerable due in the "bridge" chapter. Insofar as he used "satisfaction" as his guiding idea, the word "substitution" does not precisely encapsulate his theme. However, his carefully argued position has, not inaccurately, come to be associated with the emergence of substitution as a *dominant* way of talking about the cross in Protestantism. Anselm's rationalistic and scholastic way of arguing his case had tremendous influence, and it opened the way to subsequent trends in the interpretation of the cross that eventually led to unfortunate consequences.

Christus Victor motif in both Greek and Latin Fathers has been widely assumed by many since Aulén, so it may come as a surprise to learn that "the main stream of Greek soteriology in the fourth century" was neither incarnation nor *Christus Victor,* but "doctrines which interpreted Christ's work in terms of a sacrifice offered to the Father" (Kelly, *Early Christian Doctrines,* 384).

41. *Summa Theologiae* IIIa, q. 52, a. I, c.

This did not happen right away, however. Calvin, in particular, handled the motif of substitution with great authority and massive knowledge of Scripture and the Fathers.

Martin Luther

In much of Protestantism, the *Christus Victor* theme that was so prominent in Luther was reduced in importance, with the greater emphasis being put on justification by faith and imputed righteousness. Aulén succeeded in redirecting attention to Luther's robust proclamations: "Christ's victory . . . the overcoming of the Law, of Sin, our flesh, the world, the devil, death, hell, and all evils; and this victory he has given to us."[42] In his preface to the New Testament Epistles, Luther writes, "In these books [John, I Peter, and Paul's Epistles] you will find a masterly account of how faith in Christ conquers Sin, Death, and Hell; and gives life, righteousness, and salvation. *This is the true essence of the gospel.*"[43]

These are only two examples among thousands in which Luther champions the gospel of the victorious Christ. No one has ever done it with more ringing personal conviction. However, it is a mistake to limit Luther to this one theme. Using his Galatians commentary as our illustrative text, we find an astonishingly wide range of images. In just a few pages dealing with Galatians 1:4 and 3:13, we find references to ransom, redemption, price, scapegoat, satisfaction, sacrifice, Satan, the wrath of God, the justification of the ungodly, Christ as mediator, our sins nailed to the cross (as in Col. 2:14), the paschal lamb, substitution (with Isa. 53 specifically quoted), and of course the prominent *Christus Victor* theme.[44] Aulén quotes at length a passage from the commentary on Galatians where Luther treats 3:13 ("Christ became a curse for us"), and it certainly is a resounding declaration of the *Christus Victor* theme in Luther's most vigorous style. He typically refers to the "combat" that Christ undertook against Sin, the Law, Death, and the devil. However,

---

42. Martin Luther, *Commentary on the Epistle to the Galatians* (1535) (Wheaton, Ill.: Crossway, 1998), 1:1.

43. From the first edition (1522) of the *Preface to the New Testament*.

44. Jaroslav Pelikan, who of all people would have known, remarks on the "heterogeneity of Luther's pictures of the redemptive work of Christ," and warns that the way forward in interpreting this multiplicity is precisely "*not* to reduce all the mutually contradictory language to any single theory, not even to the 'classic idea' [the *Christus Victor* theme is called 'classic' by Aulén because it was so prominent in the first thousand years]" (foreword to the paperback edition of *Christus Victor: An Historical Study of the Three Main Types of the Idea of the Atonement* [New York: Macmillan, 1969], xvi). This precisely states the aim of the present volume.

Luther's reflections on this "combat" suggests that *the way that Christ became the Victor was through his death on our behalf and in our place.* The collision of the two antagonists came to its climax on the cross.

Luther repeatedly emphasizes the submission of Christ to the accusation of the Law, that we might be freed from condemnation. "The Law . . . was against us cursed and damned sinners," but it set itself above all against Christ — "It made him guilty before God of the sins of the whole world [and] condemned him to death, even to the death of the Cross."[45] The word "substitute" is not used, but the idea is clearly present. In another typical passage from this section, Luther writes that Christ "put upon himself our person, made himself subject to the Law." It strains at logic to argue that he did not do this "in our place." A passage on Galatians 3:13 should make the point:

> For [Christ] being made a sacrifice for the sins of the whole world, is not now [on the cross] an innocent person and without sins . . . but a sinner, which has and carried the sin of Paul, who was a blasphemer, an oppressor, and a persecutor; of Peter, who denied Christ; of David, who was an adulterer, a murderer, and caused the Gentiles to blaspheme the name of the Lord: and briefly, who has and bears all the sins of men in his own body, that he might make satisfaction for them with his own blood.[46]

Throughout his commentary on Galatians, Luther rings the changes on this theme: the Son of God offers himself up as Adam, the man of sin, condemned under the Law. This is the recapitulation theme we will examine in chapter 12. In that sense he has substituted himself for the original Adam — that is to say, for us all.

John Calvin

Calvin is known for his emphasis on the motif of substitution. Since Calvin has acquired an undeserved bad name among many in the churches, the link between him and the motif may have contributed to a general dislike of substitution in some circles. His numerous detractors frequently fail to understand how deeply pastoral his theological concerns are. He addresses himself to "trembling consciences." All his work is suffused with his desire that Christians should be free from anxiety about their standing before God. Christ was appointed to "care for the consciences of his people" so that we

45. Luther, *Galatians,* on Gal. 4:4.
46. Luther, *Galatians,* on Gal. 3:13.

might live in "untroubled expectation of judgment."[47] Everything that he says about Christ should be seen in this light.

Although Calvin and Anselm would seem to be close partners, their methods could not be more different. Even those who most appreciate Anselm are likely to admit that his presentation, though as pastoral in intent as Calvin's, suffers from an excess of schematic rationalism. Calvin, compared to Anselm, is more a preacher and storyteller. Here, for instance, he captures the general idea of substitution without insisting literally or woodenly upon it: "Thus we perceive Christ representing the character of a sinner and a criminal, while, at the same time, his innocence shines forth, and it becomes manifest that he suffers for another's, and not his own, crime" (2.16.5).

To understand Calvin further on substitution, we need to return briefly to the biblical theme of the wrath of God.[48] We must strenuously try to understand that Calvin is not referring to an enraged, vindictive old man in the sky (or on earth, for that matter, as though Zeus or Odin were striding the globe). It is essential to read "the wrath of God" as *symbolic language.* It is a figurative way of expressing the eternal opposition of God to all that would hurt and destroy his good creation.[49]

One of the principal problems with substitution is the way that it so easily lends itself to a coarse interpretation. A reader who glances over key passages in the *Institutes* will quickly spot phrases and sentences that appear

47. All quotations from Calvin in this paragraph are from the *Institutes* 2.16.5. The translation used is *Institutes of the Christian Religion*, ed. John T. McNeill, trans. Ford Lewis Battles, Library of Christian Classics (Philadelphia: Westminster, 1960).

48. There are, to be sure, many difficulties for the reader of today. Calvin's language often grates against modern sensibilities. For instance, he speaks of "the wrath and vengeance of God" and "God's wrath and hostility." He refers to appeasement, satisfaction, judgment, punishment, and vengeance (2.26.1). The human being is "an heir of wrath, subject to the curse of eternal death . . . the slave of Satan, captive under the yoke of sin, destined finally for a dreadful destruction." The Son "has taken upon himself" the "righteous vengeance" of God (2.16.5). Some are so put off by this language that they find it difficult to work through it to Calvin's underlying meaning; they don't understand that this wrath and vengeance are directed essentially against Sin understood as a destroying power, not against helpless individuals, let alone his Son.

49. Calvin knows that much of what he writes sounds anthropomorphic and crass. He uses the Old Testament sacrifices as *figures* for the atonement wrought by Christ. A careful reading shows that he does not mean this *literally*. The Old Testament sacrifices were "like" their archetype in Christ. We should not be misled by Calvin's dogmatic, assertive tone; he is groping for the right way to say all these things, and he recognizes the inadequacy of his language. Hence his use of "as it were," and "somehow" (e.g., our sin is "somehow" transferred to the Son). He even refers to the cross as a "symbol," even though it is obviously a material object (2.16.6-7). In these various ways he indicates that "the old figures" (2.17.4) can only point beyond themselves to an infinitely greater complex of meaning.

to support the theological errors that we want to avoid. For instance, in this passage Calvin speaks of appeasement: "No one can descend into himself and seriously consider what he is without feeling God's wrath and hostility toward him. Accordingly, he must anxiously seek ways and means to appease God — and this demands a satisfaction" (2.16.1).

Calvin wants us to understand how fatally serious the breach is between humanity and God. Paul's depiction of the wrath of God in Romans 1:18–3:19 is very much in the picture here. "God, who is the highest righteousness, cannot love the unrighteousness that he sees in us all" (2.16.3). This idea, that God cannot love us "just as we are," is deeply offensive to many Christians today who have been weaned on "self-esteem." And yet "because the Lord wills not to lose what is his in us, out of his own kindness he still finds something to love" (2.16.3). It is worth the extra work to understand Calvin's language about the breach between sinful humanity and righteous God as a corrective to our narcissism.

God's "wrath and hostility" cause anxiety in the conscientious soul, but Calvin wants us to understand that the "means to appease" do not lie within us and that it is a waste of time to seek them from ourselves. He wants us to turn to God for those means. What God loves in us is not our unredeemed selves (which, today, we are constantly urged to regard with "esteem"). What God loves in us is *what we will become as he carries out his work of regeneration in us.* Beginning in 2.16.1, Calvin launches an argument that creates considerable suspense for anyone who cares about what the crucifixion means. In 2.16.2, he quotes Romans 5:10, Galatians 3:10, and Colossians 1:21-22. Each of these verses contains an "until" that makes it sound as if the Father was disposed to condemn us "until" the interposition of Christ. It's safe to say that most people, reading this, would be inclined to understand it to mean that something took place in time that resulted in an alteration in the Father's mind. Calvin, however, in his intellectually sophisticated way, explains that these sorts of expressions are not to be taken literally: "Expressions of this sort have been accommodated to our capacity that we may better understand how miserable and ruinous our condition is apart from Christ. For if it had not been clearly stated that the wrath and vengeance of God and eternal death rested upon us, we would scarcely have recognized how miserable we would have been without God's mercy, and we would have underestimated the benefit of liberation" (2.16.2).

Calvin also cautions us that "expressions of this sort" about what happened in Christ must be "tempered [by the Spirit] to our feeble comprehension."[50] Theologians today would be careful to avoid even a hint of such imagery. Has Calvin led us into a trap? This is part of the suspense as we read on. If we have been alert, though, we will note that Calvin has already suggested the direction he will take in another "until" passage: "We must see . . . how fitting it was that God, who anticipates us by his mercy, should have been our enemy until he was reconciled to us through Christ. For how could he have given in his only begotten Son a singular pledge of his love to us if he had not already embraced us with his free favor?" (2.16.2).

These two sentences encompass the paradox. The reader may be confused, but Calvin is far too shrewd a thinker to be unaware of what he is doing here. First he says that the Father was our enemy "until" the Son reconciled *him* to *us* (the language of propitiation), and then he seeks our assent to the direction he is going by asking a rhetorical question: How could the Son's life and death be a sign of his love instead of his enmity unless the Father "embraced us with his free favor" *first* and *then* gave the Son? How is this paradox "fitting"?

A high point in Christian theology is now reached in the *Institutes* (2.16.1-4). The careful reader is wondering if Calvin hasn't painted himself into a corner by appearing to say that the Father had to be reconciled to us by the historic event of the crucifixion. Both of the errors we have defined seem to be holding the field here: the Father and the Son seem to be separated, and we seem to see an alteration in the Father. We sense that something fundamental is threatened when we read, "It was fitting that God . . . should be our enemy, until he was reconciled to us through Christ."[51] The reader will almost certainly assume that a temporal change has occurred within God.

But Calvin has anticipated all of this. In one breathtaking stroke in paragraph 4, addressing the problem that seems to result from his comparison of John 3:16 and Romans 5:10, he sweeps away all the misunderstandings, quoting Ephesians 1:4-5 to the effect that the loving purpose of God was "before the creation of the world." Then, rather charmingly, he writes, "But to render these things more certain among those who require the testimony of the ancient church, I shall quote a passage of Augustine where the very

---

50. Some may protest that Calvin's "expressions" may not have been tempered enough! It takes considerable effort to understand how Calvin actually means us to understand the expressions. Many readers today will be tempted to conclude that the caricatures of Calvin are true, that the Son's suffering was necessary to "appease" the Father's "wrath and vengeance." If Calvin were writing today, he would have to use different wording to make his points. We will shortly see that Calvin's most important revisionist, Karl Barth, abandons this sort of language.

51. The average reader today would likely overlook the phrase elided here, "who anticipates us by his mercy."

thing is taught." Here is the quotation, from Augustine of Hippo (fifth century) via John Calvin (sixteenth century):

> God's love is incomprehensible and unchangeable. For it was not *after* we were reconciled to him through the blood of his Son that he began to love us. Rather, he has loved us before the world was created. . . . The fact that we were reconciled through Christ's death must not be understood as if his Son reconciled us to [the Father] so that he might now begin to love those whom he had hated. Rather, we have already been reconciled to him who loves us, with whom we were enemies on account of sin. The apostle will testify whether I am speaking the truth: "God shows his love for us in that while we were still sinners Christ died for us" [Rom. 5:8]. Therefore he loved us even when we practiced enmity toward him and committed wickedness. Thus in a marvellous and divine way he loved us even when he hated us. For he hated us for what we were that he had not made; yet because our wickedness had not entirely consumed his handiwork, he knew how, at the same time, to hate in each one of us what *we* had made, and to love what *he* had made.[52]

Perhaps, with that, we are in a better position to receive Calvin's doctrine of substitution conveyed in this simple summary of Galatians 3:13-14: "The cross was accursed, not only in human opinion but in God's law (Deuteronomy 21:23). Hence, when Christ is hanged upon the cross, he makes himself subject to the curse. It had to happen in this way in order that the whole curse — which on account of our sins . . . lay upon us — might be lifted from us, while it was transferred to him" (2.16.6).

Penal Substitution in Late Reformed Scholasticism

Protestant scholarship after Calvin took a different turn. The substitution model evolved into a more programmatic presentation than anything in Calvin's writings, let alone in the New Testament. The model, as it developed, especially in the Reformed tradition, can be summarized as follows:

- As a result of the original sin of Adam, the entire human race has been mired in sin and has incurred the wrath of God.

---

52. Augustine, *John's Gospel* 110.6, quoted in Calvin's *Institutes* 2.16.5, emphasis added. When Augustine uses the word "hate," he means something like "implacably set against." He certainly does not mean "hate" in the sense of a human emotion.

- God cannot overlook sin as though it had not occurred. Sin must be punished.
- Jesus, the only-begotten Son of God, entered into the place of sinners and took the punishment on himself.
- On the cross, particularly as shown in the cry of dereliction, Jesus submitted to the curse upon sin and underwent God's judgment.
- By deflecting the wrath of God onto himself, Jesus took it away from humanity.

This developed model of the so-called substitutionary atonement is especially associated with nineteenth-century Protestant and evangelical circles, especially in the Reformed tradition. It was powerfully disseminated by Charles Hodge (1797-1878) during his fifty years at Princeton Theological Seminary, and it remains standard in some conservative-evangelical circles (though it has been losing ground lately). Today, however, a consensus is emerging, even within some conservative Protestant circles in America, Canada, and Great Britain, that the model of penal substitution as it has been widely taught in the nineteenth and twentieth centuries should be rethought and revised.

Indeed, there is good reason to question the biblical character of the model. For instance, Hodge used expressions like "forensic penal satisfaction," which does not sound remotely like anything in Scripture.[53] The preachers and teachers of penal substitution forced the biblical tapestry of motifs into a narrowly defined, schematic, rationalistic — and highly individualistic — version of the substitution motif derived in part from Anselm, whose rationalistic approach, it must be admitted, had an ill effect. This insensitive use of Anselm has been largely, though not entirely, responsible for the scorn heaped upon his work by those who have turned away from the "forensic penal" model. It is unfortunate that this misappropriation of Anselm has been thus overemphasized, because it has been more difficult to gain a hearing for him as a result. However, Anselm *never* used language like this: "When the Lord suffered, the Wrath of God was poured out in such measure upon him, that the Father was satisfied."[54] Such statements easily lead into both of the errors we have identified, separating the Father from the Son and suggesting a change in the Father (not to mention a truly distressing view of the Father). A more sophisticated version of these misreadings

---

53. Charles Hodge, *Systematic Theology,* vol. 2 (Grand Rapids: Eerdmans, 1981), 488.

54. David Clark, "Why Did Christ Have to Die?" *New England Reformed Journal* 1 (1996): 35-36.

of Anselm presents a God violently divided within God's self — his wrath against his mercy — thus destroying his unity. It is no wonder that there has been so much outcry against these distortions.[55]

2. Objections to the Penal Substitution Model

In the section on Calvin, above, we noted the most important errors in the substitution model as it is sometimes (not always) presented. Here are further criticisms of the motif, some more telling than others. None of these objections would have been as strong without the single-minded focus on "forensic penal substitution" that prevailed in Protestant scholasticism. They are listed in more or less ascending order of importance.

It Is "Crude"

A word often used to describe penal substitution is "crude."[56] The word comes from the Latin *crudus,* meaning "raw." It has several meanings in English: primitive, lacking in finish, unrefined, immature, wanting grace and taste. Might this be an aesthetic judgment, or even a subtle class distinction? It has sometimes seemed so. The widespread use of the word "crude" in the context of atonement doctrine suggests distaste not only for content, but also for a *style* of proclaiming the cross associated with appeals to less educated, more credulous groups of people gathered in backcountry churches. It is tempting to conclude (especially in the case of Anglicans)[57] that the critics are objecting as much to form as to content.[58] Whether this is a fair

55. See, for instance, J. Denny Weaver, *The Nonviolent Atonement* (Grand Rapids: Eerdmans, 2001). See also an essay by David Eagle, another Mennonite theologian: "Anthony Bartlett's Concept of Abyssal Compassion and the Possibility of a Truly Nonviolent Atonement," *Conrad Grebel Review* 24, no. 1 (Winter 2006): 66. The Mennonite commitment to nonviolence sometimes leads to a tendency to see violence where there is none.

56. Bryan Green, a celebrated Anglican evangelist (1901-1993), made a point of saying, "Crude theories of the atonement do not attract me." He was consciously differentiating himself from evangelicals in the Church of England who until quite recently made a particular way of teaching the "substitutionary atonement" a crucial test of theological "soundness."

57. Anglicans are often satirized for their emphasis on taste. If anyone is looking for someone to lampoon on those grounds, I confess that I stand near the head of the line.

58. The critique best known to two generations of Episcopal seminarians was that of John Macquarrie, whose *Principles of Christian Theology* was regularly assigned. We should note his objections. "This view of the Atonement . . . even if it could claim support from the Bible or

judgment or not, the point was made at length in chapter 2 that nothing in religious history can approach *crucifixion* for *crudeness.*

However, there is certainly ample evidence from the popular preaching of the nineteenth and twentieth centuries that when substitution is tightly identified with a system of "merit" and a transfer of merit from Christ to us, it can indeed become a "crudely transactional idea of atonement."[59] It is not uncommon, even today, to hear presentations of the atonement that are startlingly literal-minded, as though God had an actual pair of scales in his hand, or was making a list in columns, weighing our merits against our demerits, with bad results for us.[60] Reductionistic treatments of this sort have given the satisfaction concept a bad name, and since satisfaction has attached itself to substitution, both have suffered. The reaction against these versions of the *theologia crucis* is now so widespread that we may expect a continuing turn away from them even at the level of the grassroots revival meeting.

It Keeps Bad Company

Over the years, many penal-substitution adherents have appeared to relish the idea of the sufferings of the unredeemed. It can be argued that there is a certain "Calvinist temperament" that is overly focused on the "penal" aspect.[61] This is a fair critique and should be taken seriously, though it does not by any means always apply.

---

the history of theology would have to be rejected because of the affront it offers to reason and conscience." Note that Macquarrie (in whose class I read Hegel) makes reason and conscience, not Scripture or tradition, his norm, and in that sense speaks from a perspective quite different from the one espoused in this book.

59. C. F. D. Moule, "The Energy of God: Rethinking New Testament Atonement Doctrines" (Sprigg Lectures, Virginia Theological Seminary, Alexandria, Virginia, March 1-2, 1983, audiotape).

60. The use of the term "merit" is not always misleading. There are, for instance, several different ways of understanding Thomas Cranmer's eucharistic words (1928 Book of Common Prayer, 81), where the celebrant asks that God would receive us at the Lord's Table "not weighing our merits, but pardoning our offenses." This great phrase was eliminated in the 1979 revision, no doubt because the revisers did not like to speak of "merits" with its suggestion of the discredited balance-sheet approach to atonement. However, those who regret the absence of these words understand them as the ground of human hope — not in a literal, transactional sense, but in confidence that the righteousness of Christ has become our only secure righteousness. Paul states this with great clarity in Rom. 5:19 and 10:3-4.

61. The Cameronians, or Covenanters, of seventeenth-century Scotland would be an example of Calvinism at its most ferocious (yet there is much to admire in their intimate knowledge and love of Scripture). Walter Scott's novels of the Cameronians, *The Heart of Midlothian* and *Old Mortality,* give a vivid portrait.

It Is Culturally Conditioned

This familiar argument is typical of our time, because intellectual currents have taught us that texts reflect power struggles and must be read against their social and cultural background. Thus it is said that Anselm is obsolete because of his setting in feudalism, and penal substitution cannot be viable today because it is based in nineteenth-century concepts of justice. There is certainly some merit in understanding context, but how much should we allow it to guide our assessment of a theological text or doctrine? It is possible to exaggerate the influence of cultural context. *The Iliad* still speaks to soldiers on the battlefield; Madame Bovary has her counterparts among the "desperate housewives" of today; Marcel Proust understood Freud without Freud . . . and so forth. Moreover, negative judgments about cultural conditioning often derive from an indiscriminate cultural "tolerance" without reference to what is actually happening. We are learning that multiculturalism brings its own problems, and that not all cultural customs are equal.[62]

A substantive argument against the motif of atonement and substitution is that people in other cultures around the world do not see themselves in the categories we have been discussing — guilt, incapacity, bondage, shame, failure, defeat.[63] Yet the more one hears this, the more the categories seem to pop up. Here is an example that originated in American comic-book culture and spread around the world.[64] In a highbrow essay-review of *Spider-Man,* the blockbuster movie of 2002, Geoffrey O'Brien, editor in chief of the Library of America, harks back to the original comic of 1962:

> The crucial plot point in the original episode was that Peter Parker's initial burst of unwonted arrogance on receiving his spider powers led . . . to the death of his beloved Uncle Ben. *The notion of a moral lapse* (his momentary hubris) that *could never really be atoned for* gave the comic book its air of perpetual dissatisfaction; being Spider-Man was . . . a perpetual reminder to the hero of his own shortcomings, *a kind of penance.* There was always the possibility that he would fail again, and so he was *con-*

---

62. The most obvious cases in point are the customs of female genital mutilation and of "honor killings" of women.

63. This point, as far as it goes, is well presented in Green and Baker, *Recovering the Scandal of the Cross.*

64. In the much-praised 2005 film *Syriana,* young Pakistani men working in the Middle Eastern oilfields are shown discussing *Spider-Man* when they are not studying the Koran.

demned to a vigilant monitoring of his own reactions and impulses. In such a situation an unqualified sense of triumph was by definition impossible. In its own goofy way, *The Amazing Spider-Man* acknowledged *the tragic sense of life.*[65]

This remarkable paragraph from a secular journal incorporates much of what we have been trying to say all along. Moreover, it mirrors in an almost uncanny way the struggle of Martin Luther to monitor his behavior and his consequent discovery that an "unqualified sense of triumph" is "by definition impossible," and can only be experienced through the victory of Christ. It is certainly true that, under Luther's influence, "the introspective conscience of the West" has been artificially superimposed upon the biblical narrative with a corresponding overemphasis on the plight of individual sinners.[66] In his reference to the "tragic sense of life," however, O'Brien means to set the guilt of one individual into its context, that of ubiquitous human failure. In great novels of universal significance such as those of Joseph Conrad, the same dynamic is revealed. Conrad's narrator Marlow tells stories showing that the guilt and shame of one man *(Lord Jim)* are made to stand for us all, and the guilt of the British Empire *(Heart of Darkness)* is drawn into the larger saga not only of the individual soul but also of cosmic entrapment in "the infernal stream . . . of darkness."

If this be "Western," make the most of it.

It Views the Death as Detached from the Resurrection

No account of substitution should be given without the "sure and certain hope" of the resurrection of Jesus Christ from the dead.[67] The benefits of his substituting himself for us, or exchanging places with us, cannot be appreciated, let alone preached, without the victory of Christ over the Powers of Sin and Death. This is an indispensable link between the *Christus Victor* theme and the substitution theme. In his exchange with us, he brings us over from death into life, from sin into righteousness. The resurrection is the

---

65. Geoffrey O'Brien, "Popcorn Park," *New York Review of Books,* June 13, 2002, emphasis added. O'Brien thinks that the movie pushes these themes in too ponderous a fashion, but there can be no doubting his conviction that they remain utterly contemporary.

66. The reference is to a famous essay by Krister Stendhal, "The Apostle Paul and the Introspective Conscience of the West."

67. "Sure and certain hope": Committal at the grave, Burial of the Dead, 1979 Book of Common Prayer, 485, 501.

"first fruit" of the age to come, the sign *within* history of the *trans*historical purpose of God. By this power alone are we enabled to confess the faith of Christ crucified on our behalf and in our place.

It should therefore be affirmed with no ambivalence or ambiguity whatsoever: ours is an Easter faith. One of the defects of Mel Gibson's worldfamous but deeply flawed film *The Passion of the Christ* is that it focuses exclusively and in detail on the suffering and death. Christ's resurrection appears in so glancing and obscure a fashion that it might as well not be there at all. It cannot be said too often: if Christ was not raised from the dead, we would never have heard of him. Tens of thousands were crucified in the Roman era; of all of these, the name of Jesus of Nazareth is the only one known to us. He was consigned to the oblivion designed by Rome for crucified victims, but within weeks was proclaimed as the name above all names (Acts 4:12). "If Christ has not been raised, your faith is futile and you are still in your sins" (I Cor. 15:17).

However, in interpreting the cross and resurrection for the church, it is important to understand that the resurrection from the dead did not *cancel out* the crucifixion; it *vindicated* the crucifixion. The resurrection enabled the first disciples to understand what the death had accomplished, and the preaching of the cross by Paul is grounded in that new and revelatory connection.[68]

It Is Incoherent: An Innocent Person Cannot Take on the Guilt of Another

This is a rationalistic objection; or, to put it another way, it is a literal-minded one. Christ does not take our guilt upon himself in any way that can be described in ordinary human terms; it is not logical in that sense, and analogies are doomed to inadequacy. Like so much of Scripture, the idea in Isaiah 53 that "the Lord has laid on him the iniquity of us all" is *poetic* truth, to be received in faith; it is not a statement that we can rationally explain.[69] When Paul writes that "[God] made him [Jesus] to be sin who knew no sin," we cannot apprehend such a statement as though it were a philosophical proposition. It speaks to us of reality, but in another fashion and from another

---

68. Here again is the central importance of Paul, whose "word of the cross" gives us what might have been overlooked if we had only the preaching in the book of Acts.

69. Handel's setting of this line, in *Messiah*, most eloquently creates a confessional mood in which the mysterious saying strikes the heart not with its logical coherence, but with its essentially kerygmatic truth.

perspective. God in three persons is acting here; that, too, is a conception beyond the categories of human religion.

It Glorifies Suffering and Encourages Masochistic Behavior

In the 1980s and 1990s, feminist theologians raised this objection in a number of forms.[70] They maintained that the narrative of substitution glorifies passive suffering and has done untold damage to women over the centuries.[71] They referred to substitution-based models of the cross as "divine child abuse," a phrase that has achieved much currency. If attention paid to this critique is any criterion, it has been very successful; most recent interpreters have felt obliged to respond to it. However, it seems that this particular objection has already had its day, so widespread has been the reaction — including reaction from other women theologians. Its greatest success, therefore, has been as a corrective.

It is not "Anselmian" doctrine or even penal substitution that has stood behind the suffering of women at the hands of patriarchal society. Other scriptural passages lie behind the idea that women's lot is to endure without complaint; for instance, the curse laid upon Eve as she is expelled from the Garden of Eden, or the "household rules" (Eph. 5:21-33; Col. 3:18–4:1; I Pet. 3:1-7), or the well-known passage in I Peter that urges obedience to Christ's example ("Christ also suffered for you, leaving you an example, that you

---

70. See especially the collection of essays in Joanna Carlson Brown and Carole R. Bohn, eds., *Christianity, Patriarchy, and Abuse: A Feminist Critique* (New York: Pilgrim Press, 1989).

71. Darby Kathleen Ray writes from a feminist perspective: "The implied model of relationship based on the unilateral power of one over another not only mirrors situations of systemic violence and personal abuse, but also offers them divine sanction" (*Deceiving the Devil: Atonement, Abuse, and Ransom* [Cleveland: Pilgrim Press, 1998], 35). She is not entirely set against some form of atonement. Her focus on "unjust relationships and policies" is a theme that makes apocalyptic interpretation appealing to those who want to move past individuals to structures and systems — a position espoused here. However, she sees "the problems of today's atonement orthodoxy" (rather narrowly and unsympathetically understood) as "theological violence" (130). She identifies the "patristic model" (*Christus Victor,* essentially) as the one to have. There is much here to be affirmed. What is being argued in these pages, however, is that it is a grave mistake to isolate one model and exclude all the others. That is what the penal substitution devotees did for a long time; if the *Christus Victor* model were to crowd out the other motifs, it would be impoverishing. There is such richness in the combination of motifs. "Here was no common evidence of his incomparable love toward us: to wrestle with terrible fear, and amid those cruel torments to cast off all concern for himself that he might provide for us" (Calvin, *Institutes* 2.16.5).

should follow in his steps" [2:21]).[72] Numerous passages of this nature surely have had more to do with the subjugation and suffering of women, slaves, and children than theories of atonement.[73]

The topic of "divine child abuse" has by now been thoroughly worked over.[74] The salutary result of this rethinking is that we can never again read certain statements in the tradition in the same way. All of us, across the spectrum of theological opinion, have been well reminded to be much more careful in the future to avoid language that appears to separate Father and Son.[75]

It Is Too *"Theoretical," Too Scholastic and Abstract*

It is argued that the language of logical necessity (as in Anselm) seems to rob grace of its unconditional character. Gustav Aulén objected to a view of the

---

72. Indeed, if this passage from I Peter is examined in this context, it would be the Abelardian, "exemplary" model that would be indicted, not substitution.

73. The point made by womanist theologian Delores Williams that the concept of Jesus as a *surrogate* is offensive to African American women is more persuasive to me than any of the white feminist objections to substitution (*Sisters in the Wilderness: The Challenge of Womanist God-Talk* [Maryknoll, N.Y.: Orbis, 1993], 162-65). However, from my not inconsiderable experience of black female Christians, this rather rarefied problem of interpretation does not seem to trouble the typical churchgoing African American woman. And too, Williams insists that the active agency in Jesus' death was human evil. There is an important sense in which this is true; many complaints about violence in the substitution motif blame God exclusively for the crucifixion, ignoring the role of human (and demonic) evil. The problem is with the other half of Williams's proposal; she wants to keep God out of the death of Jesus altogether. This means that Jesus died *purely* as a victim, accomplishing nothing by his death. (On the positive side, Williams's insistence on the value of Jesus' *life* preserves the link between incarnation and atonement that is omitted from so many accounts of penal substitution. On the unity of incarnation and atonement, see T. F. Torrance, *The Mediation of Christ,* rev. ed. [Colorado Springs: Helmers and Howard, 1992; orig. 1983], 40-41; see also Christopher Morse, *Not Every Spirit,* in which he speaks consistently of Jesus' "life span" rather than his death in isolation.)

74. J. Denny Weaver does a good job of surveying the discussion in *The Nonviolent Atonement.* His proposal of "narrative *Christus Victor*" is very much along the lines of what I am espousing in this book. I do not at all agree, however, with his rejection of Anselm's project (which he calls "satisfaction atonement"). An even more serious objection is that his displacement of the divine agency moves us out of the biblical worldview altogether.

75. To give one example: a sentence by Herman N. Ridderbos, speaking of "the divine judgment executed *upon* him [Jesus]," would be better worded "*through* him." Ridderbos almost certainly did not intend to posit a division between the Father and the Son, but the preposition "upon" can be construed in a way he probably did not mean ("The Earliest Confession of the Atonement in Paul," in *Reconciliation and Hope: New Testament Essays on Atonement and Eschatology,* ed. Robert Banks [Grand Rapids: Eerdmans, 1974]).

atonement deriving from, or related to, Anselm because "it has a rational-izing character; in fact, it gives a rational explanation of the atonement. . . . Satisfaction is treated as rational necessity, the only possible method by which Atonement can be effected."[76]

The notion of "necessity" can be used in several ways, some more theo-logically helpful than others.[77] Calvin uses the word negatively in order to emphasize the willingness of the Son: "For he was not compelled by violence or *necessity,* but was induced purely by his love for us and by his mercy to submit to it."[78] The difficulty with "necessity" in the context of the cross is the idea that God is subject to external logic rather than love for his fallen creation.[79] When presented in *narrative* form, the motif of substitution has unparalleled warmth. However, it is true that some presentations of penal substitution seem to owe more to logic than to biblical narrative, and the intent here is to turn in the opposite direction.[80]

76. Gustav Aulén, *Christus Victor: An Historical Study of the Three Main Types of the Idea of the Atonement* (New York: Macmillan, 1969; orig. 1931), preface to the paperback edition; also p. 128. The charge of mechanization or abstraction is particularly associated with Vincent Taylor, who thought that substitution portrayed an automatic transfer independent of the faith-union of the believer with Christ, resulting in new life. (How this would be true of the substitution model and not of the *Christus Victor* model is not clear, since the *Christus Victor* model can also be construed as having happened, so to speak, over the head of the believer.) Jaroslav Pelikan, for his part, combines the accusation of abstraction with that of crudeness; speaking of the ap-proach of the nineteenth and twentieth centuries, he calls it "the mechanization of Redemption by a vulgarized orthodoxy" (in introduction to paperback edition of *Christus Victor*).

77. Karl Barth is an excellent guide through this thicket, showing how "necessity" can be used in two ways. Repeatedly, he asserts that God does not act out of necessity: "We cannot establish in principle from any side that it [the incarnation] *must be* so, that God *had to* [come to our aid]." But then Barth, speaking as though he were trying to help Anselm out of a diffi-culty, writes that "if we can speak of a necessity of any kind here, it can only be . . . because it is derived from and is posited by God" (*CD* IV/1, 213). In other words, we cannot speak of any abstract logical force working from the outside upon God. If there is any necessity, it is the necessity of God being God, faithful to God's own nature. This is a classic Barthian argument: metaphysical necessity cannot have anything to do with God, whose essence is freedom and who cannot be grasped by any human logical or rational human construction.

78. Calvin, *Institutes* 2.16.12, emphasis added.

79. *Cur Deus Homo?* is easy to misread that way, but no one reading Anselm's prayers could imagine him intending such a mistake.

80. Here is an example of nineteenth-century penal substitution: "If God wants to heal us all he has to do is say 'Be healed!' Benevolence therefore cannot be his sole motive in punishing. God's motive must be not merely remedial but retributive. . . . Behind and beneath all these legitimate and benevolent policies is God's fundamental judgment, that sin is to be punished because it deserves to be, because impartial justice requires due penalty, just as it demands reward for virtue" (Robert L. Dabney, *Christ Our Penal Substitute* [Richmond, Va.: Presbyte-

It Depicts a Vindictive God

A contemporary French writer, Antoine Vergote, asks, "Can one imagine a more obsessional phantasm than that of a God who demands the torturing of his own son to death as satisfaction for his anger?"[81] This is the accusation in an extreme form, and unfortunately, many distortions in nineteenth- and twentieth-century presentations of the gospel have understandably called forth this critique. Earlier in this book, this version of the atonement was repudiated, not only as an interpretation of Anselm and a too-literal conception of the wrath of God, but also, and more to the point, as a wholesale miscasting of Trinitarian doctrine. In this objection by Vergote and numerous others similar to it, there is no hint that the Father and the Son are acting as one.[82] Yet this caricature is widely offered as though it were a responsible critique, intended to protect the tender-minded from the atrocities of scholastic theologians. Christian theologians and preachers have much to answer for in this regard, since the dangers in the "penal substitution" model were ignored for a long time.

It Is Essentially Violent

This is a particularly interesting objection. In recent years, many complaints about the substitution model have focused on "violence."[83] It is not always

---

rian Committee of Publication, 1898], 43-46). Reading this today, one immediately notices its overly rationalistic form, characterized by words and phrases like "cannot be" and "must be," "requires" and "demands." Anselm, for all his scholasticism, never sounds like this. One also suspects that Dabney's account is being driven by concerns that are not primary in the biblical narrative, particularly a fondness for the notion of punishment (Emily Dickinson was right to complain about preachers who seemed to enjoy the subject of perdition).

81. Quoted in Anthony W. Bartlett, *Cross Purposes: The Violent Grammar of Christian Atonement* (Harrisburg, Pa.: Trinity, 2001), 4 n. 4.

82. Particularly noticeable in the construal of substitution as the action of a sadistic Father is the absence of any perception that the torturing to death of the only Son is related to the fall of Adam. In these critiques, there is no suggestion that *the torturers themselves* might be playing a part here, even if "they know not what they do" (Luke 23:34). Anyone seeking to caricature the crucifixion as the hateful action of a vindictive father does not understand what is happening: namely, the justification of the *ungodly* (Rom. 4:5; 5:6-9). In these critiques there is always more than a hint that the critic does not include himself or herself among the perpetrators. This will be examined further in the concluding chapter.

83. Books influenced by these currents or addressing these issues have titles or subtitles such as *The Violent Grammar of Atonement* (Bartlett), *The Nonviolent Atonement* (Weaver), *Violence, Hospitality, and the Cross* (Boersma). Bartlett and Weaver are at odds with Boersma,

clear why the cross is being construed in precisely this way. Obviously, a person who is crucified has suffered from violence, but violence is not the only thing being suffered — nor is violence the aspect of Christ's death most featured in the New Testament. In fact, the New Testament pays little or no attention to the physical aspects of crucifixion. Instead, it focuses on shame (Heb. 12:2), contempt and mockery (Luke 23:11), scandal and foolishness (I Cor. 1–2), Jesus' blamelessness (Luke 23:13-25, 39), and his dereliction or Godforsakenness (Matt. 27:46; Mark 15:34; II Cor. 5:21) — anything and everything but the physical details.

In recent interpretation, Mennonite theologians, disciples of René Girard, feminists, and others have focused on the "violent grammar of atonement."[84] This critique takes two forms:

1. The substitution motif provides a rationale, even an encouragement, for Christians to commit violence.
2. The substitution-satisfaction theme, specifically as laid out by Anselm and elaborated later in models of penal substitution, introduces an element of violence into the being of God.

The first is the easier of the two objections to refute. It does not make sense to single out the substitution theme for blame in this regard. Surely the *Christus Victor* motif provides just as much if not more fuel for aggression than does the substitution motif, given the violence ever ready to erupt in human nature; the concept of Christ as a conquering hero lends itself all too easily to a Crusader mentality.[85] Constantine's motto, *In hoc signo vinces,* has had a bloody history.[86] When Christians brandish the cross as a weapon

---

but as Joseph Mangina points out, in the work of all these authors, "the 'violence' thematic tends to occlude everything else" (Mangina, review of *Violence, Hospitality, and the Cross,* by Hans Boersma, *Scottish Journal of Theology* 61, no. 4 [2008]: 494-502).

84. Bartlett, *Cross Purposes: The Violent Grammar of Atonement.*

85. Hans Boersma makes some of the same points about *Christus Victor* and the Constantinian dispensation (Boersma, *Violence, Hospitality, and the Cross: Reappropriating the Atonement Tradition* [Grand Rapids: Baker Academic, 2006], 154-58).

86. The emperor Constantine, according to legend, had a vision of a cross and the motto *in hoc signo vinces* — "in this sign conquer." He adopted this as his military standard. Under Constantine, persecution of Christianity ceased, and the faith became "established." The question about the genuineness of Constantine's conversion has never been satisfactorily settled; in any case, he could hardly have understood the true meaning of the death of Christ, since he adopted the cross design as his personal battle flag. In our "post-Constantinian" era, the achievements of Christendom under Constantine appear much less glorious than they once did. The widely popular hymn "Lift High the Cross," with its words "led on their way by this

or sign of conquest, it is not a "theory of atonement" that they carry with them into violent battle.[87] Support for their actions would more likely be found in such passages as the story of Joshua's conquests, or the exploits of David, or Gideon and the Midianites.[88] The Constantinian cross *per se* has no theological content. It is no different from the hammer and sickle or any other motif in that respect. It signifies the group and its mission, whatever that might be. Human nature being what it is, the gross incongruity of the cross used in this way does not occur to its bearers. When the Serbian Orthodox erected crosses during the Bosnian conflict to signify their "victories"

---

triumphant sign / the hosts of God in conquering ranks combine," strikes me as a "Constantinian" or "Crusader" hymn, especially in the version used in the Episcopal hymnal (some original verses are omitted). As it is presently sung, there is no sense of tension or struggle. Another problem in the hymn is that the cross is extolled as a "triumphant sign." This is not wrong; we have already seen in the Passover chapter and the *Christus Victor* chapter that triumph is a major aspect of Christ's work. In the hymn, however, there is no corresponding hint of price or cost, nor is there any suggestion of what it would mean to "lift high the cross" except to carry it in a triumphal procession, which is usually what is happening when the hymn is being sung.

87. In *Cross Purposes,* Anthony W. Bartlett argues at length (from a Girardian perspective) that the "violence" inherent in a substitutionary interpretation of the crucifixion has produced a violent strain of Christianity and provided a rationale for holy war. He believes that the Anselmian train of thought led directly to the Crusades and to a general enthusiasm for "righteous" military causes in Christian culture. I find this strained and tendentious. Episodes from recent history serve as a counterweight to this view. Violence-prone groups will seize upon religious slogans in situations having nothing to do with atonement theory. The 9/11 terrorists shouted "Allahu Akbar" (God is great) before they crashed the planes into the Twin Towers. In 2013, fanatical sword-wielding Buddhist groups began attacking Muslim Rohingya neighborhoods in Myanmar (someone noted that "violent Buddhist" was an oxymoron). In 2011, Nigerian Christian rioters wrote "Jesus is Lord" onto the ruins of a burned mosque (Adam Nossiter, "Election Fuels Deadly Clashes in Nigeria," *New York Times,* April 24, 2011). In such cases the religious signs and words are without content; they have been unthinkingly (and fanatically) appropriated as cultural symbols with little more reference to their deeper meaning than if they had been swastikas.

88. In an extraordinarily interesting section on the "Germanization" of Christianity in the early medieval period (*Cross Purposes,* 95-139), Bartlett quotes from both a Crusader sermon and the *Heliand,* the ninth-century Old Saxon epic. These passages strikingly support the thesis that Christianity was co-opted by the Germanic warrior culture, leading to the Crusader mentality (Bartlett cites G. Roland Murphy, *The Saxon Saviour,* and James C. Russell, *The Germanization of Early Medieval Christianity*). I find this persuasive, and there is much to admire in Bartlett's critique of the Christian warrior cult, which is frighteningly alive in our own time. However, even though the Crusader sermon he quotes does seek to whip up the knights with imagery of the crucified Christ, this tactic is not materially different from the role played by "martyrology" in other situations where the death of a hero is summoned up to inflame martial passions. In all Bartlett's discussion, no consequential connection whatsoever is made to the motif of substitution. Bartlett comes close to blaming Anselm for the Crusades, for reasons I find fatally unsympathetic to the spirit of Anselm.

over Muslim communities, they were not thinking of "the violent grammar of atonement," but were simply — and barbarically — glorying in their supremacy.[89] Such examples should make any true Christian weep for shame; but there is no rhyme or reason for assigning the blame to one or another model of atonement.

The second objection about violence within the Godhead requires more attention and focus. We have sought repeatedly to explain that any model requiring us to split the Father from the Son violates the fundamental Trinitarian theology of God and must be renounced. Equally central is the assertion that God does not change; least of all does he change as a result of the self-giving of the Son.[90] This is a central affirmation. The event of the cross is the enactment *in history* of an *eternal* decision within the being of God. God is not changed by the historical event but has always been going out from God's self in sacrificial love. The being of God also includes his opposition ("wrath") to all that stands against his love. God's "wrath," or his "violence," if you will, is not to be understood literally, as though he were choosing specific moments to unleash his rage and other specific moments to withdraw it. God's judgment on Sin and Death — incarnated in the Son's life, death, and resurrection — is in place within his being from before all time. God is against all that is not part of his purpose; that is the meaning of his "wrath."

It seems perverse to argue that the theme of substitution assigns violence to the being of God. If the Son of God submits to a violent death by "the hands of sinners" (Matt. 26:45), how is that violence in the being of God? God is not committing violence. God in the person of the incarnate Son is himself a willing and purposeful victim of the violence that entered the creation as a result of the fall of Adam. How is this a sign of violence within God? The violence that we see in the crucifixion is the work of the Enemy.

It Is Morally Objectionable

This criticism is dependent on the conviction that the substitution motif requires us to focus on punishment and retribution. Insofar as "crude" inter-

---

89. Roger Cohen, "In a Town 'Cleansed' of Muslims, Serb Church Will Crown the Deed," *New York Times,* March 7, 1994.

90. Anthony Bartlett tries strenuously to show that the crucifixion marks the turn of the ages in specific New Testament apocalyptic terms, but he undoes his own argument by saying in the end that "Christ's final surrender had a determinative effect on the history of God" (*Cross Purposes,* 227-28). J. C. Beker and Ernst Käsemann would not recognize themselves as they appear in his book.

pretations emphasize the details of Christ's sufferings as though they were specifically inflicted by the Father as part of a transaction, this is a fair critique.[91] However, there is more than one way to construe the motif. As we proceed, two seemingly contradictory points will be argued:

1. We will look at the concept of *impunity* in order to show that the idea of penalty cannot be altogether excluded in a moral order.
2. We will look at Karl Barth's account of substitution, which, while it does not exclude penalty, operates in another frame of reference where punishment and retribution become irrelevant.

It Does Not Develop Christian Character

This view is put forward by various contemporary critics of the substitution motif. J. Denny Weaver, for example, argues that whereas the *Christus Victor* theme rallies Christians to resist social evil, the models supposedly derived from Anselm (according to this view) encourage passivity.[92] If this notion were applied exclusively to the so-called Christian Right in America, one might be tempted to agree, but it cannot be maintained when theologians and biblical scholars in other countries are included. There has been a strong thrust toward resistance and social justice in many Reformed circles where substitution is a theme.[93] Even in conservative churches, the passion of many

91. An example can be seen in Robert Duvall's superb movie *The Apostle,* where the Pentecostal preacher holds up a small child's hand to dramatize the Father's piercing of the Son's hand with nails.

92. See also Green and Baker, who state: "This particular way of portraying the significance of Jesus' death has had little voice in how we relate to one another in and outside of the church or in larger, social-ethical issues" (*Recovering the Scandal,* 31). But can it actually be shown that the *Christus Victor* model (or any other) is more effective in this regard? Why would we not want to follow the pattern of sacrificial sin-bearing set for us by the Son of God? Would this not lead us to think of bearing the burdens of others, in their place if necessary? I am not persuaded by this argument.

93. The Reformed tradition, deriving from Calvin, has produced many courageous, self-sacrificing Christians. For instance, several members of the devoutly Calvinist ten Boom family of Haarlem in the Netherlands lost their lives in Nazi camps because they hid Jews (*The Hiding Place,* by Corrie ten Boom, tells the story). The French Protestants of the Cévennes hid many Jews all during World War II (*Lest Innocent Blood Be Shed,* by Philip Hallie). Karl Barth, with his commitment to substitution, was the author of the Barmen Declaration against Hitler. Dutch Calvinism lent itself to apartheid in South Africa, but — and this is the point — *it also contained within itself resources to resist apartheid,* declaring it to be a theological heresy in the remarkable Belhar Declaration of 1986 (which should be much better known). Reformed

evangelicals to resist evil is notable, although, to be sure, the evils they resist are not the evils their critics have in mind![94]

It is tempting to view this particular criticism as self-serving, in a subtle sense. The argument shapes up as a version of "my branch of the church has behaved better and been more righteous than yours." This in itself undermines the radicality of the cross, where all such distinctions become meaningless (Rom. 3:23) and the line between good and evil is seen to run through each person. Can it really be shown that abandoning the substitution motif results in more resistance and more charity? If one believes that the very essence of God is shown forth in the Son's death on our behalf *and in our place,* then the logical outworking of this faith would be a style of living for others, even taking their place if necessary. How does the motif of substitution *not* teach that?[95]

It Is Too Individualistic

This is one of the most important criticisms of the way that the substitution motif has been used in the church, and it must be incorporated into any revised account of the theme. God in Christ was and is calling to himself *a people,* not discrete individuals one by one. The *telos* (goal, end) of God's purpose in the incarnation, life, death, resurrection, and ascension of Jesus Christ was indeed for the deliverance of his people (as in the Passover and exodus), but his design did not end there. The deliverance was for a purpose: the creating of a holy people, a royal priesthood (Exod. 19:6; I Pet. 2:9). God is the one "who loves us and has freed us from our sins by his blood and made us a kingdom, priests to his God and Father" (Rev. 1:5-6). Those who know themselves to be liberated in Christ will also understand that they are not

---

ethicist Paul L. Lehmann *(Ethics in a Christian Context),* for whom sociopolitical engagement was a dominant theme, was an avowed believer in the theme of substitution. The Reformed theologian George Hunsinger, a supporter of substitution/exchange, was a founder and leader of the National Religious Committee against Torture (NRCAT). The list could go on and on.

94. I am thinking of such causes as human trafficking, famine, Ebola, refugees, and persecuted Christians around the world.

95. Ephraim Radner, in his theological commentary on Leviticus, writes, "Substitution as a theory of atonement attempts to describe the mechanism by which Christ redeems us; but it does not explain, let alone establish, the fact of our concrete destiny in Christ" [*Leviticus,* Brazos Theological Commentary on the Bible [Grand Rapids: Brazos, 2008], 171 n. 10). Why does it not? If the Son of God exchanges himself for us (a form of substitution), does that not point toward our incorporation into Christ by the power of the resurrection from the dead (Rom. 6:1-4)? And why would we not want to imitate the Lord out of simple gratitude?

isolated individuals, but part of a "cloud of witnesses" (Heb. 12:1). The new community called into being by the Spirit understands that it lives *corporately* within the world as an image of Christ's incarnate love for the world.

The manner in which the motif of substitution has been used to focus on the salvation of individuals one at a time, with a resulting neglect of the Christian community and its vocation, has been a major error. In our time there is a significant movement from both ends of the ecclesiological spectrum to correct this mistake. However, the overemphasis on individuals cannot by any means be blamed exclusively on the motif of substitution. There were massive shifts in Western thought and culture in the eighteenth and nineteenth centuries that facilitated the displacement of the idea of community from the center to the periphery of Christian proclamation, supplanted by a focus on the supposedly autonomous individual. This has been widely noted in numerous sociological studies. American history and culture, in particular, foster individualism in a way that has been difficult to dislodge from the way that American Christians perceive their redemption.

It Is Controlled by an Emphasis on Punishment

This criticism arises out of a theme in our present culture, which rejects the notion of a punitive God. The whole idea of punishment evokes an image of a wrathful nineteenth-century father rolling up his sleeves and reaching for the rod. The archetype of the angry father is permanently and frighteningly lodged in the human psyche and cannot be displaced in this life. Fortunate indeed is the person who was raised in a family where the father was emotionally present to each of his children in such a way that his chastisement was received as a facet — only one small facet — of his love (as in Prov. 3:11-12 and Heb. 12:6).

It would be a mistake, however, to construe the *theological* concept of punishment solely according to this wrathful image. We need to look once more at the concept of *impunity,* which was discussed in chapter 3.[96] This will help us understand the need to retain punishment, or penalty, in our constellation of ideas about God and the cross of Christ. "Impunity" (Latin *impunis*) means exemption from punishment.

---

96. In the riveting testimony of Sister Dianna Ortiz, who suffered terrible torture in Guatemala, she stressed the importance of the concept of impunity. Where there is impunity, as in her case, cruelty can only flourish. The SPE (Stanford Prison Experiment), conducted by Philip G. Zimbardo in an atmosphere of impunity, has already been discussed in chapter 10.

A word more commonly used to describe a condition of impunity is "lawlessness." The American "Wild West" has been popularly called "lawless," but because the western movies of the classic era bestow mythic stature upon the heroic figure who cleans up, the concept of truly lawless impunity does not become real to us through that medium. To understand impunity we need to look around us at the world today. An example would be the pervasive atmosphere in the Amazon in the early twenty-first century. Terrible atrocities are carried out by large monied interests with no consequences for the perpetrators — men castrated, a nun murdered, laborers "disappeared." A local community organizer, in despair, testified that it was "a culture of impunity."[97] In 2011, testimony about the U.S. Army's Stryker brigade during the Afghan war portrayed a culture of impunity within the unit, involving not only the enlisted men but also the structure of command, which resulted in the cold-blooded killings of civilians for fun.[98] Indeed, in recent years one has the impression that the word "impunity" occurs in the news more often than it used to. Conflicts and conditions all over the globe, from Congo to Turkmenistan to the Chinese takeover of Tibet, have forced us to think more intentionally about this factor.

The idea of punishment cannot be entirely eliminated, and indeed must not be.[99] It lies behind such important New Testament passages as "[God] made him to be sin who knew no sin" (II Cor. 5:21); "he himself bore our sins in his body on the tree" (I Pet. 2:24); "having become a curse for us" (Gal. 3:13); and "My God, my God, why hast thou forsaken me?" (Matt. 27:46 and Mark 15:34) — not to mention "upon him was the chastisement that made us whole" (Isa. 53:5). Perhaps the best way of construing the idea of punishment in our time is in terms of exclusion or rejection. If God is to exclude violence and injustice from his coming kingdom, something has to be done about violence and injustice and every other form of enmity that

---

97. Julie McCarthy, "Reporter's Notebook: Violence in the Amazon," NPR interview with Bishop Dom Earwin, June 7, 2008.

98. William Yardley, "Soldier Is Given 24 Years in Civilian Afghan Deaths," *New York Times,* March 24, 2011.

99. Any culture that *excludes punishment,* if there were such a thing, would produce countless victims who have no redress. Stanley Hauerwas, never one to shrink from controversy, has argued that punishment plays an important role within the church itself (*Performing the Faith: Bonhoeffer and the Practice of Nonviolence* [Grand Rapids: Brazos, 2004], 189-200). The challenge in discussing punishment in the context of the cross is to set it within the proclamation that a new reality has invaded the world of impunity and set it right — proleptically to be sure, but definitively. God has done this by abolishing the reign of the Powers (Rom. 6:9-14) and the tyranny of the Law (Gal. 3:19-26).

seek to thwart God's purposes. These things are manifestations of the reign of Sin and Death, and they cannot be overlooked or ignored — although many construals of salvation attempt to do so. Again, the word *dikaiosyne* (familiarly known as "justification," but better rendered "rectification") is central, for it encompasses *both* righteousness *and* judgment. It is the action of God to make right what is wrong, and that means that some form of final rejection must take place.

In the crucifixion and its vindication in the resurrection, we see how every Power that wars against God has been and will be overcome and ultimately annihilated. It does not take a great stretch of the imagination to grasp how this may be linked with the cry of dereliction. In this sense, we may say that Jesus Christ absorbs into himself the divine sentence against Sin and Death. When Paul says "God made him to be sin," he can be understood to say that in the tormented, crucified body of the Son, the entire universe of Sin and every kind of evil are concentrated and judged — not just *forgiven,* but definitively, finally, and permanently *judged and separated* from God and his creation.[100]

A Final Objection: Forensic Imagery Excludes the New Testament Apocalyptic Viewpoint

Many versions of the substitution motif depend for their force on forensic imagery.[101] The most substantively biblical of all the objections to substitution is therefore made from an apocalyptic perspective. This argument does not play a part in the antipathy toward substitution in the mainline denominations, largely because the recovery of the apocalyptic outlook of the New Testament has not yet percolated down into the local churches.

In this significant critique of substitution, the forensic motifs are held to be insufficient *not* because they focus on punishment or recommend masochistic suffering or encourage violence. These concerns are peripheral to the *principal* objection, which is that the forensic scenario is not only too much focused on single individuals, but — more to the point — does not depict a cosmic battle with an active Enemy. The determining apocalyptic perspective of the New Testament in general and the apostle Paul in partic-

---

100. Christopher Morse writes of God's "eternal subjection" of the work of the Enemy, who is "ultimately defeated and rejected" by God (*Not Every Spirit: A Dogmatics of Christian Disbelief* [New York: Trinity, 1994], 340).

101. See chapter 8, "The Great Assize."

ular depends on our envisioning a tripartite contest involving not only God and his rebellious creation, but also the actively hostile occupying Powers.[102]

However — and this is central to the argument of this volume — the forensic motif so familiar in many evangelical circles and the apocalyptic worldview of the New Testament are not mutually exclusive. They can be allowed to enrich one another. The problem arises when forensic imagery is given *precedence* over other imagery, especially *Christus Victor,* and is allowed to obscure it. When this happens, the single individual with his solitary guilt looms over the conceptual landscape, leaving no space for the drama of the cosmic struggle in which the new, living organism called the body of Christ joins forces with the unseen heavenly host on the frontier where the doomed and dying old aeon meets God's age to come. If the image of the law court is allowed to predominate, as it does in most of the substitutionary scenarios, we can find ourselves mired in a world of "binary discourse" and "score-settling" that leads to many of the abuses cited above.[103] It is essential, especially now in our own time, which is uniquely shaped by interrelated global forces, that we not understand substitution in purely or even primarily individualistic terms.

Summing Up the Critiques

The penal-substitution model as it was taught in so-called Protestant orthodoxy needs a thorough overhaul. However, *rethinking* the substitution motif does not mean *eliminating* it.

The essential, underlying reason for the present hostility toward the substitution motif is quite possibly not found in most of the above critiques. If the critiques were friendly, they would be accompanied by proposed reworkings of substitution. Instead, the critiques have generally — though not quite always — been accompanied by wholesale rejection of the theme. It is difficult to avoid the conclusion: a good deal of the opposition to the substitution motif is rooted in an aversion to its fundamental recognition of the rule of Sin and God's judgment upon it.

We therefore turn to the best modern reworking of the motif of substitution, one that has not yet been surpassed: that of Karl Barth.

102. This was also discussed earlier in the section on forensic versus cosmological apocalyptic in chapter 8.

103. Martinus C. de Boer, especially in his recent commentary on Galatians, differs from Martyn with regard to the forensic theme. Martyn turns away from it, but de Boer wants to include it in the equation as long as the apocalyptic scenario remains primary.

3. Karl Barth and "The Judge Judged in Our Place"

The most serious deficiency in the current debate about the substitution motif, and the concept of the atonement in general, is the lack of engagement with Karl Barth on the subject. American Christianity has never had a "Barthian" period. In many of the seminaries that prepare clergy, especially but not exclusively "evangelical" ones, students are not required to come to terms with this towering figure. It is remarkable that many books on the subject of the crucifixion mention Barth not at all, or only in a glancing way. No enduring critique of substitution can be sustained without coming to terms with his presentation, and it is strange that so many interpreters have failed to do so.[104]

Barth's treatment is found in volume IV/1 of his *Church Dogmatics,* in the long section called "The Judge Judged in Our Place." Together with its equally long bracketing sections, "The Way of the Son of God into the Far Country" and "The Verdict of the Father," it is the most comprehensive, most scriptural, most balanced — and at the same time most original — treatment that we have, particularly in contrast to many in the "Protestant orthodox" tradition.[105] Karl Barth's presentation could not be more different from these.[106] Difficult though his dense text assuredly is, the warmth,

---

104. Among recent studies, Hans Boersma's *Violence, Hospitality, and the Cross,* and *Recovering the Scandal of the Cross* by Green and Baker, are conspicuous examples of otherwise excellent books in which Barth is ignored, which in my judgment weakens their arguments considerably. I am not sure that Scot McKnight fully grasps the importance of substitution in his otherwise splendid manifesto, *A Community Called Atonement.* He sets out a good many of the same points that are being made here, but like so many other critics of substitution, he seems not to have grappled with it in its most profound, least tendentious form. I do not mean to suggest that Barth has no *tendenz* (what we might call an "agenda"); but no theologian has ever wrestled harder, over a period of decades, to keep his personal biases subject to the prior address of the Word.

105. When doing research for this book, I found the patristic and Reformation material surprisingly fresh, but some of the fine distinctions that emerge in the proliferating accounts of Christ's atoning death in the nineteenth and twentieth centuries are quite literally stupefying to the nonspecialist. After years spent examining some of these accounts with little to show for it, I came upon the "Atonement" entry in the celebrated eleventh edition of the Encyclopaedia Britannica, written by the learned Professor Dr. W. H. Bennett, M.A., D.D., D.Litt. (Cantab.). It was at that point that I threw up my hands and determined to go with Barth's narrative treatment.

106. Barth is careful to declare that his position, "in contrast to certain one-sided elements in earlier dogmatic conceptions," is based on the whole of the New Testament witness, not just selected portions (*CD* IV/1, 231). The cross should not be isolated from the incarnation; the life and death are a seamless whole. A good many of the abuses of the substitution theme have

energy, and absence of academic jargon, together with its thoroughgoing overhaul of Calvin, commends it above any other discussion of the motif of substitution.

A good way to introduce Barth on this subject is to look at his own short summary in his little book *Dogmatics in Outline,* an exposition of the Apostles' Creed. He writes, "Man's reconciliation with God takes place through God putting Himself in man's place and man's being put in God's place, as a sheer act of grace. It is this inconceivable miracle which is our reconciliation."[107]

A Narrative Approach

For Karl Barth, the entire story of Jesus Christ, from birth to death and resurrection, is atonement. Barth expounds Christ as our representative and substitute, using the two words interchangeably.[108] As a true inheritor of the Greek Fathers, he does this within the context of the incarnation and the three persons of the Trinity. He does this without the slightest hint of a "theory." In his description of Christ's atoning work, he eschews abstractions and focuses on the passion narratives themselves. Barth's multivolume *Church Dogmatics* is not easy reading, but it helps, when beginning, to understand that his treatment of Christ's death is in *narrative* form.[109]

---

arisen because the overly rationalized version of it overwhelmed the interpretive landscape. Barth's targets here are the Reformed scholastics that we identified earlier. (I remember being startled when I attended a worship service on the first Sunday after Easter at an old-line "penal substitution" church and the sermon was about the cross instead of the resurrection!)

107. Karl Barth, *Dogmatics in Outline* (New York: Harper Torchbooks, 1959), 115.

108. Some have argued that representation and substitution are two separate motifs. This has been a theme in Anglo-Saxon theology; Horace Bushnell, P. T. Forsyth, and F. D. Maurice have argued variously that they are not the same. Bushnell preferred to speak of "vicarious" suffering, which has been seen by some as an alternative to substitution. F. D. Maurice eschews the word "vicarious," wanting to rid the atonement of any suggestion that there is a transfer of guilt and punishment to Christ on the cross — an objection to which we may assent up to a point; Maurice wished to move the idea of substitution out of the penal category into the context of the incarnation. Maurice thought he was rejecting the substitution motif when he wrote: "Christ indeed bore instead of us what we could not ourselves bear — but it was not by a transference of penalty to him for us as a substitution, so much as by his coming into our region which lies under the divine wrath and from the midst of it making the perfect acquaintance of that wrath as our representative" (*The Doctrine of Sacrifice Deduced from the Scriptures* [London: Macmillan, 1893], 179). As much as Maurice wants to renounce the idea of substitution in favor of representation, it is ultimately, as Barth seems to say, a distinction without a difference.

109. Indeed, he refers to it as *Sage* (German for "saga") in various places in the *CD.* His

Although the complexity of his presentation often disguises his method, he is essentially *telling the story* of salvation. The passion of Christ is an *event,* and the proper mode of communicating it is *narrative;* thus Barth, as always, demonstrates his commitment to the task of preaching and teaching in the church. "Will it preach?" is the question he seems always to be asking himself as he works. It is curiously and paradoxically fitting that this least "subjective" of theologians should depict the passion of Christ in an emotional and moving way, as a preacher might. We are invited to behold the cross, and to tremble. The Isenheim altarpiece is the illustration, and the cry of dereliction is the sound track.[110]

The Biblical Narrative of Salvation

It is significant that Barth does not begin his mighty work of dogmatic theology with the fall from the Garden of Eden. He begins with the doctrine of the Word of God and its power, then takes up the doctrines of God and of creation. Not until volume IV does he deliver a full exposition of the cross. In other words, the judgment of God is preceded by the grace of God. The Epistle to the Romans follows the same pattern: Paul preaches the gospel (Rom. 1:1-17) *before* he turns to his long section on the wrath of God.

Barth uses imagery from the parable of the prodigal son, who left his father's house to go into a "far country" (Luke 15:13). He makes this a framework for the journey made by the Son of God through his incarnation into the world of sin and death. The Old Testament drama sets out the rupture that has occurred between God and his creatures. Barth calls this "the antithesis" between the righteous God and the suffering that has resulted from humanity's fall. Only if we understand this chasm between our Creator and ourselves can we fully assimilate the gospel declaration: "In the passion story of the New Testament this antithesis is done away. It is God Himself who

---

careful differentiation between "myth, saga, fable, legend, and anecdote" in III/1 (Edinburgh: T. & T. Clark, 1958), 81-94, contributes to the discussion about "myth" especially in Gen. 1–3. Barth's preference for "saga" rather than "myth" is based on his conception of the creation story as "an intuitive and poetic picture of a pre-historical reality of history which is enacted once and for all within the confines of time and space" (81).

110. Throughout his life, Barth kept a reproduction of Matthias Grünewald's Isenheim altarpiece in his study. Of all the Old Masters, Grünewald offers the most gruesome illustration of the crucified body of Christ. Barth identified himself with John the Baptist's large index finger pointing to the crucified One, with the inscription, "He must increase and I must decrease."

takes the place of the former sufferers and allows the bitterness of their suffering to fall *upon Himself.*"[111]

As soon as Barth makes this clear reference to substitution, he moves into the language of apocalyptic, with its envisioning of the "far country" not as a geographical or even mythical location, but as an apocalyptic one: "God gives Himself to this most dreadful of all foreign spheres" (175). Implicit here is the notion of a competing realm, ruled by a "foreign" Enemy — an indispensable feature of New Testament apocalyptic theology.[112]

Then, with the encompassing embrace of multiple biblical themes that typifies his work, Barth draws Israel into his narrative to show how grace and love *preceded* God's judgment and *remained operative,* though hidden, behind his judgment upon their apostasy: "What took place on the Cross of Golgotha is the last word of an old history and the first word of a new. God was always the One whose condescension showed itself to be unlimited in the suffering and death of the man Jesus. He is the same God who was truly gracious to Israel in the hiddenness of His love in the form of His righteous wrath" (176).

One of Barth's great contributions to the Reformed tradition, which has emphasized the wrath of God against sin, is his clarification on this point. Throughout *Church Dogmatics,* he insists that God's judgment is entirely enclosed by his mercy.

The Incarnation as the Original Substitution

No feature of Barth's discussion is more important than the consistency of his perspective on the cross from within the totality of the incarnation. "The Almighty exists and acts and speaks here in the form of One who is weak and impotent, the eternal as One who is temporal and perishing, the Most High in the deepest humility. The Holy One stands in the place and under the accusation of a sinner with other sinners. The glorious One is covered with shame. The One who lives for ever has fallen a prey to death" (176).

Barth's mode in passages like this is simple storytelling. There is nothing theoretical here, nothing "logical" or propositional. Instead, Barth plainly sets forth the astonishing contrasts that we see in the birth, life, and death of the

111. Barth, *CD* IV/1, 171, emphasis added. Notice how clearly Barth shows that the Father and the Son are one, with the word "Himself." The page references in the following text are to *CD* IV/1.

112. This is not to suggest that Barth was conscious of what would become a self-styled movement. However, this most biblical of theologians has been recognized by virtually all who are interested in apocalyptic theology, from Käsemann on, as a major figure in this way of thinking and seeing.

Son. He does not speak here simply of the crucifixion but of the entire span of Jesus' life "under the accusation of a sinner with other sinners." He was "a prey to death" as soon as he was conceived in the womb of his human mother.

God as the Acting Subject

In the next passage we encounter the crucial matter of *agency*. Barth consistently holds that God is the acting subject in all that happens through his Son. This is one of the most important affirmations in this book as well: *God is doing this.*

> Even in the form of a servant, which is the form of His presence and action in Jesus Christ, we have to do with God Himself in His true deity. . . . The humility in which He dwells and acts in Jesus Christ is . . . that which He is in Himself, in the most inward depth of His Godhead. . . . The truth and actuality of our atonement depends on this being the case. The One who reconciles the world with God is necessarily the one God Himself in His true Godhead. Otherwise the world would not be reconciled with God. (193)

In the following pages Barth argues for a contradiction: Jesus is no less God in the incarnation and on the cross than he is in the eternal Godhead. *God must be seen to be undertaking the atonement himself.* "He acts as Lord over this contradiction [i.e., undergoing his own judgment] even as He subjects Himself to it. . . . He is not untrue to Himself but true to Himself in this condescension, in this way into the far country" (273). Notice how Barth sticks to his narrative structure, extending his identification of the Son of God with the prodigal son who went "into the far country."

If any doubt were to remain about who is the responsible agent in this narrative of Christ's life and death, it is banished with this passage:

> It is a matter of determining the acting subject of the reconciliation of the world with God . . . when we have to do with Jesus Christ we are dealing with the author and finisher of this work, with . . . the One who has taken upon Himself and away from the world the enmity of the world against God and the curse which rests upon it, with the One who accomplishes the ineluctable judgment of the world in such a way that He Himself bears it in order to bear it away. . . . *Everything depends upon our seeing and understanding as the New Testament does that He is the acting subject in this work.* (197, emphasis added)

Barth, the Christus Victor *Theme, and the Plan of This Book*

Barth is well aware of the *Christus Victor* theme and works it easily and without strain into his overall presentation. He speaks of "spheres," indicating his grasp of New Testament cosmology. He sees Sin and Death as Powers, perhaps not in the thoroughgoing way that many Pauline scholars would today, but recognizable as such nonetheless, writing that Christ makes "the offering of His life to the powers of death" (252). In his rich presentation, he combines martial *Christus Victor* language with substitution when he speaks of "the victory which has been won for us, in our place, in the battle against sin" (254).

In Barth's narrative, Christ was able to take our place as the sinless One because "He was free from the basis of all sins" (258). Note the unusual way in which Barth puts this. Instead of saying he was free from all sin, he speaks of *the basis of all sins.* In other words, Jesus arrived in the world from the sphere of God's rule, which is not only outside the rule of Sin but also sovereign over it. The Messiah's locus of power is the only point from which a weapon could be wielded that would dislodge Sin and reverse Satan's usurpation. If there were any doubt about the implications of Barth's thinking about the demonic dimension, it is dispelled by the long account of the temptation a few pages later. If Christ had made an agreement with the devil, then the world would have been "ostensibly ruled by Christ but secretly by Satan." "Jesus has to do continually with the kingdom of darkness." Barth explicitly explains Gethsemane in terms of the demonic. He says that the world is Satan's "sphere of influence." With vivid narrative power he shows us how Christ, in the Garden, saw that he would not only be *alone* as he died but would be *given over to the power of Satan* working through his human instruments. "The convulsion of that hour" in Gethsemane shows us something of the horror of seeing Satan triumphant (258-66).[113]

Jumping ahead briefly in "The Judge Judged in Our Place," we find Barth concluding with a long section of fine print in which he argues that the theme of substitution — especially in its significance "for us" and "for sin" — subsumes all the others. It would be a mistake, however, to discount Barth because he gives such prominence to "the substitutionary atonement." His survey of the other motifs is thorough. He seeks to give the ransom image its place in the whole, though he thinks it minor. He wants to rehabilitate "satisfaction" in biblical terms.[114] He refers to *Christus Victor* as the "military"

---

113. There are important similarities between Barth's treatment of Gethsemane and Raymond E. Brown's apocalyptic interpretation (see chap. 9, "The Apocalyptic War").

114. In Barth's long analysis of the "cultic" imagery (discussed in this book in chap. 6,

theme, and specifically insists that the *Christus Victor* image represents "a particular truth" and must receive its due.[115] It is the argument of this book that, just as Barth does not disparage the other themes, and notes that "the different groups of terms cut across each other very frequently," it is essential — especially for preachers — to pursue a type of interpretation and exposition that allows this sort of crosscutting to happen frequently (*CD* IV/1, 274). Preachers of the past who knew vast amounts of the Old and New Testaments by heart did this crosscutting instinctively, as a matter of course, for Scripture interprets itself *(Scriptura sui interpres)*.

The Unwitting Participation of the Ungodly

In the beginning of the section that deals directly with the crucifixion, "The Judge Judged in Our Place," Barth returns to the narrative of God's dealings with Israel in order to open up the story to the Gentiles:

> God . . . did not regard it as too mean a thing, but gave Himself fully . . . as the God of the needy and rebellious people of Israel, to be born a son of this people, to let its wickedness fall on Him, to be perfected by it, but in its place and for the forgiveness of its sins to let Himself be put to death by the Gentiles — and by virtue of the decisive cooperation of the Gentiles in His rejection and humiliation to let Himself be put to death in their place, too, and for the forgiveness of their sins. (214)

"The Blood Sacrifice"), he puts the best face possible on Anselm's term "satisfaction" by saying simply that in the cross, "satisfaction — *that which suffices* for the reconciliation of the world with God — has been made *(satis fecit)*." Barth regards the imagery of blood sacrifice as very important and shows how it fits into his overall category of substitution: "This Priest [as in the Epistle to the Hebrews] is not only the One who offers sacrifice but also the sacrifice which is offered; just as He is also the Judge and the judged. He does not offer anything else. . . . He simply offers Himself. He does not pour out the blood of others, of bulls and calves, to go into the Holiest with this offering. It is a matter of His own blood, of the giving of His own life to death" (*CD* IV/1, 276-77, emphasis added). Note Barth's deeply scriptural approach, particularly characteristic of this section of the *Church Dogmatics*.

115. Barth uses representation and substitution interchangeably. New Testament scholar J. D. G. Dunn argues that substitution does not preserve the agency of the Father. (How is that so? Certainly it is not true of Barth's discussion, where the Father and the Son are acting together.) Dunn prefers "representation." However, he says, "The animal must be holy, wholly clean precisely so that priest and sinner may be certain that its death is not its own, that it does not die for any uncleanness of its own." If not its own, then whose? Doesn't that imply substitution? Dunn, "Paul's Understanding of the Death of Jesus," in *Reconciliation and Hope,* 136.

In this passage Barth is explicit about the "decisive cooperation" of the Gentiles in the execution of the Son. He is moving toward a clear statement of the role of the perpetrators in the drama of the death of Christ "in their place, too." Thus the substitution clearly takes place "for us" not only in the sense of "for our benefit" but also in the sense of "in the place of" the actual executioners. Every Christian is summoned to see herself among the perpetrators for whom Christ has substituted himself. "He takes our place when we become sinners, when we become His enemies, when we stand as such under His accusation and curse, and bring upon ourselves our own destruction" (216). To this day, as we look around us at the self-destructive tendencies in the world that destroy good and hopeful things — from broken levees to derelict housing projects to botched aid operations to failed nation-building — we see the Lord standing in the place where the fiascoes are happening, not only in the place of those victims who are made to suffer but also and most radically in the place of the delinquents, collaborators, transgressors, and perpetrators. This, in part, is what it means to say with the apostle Paul that he *justifies the ungodly.* These words about how Christ takes our place are meant not only for everyone without exception; they are also meant to strike the heart of each individual with a piercing joy as we recognize ourselves among those sinners and enemies who, without his intervention, would "bring upon ourselves our own destruction."

The Substitution Theme Set Forth

When Barth, a few pages later, asks the question, "But what did take place?" he does not mean Golgotha only, but the entire story of the downward journey of the Son "into the far country." He then sets out the substitution theme in the most straightforward, bare-bones way: "At this point we can and must make the decisive statement: What took place is that the Son of God fulfilled the righteous judgment on us men [*sic*] by Himself taking our place as man and in our place undergoing the judgment under which we had passed. That is why He came and was amongst us. In this way, in this 'for us,' He was our Judge against us" (222).[116]

Nothing here sounds at all like the overwrought penal-substitution presentations of "Protestant orthodoxy." The emphasis is always on the "for us

---

116. Barth's habitual use of the generic "man" was acceptable usage in English for many hundreds of years. The modern reader is asked to get past this in order to appreciate Barth. This is the only time that I will use *sic.*

[*pro nobis*]." Even as he is the Judge, he is first and last "for us." He was for us *before* he was against us, and for us *even as* he was against us — *pro nobis* first, last, and always.

Barth then takes us through the New Testament narrative. All the Synoptics present Christ as the coming Judge in the preaching of John the Baptist, and we see him as an assertive, active master and leader all during his ministry. Then when the passion narratives begin, suddenly

> Jesus no longer seems to be the subject but the object of what happens. There is, in fact, a complete reversal, an *exchange of roles.* Those who are to be judged are given space and freedom and power to judge. The Judge allows Himself to be judged. . . . [T]he accusation, condemnation and punishment to which it refers all fall on the very One on whom they ought to fall least of all, and not at all on those on whom they ought to fall. The most forceful expression of this scandalous contrast is the Barabbas episode in which a murderer is in every respect acquitted instead of Jesus, and Jesus is condemned to be crucified *in his place.* . . . He is not dying a hero's death, but the death of a criminal. (226, emphasis added)

Barth's diction and syntax are complex and old-worldly, employing a great deal of what may appear to be unnecessary repetition, so it is easy to miss the essential simplicity of what he is saying. No other theologian of his stature does it quite this way. Behind all the looping sentences is a childlike trust in the Spirit who guided the formation of the biblical story, and in the Evangelists and apostles whose sole motivation was their faith in their great Subject and their desire to make him known. Barth tells the story not to convince us rationally, but to win us over to see ourselves in it.

The Meaning of "For Us"

For Barth, the central declaration is *pro nobis,* "for us." "All theology . . . depends upon this *theologia crucis.* And it depends upon it under the particular aspect [of] the doctrine of substitution." He could hardly be more emphatic, saying, "this is the place for a full stop" (273). Everything that the Son of God has done during the entire span of his life from incarnation to crucifixion was done *for us.* No one in creation has ever been able to be "for us" in the way that he is, for he is begotten of the Father, not created. Again, remember that the substitution theme is worked out by Barth in terms of the whole story of the incarnate One:

Jesus Christ "for us" means that . . . this one true man Jesus Christ has taken the place of us men . . . representing us without any co-operation on our part.[117]

. . . [W]e look back to the fact that this One has acted as very man and very Son of God, that He has acted as our representative and in our name, that His incarnation, His way of obedience has . . . fulfilled as its ultimate meaning and purpose the fact that He willed to do this and had done it: His activity as our Representative and Substitute. (230)

Barth amplifies the meaning of substitution in a manner far removed from the schematic style of "the earlier dogmatic conceptions." He does not think of it as a "conception" at all; he seeks to describe the great exchange in terms that engage our personal attention:

In the New Testament the words *anti, huper,* and *peri* are used to bring out the meaning of this activity [as Representative and Substitute] of Jesus Christ. . . . [T]hese prepositions speak of a place which ought to be ours, that we ought to have taken this place, that we have been taken from it, that it is occupied by another, that this other acts in this place as only He can, in our cause and interest, that we cannot add to anything that He does there because the place where we might do so is occupied by Him, that anything further which might happen can result only from what is done by Him in our place and in our cause. (230)

Putting the Penal Theme in Its Rightful Place

Barth continues to differentiate his treatment of substitution from the "older presentations of the doctrine of atonement" (273).[118] He saw, before many others in his tradition did, that these "older presentations" in the Reformed scholastic tradition allowed a rigidly schematic concept of penal substitution to become an *idée fixe,* crowding out all the other biblical models. Barth saw

117. What Barth means to stress here is the implication of all of humanity in the execution of Jesus. Another way of putting this would be to say that since every human being lives under the rule of Sin and Death, we were incapable of "cooperating" with our Redeemer until he liberated us.

118. Here he means largely the seventeenth-century Calvinists. He defines them further by adding, "especially those which follow Anselm of Canterbury." Barth, ordinarily a defender of Anselm, is distancing himself from this (mis)interpretation of Anselm. Anselm himself proposes satisfaction instead of punishment (see pp. 153-59 above, especially n. 28 on p. 159).

the error in this, not only because it was insensitive to the richness of the biblical imagery, but also because it focused on punishment in an unhealthy way. Barth does not want to do away with penalty altogether, but he moves it away from the center to the periphery:

> The concept of punishment has come . . . from Isaiah 53. In the New Testament it does not occur in this connection. But it cannot be completely rejected or evaded on this account. My turning from God is followed by God's annihilating turning from me. When it is resisted His love works itself out as death-dealing wrath. If Jesus Christ has followed our way as sinners to the end to which it leads, in outer darkness, then we can say with that passage from the Old Testament that He has suffered this punishment of ours. But we must not make this a main concept. (253)

The way Barth works with the concept of "death-dealing wrath" is both abstract and narrative, at the same time. He is thinking of the *idea* of God's wrath as the way that God's love is felt when resisted, but he casts it in dramatic terms with a warmth and literary flair often lacking in the "older presentations." In this paragraph, the frightening image of God's "annihilating" turning-away is taken up into the picture of Jesus going into outer darkness in our place. There is much in that picture in addition to "punishment." The "no" of God to Sin is punishment enough. The Son, acting as one with the Father, absorbs that negation to the last extremity.

Accompanying the above passage, which is in Barth's small print, are the lines that form the heart of his presentation:

> The very heart of the atonement is the overcoming of sin: sin in its character as the rebellion of man against God, and in its character as the ground of man's hopeless destiny in death. It was to fulfil this judgment on sin that the Son of God as man took our place as sinners. He fulfils it [the judgment] as man in our place, by treading the way of sinners to its bitter end in death, in destruction, in the limitless anguish of separation from God. . . . We can say indeed that He fulfils this judgment by suffering the punishment which we have all brought on ourselves. (253)

"The decisive thing," he writes, is not that we are spared punishment, though "this is true, of course." The decisive thing is that in Jesus Christ God himself has put an end to Sin and to our imprisonment under the reign of Sin. Barth, characteristically, insists on the point that Jesus *has taken the place of* the man of sin ("Adam," as in Rom. 5), but the emphasis is not on the penalty suffered. Surely, it *is* suffered — no dispute there — but Barth throws all the weight on the undoing of Sin. This whole section reinforces the significance of Christology — none of it works unless the crucified One is the incarnate second person of the Trinity. On the cross, we see the only-begotten Son of God delivering sinful humankind ("Adam") over to destruction *in God's own person,* as the Son submits to the curse that lay upon us on account of Sin, Death, and the Law. Thus the substitution motif has been freed from its doctrinaire prison, thoroughly reworked, and greatly expanded in terms of *Christus Victor* and of recapitulation.[119] In the final analysis, though Barth is obviously an enthusiastic exponent of the substitution motif, he has recast the model with great originality. Even though Barth does not speak of Sin as an apocalyptic Power in precisely those words, clearly he thinks of it in that way.

The Theme of Displacement

Barth's originality is also shown in his concept of displacement, or deposition. As the story of the primordial couple in Genesis 2–3 makes clear, our "original sin" was to set ourselves up as judges, that is, capable of determining good and evil on our own. In this presumption of ours we are radically in error. The usurpation of the role that belongs to God alone has led to the bondage of all creation (Rom. 8:20-23). Therefore the invasion of creation by God in Christ means that we have been radically displaced, deposed from our self-made throne or bench where we sit and judge others in order to shore up our restless need to prove our own righteousness. We want to "pronounce ourselves free and righteous and others more or less guilty." We enjoy this role. But in the cross we see that we have been "displaced" by the one who is truly the Judge and is at the same time "radically and totally for us, in our place" (231-32). "For where does our own judgment always lead? To the place where we pronounce ourselves innocent . . . that is how we live. And that is how we can no longer live in the humiliating power of what took place in Jesus Christ. We are threatened by it because there is a complete turning of the tables. He who has acted there as Judge will also judge me, and He and not I will judge others" (233).

---

119. "The man of sin was taken and killed and buried in and with Him on the cross . . . [*thereby*] reopening the blocked road of man to God" (254). This is an interpretation of the story of Adam and Christ in Rom. 5, and as such is closely bound together with the theme of recapitulation — as we shall shortly see in the next chapter.

It is possible to argue that the demonic third party so crucial to the *Christus Victor* scenario is not in the picture here. However, the imagery of displacement/dislodgement/deposition implies a coup. To displace humanity from its self-erected seat of judgment, God must act aggressively, with "humiliating power."

This is a compelling diagnosis of the human condition and our resistance to the whole concept of substitution. We do not want to give up our place as judge. Barth specifically defines the primal human sin as making ourselves judges in order to exculpate ourselves and condemn others. This is pictured in the instantaneous response of Adam and Eve, who, after eating the forbidden fruit of the knowledge of good and evil, begin blaming each other and the serpent in order to hang on to the illusion of innocence — an innocence irreparably lost. We have usurped God's place as the only true Judge, and therefore the substitution must happen at that particular juncture. An invasive, displacing movement on God's part is clearly indicated, but paradoxically, it is the invasion that liberates even as it humiliates. Barth writes of this with the joy that often characterizes his work:

> The second effect of Christ's action (the first being the deposition and overturning of man) is an immeasurable liberation and hope . . . a heavy and indeed oppressive burden is lifted from us when Jesus Christ becomes our Judge. . . . It is a constraint always to have to be convincing ourselves that we are innocent, we are in the right [and] others are in one way or another in the wrong. . . .
>
> We are all in process of dying from this office of Judge which we have arrogated to ourselves. It is therefore a liberation that . . . [in Christ] we are deposed and dismissed from this office because He has come to exercise it *in our place.* . . .
>
> I am not the Judge. Jesus Christ is the Judge. The matter is taken out of my hands. And that means liberation. A great anxiety is lifted, the greatest of all. I can turn to other more important and more happy and more fruitful activities. I have space and freedom for them in view of what has happened in Jesus Christ. (233-34, emphasis added)

Barth then speaks of hope in the Last Judgment. The One who is the true Judge has already decided *for us,* and will decide for us in the last day. Barth links this with the incarnation by saying that God's action in Christ "was already decided when the Word became and was flesh." Therefore we may look forward to the ultimate decision of the Judge "with a terror-stricken joy."

The **effect** of the substitutionary, displacing, deposing activity of Christ is further described by Barth much later in the volume, in "The Act of Faith" section: "I myself, the man of sin, who has not and will not overcome himself, am the one who finds that he is overcome in Him. My proud heart is vanquished. My proud thoughts and words and works as they flow from that heart are vanquished. The man of sin is vanquished . . . removed, destroyed, put to death. That is the substitutionary being and activity of Jesus Christ. . . . That is what He has done for me in His death and what, again for me, is shown to be done in His resurrection" (770).

The Eternal Decision Played Out on Earth: Apocalyptic Transvision

If we make certain links between Barth and the theme of chapter 9, "The Apocalyptic War," we can spot another original feature of Barth's discussion of the meaning of Christ's life and death "for us." This inquiry follows along the lines of Barth's exposition of the agony in Gethsemane as the turning point of Jesus' life and mission. In the prepassion part of the four Gospels' narratives, he is "the divine *subject* of the judgment on man," for in his ministry Jesus speaks and acts as one with power to judge and dispose. From Gethsemane onward, however, he becomes the *object* of this judgment, the one who is himself disposed of — the Judge judged in our place. "If the judgment [of God on sin] is fulfilled at all . . . then it is with this reversal. Jesus represents men at the place which is theirs according to the divine judgment, by putting himself in the place which is theirs on the basis of and in accordance with their human unrighteousness" (238).

Barth then gives us another of his characteristic formulations, which, in this case particularly, helps us to understand the mysterious relationship between what is happening on earth and what is happening in "heaven," that is to say, the sphere of divine power. In the context of the persistent question about whether Jesus really was abandoned by God in his death, Barth explains that the anguish suffered by the Son in Gethsemane, as he begs for the "cup" to be taken away from him, "yet not my will, but thine," is *a replaying in history* of *the eternal decision within the Godhead* (238-39).[120] If the Father abandons the Son, it is with the Son's will and permission, for the two are one.

120. Barth fills out this insight by asserting, in remarkably anthropomorphic imagery, that this eternal decision was made only with the greatest difficulty and struggle. Some years later, Hans Urs von Balthasar expressed some of this in a similar way: "The experience of being abandoned by God, in which Jesus endures the condition of the sinner before God, emanates in its inscrutability . . . from a Trinitarian transaction of consent *within history* between the Father and the Son in the Holy Spirit" (quoted by George Hunsinger, *Disruptive Grace,* 30).

Here is a sort of double vision where the theologian sees on two levels at once. This can be called "transvision," that is, seeing *through* the events of the present into the transcendent purpose of God. Where there is transvision of the sort that we find in the Bible,[121] we may see a hint of the perpetual interplay between freedom and predestination, earth and heaven, the now and the not yet, doctrine and ethics, that lies behind so much of the Scripture's message about human responsibility.

Conclusions about Barth's Teaching on Substitution

Almost from the beginning of this volume, we have been guided by the biblical picture of human nature, so well understood by the great literary writers and so much resisted by today's purveyors of self-help. The biblical figure of "Adam" personifies the ubiquitous human fixation on the idea of its own innocence and the refusal of God's right to be our Judge. Consequently we live with a delusion, insatiable in its demands and demonstrably false: the delusion that we can live free of the deeply lodged power of Sin in our lives. This is less a failure of *anthropo*logy than of *theo*logy — it is a tragically insufficient grasp of who *theos* (God) is in relation to the creation. We have seen that where there is no knowledge of God, there is no knowledge of Sin.[122] In the biblical record, the response of human beings to the appearance of God (in the guise of an angel, a burning bush, a whirlwind) is always the same — fear and terror. When Simon Peter sees the miraculous draught of fish, instead of exclaiming over the bounty, he falls to his knees and says, "Depart from me, for I am a sinful man, O Lord" (Luke 5:8). The huge catch of fish is the occasion for a theophany. The Lord's gracious response is exactly the same as that of the biblical angels who come directly from the presence of God: "Fear not."[123] Without that merciful reassurance,

121. The prophets operate via transvision a good deal of the time (for instance, Isa. 40:3-8), but a particularly dramatic narrative of transvision is II Kings 6:8-17, the story of the siege of Dothan by the Syrians.

122. Robert Oppenheimer, the famous physicist and a chief inventor of the atomic bomb, gave a lecture to his fellow scientists in which he said these words: "In some sort of crude sense which no vulgarity, no humor, no overstatement can quite extinguish, *the physicists have known sin; and this is a knowledge which they cannot lose*" (*Time*, July 29, 1985, emphasis added). This is a remarkable formulation. Oppenheimer (a Jew and a very conflicted person) clearly had some sense of God, however unacknowledged, or he could not have said this.

123. During the struggle for freedom from Stalinism in Poland, the Polish Pope John Paul II habitually greeted the Polish people, members of Solidarity, priests, and other resisters with "Be not afraid!"

the human being would be annihilated by the burning holiness of God. This sense of the *distance* between God and his creation must always be *held in tension* with the intimate *closeness* of the personal God who draws near to us in grace, or else we are in danger of having no god except the one we have fashioned to suit ourselves.

It seems likely that the current popularity of the *Christus Victor* model in its most stripped-down form is based on a belief that it offers, in place of Sin, a more palatable view of Evil (and/or Death) as an impersonal force threatening humanity. This move is not only biblically impossible but also pastorally irresponsible, since it encourages people to live in denial about humanity's responsibility concerning the origins of Sin. It is not just a matter of being rescued from impersonal forces; it is Sin that has unleashed these forces.[124] While it is essential to affirm the strength of the *Christus Victor* model in its depiction of Powers with an identity and existence of their own, it is equally necessary to understand that we humans are *accountable for* all these evils even as we are *held prisoner by* them.

This is, perhaps, a subtle point. We need to hold two seemingly contradictory propositions in our minds at once when talking about our relationship to Sin. This can be stated colloquially: *first,* "the devil made me do it"; *second,* I am guilty just the same. We are victims of cosmic evil powers, yet we as individual sinners bear a burden of responsibility. How can both these things be true? Freud is helpful here. We cannot help ourselves, Freud taught; we are at the mercy of various impulses and drives that were set in motion by family patterns before we were born. This aspect of Freud's system is well enough known to be caricatured on a regular basis. What is less well understood is that Freud never sought to *exonerate* the patient; rather, he sought to *understand* in order to help release the patient from irrational behavior.[125] There is much to be learned from Freud about the unconscious and its role in what we think are our "choices." Recognizing this paralysis in ourselves is a leap forward in understanding the dimensions of our ancient bondage and our new freedom in Christ.

Barth has rescued the substitution motif from "theory" and has restored

---

124. In the chapter on the descent into hell we attempted to elucidate the presence of the serpent in the Garden as a metaphor that allows us to make seemingly contradictory assertions. (1) Though God did not create evil, so that it has no existence of its own, it appeared in the Garden prior to the human decision to disobey. (2) "Adam" and "Eve," standing in for each and all of us, are nevertheless responsible beings whose original fault has brought the entire human race into bondage (as Paul explains in Rom. 5:12-21).

125. Here I acknowledge a debt to lectures by Cyril C. Richardson and conversations with Dorothy Martyn.

it to us in the form of the biblical story. In the following summation we can see the very heart of Barth's conception:

> The passion of Jesus Christ is the judgment of God in which the Judge Himself was the judged. And as such it is at its heart and center the victory which has been won for us, in our place, in the battle against sin. By this time it should be clear why it is so important to understand this passion as *from the very first the divine action* . . . the radical divine action which attacks and destroys at its very root the primary evil in the world; the activity of the second Adam who took the place of the first, who reversed and overthrew the activity of the first in this world, and in so doing brought in a new man, founded a new world and inaugurated a new aeon.[126]

Is Barth right when he insists that we are "to understand this *passion* as from the very first the divine *action*"? As we regard the crucified One, who is the chief actor?

4. The Matter of Agency

By now, it should be obvious that a major thesis of this book is the divine agency. Barth lays it out in the quotation just above. If the Bible is to be understood in its own terms, it cannot be fairly understood any other way. From beginning to end, the principal acting subject is God. Therefore there can be no retreating from the foundational statement: "In Christ God was reconciling the world to himself" (II Cor. 5:19). But does that mean that the crucifixion was itself an act of God? or was it an act of Satan? or was it the result of human evil? Those are the three agencies in the New Testament, in descending order of power.

The four passion narratives in the Gospels are designed, through extensive use of citations from the Old Testament, to show that God is at work at every turn to carry out his plan. Paul makes the narrative explicit: "If any one is in Christ, he is a new creation; the old has passed away, behold, the new has come. *All this is from God,* who through Christ reconciled us to himself . . . that is, in Christ God was reconciling the world to himself, not reckoning their trespasses against them" (II Cor. 5:17-19).

A persuasive case can be made that "All this is from God" is the theme

126. Barth, *CD* IV/1, 253-54, emphasis added.

of the entire Corinthian correspondence.[127] Indeed, there is a sense in which it is Paul's primary message throughout his ministry. His is a profoundly *theo*logical, *theo*centric gospel, just as much as it is christocentric.[128] In passages like the one above, the doctrine of the Trinity is implicit, with each of the persons actively at work.[129] Moreover, as God was in Christ, Paul can — and does — say that God is also powerfully at work in himself, the apostolic messenger.

The question of agency is a primary one in Christian theology and practice. It is vital for the purposes of this study that we clarify the matter. Who is acting in the world to reconcile humanity to God and human beings to one another, and who was the active agent in the crucifixion of Jesus? These two questions are related. Here in the context of the substitution motif, the matter of agency is critical. Who is in charge at Golgotha? Perhaps even more to the point, who is in charge in the Garden of Gethsemane?

Various answers have been given to this question. To begin with, "we" — meaning all human beings, not just "the Jews" or "the Romans" — can be seen as the agents. Famous hymn texts incorporate this idea, so that the person who is singing confesses his complicity in the crucifixion: "'Twas I, Lord Jesus, I it was denied thee, I crucified thee"; "Died he for me, who caused his pain? For me, who him to death pursued?"[130]

On a different tack, recent Anabaptist theologians, together with critics of atonement theory from feminist and womanist perspectives, have sought to remove agency from God altogether and give it to the demonic powers.[131] This is not altogether wrong, to be sure; J. Louis Martyn argues persuasively from Galatians 3:13 that the Law is the secondary agent:

> The promissory blessing of God that had been waiting in the wings met the curse of the Law for the first time at the cross. As Paul hears Deuteronomy 21:23 (Galatians 3:13), it was the Law, not God, that pronounced its curse on the crucified One, and the one thus cursed by the Law was

127. The Corinthian congregation held themselves and their spiritual vitality in high regard.

128. In the undisputed letters of Paul, he refers to "God" almost as many times as "Christ" or "Jesus." The Spirit also gets well over a hundred references.

129. Paul's theology of the Holy Spirit is as powerful as John's or Luke's — Rom. 8 is the *locus classicus.*

130. Johann Heermann (1585-1647), "Ah, Holy Jesus, How Hast Thou Offended?"; Charles Wesley (1707-1788), "And Can It Be That I Should Gain?"

131. Weaver, *The Nonviolent Atonement,* sums up these positions.

in fact God's Christ.[132] It was in the cross that the apostle came to see a momentous fact about the Law: its cursing voice is not the voice of God. But he saw also that that voice was robbed of its power when, approved by God in his Law-cursed death, Christ *embodied* the Law's curse, for *in that embodiment* Christ vanquished that curse, freeing the whole of humanity from its power.[133]

In the final analysis, however, the Gospels and the witness of Paul overwhelmingly testify to the primary action of *God* in the crucifixion of Christ. As a conclusion to this chapter, we turn to a sermon of Lancelot Andrewes (1555-1626) that offers a clear perspective, not only on this question of agency, but also on the theme of substitution.

5. Substitution and Agency in a Sermon by Lancelot Andrewes

The sermons of the great Anglican divines of the seventeenth century can only inspire awe and wonder in present-day students of language and church history. Unfortunately, the syntax of Shakespeare and the King James Version, of John Donne and Lancelot Andrewes, has become difficult for today's average reader. Moreover, the sermons of Donne and Andrewes are *biblical* in a sense that preachers of today cannot hope to emulate, for congregations today would not sit still for the learned, intricate reflections of these mighty intellects, even though their sermons are so admirably harnessed to the *ministerium Verbi divini* (service of the divine Word).

It is both humbling and instructive, however, for us to make the necessary effort to read some of these masterpieces. In a Good Friday sermon called "Never the Like Was," Bishop Andrewes expounds a verse from Lamentations, "Consider and behold, if ever there was sorrow like my sorrow, which was done unto Me, wherewith the Lord did afflict Me in the day of the fierceness of His wrath."[134] In this long sermon about the passion of Christ,

---

132. Gal. 3:13: "Christ redeemed us from the curse of the law, having become a curse for us — for it is written, 'Cursed be every one who hangs on a tree' [from Deut. 21:23]."

133. J. Louis Martyn, *Galatians*, Anchor Bible 33A (New York: Doubleday, 1997), 326, emphasis added. This reference to *embodiment* can readily be linked to the passages from Barth quoted just above. Note that Martyn capitalizes Law to indicate its status as one of the Powers.

134. 1604 Sermon on Lamentations 1:12, in *Ninety-six Sermons of the Right Honourable and Reverend Father in God, Lancelot Andrewes* (Oxford and London: James Parker and Co., 1832), 139-58; quotations are taken from this edition. Page numbers of the sermon in the 1841 edition are 138-57. The capitalization in this translation of Lamentations (which Andrewes

Andrewes interleaves all the biblical imagery that we have surveyed, and more besides. Of particular interest is the way he develops the theme of substitution without looking over his shoulder at Anselm, let alone veering off into a schematic penal version. He states his subject, weaving in the motifs of ransom, price, and blood sacrifice: "His Passion, Who this day poured out His most precious Blood, as the only sufficient price of the dear purchase of all our redemptions." When we read a sentence like that, it seems perverse to complain about possible errors in the imagery.

Agency: God as Acting Subject in Andrewes

Particularly noteworthy is Andrewes's elucidation of *agency* in the crucifixion of Christ. We have just considered Martyn's suggestion that the curse that fell upon Jesus (Gal. 3:13) was the Law.[135] If we stretch this a bit to hook the Law to Sin as Paul does in Romans 7:8-11, we can say that Andrewes supports this assignment of agency to the Law, in a sense, even as he places it in a threefold setting. He speaks of three causes at work in the *unique ("never the like was")* suffering of Christ.

Andrewes skillfully begins by suggesting to his congregation that the first cause was "the power of darkness . . . wicked Pilate, bloody Caiaphas, the envious Priests, the barbarous soldiers" (note that he specifically avoids blaming "the Jews"). Then he quickly moves to assert that this is *theo*logically deficient: "We are too low by a great deal, if we think to find [the cause] among men. *Quae fecit Mihi Deus,* 'it was God that did it.' An hour of that day was the hour of the 'power of darkness'; but the whole day itself, it is said here plainly, was the day of the wrath of God."[136]

Notice how finely Andrewes distinguishes between the power of Satan,[137] which is given its causative moment ("an hour of that day"), and the

---

was using) is a clue to the christological move he was making. (Not incidentally, he mastered Hebrew as well as a dozen other languages.) Andrewes is anything but naïve in doing this. He specifically cites New Testament typology and the Fathers to argue that Christ has taken the Old Testament words and types unto himself. I am grateful to Ellen Davis for bringing this sermon to my attention.

135. It has already been emphasized that the Law cannot be detached from the Lawgiver. This dialectic requires conceptual dexterity and a willingness to live in the paradox — as in the case of evil being dependent upon God yet not part of creation, discussed in chapter 10.

136. Though we cannot quote the entire sermon here, Andrewes takes great pains to keep the persons of the Trinity together so that we do not think of the Son as the victim of the Father.

137. The power of darkness and the power of Satan are essentially the same in the Gospels.

overarching plan of God ("the whole day itself"). Within the great eschatological drama, Satan plays a strictly circumscribed role. Sin and Satan are secondary agents and must operate within the limits God allows.

Andrewes is intent to show that the power of Sin (with its co-opted servant the Law) over human beings includes particularly the congregation listening to the sermon. He quotes Paul: "*Cum inimici essemus,* saith the Apostle; *we* were His enemies" (Rom. 5:8). Andrewes avoids making Sin the first cause of the action of God by putting the wrath of God before it. Sin, the secondary cause, provoked God's wrath, the first cause. But far more, it was love, the third agency, that caused Christ's suffering for our sake. "So have we the causes, all three," Andrewes continues:

1. Wrath in God
2. Sin working in ourselves
3. Love in Him

This nicely shows how we can make distinctions among the causes of the crucifixion, making certain that "we" are seen as perpetrators, yet in no way removing God as first cause, and the love of God in particular. For all his attention to the role of Sin and the "power of darkness," Andrewes never lets go of God as acting subject.

The Theme of Substitution in Andrewes

Most striking for the purposes of this chapter is Andrewes's unabashed use of the motif of substitution.[138] He does it as though it were the most natural thing in the world, without forcing it or insisting on it or incorporating it into a "theory."

> There is no way to preserve God's justice and Christ's innocency both, but to say of Him as the Angel said of Him to the Prophet Daniel, "The Messiah shall be slain, but not for Himself."[139] Not for Himself? For whom then? For some others. He took upon Him the person of others.

---

138. Andrewes is generally considered anti-Calvinist compared to some of his Anglican contemporaries, for instance, the Archbishop of Canterbury John Whitgift (c. 1530-1604). This is all the more reason we should pay attention to his presentation of the substitution motif.

139. Dan. 9:26. Andrewes gives the passage the church's traditional messianic interpretation.

> Pity it is to see a man pay [for what] he never took; but if he will become a surety, if he will take on him the person of a debtor, so he must. . . . And so Christ, though without sin in Himself, yet as a surety, as a sacrifice, may justly suffer for others, if He will take upon Him[self] their persons.

Andrewes then quotes Isaiah 53, not worrying about misappropriating it as we might today. He wants us to know that Isaiah repeats his message seven times in seven different ways in verses 4-6, lest we miss the point: *The Lord has laid on him the iniquity of us all.* Andrewes emphasizes "all," and includes even those who "pass by" and do not "regard" the world-transforming event. This suffering is for them too. He has taken their persons, also, upon himself, whether they regard him or not.

Andrewes follows this with a passage evoking the theme of substitution as vividly as anyone ever has, in a passionate appeal to the congregation to hear itself personally addressed by the living Word:

> The short [of it] is, it was we that for our sins, our many great and grievous sins . . . should have sweated this sweat and have cried this cry; should have been smitten with these sorrows by the fierce wrath of God, had He not stepped between the blow and us, and latched it in His own body and soul, even the dint of the fierceness of the Wrath of God. . . .
>
> Which bringeth home this our text to us, even into our own bosoms, and applieth it most effectually to me that speak and you that hear, to every one of us, and that with the Prophet Nathan's application: *Tu es homo,* "Thou art the man."[140]

Our Personal Involvement in the Substitution

The *Christus Victor* theme has been criticized for taking place over our heads, so to speak, without our involvement. In an important sense this is true of substitution and the other motifs as well. *God did this for us without our assistance or cooperation.* The images express this variously: we were dragged out of Egypt into the desert kicking and screaming; we were hostages unable to free ourselves; we were guilty and sentenced to death. Paul underscores this: while we were *still helpless,* "Christ died for the ungodly" (Rom. 5:6). We need to make a full stop here, on the issue of agency. Our salvation and

---

140. The elided text, which clearly affirms the responsibility *of Christians* in the death of Christ, is relevant to the subject of Christians and Jews.

reconciliation have been accomplished *by God as acting subject* from start to finish. He has brought us from death to life. "Even when we were dead through our trespasses, [God] made us alive together with Christ" (Eph. 2:5).

However, we are both *involved* and *implicated* in Christ's work.[141] Although God brings into being a new *community,* the idea of substitution has a unique power to involve us *personally,* emotionally, at the gut level. We have already stressed the communal nature of God's redeemed people over against a hyperindividualistic interpretation of the cross, but we must not lose sight of the individual and the summons to the conversion and discipleship of individuals. One of the most striking characteristics of Jesus as he went about his ministry was his personal address to individual men and women — calling them by name, speaking to the intimate circumstances of their lives, addressing each one in his or her singularity. Of all the motifs, it is substitution that most directly addresses the individual's involvement, expressed by the line in Heerman's hymn, "I crucified thee."

The theme of substitution allows full scope for us to understand the depth and completeness of Christ's involvement in the human condition. From this perspective, it is truly hard to understand why there is so much resistance to it. How does it make the self-sacrifice of Christ more palatable to say that he gave himself only *for our benefit,* rather than *in our place?* Even if it is construed exclusively as a victory over the Powers — as in the *Christus Victor* motif — does that explain why the Son of God had to undergo *crucifixion* to defeat Sin, Death, and the devil? Does it not require some suspension of disbelief in any case? Why should we resist the most obvious sense of the words "for us" and "for me" in the case of Jesus on the cross? Since he clearly did not deserve what happened to him, why is it not right to conclude that we should have been there instead of him? Is that not the most basic sort of human reaction? We have all heard of people saying, "It should have been me instead of him." Why should we want ruthlessly to eliminate such thoughts concerning Christ on the cross? The plain sense of the New Testament taken as a whole gives the strong impression that Jesus gave himself up to shame, spitting, scourging, and a degrading public death before the eyes of the whole world, not only *for our sake* but also *in our place.*[142]

---

141. Gerhard O. Forde, "Caught in the Act: Reflections on the Work of Christ," *Word and World* 3, no. 1 (Winter 1983): 22-31.

142. All four passion narratives place great emphasis on the disciple Peter's blatant triple denial of the Master who loved him so unconditionally. In view of this appalling behavior, how could Peter *not* think of Jesus as one who suffered instead of him, in his place — "It should have been me instead of him"? When Peter "wept bitterly" (Luke 22:62), is it just because Jesus' searching gaze at the crowing of the cock reveals to him that he is a craven coward and

This gospel message has incomparable pastoral effects, offering not only consolation and peace, but also freedom and life. When the apostolic message is personally appropriated, it calls forth an active faith. More than any other theme, even that of sacrifice (from which it cannot be disentangled), this particular news evokes a sense of personal gratitude and emotional commitment. This *evangel* has a very specific outcome: it shows how Christ *assumed the weight* of sin and guilt that lies upon the human spirit precisely in the moment that *the weight is lifted,* and it therefore powerfully evokes from us a sense of thanksgiving so profound that we no longer need to avoid accountability, but gladly embrace it. As Colin Gunton puts it, quoting the *Epistle to Diognetus* (second century): "'Oh sweetest exchange! . . . The sinfulness of many is hidden within the Righteous One, while the righteousness of the One justifies the many that are sinners.' . . . Not here some grim balancing of accounts, but rejoicing in a liberation. The Son of God has given himself to be where we were so that we might be where he is, participants in the life of God."[143]

6. Some Conclusions

Substitution and Christus Victor

In view of our earlier, sweeping affirmation of the earliest Christian confession as our lodestar ("Jesus is Lord" — *Kurios Iesous* — I Cor. 12:3) and *Christus Victor* as the all-encompassing motif, it may seem contradictory to say, in this chapter, that *substitution* is the indispensable theme. A certain amount of conceptual elasticity is needed here; the intention is to lock the two together rather than making them competitive or mutually exclusive. There are several advantages to be gained by doing so.

First, *the apocalyptic drama* is the nonnegotiable context for the substitution model and all the others as well. It is the thought-world from which

---

deliberate liar? Is it not also his realization that he has been a betrayer little better than Judas and therefore deserving of condemnation, yet it is his guiltless Master who is condemned? We may want to avoid the term "substitution," but it is hard to see what is gained by suppressing the clear idea that the innocent Jesus is suffering while the guilty Peter goes free.

143. Colin Gunton, *The Actuality of Atonement: A Study of Metaphor, Rationality, and the Christian Tradition* (Grand Rapids: Eerdmans, 1989), 140. If it is necessary to give up the term "substitution" in favor of some other term like "exchange," as Gunton does here, or "vicarious representation," so that the incomparable news can once again ring forth from our pulpits, then so be it; but we are arguing here that the power in the word "substitution" should not be abandoned because of the word's misuse.

the entire New Testament was written. The incarnate Son arrived not in neutral territory, but in a realm occupied by an Enemy power.

Second, *the way in which* Christ became the apocalyptic victor was *through the substitution*.[144] The *Kurios* could have achieved his victory in some other way, but God chose *this* way. The incarnate One exchanged his glory for the shame of the cross (Heb. 12:2) from the very beginning of his life, being born in shameful circumstances, his infancy mortally threatened by a tyrant, branded an impostor by the religious authorities from the first (Luke 4:28-29), being without a place to lay his head throughout his ministry (Matt. 8:20; Luke 9:58), meeting with hostility everywhere he went. The shame he endured is often expressed in terms of *exchange,* closely related to substitution: being in the form of God, he exchanged his glory for the form of a slave, exchanging his riches for our poverty, his righteousness for our unrighteousness, even to death on a cross. That is the manner in which he won the victory — "therefore God has highly exalted him" (Phil. 2:9; cf. II Cor. 8:9; I Pet. 3:18).

Third, there is a *correspondence* between Christ's death, the Law (the Torah, or "the commandment"), and the human condition under the Law. We have previously seen that although the Law, originating in God, is "holy and just and good" (Rom. 7:12), it was appropriated by Sin, twisted out of shape, and used as a weapon of destruction (7:5, 8-11). Christ suffers and dies under the combined assault of these annihilating Powers. He is condemned and put to death under the Law.

The accursed, Godforsaken death suffered by Jesus was, in some way that we cannot fully articulate, the death that should have been ours, a death under the cursing voice of the Law wielded as a weapon by the Power of Sin.[145] The incarnate Son took our place under the sentence of Death, the third Power in this unholy trinity.

144. In saying this I do not mean to neglect the other motifs such as blood sacrifice, but I read them as subsidiary and supportive.

145. J. L. Martyn distinguishes between the "two voices" of the Law, one cursing and one promising ("A Formula for Communal Discord!" in his *Theological Issues in the Letters of Paul* [Edinburgh: T. & T. Clark, 1997], 267-78, and *Galatians,* 506-12). The "cursing voice of the Law" is the handmaiden of Sin. The "promissory voice of the Law," on the other hand, was preached — in one of Paul's more audacious insights — *ahead of time, before Sinai,* to Abraham — the "father of [us] all" (Rom. 4:11; Gal. 3:8, 14-16). The cursing voice is that of enslavement; the promissory voice is that which begets the free "children of promise" (Gal. 4:21-31; 5:6-14). It was the cursing, condemning voice of the Law that was conclusively defeated on the cross. Marilyn McCord Adams writes, "If God in Christ crucified becomes curse, the power of curse is cancelled: curse cannot exile us from God any more. Likewise, if Christ is made sin for us, sin loses its power to separate us from the love of God" (*Horrendous Evils and the Goodness of God* [Ithaca, N.Y.: Cornell University Press, 1999], 99).

William Blake, in his poem "Jerusalem," captures this perfectly:

When Satan first the black bow bent
And the Moral Law from the Gospel rent,
He forg'd the Law into a sword,
And spill'd the blood of Mercy's Lord.[146]

Note that Blake, like Paul, depicts Satan as the agent that severed the Law from the gospel.[147] As we saw in chapter 10, this is a pictorial way of maintaining the goodness of the commandment while keeping its perversion separate from the direct will of God. Paul describes the consequence: "The very commandment which promised life proved to be death to me" (Rom. 7:10). Paul says "me" (and he may very well be thinking autobiographically here), but he is using "me" as a stand-in for all humanity under "Adam." Since the Law has been commandeered by Sin, the unaided human being cannot make the commandment work properly; the often-invoked "law of unintended consequences" bears witness to this. "I do not do the good I want, but the evil I do not want is what I do" (Rom. 7:19).[148]

The purpose of emphasizing the death-dealing role of the Law is to show how the obscene, accursed character of crucifixion is linked to the demonic perversion of the gracious Law of God. *This was the death that Satan designed for all of us.* Focusing exclusively on *Christus Victor* would encourage us to avoid the substitution theme with its clear and intimately personal link to Sin and Death. The Son could have offered himself to some other death, such as beheading, but as we have seen, that was a *citizen's* death, not a *slave's* death. Christ suffered as a slave *in our place,* for it was we, not he, who were the slaves to Sin.

Fourth, the "great exchange" made by Christ on the cross as our substitute was a descent into perdition for him, a deliverance from condemnation for us. Hence the special importance of the cry of dereliction —

---

146. I do not remember who first brought Blake's quatrain to my attention, but its striking encapsulation of Romans has been noted by others than myself.

147. Calvin, in teaching "the third use of the Law . . . being also the principal use, and more closely connected with its proper end," shows how this work of the Enemy is undone by the Spirit as the Law and the Gospel are reunited in a new relationship as a result of the work of Christ (*Institutes* 2.7.6-17). "If you are led by the Spirit you are not under the law" (Gal. 5:18).

148. In the middle of the decade 2010-2020, some particularly depressing studies showed that much foreign aid to countries afflicted with natural disasters, war, famine, the Ebola virus, and other ills was counterproductive because of waste, incompetence, corruption, and failure to understand other cultures. Good intentions really do seem to pave the way to hell sometimes. Hence, the maxim, "No good deed goes unpunished."

"My God, my God, why hast thou forsaken me?"[149] We cannot plumb the depths of this cry — more like a shriek or abysmal groan — for truly it comes as Christ descends into the hell from which he delivers us. In this cry, however, we hear something of what it meant for our Lord "to become sin." Paul's mysterious utterance in II Corinthians 5:21, "[God] made him to be sin who knew no sin," has never been fully understood, but many commentators have noted its relationship to the cry of dereliction. God made Jesus to be sin even though he knew no sin, and in that indescribably terrible and unique transaction, Jesus apparently felt the full force of utter separation from the Father. That is what he underwent in order to remake our human nature — not to improve it, not to accept it, not even to perfect it, but to reengender it altogether. He "became sin"; we "become the righteousness of God."[150]

These four points are intended to show *how* the two predominant motifs are interlocked.

7. Summary

The theme of substitution

- properly arises *out of the biblical narrative,* where it appears in various contexts as part of an organic whole.[151] It appears as a theme wherever the Greek words *huper* (for) and *peri* (on account of) are used to declare the meaning of Christ's death.
- is best understood as *an underlying motif* supporting the other themes, illuminating them and being illuminated by them, not in isolation from the overall biblical narrative or in competition with other motifs.[152]

149. Barth devotes an extraordinary amount of attention to this "word from the cross" in *CD* IV/1. Only John 1:14 gets more attention ("The Word became flesh and dwelt among us"). The special emphasis on these two verses is a sign of Barth's emphasis *not only* on the cross *but also* on the incarnation.

150. Because of the exchange Christ has made with us, we now participate in his righteousness.

151. See also Hans Urs von Balthasar, *Theo-Drama: Theological Dramatic Theory,* vol. 4 (San Francisco: Ignatius, 1994), for a similar angle on the cross of Christ.

152. The following passage from Brevard Childs's *Biblical Theology of the Old and New Testaments: Theological Reflection on the Christian Bible* (Minneapolis: Fortress, 1993) is relevant because he argues for the primacy of the substitution theme in spite of the predominance of the *Christus Victor* motif in much commentary today: "There can be little question but that both testaments use the imagery of combat and liberation to portray the work of God and

- should be interpreted in the context of *the entire incarnate life* of the Son of God, a life that from the beginning was set on a path to the cross.
- is more closely linked with the *virtually ubiquitous biblical teaching about God's judgment upon Sin* than any other motif, however much our culture may wish to avoid this unpleasant truth about itself.
- was unself-consciously present, together with "the blood," in homiletical exposition not only in evangelical circles but also in "catholic" Anglicanism (used as an illustration).
- lends itself most particularly to the proclamation of *the justification of the ungodly,* the subject of the closing chapter of this volume.

But what difference does it make to us, finally, that Christ died in our place? Does this belief call forth tears of self-indulgent repentance and little else? Does it not reveal something to us that we would rather not behold? Do we not see, at Golgotha, something altogether new about who is the victim and who are the perpetrators, something about the inclusive nature of human depravity? And does this revelation not "create in me a clean heart, O God, and put a new and right spirit within me," as the psalmist implores?[153]

The death of Jesus on the cross is God in three persons acting *together,* with one will, for one purpose — to deliver all humanity from the curse of Sin and its not-so-secret weapon, the Law. Jesus, the representative man, our substitute, not only *shows us how* human will can align itself with the will of God, but also *makes it happen, in his own incarnate person;* and then, in the greatest act of love that has ever taken place, he gives his own person back to us, crucified and raised from the dead, the firstfruits of all who belong to him. "For you have died, and your life is hid with Christ in God. When Christ who is our life appears, then you also will appear with him in glory" (Col. 3:3-4).

The hymn by Johann Heermann, "Ah, Holy Jesus, How Hast Thou Offended?" is typically sung on Palm Sunday and Good Friday in the Episcopal Church. The words indicate as clearly as possible that Jesus on the cross is

---

Christ in freeing humanity from the powers of sin and evil. However, the theological issue still remains to be discussed to what extent such imagery can be said to support an independent and self-contained theology of Christ's redemption in any way comparable to the themes of justification and sacrificial atonement. Could it be that the significance of this imagery lies in an important dimension to which this language points *within* the *more central* New Testament focus on justification, atonement, and reconciliation which is firmly grounded in a Christological affirmation?" (518, emphasis added).

153. Ps. 51, tellingly, is appointed to be read on Ash Wednesday.

there in our place. The words in their extraordinary devotional effectiveness carry the day and are beyond criticism. It is as though the hymn, sung in response to the reading of the passion narrative, stops all argument:

> Lo, the Good Shepherd for the sheep is offered;
> The slave hath sinnèd, and the Son hath suffered;
> For our atonement, while we nothing heeded,
> God interceded.

CHAPTER TWELVE

Recapitulation

We think that Paradise and Calvarie,
Christ's Crosse and Adam's tree, stood in one place.
Looke, Lord, and finde both Adams met in me;
As the first Adam's sweat surrounds my face,
May the last Adam's blood my soul embrace.

JOHN DONNE[1]

The motif of *substitution* is closely allied with the notion of *representation,* although it is not precisely the same.[2] It is also compatible with the un-impeachable model of *recapitulation.* To this final motif in our list of New Testament themes we now turn.

This model is presented last in the sequence. There is little controversy

---

1. John Donne, "Hymn to God, My God, in My Sickness," available at Poetry Foundation Web site.

2. The central notion in substitution, that Christ actually suffered what we should have suffered, is not quite so apparent if the concept of representation is in the foreground. About recapitulation, Morna Hooker proposes a point that we have been circling throughout the previous chapter: "It is not . . . a case of Christ and the believer *changing places,* but of the believer *sharing in Christ's life*" (*Not Ashamed of the Gospel: New Testament Interpretations of the Death of Christ* [Grand Rapids: Eerdmans, 1994], 33). This is a helpful redirecting of some of the more distorted uses of the substitution theme. In shifting emphasis from substitution to participation, she wants to show how we are not so much acquitted of guilt by the cross (the emphasis of so many penal substitution models) as we are incorporated into the life of the crucified Christ. While this is an emphasis of great importance and should not be neglected, it does not fully take account of Jesus' brutal, obscene, and shameful public death. It is neither necessary nor desirable to choose one motif exclusively and reject the others, as is argued throughout this book.

surrounding this theme. It arises out of the apostle Paul's extraordinary presentation of Christ as the new Adam in Romans 5, and therefore has all the advantages of narrative over "theory." Moreover, the theme of recapitulation can be understood as incorporating all the others. In the foregoing chapter on substitution, we discussed how, by reenacting the life history of "Adam," Christ puts himself in Adam's place — that is, the place of all humanity individually and collectively.

Is there anyone alive over fifty who would not want to live his or her life over again in order to correct the mistakes, avoid the wrong turns, undo the damage, maximize the opportunities, recover the wasted time, repair the broken relationships, restore the lost future? More important still, would we not wish to see great wrongs wiped out — all the mass murders, child abuse, destruction of cultures and populations, despoliation of nature, and all the other miseries and atrocities of history rectified and the memory of them obliterated? In Christ, Paul is telling us, not only will all this happen in the eschatological age, but also the power of what Christ has accomplished for us and the whole creation is active in our lives even now as we put our trust in his remade humanity.

Recapitulation is the oldest of the biblical themes to appear consistently in the Church Fathers. This excerpt from Kelly's *Early Christian Doctrines* explains its content and significance:

> Running through almost all the patristic attempts to explain the redemption there is one great theme which provides the clue to the fathers' understanding of the work of Christ. This is the ancient idea of *recapitulation* which Irenaeus derived from St. Paul, presenting Christ as the *representative* of the entire race. Just as all men were somehow present in Adam, so they are . . . present in the second Adam, the man from heaven. Just as they were involved in the former's sin, with all its appalling consequences, so they . . . *participate in* the latter's death and ultimate triumph over sin, the forces of evil, and death itself. Because, very God as He is, He has identified Himself with the human race, Christ has been able to act on its behalf and in its stead; and the victory He has obtained is the victory of all who belong to Him.[3]

3. J. N. D. Kelly, *Early Christian Doctrines* (New York: Harper and Row, 1959), 376-77, emphasis added. The elided words in Kelly are "or can be" and "can." This runs counter to Paul, who does not use that sort of "possibility" language. All men are present in the second Adam, period. Their ultimate destiny is in the hands of God. When Paul is in his most expansive mode, as for instance in "As in Adam all die, even so in Christ shall all be made alive" (I Cor. 15:22), he does not qualify *pantes*, "all." He does not say "*can be* made alive." See also Rom. 11:26 ("all

In one short passage Kelly makes use of three key concepts: *representation, recapitulation,* and *participation.* Note also the substitution motif in the words "in its stead." He then adds, "All the fathers, of whatever school, reproduce the motif."[4] No wonder that, in these times of increasing respect for the patristic period, recapitulation is gaining in esteem.[5] It has the advantage of being very early, making its appearance in the anti-gnostic polemic of the first great theologian of the postapostolic church, Irenaeus, who drew deeply from the well of Romans 5:15-21 for his doctrine of recapitulation.[6]

Irenaeus (c. 130–c. 200), bishop of Lyons, is an impressive person in Christian history. Even though we do not have his works in their original Greek but only in a Latin translation, his essential qualities clearly come through. He writes not as an academic but as a pastor with love for his flock, wishing above all to strengthen them in the true faith and to ward off the ever-present lure of gnostic spirituality (which he satirizes quite amusingly). He presents the essentials of the faith in powerfully simple affirmations, anticipating the Nicene Creed and setting out the terms in which Christian doctrine would be discussed for centuries to come. It is remarkable how fresh he sounds even today.[7] Irenaeus's teaching about re-

---

Israel will be saved") and especially 11:32 ("God has consigned all men to disobedience, that he may have mercy upon all").

4. For example, Augustine quotes Ambrose: "I fell in Adam, in Adam was I expelled from Paradise, in Adam I died; and [God] does not recall me unless He has found me in Adam . . . Christ's flesh, however has condemned sin . . . which by dying He crucified, that in our flesh there might be justification through grace, where previously there was impurity through sin." Augustine, *On the Grace of Christ, and on Original Sin* 2.47.

5. Almost a thousand years after Irenaeus, Anselm restated his basic theme: "As death came upon the human race by the disobedience of man, it was fitting that by man's obedience life should be restored" (*Cur Deus Homo?* 1.3). Another thousand years separates Anselm from modern theologians, yet the theme is as fresh as ever: "Jesus' perfect obedience . . . embodies a reversal of every other human narrative or life-story" (Stephen W. Sykes, *The Story of Atonement,* Trinity and Truth Series [London: Darton, Longman, and Todd, 1997], 16).

6. Irenaeus's term *anakephalaiosis* is usually translated "recapitulation" (from the Latin), but it can also be understood as "summing up" or "regathering" because it does not mean simply "repetition." Ephraim Radner writes in his commentary on Leviticus, "Jesus holds within himself all of history and all of its forms. . . . All of this, in Christ, is brought into its reconciled order under and in unity with God" (*Leviticus,* Brazos Theological Commentary on the Bible [Grand Rapids: Brazos, 2008], 288-89). That is a good definition of recapitulation as Irenaeus sees it.

7. A caveat for nonspecialists: Irenaeus is best read selectively. His editor Edward Rochie Hardy refers to "islands of brilliance in a work which pursues its turgid way" through sometimes tedious rhetorical refutations of fantastic gnostic constructs (introduction to section on Irenaeus in *Early Christian Fathers,* ed. Cyril C. Richardson, Library of Christian Classics [Phil-

capitulation has been taken up enthusiastically by many who are rethinking the meaning of Christ's death in the context of his incarnation, ministry, and resurrection.

Irenaeus was able to draw out the implications of Romans 5:12-21 early in the life of the church with an insight that has seldom been excelled in church history. The whole human race, he saw *via* Romans 5, is implicated in the original act of disobedience described in the great myth of Genesis 2–3.[8] The significance of "Adam," as we have already seen, is metaphorical; the name gathers up into itself the solidarity of all human beings under the rule of Sin.[9] "We" are "Adam," and "in Adam all die" (I Cor. 15:22). This is a central declaration of the Christian faith. From this it follows that Christ enters into battle with the Powers and, in Irenaeus's encompassing expression, "overcomes through Adam what had stricken us through Adam."[10]

Paul's Story of the Two Adams (Reprise)

We examined Romans 5:12-21 at length in chapter 9, and the reader can refer to the section in that chapter called "The *Kurios* as *Christus Victor* in Romans 5 and 6" in tandem with this one. Ricoeur throws a spotlight on the originality of Paul when he discusses Genesis 2–3: "Adam . . . remained a mute figure for practically all of the writers of the Old Testament . . . [the myth of Adam] remained in a state of suspended animation, so to speak, until St. Paul revived it by making it parallel to the second Adam, Jesus Christ."[11] In Romans 5, the forgotten cosmic significance of the Adamic story is recovered and reversed by the apocalyptic event of Jesus Christ.

We looked at Paul's parallels earlier, but in a different context. In chapter 9 we were focusing on Christ as conqueror at the turn of the ages. Here, we point out the parallels from a different perspective as we trace the story of the second Adam:

---

adelphia: Westminster, 1953], 344). Even so, there are many accessible passages, and Irenaeus's satirical remarks directed at Gnosticism are particularly pertinent today.

8. Paul himself may not have believed that there were actual persons named Adam and Eve; in any case, such a belief is in no way necessary.

9. In Eph. 1:10, the Greek word *anakephalaioo* is awkwardly translated "to head up" (*ana*, "up"; *kephale*, "head"). In Irenaeus the idea seems to be that whereas Adam stands at the head *(kephale)* of the line of unregenerate humanity, Christ is now the head of redeemed humanity.

10. Irenaeus, *On the Apostolic Preaching* 16.68.

11. Paul Ricoeur, *The Symbolism of Evil* (Boston: Beacon Press, 1967), 6. The myth came into its own when Paul appropriated it.

Judgment → one sin → condemnation
    is contrasted with
Gift → many sins → justification

And in 5:17:

Adam's trespass → Death reigned
    is contrasted with
Christ's grace and righteousness → reign in life

In 5:18 Paul restates and summarizes:

One trespass → condemnation for all
    is contrasted with
One act of righteousness → justification and life for all

Paul repeats these contrasting parallels numerous times, as we saw in chapter 9, to build up his case, using his typical "how much more" structure to show that God's action in Christ is infinitely greater than all the calamities that followed upon the disobedience of Adam.

Irenaeus puts it like this:

[Christ] when he became incarnate, and was made man, began anew the long line of human beings, and furnished us, in a brief, comprehensive manner [*in compendio*] with salvation; so that what we had lost in Adam — namely to be according to the image and likeness of God — we might recover in Christ Jesus. (*Adversus haereses* 3.18.1)

God recapitulated in himself [*in seipso recapitulavit,* "summed up in himself"] the ancient formulation of man, that he might kill sin, deprive death of its power, and vivify man. (3.18.7)

So did he who was the Word, recapitulating Adam in himself, rightly receive a birth, enabling him to gather up Adam [into himself] . . . that the very same formation should be summed up [recapitulated] in Christ. (3.21.10)

Like virtually all the important Christian thinkers prior to the post-Enlightenment and modernist milieu that dominated biblical studies until the second half of the twentieth century, Irenaeus moved easily among various images of what Christ accomplished. Because he was able to appropriate the conceptual world of the New Testament without the "scientific" scruples that reigned until recently, he adopted much of the New Testament cosmology: "He [Christ] therefore completely renewed all things, both taking up the battle against our enemy, and crushing him who at the beginning had led us captive in Adam" (5.21.1).

There is much for us to notice here. Recapitulation is not to be understood simply as Christ reliving the human story and making right decisions instead of wrong ones.[12] Unlike most modern interpreters, Irenaeus speaks quite naturally of the third party, the Enemy, who had largely gone missing from mainstream New Testament interpretation until the twentieth century. Irenaeus also comes close to personifying Sin and Death, as Paul does — sin has to be crushed, death has to be deprived of its power. Understood this way, his doctrine of recapitulation, blossoming out of Romans 5, is interwoven with the *Christus Victor* theme in its fullest context, that of God's apocalyptic war against "him who at the beginning had led us captive in Adam."

In the last verse of the Adam-Christ passage (Rom. 5:21), Paul evokes the collision between two kingdoms and two lords. He does this by setting up two more parallel contrasts. Notice how the word for kingdom *(basileia)* appears in the form of a *verb,* in order to show that we are talking here about two active agents with rival dominions:

Just as Sin reigned [verb, *basileuo*] in Death,
So also grace might reign [verb, *basileuo*] through righteousness. . . .

---

12. I intend this polemically. Everyday use of the terms "good/right choices" versus "bad/wrong choices" is characteristic of American culture in our time. This emphasis on choice sounds suspiciously Pelagian; it does not sit well with the Pauline/Augustinian view that our wills are bound. A good deal of work has been done in the secular social sciences to undermine the notion of "free" choice (Gary Gutting, a professor of philosophy at Notre Dame, surveys the landscape in the opinion pages of the *New York Times,* October 19, 2011). Speaking biblically and theologically, it is only by the grace of God that we are enabled to make the "good choices" that are being urged on us by those without any sense of Christian formation. When the talented singer-songwriter Amy Winehouse died, many said that she "made bad choices." Not so; she was in the grip of the demonic power of substance abuse. The suggestion that someone has made bad choices sounds patronizing and distancing, as though the speaker cannot imagine having such problems. Interestingly, I do not remember anyone saying that the great actor Philip Seymour Hoffman had made "bad choices." Everyone seemed to recognize that he was driven, that he had been swallowed up by a power beyond his control.

In case there is any doubt about who is victor in this conflict, Paul, in a fine rhetorical move, departs from his exact parallelism to add an additional phrase, thereby bringing the series of contrasts to a ringing conclusion: "So that . . . grace also might reign through righteousness to life eternal *through Jesus Christ our Lord (Kurios).*"

The comprehensive reach of Romans 5:12-21 is uniquely powerful — uniquely inclusive, if you will. *This is our story.* As Käsemann writes, "The person curved in upon himself who undergoes the fate of Adam exists everywhere."[13] If there were any doubt about our powerlessness in the face of Sin, we need only think of the reign of Death and try to imagine ourselves winning *that* battle. Death is indeed a dominion — a *basileia* — and no other religious hope has ever offered a definitive declaration of total victory over the domain of death equal to that of the biblical story. If Jesus is Lord, the challenge for us is to participate in his victory even now in this "present evil age" (Gal. 1:4). The theme of *participation,* so closely related to recapitulation, follows upon the story of Adam and Christ, as Paul develops it in Romans 6 and elsewhere. The inseparable connection between the *theologia crucis* — the theology of the cross — and the cruciform life of the Christian community is apparent in this connection. "We have the mind of Christ," Paul declares to the Corinthians directly following his most impassioned exposition of the *theologia crucis* (I Cor. 2:16).

Baptism in Romans 6

Immediately following the Adam-Christ passage in Romans 5, Paul moves the whole conversation about the second Adam into the realm of baptism. The word "realm" *(basileia)* reflects the deutero-Pauline text in Colossians that is generally agreed to be a fragment of an earlier baptismal hymn: ". . . giving thanks to the Father, who has . . . delivered us from the dominion of darkness and transferred us to the kingdom [*basileia*] of his beloved Son" (Col. 1:11-13). Anyone following the discussion thus far will recognize this transfer of *basileia* — this translation of the newly baptized believer from one domain to another by the power of God. This is pure New Testament apocalyptic. Baptism is not a simple bestowing of blessing. It signifies a radical shift of aeons, a snatching of the baptized person out of the Enemy's clutches, and a transfer into the age to come.[14]

---

13. Ernst Käsemann, *Commentary on Romans* (Grand Rapids: Eerdmans, 1980), 209.

14. The apocalyptic language of *transfer* in Colossians is not like the concept of a "journey"

Romans 6 begins with Paul anticipating the question, "How then shall we live?" If it is true, as Paul proclaims, that our salvation has been entirely won by the second Adam, then what difference does baptism make? Why not simply continue our lives as enthusiastic sinners? This is Paul's opportunity to explain that we have "died to sin": "Do you not know that all of us who have been baptized into Christ Jesus were baptized into his death? We were buried therefore with him by baptism into death, so that as Christ was raised from the dead by the glory of the Father, we too might walk in newness of life" (Rom. 6:3-4).

There is an "objectivity" about this that, in fact, characterizes every one of the atonement models we are considering.[15] Following Romans 6, we learn that the *objective fact* of our redemption is the force driving all *subjective response to* and *consequent imitation of* Christ. If we are objectively buried by baptism into Christ's death, then there is a resulting objective reorientation of our lives and our wills as those "who have been brought from death to life" (6:13). Our old Adam, Paul says in effect, has been crucified with Christ (6:6).[16] Indeed, he says this explicitly of himself in unusually personal terms in Galatians 2:20, "I have been crucified with Christ; it is no longer I who live, but Christ who lives in me. . . ."[17]

The Obedience of Faith in Romans 5 and 6

Obedience is a central component of Irenaeus's recapitulation model. It is the obedience of Christ that engenders and shapes our obedience and faith. In view of the death grip of Sin on human beings, however, how is this to be appropriated? It is tempting to glide past the continuing presence of the Powers into the idea of imitation. Since Paul's story of the first and second

---

as is so often imagined. The action of the Holy Spirit in baptism is immediate and not dependent upon the baptizand's progress toward a spiritual goal.

15. This may even be true of the "subjective" model associated with Abelard. There has to be some sort of objective moment in the story of the cross that evokes the love of the believer and the motivation to wish to imitate Christ.

16. Romans 6:6 states the idea in Paul's most characteristic terms: "We know that our old self was crucified with him so that the sinful body might be destroyed, and we might no longer be enslaved to sin."

17. It is important to go on to read Paul's full sentence here. He shows how life in Christ is not an "imitation," but an outworking of Christ's recapitulation of the life of "Adam" — in his incarnate life, and supremely in his death: "I have been crucified with Christ; it is no longer I who live, but Christ who lives in me; and the life I now live in the flesh I live by [the faithfulness of] the Son of God, who loved me and gave himself for me."

Adam was the seed for Irenaeus's whole idea of recapitulation, we need to get the right fix on Paul's train of thought.

In the primal event, "Adam" was disobedient. The character of the disobedience is drawn as broadly as possible in Genesis 2–3: rebellion against the good purpose of God. Because of that catastrophic primordial event of disobedience, the whole consequent history of humankind has been a saga of estrangement and folly. There is no area of human personality that is not infected by Sin. It has penetrated the human DNA, so to speak.[18] It was into precisely *this human condition* that the Son of God became incarnate. Paul refers to this human predicament no fewer than five times in five verses: "Many died through one man's trespass . . . the judgment following one trespass brought condemnation . . . because of one man's trespass, death reigned through that one man . . . one man's trespass led to condemnation for all men . . . by one man's disobedience many were made sinners" (Rom. 5:15-19). Notice the chain of references to judgment, condemnation, and the reign of Death; this is the unredeemed human condition. Redemption, therefore, involves a radical reconstituting of human nature.[19]

In Romans 5, this radical remaking was accomplished by the incarnate Christ, who rewrote the history of Adam by being obedient to the Father in every stage of his earthly life.[20] Paul's gospel is modeled, not on *human pos-*

---

18. Obviously, this is not biological fact. It is metaphor, used to suggest what Calvin's much-misunderstood concept of "total depravity" is meant to convey. No component of human existence remains untouched by the Fall. Contrary to much religious and "spiritual" teaching unmoored from the Judeo-Christian tradition, there is no pure, untouched "spiritual" core, impervious to Sin, at the center of human personality. We must be remade from the inside out — as Christ took upon himself full humanity in the incarnation.

19. The recapitulation motif is not found only in Romans. Matthew's Gospel, for example, suggests recapitulation at several points. By chapter 4, Matthew has fully presented Jesus as Son of God and Messiah of Israel. He saves his people from their sins (the name Jesus itself meaning "God saves" — Matt. 1:21), and he does so by being perfectly obedient to God, reversing the disobedience of Israel — beginning with his baptism "to fulfil all righteousness" (Matt. 3:15). J. D. Kingsbury, in his commentary on Matthew, writes, "In that these temptations are antitypical to those experienced by the Israelites in their wanderings from Egypt to Canaan, Jesus is portrayed as *recapitulating* in his person this history of Israel, who had also been designated by God as his son (Exodus 4:22-23). But whereas Israel son of God broke faith with God, Jesus Son of God renders to him perfect obedience" (*Matthew,* Proclamation Series [Philadelphia: Fortress, 1977], 40).

20. Because of this emphasis on lifelong conformity with the will of God, Irenaeus's model of recapitulation has been linked to the Abelardian moral-influence theme. To be sure, it is well suited to the motif of the "imitation" of Christ in his lifelong obedience. However, moving toward an emphasis on recapitulation as "exemplary" immediately after expounding Rom. 5:12-21 would be badly to misunderstand Paul. For example, Jaroslav Pelikan, *The Christian Tradition:*

sibility and potential, but on *the power of God.* This affirmation is an essential foundation for the entire Augustinian line of development in Christian theology. The neglect of Paul in the churches today — in mainline and evangelical churches alike — results from our deep-seated human resistance to this one most basic point. The story of Adam and Christ is a story of *incapacity* on the part of Adam and *potency* on the part of God.

Paul's concept of the "obedience of faith" is a notable theme that opens and closes the letter to the Romans, but Paul is not exhorting his readers to "imitate" Christ's obedience in the way that is ordinarily understood. Paul uses the phrase "the obedience of faith" only twice, but the way he uses it is meant to fix our attention.[21] The phrase appears in a striking way to bracket his lengthy argument, once at the beginning of the letter (1:5) and again at the very end (16:26). Most important is the sentence construction. In both cases, "the obedience of faith" is to be "brought about." This is not the syntax of *exhortation* or *imitation;* this is the syntax of *proclamation* and *promise.*

A concept of "two ways" was widely held across the Hellenistic world and deeply embedded in Hellenistic Judaism.[22] In any doctrine of two ways, the human being is presented with a choice. Much of the Old Testament appears to be constructed according to this setup. Deuteronomy 11:26-28 presents, as it were, two ways between which the human being is to choose. The familiar verse in Joshua 24:15 encapsulates this: "Choose this day whom you will serve . . ." This is a strong theme in the early Old Testament, and given the tendency of human beings to believe in their power of choice, it is the default position for most of us. The overall controlling narrative of the two Testaments taken together, however, is the Abrahamic one, in which Israel — and by extension the church — is chosen and guaranteed by the unconditional, prevenient promise of God. It is the Abrahamic covenant, not the Mosaic–Mount Sinai one, that overwhelmingly dominates the New

---

A History of the Development of Doctrine, vol. 1, *The Emergence of the Catholic Tradition (100-600)* (Chicago: University of Chicago Press, 1975), 144-46: "Christ became the example for men, as Adam had been the example for Christ." Pelikan seems to see the insufficiency here, for he goes on to clarify: "Christ was not only the example, but the exemplar and prototype of the image of God according to which man had been created." "Example," he seems to suggest, is too weak, so he offers "prototype," which is more in line with Rom. 5 (Hebrews offers "pioneer": 2:10; 12:2). To say that Christ was our *representative* is even more in line with Rom. 5, since it carries with it the sense of Christ interposing himself as he displaces "Adam."

21. Paul Minear's monograph *The Obedience of Faith* makes this point early in order to emphasize the importance of the theme for Paul in light of what he may have heard about conditions in the church in Rome.

22. On the doctrine of the two ways, see J. Louis Martyn, "The Apocalyptic Gospel in Galatians," *Interpretation* 54, no. 3 (July 2000): 247-52.

Testament. This requires us to read the Old Testament differently, through the eyes of Deutero-Isaiah and the other postexilic prophets, where the emphasis is almost exclusively on *what God will do* whether his people make right choices or not. From the perspective of Paul, this reads back retroactively into the earlier portions of the Old Testament, so that he quotes freely from the Pentateuch with no sense of strain.[23]

The New Testament cosmology, most clearly displayed in Paul's letters but present to a greater or lesser degree in the Gospels and the other epistles as well, presents us not with *two ways* of life, but with *two kingdoms* — two spheres of power. Paul depicts "Adam" under the tyranny of the "flesh" (*sarx* — the domain of Sin and Death) and therefore unable to exercise good inclinations in freedom even when ardently desired (Rom. 7:15-24).[24] It is the entrance of the incarnate Son fully into the life of "Adam" that inaugurates the new life of perfect obedience. When this is understood as recapitulation, it becomes clear that whereas life in Christ results in obedience, this "obedience of faith" (Rom. 1:5; 16:26) is not accomplished by a human choice of one of two ways.[25] There is

23. And indeed, the emphasis on God's prevenient action is already present in Deuteronomy for those who are looking for it: "And the Lord your God will circumcise your heart and the heart of your offspring, so that you will love the Lord your God with all your heart and with all your soul, that you may live" (Deut. 30:6). Paul saw it there; ignoring the passages about human choice ("the righteousness based on the law") and the "two ways" in chapter 30, he seizes upon 30:11-14 and quotes the whole thing in Rom. 10:5-13 to expound the "righteousness which is by faith."

24. The rabbis later went in another direction, similar to the "two ways" of Hellenism, with the teaching of the two inclinations: the *yetser ha-ra* (evil inclination) and *yetser ha-tov* (good inclination). *The Jewish Annotated New Testament,* in expounding Rom. 7:15, calls upon the two inclinations to illuminate Paul's statement, "I do not do what I want; I do the very thing I hate." So far so good. This could certainly be interpreted as a description of the evil inclination warring against the good one. The similarity ends there, however. The rabbis taught — and still teach — that the Law was given so that by the *yetser ha-tov* we would be able to overcome the *yetser ha-ra.* Paul's whole point is that this cannot be, since even our good inclinations are captive to the law of Sin (Isa. 64:6). Romans 7:9-11 is therefore likely to be Paul's reflections on his own *bar mitzvah,* when he become a "son of the commandment." From his new perspective as "slave of Christ," Paul sees that "the commandment which promised life proved to be death to me." At the very moment that he makes this confession, the believer is already saying, "Thanks be to God through Jesus Christ our Lord!" (Rom. 7:24-25). Indeed, the confession would be impossible without the radically reempowering thanksgiving.

25. Rowan Williams, in a discussion of Christian martyrdom, reflects on the nature of Christian obedience. Polycarp's willingness to be thrown to the mob (A.D. 156) was grounded in his knowledge of himself as "the receiver of free salvation." His obedience to Jesus as king, Williams writes, "is rooted in his confidence that Jesus has saved him, that Jesus has made him the gift of his [Polycarp's] life. The power that counts for the martyr is a power that *bestows life,* not a power that *simply commands.* . . . [T]he martyr can maintain loyalty to Jesus under the

a decisive difference between a call to obey and a transfer to a new world order. In the New Testament cosmology, the life of Jesus culminating in his crucifixion and resurrection is the inaugural event of the age to come, the reign of God to which all newly-begotten baptized believers belong by adoption and grace. It is only out of this completely new arrangement that obedience is engendered, by the power of the Holy Spirit. It was this sort of obedience that Abraham was able to pursue "ahead of time" (or "beforehand" — Gal. 3:8) according to the promise of God (Rom. 4:1-22). It is this obedience that is ours through the reckoning *(logizomai)* of God to us (Rom. 7:23-25). This is entirely compatible with Irenaeus's teaching about recapitulation.

Obedience in the Life of Christ the Lord

The theme of obedience arises out of the confession of Christ as *Kurios* — "Lord."[26] There is a powerful connection here in the Greek that readers who know no Greek can easily grasp. Each of the two spheres of power has its *kurios* or *kurioi.*[27] The verb form *kurieuo,* to "lord it over," is used in Romans 6:9, where Paul declares that Death no longer "lords it over" Christ, and in 6:14, where he states the corresponding truth that Sin no longer "lords it over" the baptized believer. "To lord it over" can have its true meaning only when we understand who the "Lord" is. It is the Lord Jesus Christ who brings us out of the orbit of the Powers into the orbit of his own obedience. Our universal condition, being born into "Adam," means to be under the lordship of Sin and Death; in Christ, however, Sin and Death can no longer "lord it over" us. Their rule has been displaced by the righteousness of God in Jesus Christ the *Kurios.* To be "lorded over" by Jesus Christ is to be truly free for the first time.[28]

---

most appalling threats, because something has been *imparted,* not ordered" (*Christ on Trial: How the Gospel Unsettles Our Judgement* [Grand Rapids: Eerdmans, 2000], 99-100, emphasis added, and I have made a minor change in the punctuation). Christian obedience arises out of freedom, the freedom that comes from Christ's unconditional gift of life — given, as expounded in the main text, through his subjection of himself in perfect obedience to the Father in his recapitulation of the story of disobedient Adam. Read through this lens, I John conveys the same message: the command (to love) and the incorporation of the believer into Christ are one and the same thing.

26. About obedience, Anselm says almost the same thing as Irenaeus at times: "As death came upon the human race by the disobedience of man [Adam], it was fitting that by man's [Christ's] obedience life should be restored" (*Cur Deus Homo?* 1.3).

27. Ricoeur calls them "two ontological regimes" (*The Symbolism of Evil,* 235 n. 1).

28. The Gospel of John uses this language as freely as does Paul. "Jesus answered them,

Here is the relevant passage, beginning at 6:16, with certain words highlighted for emphasis:

> Do you not know that if you yield yourselves to any one as *obedient slaves,* you are *slaves* of the one whom you *obey,* either of sin, which leads to death, or of *obedience,* which leads to righteousness? But thanks be to God, that you who were once *slaves* of sin have become *obedient from the heart* to the standard of teaching to which you were committed, and, having been *set free* from sin, have become *slaves of righteousness.*

Paul's language in Romans 6, which seems to be about slavery and obedience, is actually about deliverance and freedom. This is not easy to illustrate, since our entire culture is oriented toward individual freedom and the celebration of throwing off shackles. It is not so simple as that, however; we must look more closely at the way we understand this freedom. A freedom that involves intense struggle against malign impulses does not always fit into our cultural definition of freedom. The man who is an alcoholic is theoretically free to take a drink or not take one, but no recovering alcoholic thinks that way. He knows himself to be in thrall to death-dealing impulses. His counterpart, the nonalcoholic, is a person who is not a slave to that particular form of bondage. Does that mean that the sober man has "made good choices"? Not so; either he does not particularly enjoy an excess of liquor, or he has had strong role models in his life, or he has such a low tolerance for alcohol that it presents no temptation for him. The recovering alcoholic has no such freedom in this area of his life; he understands what Martin Luther called, in his classic treatise, "the bondage of the will."

Our culture, with its love of transgression, mistakes one kind of freedom for another. "The freedom we have in Christ Jesus" (Galatians) is not like the freedom to cross cultural boundaries and grab at whatever we want; such "freedoms" are simply exchanges of one type of bondage for another. We are still driven by our desires. Freedom in Christ is to be released from perpetual inner conflict into "the glorious liberty of the children of God" (Rom. 8:21) where we are enabled to live, not by our own tyrannical wishes, but for the love of others. This is what true obedience to God is like. It is a gift to us *from inside our own human nature,* through the believer's incorporation into the life of the second Adam. Irenaeus writes, "Thus, in this way, He gloriously

---

'Truly, truly, I say to you, every one who commits sin is a slave to sin. The slave does not continue in the house for ever; the son continues for ever. So if the Son makes you free, you will be free indeed'" (John 8:34-36).

accomplished our salvation and . . . *dissolved the old disobedience* . . . [by] recapitulating these things in Himself in order to obtain life for us."[29]

The phrase "law of liberty," which James uses twice (James 1:25; 2:12), gives us another hint. "Law" and "liberty" sound as if they cancel one another out, but in Christ they are the same thing. Being perfectly free does not mean the opportunity to make choices, whether rebellious or obedient; it means being relinquished from the necessity of making choices at all, because one has been delivered into a realm where there is no obstacle whatsoever to complete human flourishing, and no possibility of anyone encroaching on anyone else. Being a slave of Christ the *Kurios* must be something like that, though it is far beyond what can be suggested by mere human analogies.

Link between Incarnation and Crucifixion in Romans 8

In the theology of the cross, the theme of recapitulation ranks high in value. However, there is one problem. Recapitulation alone cannot fully account for the nature of crucifixion. Compelling as Irenaeus's account is, it does not incorporate and make sense of the factor of Christ's gruesome death. This is the lacuna — the blank space begging to be filled — in much of what has been written in church history about the cross. The scandal, the hideousness, the obscenity, and above all the shame and dereliction inherent in the manner of Jesus' death have been passed over in silence more often than not.

Irenaeus does speak of Christ's suffering, and of his blood, and in that way he aligns himself with the New Testament, but these motifs are not central for him. The particular nature of the suffering does not come fully into focus in models that focus largely on the incarnation, or even on Jesus' "death," if the *manner* of his death is left unspecified.[30] Recapitulation is sometimes called the "physical" model of atonement because, as some read Irenaeus, it is the incarnation itself that brought about redemption. In this construal of recapitulation, it seems that the crucifixion of Christ was incidental to his incarnate life and was essential only to make way for the resurrection.[31] That leaves the problem of crucifixion, as gruesome method, unaddressed.

---

29. Irenaeus, *On the Apostolic Preaching* 1.37, emphasis added.

30. As we saw earlier, when Paul appropriated an already existing testimony about Christ in Phil. 2:5-11, he added the words "death *on a cross*" so as to fix attention on the particular *manner* of the death.

31. For example, Hastings Rashdall, *The Idea of the Atonement in Christian Theology* (London: Macmillan, 1919), 238.

Romans 8:3 offers a clue to the problem, though it is difficult to translate: "The Law was powerless through the weakness of the sinful nature [*sarx*], so God, sending his Son in the likeness of sinful nature [*sarx*], of sin and concerning sin, condemned sin in the flesh [*sarx*]."[32]

Notice the audacious way Paul gives a double meaning to *sarx:* it refers metaphorically to sinful human nature in general, and it refers also, and equally, to the literal, material flesh of Jesus.[33] The sentence is convoluted and very difficult to translate, but the basic idea can be explained in this way: Jesus, beginning with his incarnation, did what was impossible via the Law: he took on sinful human nature ("Adam") precisely in its "weakness" — its inability to fulfill the righteous demands of the Law — and by his obedience nullified its punishing, condemning effects. This was done precisely in the incarnate flesh of the Son.[34]

---

32. Paraphrastic translation mine. Here is more of the Greek: "The Law was powerless [*adunatos,* meaning also 'impossible'] through the weakness of the sinful nature [*sarx,* usually — and misleadingly — translated 'flesh'], so God, sending his son in the likeness [*homoioma*] of sinful nature [*sarx*], of sin and concerning sin [*hamartias kai peri hamartias*], condemned sin [*katekrinen ten hamartian*] in the flesh [*sarx*]." None of the English translations are entirely satisfactory. The NRSV makes a good stab at it: "God has done what the law, weakened by the flesh, could not do: by sending his own Son in the likeness of sinful flesh, and to deal with sin, he condemned sin in the flesh." The most difficult problem is how to translate *hamartias kai peri hamartias*. Instead of "for sin" or "concerning sin," Käsemann, in his commentary on Romans, translates it "as an expiatory sacrifice." This seems a stretch, but he is making the same move as the similar, though less pointed rendering "as a sin offering," which is also given in the KJV and NRSV as an alternative. *Peri hamartias* was regularly used in the LXX as an equivalent for a Hebrew word that sometimes meant "sin" and sometimes "sin offering."

33. C. K. Barrett helpfully renders *sarx* in this context as "the form of flesh that has passed under sin's rule" (*A Commentary on the Epistle to the Romans,* Harper's New Testament Commentaries [New York: Harper and Row, 1957], 153).

34. The word *homoioma* (likeness) is suggestive and, with its possible suggestion of Docetism, has been much discussed. The doctrine of the incarnation is at stake here. Was he simply in the "likeness" of *sarx*? Since in Phil. 2:6-7 Paul explicitly says that the Son emptied himself and took the form of a human being, this hardly seems likely. J. D. G. Dunn surveys the critical landscape and concludes, "The fundamental thought is added that God achieved his purpose for man . . . by working through man in his fallenness, letting sin and death exhaust themselves in this man's flesh, and remaking him beyond death as a progenitor and enabler of a life according to the Spirit. Hence, whatever the precise force of the *homoioma,* it must include the thought of Jesus' complete identification with 'sinful flesh' . . . a docetic interpretation can claim no adequate support in the text" (*Romans 1–8,* Word Biblical Commentary 38A [Dallas: Word, 1988], 421). In a chapter on Chalcedonian Christology, Marilyn McCord Adams writes: "This value [rectification of horrors] cannot be obtained by [God's] sending someone else, however exalted. It is *God's* becoming a human being, experiencing human nature from the inside, from the viewpoint of a finite consciousness" that accomplishes the defeat of evil (*Hor-*

The dominion of Sin over human nature was decisively condemned and conclusively rejected by God.[35] The most obvious Pauline links here are two crucial verses, II Corinthians 5:21 and Galatians 3:13:

- For our sake *(huper hemon)* he [God] made him [Christ] to be sin *(hamartian epoiesen)* who knew no sin.
- Christ redeemed us from the curse of the law, having become a curse for us *(huper hemon).*

God "made him to be sin." The syntax is strange. What exactly does Paul mean by this? We can't say for sure, but it must be something analogous to "having become a curse for us." Was Jesus "made sin" and "a curse" throughout his life? His sin*less*ness is a cardinal aspect of his being; yet he was "sent in the likeness of sinful flesh [the incarnation]."[36] This is a conundrum that, in the last analysis, we can only affirm by faith.[37] All our related discussion thus far, however, leads to this conclusion: there is no sensible way to understand when and how this *accursedness,* this *condemnation,* took place unless we think of it beginning with the agony in Gethsemane and continuing through the cry of dereliction to the accursed death. How else was sin "condemned in the flesh" if not then and there?[38]

We are taking this further than Irenaeus did in order to show that there

---

rendous Evils and the Goodness of God [Ithaca, N.Y.: Cornell University Press, 1999], 168). The connection to recapitulation is clarified when she identifies God's identification with human beings and God's participation in horrors as the crucial factor in the overcoming of horrendous evil. "It is shown by the gospel to be the one thing necessary for human deliverance."

35. Note that he does not take on *unfallen* human nature, but *sinful* human nature. "That which is not assumed is not healed" (Gregory of Nazianzus, *Epistle* 101.32).

36. A further problem has to do with the seeming contradiction between two verses in which God the Father seems to be the active agent: "sending *(pempsas)* his Son in the likeness of human *sarx*" (Rom. 8:3) and "God made him to be sin" (II Cor. 5:21); and two other verses where the acting subject appears to be the second person: Phil. 2:7-8 wherein Christ "emptied himself, taking the form of a slave," and, somewhat more ambiguously, Christ "having become a curse for us" (Gal. 3:13). Such apparent contradictions must be held together in the ever-challenging vocation of proclaiming the Trinity in its undivided unity.

37. Dietrich Bonhoeffer has called this "the central problem of Christology" (*Christ the Center* [New York: Harper and Row, 1960], 107).

38. It is the sinful human nature *(sarx)* assumed by the incarnate Son that is condemned on the cross. Does this mean that the human nature of Christ was divided from his divine nature (the Nestorian heresy)? A full analysis of the christological issues at stake here cannot be provided in this space, but we hazard this affirmation: the Son in his eternal being is not condemned. When the matter is put this way, we avoid the problem of dividing the Father from the Son.

is a way to understand recapitulation not only in light of Romans 5 but also with reference specifically to the Godlessness of the cross.[39] The ideas of substitution, representation, and exchange are present in these additional passages from Paul's letters as well. The motifs overlap, as they so frequently do in the New Testament. As for the Gospel narratives, they do not lead us to think that sin is being condemned in the flesh of Jesus throughout his entire life — he is depicted both opposing it and forgiving it while healing and restoring sinners — so there is no point in his ministry where we can say "there!" until we arrive at Gethsemane. The life and ministry, described in the Gospels, *point toward* his assuming this unique burden; in that sense, they are the necessary prologue. The formal solemnity of the three passion predictions in the Synoptic Gospels (and several more in the Fourth Gospel) and the length and gravity of the four passion narratives themselves surely lead us to understand that the cross is the culmination of the Messiah's mission. The trajectory of the story, taken together with the horror of crucifixion, leads us to the conclusion that the hideous Godforsakenness of Christ's public execution *corresponds to* the soul-destroying nature of Sin at its utmost reach, even as God renounces Sin and executes final judgment upon it.

Jesus Christ has undergone our humanity in its completeness, all the way to the last extremity. He has become *the* representative human being. But we must understand what is meant by "representative." The Son of God has not represented us as a congressman represents the people in his district. Furthermore, although it is true that Jesus "represents" us before the bar of the Last Judgment and is therefore called our Advocate *(parakletos),* even this important forensic metaphor from the Fourth Gospel cannot entirely convey the totality of Jesus' representation of us upon the cross. Morna Hooker argues that the theme of substitution, *taken by itself,* does not go far enough because it does not spell out the way in which Christ brings us along with him from death into life, from the domain of the Enemy into the forthcoming age of God.[40] As far back as Irenaeus and further still to Paul and John, Christian thinkers have understood that God in Christ somehow incorporated the entire history of the human race in his one truly human *(vere homo)* person and, in doing so, made us participants in his eternal victory.[41]

Furthermore, it is in the Son of God's assuming the consequences of

---

39. The issue of Godlessness, which is addressed in chapter 2, did not arise for Irenaeus. Like many of the early fathers of the church, he did not address all the aspects of Christ's death.

40. Hooker, *Not Ashamed,* 36.

41. Paul is by no means the only one to see this. In its own way, the Fourth Gospel uses the image of the vine and the branches to say something similar about our incorporation into Christ (John 15:1-11). I John emphasizes participation and incorporation (4:12-13, 15-16).

Adam's disobedience that God is most distinctly God, most clearly *not us.* *We would not and could not have done it.* It is crucial to understand that the transaction taking place as the Messiah suffers and dies was — and is — *beyond our capacity.* We cannot "imitate" this unique action. In that sense, yes, we were passive as it happened. We were prisoners of war in the territory of the Enemy. The cross was the divine invasion of that territory, once and for all. This is an extension of Irenaeus; whatever we mean by recapitulation, it must include this cosmology if it is to incorporate the whole of the New Testament picture. All the New Testament writers without exception assume, to a greater or lesser degree, this presupposition.

The Power of Life in the Spirit

Romans 8 is directly related to the theme of recapitulation, for it expounds the subject of life in the Spirit. Notice especially the consequence Paul draws from the verse already citied, 8:3 — "[God] condemned sin in the flesh *(sarx).*" Verse 4 continues: "*in order that* the righteous requirements of the law might be fully met in us, who do not live according to our sinful nature but according to the Spirit."[42]

This is the consequence, we can confidently say, of the reenactment of the human story (Adam) by Jesus Christ. The righteous requirements of the Law have been met *in him* in order that the righteous requirements of the Law might be met fully *in us.* This declaration by Paul is breathtaking in its precise correspondence with the idea of recapitulation and its outcome. But there is more. We have emphasized that Paul's gospel is not about *human potential* or *human possibility* but about the *power of God.* Here in Romans 8:4 is a clear illustration. Our own "recapitulation," the new life in Christ, is only *possible* through the *power* of the third person of the Trinity, the Holy Spirit. The next twenty-three verses expound the powers of the Spirit, and that section comes to a climax with the Spirit interceding for the saints according to the will of God (Rom. 8:27).

In other words, the power of the obedience of the Lord (the *Kurios*) has the corresponding Spirit-power to bring us along with it. This is emphasized

---

42. This NIV rendering makes it particularly clear that the Spirit is the active agent in doing this work in us of meeting the requirements of the law. However, in verses 5-17 the NIV goes astray by translating *sarx* as "your" sinful nature and "their" sinful nature instead of just "the flesh" or "the sinful nature." It makes it sound like an individual problem and not a Power. Unless one is truly a master of the Greek (full disclosure here), it's important to work with a number of translations as well as the original.

in a remarkable way in 8:11 where Paul puts all three persons of the Trinity *into one verse* not once but *twice,* saying in essence that the *Spirit* of the *Father* who raised the *Son* from the dead now indwells the baptized believer and "will also quicken your mortal bodies by [the same] Spirit" (KJV). In a cursory reading, it is easy to miss the repetition with which Paul intends to convey the mighty action of *God,* who, in *Christ,* by the *Spirit,* has brought into being a new Adam, a new humanity. This is the great set of events that bestows upon us nothing less than the righteousness of God for the living of our lives.

Recapitulation as "Takeover"

The baptized Christian has no righteousness of her own, and yet the righteousness of God is already hers, not because of what she has accomplished or will accomplish on her own, but because she is now "in Christ." Being "in Christ" (a phrase used in this sense about forty times in the undisputed letters of Paul) is certainly related to the idea of recapitulation. It can have a temporal meaning, as in Paul's acknowledgment of Andronicus and Junia (or Junias), who "were in Christ before me" (Rom. 16:7).[43] Sometimes it has an ethical meaning (Phil. 2:1, 5; Rom. 12:5; Philem. 8, 20). Most often, and most fundamentally, it refers to the eschatological *status* of the believer, who has been *incorporated into Christ* by grace through faith.[44]

43. These apostles are, unfortunately, otherwise unknown to us. It is now argued by many that Junia(s) may have been a woman, but this remains a matter of dispute. A balanced examination of the subject is at https://bible.org/article/junia-among-apostles-double-identification-problem-romans-167.

44. A brief summary of the concept of *theosis* (deification) is appropriate here. The idea is prevalent in Eastern Orthodoxy and in recent years has been taken up by some in the Western churches with much enthusiasm but insufficient understanding. To be sure, *theosis* is easy to misunderstand. The principal source in Scripture is II Pet. 1:4, which speaks of Christians escaping from the world's corruption and becoming "partakers of the divine nature." This one reference in the relatively obscure second Petrine epistle is asked to carry a lot of weight. A more prominent idea is that of Paul, who speaks frequently of being "in Christ." What is meant by this? It is not uncommon to hear people defining *theosis* as "God became man so that man might become God" (Athanasius, *De incarnatione* 54.3; Patrologia graeca 25:192B), and this statement is in the Roman Catholic catechism (460.79), but this can encourage a careless appropriation of the idea. In his commentary on II Peter, Douglas Harink has thoroughly reviewed the relevant material from Eastern and Western sources. Although many Orthodox insist that deification does not mean that "man becomes God," a close examination of Maximus the Confessor suggests that he does step across a line into elevating human nature "over its proper limits" (Doug Harink, *1 and 2 Peter,* Brazos Theological Commentary on the Bible

The Christian life of obedience is, therefore, not a pilgrimage toward a goal, as is commonly supposed. It is a witness or signpost to that *telos* (end, goal) that has already been achieved by Christ the *Kurios* and will be consummated in the last day by the action of God (the parousia, or second coming). The righteous, justifying action of God and the faith that is engendered by its powerful activity are the two effective agents that call forth the obedience. The next passage illustrates this "become what you already are" theme of Paul: "Do not yield your members to sin as instruments of wickedness, but yield yourselves to God as men who have been brought from death to life, and your members to God as instruments of righteousness. For sin will [not lord it] over you *(kurieusei)*, since you are not under law but under grace" (Rom. 6:13-14).

Note the transfer from one *kurios* (Sin) to another. "Grace" and "faith" frequently serve in Paul's letters as synonyms for Christ, so the word *hupo*, "under" ("not under Law but under grace"), signifies the translation of Christians from the realm of Sin and Death to the realm of the one true *Kurios*. In his gracious *basileia* (domain) there cannot be any other *kurios* to "lord it over" us like a slave master. All our "members" (*melos*, every constituent part making up the self) have *already been brought* from death to life by baptism.

Morna Hooker has well understood Paul's teaching about dying to sin and being raised to new life in terms of recapitulation. She cites Galatians 2:20: "It is no longer I who live, but Christ who lives in me; and the life I now live in the flesh I live by faith in the Son of God . . . ," and then expounds it this way: "It seems to be a case of Christ taking over our lives and living in our place."[45] In other words, the acting subject is Christ, not the faithful person *per se*. Hooker, in elaborating, repeats the "takeover" theme in a vivid way: "[I]n some mysterious sense, the whole of humanity

---

[Grand Rapids: Brazos, 2009], 141-45). John Meyendorff also, though he writes that "there cannot be any participation in divine essence by man" (*Byzantine Theology: Historical Trends and Doctrinal Themes* [New York: Fordham University Press, 1974], 164), is not as scrupulous about maintaining that point as Protestant theologians would be, especially in view of the loose way that *theosis* is being defined in some gnostically inclined circles in the churches today. Harink commends Bruce McCormack's essay, "Participation in God, Yes; Deification, No," in a 2004 Festschrift for Eberhard Jüngel (in German). *Theosis,* even when interpreted as carefully as just indicated, is really not the most helpful way to understand the larger picture of *incorporation into* Christ as in John 15 and in Paul. The best way to think about this from Paul's point of view is that God's children will be "glorified" — "heirs of God and fellow heirs with Christ, provided we suffer with him in order that we may also be glorified with him" (Rom. 8:17; see also 8:30). This preserves the promise without crossing the line between created and uncreated life. (My thanks to George Hunsinger for this insight.)

45. Hooker, *Not Ashamed,* 30.

died on Calvary. . . . He dies for us, but that means that we die with him. He was raised, and raised with such power that our lives are now taken over by him."[46]

This certainly sounds like what Paul describes in Romans 8. Hooker emphasizes *participation,* another useful word for us as we continue to think about being raised into ("taken over by," "constrained by") the life of righteousness.

Indicative and Imperative: Being Transformed

In Romans 12, Paul begins with "I appeal to you *therefore,* brethren . . ." Whenever we see the word "therefore," we need to look back to what precedes. The passage preceding Romans 12:1-2 is the doxology that concludes Paul's ruminations about the Jews and the most nearly universal proclamation he ever made. The emphasis on the divine agency could not be more unequivocal: "From him [God] and through him and to him are all things. To him be glory for ever. Amen."

This immediately precedes "therefore." It is followed by "I appeal to you *therefore,* [brothers and sisters], by the mercies of God, to present your bodies as a living sacrifice, holy and acceptable to God, which is your spiritual worship."

Romans 12, filled with imperatives, is much misunderstood because it is so frequently lifted out of its setting, with "therefore" ignored. In writing about the new life in Christ, Paul contrasts two words in their passive forms, indicating that there is a power at work in redeemed human nature that is beyond human possibility. The words are "conformation" *(suschematizo)* and "transformation" *(metamorphoo):* "Do not be *conformed* to this world but be *transformed* by the renewal of your mind, that you may prove what is the will of God, what is good and acceptable and perfect" (Rom. 12:2).

This verse is typically preached as if it heralded a break in Paul's thought, being popularly construed as Paul's move from *kerygma* (proclamation) to *didache* (instruction, or exhortation). This does not do justice to the radical nature of Paul's gospel, and it drains off much of the impact of what has gone before; indeed, it undermines it. Chapter 12 is grounded so firmly in the previous exposition that it cannot, or should not, be separated from it. Note the word "metamorphosed" (*trans*formed). *Con*formation is being

46. Hooker, *Not Ashamed,* 36.

contrasted with *trans*formation. *Con*-form-ity suggests being *formed with,* or *by,* this age of Sin and Death — being shaped by it and therefore lacking freedom — the situation personified in chapter 5 as "Adam." How do we escape such captivity? A typical response to this question would be to urge greater religious or moral effort, but that is not the gospel. How then are we to understand the source of transformation?

The Greek word translated "renewal" here means something much more drastic than "renewal" in common English use. Paul's word *anakainosis* is not used here to mean simply "refreshing" or "rejuvenating." It means being completely taken over. It means *to "become the righteousness of God"* — a transformation that only God can generate — as in II Corinthians 5:21 ("For our sake he made him to be sin who knew no sin, so that in him we might become the righteousness of God"). This is not a process that God begins in us, followed by his stepping aside to observe how we will respond. God is *in* this from first to last, because to be "in Christ" is to be continually made new by the power of the Spirit. For this reason, the word often used in the eighteenth and nineteenth centuries, "regenerate," is really more accurate and effective than "renewed."[47]

Put another way, renewal, in Paul's gospel, can be defined also in terms of *dikaiosyne,* not simply to be *declared* righteous (as in the common understanding of *dikaiosyne,* translated as "justification") but to be actually *made* righteous by the rectifying power of God. It should be clear by now that this making-right, or rectification, is not a *process.* It is *already true,* in Christ; but it is true *eschatologically,* from the perspective of the End. The now–not yet dynamic is operative here, as always. As yet we do not see ourselves or the world made right. However, because the end-time is already present in power by the Spirit, there is an "already" quality about this proclamation of "becoming the righteousness of God." It really is quite true to say that the

---

47. "Begotten from above" or "regenerate from above" is the better way of translating *gennethe anothen,* familiarly translated "born again" in John 3:3. Though the Fourth Evangelist's way of telling the story is very different from Paul's, the begetting from above is essentially the same action of God that Paul speaks about when he refers to *metamorphosis,* being "in Christ," having the "mind of Christ." It is the way we "become the righteousness of God." We receive these blessings of new life by the gracious action of God from the transcendent sphere of power that has broken into this one, overthrowing the "ruler of this world" (John 12:31; 14:30; 16:11). Hence, in the prologue of John's Gospel, we read that the Word-made-flesh "gave power to become children of God; who were born, not of blood nor of the will of the flesh nor of the will of man, but of God" (John 1:12-13). It is in this context that Jesus speaks of the vine and branches in John 15. Its concept of "abiding" in Christ is not unlike Paul's being "in Christ." Both of these apostolic voices teach that we are taken up into the life of God (see previous note on *theosis*).

gospel tells us, "become what you already are." The First Epistle of John puts it well: "Beloved, we are God's children now; it does not yet appear what we shall be, but we know that when he appears we shall be like him" (I John 3:2). The words "we know" convey the certainty that we have in the promise even though it is "not yet."

As before, what may sound to us today like an imperative ("be transformed") is actually a sort of description of something that has already happened in Christ. Romans 12 is preceded not only in the literal sense by the preceding chapters, but by the story of Christ Jesus, the second Adam, and our incorporation into his reign through the baptismal "takeover." The imperative is not only *dependent upon* but *organically produced by* the indicative, or declarative, proclamation: you have died with Christ; you have now been transferred into the new sovereignty *(basileia)* with its guarantee of participation in the righteousness of God.

Recapitulation, Substitution, and Incarnation in Gospel Preaching

No one has shown the relation of recapitulation and substitution better than T. F. Torrance in his little book designed for pastors and lay leaders, *The Mediation of Christ.* He insists that *substitution* and *representation* (virtually synonymous, in his treatment, with *recapitulation*) must be held together, and goes on to show how this is done. His argument rests upon the truth that Christ acts "in our place, in our stead, on our behalf," and he interprets this as recapitulation — as Christ reliving the story of Adam "out of the ontological depths of our actual human being."[48] Hence the absolute necessity of the doctrine of the incarnation. The Son of God secures our redemption, not over against us as a divine being, but restoring our human nature to the righteousness of God *from within* the depths of our unrighteousness. Thus he restores us to righteousness not in our own religious accomplishments (faith, prayer, spirituality, personal commitment, good works), such as they are, but in "the incarnate medium" of his own righteousness.[49] Another way of putting this is to say that we are not saved by any will or decision of our own. Our rebellious, egocentric, and disloyal human wills have been established "on an entirely different basis by being

48. "Out of our actual human being" could also be defined as "out of our flesh [*sarx*, the sinful human nature]." In either case, it is an intensely incarnational expression.

49. T. F. Torrance, *The Mediation of Christ,* rev. ed. (Colorado Springs: Helmers and Howard, 1992; orig. 1983), 94.

replaced at that crucial point by Jesus Christ himself."[50] Again, it is the "takeover" theme.

In a passage directed to preachers, Torrance challenges his readers to come to grips with true gospel proclamation, rejecting its counterfeits. He distinguishes between "unevangelical" preaching, which emphasizes human acting and deciding, and true "evangelical" preaching. He uses these terms not at all in the way Americans use them today, but directly in relation to the unconditional nature of what God has done for humanity. In his summary of the gospel message, Torrance further describes the relation between recapitulation and substitution, speaking not only directly to believing individuals but, at the same time, to the whole people of God and, indeed, to the whole created order:

> From beginning to end what Jesus Christ has done for you he has done not only as God but as man. He has acted in your place in the whole range of your human life and activity, including your personal decisions, and your response to God's love, and even your acts of faith. He has believed for you, fulfilled your human response to God, even made your personal decision for you, so that he acknowledges you before God as one who has already responded to God in him, who has already believed in God through him, and whose personal decision is already implicated in Christ's self-offering to the Father, in all of which he has been fully and completely accepted by the Father, so that in Jesus Christ you are already accepted by him.[51]

> [I]t is not upon my faith, my believing, or my personal commitment that I rely, but solely upon what he has done for me, *in my place* and *on my behalf,* and what he is and always will be as he *stands in for me* before the face of the Father.[52]

50. Torrance, *The Mediation of Christ,* 93.

51. Torrance, *The Mediation of Christ,* 94. Torrance's mode of presentation in *The Mediation of Christ* is to expound the gospel without quoting any specific biblical passages. Still, it is surprising that he does not refer, specifically, to the Adam-Christ story, since it seems certain that it lies behind all that he says about Christ redeeming us out of the very ontological center of our humanity. In any case, his exposition of substitution is to be distinguished from the late Reformed scholasticism of his ancestry, in this crucial respect: in that earlier Protestant theology, an elaborately worked-out forensic substitution became so dominant that it left no room for the other important models. It is precisely the argument of this book that substitution should take its place within the whole tapestry of motifs rather than crowding them out.

52. Torrance, *The Mediation of Christ,* 94-95. Emphasis is added to show how readily he incorporates the imagery of substitution, recapitulation, participation, and incorporation.

Invasion of the Enemy's Territory

There is something missing in Torrance's otherwise superb presentation of the gospel message. He does not refer to the Enemy, who is the third party in the apocalyptic New Testament drama.[53] When Christ recapitulated the life of "Adam," as Torrance presents it, he worked from inside human nature (incarnation) "so that in him we might become the righteousness of God" (II Cor. 5:21). The full biblical picture, however, requires us to see that this reenactment (recapitulation) of the *dikaiosyne theou* could not be accomplished without Christ's engaging the hostile occupying Powers who hold Adam and the entire created order in bondage. Here we recall the story of the temptation in the wilderness, the exorcisms that play such an important role in the Synoptic Gospels, and the repeated emphasis on "the ruler of this world" in the Fourth Gospel. All the New Testament authors assume the presence and power of an occupying Antagonist, an "evil intelligence," to use Flannery O'Connor's term, who is determined to maintain an enslaving grip on the *kosmos* and every creature in it.[54] A full biblical understanding of the theme of recapitulation requires us to hold this scenario in our minds.

In Matthew's version of the baptism of Jesus, John the Baptist initially protests that he is not worthy to baptize the one "mightier than" he, but Jesus overcomes his scruples by saying that he comes to Jordan "to fulfil all righteousness" (Matt. 3:15). Jesus' utterance has been much puzzled over, but surely it gives meaning to the recapitulation motif and its connection to the *dikaiosyne theou*. This righteousness of God is what the Son of David (Matthew's usual messianic title) freely brings to the unrighteous human race, enslaved to the Powers. The baptism of Jesus is the Messiah Jesus' symbolic assuming of our sinful nature, in order to act from within "to bring many sons [and daughters] to glory" (Heb. 2:10).[55]

Even more to the point, however, we may see the baptism of Jesus as the first public indication that he has entered upon his recapitulation of the story

53. I have been advised that Torrance does make moves in this direction in some of his posthumously published lectures.

54. The use of the personal pronoun "he" rather than "it" (not to mention "she") to denote Satan, or the "evil one" (I John 2:13, 14), is important because it indicates the personal nature of the "evil intelligence" determined to defeat the purposes of God. See chapter 10. (O'Connor describes Satan as an "evil intelligence" in a letter to John Hawkes; *The Habit of Being* [New York: Farrar, Straus and Giroux, 1979], November 20, 1959.)

55. It is much to the point that Hebrews continues with a further suggestion of incorporation: "For he who sanctifies and those who are sanctified have all one origin. That is why he is not ashamed to call them brethren" (Heb. 2:11).

of Adam.[56] He undergoes the baptism that all his subsequent disciples will receive, thus setting in motion his life's offering not only *on our behalf* but also *in our place.* In all three Synoptics, the event that follows immediately upon Jesus' baptism is the head-to-head confrontation of Jesus and Satan in the wilderness. We have seen earlier that baptism is (among other things) an exorcism of the demonic powers from their hold on the baptizands; here, the baptizand Jesus steps in between Satan and his prey to confront the Enemy, undergoing all their temptations as their representative and emerging as victor in their place — even though, as we know, the victory is only provisional at this point.

It is highly significant that Satan, in the wilderness temptation, is the first to call Jesus by the title "Son of God" in Matthew's Gospel (4:6), a deliberate move by the Evangelist in unfolding his powerful christological presentation. All three Synoptics emphasize the presence of Satan as the great Antagonist who knows exactly who Jesus is and why he has come. In Mark, the confrontation with Satan in the first exorcism (Mark 1:21-28) is a recognition scene. "What have you to do with us, Jesus of Nazareth?" cry out the demons. "Have you come to destroy us? I know who you are, the Holy One of God." Jesus' aggression into the territory of the Enemy is sharply delineated by the Second Evangelist's special use of the word "immediately" *(euthus)*. Mark shows Jesus in powerful motion and gives the impression of great force as the demons are banished by Jesus' mere word. The onlookers murmur, "What is this? A new teaching! With authority he commands even the unclean spirits, and they obey him" (Mark 1:27). Luke alone has the highly suggestive detail that Satan, after failing in the wilderness, departs from Jesus "until an opportune time" (Luke 4:13). The "second Adam" will be bedeviled (literally) all through his human life just as we are, but uniquely so in Gethsemane, the "opportune time" of confrontation and decision.[57] R. E. Brown writes that in Gethsemane "the inbreaking of God's

56. A literal-minded person might protest that Adam was never baptized! But as Paul shows in Rom. 6, baptism is itself the initiation into the new story that the new Adam is writing in his human flesh. "Yield yourselves to God as men who have been brought from death to life, and your members to God as instruments of righteousness *(dikaiosyne)*" (Rom. 6:13). This can only be true for us because the Son of God has been the pioneer (Heb. 2:10; 12:2); he has blazed the trail, so to speak. He has made "the rough places plain" (Isa. 40:4 KJV) as he has gone this way before us.

57. No one knows if the details about the angel and the bloody sweat in Luke 22:43-44 are original, but even if they are not, it seems clear that Luke means the agony in Gethsemane to be the "opportune time" when Satan returns to assault Jesus in full force. Luke's use of the eschatological word *peirasmos* is the key here. The usual translations "temptation" and "trial" (as in the Lord's Prayer) do not sufficiently convey the apocalyptic force of the *peirasmos* in

kingdom involved a massive struggle with diabolical opposition."[58] The story of recapitulation is not complete without this essential biblical component.

George Herbert (1593-1633) was not only a preeminent poet but also a true biblical theologian. "Sin placeth me in Adam's fall," he wrote, speaking for every one of us.[59] His poem "Assurance" manages to tell the story of recapitulation in terms of the individual's conflict with demonic opposition. He evokes his own internal struggle against "spiteful bitter thoughts" and his fear of judgment. He is unable to stave off these assaults by his writing. In the face of these "cold despairs," he resolves to go to the Father with his "gnawing pensiveness" that threatens to "raise devils":

> . . . O most gracious Lord,
> If all the hope and comfort that I gather
> Were from myself, I had not half a word,
> Not half a letter to oppose
> What is objected by my foes.
>
> But thou art my desert:
> And in this league, which now my foes invade,
> *Thou art not only to perform thy part,*
> *But also mine. . . .*[60]

It's all here: the bondage of the human being to his own unbidden thoughts, the invasion of the accusing demons, the inadequacy of human opposition to this invasion, the presence of fear and despair, the turn to the Father, the confession of his own insufficiency in this struggle, the confident declaration that "thou art my desert,"[61] and then the breathtaking assertion that Jesus Christ plays not only his own part as the Redeemer *"but also mine."* Thus he affirms that Christ, in his own "part" as Son of God, takes

---

Gethsemane — the ultimate confrontation between the power of "the present evil age" (Gal. 1:4) and the power of the age to come. See Raymond E. Brown, *The Death of the Messiah: From Gethsemane to the Grave; A Commentary on the Passion Narratives in the Four Gospels,* 2 vols. (Garden City, N.Y.: Doubleday, 1994), 1:186.

58. Brown, *Death of the Messiah,* 1:234.

59. From "Faith," in *The Complete English Poems,* ed. John Tobin (London: Penguin Books, 1991), 44.

60. George Herbert, "Assurance," in *The Complete English Poems,* emphasis added. Archaic meaning of "objected" — to oppose or interpose, hence, the "objective" (not subjective) fact of devilish interference with his attempts to banish his "spiteful bitter thoughts."

61. In this context, "desert" does not mean "that which is deserved," but something more like "excellence" or "worth," and includes the idea that Christ is his destiny.

over the additional role of all flesh (Adam) and thus overcomes the Enemy from within. He does this not only on behalf of the individual poet George Herbert but also (as the poem continues) for the deliverance of the entire *kosmos* even unto the last things, "when rocks and all things shall disband." Most wonderful of all, he enables Adam (ourselves) to participate: "What for itself love once began, / Now love and truth will end in man."[62]

The Link to the Nature of Crucifixion

Along with the absence in Irenaeus of emphasis on the great Enemy, which we identified above, this Church Father also failed to emphasize the gruesome and accursed manner in which the Son of God died. Indeed, this second factor is largely absent from the Fathers altogether. It is tempting to suggest that only in our own age has it been forced to our attention. In studies of modern concepts of evil, it has become apparent that the genocides of the twentieth century have changed the moral landscape. We think of evil now in a new way, not just as a sum of individual episodes, but as a force with a life of its own. Radical evil is now seen in a larger context, and moreover, the new media have brought atrocities to our attention in a way that was impossible before. Is it not possible, therefore, that this neglected aspect of the death of Christ is now for the first time becoming a necessary part of confronting what we now know about the human capacity for radical evil? Had he died in a more merciful, less deliberately dehumanizing way, it would not be possible to see in his death the sum of all horrors.

This does not mean that the extreme nature of crucifixion cannot be understood in individual lives. Quite the contrary. A man whose wife died of cancer after a prolonged and agonizing period of what seemed utterly fruitless and cruel suffering kept a journal of their two-year ordeal. As they searched for some shred of redemptive meaning, it helped them to realize that Jesus was not only crucified, but also, according to Roman custom, scourged within an inch of his life beforehand. The apparently unnecessary and excessive maliciousness of this was, for them, an indication that the Lord had undergone a multiplication of superfluous suffering like their own.

Corrie ten Boom, the first female watchmaker of a family of devoutly

---

62. "End" here has the sense of *telos* (end or goal). Thus, love and truth will be perfected in man according to God's purposes. This little analysis does not even begin to address the subtleties and complexities of Herbert's poem, but I wanted to show how it combines the victory over Satan with the recapitulation motif.

Christian watchmakers in Haarlem in the Netherlands, lost all her family in the Nazi camps when it was discovered that they were hiding Jews. In her memoir, *The Hiding Place,* she recalls how at Ravensbruck the prisoners were required to strip every Friday for the "recurrent humiliation" of so-called medical inspection, where the naked prisoners standing in line were not allowed to use their hands to cover themselves but had to stand erect with hands by their sides. One Friday as Corrie stood behind her frail and dying sister Betsie, the thought came to her: "He hung naked on the cross." She whispered to Betsie, standing in front of her, "They took His clothes, too." Betsie received comfort and strength from this.[63] The details of the degradation of Jesus do make a difference. "The offence caused by Jesus Christ is not his incarnation — that indeed is revelation — but his humiliation."[64]

It is striking, therefore, that this unique feature of the death is so seldom included in preaching and teaching, as though indeed we were afraid to go where Jesus has gone. The repugnant, brutal, and dehumanizing aspect of crucifixion must be included in any study of the meaning of the cross of Christ. It is not easy to do this without crossing over into the merely prurient and sensational, but with care and sensitivity, the point can be made that there is a *correspondence* between the horrors of crucifixion and the nature of the Sin that is being fully unleashed in those horrors, precisely as Sin is being overcome in the torment of the Savior. In order for God truly to overcome the very worst, the Son underwent the very worst. "What is not undergone is not overcome."[65]

Recapitulation and Ethics: Incorporation into the Righteousness of God

Emphasizing recapitulation as "takeover" requires us to affirm that such a deliverance of humanity from the captivity of Sin, Death, and the Law effects a genuine ontological transformation in believers, a dynamic reality that is

63. Corrie ten Boom gives the context (in her as-told-to memoir): "I had not known, I had not thought . . . the paintings, the carved crucifixes showed at the least a scrap of cloth. But this, I suddenly knew, was the respect and reverence of the artist. But oh — at the time itself, on that other Friday morning — there had been no reverence. No more than I saw in the faces around us now [in Ravensbrück]" (*The Hiding Place* [Old Tappan, N.J.: Revell, 1971], 195-96).

64. Bonhoeffer, *Christ the Center,* 46.

65. This is my paraphrase of the often-quoted line by Gregory of Nazianzus, concerning the full humanity of Christ: "What is not assumed is not healed" (alternatively, "What has not been assumed has not been healed"). *Epistle* 101.32. See also p. 551 n. 35.

not simply a general amnesty or legal fiction. This is a matter of ethics. The story of Adam and Christ cannot be understood in its full dimensions without a grasp of what is meant by the righteousness of God *(dikaiosyne theou)*. We have seen throughout these pages that God's righteousness is not simply an aspect of God's character, nor is it exclusively a relational term; it is a *Power*. We have argued that the English word "rectification," as a translation of *dikaiosyne,* is better than the word "justification." Since Luther, justification has traditionally been interpreted among Protestants as imputed righteousness, but this does not sufficiently convey God's actual *power to make right all that has been wrong* throughout the entire sorry history of "Adam."[66] It is this *rectifying power* of the *dikaiosyne theou* that constitutes the eschatological Christian hope.[67] It is not just a reinstatement of individual believers. It is a recapturing of the entire history of the created order and a remaking of it so that in the final day, even the memory of its captivity will be obliterated forever in the glory of the City of God that is to come (Rev. 21:1-5).

The word "incorporation" is a companion to the motif of recapitulation, since it identifies what recapitulation has accomplished in the human story. Incorporation is a valuable word to use because it requires God to be its active agent. In the self-offering of God through his Son, God's servants are incorporated (Latin *in* — "to take into"; *corpore* — "one body") into the body of Christ. "Incorporation" is a far more gentle word than "invasion," but many students of Paul's thought have used the imagery of invasion to make clear that the action of God in rectification involves nothing less than our death and resurrection. Christ's recapitulation of the human story does not simply *invite us into* the divine life. There is an *objective reality* about it; it has happened over our dead bodies, so to speak. In the passage immediately

66. Douglas Campbell, in *The Deliverance of God,* seeks to demolish what he calls "justification theory" and in so doing mounts a full-blown reworking of the "Lutheran" view from an apocalyptic perspective.

67. Julian of Norwich famously wrote that "all shall be well, and all shall be well, and all manner of things shall be well" (*Revelations of Divine Love* 27). This saying is much cherished, and is a truthful expression of the Christian hope — up to a point. Taken out of context, however, it falls short of a fully articulated statement of the promised future because "all manner of things" can be construed as the acting subject (not that Julian meant it that way). Romans 8:28 presents a very similar choice. It can be (and often is) translated as "we know that all things work together for good to them that love God." However, translators who have respected the trajectory of Paul's preaching translate it "We know that in everything God works for good with those who love him" (RSV; NRSV offers this as an alternative). In the latter rendering, *God* is the acting subject, not "all things." It is not "all things" that work to "be well." It is *God* who will make all things well. This is a crucial distinction, and lies at the heart of both *righteousness* and *recapitulation;* in both, the essential agency is God's.

following the Adam-Christ exposition in Romans, Paul explains that "all of us who have been baptized into Christ Jesus were . . . buried therefore with him by baptism into death." The forceful language of a "takeover" is not out of place here: "We know that our old self was crucified with him so that the sinful body might be destroyed, and we might no longer be enslaved to sin. . . . For we know that Christ being raised from the dead will never die again; death no longer has dominion over him. . . . So you also must consider yourselves dead to sin and alive to God in Christ Jesus" (Rom. 6:6, 9-11).

The theme of recapitulation is remarkably expanded and deepened by Paul in this passage about baptism. Christ's "takeover" of "Adam" in his own crucified human flesh means that he is able to bring "Adam" out of the grave as forcibly and decisively as does the risen *Kurios* in the old paintings of the harrowing of hell. Death has no more dominion over the risen Lord; Death has no more dominion over those he delivers.

We have been incorporated into Christ's crucifixion, and into his resurrection — both equally.[68] There are times when Paul's language is strikingly participatory, as in Galatians 2:20: "I have been crucified with Christ; it is no longer I who live, but Christ who lives in me." In view of the minuscule number of persons who can be said to have lived "Christlike" lives, however, this bears some looking into. What sort of ontological transformation occurs in the lives of those in whom Christ is said to live?

Colin Gunton expands on this matter in relation to "the theology of Irenaeus, whose concept of recapitulation enabled him to form a link between the way in which Jesus lived out the human story in a victorious way and the continuing of his victory in the life of the Church. He is true to the insight of the New Testament writers that talk of a past victory is *not to be isolated from matters of present practice.*"[69]

Those who according to Paul are "in Christ" are called to a particular way of life that shows forth the power of his name, the boundless riches of his love, the merits of his death, and the sure and certain hope we have in his resurrection. This way of life is cruciform — that is to say, it bears the marks of Christ's crucifixion ("Henceforth let no man trouble me; for I bear on my body the marks of Jesus" — Gal. 6:17). The Christian life involves suffering — not the ordinary suffering that comes to everyone, but the particular

---

68. This is forcefully repeated in Col. 2:12: "You were buried with him in baptism, in which you were also raised with him through faith in the working of God, who raised him from the dead."

69. Colin Gunton, *The Actuality of Atonement: A Study of Metaphor, Rationality, and the Christian Tradition* (Grand Rapids: Eerdmans, 1989), 57.

affliction that must come to those who bear witness to the Lord's death. "For the sake of Christ, then, I am content with weaknesses, insults, hardships, persecutions, and calamities; for when I am weak, then I am strong" (II Cor. 12:10). The transformative thought here is the juxtaposition of the words "weak" and "strong." The suffering endured by Christian witnesses does not come from a place of weakness, but from a place of strength. That is the difference between Christian suffering and masochism.

Peter's injunction to the church illuminates the nature of suffering "under that name" that is above all names in power and glory (Acts 4:5-12): "But rejoice in so far as you share Christ's sufferings. . . . If one suffers as a Christian, let him not be ashamed, but under that name let him glorify God. For the time has come for judgment to begin with the household of God" (I Pet. 4:13, 16-17).

Here, Christ's sufferings are explicitly linked with judgment. When the church ("the household of God") enacts her proper role, she voluntarily comes under the same judgment that her Bridegroom suffered when he underwent an accursed death (Gal. 3:10-13). The Christian will never die a truly godforsaken death, however, whatever the circumstances, because Christ has undergone such a death in our place. He has lived out — recapitulated — the fate of condemned humanity to the last frontier of the demon-haunted *kosmos,* and in doing so has brought us over from eternal bondage and condemnation into the eternal realm of the righteousness of God.

Therefore, because we are confident in Christ's triumph over the destroying Powers, we can say with Paul that "God has not destined us for wrath, but to obtain salvation through our Lord Jesus Christ" (I Thess. 5:9). Salvation comes not from human effort, least of all religious effort, but by the power of God at work in us through the "implanted word" (James 1:21) and the Spirit that pours the love of God into our hearts (Rom. 5:5). The much-misunderstood concept of "predestination" finds its proper place here: "Those whom [God] foreknew he also predestined to be conformed to the image of his Son" (Rom. 8:29).[70] This concept of being conformed to Christ

---

70. There is a strong note of this predestined conformity in Ephesians and Colossians. See Eph. 1:3-5: "Blessed be the God and Father of our Lord Jesus Christ, who . . . chose us in him before the foundation of the world, that we should be holy and blameless before him. He destined us in love to be his sons through Jesus Christ, according to the purpose of his will." The link between predestination, or election, leads to a summons to become what you already are. "We are to grow up in every way into him who is the head, into Christ" (Eph. 4:15). You have already died, in Christ, to the demonic powers, the author of Colossians reminds his flock; why do you live as if you had not (Col. 2:20)? "You have died, and your life is hid with Christ in God" (Col. 3:3). There is a certainty about all this that engenders moral courage.

is central, not only to the story of recapitulation but also to Christian ethics.[71] We are all being "changed into [Christ's] likeness," for "this comes from the Lord who is the Spirit" (II Cor. 3:18), and "when he appears we shall be like him" (I John 3:2). We can truly say that we are to "become what we already are," then, for the fruits of the Spirit are already at work (Gal. 5:22-23).

The grammatically challenging sentence of Paul, "For our sake he made him to be sin who knew no sin, so that in him we might become the righteousness of God" (II Cor. 5:21), links us *ontologically* to the *dikaiosyne theou*. This happens, not through works of our own, it hardly seems necessary to say, but "in him." The benefits of the crucifixion of Christ are already at work in the community of believers to shape their behavior — not by mere imitation, but by the power of God, who preserves for us our inheritance in his age to come (I Pet. 1:5). It is the sufferings of the church for Christ's sake that link her to her Lord's death. It is the Spirit that enables her to "share Christ's sufferings" (I Pet. 4:13) and to live "no longer by human passions but by the will of God" (I Pet. 4:2).

In the mainline churches of our times, there is no lack of exhortation to a life "worthy of the calling to which [we] have been called" (Eph. 4:1). Countless sermons are built around the phrase "we are called to [be more inclusive, give more generously, embrace the Other, work for peace, minister to the needy, feed the poor, cultivate tolerance, seek justice, show hospitality, and so forth]." What is often missing from such exhortations is the powerful proclamation of the One who is doing the calling, who has ratified our calling in his own blood, who has entered upon the life of "Adam" in order to defeat *from inside human nature* the work of the Enemy. This is the resounding, foundational gospel message on which the life of the church is built, proclaimed in numerous biblical messages:

> You were buried with him in baptism, in which you were also raised with him through faith in *the working of God,* who raised him from the dead. (Col. 2:12)

> For you have died, and your life is hid with Christ in God. When Christ who is our life appears, then you also will appear with him in glory. (Col. 3:3)

> We have seen and testify that the Father has sent his Son as the Savior of the world. Whoever confesses that Jesus is the Son of God, God abides

---

71. Here Paul speaks of "conformity to Christ." In Rom. 12:2 he uses "conform" as conformity to the *world*, contrasting it with being transformed by the mind of Christ.

in him, and he in God. So we know and believe the love God has for us. God is love, and he who abides in love abides in God, and God abides in him. In this is love perfected with us, that we may have confidence for the day of judgment, *because as he is so are we in this world.* (I John 4:14-17)

These passages speak of recapitulation in the distinctive voices of their different authors. They set out their versions of the Adam and Christ story most fully laid out by Paul. They speak of our assimilation to the life of Christ, not by any doing of our own — least of all any godliness of our own — but by "the working of God."

We do not hear enough of the working of God nowadays, though we hear a good deal about our own working — especially our religious working. The message of the gospel, however, is not that of building the kingdom as though we were subcontractors or even free agents. The New Testament tells a different story. We are able to participate in the working of God only because of his self-immolation on our behalf and in our place. It is not our spiritual journey that lies at the center of our faith; it is "the way of the Son of God into the far country," as Barth calls it, claiming the language of Jesus' parable in Luke 15:13. It is the journey of the incarnate One to us that enables our participation in the redemptive working of God. If this story is not told every time the people of God are enjoined to get busy, then we are no longer hearing the gospel.

John writes that love is perfected in us "because as [Christ] is so are we in this world" (I John 4:17). That does not mean simply "being Christ to one another." That familiar notion is not wrong, exactly, but it implies a simple, imitative moralism with no sense of either our incapacity or the demonic forces arrayed against us.[72] John reassures his readers that they need not fear the coming judgment. The implication is that condemnation was our rightful destiny until Christ recapitulated our story and took the judgment upon himself. Without the full story of the Son of God and his accursed Godforsaken death, there is no good news, only another "way" to choose from, such as the *Didache* recommended almost two thousand years ago. The *Didache* did not make it into the New Testament, for very good reasons: it does not tell the story of Adam and Christ; it has no apocalyptic atmosphere; and its offer of a Way of Life and a Way of Death assumes a world still uninvaded by the power of the age to come. Without the story of Christ and Adam undergirding the

---

72. "Lo, the hosts of evil round us / Scorn thy Christ, assail his ways," wrote Harry Emerson Fosdick (a "liberal" preacher not ordinarily associated with apocalyptic theology) — "From the sins that long have bound us / Free our hearts to faith and praise."

teaching of the church at every point, appeals to "be Christ to one another" are not materially different from moral exhortation. The apostolic message speaks of our having "the mind of Christ" (I Cor. 2:16), being "like him" (I John 3:2), and "being changed into his likeness" (II Cor. 3:18), but this is true *only* insofar as he has entered the life of his utterly, irredeemably lost creation and rewritten its wretched story in his own flesh and blood. Never is it more necessary to say *sola gratia* (by grace alone) than here.

What the church needs to hear is the radical message of the good news not only for the well-meaning and the well-intentioned but also for those who plan to do harm, or drift into doing harm, or lead others into doing harm. And that, in the final analysis, includes every one of us. We were children of wrath, we were dead in our sins (Eph. 2:1-3). The Son of God did not come to make good people better but to give life to the dead.

The performance artist Laurie Anderson wrote a song called "My Eyes" in which she sang:

> If I were queen for a day
> I'd give the ugly people all the money
> I'd rewrite the book of love
> I'd make it funny.[73]

This is what Jesus did. He rewrote the book of love. We are the "ugly people" who put Jesus on the cross, but he is going to give us all his riches nevertheless. Paul said exactly the same thing in a different way: "You know the grace of our Lord Jesus Christ, that though he was rich, yet for your sake he became poor, so that by his poverty you might become rich" (II Cor. 8:9). What Paul wants us to remember is that now we have this mind among ourselves, that we have in Christ Jesus (Phil. 2:5). Because *he has rewritten the story,* we are no longer prisoners of our worst selves, nor of the evil powers that would destroy us. At any moment of our lives, God may break through with yet another miracle of rewriting. And laughter will resound from the farthest reaches of the created universe: "Rejoice in the Lord always; again I will say, Rejoice" (Phil. 4:4).

---

73. "My Eyes," from the album *Strange Angel* (1989). Ms. Anderson was still working with this same idea when interviewed nearly twenty years later: "I want to tell a better story," she said, "a truer story." Culture critic Edward Rothstein expands on this: "She inverts one story to tell another." *Mutatis mutandis,* that's quite a good riff on the Adam passage in Rom. 5. Moreover, the Enemy is not entirely missing from this narrative. The story Ms. Anderson was "inverting" in 2008 is the invasion of Iraq and the "chaos and havoc" that resulted. *New York Times,* July 29, 2008.

Condemned into Redemption:
The Rectification of the Ungodly

Rise heart; thy Lord is risen. Sing his praise
  Without delayes,
Who takes thee by the hand, that thou likewise
  With him may'st rise;
That, as his death calcinèd thee to dust,
His life may make thee gold, and much more, just.

GEORGE HERBERT, "EASTER"[1]

This final chapter begins as did the first one, with the affirmation that Christianity is unique.

The first element of this uniqueness is that the Christian faith glorifies as Son of God a man who was degraded and dehumanized by his fellow human beings as much as it is possible to be, by decree of both church and state, and that he died in a way designed to subject him to utmost contempt and finally to erase him from human memory.

The second unique feature of the Christian gospel, the subject of this chapter, is its central message of *the justification of the ungodly* (Rom. 4:5; 5:6). In this, the biblical story differs radically from any other religious, philosophical, or ethical system ever known. Every other system, including rabbinic Judaism and some varieties of gnostic teaching from within Christianity itself, assumes some sort of distinction between godly and ungodly, righteous and unrighteous, spiritual and unspiritual. In its radical form, the Christian gospel declares, "It is written, 'None is righteous, no, not one; /

---

1. George Herbert, "Easter," in *The Complete English Poems,* ed. John Tobin (London: Penguin Books, 1991).

571

no one understands, no one seeks for God'" (Paul is quoting from the Old Testament) and "there is no distinction; since all have sinned and fall short of the glory of God" (Rom. 3:10-11, 22-23).

This cuts against the grain of all religious and moral thinking. When the *kerygma* — the apostolic message — is understood as presented here, in its most radical biblical terms, it can no longer be called "religion." The claims of religion are, in a sense, similar to the claim of the earliest temptation: "You will be like God" (Gen. 3:5). Religion, in its multifaceted and almost infinite forms, instructs us in spiritual development, offers means of approaching the divine, teaches us how to become godly, and promises blessing to those who succeed. The only provision in religion for the *un*godly is to turn to religion. There is no good news in religion for those who have not turned or cannot turn. A crucial aspect of the radical newness of the Christian gospel is the word it speaks precisely to those "without God in the world" (Eph. 2:12).

Religion is recognizably "religious." Contrarily, if the gospel could be explained in ordinary "religious" terms, then it would be no longer *moros* ("foolishness" — I Cor. 1:18, 23), *skandalon* ("stumbling block" — Gal. 5:11), or *proskomma* ("obstacle" — Rom. 14:13, 20). The story of the arrest, trial, passion, and crucifixion of Jesus is not a "religious" story. A phrase familiar to generations of seminary students — "the scandal of particularity" — is especially pertinent here. The climax of the gospel story has far too many particularities to be "spiritual" — it takes place in the midst of political and socioeconomic life, it is shocking and violent, it threatens and alienates established religious authorities, it reveals the significance of God's unaccountable election of the Jews, and its central personage makes unnerving claims about himself and his relationship to his own religious milieu.

Anyone seeking to understand the cross of Christ must face certain frustrations. The narratives, images, and motifs used by the New Testament writers do not always sit together comfortably. The variants in the Gospels and Epistles as they testify to the death and resurrection of Christ show that it was necessary to use a multiplicity of perspectives to convey the unique import of the event. As this tapestry of images and motifs shows, its riches are humanly unfathomable and there is no single way of understanding it. And yet our faith calls for understanding and proclamation, and this can only be done by giving full attention to the way the authors of the biblical material made use of an extraordinary variety of motifs.

Religious Distinctions versus the Universal Gospel

Everything in this volume has been oriented toward this final chapter. The problem of "the ungodly" has been hanging over these many chapters from the beginning. There have been repeated references to the problem of perpetrators, collaborators, passive bystanders, and all others who have participated in the domain of Sin. Any view of deliverance, atonement, redemption, salvation, or reconciliation that does not account for perpetrators is ultimately to fall short of a truly "inclusive" gospel, for which of us can be certain that under certain circumstances beyond our control we might not fall into that category?

In this final chapter, therefore, we take up the theme of the rectification of the ungodly in earnest.[2] A full treatment of the theme has been held back until now, as a strategy for emphasizing it as the *telos* (goal, consummation) toward which God moves the universe. There is something new here in biblical theology.[3] Very much to this point is the difficulty faced by the great Thomas Aquinas, who, in his mighty system, was perplexed by the problem of unbaptized children and unbelieving adults. Nicholas R. Ayo, translator and editor of Thomas's sermons, figuratively throws up his hands, writing, "The Middle Ages simply did not know what to do with the unbeliever." Then, in a seemingly offhand but enormously suggestive comment, Ayo concludes that Thomas's logic did not take sufficient account of *"the infinite resourcefulness of the God who wishes to save everyone."*[4]

2. The subject was partially treated in the section called "Sacrifice on Behalf of the Ungodly" in chapter 6, and the reader is referred back to that discussion.

3. Though, to be sure, it was adumbrated by Origen and others. Not since Paul's day, however, has the rectification of the ungodly received as much attention as now.

4. Nicholas R. Ayo, in *The Sermon-Conferences of St. Thomas Aquinas on the Apostles' Creed*, ed. and trans. Nicholas R. Ayo, C.S.C. (Eugene, Ore.: Wipf and Stock, 1988), 77. Bernard of Clairvaux may be an exception to this. In the *Paradiso*, Dante has Bernard saying that the unbaptized child must remain in Limbo. But Bernard himself wrote to Hugh of St. Victor, "We must suppose that the ancient sacraments were efficacious as long as it can be shown that they were not notoriously prohibited. And after that? It is in God's hands. Not mine be it to set the limit" (Bernard of Clairvaux, to Hugh of St. Victor, as quoted in Mark Jay Mirsky, *Dante, Eros, and Kabbalah* [Syracuse, N.Y.: Syracuse University Press, 2003], 180 n. 17). Paul Rorem observes that the quotation seems to be a loose English paraphrase of a sentiment associated with Bernard and used by Hugh. Rorem comments on the Bernard-Hugh correspondence in his book *Hugh of St. Victor* (Oxford: Oxford University Press, 2009) in the section on Hugh's *De Sacramentis* (82-85), and gives extensive references in the bibliography.

Moving back to the patristic period, we should note Origen's well-known conception of the restoration of all things (*apokatastasis ton panton* in the Greek text of *De principiis* 2.10). The imagery of a refining or purgatorial fire plays a large role in this conception. He cites Mal.

It is precisely God's infinite resourcefulness that undergirds the rectification of the ungodly. The apostle Paul, in Romans 11, proclaims ahead of time that God knows things that neither the Middle Ages nor our own age knows except by revelation, and furthermore that God holds unbelievers in his purpose. If we grant this, Ayo's remark points us toward a vision like Paul's, in which the victorious Messiah obliterates the reign of the Enemy on behalf of many who lie beyond the bounds of Christian fellowship as it is ordinarily understood. This, Jesus knew, would present problems not only for Thomas Aquinas but also for his own disciples. That is the context for the parable of the laborers in the vineyard. The workers who had been in the fields all day were paid no more than the latecomers. Upon receiving their wages, the former "grumbled at the landowner, saying, 'These last worked only one hour, and you have made them equal to us who have borne the burden of the day and the scorching heat.' But he replied to one of them, 'Friend, I am doing you no wrong; did you not agree with me for a denarius? . . . I choose to give to this last as I give to you. Am I not allowed to do what I choose with what belongs to me? Or do you begrudge my generosity?'" (Matt. 20:11-15).

It is significant that this parable is immediately followed in Matthew by this passage: "And as Jesus was going up to Jerusalem, he took the twelve disciples aside, and on the way he said to them, 'Behold, we are going up to Jerusalem; and the Son of man will be delivered to the chief priests and scribes, and they will condemn him to death, and deliver him to the Gentiles to be mocked and scourged and crucified, and he will be raised on the third day'" (Matt. 20:17-19).

The link between the humiliation of the Messiah and the seemingly unfair distribution of wages in the parable is certainly meant by Matthew to push the boundaries of those who had ears to hear. The generosity of the landowner, who, like God, is "no respecter of persons" (Acts 10:34 KJV), calls forth a ubiquitous human reaction — resentment, jealousy, lack of generosity — which, we are to understand, is one aspect of the human condition

---

3:2-3 (the refiner's fire), which is certainly a key text for our consideration of the future of sinners (i.e., all of us). Gregory of Nyssa seems to draw upon Origen's idea, citing I Cor. 15:28, "When all things are subjected to him, then the Son himself will also be subjected to him who put all things under him, *that God may be everything to every one.*" A major difference between *apokatastasis* in Origen and Paul's pushing toward the outward limits in Rom. 11:32 is the far more radical apocalyptic context of Paul's thought-world. Origen's conception has a Platonist shading (not to mention a Pelagian tinge), but in Paul, there is no question of a salvageable soul or spirit to rely upon. The entire human being having been given over to the flesh *(sarx)* is transfigured by the Spirit *(pneuma)* entirely by the righteousness of God. "For God has consigned all men to disobedience, that he may have mercy upon all."

that Jesus bears in his own body as he goes to his trial, condemnation, and death by torture. This link between the parable and the cross is vital. The generosity of God means the crucifixion of the Son. The justification of the ungodly involves judgment upon those who do not, or will not, or cannot participate in the scandalous generosity of God. Yet that is not the end of their story; it remains open-ended, like that of the elder brother of the prodigal son who is mired in self-pity but not hopelessly beyond the reach of the righteousness of God (Luke 15:25-32).[5]

Readers who have followed the discussion thus far will recall the extensive treatment of *dikaiosis,* ordinarily translated "justification," and its relationship to the righteousness *(dikaiosyne)* of God in the Old Testament. More than one biblical theologian has pointed to Paul's references to the justification of the ungodly (Rom. 4:5 and 5:6) as the heart and soul of the Christian gospel.[6] There is a presupposition behind this. The revelation of God in the Bible is simultaneous with the revelation of ourselves as fallen creatures, separated from our loving Creator, helpless in bondage to Sin and Death. As we have seen, the knowledge of Sin is a *consequence* of the knowledge of the grace of God, not a *precondition* of it. Therefore, in one of those paradoxes in which Christianity abounds, to speak of "the ungodly" is already to speak of ourselves under the rule of grace. Isaiah and Simon Peter, to name only two of many biblical personages, did not know that they were among the ungodly until they were *already safely within* the call and purpose of God (Isa. 6:5; Luke 5:8).

5. Robert Farrer Capon, in his typically outrageous style, writes that the elder brother's problem is that he is not dead. The father comes out to speak tenderly with him, but "since grace works only on the dead, this is a false start. This boy's precise problem is that he refuses to be dead, that he is frantically trying to hold what passes for his life in some kind of gimcrack order" (*The Parables of Grace* [Grand Rapids: Eerdmans, 1988], 142-43).

6. Toward the end of his life, the noted British scholar F. F. Bruce was interviewed about the relationship of academic study to evangelical faith and the central meaning of the gospel. Bruce, a towering figure in biblical theology by any standard, was never easy to categorize, since, unlike many evangelicals, he was respected by other biblical theologians from various points on the ecclesiastical and theological spectrum. When Bruce was asked by the interviewer why he objected to being called a "conservative evangelical," he replied, "Conservatism is not the essence of my position." "What do you mean by 'evangelical'?" asked the interviewer. Bruce responded, "An evangelical is someone who believes in the God who *justifies the ungodly* [Rom. 4:5]. To believe in Him, and nothing more or less, is to be evangelical." He said further, "Anything that begins to allow for an element of human merit or human achievement in the work of salvation is, to that extent, non-evangelical." This is not at all the way that evangelicalism is defined in America, but Bruce (a Scot and lifelong member of the Plymouth Brethren) was not giving a sociological definition. His focus was exclusively *theo*logical. He was identifying the essence of the *evangel,* the *kerygma* that defines the relationship between God and humanity (*St. Mark's Review,* Spring 1989).

"Religion" does not define all human beings on the same level of need before God. Religion may see everyone on the same level of spiritual potential, yes; but this is precisely what the gospel does not do, because the gospel is not about human potential. The figure of Abraham in Romans 4 is the archetype here. He was not a religious prodigy — quite the contrary. Abraham's importance, as Douglas Harink has written, has nothing to do with what we like to think of as "human potential." As a bearer of the promise that he will have descendants as numerous as the stars, Abraham — an elderly man with a barren wife — has *no human potential*.[7] Paul emphasizes that Abraham was chosen *before* he was circumcised (Rom. 4:10-11), which is Paul's way of saying that Abraham brought nothing to the bargain; his election by God was *ex nihilo* (out of nothing).[8] This startling announcement lies at the heart of the biblical picture of God. This is the foundation of all that Paul says about justification; it buttresses what Paul means when he says "there is no distinction" (Rom. 3:22-23).

In religion, as in every other human enterprise, there is always some underlying distinction. Because of this ubiquitous tendency to divide, the mainline churches have sought to oppose it by speaking about inclusion and radical hospitality. Several decades of this emphasis have taught us — rightly — to reject any sort of discrimination or separation by race, class, creed, nationality, gender, ability, sexual preference, and so forth. There is a subtle difficulty, however. Congregations are claiming for human beings what is possible only for God. No congregation can include everyone. No self-identified inclusive and welcoming church can live up to this assessment of itself. Many a person who has attended a church advertising radical hospitality has come and gone from church coffee hours without being greeted by anyone. There are many categories of people who have not been welcomed in churches. The congregation that makes a place for torchbearers with Down syndrome might fail to embrace an unwashed, unmedicated, disruptive man off the street. The parish that welcomes a transgendered person might give up on a woman with

---

7. This phrase, "no human potential," comes from an unpublished sermon by Douglas Harink, preached at First Baptist Church, Edmonton, Alberta, August 27, 2006. Abram and Sarai, a couple who have not been able to conceive a child, are "picked out" by God not because of their "hidden human potential" but "precisely because they have no potential." Isaac is not conceived until Sarai/Sarah is decades beyond childbearing age.

8. It is of great importance that God's covenant with Abraham was undertaken by God alone without Abraham's participation. Paul does not refer to the ancient, eerie story of the smoking firepot in Gen. 15:17-21, but it is a most dramatic illustration of God *unilaterally* initiating and ratifying the covenant with Abraham by playing the part of *both* the covenant partners — the weaker one as well as the stronger one.

a narcissistic personality disorder. Members of a congregation who do not hold all the views currently designated as correct will find themselves marginalized, even insulted. Despite the good intentions of congregations that proclaim themselves as diverse, welcoming, and inclusive, the fact remains that no one and no group can be, in this life, all-embracing. There will always be someone for whom the sign "The Episcopal Church welcomes you" will be a mockery. There will always be some who, despite the United Methodist Church's claim to have "open hearts, open minds, open doors," will find a less than open-hearted welcome.[9] Sometimes this will be because of serious disability or annoying personality, and sometimes because of deeply held beliefs that run counter to the prevailing orthodoxy.[10] Therefore new types of exclusions replace the old, more obvious race- or class-based types. It is part of sinful human nature that this is so.

The crucifixion of Jesus Christ puts an end to all these religious categories that separate people from one another. There is no one who is not guilty of perpetrating something on someone at some point.[11] We spend a good deal of psychic energy (often unconsciously) in keeping a mental balance sheet, so that one person's failure in a personal relationship is not seen as equal to another person's act of vicious assault. In Paul's words, however, "there is no distinction" (Rom. 3:22). We must find a way to talk theologically about persons both righteous *and* unrighteous, spiritual *and* unspiritual, religious *and* irreligious — and perhaps especially about people who have wasted their "human potential." Above all, we must account for victims and perpetrators alike. If we cannot do this, then it is not the *evangel.*

Unintentional versus "High-Handed" Sin in the Old Testament

Thoughtful readers of the Bible with the ungodly in mind will notice right away that the Old Testament is packed with references to the woeful destiny of the ungodly (also called the unrighteous). A couple of examples from among many hundreds of verses will illustrate this:

9. All these examples are taken from real-life situations involving real people and real churches.

10. Evangelicals (even "liberal" evangelicals) have experienced discrimination, disdain, and even exclusion from within the mainline churches for decades.

11. In Robert Penn Warren's novel *All the King's Men,* the politician Willie Stark orders a former reporter, now in his pay, to "get something" on a judge. The reporter protests that the judge is such a model of probity that there is nothing to be got. Stark responds, "There is something on everybody."

God will scatter the bones of the ungodly;
> they will be put to shame, for God has rejected them. (Ps. 53:5)

"Both prophet and priest are ungodly;
> even in my house I have found their wickedness, says the Lord.
Therefore . . . I will bring evil upon them
> in the year of their punishment, says the Lord." (Jer. 23:11-12)

In the Priestly Code of the Pentateuch, there is no provision for the person who commits sin "with a high hand . . . ; his iniquity shall be upon him" (Num. 15:30-31). The Levitical sacrifices were provided for those who sin "unintentionally" (NRSV). This sharply poses the problem of perpetrators. If indeed Christ died "for sin," as the New Testament repeatedly proclaims, and if that death has universal significance "once for all," as Hebrews declares, then there must be some provision for the "high-handed."

The definition of a high-handed perpetrator has changed since biblical times. Our notions today of "the ungodly" or, alternatively, "the unrighteous" are quite different from those in the Old Testament, or for that matter in the Judaism of Jesus' day. When we think of the truly ungodly, we tend perhaps to think not so much of habitual violators of God's covenant faithfulness, but rather of archetypally evil figures such as Pol Pot or, on a smaller scale, defiant and unrepentant serial killers. We suggested earlier that there may be a few psychopaths who are not really human at all, and it is not humanly possible to imagine a proper fate for them.[12] Far more challenging and significant are the questions about "ordinary" people who become involved in a network of sin and evil: young American men in a poorly led military unit who become rapists and murderers; high school football players who are swept up in a brutal attack on a developmentally vulnerable girl; corporate executives who encourage and then cover up ravenous practices that lead to disastrous consequences for the entire economy. These everyday events are easily brushed aside, and are passed over more often than not, because we are willing to make allowances for circumstances, culture, or tribe (platoon, sports team, business associates). Is there a line drawn by

---

12. Although Will Campbell, in his book *And Also with You,* has tried. No white person was more aware of the horrors of white racist violence in the Deep South, or more involved in the civil rights movement at risk of his life, yet he is able to envision the redemption of the demonically possessed Sam Bowers (head of the KKK), and even of Hitler, in a mostly-but-not-entirely-fantastic scenario at the end of the book, where Golda Meir (playing the part of a hound of heaven) chases Hitler around "the pinnacles of heaven" for aeons until she succeeds in pinning a yellow star on him.

God somewhere between righteous and unrighteous, godly and ungodly? How are we to know which side of that line, if there is one, we ourselves are on? How do we judge others? It has become the norm in our day to renounce "judgmentalism" (a word unknown until very recently), and yet we all do make judgments at some point, whether we recognize it or not — even if only against those we deem judgmental.[13]

It therefore becomes problematic even by Old Testament standards to delineate between the righteous and the unrighteous. *This difficulty is noted in the Old Testament itself.* It is an indispensable rule of biblical interpretation that the Bible, when studied thoroughly and canonically, is filled with self-correction. Certain key passages in the Old Testament look forward to the radical erasure of distinctions. We have already noted Isaiah 64:5-7. The apostle Paul saw *in the Hebrew Bible* itself the foundation for his truly inclusive declaration that all human beings are under the power of Sin. In Romans 3:9-12 he writes, quoting Psalm 14:1-3:

I have already charged that all men, both Jews and Greeks, are under the power of sin, as it is written:

"None is righteous, no, not one;
no one understands, no one seeks for God.
All have turned aside, together they have gone wrong;
no one does good, not even one."[14]

The great literary writers are our best teachers concerning human nature. The Turkish novelist Orhan Pamuk won the Nobel Prize in 2006. Later that year, he delivered the Arthur Miller Freedom to Write lecture to the PEN society of writers. Here is part of what he said: "I am, after all, a novelist, the kind of novelist who makes it his business to identify with all his characters, especially the 'bad' ones . . . living as I do in a world where, in a very short time, someone who has been a victim of tyranny and oppression can suddenly become one of the oppressors."[15]

---

13. Chapter 3 ("The Question of Justice") and chapter 10 ("The Descent into Hell") examined these issues at some length.

14. See also Pss. 53:1-3; 143:2.

15. Orhan Pamuk, "Freedom to Write," *New York Review of Books*, May 25, 2006. Along similar lines, novelist Jonathan Franzen, writing admiringly of Nobel Prize–winner Alice Munro, has this to say: "If you're unhappy about the hatred that's been unleashed in your heart, you might try imagining what it's like to be the person who hates you; you might consider the possibility that you are, in fact, the Evil One yourself; and if this is difficult to imagine, then you

If this is what the writer of literary fiction is able to do with the personages that he creates, how much more the loving Creator himself? Has not our Lord Jesus done exactly this, identifying himself with — indeed, putting himself in the place of — "all his characters, especially the 'bad' ones"? Note that Pamuk is not writing about absent-minded, unintentional sins — the kind provided for in the Levitical sacrifices. He has in mind not only the passive collaborators but also the "high-handed" perpetrators, the worst among us, precisely the ones who might in other circumstances have been counted among the best of us.

And yet even the greatest novelists can only summon us to understand and, possibly, to forgive the high-handed perpetrator. The novelist cannot right wrongs. Only God can execute a regime change in which the tyrannical Powers are displaced and overthrown. This is the story of the purpose of God, "which he set forth in Christ as a plan for the fulness of time, to unite all things in him, things in heaven and things on earth" (Eph. 1:9-10).

Rectification as Change of Regime

The term "regime change" emerged from an unsavory political context, but as an approximation of what the righteousness of God is able to do, we can capture it for the service of the apocalyptic drama.[16] The old regime, in which the Powers of Sin and Death rule over the human race, will be definitively vanquished and "the creation itself will be set free from its bondage to decay" (Rom. 8:21). This means that there is a new future in which those things that are possible only with God will become the only ultimate reality.

Paul speaks of regime change in many places in his letters. One of the most important is Romans 13:12-14. "The night is far gone, the day is at hand. Let us then cast off the works of darkness and put on the armor of light; let us conduct ourselves becomingly as in the day. . . . Put on the Lord Jesus Christ, and make no provision for the flesh, to gratify its desires." In Romans 13 and 14, Paul's use of the word *Kurios* (Lord) is a key to his entire gospel of regime change, but this will not be obvious unless one is looking closely. Take verse 4 in chapter 14, for instance: "Who are you to judge someone

---

might try spending a few evenings with [Alice Munro]" (Jonathan Franzen, *New York Times Sunday Book Review,* November 14, 2004).

16. The administration of George W. Bush used the term to refer to the goals of the preemptive war against Saddam Hussein in Iraq. I thought that I had appropriated the term on my own, but in looking through my notes from a conference on Romans in Princeton in May 2012, I see that I derived it from a lecture by Susan Eastman.

else's servant? To his own *kurios* (master) he stands or falls. And he will stand, for the *Kurios* (Master or Lord) *is able* to make him stand" (NIV).

This is classic Pauline preaching. The apostle seems to be issuing a rather peremptory put-down of a "judgmental" person, but in fact he is preaching the gospel of regime change. The whole following section seems to be instruction in ethical behavior, and it has often been characterized that way (as *paraenesis*), but it would be a mistake to construe it that way without noticing that it has the tightest possible relation to the shift of *kosmos*. This becomes apparent when we see that Paul keeps using the word *kurios* in 14:4-14. Here is the central point: *the change in regimes that Paul describes as night and day in 13:12 has been effected by Christ.* The whole structure of the gospel is founded on and built upon the Lordship of the crucified, risen, victorious Christ, who is able to make his servants stand and not fall.[17]

True Inclusion

When the word *dikaiosis* is translated as "rectification," the radicality of Paul's preaching of the *Christus Victor* theme becomes more clear. Any reader of this volume will be aware of the strong support given, up to a point, to the "social gospel," which, in recent decades, has been taken up virtually without reservation in the mainline denominations. However, as we have repeatedly observed, there is something missing in the social gospel and its close cousin, liberation theology. For all their considerable biblical resonances, they are not inclusive enough. The various versions of liberation theology tend to encourage a distinction between the guilty and the innocent. Here again, it is often necessary for thinking Christians to hold two contradictory positions at once. In this case, it is quite possible to champion God's "preferential option for the poor" and at the same time agree with Flannery O'Connor that "we are *all* the poor."[18] Hans Küng manages this quite handily when he writes, "Nowhere did it become more evident than in the Cross that this

17. In regard to being set on one's feet, one of the most dazzling (albeit mysterious) passages in Scripture is the inaugural vision of Ezekiel. It concludes in this way: "Such was the appearance of the likeness of the glory of the Lord. And when I saw it, I fell upon my face, and I heard the voice of one speaking. And he said to me, 'Son of man, stand upon your feet, and I will speak with you.' And when he spoke to me, the Spirit entered into me and set me upon my feet; and I heard him speaking to me" (Ezek. 1:28–2:2). It is the Spirit of the Lord that makes a man stand.

18. Flannery O'Connor, Letter to "A," September 15, 1955, in *The Habit of Being* (New York: Farrar, Straus and Giroux, 1979), 103, emphasis added.

God is in fact a God on the side of the weak, sick, poor, underprivileged, oppressed, *even of the irreligious, immoral and ungodly.*"[19]

Truly inclusive assessments of humanity are frequently found in the accounts of those who have suffered under totalitarian regimes. Primo Levi coined the phrase "the gray zone" to describe extreme circumstances in which it became impossible to separate the righteous from the unrighteous.[20] Jan T. Gross, in his influential book about a particularly terrible atrocity in Poland during the Nazi era, wrote: "Can one, as a group with a distinctive collective identity, be *at the same time a victim and a perpetrator?* Is it possible to suffer and inflict suffering at the same time? In the postmodern world the answer to such questions is very simple — of course it is possible."[21]

The reluctance to take a hard look at these assertions in the churches' present mood of undifferentiated affirmations has only exacerbated the destructive separations and divisions among us. Various mainline constituencies vie with one another for who can be more diverse and inclusive, or less like the so-called Christian Right — while the Right does the same sort of thing, with different issues, from their position. An apocalyptic interpretation of the Bible, however, when it is most true to the Bible's own internal clues, will stress the common plight of all humankind, for it is the one thing that binds us together.[22] The New Testament writers were attuned to those internal biblical clues (it is easy to forget that the Hebrew Scriptures were the only Bible that the New Testament Christians had). Paul's phrase "the justification [rectification] of the *ungodly*" seems to contradict such lines in the

19. Hans Küng, *On Being a Christian* (New York: Doubleday, Image Books, 1984), 435, emphasis added.

20. Primo Levi, *The Drowned and the Saved* (New York: Vintage Books, 1988), title of chap. 2 (36-69).

21. Jan T. Gross, *Neighbors: The Destruction of the Jewish Community in Jedwabne, Poland* (Princeton: Princeton University Press, 2001), 144, emphasis added. This book describes a hands-on massacre that occurred in Poland early in World War II. The Jewish half of the population of a town in Poland was murdered by the Gentile half. Gross has shown that it was not the Germans but the local Polish population who enthusiastically herded their Jewish neighbors into barns and burned them alive, throwing bound bundles of small children into the fires with pitchforks. Gross quotes the philosopher Eric Voegelin, who writes that evil regimes are able to recruit "the simple man who is a decent man as long as the society as a whole is in order but who then goes wild, *without knowing what he is doing,* when disorder arises somewhere and the society is no longer holding together" (Gross, 156-57, emphasis added).

22. Sometimes it seems that the people who have made the most effort to understand the extreme right-wing Christian sector are not "liberal" Christians at all, but journalists and writers. Jeff Chu, in his book about being a gay Christian, *Does Jesus Really Love Me?* goes to remarkable lengths to portray the members of the infamous gay-baiting Westboro Baptist Church in a sympathetic light. "What God Wants," review of Chu's book, *New York Times,* April 11, 2013.

Psalms as this: "Know that the Lord has set apart the *godly* for himself" (Ps. 4:3). And yet it is precisely in the Psalms that Paul finds confirmation for the central insight that "none is righteous, no, not one."[23] It is essential to read the Scriptures with close attention to these cross-references, on the principle that the Bible interprets itself. Otherwise, we are certain to fall back into the universal human trait of seeking to demonstrate our own innocence.

> There are those who are pure in their own eyes
> > but are not cleansed of their filth. (Prov. 30:12)

> All the ways of a man are pure in his own eyes,
> > but the Lord weighs the spirit. (Prov. 16:2)

It is precisely this state of affairs — universal human nature caught in the web of Sin yet universally concerned to vindicate itself — that is addressed by the righteousness of God.

The Righteousness of God in the Psalms

Reading the Scriptures from the perspective of God's apocalyptic in-breaking can be illustrated from such Old Testament passages as Psalm 25 (*Ad te, Domine, levavi:* "to thee, O Lord, I lift up my soul"). As in many psalms, the faithfulness of God is extolled:

> All the paths of the Lord are steadfast love and faithfulness,
> > for those who keep his covenant and his testimonies. (Ps. 25:10)

This in turn raises a question. Who fits the description, "those who keep his covenant"? Who can claim that she has done this? Who can be

---

23. For two hundred years and more in America, the use of a General Confession in the Christian liturgy offset this universal human characteristic. The General Confession used during Morning Prayer in the Episcopal Church was part of common speech ("We have erred and strayed from thy ways like lost sheep . . . we have followed too much the devices and desires of our own hearts"). The prayer encouraged the faithful to understand themselves as part of a commonality in Sin. A weaker version of the General Confession in the revised Book of Common Prayer has never caught on in the same way, and since the disuse of Morning Prayer on Sunday morning, it has not held the same position of prominence and authority in the church. The newer prayers of confession used in the mainline churches lack the power of expression and the unconditional universality that distinguished the older versions.

certain that his life has been one of covenant fidelity? In the Judaism of Jesus' time, as we have noted several times, it seems to have been assumed that covenant faithfulness was within the reach of human beings *even without* a radical incursion of God's rectifying power. Paul the Pharisee certainly thought so, prior to his conversion (Phil. 3:4-6). This is a view later associated with Pelagius, whom Augustine mocked for "believing that so great are the powers of our nature, which he is in such a hurry to exalt, that even without the help of the Holy Ghost the evil spirit can be resisted — less easily it may be, but still in a certain measure."[24] Though in theory Augustine "won" this debate, he did not succeed in eliminating Pelagius's view; it has persisted ever since as most Christians' default position.[25] The more serious one is about spiritual and ethical development, the more "Pelagian" one tends to become, so great is the temptation to think that one is making moral and spiritual progress. The psalmist, however, expresses unease:

> For thy name's sake, O Lord,
>> pardon my guilt, for it is great. (Ps. 25:11)

This is followed by the comforting affirmation that God will instruct and guide his servants:

> The friendship of the Lord is for those who fear him,
>> and he makes known to them his covenant.
> My eyes are ever toward the Lord,
>> for he will pluck my feet out of the net. (vv. 14-15)

Yet still the psalmist knows himself to be on shaky ground, begging for aid:

> Turn thou to me, and be gracious to me;
>> for I am lonely and afflicted. . . .
> Consider my affliction and my trouble,
>> and forgive all my sins. (vv. 16-18)

---

24. Augustine, *Treatise on the Grace of Christ* 28.27-28.

25. Not only is it a default position, but also for some, in recent years, it is a chosen position. There is presently a movement to reinstate Pelagius and Pelagianism as a preferred choice, particularly among those with "Celtic" leanings. John Philip Newell has supported this move in his numerous popular books, especially *Listening to the Heartbeat of God* (Mahwah, N.J.: Paulist, 1997).

This psalm, like the Bible as a whole, can be read in two basically different ways. Is God a helper to those who help themselves? Or is God the helper
of the helpless? Put another way, *whose righteousness* has saving power? *God*
is the active agent throughout the psalm, the subject of virtually all the verbs:
God "makes known," he "plucks out of the net," he "turns to" the afflicted
one, he "relieves troubles," he "brings out of distress." The psalm ends with
these lines:

> Oh guard my life, and deliver me;
>> let me not be put to shame, for I take refuge in thee.
> May integrity and uprightness preserve me,
>> for I wait for thee.
> Redeem Israel, O God,
>> out of all his troubles. (vv. 20-22)[26]

Here, the psalmist does not refer to *his own* "integrity and uprightness,"
but to God's. The righteousness of God — a strong theme in the Hebrew
prophets — not only supports but also *engenders* integrity and uprightness
among human beings. Paul sees this as the foundation of all that he reads in
the Scriptures.[27] The redemption of Israel "out of all his troubles" is precisely
what God has done in Christ. Whatever integrity and uprightness may be operative, they are operative as the righteousness of God.[28] The psalmist must
live in the midst of enemies and dangers, but awaits the Lord's saving acts.

Psalm 69 (*Salvum me fac:* "Save me, O God") has a similar trajectory, beginning with an individual *in extremis* and expanding into a vision of promised
redemption. Because of verses 20-21, this psalm is associated with Good Friday:

> Insults have broken my heart,
>> so that I am in despair.

26. "Israel" in the New Testament can sometimes mean the Jews — as for instance in Rom.
9:3-5 and 11:25 — but more often, for Paul, it has a universal application to the entire people of
God, Jews and Gentiles alike ("the Israel of God," as Paul calls it, God's "new creation" — Gal.
6:15-16). Thus the redemption of the eponymous "Israel . . . out of all his troubles," as in the
psalm quoted, has both a particular and a universal meaning.

27. Käsemann, in his breakthrough essay "The Righteousness of God in Paul," has helped
us to see that *dikaiosyne theou,* "the righteousness *of God,*" is qualitatively different from a virtue
or an attribute of God. The righteousness of God is *the power of God for salvation* (Rom. 1:16-17).

28. As Simon Gathercole puts it, "God is the sole operator in salvation. . . . It is not that
we have accomplished some successful law-observance that needs to be topped off by God to
make a full quota. . . . God acts so that it is obvious to all that he alone does the whole saving
work" (Rom. 11:6) ("What Did Paul Really Mean?" *Christianity Today,* August 2007).

> I looked for pity, but there was none;
>> and for comforters, but I found none.
> They gave me poison for food,
>> and for my thirst they gave me vinegar to drink.

And yet, these verses are immediately followed by imprecations:

> Let their own table before them become a snare. . . .
> Pour out thy indignation upon them,
>> and let thy burning anger overtake them. . . .
> Add to them punishment upon punishment;
>> may they have no acquittal from thee. . . .
> Let them not be enrolled among the righteous. (vv. 22-28)

This poses the question of victims and perpetrators quite bluntly. It is the victim who speaks in the psalm, and unlike Jesus, who prayed for the forgiveness of his tormentors, the victim prays for their condemnation and exclusion. He appeals to God's justice and demands a forensic sentencing. What are we to make of this?

A canonical reading informed by New Testament apocalyptic will see the final verses of Psalm 69 as determinative of the whole. Enmity, retribution, and condemnation are not the last word. The psalm ends with praise, putting it all into God's hands, encompassing all those whom God will choose to bless, trusting in his inalienable righteousness. Thus the Old Testament, when read in the light of the New, is filled with testimony to God's victory over all that darkens the human heart.

> Let heaven and earth praise him. . . .
> For God will save Zion
>> and rebuild the cities of Judah;
> and his servants shall dwell there and possess it;
>> the children of his servants shall inherit it,
>> and those who love his name shall dwell in it. (vv. 34-36)

The Depth of the Human Predicament and the *Dikaiosyne* of God

This faith in the righteousness of God calls for a new view of human nature, one that refuses to make hard-and-fast judgments about who is godly and who is not. In Herman Melville's towering masterpiece, *Moby Dick,* the ship

Pequod is a microcosm of humanity. The epic tale is loaded with references to the universal human predicament. Early on, Ishmael says, "In the scales of the New Testament . . . who ain't a slave?" The famous sermon by Fr. Mapple, delivered from a pulpit shaped like a ship's prow, is addressed to the pastor's "beloved shipmates" and emphasizes the preacher's solidarity with them in peril. Later, the "savage" Queequeg says, "It's a mutual, jointstock world. We cannibals must help these Christians." Ishmael declares, "Heaven have mercy on us all, Presbyterians and Pagans alike, for we are all somehow dreadfully cracked about the head, and sadly in need of mending."

Melville's mysterious novel is many things, but it can be said for certain that it is absorbed with the theocentric themes of Calvinist New England even as its author strives against the Calvinist God and the faith of his fore-bears. John Calvin famously wrote of the universal, "total" depravity of the human will.[29] We could get a better hearing for Calvin today if we chose in-stead the words of Ishmael to describe the human plight — "sadly in need of mending." Not just in need of *forgiveness,* mind you, but of *mending* — rectifi-cation. In no other way can God's justice be worked out on a universal plane.

We have noted the deep-seated resistance to the idea of judgment that has predominated in the mainline churches for many decades. Judgment has been largely edited out of the lectionaries and is absent from most preach-ing. And yet, in spite of the call for a loosely conceived "tolerance" that is so characteristic of our times, there remains a deep sense in our communities of a need for judgment in cases that profoundly offend community sensi-bilities. The call for justice and righteousness is indestructibly embedded in the Judeo-Christian tradition, and can be seen most clearly when that identity is shaken by examples of human depravity. Here are two examples from a Jewish milieu.

A *New York Times* reporter writes:

> A great deal of soul-searching went on in the American Jewish community when it was learned that Bernard Madoff, a Jew, had perpetrated one of the most, if not the most, colossal financial frauds of all time. It was, said Rabbi David Wolpe of the Los Angeles Sinai Temple, "theft on a global scale."
>
> Rabbi Wolpe said that he did not believe Mr. Madoff could ever make

---

29. Calvin never meant "total" in the sense of all-pervasive wickedness. He meant that there was no component of human being, no corner of the self, that we could retreat to and trust to be untouched by the power of sin. "No part is immune from sin" (*Institutes* 2.1.9). Contrast the gnostic tendency to seek a pure, inner, spiritual core in which to rest.

amends. "It is not possible for him to atone for all the damage he did," the rabbi said, "and I don't even think that there is a punishment that is commensurate with the crime, for the wreckage of lives that he's left behind. The only thing he could do, for the rest of his life, is work for redemption that he would never achieve."[30]

The rabbi's assessment is striking for three reasons:

1. The conception of a global-scaled crime
2. The need for "a punishment commensurate with the crime"
3. The impossibility of atonement in such a case

Despite the continual protests of many in the church who say that atonement is an obsolete concept, the word is enshrined in Judaism as Yom Kippur, the Day of Atonement. But Bernie Madoff, as a particularly villainous perpetrator, has gone so far in ungodliness that the rabbi categorizes him as one who has no hope of "achieving" redemption. Each person reading these lines will have his or her own idea of an unforgivable crime. The underlying thought is that *the damage done can never be made right.* The "achieving" of redemption may be possible for smaller offenders, the rabbi obliquely suggests, but not for a crime on this scale. But how are the weights on this scale to be measured? How many people's investments must be destroyed to tip the scale — a hundred? a thousand?

The Jewish community has every right to be protective of its ingrained, God-given concern for ethics and compassion. The problem among Jews and Gentiles alike, however, is the tendency for those who observe and comment upon wrongdoing to separate themselves from the category of ungodly perpetrator. This is the universal human way. It is our means of shoring up our dearly held conviction that we, the godly, are in a different position from the ungodly. This self-protective stance is enshrined in Jesus' parable of the Pharisee who prayed, "God, I thank thee that I am not like other men," contrasted with the tax collector who cried out, "God, be merciful to me a sinner." It is the tax collector who "went down to his house justified rather than the other" (Luke 18:9-14). The thrust of Luke's parable of justification is extended *ad infinitum* by Paul's cosmic conception of what the *dikaiosyne* of God can accomplish.[31]

---

30. Robin Pogrebin, "In Madoff Scandal, Jews Feel an Acute Betrayal," *New York Times,* December 23, 2009.

31. Luke's word is *dedikaiomenos* — the same word-group as *dikaiosyne.* It is generally

The second example from a Jewish context illustrates, in a different way, our difficulty in understanding how close under the surface the capacity for wrongdoing, even for wickedness, lies in all of us, and how universal is our temptation to isolate the perpetrator as someone different from ourselves. An article on the front page of the *New York Times* told of seven Israeli teenagers who had been arrested on charges of attempting to lynch several Palestinian youths. One of the suspects was a thirteen-year-old girl. A fifteen-year-old suspect was heard to say, "For my part he can die, he's an Arab. If it was up to me, I'd have murdered him." In one of the Israeli newspapers, a commentator asked, "Where on earth does a *bar-mitzvah*-aged child find so much evil in himself?"[32]

That question sums up a good deal of the argument of this chapter, and it illustrates the willful blindness of all human beings — *Gentiles and Jews alike* — to the enormity and ubiquity of Sin. We should not be surprised that there is evil "in" any human being. We should not expect to see some great accession of righteousness to occur with the bar mitzvah or any other "call to the commandment." We should not continue to be perpetually surprised that people "find so much evil" within themselves and others. We should never cease to be shocked, grieved, even enraged — but we should never be surprised, for "all men, both Jews and Greeks, are under the power of sin" (Rom. 3:9).[33]

These two illustrations show how even Judaism, by the grace of God the most indestructible of all cultures, begotten from the direct action of God in electing Israel, will choose a way of reading its own Scripture that is common to Christians as well, through the Pelagian default — the assumption that righteousness is actually within reach of the human will.[34] We return to the

---

agreed that this, Luke's only use of the word-group, does not carry the same freight as it does in Paul's thought-world.

32. Isabel Kershner, "Young Israelis Held in Attack on Arab Youths," *New York Times,* August 21, 2012.

33. Martin Luther King is a modern hero, memorialized everywhere, but he was also one of those who understood the bondage of Sin; his internal struggles undercut any tendency he had for self-glorification. "King was deeply aware of the power of evil, and he never suggested that it was mainly institutional nor primarily in the enemy's camp. He knew that darkness camped in the human heart, on both sides of the battle line" (Tim Stafford, review of *Parting the Waters,* by Taylor Branch, *Christianity Today,* June 16, 1989).

34. In a gathering at Union Theological Seminary in the late 1970s, Rom. 7 was being discussed. To the genuine astonishment of some of the Christian scholars present, Shaye J. D. Cohen (then dean and professor of Jewish history at the Jewish Theological Seminary, later professor at Harvard) expressed incomprehension. He said he genuinely did not recognize Paul's description of the human being in captivity to Sin and the Law. Several who were pres-

psalmist who sets before us a multidimensional view of the human being buffeted by a variety of forces both within and without, always alien to the righteousness of God. The Bible does not shrink from presenting our more unattractive — yet entirely understandable — thoughts. The psalmist does not conceal his rage against those who persecute him. Clearly he thinks of himself as one of the righteous:

> Let them be blotted out of the book of the living;
>> let them not be enrolled among the righteous. (Ps. 69:28)

As the psalm moves to its conclusion, however, the singer seems to calm down and recognize himself among those who are dependent upon the mercy of God:

> For the Lord hears the needy,
>> and does not despise *his own that are in bonds.* (69:33)

From the perspective of "the power of God for salvation" (Rom. 1:16), the reference to "his own that are in bonds" is a move away from the division of righteous from unrighteous, godly from ungodly. The psalmist shifts from asking that our enemies be written out of the book of the righteous to recognizing that all of us, even God's "own," are in bondage to Sin and in need of deliverance by a greater Power. In this way, the Old Testament prefigures and bears witness to the New.

The best definition of the righteousness of God is the simplest one: it is the power of God to make right what has been wrong. And what has been wrong since "Adam" is the captivity of the entire human race to Sin, Death, and the judging and condemning voice of the Law. It is not really possible to grasp the full meaning of rectification *(dikaiosis)* without an understanding of the way that Sin hijacked the Torah. People who quote the popular saying "No good deed goes unpunished" are humorously but ruefully acknowledging — without realizing it — the power of Sin to twist the Law. Paul Meyer, in an influential essay with the suggestive title "The Worm at the Core of the Apple," puts this into clear terms:

---

ent that evening remember this. It illustrates the point we have repeatedly made about the difference between those Jews and Christians who believe that obedience to the Law is actually possible and those who, reading Scripture with the eyes of Paul (and Augustine and their descendants), believe that it is *humanly* impossible (but "with God all things are possible" — Matt. 19:26; see also Mark 9:23; 10:27; 14:36).

The experience of the demonic power of Sin to use the Mosaic law to effect just the opposite of what its devoted adherents expect, *even and especially when it is obeyed,* manifests not only the sinister nature of Sin itself (Romans 7:13) but also how profoundly the religious self is "sold" under it and indeed possessed by it (Romans 7:14-20). God's own good law takes on a quality and character opposite to that which a person knows to be true, so that the religious self is put in the wretched position of serving Sin in its very service of God. Two thousand years of Christian history have shown that in the presence of this power there is no distinction between the "godly" and the "ungodly." [Romans 7] is part of Paul's explanation of why God sent God's own Son, on behalf of all, to deal with Sin as the law could not (Romans 8:3-4).[35]

It is not possible to see how this is true without radical conversion, that is, without the overturning of human pretension that accompanies an unconditional accession of grace. The writer Mark Richard pays homage to Flannery O'Connor in his memoir *House of Prayer No. 2,* as he shows how convenient it is to project wickedness out of the self onto others (when he says "you" he is actually speaking of himself): "The people you met so far [in Hollywood] were more interested in television shows and movies in which people of faith protected souls by fighting teen idol agents of Satan, fire-breathing dragons, Muslim hordes, and super-secret cells within the government. The problem is that, like your favorite writer Flannery O'Connor, you believe the biggest threat to your soul is *you.*"[36]

How different that is from "God accepts you just as you are"!

Radical Hospitality or Complete Makeover?

"God accepts (or loves) you just as you are" has been one of the most frequently used slogans in the church of our day. It has been uttered frequently enough to almost qualify as Scripture, and is often offered up as the essence of the gospel.[37]

---

35. Paul W. Meyer, "The Worm at the Core of the Apple," in *The Conversation Continues: Studies in Paul and John in Honor of J. Louis Martyn,* ed. Robert T. Fortna and Beverly K. Gaventa (Nashville: Abingdon, 1990), 80, emphasis added.

36. Mark Richard, *House of Prayer No. 2: A Writer's Journey Home* (New York: Nan A. Talese, 2011), 190.

37. Paul Tillich's celebrated sermon, "You Are Accepted," in *The Shaking of the Foundations,* certainly contributed to the popularity of this version of the gospel.

But what exactly is meant by acceptance?[38] What is the love of God in its fullest dimensions?

The "just as I am" language was strongly reinforced in the twentieth century by the powerful hymn that Billy Graham always used for his altar calls, "Just as I Am." The words of the hymn, however, contain something rather more than what is understood by the phrase in general use today.

> Just as I am, without one plea
> But that thy blood was shed for me
> And that thou bidd'st me come to thee,
> O Lamb of God, I come. . . .[39]

This specific reference to the blood of Christ puts the phrase "just as I am" in a rather more challenging context. In the hymn, the hospitality — the welcome — of God is indeed extended to the "poor, wretched, blind" sinner, conscious of "fightings and fears within, without," but always *within the confession of Christ crucified.* Thus the divine welcome already carries with it the implicit presence of righteous judgment. The crucifixion of Christ is incomprehensible unless we understand it in the context of divine justice. When we are reminded — as we repeatedly have been in these pages — that God's *justice* and God's *righteousness* are the same thing *(dikaiosyne),* we can see that there is something more involved here than mere acceptance

---

38. The Joint Declaration on the Doctrine of Justification (JDDC), issued and signed by the Lutheran World Federation and the Roman Catholic Church in 1999, was a remarkable achievement, but it did not go far enough. Take, for instance, this concluding statement in the declaration: "Together we confess: By grace alone, in faith in Christ's saving work and not because of any merit on our part, we are accepted by God and receive the Holy Spirit, who renews our hearts while equipping and calling us to good works." As welcome as this is, this statement has two significant theological and interpretive problems: the word "accepted" and the word "calling." The word "accepted," even with the qualifications in the last part of the sentence, is too weak to convey the force of *dikaiosis* (justification/rectification). The word "equipping" is strong (its biblical precedent is *katartismos:* Eph. 4:12), but the sequence should be reversed to read "calling and equipping" to show that it is God who not only does the calling but also does the equipping. The word "calling" (*klesis* — Eph. 4:1) is typically used in contemporary preaching as though it were synonymous with "invitation." Thus the powerful agency of God in *dikaiosis* is — perhaps unintentionally, but with no less serious theological consequences — shifted to human agency and choice. If sermons end, as they often do, with words such as "We are called to [fill in the blank]," the unconditional quality of the gospel announcement is lost and an appeal to human decision is substituted. If God is truly in charge of his own plan of redemption, then any suggestion that human agency is determinative is theologically fatal to the entire enterprise.

39. Hymn, "Just as I Am," by Charlotte Elliott (1835).

— or, as we might say today, mere "tolerance." There is a limit to what can be accepted or tolerated, even by flawed human beings, let alone by God. Something has to be made right, justified, *rectified (dikaiosis)*.

A declaration of amnesty does not solve the problem of guilt. Something must be done to rectify the situation in order for justice to be served and redemption achieved, something "commensurate with the crime." We may extrapolate from this something not entirely unlike what Anselm means by "satisfaction" — not in his scholastic, schematic terms, but throwing a spotlight on the correspondence between the *ponderis peccatum* (weight, or gravity, of sin) and the nature of Christ's gruesome death.

Even more than this, however, is the promise of a complete transformation of human nature by Christ's victory over the Power of Sin. "Acceptance" is the least of it. Any serious reading of the Old Testament must point to an understanding of God, not superseded, which cannot benignly coexist with us in our condition under Sin. The distinguished writer Julian Green, the first American ever to be elected to the Académie Française, was a devout Roman Catholic. At the age of ninety, he spoke of aspects of his earlier life as a sort of crucifixion, and told an interviewer that "he could now, after a long struggle, await death with serenity." He was looking forward, he said, "to standing before God . . . finally to know exactly who I am, free of all the illusions, the little lies, knowing I am going to purgatory, and knowing I will be very happy."[40] We don't have to believe in a detailed medieval version of Purgatory to respond to this. The essential idea is present in the final, climactic book of the Old Testament; like the corrupt sons of Levi, we will all pass through the refiner's fire: "But who can endure the day of his coming, and who can stand when he appears? For he is like a refiner's fire and like fullers' soap; he will sit as a refiner and purifier of silver, and he will purify the sons of Levi and refine them like gold and silver, till they present right offerings to the Lord. Then the offering of Judah and Jerusalem will be pleasing to the Lord" (Mal. 3:2-4).

The placing of Malachi at the end of the Christian Old Testament was an inspired move by the early Christian church. The Tanakh (Hebrew Scriptures) closes with the Wisdom literature (the Writings), but the Old Testament was shaped in an apocalyptic direction, so that it ends not with the Writings but with the Prophets and, in the very last two verses, "the great and terrible day of the Lord" (Mal. 4:5). The final words of the Old Testament are in the form of promise, though not without a potent reminder of the curse that lies over God's people. These verses undercut any notion

40. Richard E. Nicholls, obituary of Julian Green, *New York Times,* August 18, 1998.

that the human predicament can be resolved by mere "acceptance." Instead, there is creation *ex nihilo,* the resurrection of the dead.

The righteousness of God, the *dikaiosyne theou,* burst forth from the tomb on the day of the resurrection of the Redeemer. "As in Adam all die, even so in Christ shall all be made alive." The human race is redeemed, not by "acceptance," but by death and resurrection. This is the fullness of the message of Easter Day.

The Rectification of Horrors

If the doxology in Romans 11:33-36 is lifted out of its context, it cannot be fully understood. Paul has just finished putting himself and his hearers through an intense investigation into the most serious division facing the church in his own time. His struggle, largely neglected by Bible readers for two thousand years, awaited its moment: namely, the failure of the Christian churches to protect the Jews of Europe in the heart of Christendom. For this failure, there can be no talk of anything redemptive from a strictly human perspective. We cannot compensate even for one, let alone six million.

We therefore return to Christ's descent into hell and Marilyn McCord Adams's term, "horrendous evils." That even one family should be destroyed in ghastly circumstances while the churches stand by, or assist, is intolerable. That millions of families are exterminated in full view is unthinkable, yet we must think it. If the justification of the ungodly is indeed at the heart of the Christian gospel, we must admit that this salvation — this righting of all wrongs by God — must mean something far more than the forgiveness of individuals for individual offenses.

The Austrian-born essayist Jean Améry, who survived Nazi torture at a terrible price, wrote of a meeting he attended after the war was over: "The Jews who in that hour were already trembling with the pathos of forgiveness and reconciliation, whether their name was Victor Gollancz or Martin Buber, were . . . distasteful to me . . . gushing about reconciliation."[41]

---

41. Jean Améry, *At the Mind's Limits: Contemplations by a Survivor of Auschwitz and Its Realities,* trans. Sidney Rosenfeld and Stella P. Rosenfeld (Bloomington: Indiana University Press, 1980), 94. Jean Améry, born Hanns Chaim Mayer, was the son of a Jewish father and Catholic mother. Raised Roman Catholic, he considered himself a Christian but also a Jew insofar as he bore the Auschwitz number on his arm. He was held for a time in Fort Breendonk, not one of the best-known of the Nazi prisons but acknowledged to be one of the very worst for its tortures. I first learned about Breendonk from W. G. Sebald's novel *Austerlitz* (New York: Modern Library, 2001), 19-27. Jean Améry's book about the Third Reich and its horrors

As we have repeatedly urged in these pages, reconciliation can be premature, and forgiveness is not enough.[42] As we discussed in the chapter on Christ's descent into hell, there are evils that cannot be redressed by any means this world has to offer. *It is necessary to think in terms of means from beyond this world.*

During the decade 2000-2010, a furious controversy arose that we might file under the title "Hitler's Baby Pictures." The view of Hitler that prevailed for fifty years after World War II was essentially that of monster, demon, evil incarnate. In the early twenty-first century, however, a spate of books and documentaries has appeared that examines (or purports to examine) Hitler's early life — his failed artistic endeavors, his dog Blondie, his niece Geli, his purported undescended testicle, the possibility that he was a repressed homosexual (the "pink Führer"), and so forth, in order to "explain" him. Ron Rosenbaum, who began "raging against explanation" of Hitler in 1995, continues to raise *"the forbidden possibility of having to forgive Hitler."*[43]

It is precisely these implications that we raise once again in this final chapter. There may be some monsters in history who are, or were, not really human beings at all. Perhaps we should entertain the idea that they were purely agents of Satan. In such a case, following the logic of the argument in this book, not only will their persons be annihilated, but also, and more important, the memory of them will be annihilated. No recollection of them or of their works will remain; it will be as though they and their monstrous deeds had never been. Thus we round out the classic doctrinal affirmation about absolute evil: in the End, it will be seen that it had no ontological existence.

Mary Bell, whose story is told by journalist Gitta Sereny in her book *Cries Unheard* (a highly suggestive title),[44] was eleven years old when she

---

is widely considered among the very best of its genre. Much of it illustrates the themes in these pages. For instance, he writes that the Nazi regime was one of sadism — the wish "to nullify the world." His book is entitled *Jenseits von Schuld und Sühne* ("Beyond guilt and atonement") — less strikingly called *At the Mind's Limits* in English.

42. This subject was introduced in chapter 3 ("The Question of Justice").

43. Julie Salamon, "Is a Demon Humanized No Longer a Demon?" *New York Times,* February 2, 2003. Along these lines are the musings of the Dalai Lama, whose reflections on the childhood of Stalin seem to suggest that if only he could have been persuaded to remember his mother's love, he might have been less ruthless (Dalai Lama, with Howard C. Cutler, *The Art of Happiness: A Handbook for Living* [New York: Riverhead Books, 1998], 123). Ron Rosenbaum's "rage against explanation" is fully explored in his book *Explaining Hitler: The Search for the Origins of His Evil* (Philadelphia: Da Capo Press, 1998), preface and afterword by Ron Rosenbaum, 2014.

44. Gitta Sereny, *Cries Unheard: Why Children Kill: The Story of Mary Bell* (New York: Metropolitan Books, 1999), 339.

killed a four-year-old boy and then a three-year-old boy.[45] *Cries Unheard* is an examination of Mary Bell's background, painstakingly reconstructed in conversations between Sereny and her subject-collaborator thirty years after the crime. The two of them together present a story of moral accountability held in tandem with a hope for redemption. Mary's unwavering insistence on her own guilt is extraordinary; she refuses to excuse it by referring to her own "cries unheard" during the atrocities perpetrated on her by her own mother. *"Nothing can justify* [note the word] *what I did,"* she says to Sereny. *"Nothing."*

Sereny observes: "Nothing can remove it [the guilt] and the sadness for what she has done. . . . She allows herself no mitigation, and in her despair for an answer has repeatedly said, 'There are many unhappy, very disturbed kids out there who don't end up robbing families of their children.'"

Gitta Sereny's collaboration with Mary Bell serves a summary purpose here as we approach the end of this book. "Nothing can justify what I did. Nothing." Notice the use of the word "justify" — *dikaioo.* There is absolutely nothing that can be done from this sphere of reality that can overcome horrors and rectify — make right — everything that has been wrong. Yet this is precisely what is promised by the *dikaiosyne theou,* the righteousness and justice of God.

Penultimate Judgment, Ultimate Rectification?

There is certainly a strong thread of condemnation for the ungodly throughout the New Testament; one could hardly miss it.[46] Clearly this is meant to be taken with utmost seriousness. Often overlooked, however, is a counterthread, one that seems to suggest that the number of those who will inherit Christ's redemption is equal to the number who have inherited Adam's fall (I Cor. 15:21-22; II Cor. 5:14-15; Rom. 5:15-19). Throughout the authentic letters of Paul, there is a dialectic between judgment upon intractable sin and a larger redemption that in certain key passages (especially Rom. 11:32) seems to push the margins out toward some sort of universal vision. Joel Marcus has found something along these lines even in the Pastoral Epistles, enlarging a suggestion made in Martin Dibelius's commentary on the Pastorals.[47]

45. Sereny's respected, if controversial, writing career has been noted for its unsentimental analysis of the lives of evildoers.

46. Admittedly, this theme of Scripture has been so thoroughly suppressed in the mainline churches today that only those who actually read the Bible might come across it.

47. Martin Dibelius and Hans Conzelmann, *The Pastoral Epistles,* Hermeneia (Philadelphia: Fortress, 1972), 109. Marcus comments on the hymn-like passage in II Tim. 2:11: "[The

In II Timothy 2:11-13, a saying appears, with four couplets:

If we have died with him, we shall also live with him;
if we endure, we shall also reign with him;
if we deny him, he also will deny us;
if we are faithless, he remains faithful — for he cannot deny himself.

This unusual passage reverses the three conditional "if-then" couplets by a final, unconditional "because-therefore" one. There is a suggestion of a penultimate judgment taken up into the ultimate faithfulness of God — penultimate judgment in the service of ultimate redemption.[48] This concept is clearly present in the case of the incestuous man in I Corinthians 5:5; he is to be delivered to Satan in order that he may be saved in the day of Christ Jesus.[49]

A Power from Somewhere Else

"With men it is impossible, but not with God; for all things are possible with God." This saying of Jesus, which appears in all the Synoptic Gospels (Matt. 19:26; Mark 10:27; Luke 18:27), points us emphatically beyond human justice and human forgiveness. Forgiveness is a divine action in which human beings can participate, but a complete remaking of the *kosmos* is an action that can be performed only by God. It is common to hear, in motivational materials, of

---

author] does not want to say anything which diminishes the seriousness of sin, but he is also convinced of God's ultimate victory over human perversity, a victory which he has already begun to display in the justification of the ungodly" (Joel Marcus, unpublished paper in my possession, from "The Paul Group" at Union Theological Seminary circa 1977. Quoted by permission).

48. Dibelius interprets this in terms of "formal recompense" or "formal retaliation" (God's rightful and deserved judgment upon sin) and the coexistent "suppression" by God of that formal retaliation. He underscores his exposition by citing a passage from Qumran that has often been quoted in the context of the righteousness of God: "And I, if I stagger, God's mercies are my salvation forever; if I stumble because of the sin of the flesh, my justification is in the righteousness of God which existed forever" (from the Qumran *Community Rule,* formerly known as *The Manual of Discipline* [1QS 11:11-12]). Ernst Käsemann also quotes this, in his famous essay "The Righteousness of God in Paul," to show that the *dikaiosyne theou* was present before Paul picked it up. Käsemann then adds, "the significance of this statement is for the most part not perceived," which is an understatement, but it is a surprise and an encouragement to see it in the largely legalistic and perfectionist writings of the Jewish apocalyptic sect at Qumran.

49. The use of "flesh" and "spirit" in I Cor. 5:5 does not refer to "body" and "soul" but to *sarx* and *pneuma* in Paul's special usage, referring to the two dominions — Sin and Death versus the Lordship of Christ.

individuals "changing the world." Certainly it is true that certain individuals have helped to change the world. Martin Luther King would be a particularly striking example; yet no person has ever urged more insistently and more steadfastly that he was merely an instrument of the invincible purpose of God. Those who marched and demonstrated with him, repeatedly risking their lives, knew that they, too, were participating in God's plan. Human agents can administer justice, up to a point, and human forgiveness can certainly — and often does — carry with it the power of God. But actual *rectification — making right what has been wrong so that the wrong no longer exists — is impossible for human beings.* The coming of the Day of the Lord (Old Testament), the new creation (Second Isaiah and Paul), the kingdom of God (the Synoptic Gospels), eternal life (John), the new Jerusalem (Revelation) will not be accomplished through human means, but only through the working of God.

The key verse to remember as we begin to develop our final theme is in Romans 4, where Paul sets out Abraham as "the father of us all." The verse that stands out in its uncompromising radicality is 4:17, where Abraham is called into "the presence of the God in whom he believed, who gives life to the dead and *calls into existence the things that do not exist.*"

The significance of this verse cannot be overstated. The African American churches are fond of saying that God makes a way out of no way. That is not just a figure of speech. The God who creates out of nothing was there before we thought of him. The skeptic asks if God exists, but the Holy Scriptures bear witness to the God who was present from before there was such a thing as "existence." We need to hear more of the *aseity* ("being from itself") of God in our churches.[50] What the church needs is a renewal of faith in the God who is not an easily dismissed product of human wishes, longings, and fears but was already God in three persons before there were ever any human beings to ask if there was a god.

> Thus says the Lord . . . :
> "I am the first and I am the last;
>   besides me there is no god.
> Who is like me? Let him proclaim it,
>   let him declare and set it forth before me. . . .
> Fear not, nor be afraid;
>   have I not told you from of old and declared it?" (Isa. 44:6-8)

---

50. The *aseity* of God means that God exists from God's self alone. In classical Christian doctrine, this distinguishes God from all created beings, who must derive their existence from him.

Therefore, we may extrapolate as follows: the God who is able to create out of nothing is able to create faith where there is no faith, righteousness where there is no righteousness, life where there is only the finality of death. By now the reader will readily see the connection between these affirmations and the crucifixion. *On the cross, the disciples' faith was destroyed.* Perfect righteousness was consigned to nothingness by an unholy collusion of the "godly" (the religious establishment) and the "ungodly" (the imperial Gentile authorities). The Giver of eternal life was put to death and consigned to hell.

> But now is Christ risen from the dead. . . . For as in Adam all die, even so in Christ shall all be made alive. (I Cor. 15:20, 22 KJV)

> Thou wilt not leave my soul in hell, neither wilt thou suffer thine Holy One to see corruption. (Acts 2:27 KJV)

A wondrous poem of Christopher Smart, whose life in eighteenth-century London was a sad wreck because of debt and purported mental illness, evokes with surpassing emotion and originality the resurrection of the crucified One as creation *ex nihilo*. Here are the two final verses:

> His enemies had sealed the stone
> As Pilate gave them leave,
> Lest dead and friendless and alone
> He should their skill deceive.

> O Dead arise! O Friendless stand
> By Seraphim adored!
> O Solitude again command
> Your host from heaven restored![51]

The Righting of All Wrongs

In September 2013, to note the fortieth anniversary of the Chilean military coup that inaugurated the brutal regime of General Pinochet, the *New York*

---

51. "Awake, Arise, Lift Up Your Voice," hymn by Christopher Smart (1722-1771), Episcopal Hymnal, #212. It is not clear whether Smart was actually mentally ill or not, but despite his connections in London's literary circles, he was miserably held in both mental asylums and debtor's prisons.

Times ran an article about the political murder of Victor Jara, a Chilean theater director and songwriter, beloved in his country. Being a leftist with a
special concern for the oppressed, he was a victim of the September 11, 1973,
coup. Beaten and tortured, his body was found dumped on the ground with
forty-four bullet wounds. Today, the arena where thousands were held after
the coup is named Victor Jara Stadium, but the officer charged with murdering him lives as an American citizen in Deltona, Florida. Jara's wife has
fought for forty years to get justice, seeking damages for numerous crimes,
including extrajudicial killing and cruel, inhuman, and degrading treatment.
She is very clear that she is not after money. "There's no money that can cure
the damage that has been suffered," she said. After 1973, her life was totally
upturned and taken over by a search for justice that can never, in this life,
be truly fulfilled.[52]

In his study of the righting of wrongs, Miroslav Volf is able to maintain the tension between imperfect human witness in "the present evil
age" (Gal. 1:4) and the completeness of God's final purpose in the last
day. In doing so, he combines the relational and the juridical aspects of
dikaiosis (rectification) in remarkable ways. For example: "The Last Judgment is a social event; it happens not simply to individuals but between
people. Human beings are linked by many ties to neighbors near and far,
both in space and in time. We wrong each other and rightfully have cases
against each other. At the Last Judgment God will settle all these 'cases' —
which involve all offenses against God, too, since any wrongdoing against
a neighbor is also an offense against God. *Ultimately, God will right all
wrongs.*"[53]

The Christian life is lived in the embrace of this promise, which is exponentially more regenerative than either a declaration of pardon or a general amnesty. The Bible begins with the Word of God bringing a world into
being ("and God said, 'Let there be light'; and there was light" — Gen. 1:3),
and everything that follows from Genesis to Revelation proceeds from that
creating power. Only the Word of God, incarnate in Christ, is able to "right
all wrongs" in a new creation. Only through God's final judgment upon Sin
and Death can they be annihilated as though they had never existed. As

52. Pascale Bonnefoy, "Chilean's Family Files Suit in US over His Torture and Death in
'73," *New York Times,* September 5, 2013. U2 recorded a song in 1987 called "One Tree Hill."
It has a biblical, apocalyptic note. The relevant lines are: "Jara sang his song, a weapon in the
hands of love / You know his blood still cries from the ground" (The Joshua Tree, Island Records, 1987). Thanks to Robert Dean for this reference.

53. Miroslav Volf, *The End of Memory: Remembering Rightly in a Violent World* (Grand
Rapids: Eerdmans, 2006), 180, emphasis added.

outlined in the previous chapter, this victory is achieved by God through recapitulation, as Jesus Christ, inhabiting the life of the old Adam from the inside (Rom. 5:12-21), has personally carried humanity "through the Red Sea waters."[54] And, as Paul sums up one of his major themes, "All this is from God" (II Cor. 5:18); in other words, the deliverance of the creation from its bondage (Rom. 8:19-22) through Christ is not a work owing anything to human capability. Because of the old Adam's condition in universal captivity, it all has to be, and has been, accomplished by God alone. Lesslie Newbigin, in one simple but potent sentence, echoes Paul: "The author of our salvation is God."[55]

The Role of Faith and Human Righteousness

Hanging over everything being said about the power of God for salvation are these two questions: What does it mean to believe in Christ as the Savior of the world, the One whose birth, life, crucifixion, and resurrection inaugurated the age to come? What of those who reject him?

There is ample evidence in the New Testament that Jesus himself requires personal commitment from all who would be saved by him — and a world of missionary endeavors is based in the Great Commission (Matt. 28:19) — and that salvation is from Christ alone. The most obvious extrapolation from this is to declare that human beings must come to faith in Christ if they are to be saved. If the wonder and miracle of faith in Christ is dismissed as unnecessary and unimportant, then the dynamic, outgoing, evangelistic pulse of the gospel is negated and Christianity becomes a feeble shadow of itself. There is, however, a further question. How do people come to faith in

---

54. From an Easter hymn, "Come, Ye Faithful, Raise the Strain." Original text by John of Damascus, eighth century. Translation by John Mason Neale (1818-1860). Dietrich Bonhoeffer, in his Nazi prison during Advent, drew strength from the words of hymns he had memorized. A Christmas hymn by Paul Gerhardt has these words, spoken by the Christ child: "Calm your hearts, dear friends; / whatever plagues you, / whatever fails you, / I will restore it all." Bonhoeffer writes, "What does that mean, 'I will restore it all'? Nothing is lost; in Christ all things are taken up, preserved, albeit in transfigured form. . . . Christ brings all this back, indeed, as God intended, without being distorted by sin. The doctrine originating in Ephesians 1:10 of the restoration of all things, *anakephalaiosis — recapitulatio* (Irenaeus), is a magnificent and consummately consoling thought. . . . No one has been able to express this with such simplicity and childlikeness as P. Gerhardt in the words he places in the Christ child's mouth: 'I will restore it all' " (*Letters and Papers from Prison*, ed. Eberhard Bethge, enlarged ed. [New York: Macmillan, 1972], 229-30).

55. Lesslie Newbigin, *Sin and Salvation* (London: SCM, 1956), 56.

Christ? And what might prevent them from coming? Is faith a "work" that, in the end, saves the Christian? This is the struggle Paul has in Romans 9–11 when it is becoming apparent to him that his "kinsmen by race," the Jews, will not come to the faith in any numbers (Rom. 9:3). In these chapters, we see Paul undergoing a titanic inner conflict. The themes that tie together the entire letter to the Romans are those of the righteousness of God and the Lordship of Christ. In the providence and purpose of God, even unbelief can play a role.

This concept of the righteousness of God, with its power to rectify all things unconditionally, rests upon a foundation that can be supplied by any number of major passages in the Old Testament. The story of Noah (Gen. 6–9), the visions in Ezekiel (11:16-20 and 34:11-31), and the new covenant passage in Jeremiah (31:31-34) can be seen to point the way ahead. In each of these sources, the wrath of God is present in terror, in judgment, and in devastation; yet it is transcendently clear that God's punitive actions are *in the service of his salvation*. The Noachic covenant precedes both the Abrahamic and Mosaic covenants in its sweeping promise to "every living creature of all flesh that is upon the earth" (Gen. 9:16). Even though "the imagination of man's heart is evil from his youth" (8:21), God nevertheless makes his "everlasting covenant" in the sign of the rainbow (9:16).[56] Jeremiah also knows that God's people

> "have no understanding.
> They are skilled in doing evil,
>   but how to do good they know not." (Jer. 4:22)

Yet his prophecy is unconditional in its promise of a new covenant that is not like "my covenant which they broke," but will be written in their hearts (Jer. 31:31-32).

Ezekiel in particular, though little read or studied in the mainline churches, is an astonishing book. To be sure, its more lurid scenes are hard to take if read literally. However, the pictorial and literary imagery of the book, harsh as it often is, drives the essential theological message, breathtaking in its scope and in its utter commitment to the righteousness of God and its power to make all things new. God's people are "condemned into redemption."[57] The dry bones passage (Ezek. 37:1-14) is the most well-known, but

---

56. The Abrahamic covenant is in Gen. 12:2-3; the Mosaic covenant is found in Deut. 5 and 29.

57. William Shakespeare, *All's Well That Ends Well.*

it loses much of its stunning impact when it is taken out of its context. Only in its setting of wholesale judgment on the people for their apostasy and faithlessness does the resurrection of the dry bones fully display the power of the Spirit of God — for these bones are not just dead, they are *dead in sin*. Interspersed with Ezekiel's prophecies of God's vengeance, the refrain is heard: "A new heart I will give you, and a new spirit I will put within you; and I will take out of your flesh the heart of stone and give you a heart of flesh. And I will put my spirit within you, and cause you to walk in my statutes and be careful to observe my ordinances. . . . You shall be my people, and I will be your God" (Ezek. 36:26-28). Throughout the forty-eight chapters of Ezekiel this note is sounded: God himself is able to remake the hearts of his people, and he promises unconditionally to do so irrespective of their (luxuriantly described) apostasy.

This does not mean that God simply "forgives and forgets" sin. What God says in Jeremiah 31:34 — "I will forgive their iniquity, and I will remember their sin no more" — needs to be understood according to the Old Testament concept of "remember." It does not mean "to put out of mind," which is beyond possibility for humans. Remembrance, in biblical terms, is the action of God. When, in prayer, God is asked to "remember" someone, the plea is that God will take action on behalf of that person. Reading Jeremiah 31:34 through Paul means that God will take action to rectify his people's wholesale violation of his commandments by breaking the bonds of Sin, and to obliterate not only the consequences of Sin but also the memory of it, so as to consign the activity of the evil Powers permanently to its proper status of nonexistence. The unrepentant monsters of history who, like Pol Pot, died peacefully in their beds will be either utterly transfigured or annihilated altogether, for no one is beyond the reach of God's power.

> "Remember not the former things,
>   nor consider the things of old.
> Behold, I am doing a new thing." (Isa. 43:18-19)

This is rectification: God in his righteousness will make right all that has been wrong. This is the very promise of God that the "former things" will be obliterated and no memory of them will remain. And here is the staggering irony: all this is accomplished in the death of Jesus Christ by crucifixion, the method that was especially designed to erase the memory of its victims as though they had never existed.

Such is the power of the God who raises the dead.

Jacob and Esau as Archetypes of God's Purpose in Romans 9–11

Early on in these pages, we flagged the story of the two brothers Jacob and Esau for future reference.[58] In that earlier context, the theme was God's love and care for a man (Esau) he had provisionally rejected. As readers, we find this pleasing, since Esau was abominably treated for no good reason by his mother and by Jacob. However, Paul's reference to Jacob and Esau in Romans 9 pushes the boundaries in a far more radical, more challenging direction. To understand the full ramifications of *dikaiosis* (justification/rectification), we need to grapple with this most audacious part of Paul's gospel.

In Romans 9–11, Paul wrestles intensely with the question of the resistant Jewish community. Was not the Messiah of Israel destined to appear among his own people? Were they not prepared especially to receive him? How then to account for their renunciation of God's anointed? Paul, himself part of the Jewish elite who in a fateful encounter has been commandeered by the Lord, is genuinely agonized that his fellow Jews are not being converted to the gospel. He feels so keenly about this that he, like Moses before him (Exod. 32:32), is ready to put his own salvation on the line (Rom. 9:3).

Remarkably, however, Paul scarcely draws breath before he is lifted out of his distress in contemplation of God's unlimited purposes. As soon as he starts thinking about the Jews and their obduracy, he is led out of despair into rhapsody and self-forgetful praise: "They are Israelites, and to them belong the sonship, the glory, the covenants, the giving of the law, the worship, and the promises; to them belong the patriarchs, and of their race, according to the flesh, is the Christ. God who is over all be blessed for ever. Amen" (Rom. 9:4).[59]

---

58. The essential Jacob-Esau story is found in two parts, Gen. 25:19–28:22 and 32:6–33:17. Paul is working with the narrative typologically. From a purely literary and human perspective, the anguish of Esau when he is deprived of his beloved father's blessing is one of the most emotional portions of the Old Testament. The depiction of the reunion of the brothers in chapter 32 is very moving also.

59. What is the role of the covenant with Israel in Paul's theological perspective? The group of scholars conveniently but somewhat inaccurately championing the "New Perspective on Paul" tend to place great store in the continuity of the covenant with Israel. Yet it is remarkable how rarely Paul refers to God's covenant with Israel in specific terms. It is often argued that it is in the background of his thought all the time; but why then would he rather conspicuously avoid referring to it? This particular passage suggests the place he assigns to it in his overall presentation — he acknowledges "the covenants" (plural *diatheki*) along with other precious gifts of God, but his inclusion of "the giving of the law" suggests his nuanced relationship to them. (One of his very few references to "covenant" is in Christ's words of institution ["this cup is the 'new' covenant in my blood"] in I Cor. 11:25, words that undoubtedly

As he is recalled to the omnipotence of God, Paul continues to work out the challenge of Jewish unbelief from another perspective. He shows how the promise to Abraham has been enlarged to bring in those who were previously excluded. In Romans 9, the "children of the flesh" are the legitimate descendants of Abraham, and the "children of the promise" are the illegitimate Gentiles: "But it is not as though the word of God had failed. . . . It is not the children of the flesh who are the children of God, but the children of the promise are reckoned as descendants" (Rom. 9:6, 8).

Then we meet Jacob and Esau once again. Paul is actually quoting not Genesis, where the original Jacob-Esau story appears, but none other than our friend Malachi, who speaks of God's doom upon Esau, who has been exiled "beyond the border of Israel" (Mal. 1:5). To be sure, Paul's midrashic use of Malachi 1:2-3 is freewheeling by the standards of interpretation today. The apostle takes the passage from the Old Testament prophet and turns it into an eschatological declaration having little to do with the way Malachi uses it. In spite of this apparent interpretive liberty, however, Paul's locating of Jacob and Esau in the apocalyptic scenario is not altogether against the spirit of the book of Malachi, which projects a distinctly transnational image of the reign of God (Mal. 1:11, 14b), and — as noted above — closes the canonical Old Testament with an evocation of "the day when I [the Lord] act."

What Paul is grappling with here is the whole notion of a sharp division between the righteous and the unrighteous, the chosen (Jacob) and the rejected (Esau). Behind this language of election lies Paul's conviction that there is no such ultimate division between persons or groups of persons. Admittedly, the ending of Malachi does seem to posit a clear separation of this sort, for the Lord says, "On the day when I act . . . you shall distinguish between the righteous and the wicked" (Mal. 3:17-18). Once again, even as Paul calls upon Malachi, he is out ahead of us, because he is working within the declaration of Romans 3:10 that "all men, both Jews and Greeks, are under the power of sin." Paul accepts the category of righteous and unrigh-

---

had already become hallowed by use in the very earliest congregations. The very language of "new covenant," sharply distinguished from the old covenant, derives from the very important eschatological passage in Jer. 31:31-34.) Paul typically refers to the *promise* made to Abraham, rather than the *covenant* with Abraham. This usage is notable in Rom. 4 and Gal. 3:18. It seems likely that Paul deliberately chooses to de-emphasize *covenant* in favor of *promise,* in order to accentuate the newness and, more, the discontinuity of what God has done in bringing the entire previous world-order, including that of religion, through crucifixion into resurrection. Though Paul is at pains to claim the Old Testament story, he brings it into the service of the new event of Christ — as in Rom. 4 and 5 and also Gal. 3:6-18 and 4:21-31. The presentation in Rom. 5, which we have discussed thoroughly in two places in this book, is unique to Paul.

teous, godly and ungodly, but — and here is the point — he insists that, as we have seen repeatedly in these pages, *the line runs through each person.*

"Jacob I loved, but Esau I hated." Paul is quoting from Malachi 1:2-3. The context in Malachi seems to suggest that God rejects Esau's people permanently and that this rejection conclusively shows that the Lord is great *"beyond the border of Israel"* (Mal. 1:5). Paul, however, takes this and turns it on its head. The Lord is indeed great beyond the borders of Israel, as Paul's own mission to the Gentiles was dramatically proving, but now the apostle needs to show that the Lord is great *within* the boundary of Israel as well, and he forthrightly declares that this is indeed so: "I ask, then, has God rejected his people? By no means! . . . God has not rejected his people whom he foreknew" (Rom. 11:1-2).

God's Offensive Choices

It is therefore within the context of God's irreversible election of the Jews that the Jacob-Esau dynamic is played out. Paul is struggling to figure out how there might be a divine purpose in the seemingly inexplicable behavior of the Jews. Strange and contradictory as it may seem, unbelief apparently plays a part in the plan of redemption. It is at this point that Paul, with his unique audacity, retrieves numerous baffling passages from the Old Testament that speak of *stubborn resistance occurring precisely within the ultimate purpose of God.* Words derived from Isaiah give the idea:

> "God gave them a spirit of stupor,
> eyes that should not see and ears that should not hear,
> down to this very day." (Rom. 11:8, derived from Isa. 29:10)[60]

60. The commission given to Isaiah by God in chapter 6 is even more explicit than 29:10:
"Go and say to this people:
'Hear and hear, but do not understand;
see and see, but do not perceive.'
Make the heart of this people fat,
    and their ears heavy . . .
lest they see with their eyes
    and hear with their ears." (Isa. 6:9-10)
This passage is quoted in the New Testament five times, more than any other Old Testament text — once in each of the four Gospels, and once in Acts. Yet the actual words of the commission are virtually always omitted from public readings of Isaiah's famous vision in the Jerusalem temple. The idea that God elects some, not all, to faith has always been a strong pill to swallow. Yet many a preacher can testify that when the transcendent moment of saying "Here am I; send

Romans 9–11, once ignored, is now being reconsidered as close to the heart and center of Paul's gospel. In view of the widespread neglect of these chapters in Christian history, this new development in interpretation is extraordinary — and its cause is excruciating to think about, since it was the destruction of Europe's Jews that thrust these chapters back into view. Paul's utterly original inquiry into the relation of Christians and Jews is essential for filling out the picture of the purpose of God for the *un*godly. To begin with, *the godly* in Paul's context would be, precisely, the Jews. It is the Gentiles who are the *un*godly, the *un*spiritual, the *un*righteous. Issuing a spoiler alert, we may say that as Paul's train of thought unfolds to its climax, the term "ungodly" comes to embrace all humanity. The Jacob-Esau dichotomy therefore becomes no dichotomy at all, but a summation of God's dealings with the entire human race in its twinned identity — simultaneously *both* reprobate *and* elect.

Paul continues to spin out his line of thinking. If it is the case that no one is righteous, then what is the meaning of God's seemingly arbitrary choice of one person (Jacob) over another (Esau) when there is no clear reason for this choice? Paul's conclusion to this question, so clearly relevant to the presenting problem of Christians and Jews, has often been overlooked in spite of its crucial importance: it is "in order that God's purpose of election might continue, *not because of works* [since neither had done anything either good or bad] *but because of his call*" (Rom. 9:11).

Paul is moving toward the question of whether God has deliberately chosen the Gentiles to "supplant" Israel.[61] He continues this way: "When Rebecca had conceived children by one man, our forefather Isaac, though they were not yet born and had done nothing either good or bad, . . . she was told, 'The elder will serve the younger.' As it is written, 'Jacob I loved, but Esau I hated'" (Rom. 9:10-13).

Surely this will strike any modern reader as outrageous. But not only the modern reader! Paul has anticipated the protests:

> What shall we say then? Is there injustice on God's part? By no means! For he says to Moses, "I will have mercy on whom I have mercy, and I will have compassion on whom I have compassion." *So it depends not upon man's will or exertion, but upon God's mercy.* For the scripture says to Pharaoh, "I have raised you up for the very purpose of showing my power in

---

me" is past, she must wrestle for the rest of her preaching life with the fact that the good news of Jesus Christ frequently falls on deaf ears.

61. The name Jacob means "one who supplants."

you, so that my name may be proclaimed in all the earth." So then he has mercy upon whomever he wills, and he hardens the heart of whomever he wills. (Rom. 9:14-18)

It is instructive to note how difficult and challenging — indeed, how offensive — this gospel of Paul's has been over the centuries. Many expository preachers and other interpreters have skipped over chapters 9–11 as though they scarcely existed.[62] Moreover, many Christians mistakenly still try to separate the so-called "New Testament God" from the supposedly benighted "Old Testament God." Paul, in contrast, is at pains to show that it is precisely the God of the Hebrew people who is acting in Jesus Christ. The Father of Jesus is the same God who elected Abraham, who showed his power in Pharaoh, who favored Jacob over Esau, who chose Israel out of all the peoples of the earth, who in the fullness of time extended that election and that choice *to the ungodly.*[63]

Paul knows that this radical proclamation of God will be resisted — Americans are not the first to believe in the autonomous human being! Undaunted, he continues:

Who are you, a man, to answer back to God? Will what is molded say to its molder, "Why have you made me thus?" Has the potter no right over the clay, to make out of the same lump one vessel for beauty and another for menial use? What if God, desiring to show his wrath and to make known his power, has endured with much patience the vessels of wrath made for destruction, in order to make known the riches of his glory for the vessels of mercy, which he has prepared beforehand for glory, even us whom he has called, not from the Jews only but also from the Gentiles? (Rom. 9:20-24)

In this whole section, Paul repeatedly warns against self-righteousness. He says things like "do not boast over the branches," "do not become proud, but stand in awe," "lest you be wise in your own conceits" (11:18, 20, 25). The radical leveling of which he has spoken throughout Romans, beginning with

---

62. Alexander McLaren, the great nineteenth-century preacher (a Scot who spent his preaching life in England), is an example. His multivolume collection of expository sermons from the whole Bible includes not one sermon on Rom. 9–11.

63. It is remarkable that Paul never mentions Moses in connection with the covenant (in fact, as we have seen, he hardly mentions the covenant at all). In the analysis of the story of the binding of Isaac, we began to see how Paul goes back to Abraham to make clear that the promise of God was unconditional and not linked to failure under the Law.

1:16 and coming to a provisional climax in 3:22 ("there is no distinction"), is now becoming the center of a vision of the entire *kosmos* transformed by the righteousness of God, the *dikaiosyne theou*.[64]

Paul on the Summit

It takes some imagination, perhaps, to see how in chapters 9–11 Paul is beginning to rise to heights yet unreached, because for generations Christians have been accustomed to thinking of the great summarizing passage at the end of Romans 8 as the climax of the whole letter, not realizing that Paul goes straight on to even greater heights as he challenges the problem of unbelief. Many passages in Paul's letters display his passion for what he is unfolding; that is nowhere more true than here. His argument rises in a crescendo to the conclusion of chapter 11, arguably the most encompassing affirmation in the entire Bible.

What Paul sees and proclaims in all his letters is "the power of God for salvation." He invokes it when he sets out his theme in Romans 1:16-17. It is in Romans 9–11, however, that this theme find its most universal expression. Salvation *(soteria)* in Paul's letters is not to be understood simply in the way that we so often hear it used in American Christianity, as the rescue of first one person, then another, individual by individual, as those persons put their faith in Christ. When the individual is exclusively emphasized, serious theological, ecclesiological, and — not least — geopolitical errors ensue. As Paul develops his message in Romans, the individual Christian does not lose his individual preciousness, but is taken up into the new family of believers and ultimately into the cosmic plan of God. Verse 11:32 is as radically "inclusive" a statement as the Bible contains: "For God has consigned all men to disobedience, that he may have mercy upon all."

Following this utterance, which must have seemed to Paul after his long

---

64. We must approach these passages in Paul's letters (notably Rom. 11) with restraint. He does seem at times to break out into a universal vision that "all" will ultimately be taken up into the life of the eternal age: "As in Adam all die, so also in Christ shall all be made alive" (I Cor. 15:22). Whether this is universal salvation or not, we are unable to say — though we are permitted to hope for it (Karl Barth, *Church Dogmatics* IV/3, 477-78). What is certain is that there will be a conclusive judgment upon Satan and all his works, and a definitive and final separation of good from evil in the City of God: "Behold, the dwelling of God is with men. He will dwell with them, and they shall be his people, and God himself will be with them; he will wipe away every tear from their eyes, and death shall be no more, neither shall there be mourning nor crying nor pain any more, for the former things have passed away" (Rev. 21:3-4).

struggle like a word coming directly from the Creator himself, he seems utterly taken over by a vision beyond human capacity — and perhaps he was aware of this, since he breaks out into doxology as the only possible response to what he has just been led to utter:

> O the depth of the riches and wisdom and knowledge of God! How unsearchable are his judgments and how inscrutable his ways!
>
>> "For who has known the mind of the Lord,
>>   or who has been his counselor?"
>> "Or who has given a gift to him
>>   that he might be repaid?"
>
> For from him and through him and to him are all things. To him be glory for ever. Amen. (Rom. 11:33-36)

Summary

Forgiveness is not enough. Belief in redemption is not enough. Wishful thinking about the intrinsic goodness of every human being is not enough. Inclusion is not a sufficiently inclusive message, nor does it deliver real justice. There are some things — many things — that must be condemned and set right if we are to proclaim a God of both justice and mercy. Only a Power independent of this world order can overcome the grip of the Enemy of God's purposes for his creation.

Jesus Christ, "the heir of all things" (Heb. 1:2), offered himself to be the condemned and rejected Righteous One. Giving himself up in full knowledge — after Gethsemane — of what would happen to him, and in perfect union with his Father, he went to Golgotha carrying his own cross, upon which he was nailed, "despised and rejected by men" (Isa. 53:3). At the historical time and place of his inhuman and godless crucifixion, all the demonic Powers loose in the world convened in Jerusalem and unleashed their forces upon the incarnate Son of God. Derelict, outcast, and godforsaken, he hung there as the representative of all humanity, and suffered condemnation in place of all humanity, to break the Power of Sin and Death over all humanity.

None of this would avail against the world's evil were it not for the righteousness of God, the *dikaiosyne theou*. The power of God to make right what has been wrong is what we see, by faith, in the resurrection of Jesus

Christ on the third day. Unless God is the one who raises the dead and calls into existence the things that do not exist, there cannot be serious talk of forgiveness for the worst of the worst — the mass murders, tortures, and serial killings — or even for the least of the worst — the quotidian offenses against our common humanity that cause marriages to fail, friendships to end, enterprises to collapse, and silent misery to be the common lot of millions. "All for sin could not atone; thou must save, and thou alone." This is what is happening on Golgotha. All the manifold biblical images with their richness, complexity, and depth come together as one to say this: the righteousness of God is revealed in the cross of Christ. The "precious blood" of the Son of God is the perfect sacrifice for sin; the ransom is paid to deliver the captives; the gates of hell are stormed; the Red Sea is crossed and the enemy drowned; God's judgment has been executed upon Sin; the disobedience of Adam is recapitulated in the obedience of Christ; a new creation is coming into being; those who put their trust in Christ are incorporated into his life; the kingdoms of "the present evil age" are passing away and the promised kingdom of God is manifest not in triumphalist crusades, but in the cruciform witness of the church. From within "Adam's" (our) human flesh, the incarnate Son fought with and was victorious over Satan — on our behalf and in our place. Only this power, this transcendent victory won by the Son of God, is capable of reorienting the *kosmos* to its rightful Creator. This is what the righteousness of God has achieved through the cross and resurrection, is now accomplishing by the power of the Spirit, and will complete in the day of Christ Jesus.

And Finally

The greater part of the discussion in these pages has focused upon the communal, corporate, and cosmic significance of the cross of Jesus Christ. However, let no reader think that the apocalyptic and universal dimensions of the gospel message leave no place for the faith and confidence of the individual believer. Several times in this book the reader has encountered an intimately personal testimony by the apostle Paul in his letter to the church in Galatia. For writer and readers alike, these words can be our heart's comfort and joy, for now and for all the days to come, whatever befalls: "I have been crucified with Christ; it is no longer I who live, but Christ who lives in me; and the life I now live in the flesh I live by faith in the Son of God, who loved me and gave himself for me" (Gal. 2:20).

The author of this volume concludes by making this confession together with Christopher Smart:

Awake, arise, lift up your voice,
let Easter music swell;
rejoice in Christ, again rejoice
and on his praises dwell.

Oh, with what gladness and surprise
the saints their Savior greet;
nor will they trust their ears and eyes
but by his hands and feet,
those hands of liberal love indeed
in infinite degree,
those feet still free to move and bleed

for millions,

and for me.[65]

Amen.

---

65. Hymn by Christopher Smart (1722-1771), final five words separated and italicized for emphasis.

Bibliography

For commentaries on specific books of the Bible, see pages 631-35.

Achebe, Chinua. "An Image of Africa: Racism in Conrad's 'Heart of Darkness.'" *Massachusetts Review* 18 (1977).

Achtemeier, Elizabeth. "Righteousness in the Old Testament." In *The Interpreter's Dictionary of the Bible.* New York: Abingdon, 1962.

Achtemeier, Paul. "Righteousness of God in the New Testament." In *The Interpreter's Dictionary of the Bible.* New York: Abingdon, 1962.

Adams, James Rowe, ed. *The Essential Reference Book for Biblical Metaphors: From Literal to Literary.* 2nd ed. Dallas: Word, 2008.

Adams, Marilyn McCord. *Horrendous Evils and the Goodness of God.* Ithaca, N.Y.: Cornell University Press, 1999.

Adams, Marilyn McCord, and Robert Merrihew Adams, eds. *The Problem of Evil.* Oxford: Oxford University Press, 1990.

Alison, James. *Knowing Jesus.* Springfield, Ill.: Templegate, 1994.

———. *The Joy of Being Wrong: Original Sin through Easter Eyes.* New York: Crossroad, 1998.

———. *Raising Abel: The Recovery of the Eschatological Imagination.* New York: Crossroad, 2000.

Allison, Dale. *The End of the Ages Has Come: An Early Interpretation of the Passion and Resurrection of Jesus.* Philadelphia: Fortress, 1985.

———. *Studies in Matthew: Interpretation Past and Present.* Grand Rapids: Baker Academic, 2005.

———. *Reconstructing Jesus: Memory, Imagination, and History.* Grand Rapids: Baker, 2010.

Allison, FitzSimons. *The Rise of Moralism.* London: SPCK, 1966.

Améry, Jean. *At the Mind's Limits: Contemplations by a Survivor on Auschwitz and Its Realities.* Bloomington: Indiana University Press, 1980.

Andrewes, Lancelot. *Ninety-six Sermons of the Right Honourable and Reverend Father in*

God, Lancelot Andrewes. Oxford and London: James Parker and Co., 1832. Available online at https://archive.org/details/ninetysixsermono202andrgoog.

Anselm of Canterbury. *The Prayers and Meditations of Saint Anselm with the Proslogion.* London: Penguin Books, 1973.

―――. *St. Anselm, Basic Writings.* Translated by S. N. Deane. La Salle, Ill.: Open Court, 1974.

Antwi, Daniel J. "Did Jesus Consider His Death to Be an Atoning Sacrifice?" *Interpretation* 45 (January 1991).

Aquinas. Thomas. *The Sermon-Conferences of St. Thomas Aquinas on the Apostles' Creed.* Edited and translated by Nicholas R. Ayo, C.S.C. Eugene, Ore.: Wipf and Stock, 1988.

Ash, Timothy Garton. "The Truth about Dictatorship." *New York Review of Books,* February 19, 1998.

Athanasius. *On the Incarnation.* Crestwood, N.Y.: St. Vladimir's Orthodox Theological Seminary, 1953-1978.

―――. *Orations against the Arians.* Cambridge Library Collection. Cambridge: Cambridge University Press, 2014.

Auden, W. S. *Selected Poems.* Edited by Edward Mendelson. Expanded 2nd ed. New York: Vintage Books, 2007.

Augustine. *Confessions and Enchiridion.* Edited by Albert Cook Outler. Library of Christian Classics. Philadelphia: Westminster, 1955.

―――. *On Grace and Free Will* and *On Forgiveness of Sins, and Baptism.* In Select Library of the Nicene and Post-Nicene Fathers of the Christian Church, edited by Philip Schaff, ser. 1, vol. 5. Grand Rapids: Eerdmans, 1971.

―――. *The City of God* and *On Christian Doctrine.* In Select Library of the Nicene and Post-Nicene Fathers of the Christian Church, edited by Philip Schaff, ser. 1, vol. 2. Grand Rapids: Eerdmans, 1973.

Aulén, Gustav. *Christus Victor: An Historical Study of the Three Main Types of the Idea of the Atonement.* Foreword by Jaroslav Pelikan. New York: Macmillan, 1969; orig. 1931.

Balthasar, Hans Urs von. *Dare We Hope "That All Men Be Saved"? With a Short Discourse on Hell.* San Francisco: Ignatius, 1988.

―――. *Theo-Drama: Theological Dramatic Theory.* San Francisco: Ignatius, 1994.

―――. *Mysterium Paschale: The Mystery of Easter.* San Francisco: Ignatius, 2000; orig. German ed., *Theologie der Drei Tage,* 1970.

Banks, Robert, ed. *Reconciliation and Hope: New Testament Essays on Atonement and Eschatology.* Grand Rapids: Eerdmans, 1974.

Barmen Theological Declaration (1934): The Book of Confessions, Study Edition. Louisville: Geneva, 1999.

Barrett, C. K. "New Testament Eschatology." *Scottish Journal of Theology* 6 (1953): 136-55, 225-43.

Barth, Karl. *Church Dogmatics.* 13 vols. Edinburgh: T. & T. Clark, 1956-1975.

―――. *Dogmatics in Outline.* New York: Harper Torchbooks, 1959.

―――. *Fides Quaerens Intellectum: Anselm's Proof of the Existence of God in the Context of His Theological Scheme.* London: SCM, 1960; German orig. 1930.

———. *Learning Jesus Christ through the Heidelberg Catechism.* Grand Rapids: Eerdmans, 1964.

———. *Deliverance to the Captives.* First paperback ed. New York: Harper and Row, 1978.

Barth, Markus. *Justification.* Grand Rapids: Eerdmans, 1971.

Bartlett, Anthony W. *Cross Purposes: The Violent Grammar of Christian Atonement.* Harrisburg, Pa.: Trinity, 2001.

Beker, J. Christiaan. *Paul the Apostle: The Triumph of God in Life and Thought.* Philadelphia: Fortress, 1980.

———. *Paul's Apocalyptic Gospel: The Coming Triumph of God.* Philadelphia: Fortress, 1982.

———. *Suffering and Hope: The Biblical Vision and the Human Predicament.* Philadelphia: Fortress, 1987.

Belhar Declaration of 1986. www.pcusa.org/resource/belhar-confession/.

Bell, Daniel. *The Economy of Desire: Christianity and Capitalism in a Postmodern World.* Grand Rapids: Baker Academic, 2012.

Berkhof, Hendrikus. *Christ and the Powers.* Translated by John Howard Yoder. Scottdale, Pa.: Herald, 1962.

Berkhof, Louis. *Systematic Theology.* Grand Rapids: Eerdmans, 1996.

Berkouwer, G. C. *Sin.* Grand Rapids: Eerdmans, 1971.

———. *The Work of Christ.* Grand Rapids: Eerdmans, 1980.

Bernard of Clairvaux. *Life and Works of Saint Bernard, Abbot of Clairvaux.* Translated and edited by Samuel J. Eales. London: John Hodges, 1896.

Bethge, Eberhard. *Dietrich Bonhoeffer: Man of Vision, Man of Courage.* New York: Harper and Row, 1970.

Black, C. Clifton. "The Persistence of the Wounds." In *Lament: Reclaiming Practices in Pulpit, Pew, and Public Square.* Louisville: Westminster John Knox, 2005.

Bloesch, Donald G. *Essentials of Evangelical Theology.* 2 vols. Peabody, Mass.: Hendrickson, 1978.

———. *Jesus Christ: Savior and Lord.* Carlisle: Paternoster, 1997.

Blumhardt, Johann Christoph, and Christoph Blumhardt. *Thy Kingdom Come: A Blumhardt Reader.* Edited by Vernard Eller. Grand Rapids: Eerdmans, 1980.

Bockmuehl, Markus, ed. *The Cambridge Companion to Jesus.* Cambridge: Cambridge University Press, 2001.

Boff, Leonardo. *Passion of Christ, Passion of the World.* Maryknoll, N.Y.: Orbis, 1987.

Bonhoeffer, Dietrich. *Life Together.* New York: Harper and Row, 1954.

———. *Ethics.* Edited by Eberhard Bethge. New York: Macmillan, 1955.

———. *Christ the Center.* New York: Harper and Row, 1960.

———. *The Communion of Saints: A Dogmatic Inquiry into the Sociology of the Church.* New York: Harper and Row, 1963.

———. *The Cost of Discipleship.* New York: Macmillan, 1963.

———. *No Rusty Swords.* Fontana Library. New York: Harper and Row, 1970.

———. *Letters and Papers from Prison.* Edited by Eberhard Bethge. Enlarged ed. New York: Macmillan, 1972.

Bornkamm, Günther. *Jesus of Nazareth.* New York: Harper and Row, 1960.

————. *Early Christian Experience.* New York: Harper and Row, 1969.

————. *Paul.* New York: Harper and Row, 1971.

Braaten, Carl E., and Robert W. Jenson, eds. *Sin, Death, and the Devil.* Grand Rapids: Eerdmans, 2000.

Branch, Taylor. *Parting the Waters: America in the King Years, 1954-63.* New York: Simon and Schuster, 1988.

————. *Pillar of Fire: America in the King Years, 1963-65.* New York: Simon and Schuster, 1998.

————. *At Canaan's Edge: America in the King Years, 1965-68.* New York: Simon and Schuster, 2006.

Bright, John. *A History of Israel.* Philadelphia: Westminster, 1972.

Brock, Rita Nakashima, and Rebecca Ann Parker. *Proverbs of Ashes: Violence, Redemptive Suffering, and the Search for What Saves Us.* Boston: Beacon Press, 2001.

Brown, Alexandra R. *The Cross and Human Transformation: Paul's Apocalyptic Word in I Corinthians.* Minneapolis: Fortress, 1995.

Brown, Joanna Carlson, and Carole R. Bohn, eds. *Christianity, Patriarchy, and Abuse: A Feminist Critique.* New York: Pilgrim Press, 1989.

Brown, Peter. *Augustine of Hippo: A Biography.* New edition, with epilogue. Berkeley: University of California Press, 2000.

Brown, Raymond E. *The Birth of the Messiah: A Commentary on the Infancy Narratives in the Gospels of Matthew and Luke.* Garden City, N.Y.: Doubleday, 1977.

————. *The Death of the Messiah: From Gethsemane to the Grave; A Commentary on the Passion Narratives in the Four Gospels.* 2 vols. Garden City, N.Y.: Doubleday, 1994.

————. *Introduction to the New Testament.* New York: Doubleday, 1997.

Brown, Robert McAfee. *Making Peace in the Global Village.* Philadelphia: Westminster, 1981.

Brown, Sally A., and Patrick D. Miller, eds. *Lament: Reclaiming Practices in Pulpit, Pew, and Public Square.* Louisville: Westminster John Knox, 2005.

Bruce, F. F. "Justification by Faith in the Non-Pauline Writings of the New Testament." *Evangelical Quarterly* 24 (1952): 66-77.

Browning, Christopher R. *Ordinary Men: Reserve Police Battalion 101 and the Final Solution in Poland.* 2nd paperback ed. with afterword. New York: HarperPerennial, 1998.

Bultmann, Rudolf. *Theology of the New Testament.* 2 vols. New York: Scribner, 1951, 1955.

Buruma, Ian. "Who Did Not Collaborate?" *New York Review of Books,* February 24, 2011.

————. "From Tenderness to Savagery in Seconds." *New York Review of Books,* October 13, 2011.

————. "The Hell of Victory." *New York Review of Books,* November 24, 2011.

Calvin, John. *Institutes of the Christian Religion.* Edited by John T. McNeill. Translated by Ford Lewis Battles. Library of Christian Classics. Philadelphia: Westminster, 1960.

————. *Calvin's Commentaries.* Edited by David W. Torrance and Thomas F. Torrance. Translated by William B. Johnston. Grand Rapids: Eerdmans, 1963.

Cameron, J. M. "A Good Read." *New York Review of Books,* April 15, 1982.

Campbell, Douglas. *The Deliverance of God: An Apocalyptic Rereading of Justification in Paul.* Grand Rapids: Eerdmans, 2009.

Campbell, Will D. *And Also with You: Duncan Gray and the American Dilemma.* Franklin, Tenn.: Providence House Publishers, Tennessee Heritage Library, 1997.

Campbell, Will D., and James Y. Holloway. *Up to Our Steeples in Politics.* New York: Paulist, 1970.

Camus, Albert. *The Fall.* Translated by Justin O'Brien. New York: Knopf, 1956.

Capon, Robert Farrer. *The Parables of Grace.* Grand Rapids: Eerdmans, 1988.

Chang, Iris. *The Rape of Nanking: The Forgotten Holocaust of World War II.* New York: Penguin Books, 1998.

Charry, Ellen. *By the Renewing of Your Minds: The Pastoral Function of Christian Doctrine.* New York: Oxford University Press, 1997.

Chartres, Caroline, ed. *Why I Am Still an Anglican.* London: Continuum, 2006.

Childs, Brevard. *Introduction to the Old Testament as Scripture.* Philadelphia: Fortress, 1979.

————. *The New Testament as Canon: An Introduction.* Philadelphia: Fortress, 1984.

————. *Biblical Theology of the Old and New Testaments: Theological Reflection on the Christian Bible.* Minneapolis: Fortress, 1993.

————. *The Struggle to Understand Isaiah as Christian Scripture.* Grand Rapids: Eerdmans, 2004.

Chopp, Rebecca S. *The Praxis of Suffering: An Interpretation of Liberation and Political Theologies.* Maryknoll, N.Y.: Orbis, 1986.

Collins, John J. *The Apocalyptic Imagination: An Introduction to Jewish Apocalyptic Literature.* 2nd ed. Grand Rapids: Eerdmans, 1998.

Cousar, Charles B. *A Theology of the Cross: The Death of Jesus in the Pauline Letters.* Overtures to Biblical Theology. Minneapolis: Augsburg Fortress, 1990.

Culpeper, Robert H. *Interpreting the Atonement.* Grand Rapids: Eerdmans, 1966.

Dabney, Robert L. *Christ Our Penal Substitute.* Richmond, Va.: Presbyterian Committee of Publication, 1898.

Dalai Lama [Tenzin Gyatso]. *The Transformed Mind: Reflections on Truth, Love, and Happiness.* London: Hodder and Stoughton, 2000.

————. *The Essential Dalai Lama: His Important Teachings.* Edited by Rajiv Mehrotra. New York: Viking, 2005.

————. *Essential Writings.* Edited by Thomas A. Forster. Modern Spiritual Masters Series. Maryknoll, N.Y.: Orbis, 2008.

————. *Becoming Enlightened.* Edited and translated by Jeffrey Hopkins. New York: Atria Books, 2009.

Dalai Lama, with Howard C. Cutler. *The Art of Happiness: A Handbook for Living.* New York: Riverhead Books, 1998.

Dale, R. W. *The Atonement.* London: Congregational Union of England and Wales, 1875; 7th ed. 1878; 26th ed. 1914.

Dallaire, Roméo. *Shake Hands with the Devil: The Failure of Humanity in Rwanda.* Toronto: Random House Canada, 2003.

Danner, Mark. *The Massacre at El Mozote: A Parable of the Cold War.* New York: Vintage, 1994. Originally constituting the entire issue of the *New Yorker,* December 6, 1993, as "The Truth of El Mozote."

———. "Rumsfeld's War and Its Consequences Now." *New York Review of Books,* December 19, 2013.

———. "Rumsfeld: Why We Live in His Ruins." *New York Review of Books,* February 6, 2014.

———. "In the Darkness of Dick Cheney." *New York Review of Books,* March 6, 2014.

———. "Cheney: 'The More Ruthless the Better.'" *New York Review of Books,* May 8, 2014.

Davis, Ellen F. "Reading Leviticus in the Church." *Virginia Seminary Journal* (Winter 1996-1997).

Davis, Joshua B., and Douglas Harink, eds. *Apocalyptic and the Future of Theology: With and Beyond J. Louis Martyn.* Eugene, Ore.: Cascade, 2012.

Day, Dorothy. *The Duty of Delight: The Diaries of Dorothy Day.* Edited by Robert Ellsberg. Milwaukee: Marquette University Press, 2008.

De Boer, Martinus C. "Paul and Jewish Apocalyptic Eschatology." In *Apocalyptic and the New Testament: Essays in Honor of J. Louis Martyn,* edited by Joel Marcus and M. L. Soards, 169-90. Sheffield: JSOT, 1989.

———. "Paul, Theologian of God's Apocalypse." *Interpretation* (January 2002).

Delbanco, Andrew. *The Death of Satan: How Americans Have Lost the Sense of Evil.* New York: Farrar, Straus and Giroux, 1995.

Denney, James. *The Death of Christ.* Edited by R. V. Tasker. London: Tyndale Press, 1951; orig. 1902.

Dillistone, F. W. *The Christian Understanding of Atonement.* Philadelphia: Westminster, 1968.

Diognetus, Epistle to. In *Early Christian Fathers,* edited by Cyril C. Richardson. Library of Christian Classics. Philadelphia: Westminster, 1953.

Donne, John. *The Sermons of John Donne.* Edited by George R. Potter and Evelyn M. Simpson. 10 vols. Berkeley: University of California Press, 1953-1962.

Dostoevsky, Fyodor. *The Brothers Karamazov.* Translated by Richard Pevear and Larissa Volokhonsky. New York: Farrar, Straus and Giroux, 1990.

Douglas, Ann. *The Feminization of American Culture.* New York: Noonday Press/Farrar, Straus and Giroux, 1998; orig. 1977.

Duff, Nancy J. "Pauline Apocalyptic and Theological Ethics." In *Apocalyptic and the New Testament,* edited by Joel Marcus and Marion L. Soards. Sheffield: Sheffield Academic Press, 1989.

———. "Atonement and the Christian Life: Reformed Doctrine from a Feminist Perspective." *Interpretation* 53, no. 1 (January 1999).

Duffy, Eamon. "A Deadly Misunderstanding." *New York Review of Books,* July 5, 2001.

Dunn, J. D. G. "Paul's Understanding of the Death of Jesus." In *Reconciliation and Hope: New Testament Essays on Atonement and Eschatology,* edited by Robert Banks. Grand Rapids: Eerdmans, 1974.

———. "The New Perspective on Paul: Paul and the Law." In *The Romans Debate,* edited by Karl P. Donfried. Revised and expanded ed. Peabody, Mass.: Hendrickson, 1991.

———. *The Theology of Paul the Apostle.* Grand Rapids: Eerdmans, 1998.

Elliott, Neil. "The Anti-Imperial Message of the Cross." In *Paul and Empire: Religion and Power in Roman Imperial Society,* edited by Richard Horsley, 167-83. Harrisburg, Pa: Trinity, 2000.

———. *The Arrogance of Nations: Reading Romans in the Shadow of Empire.* Minneapolis: Fortress, 2008.

Ellis, Peter F. *Seven Pauline Letters.* Collegeville, Minn.: Liturgical Press, 1982.

Fairweather, Eugene, ed. *A Scholastic Miscellany: Anselm to Ockham.* New York: Macmillan, 1970.

Farrer, Austin. *Saving Belief.* New York: Morehouse-Barlow, 1964.

Fenn, Richard K. *Beyond Idols: The Shape of a Secular Society.* New York: Oxford University Press, 2001.

Ffrench-Beytagh, Gonville Aubie. *Encountering Darkness.* London: William Collins Sons and Co., 1973.

Fiddes, Paul S. *Past Event and Present Salvation: The Christian Idea of Atonement.* Louisville: Westminster John Knox, 1989.

Flew, Antony, and Alasdair MacIntyre, eds. *New Essays in Philosophical Theology.* American paperback ed. New York: Macmillan, 1964.

Forde, Gerhard O. *On Being a Theologian of the Cross: Reflections on Luther's Heidelberg Disputation, 1518.* Grand Rapids: Eerdmans, 1997.

———. "Caught in the Act: Reflections on the Work of Christ." *Word and World* 3, no. 1 (Winter 1983): 22-31.

Forsyth, P. T. *The Work of Christ.* Eugene, Ore.: Wipf and Stock, 1996.

Fortna, Robert, and Beverly R. Gaventa, eds. *The Conversation Continues: Studies in Paul and John in Honor of J. Louis Martyn.* Nashville: Abingdon, 1990.

Fretheim, Terence E. *The Suffering of God: An Old Testament Perspective.* Overtures to Biblical Theology. Philadelphia: Fortress, 1984.

Frye, Northrop. *The Great Code: The Bible and Literature.* New York: Harcourt Brace Jovanovich, 1982.

Fuller, Reginald H. *The Mission and Achievement of Jesus: An Examination of the Presuppositions of New Testament Theology.* London: SCM, 1954.

———. *Interpreting the Miracles.* London: SCM, 1963.

———. *A Critical Introduction to the New Testament.* London: Duckworth, 1966.

Furnish, Victor. *Theology and Ethics in Paul.* Nashville: Abingdon, 1968.

Gathercole, Simon. "What Did Paul Really Mean?" *Christianity Today,* August 2007. Online at http://www.christianitytoday.com/ct/2007/august/13.22.html.

Gaventa, Beverly R. "You Proclaim the Lord's Death: I Corinthians 11:26 and Paul's Understanding of Worship." *Review and Expositor* 80 (1983): 380.

———. "Is Galatians Just a 'Guy Thing'?" *Interpretation* 54, no. 3 (July 2000).

———. *Our Mother Saint Paul.* Louisville: Westminster John Knox, 2007.

———, ed. *Apocalyptic Paul: Cosmos and Anthropos in Romans.* Waco: Baylor University Press, 2013.

Gaylin, Willard. *The Killing of Bonnie Garland: A Question of Justice.* New York: Simon and Schuster, 1982.

Girard, René. *The Scapegoat.* Baltimore: Johns Hopkins University Press, 1989.

————. *Violence and the Sacred.* New York: Continuum, 2005.

Goldberg, Michael. *Jews and Christians: Getting Our Stories Straight.* Valley Forge: Trinity, 1991.

Gourevitch, Philip. *We Wish to Inform You That Tomorrow We Will Be Killed with Our Families: Stories from Rwanda.* New York: Farrar, Straus and Giroux, 1998.

Gourevitch, Philip, and Errol Morris. "Exposure: The Woman behind the Camera at Abu Ghraib." *New Yorker,* March 24, 2008.

Green, Joel B. "Crucifixion." In *The Cambridge Companion to Jesus,* edited by Markus Bockmuehl. Cambridge: Cambridge University Press, 2001.

Green, Joel B., and Mark D. Baker. *Recovering the Scandal of the Cross: Atonement in New Testament and Contemporary Contexts.* Downers Grove, Ill.: InterVarsity, 2000.

Gregory of Nyssa. "An Address on Religious Instruction." In *Christology of the Later Fathers,* edited by Edward Rochie Hardy and Cyril C. Richardson. Library of Christian Classics, vol. 3. Philadelphia: Westminster, 1954.

Grieb, A. Katherine. *The Story of Romans: A Narrative Defense of God's Righteousness.* Louisville: Westminster John Knox, 2002.

Grillmeier, Aloys. *Christ in Christian Tradition.* New York: Sheed and Ward, 1965.

Gross, Jan T. *Neighbors: The Destruction of the Jewish Community in Jedwabne, Poland.* Princeton: Princeton University Press, 2001.

Gundry-Volf, Judith. "Expiation, Propitiation, Mercy Seat." In *Dictionary of Paul's Letters,* edited by Gerald F. Hawthorne, Ralph P. Martin, and Daniel G. Reid. Downers Grove, Ill.: InterVarsity, 1993.

Gunton, Colin. *The Actuality of Atonement: A Study of Metaphor, Rationality, and the Christian Tradition.* Grand Rapids: Eerdmans, 1989.

Hall, Douglas John. *Lighten Our Darkness: Toward an Indigenous Theology of the Cross.* Philadelphia: Westminster, 1976. See especially pp. 115-37.

————. *God and Human Suffering: An Exercise in the Theology of the Cross.* Minneapolis: Augsburg, 1989.

Hallie, Philip P. *Lest Innocent Blood Be Shed: The Story of the Village of Le Chambon and How Goodness Happened There.* New York: Harper and Row, 1979.

Harink, Douglas. *Paul among the Postliberals: Pauline Theology beyond Christendom and Modernity.* Grand Rapids: Brazos, 2003.

————. "Setting It Right: Doing Justice to Justification." *Christian Century,* June 14, 2005.

————, ed. *Paul, Philosophy, and the Theopolitical Vision: Critical Engagements with Agamben, Badiou, Žižek, and Others.* Eugene, Ore.: Cascade, 2010.

Hart, David B. "A Gift Exceeding Every Debt: An Eastern Orthodox Appreciation of Anselm's *Cur Deus Homo.*" *Pro Ecclesia* 7, no. 3 (Summer 1998): 330-49.

————. *The Doors of the Sea: Where Was God in the Tsunami?* Grand Rapids: Eerdmans, 2005.

Hauerwas, Stanley. "No Enemy, No Christianity: Theology and Preaching between 'Worlds.'" In *The Future of Theology: Essays in Honor of Jürgen Moltmann,* edited by Miroslav Volf, Carmen Krieg, and Thomas Kucharz. Grand Rapids: Eerdmans, 1996.

————. *With the Grain of the Universe: The Church's Witness and Natural Theology.* Grand Rapids: Brazos, 2001.

————. *Performing the Faith: Bonhoeffer and the Practice of Nonviolence.* Grand Rapids: Brazos, 2004.

Hauerwas, Stanley, and William H. Willimon. *Resident Aliens: Life in the Christian Colony.* Nashville: Abingdon, 1989.

Havel, Václav. *Open Letters: Selected Writings.* New York: Knopf, 1991.

Hays, Richard B. *The Faith of Jesus Christ: The Narrative Substructure of Galatians 3:1–4:11.* 2nd ed. Grand Rapids: Eerdmans, 2002.

————. *The Conversion of the Imagination: Paul as Interpreter of Israel's Scripture.* Grand Rapids: Eerdmans, 2005.

Hengel, Martin. *Crucifixion.* Philadelphia: Fortress, 1977.

————. *Acts and the History of Earliest Christianity.* Philadelphia: Fortress, 1979.

————. *The Atonement: The Origins of the Doctrine in the New Testament.* Philadelphia: Fortress, 1981.

Herbert, George. *The Complete English Poems.* Edited by John Tobin. London: Penguin Books, 1991.

Hersey, John. *Hiroshima.* New York: Vintage Books, 1989. Published in full in the *New Yorker,* August 31, 1946.

Hodge, Charles. *Systematic Theology.* Vol. 2. Grand Rapids: Eerdmans, 1981.

Hooker, Morna D. *Jesus and the Servant: The Influence of the Servant Concept of Deutero-Isaiah in the New Testament.* London: SPCK, 1959.

————. "Interchange in Christ." *Journal of Theological Studies* 22 (1971): 349-61.

————. "Interchange and Atonement." *Bulletin of the John Rylands University Library of Manchester* 60 (1978): 462-81.

————. *Not Ashamed of the Gospel: New Testament Interpretations of the Death of Christ.* Grand Rapids: Eerdmans, 1994.

Hultgren, Arland J. *Paul's Gospel and Mission: The Outlook from the Letter to the Romans.* Philadelphia: Fortress, 1985.

————. *Christ and His Benefits: Christology and Redemption in the New Testament.* Philadelphia: Fortress, 1987.

Hunsinger, George. *Disruptive Grace: Studies in the Theology of Karl Barth.* Grand Rapids: Eerdmans, 2000.

Hurtado, Larry W. *Lord Jesus Christ: Devotion to Jesus in Earliest Christianity.* Grand Rapids: Eerdmans, 2003.

————. *How on Earth Did Jesus Become a God? Historical Questions about Earliest Devotion to Jesus.* Grand Rapids: Eerdmans, 2005.

Husbands, Mark, and Daniel J. Treier, eds. *Justification: What's at Stake in the Current Debates?* Downers Grove, Ill.: InterVarsity, 2004.

Irenaeus. *Against Heresies.* Ante-Nicene Fathers, vol. 1. Grand Rapids: Eerdmans, 1987.

————. *On the Apostolic Preaching.* Popular Patristics Series. Crestwood, N.Y.: St. Vladimir's Seminary Press, 1997.

Jenson, Robert. *Systematic Theology.* Vol. 1, *The Triune God.* New York: Oxford University Press, 1997.

———. *Systematic Theology*. Vol. 2, *The Works of God*. New York: Oxford University Press, 1999.

Jersak, Brad, and Michael Hardin, eds. *Stricken by God? Nonviolent Identification and the Victory of Christ*. Grand Rapids: Eerdmans, 2007.

Jervis, L. Ann. *At the Heart of the Gospel: Suffering in the Earliest Christian Message*. Grand Rapids: Eerdmans, 2007.

John of Damascus. *Exposition of the Orthodox Faith*. In Select Library of Nicene and Post-Nicene Fathers, edited by Philip Schaff and Henry Wace, ser. 2, vol. 9. Grand Rapids: Eerdmans, 1973.

Judt, Tony. "The 'Problem of Evil' in Postwar Europe." *New York Review of Books*, February 14, 2008.

Julian of Norwich. *Revelations of Divine Love*. London: Penguin Books, 1998.

Jüngel, Eberhard. *God as the Mystery of the World: On the Foundation of the Theology of the Crucified One in the Dispute between Theism and Atheism*. Grand Rapids: Eerdmans, 1983.

Kähler, Martin. *The So-Called Historical Jesus and the Historic, Biblical Christ*. Philadelphia: Fortress, 1964.

Käsemann, Ernst. *Jesus Means Freedom*. Philadelphia: Fortress, 1968.

———. *New Testament Questions of Today*. Translated by W. J. Montague. London: SCM, 1969.

———. *Perspectives on Paul*. Philadelphia: Fortress, 1971.

———. *On Being a Disciple of the Crucified Nazarene*. Grand Rapids: Eerdmans, 2011.

Kay, James F. "The Word of the Cross at the Turn of the Ages." *Interpretation* 53 (1999): 44-56.

———. "He Descended into Hell." In *Exploring and Proclaiming the Apostles' Creed*, edited by Roger van Harn, 117-29. Grand Rapids: Eerdmans, 2004.

———. "He Descended into Hell." *Word and World* 31, no. 1 (Winter 2011): 17-21.

Keck, Leander. *Paul and His Letters*. Philadelphia: Fortress, 1979.

———. "Paul and Apocalyptic Theology." *Interpretation* 38, no. 3 (July 1984): 238.

———. *The Church Confident: Christianity Can Repent but It Must Not Whimper*. Nashville: Abingdon, 1993.

Kelly, J. N. D. *Early Christian Doctrines*. New York: Harper and Row, 1959.

Kierkegaard, Søren. *"Fear and Trembling" and "The Sickness unto Death."* Garden City, N.Y.: Doubleday Anchor Book, 1941, 1954; reprinted by arrangement with Princeton University Press.

Kingsbury, Jack Dean. *Matthew: Structure, Christology, Kingdom*. Minneapolis: Fortress, 1991; orig. 1975.

Kittel, G., and Gerhard Friedrich, eds. *Theological Dictionary of the New Testament*. Translated and edited by Geoffrey W. Bromiley. 10 vols. Grand Rapids: Eerdmans, 1965-1976.

Koch, Klaus. *The Rediscovery of Apocalyptic: A Polemical Work on a Neglected Area of Biblical Studies and Its Damaging Effects on Theology and Philosophy*. London: SCM, 1972.

Kovály, Heda Margolius. *Under a Cruel Star: A Life in Prague, 1941-1968*. New York: Holmes and Meier, 1997.

Koyama, Kosuke. *Mount Fuji and Mount Sinai: A Critique of Idols.* London: SCM, 1984.

Krötke, Wolf. *Sin and Nothingness in the Theology of Karl Barth.* Translated by Philip G. Ziegler and Christina-Maria Bammel. Studies in Reformed Theology and History. Princeton: Princeton Theological Seminary, 2005.

Küng, Hans. *Justification: The Doctrine of Karl Barth and a Catholic Reflection.* New York: Nelson, 1964.

―――. *On Being a Christian.* New York: Doubleday, Image Books, 1984.

LaCugna, Catherine Mowry. *God for Us: The Trinity and Christian Life.* San Francisco: HarperSanFrancisco, 1993.

Leech, Kenneth. *The Eye of the Storm: Spiritual Resources for the Pursuit of Justice.* London: Darton, Longman, and Todd, 1992.

―――. *We Preach Christ Crucified.* New York: Church Publishing, 1994.

Lehmann, Paul L. *The Transfiguration of Politics.* New York: Harper and Row, 1975.

―――. *The Decalogue and a Human Future: The Meaning of the Commandments for Making and Keeping Human Life Human.* Introduction by Nancy J. Duff. Grand Rapids: Eerdmans, 1994.

―――. *Ethics in a Christian Context.* Library of Theological Ethics. Louisville: Westminster John Knox, 2006; orig. 1963.

Lelyveld, Joseph. *Move Your Shadow: South Africa, Black and White.* New York: Times Books, 1985.

Levi, Primo. *The Drowned and the Saved.* New York: Vintage Books, 1988.

―――. *Survival in Auschwitz.* New York: Simon and Schuster, Touchstone, 1966. Italian ed. *Se questo è un uomo* ("If this be a man"; also translated "If this is a man").

Lischer, Richard. *The Preacher King: Martin Luther King, Jr., and the Word That Moved America.* Oxford: Oxford University Press, 1995.

Lochman, Jan. *The Faith We Confess: An Ecumenical Dogmatics.* Philadelphia: Fortress, 1984.

Longenecker, Bruce. *Narrative Dynamics in Paul: A Critical Assessment.* Louisville: Westminster John Knox, 2002.

Lose, David. *Confessing Jesus Christ: Preaching in a Postmodern World.* Grand Rapids: Eerdmans, 2003.

Luther, Martin. "The Bondage of the Will," "The Freedom of the Christian," and "Preface to the New Testament." In *Martin Luther: Selections from His Writings,* edited by John Dillenberger. Garden City, N.Y.: Anchor Books, 1961.

Lyttleton, Arthur. "The Atonement." In *Lux Mundi,* edited by Charles Gore. London: John Murray, 1889.

Mackintosh, H. R. *The Christian Experience of Forgiveness.* London: Nisbet, 1927.

Macleod, Donald. *Christ Crucified: Understanding the Atonement.* Downers Grove, Ill.: InterVarsity, 2014.

Macquarrie, John. *Principles of Christian Theology.* New York: Scribner, 1966.

Magill-Cobbler, Thelma. "A Feminist Rethinking of Punishment Imagery in Atonement." *Dialog* 35, no. 1 (Winter 1996).

Mangina, Joseph. "Hans Boersma's Violence, Hospitality, and the Cross." *Scottish Journal of Theology* 61, no. 4 (2008): 494-502.

Mannermaa, Tuomo. *Christ Present in Faith: Luther's View of Justification*. Minneapolis: Augsburg Fortress, 2005.

Manson, T. W. "Hilasterion." *Journal of Theological Studies* 46 (1945): 1-10.

Marcus, Joel, and M. L. Soards, eds. *Apocalyptic and the New Testament: Essays in Honour of J. Louis Martyn*. Sheffield: Sheffield Academic Press, 1989.

Margolius, Ivan. *Reflections of Prague: Journeys through the 20th Century*. Chichester: John Wiley and Sons, 2006.

Marsh, Charles. *God's Long Summer: Stories of Faith and Civil Rights*. Princeton: Princeton University Press, 1997.

Marsh, Charles, and John Perkins. *Welcoming Justice: God's Movement toward Beloved Community*. Downers Grove, Ill.: IVP, 2009.

Marshall, I. Howard. "The Meaning of Reconciliation." In *Unity and Diversity in New Testament Theology*, edited by Robert Allison Guelich. Grand Rapids: Eerdmans, 1978.

Martin, Ralph P. *An Early Christian Confession: Philippians 2:5-11 in Recent Interpretations*. London: Tyndale, 1960.

———. *Reconciliation: A Study of Paul's Theology*. Atlanta: John Knox, 1981.

Martyn, Dorothy. "Compulsion and Liberation: A Theological View." *Union Seminary Quarterly Review* 36, nos. 2-3 (Winter/Spring 1981): 119-29.

———. *The Man in the Yellow Hat: Theology and Psychoanalysis in Child Therapy*. Atlanta: Scholars Press, 1992.

———. *Beyond Deserving: Children, Parents, and Responsibility Revisited*. Grand Rapids: Eerdmans, 2007.

Martyn, J. Louis. "Epistemology at the Turn of the Ages: II Corinthians 5:16." In *Christian History and Interpretation: Studies Presented to John Knox*, edited by W. R. Farmer, C. F. D. Moule, and R. R. Niebuhr. Cambridge: Cambridge University Press, 1967.

———. *Theological Issues in the Letters of Paul*. Nashville: Abingdon, 1997.

———. "The Apocalyptic Gospel in Galatians." *Interpretation* 54, no. 3 (July 2000): 246-66.

———. "De-apocalypticizing Paul: An Essay Focused on *Paul and the Stoics* by Troels Engberg-Pedersen." *Journal for the Study of the New Testament* 86 (2002): 61-102.

———. "*Nomos* Plus Genitive Noun in Paul." In *Early Christianity and Classical Culture: Comparative Studies in Honor of Abraham Malherbe*, edited by John T. Fitzgerald, Thomas H. Olbricht, and L. Michael White. Boston: Brill, 2003.

———. "World without End or Twice-Invaded World?" In *Shaking Heaven and Earth: Essays in Honor of Walter Brueggemann and Charles Cousar*, edited by Christine Roy Yoder et al. Louisville: Westminster John Knox, 2005.

Mathewes-Green, Frederica. "The Meaning of His Suffering." http://www.frederica.com/orthodox/meaning_of_his_suffering.html.

Maurice, F. D. "On the Atonement." In *Theological Essays*. London: Macmillan, 1853.

———. *The Doctrine of Sacrifice Deduced from the Scriptures*. London: Macmillan, 1893.

Mayer, Jane. "The Black Sites." *New Yorker,* August 13, 2007.

McCarthy, Cormac. *Blood Meridian*. New York: Vintage International, 1992.

———. *The Border Trilogy: The Crossing*. New York: Knopf, Everyman's Library, 1999.

McCormack, Bruce L. "For Us and Our Salvation." In *Studies in Reformed Theology and History*, 28-29. Princeton: Princeton Theological Seminary, 1993.

⸻. "What's at Stake in Current Debates over Justification? The Crisis of Protestantism in the West." In *Justification: What's at Stake in the Current Debates?* edited by Mark Husbands and Daniel J. Treier. Downers Grove, Ill.: InterVarsity, 2004.

McDonald, H. D. *The Atonement of the Death of Christ: In Faith, Revelation, and History.* Grand Rapids: Baker, 1985.

McFague, Sallie. *Metaphorical Theology: Models of God in Religious Language.* Philadelphia: Fortress, 1982.

McGrath, Alister. *Iustitia Dei: A History of the Christian Doctrine of Justification.* 2nd ed. Cambridge: Cambridge University Press, 1998.

McKnight, Scot. *A Community Called Atonement.* Nashville: Abingdon, 2007.

Meeks, Wayne. *The First Urban Christians: The Social World of the Apostle Paul.* New Haven: Yale University Press, 1983.

⸻. "On Trusting an Unpredictable God: A Hermeneutical Meditation on Romans 9-11." In *Faith and History: Essays in Honor of Paul W. Meyer,* edited by J. T. Carroll et al., 105-24. Atlanta: Scholars Press, 1990.

Meyendorff, John. *Byzantine Theology: Historical Trends and Doctrinal Themes.* New York: Fordham University Press, 1974.

Meyer, Paul W. "The Worm at the Core of the Apple." In *The Conversation Continues: Studies in Paul and John in Honor of J. Louis Martyn,* edited by Robert T. Fortna and Beverly K. Gaventa. Nashville: Abingdon, 1990.

Michnik, Adam. "Letter from the Gdansk Prison." *New York Review of Books,* July 18, 1985.

⸻. *Letters from Prison and Other Essays.* Berkeley: University of California Press, 1987.

Minear, Paul S. "The Time of Hope in the New Testament." *Scottish Journal of Theology* 6 (1953): 337-61.

⸻. *The Golgotha Earthquake: Three Witnesses.* Cleveland: Pilgrim Press, 1995.

Moberly, R. C. *Atonement and Personality.* London: John Murray, 1901.

Moltmann, Jürgen. *The Crucified God: The Cross of Christ as the Foundation and Criticism of Christian Theology.* New York: Harper and Row, 1973.

Morris, Leon. *The Apostolic Preaching of the Cross.* Grand Rapids: Eerdmans, 1955.

⸻. "The Meaning of *Hilasterion* in Romans 3:25." *New Testament Studies* 2 (1955): 33-43.

Morrow, Lance. *Evil: An Investigation.* New York: Basic Books, 2003.

Morse, Christopher. *Not Every Spirit: A Dogmatics of Christian Disbelief.* New York: Trinity, 1994.

⸻. *The Difference Heaven Makes: Rehearing the Gospel as News.* London: T. & T. Clark/Continuum, 2010.

Moule, C. F. D. "The Energy of God: Rethinking New Testament Atonement Doctrines." Sprigg Lectures, Virginia Theological Seminary, Alexandria, Virginia, March 1-2, 1983. Audiotape.

⸻. "Punishment and Retribution: Delimiting Their Scope in New Testament

Interpretation." In *Stricken by God? Nonviolent Identification and the Victory of Christ,* edited by Brad Jersak and Michael Hardin. Grand Rapids: Eerdmans, 2007.

Nessan, Craig L. "Violence and Atonement." *Dialog* 35, no. 1 (Winter 1996).

Neuhaus, Richard John. *Death on a Friday Afternoon: Meditations on the Last Words of Jesus from the Cross.* New York: Basic Books, 2000.

Newbigin, Lesslie. *Sin and Salvation.* London: SCM, 1956.

———. *The Finality of Christ.* London: SCM, 1969.

———. *The Gospel in a Pluralist Society.* London: SPCK, 1989.

———. *Lesslie Newbigin, Missionary Theologian: A Reader.* Edited by Paul Weston. Grand Rapids: Eerdmans, 2006.

Niebuhr, H. Richard. *The Kingdom of God in America.* New York: Harper Torchbooks, 1959; orig. 1937.

Niebuhr, Reinhold. *The Nature and Destiny of Man: A Christian Interpretation.* 2nd ed. 2 vols. New York: Scribner, 1964.

Norris, Richard A. *Understanding the Faith of the Church.* New York: Seabury Press, 1979.

———, ed. *The Christological Controversy.* Sources of Early Christian Thought. Philadelphia: Fortress, 1980.

O'Brien, Niall. *Revolution from the Heart.* New York: Oxford University Press, 1987.

O'Connor, Flannery. *Wise Blood.* New York: Farrar, Straus and Giroux, 1949.

———. *The Violent Bear It Away.* New York: Farrar, Straus and Giroux, 1955.

———. *Mystery and Manners.* New York: Farrar, Straus and Giroux, 1969.

———. *The Collected Short Stories.* New York: Farrar, Straus and Giroux, 1971.

———. *The Habit of Being.* New York: Farrar, Straus and Giroux, 1979.

Origen. *De principiis.* Torchbook Edition. Gloucester, Mass.: Peter Smith, 1973.

Ortiz, Sister Dianna, O.S.U. *The Blindfold's Eyes: A Journey from Torture to Truth.* Maryknoll, N.Y.: Orbis, 2002.

———. "Theology, International Law, and Torture: A Survivor's View." *Theology Today* 63, no. 3 (October 2006).

Pelikan, Jaroslav. *The Christian Tradition: A History of the Development of Doctrine.* 5 vols. Chicago: University of Chicago Press, 1975-1991.

———. *Bach among the Theologians.* Philadelphia: Fortress, 1986.

Piper, John. *The Passion of Christ: Fifty Reasons Why Jesus Came to Die.* Wheaton, Ill.: Crossway, 2006.

Placher, William C. *The Domestication of Transcendence: How Modern Thinking about God Went Wrong.* Louisville: Westminster John Knox, 1996.

———. "Christ Takes Our Place: Rethinking Atonement." *Interpretation* 53, no. 1 (January 1999): 5-20.

Plantinga, Alvin. *God, Freedom, and Evil.* Grand Rapids: Eerdmans, 1974.

Power, Samantha. *"A Problem from Hell": America in the Age of Genocide.* New York: Basic Books, 2002.

Procksch, Otto. "The *Lutron* Word-Group in the Old Testament." In *Theological Dictionary of the New Testament,* edited by G. Kittel and G. Friedrich, translated by G. W. Bromiley, 4:329. Grand Rapids: Eerdmans, 1964-1976.

Ragaz, Leonhard. "God Himself Is the Answer." In *The Dimensions of Job: A Study and*

Selected Readings, edited by Nahum Glatzer, 130-31. New York: Schocken Books, 1969.

Raines, Howell. *My Soul Is Rested: Movement Days in the Deep South Remembered.* New York: Putnam, 1977.

Rancour-Laferrier, Daniel. "The Moral Masochism at the Heart of Christianity: Evidence from Russian Orthodox Iconography and Icon Veneration." *Journal for the Psychoanalysis of Culture and Society* 8, no. 1 (Spring 2003): 12-22.

Rashdall, Hastings. *The Idea of the Atonement in Christian Theology.* London: Macmillan, 1919.

Ray, Darby Kathleen. *Deceiving the Devil: Atonement, Abuse, and Ransom.* Cleveland: Pilgrim Press, 1998.

Rhinelander, Philip J. *The Faith of the Cross.* Paddock Lectures, General Theological Seminary, 1914. New York: Longmans, Green and Co., 1916.

Richard, Mark. *House of Prayer No. 2: A Writer's Journey Home.* New York: Nan A. Talese, 2011.

Ridderbos, Herman N. "The Earliest Confession of the Atonement in Paul." In *Reconciliation and Hope: New Testament Essays on Atonement and Eschatology,* edited by Robert Banks. Grand Rapids: Eerdmans, 1974.

Riesenfeld, Harald. "'Uper." In *Theological Dictionary of the New Testament,* edited by G. Kittel and G. Friedrich, translated by G. W. Bromiley, 8:507-16. Grand Rapids: Eerdmans, 1964-1976.

Rorem, Paul. *Hugh of St. Victor.* Great Medieval Thinkers Series. Oxford: Oxford University Press, 2009.

Rosenbaum, Ron. "Staring into the Heart of the Heart of Darkness." *New York Times Magazine,* June 6, 1995.

―――. *Explaining Hitler: The Search for the Origins of His Evil.* New York: Harper-Perennial, 1999.

Rowe, C. Kavin. *World Upside Down: Reading Acts in the Graeco-Roman Age.* New York: Oxford University Press, 2010.

Russell, Jeffrey Burton. *The Devil: Perceptions of Evil from Antiquity to Primitive Christianity.* Ithaca, N.Y.: Cornell University Press, 1977.

―――. *Satan: The Early Christian Tradition.* Ithaca, N.Y.: Cornell University Press, 1981.

―――. *Lucifer: The Devil in the Middle Ages.* Ithaca, N.Y.: Cornell University Press, 1984.

―――. *Mephistopheles: The Devil in the Modern World.* Ithaca, N.Y.: Cornell University Press, 1986.

―――. *The Prince of Darkness: Radical Evil and the Power of Good in History.* Ithaca, N.Y.: Cornell University Press, 1988.

Sanders, E. P. *Paul and Palestinian Judaism: A Comparison of Patterns of Religion.* Philadelphia: Fortress, 1977.

Schell, Orville. *Virtual Tibet: Searching for Shangri-La from the Himalayas to Hollywood.* New York: Metropolitan Books, 2000.

Schnackenburg, Rudolf. *The Church in the New Testament.* New York: Herder and Herder, 1965.

Schneider, John R. "Seeing God Where the Wild Things Are." In *Christian Faith and the Problem of Evil,* edited by Peter Van Inwagen. Grand Rapids: Eerdmans, 2004.

Schütz, John Howard. *Paul and the Anatomy of Apostolic Authority.* Society for New Testament Studies Monograph Series 26. Cambridge: Cambridge University Press, 1975.

Schweizer, Eduard. *Jesus the Parable of God: What Do We Really Know About Jesus?* Princeton Theological Monograph Series. Allison Park, Pa.: Pickwick, 1994.

Seitz, Christopher R. *Word without End: The Old Testament as Abiding Theological Witness.* Grand Rapids: Eerdmans, 1998.

———. *The Character of Christian Scripture: The Significance of a Two-Testament Bible.* Grand Rapids: Baker Academic, 2011.

Sereny, Gitta. *Cries Unheard: Why Children Kill: The Story of Mary Bell.* New York: Metropolitan Books, 1999.

Smail, Thomas A. *Reflected Glory: The Spirit in Christ and Christians.* Grand Rapids: Eerdmans, 1975.

Smit, Dirk J. *Essays on Being Reformed.* Stellenbosch, South Africa: SUN MeDIA, 2009.

Smith, C. Ryder. *The Bible Doctrine of Salvation: A Study of the Atonement.* Eugene, Ore.: Wipf and Stock, 2009.

Smith, Huston. *The Religions of Man.* New York: Harper, 1958.

Snyder, Timothy. *Bloodlands: Europe between Hitler and Stalin.* New York: Basic Books, 2010.

Sobrino, Jon. *Jesus in Latin America.* Maryknoll, N.Y.: Orbis, 1987.

———. *Jesus the Liberator: A Historical-Theological Reading of Jesus of Nazareth.* Maryknoll, N.Y.: Orbis, 1993.

Solzhenitsyn, Alexsandr. *The Gulag Archipelago.* 3 vols. New York: Harper and Row, 1973.

Sonderegger, Katherine. "The Doctrine of Justification and the Cure of Souls." In *The Gospel of Justification in Christ: Where Does the Church Stand Today?* edited by Wayne C. Stumme. Grand Rapids: Eerdmans, 2006.

Sontag, Susan. *Illness as Metaphor.* New York: Farrar, Straus and Giroux, 1977.

Soulen, Kendall. *The God of Israel and Christian Theology.* Minneapolis: Augsburg Fortress, 1996.

Southern, R. W. *Saint Anselm: A Portrait in a Landscape.* Cambridge: Cambridge University Press, 1990.

Stendahl, Krister. "The Apostle Paul and the Introspective Conscience of the West." *Harvard Theological Review* 56, no. 3:199-215. Reprinted in Stendahl, *Paul among the Gentiles* (Philadelphia: Fortress, 1976).

Stott, John R. W. *The Cross of Christ.* Downers Grove, Ill.: InterVarsity, 1986.

Stringfellow, William. *A Private and Public Faith.* Grand Rapids: Eerdmans, 1962.

———. *Count It All Joy.* Grand Rapids: Eerdmans, 1967.

———. *An Ethic for Christians and Other Aliens in a Strange Land.* Waco: Word, 1973.

———. *Conscience and Obedience: The Politics of Romans 13 and Revelation 13 in Light of the Second Coming.* Waco: Word, 1977.

Stuhlmacher, Peter. "Eighteen Theses on Paul's Theology of the Cross." In Stuhlmacher,

Reconciliation, Law, and Righteousness: Essays in Biblical Theology. Philadelphia: Fortress, 1986.

———. "Recent Exegesis on Romans 3:24." In Stuhlmacher, *Reconciliation, Law, and Righteousness: Essays in Biblical Theology.* Philadelphia: Fortress, 1986.

Sykes, Stephen W. *The Story of Atonement.* Trinity and Truth Series. London: Darton, Longman, and Todd, 1997.

Taylor, Vincent. *Jesus and His Sacrifice.* London: Macmillan, 1937.

———. *Forgiveness and Reconciliation: A Study in New Testament Theology.* London: Macmillan, 1946.

———. *The Atonement in New Testament Teaching.* London: Epworth Press, 1963.

Ten Boom, Corrie, with John and Elizabeth Sherrill. *The Hiding Place.* Old Tappan, N.J.: Revell, 1971.

Terrien, Samuel. *The Elusive Presence: Toward a New Biblical Theology.* Religious Perspectives Series. San Francisco: Harper and Row, 1978.

Tillich, Paul. *The Shaking of the Foundations.* New York: Scribner, 1948.

———. *The Courage to Be.* 2nd ed. New Haven: Yale University Press, Yale Nota Bene, 2000.

Tilling, Chris, ed. *Beyond Old and New Perspectives: Reflections on the Work of Douglas Campbell.* Eugene, Ore.: Cascade Books, 2014.

Torrance, David W., ed. *The Witness of the Jews to God.* Edinburgh: Handsel Press, 1982.

Torrance, T. F. *The Doctrine of Grace in the Apostolic Fathers.* Edinburgh: Oliver and Boyd, 1948.

———. *The Mediation of Christ.* Rev. ed. Colorado Springs: Helmers and Howard, 1992; orig. 1983.

———. *Atonement: The Person and Work of Christ.* Edited by Robert T. Walker. Downers Grove, Ill.: InterVarsity, 2009.

Tutu, Desmond. *No Future without Forgiveness.* New York: Image Books, 1999.

Van Dyk, Leanne. "Do Theories of Atonement Foster Abuse?" *Dialog* 35, no. 1 (Winter 1996).

———. "The Three Offices of Christ: The *Munus Triplex* as Expansive Resources in Atonement." *Catalyst* 25, no. 2 (1999).

Van Inwagen, Peter, ed. *Christian Faith and the Problem of Evil.* Grand Rapids: Eerdmans, 2004.

Volf, Miroslav. *Exclusion and Embrace: A Theological Exploration of Identity, Otherness, and Reconciliation.* Nashville: Abingdon, 1996.

———. "Theology, Meaning, and Power." In *The Future of Theology: Essays in Honor of Jürgen Moltmann,* edited by Miroslav Volf, Carmen Krieg, and Thomas Kucharz. Grand Rapids: Eerdmans, 1996.

———. *The End of Memory: Remembering Rightly in a Violent World.* Grand Rapids: Eerdmans, 2006.

Von Rad, Gerhard. *Old Testament Theology.* 2 vols. New York: Harper and Row, 1962; Louisville: Westminster John Knox, 1965.

Watson, Francis. "The Quest for the Real Jesus." In *The Cambridge Companion to Jesus,* edited by Markus Bockmuehl. Cambridge: Cambridge University Press, 2001.

Weaver, J. Denny. *The Nonviolent Atonement.* Grand Rapids: Eerdmans, 2001.

Weil, Simone. *Waiting for God.* New York: Putnam, 1951.

———. *Gravity and Grace.* Lincoln: University of Nebraska Press, 1952.

West, Rebecca. *Black Lamb and Grey Falcon.* New York: Penguin Books, 1994; orig. 1941.

Westerholm, Stephen. *Justification Reconsidered.* Grand Rapids, Eerdmans, 2013.

———. "Righteousness, Cosmic and Microcosmic." In *Apocalyptic Paul: Cosmos and Anthropos in Romans,* edited by Beverly R. Gaventa. Waco: Baylor University Press, 2013.

———, ed. *The Blackwell Companion to Paul.* Malden, Mass.: Wiley-Blackwell, 2011.

Westermann, Claus. *Creation.* Philadelphia: Fortress, 1974.

Whale, J. S. *Christian Doctrine.* Cambridge: Cambridge University Press, 1956.

———. *Victor and Victim: The Christian Doctrine of Redemption.* Cambridge: Cambridge University Press, 1960; orig. 1927.

White, Ronald C., Jr. *Lincoln's Greatest Speech: The Second Inaugural.* New York: Simon and Schuster, 2002.

Wilder, Amos *Early Christian Rhetoric.* Cambridge: Harvard University Press, 1971.

Wilder, Thornton. *The Bridge of San Luis Rey.* New York: HarperCollins, Perennial Edition, 1986.

Wilken, Robert Louis. *The Christians as the Romans Saw Them.* 2nd ed. New Haven: Yale University Press, 2003.

———. *The First Thousand Years.* New Haven: Yale University Press, 2012.

Williams, Daniel Day. *The Spirit and the Forms of Love.* New York: Harper and Row, 1968.

Williams, Delores S. *Sisters in the Wilderness: The Challenge of Womanist God-Talk.* Maryknoll, N.Y.: Orbis, 1993.

Williams, Rowan. *Christ on Trial: How the Gospel Unsettles Our Judgement.* Grand Rapids: Eerdmans, 2000.

Williams, Sam K. *Jesus' Death as Saving Event: The Background and Origin of a Concept.* Missoula, Mont.: Scholars Press, 1975.

Wink, Walter. *Naming the Powers: The Language of Power in the New Testament.* Philadelphia: Fortress, 1984.

———. *Unmasking the Powers: The Invisible Forces That Determine Human Existence.* Philadelphia: Fortress, 1986.

———. *Engaging the Powers: Discernment and Resistance in a World of Domination.* Minneapolis: Fortress, 1992.

Wright, N. T. *Jesus and the Victory of God.* Minneapolis: Fortress, 1996.

———. *The Scriptures, the Cross, and the Power of God: Reflections for Holy Week.* Louisville: Westminster John Knox, 2006.

———. *Paul and the Faithfulness of God.* Minneapolis: Augsburg Fortress, 2013.

———. *Pauline Perspectives: Essays on Paul, 1978-2013.* Minneapolis: Fortress, 2013.

———. *Paul and His Recent Interpreters.* Minneapolis: Augsburg Fortress, 2014.

Yoder, John Howard. *The Politics of Jesus: Vicit Agnus Noster.* Grand Rapids: Eerdmans, 1972.

Young, Andrew. *An Easy Burden: The Civil Rights Movement and the Transformation of America.* New York: HarperCollins, 1996.

Zahl, Paul F. M. *The Protestant Face of Anglicanism.* Grand Rapids: Eerdmans, 1998.
Ziegler, Philip. "Dietrich Bonhoeffer: An Ethics of God's Apocalypse?" *Modern Theology* 23, no. 4 (October 2007).
————. "Christ Must Reign: Ernst Käsemann and Soteriology in an Apocalyptic Key." In *Apocalyptic and the Future of Theology,* edited by Joshua B. Davis and Douglas Harink. Eugene, Ore.: Cascade Books, 2012.

COMMENTARIES ON BOOKS OF THE BIBLE

The works listed here are separated out from the general bibliography to highlight them as *theological* commentaries; they were particularly helpful in the preparation of this volume, and they are highly recommended for preachers. This is an idiosyncratic list and does not pretend to be exhaustive. The commentaries are arranged in order of the biblical books.

Genesis
Kidner, Derek. *Genesis: An Introduction and Commentary.* Tyndale Old Testament Commentaries, vol. 1. Downers Grove, Ill.: InterVarsity, 1967.
Sarna, Nahum. *Understanding Genesis: The Heritage of Biblical Israel.* New York: Schocken Books, 1970.
Von Rad, Gerhard. *Genesis.* Rev. ed. Old Testament Library. Philadelphia: Westminster, 1972.

Exodus
Childs, Brevard. *The Book of Exodus: A Critical, Theological Commentary.* Old Testament Library. Philadelphia: Westminster, 1974.
Sarna, Nahum. *Exploring Exodus: The Origins of Biblical Israel.* New York: Schocken Books, 1986.

Leviticus
Radner, Ephraim. *Leviticus.* Brazos Theological Commentary on the Bible. Grand Rapids: Brazos, 2008.

Deuteronomy
Miller, Patrick D. *Deuteronomy.* Interpretation Series. Louisville: John Knox, 1990.

Books of Kings
Ellul, Jacques. *The Politics of God and the Politics of Man.* Grand Rapids: Eerdmans, 1972.

Job
McKibben, Bill. *The Comforting Whirlwind.* Grand Rapids: Eerdmans, 1994.
Terrien, Samuel. *Job.* The Interpreter's Bible, vol. 3, pp. 877-1198. New York and Nashville: Abingdon, 1957.

Psalms

Mays, James L. *Psalms.* Interpretation Series. Louisville: Westminster John Knox, 2011.
Terrien, Samuel. *The Psalms and Their Meaning for Today: Their Original Purpose, Contents, Religious Truth, Poetic Beauty, and Significance.* Indianapolis: Bobbs-Merrill, 1952.
————. *The Psalms: Strophic Structure and Theological Commentary.* Grand Rapids: Eerdmans, 2002.

Proverbs

Davis, Ellen F. *Proverbs, Ecclesiastes, and the Song of Songs.* Westminster Bible Companion. Louisville: Westminster John Knox, 2000.

Ecclesiastes

Davis, Ellen F. *Proverbs, Ecclesiastes, and the Song of Songs.* Westminster Bible Companion. Louisville: Westminster John Knox, 2000.

Song of Songs

Davis, Ellen F. *Proverbs, Ecclesiastes, and the Song of Songs.* Westminster Bible Companion. Louisville: Westminster John Knox, 2000.
Jenson, Robert. *Song of Songs.* Interpretation Series. Louisville: Westminster John Knox, 2012.
Norris, Richard A. *Song of Songs: Interpreted by Early Christian and Medieval Commentators.* Church's Bible Series. Grand Rapids: Eerdmans, 2003.

Isaiah

Muilenburg, James. *Isaiah 40–66.* The Interpreter's Bible, vol. 5. Nashville: Abingdon, 1956.
Seitz, Christopher. *Isaiah 1–39.* Interpretation Series. Louisville: Westminster John Knox, 2011.
Westermann, Claus. *Isaiah 40–66.* Philadelphia: Westminster, 1977.
Wilken, Robert Louis. *Isaiah: Interpreted by Early Christian and Medieval Commentators.* Church's Bible Series. Grand Rapids: Eerdmans, 2007.

Jeremiah

Bright, John. *Jeremiah.* Anchor Bible 21. New York: Doubleday, 1965.

Daniel

Porteous, Norman. *Daniel: A Commentary.* Old Testament Library. Philadelphia: Westminster, 1965.

Minor Prophets

Birch, Bruce C. *Hosea, Joel, and Amos.* Westminster Bible Companion. Louisville: Westminster John Knox, 1997.

Mays, James Luther. *Amos: A Commentary.* Old Testament Library. Philadelphia: West-minster, 1969.

———. *Hosea: A Commentary.* Old Testament Library. Philadelphia: Westminster, 1969.

Matthew

Allison, Dale. *Matthew: A Shorter Commentary.* Grand Rapids: Baker Academic, 2005.

Gundry, Robert H. *Matthew: A Commentary on His Literary and Theological Art.* Grand Rapids: Eerdmans, 1982.

Kingsbury, Jack Dean. *Matthew.* Proclamation Series. Philadelphia: Fortress, 1977.

Schweizer, Eduard. *The Good News according to Matthew.* Atlanta: John Knox, 1975.

Mark

Marcus, Joel. *Mark 1–7: A New Translation with Introduction and Commentary.* Anchor Bible 27. New York: Doubleday, 2000.

———. *Mark 8–16: A New Translation with Introduction and Commentary.* Anchor Yale Bible 27A. New Haven: Yale University Press, 2009.

Nineham, D. E. *Saint Mark.* Pelican New Testament Commentary. Middlesex: Penguin Books, 1963.

Schweizer, Eduard. *The Good News according to Mark.* Atlanta: John Knox, 1966.

Luke

Caird, G. B. *Saint Luke.* Pelican New Testament Commentary. Middlesex: Penguin Books, 1973.

Marshall, I. Howard. *The Gospel of Luke.* New International Greek Testament Com-mentary. Grand Rapids: Eerdmans, 1978.

John

Bultmann, Rudolf. *The Gospel of John.* Philadelphia: Westminster, 1971.

Dodd, C. H. *The Interpretation of the Fourth Gospel.* Cambridge: Cambridge University Press, 1965.

Hoskyns, Edwyn Clement. *The Fourth Gospel.* Edited by Francis Noel Davy. London: Faber and Faber, 1947.

Schnackenburg, Rudolf. *The Gospel according to St. John.* 3 vols. New York: Crossroad, 1982.

Acts of the Apostles

Bruce, F. F. *Commentary on the Book of the Acts.* New International Commentary on the New Testament. Grand Rapids: Eerdmans, 1977.

Fitzmyer, Joseph A. *The Acts of the Apostles.* Anchor Bible 31. New York: Doubleday, 1998.

Pelikan, Jaroslav. *Acts.* Brazos Theological Commentary. Grand Rapids: Brazos, 2005.

Romans

Barrett, C. K. *A Commentary on the Epistle to the Romans*. Harper's New Testament Commentaries. New York: Harper and Row, 1957.

Barth, Karl. *The Epistle to the Romans*. 6th ed. Oxford: Oxford University Press, 1968.

Byrne, Brendan. *Reckoning with Romans: A Contemporary Reading of Paul's Gospel*. Wilmington, Del.: Michael Glazier, 1986.

Cranfield, C. E. B. *A Critical and Exegetical Commentary on the Epistle to the Romans*. International Critical Commentary. Edinburgh: T. & T. Clark, 1975.

Dunn, J. D. G. *Romans 1–8*. Word Biblical Commentary 38A. Dallas: Word, 1988.

———. *Romans 9–16*. Word Biblical Commentary 38B. Dallas: Word, 1988.

Grieb, A. Katherine. *The Story of Romans: A Narrative Defense of God's Righteousness*. Louisville: Westminster John Knox, 2002.

Käsemann, Ernst. *Commentary on Romans*. Grand Rapids: Eerdmans, 1980.

Minear, Paul. *The Obedience of Faith: The Purposes of Paul in the Epistle to the Romans*. Naperville, Ill.: Alec R. Allenson, 1971.

Smart, James D. *Doorway to a New Age*. Philadelphia: Westminster, 1972.

I Corinthians

Barrett, C. K. *A Commentary on the First Epistle to the Corinthians*. Harper's New Testament Commentaries. New York: Harper and Row, 1967.

Fee, Gordon D. *The First Epistle to the Corinthians*. New International Commentary on the New Testament. Grand Rapids: Eerdmans, 1987.

Hays, Richard B. *First Corinthians*. Interpretation Series. Louisville: John Knox, 1997.

II Corinthians

Furnish, Victor. *II Corinthians*. Anchor Bible 32A. Garden City, N.Y.: Doubleday, 1984.

Hays, Richard B. *A Commentary on the Second Epistle to the Corinthians*. Harper's New Testament Commentaries. New York: Harper and Row, 1973.

Hughes, Philip Edgcumbe. *Paul's Second Epistle to the Corinthians*. Grand Rapids: Eerdmans, 1962.

Galatians

Luther, Martin. *Commentary on the Epistle to the Galatians*. Wheaton, Ill.: Crossway, 1998; orig. 1535.

Martyn, J. Louis. *Galatians*. Anchor Bible 33A. New York: Doubleday, 1997.

Ephesians

Barth, Markus. *Ephesians: Introduction, Translation, and Commentary on Chapters 1–3*. Anchor Bible 34. Garden City, N.Y.: Doubleday, 1974.

———. *Ephesians: Translation and Commentary on Chapters 4–6*. Anchor Bible 34A. Garden City, N.Y.: Doubleday, 1974.

I and II Thessalonians

Gaventa, Beverly Roberts. *First and Second Thessalonians*. Interpretation Series. Louisville: John Knox, 1998.

Hebrews

Bruce, F. F. *The Epistle to the Hebrews*. 2nd ed. New International Commentary on the New Testament. Grand Rapids: Eerdmans, 1997.

Hughes, Philip Edgcumbe. *A Commentary on the Epistle to the Hebrews*. Grand Rapids: Eerdmans, 1977.

Westcott, B. F. *The Epistle to the Hebrews*. 1889. Reprint, Grand Rapids: Eerdmans, 1967.

James

Stringfellow, William. *Count It All Joy: Reflections on Faith, Doubt, and Temptation*. Grand Rapids: Eerdmans, 1967.

Epistles of John

Bruce, F. F. *The Epistles of John: Introduction, Exposition, and Notes*. Grand Rapids: Eerdmans, 1970.

Marshall, I. Howard. *The Epistles of John*. New International Commentary on the New Testament. Grand Rapids: Eerdmans, 1978.

Smith, D. Moody. *First, Second, and Third John*. Interpretation Series. Louisville: John Knox, 1991.

Epistles of Peter

Harink, Douglas. *1 and 2 Peter*. Brazos Theological Commentary on the Bible. Grand Rapids: Brazos, 2009.

Selwyn, E. G. *The First Epistle of St. Peter*. London: Macmillan, 1964.

Revelation

Caird, G. B. *A Commentary on the Revelation of St. John the Divine*. New York: Harper and Row, 1966.

Mangina, Joseph L. *Revelation*. Brazos Theological Commentary on the Bible. Grand Rapids: Brazos, 2010.

Minear, Paul. *I Saw a New Earth: An Introduction to the Visions of the Apocalypse*. Washington, D.C.: Corpus Publications, 1968.

Schüssler-Fiorenza, Elisabeth. *Revelation: Vision of a Just World*. Proclamation Commentaries. Minneapolis: Fortress, 1991.

Stringfellow, William. *An Ethic for Christians and Other Aliens in a Strange Land*. Waco: Word, 1973.

Index of Names

Index of Subjects

Major treatments are in **bold** type.

Abelardian model. *See* Subjective theme

Abraham: Abrahamic covenant, primacy of, **545-46**; hope of, 390; lack of human potential, **576**; as name of God, 10-11; and obedience of faith, **261, 265-66**; and promise to Gentiles, 99; righteousness reckoned to, 332-33; unconditional promise to, 192n60, 243, 359. *See also* Faith; Sacrifice: of Isaac

Acceptance: theological insufficiency of, **591-94**

Acquittal, 188, 336, 470; insufficiency of, 316, 329, 350, 536n2, 586. *See also* Judgment, Day of

"Adam": as archetypal figure, 13, 20, 184, **188-89**, 337n76, 419n65, 427n94, 522n124, **538n4**; in bondage to Sin, 178, 184, **200**, 203, 480, 483, 487, 517, 520, 562; as central figure in recapitulation, 13, 470n15, 537, 558, 560; and Eve, 178, 180, 184, 195, 306, 337n76, 411, 420, 519; in George Herbert, **562-63**; as "historical" figure, 184n43, 419n65, 470n14, 539n8; the "old Adam," 144, 184, 518; in Rom. 5, 200, **354-57**, 469-70; second Adam, 13, 184n43, 365, 477n25, 478, 523, 537, **539**, 543, 554, 559n51, **569-70**; story of, in John Donne, 536; universal designation, 13, 36, 177, 178, 184, 200, 227, 364, 470, 487, 518, 521, 532, 537, 539, 542, 562. *See also* Recapitulation

Advent, 45, 313-14, 387-88, 421n72. *See also* Now/not-yet dialectic

Adversary, the. *See* Enemy, the

African American churches, 14n25, 57n37, 87n36, 88n36, **115n12**, 166n44, **227-30**, 237, **384-86**, 390, 495n73, 598. *See also* Civil rights movement

Agency, **597-99**; as central issue, 494n74, **523-25, 559, 565n67**; in the crucifixion, 132, 249n38, **361-62**, 386, 415n50, **461, 511, 523-25, 526-27, 528-29**; divine, **139-40**, 161-63, 181, 218n9, 266, 280, 282, 325, **327-30, 386, 511, 513, 534, 555, 576n8, 559, 580-81, 600-601**; as indispensable idea in apocalyptic, 138, **222**, 386; in Lord's Supper, 66n63, **217-20**; in Passover Seder, 217-18; in recapitulation, **600-601**; in rectification *(dikaiosyne)*, 296; role of human, 222, **330, 342-43**, 362n34; of Scripture as Word of God, 19-21, **456, 600-601**. *See also* Participation; Powers

Agnus Dei. See Lamb of God

Akedah. *See* Sacrifice: of Isaac

Alcoholism, 341, 548

Already/not yet. *See* Now/not-yet dialectic

America: eclectic religiosity of, 10, 49, 88n36; enslaved by marketing, 190; optimism and positive thinking in, 37, 44, 45n8, 57, 69-70, **122-24**, 197, 202

Annihilation, **459-60**, 603

Anselm, 146-65; African American appreciation of, 152n13, 166n44; apocalyptic themes in, 149n9, 154, 155, 350; artistry and warmth of, 146, 149, 154; *Christus Victor* theme in, 155, 160; contemporary relevance of, 147, 165-66; controversy concerning, 146, 147n3, 158-61, 161-62, 163, 488-89, 499n88; faith seeking understanding, 147, 149, 158; and God's honor, 155, 156-57; grace of God, 156; gravity of, **192-93**; on happiness, 150-51; and inadmissibility of impunity, 148-49, 152; and patristic theologians, 160-61; punishment as "inconsolable need," 153-54; and

464n4, 489n55, 497-98; as apocalyptic warfare, 103, 275, 319, **346-47, 382**; concerning the crucifixion, 448-49, 497-500; contrasted with persuasion, **448-49**; deliverance from, 301, 308; as divine invasion, 346, 416; in God, 147n3, **168n4**, 179n4, 382, 413, **500**; "God's monopoly on," **448-50**; misuse of, 413n45, **498-500**; necessity of, 380, **412-13, 504-5**; in New Testament cosmology, 379, **380-81**, 448-50; in Revelation, **376-84**; as work of the Enemy, 500, 504-5; as work of Sin, 174, 196, 198, 202, 357. *See also* Apocalyptic war; Invasion; Kingdom of God; Nonviolent resistance

War. *See* Apocalyptic war; Violence
Wisdom: in gnosticism, **46-47**; versus power of God, **15, 85-87**
Wisdom literature, 138, 185n44, 222, 309, 593; Job, 20, **286n6, 405n22, 444-47**
Word of God: as active agency, **19-21, 20-21, 330-31, 335-36, 349n4, 456, 600-601**; canonical shaping of, as Christian Scripture, 22-23, 84n32, 140n73, 250n39, 341n85, 404n20, 579, 586, **593-94, 605**; community created by, 20; Holy Spirit interpreted by, 18n29, 23; interprets itself *(Scriptura sui interpres)*, 512-13, 583; as performative *(logizomai)*, **333-35**; as sec-

ond person of the Trinity, 19; transmitted through preaching, 30, 330; varying witnesses in, 23-24, 68n71, 185n44, 250n39, 267, 562, 568. *See also* Gospel message; *Logizomai*
"Word of the cross" (I Cor. 1:18): as apocalyptic *novum* (new thing), **90, 215n4**; cost of, 44; dearth of, in today's churches, 14-15; erases all distinctions, 54, 105; ethical impetus in, 37; and gnosticism, **69-70**; as human witness, **21-22**; as irreligious, 2n2, 18, **75-76**, 87, **104-5**; as power *(dunamis)* of God, **13-14, 18**, 19, 22, 27; as power speaking today, **288-89**; as preaching, **13-14**, 19, 23, 85, 87, 288-89; required for interpretation, 17; resistance to, 15, 70; as scandalous, 3, **14-16**, 17, 18, 21, 70, 85, **104-5**; triune God as active agency in, **18-19, 20-21, 23**; uniqueness of, 18, **19-20, 57n40**. *See also* Creation *ex nihilo;* Scandal
Works: relationship to divine agency, 330, 342, 360, 558, **569, 607**
Wrath, human. *See* Hatred
Wrath of God, 129-32, **131**, 136, 286n6; God's mercy in service of, 143, 282, **322-25, 510, 518-20**; Jesus Christ, absorbed by God in, 132, 143, 325; necessity of, **380-82, 412-13**, 449

Yetser ha-ra. See Evil inclination

Index of Scripture and Other Ancient Literature